The Law of the
International Civil Service

The Law of the International Civil Service

(*as Applied by International Administrative Tribunals*)

VOLUME II

by
C.F. AMERASINGHE
BA, LL B, Ph.D., LL D (Cantab.), LL M (Harv.);
Executive Secretary, World Bank Administrative Tribunal; Member,
Institut de Droit International; Sometime Second Professor of Law,
University of Ceylon, Colombo

CLARENDON PRESS · OXFORD
1988

Oxford University Press, Walton Street, Oxford OX2 6DP
Oxford New York Toronto
Delhi Bombay Calcutta Madras Karachi
Petaling Jaya Singapore Hong Kong Tokyo
Nairobi Dar es Salaam Cape Town
Melbourne Auckland
and associated companies in
Berlin Ibadan

Oxford is a trade mark of Oxford University Press

Published in the United States
by Oxford University Press, New York

British Library Cataloguing in Publication Data

Amerasinghe, C.F.
The law of the international civil service:
(as applied by international
administrative tribunals).
Vol. 2
1. International officials and employees
——Legal status, laws, etc.
I. Title
341.2   JX1995

ISBN 0-19-825610-8 (volume 2)

Library of Congress Cataloging-in-Publication Data

Amerasinghe, Chittharanjan Felix, 1933-
The law of the international civil service.
Bibliography: v. 2, p.
Includes index.
1. International officials and employees.
2. International administrative courts.
3. International agencies.   I. Title.
JX1995.A4685   1988   341.23'3   87-22095

ISBN 0-19-825610-8 (v. 2)

Set by Colset Private Limited, Singapore

Printed and bound in Great Britain by
Biddles Ltd, Guildford and King's Lynn

CONTENTS

SUMMARY OF CONTENTS OF VOLUME I

ABBREVIATIONS

AD	*Annual Digest of International Law Cases*
AFDB	African Development Bank
AFDI	*Annuaire français de droit international*
AJCL	*American Journal of Comparative Law*
ASIL	American Society of International Law
BIRPI	Bureaux Internationaux Réunis pour la Protection de la Propriété Intellectuelle
BYIL	*British Yearbook of International Law*
CAFRAD	African Training and Research Centre in Administration for Development
Case-Law Digest	*Case-Law Digest of the Appeals Board of the Council of Europe* (1985)
CERN	European Organization for Nuclear Research
CIEPS	International Centre for Registration of Publications in Series
CIPE	Interamerican Centre for Export Promotion
CIPEC	Intergovernmental Council of Copper Exporting Countries (Conseil Intergouvernemental des Pays Exportateurs de Cuivre)
CJEC	Court of Justice of the European Communities
EAEC	European Atomic Energy Community
EC	European Communities
ECHR	European Court of Human Rights
ECR	Reports of the European Court of Justice
ECSC	European Coal and Steel Community
EEC	European Economic Community
EFTA	European Free Trade Association
ELDO	European Space Vehicle Launcher Development Organization
EMBL	European Molecular Biology Laboratory
EPO	European Patent Organization
EPU	European Payments Union
ESA	European Space Agency
ESO	European Southern Observatory
ESRO	European Space Research Organization
EURATOM	European Atomic Energy Community
Eurocontrol	European Organization for the Safety of Air Navigation

FAO	Food and Agricultural Organization of the United Nations
FISCA	Federation of International Civil Servants' Associations
GAOR	General Assembly Official Records
IAEA	International Atomic Energy Agency
IBRD	International Bank for Reconstruction and Development
ICAO	International Civil Aviation Organization
ICCROM	International Centre for the Study of the Preservation and the Restoration of Cultural Property
ICEM	Intergovernmental Committee for European Migration
ICITO-GATT	Interim Commission for the International Trade Organization
ICJ	International Court of Justice
ICLQ	*International and Comparative Law Quarterly*
ICM	Intergovernmental Committee for Migration
ICRISAT	International Crop Research Institute for the Semi-Arid Tropics
ICSC	International Civil Service Commission
ICSID	International Center for Settlement of Investment Disputes
IDA	International Development Association
IDB	Inter-American Development Bank
IDBAT	Inter-American Development Bank Administrative Tribunal
IFAD	International Fund for Agricultural Development
IFC	International Finance Corporation
IIIC	International Institute of Intellectual Co-operation
IJIL	*Indian Journal of International Law*
ILC	International Law Commission
ILCE	Latin American Institute for Educational Communication
ILO	International Labour Organization
ILOAT	International Labour Organization Administrative Tribunal
ILR	*International Law Reports*
IMCO	Inter-governmental Maritime Consultative Organization
IMF	International Monetary Fund
IMO	International Maritime Organization
IMT	Institute for Management of Technology
IPI	International Patent Institute
IPU	International Paleontological Union
IRO	International Refugees Organization

ITU	International Telecommunication Union
JDI	*Journal de droit international*
JUNAT	Judgments of the United Nations Administrative Tribunal
LN	League of Nations
LNT	League of Nations Administrative Tribunal
NAMSA	NATO Maintenance and Supply Agency
NATO	North Atlantic Treaty Organization
OAPEC	Organization of Arab Petroleum Exporting Countries
OAS	Organization of American States
OASAT	Administrative Tribunal of the Organization of American States
OCDE	Organization of Economic Co-operation and Development
OCTI	Central Office for International Railway Transport
OECD	Organization for Economic Co-operation and Development
OECE	European Organization for Economic Co-operation
OEEC	European Organization for Economic Co-operation
OIE	International Office of Epizootics
OIT	Organization Internationale du Travail (International Labour Organization)
PAHO	Pan-American Health Organization
PAU	Pan American Union
PCIJ	Permanent Court of International Justice
PMS	Personnel Manual Statement (World Bank)
RDI	*Rivista di dirito internazionale*
TGS	*Transactions of the Grotius Society*
UIBPIP	United International Bureau for the Protection of Intellectual Property
UN	United Nations
UNAT	United Nations Administrative Tribunal
UNCIO	United Nations Conference on International Organization
UNDP	United Nations Development Program
UNECLA	United Nations Economic Commission for Latin America
UNEP	United Nations Environmental Program
UNESCO	United Nations Educational, Scientific, and Cultural Organization
UNICEF	United Nations International Children's Emergency Fund

UNIDO	United Nations Industrial Development Organization
UNIDROIT	International Institute for the Unification of Private Law
UNRWA	United Nations Relief and Works Agency
UPU	Universal Postal Union
WBAT	World Bank Administrative Tribunal
WEU	Western European Union
WHO	World Health Organization
WIPO	World Intellectual Property Organization
WMO	World Meteorological Organization
WPU	World Postal Union
WTO	World Tourism Organization
ZAORV	*Zeitschrift für auslandisches öffentliches Recht und Völkerrecht*

PART II
Specific Subjects

CHAPTER THIRTY-FOUR

Types of Appointments

INTERNATIONAL organizations do not use a single type of appointment in their practice of employment. As already seen, most organizations base their employment relationship initially on a contract of employment. It is only a few organizations, such as the European Communities and the OECD, that in general resort to a statutory instrument to create the employment relationship without any reference to the agreement of the person appointed. But even such organizations may resort to the contract of employment to engage some of their personnel. Thus, the CJEC uses the contractual method to employ temporary and auxiliary staff.[1]

The manner in which appointments are classified does not necessarily depend on the nature of the employment relationship in the organization. Those organizations that base the employment relationship on status have classifications of appointments often somewhat similar to those utilized by some organizations that base the employment relationship on a contract of employment. What is significant is that most organizations have their own individual classifications and that often there is no exact identity between the classifications of different organizations, although sometimes similarities in classification do exist.

Furthermore, there may be more than one system of classification of appointments in the same organization. Thus, apart from the standard distinction made between those appointments that are permanent and those that are not, appointments may be classified as 'locally recruited' or 'local' and 'not-locally recruited' or 'non-local',[2] or as 'temporary' and 'auxiliary'.[3] It is not proposed to examine all these classifications of appointments, although classifications and antinomies such as these are relevant to the application of the Staff Regulations and Staff Rules of the different organizations.[4] What is

[1] See the Conditions of Employment of Other Servants of the European Communities, Titles II and III: Amerasinghe (ed.), 4 *Staff Regulations and Staff Rules of Selected International Organizations* (1983) p. 59 at pp. 64 ff.

[2] See *Clegg-Bernardi*, ILOAT Judgement No. 505 [1982] (FAO); and *Hoefnagels*, ILOAT Judgment No. 506 [1982] (FAO). Both these cases refer to the Staff Rules of the FAO for the distinction: see now Staff Rule 302.4063 in Amerasinghe (ed.), 3 op. cit. (note 1 *supra*) p. 84 at p. 112.

[3] See *Fournier*, CJEC Case 106/80 [1981] ECR p. 2759; and *Laredo and Garilli*, CJEC Cases 225 & 241/81 [1983] ECR p. 347. For another distinction between 'area' and 'international' posts see *van der Valk*, UNAT Judgment No. 117 [1968], JUNAT Nos. 114–166 p. 33 at p. 40.

[4] See the cases referred to *supra* notes 2 and 3.

of basic significance is the differentiation of appointments centring around the idea of the permanent appointment and appointments that are not permanent, which is based not only on the duration of the appointment but on other factors as well. It may be noted that even those organizations that predicate their basic appointment on status as opposed to contract may within the concept of status have distinctions among appointments which involve permanency and the absence of permanency.[5]

In the UN, which is one of the oldest extant organizations, a distinction is made in the Staff Rules between permanent and regular appointments, on the one hand, and temporary appointments on the other. The permanent appointment is not defined but is intended for staff members who have demonstrated their suitability for a career as international civil servants.[6] Regular appointments are of a similar nature, being restricted to a certain category of staff members other than professional, and are described as being for an indefinite period with the capability of lasting until retirement.[7] But there is a distinction between regular and permanent appointments in so far as the Staff Regulations and Staff Rules applicable to temporary appointments which are not for a fixed term govern regular appointments.[8] Temporary appointments are of three kinds: probationary, fixed-term, and indefinite. Probationary appointments are granted to persons under 50 years of age who are recruited for career service, must be converted into permanent or regular appointments unless they are terminated during or at the end of the period of probation, and are governed by the Staff Regulations and Staff Rules applicable to temporary appointments which are not for a fixed term.[9] The fixed-term appointment has an expiration date specified in the letter of appointment, may be granted for a period not exceeding five years, and does not, according to the letter of the Staff Rule concerned, carry any expectancy of renewal or of conversion to any other type of appointment.[10] The indefinite appointment is intended for persons in special categories, does not carry any expectancy of conversion to any other type of appointment, has no specific expiration date, and is governed by the Staff Regulations and Staff Rules applicable to temporary appointments which are not for a fixed term.[11]

In the WHO the classification is somewhat different. There are permanent appointments which are career-service appointments and are without time limit and there are temporary appointments which may be on a full-time,

[5] See Staff Regulation 9 of the OECD: Amerasinghe (ed.), 5 op. cit. (note 1 *supra*) p. 1 at p. 29.

[6] Staff Rule 104.13 (a) (i): see Appendix V *infra*.

[7] Staff Rule 104.13 (b): See Appendix V *infra*.

[8] Staff Rule 104.13 (b) (ii): See Appendix V *infra*.

[9] Staff Rules 104.12 (a): See Appendix V *infra*.

[10] Staff Rule 104.12 (b): Appendix V *infra*.

[11] Staff Rule 104.12 (c): Appendix V *infra*.

part-time, or when-actually-employed basis and are either fixed-term when they are for one year or more, or short-term when they are for less than one year.[12] Any appointment for one year or more must be subject to a period of probation.[13] This is similar to the probationary appointment in the UN and such an appointment is temporary.

In the ILO there is a basic distinction between permanent appointments and those that are for a fixed term of not less than one year and of not more than five years.[14] According to the Staff Regulations the latter carry no expectation of renewal or of conversion to permanent appointments and terminate without prior notice on the termination date fixed in the contract of employment. In the Council of Europe there are probationary appointments, fixed-term appointments, and appointments of indefinite duration which are the equivalent of permanent appointments.[15]

In the case of the World Bank the basic distinction is between regular appointments which are full-time and of indefinite duration and are the equivalent of permanent appointments, fixed-term appointments which are full-time and for a specified term of one year or more in duration, temporary appointments which are full-time and for less than one year in duration, and part-time appointments.[16] Provision is also made for probation in the case of regular and fixed-term appointments.[17]

Most organizations have the concept of a permanent appointment but distinguish it from different kinds of other appointments which are not regarded as permanent.[18] In most cases the concepts of probation or probationary appointments and of fixed-term appointments which may or may not be contractual are also recognized.

Permanent appointments

The permanent appointment is fundamentally the type of appointment upon which a career in the international civil service is based, whether the nature of employment is predicated upon status or contract and whether the

[12] Staff Rule 420: Amerasinghe (ed.), 1 op. cit. (note 1 *supra*) p. 118 at p. 145.

[13] Ibid.

[14] Article 4.6 (c) and (d) of the Staff Regulations: Amerasinghe (ed.), 4 op. cit. (note 1 *supra*) p. 185 at p. 225.

[15] Appendix II Article 17, 20, and 21 of the Staff Regulations: See Appendix VI *infra*.

[16] See Personnel Manual Statement No. 2.00 of September 1977, paras. 9–12.

[17] Ibid., paras. 9 and 10.

[18] For the European Communities see Rogalla, *Fonction publique européene* (1982) pp. 81 ff. Plantey, *The International Civil Service: Law and Management* (1981) pp. 150 ff., also deals briefly with the various kinds of appointments. See also Napoletano, *La cessazione del rapporto di lavoro dei funzionari internazionali* (1980) pp. 3 ff.; where the various kinds of appointments are distinguished from a basic point of view.

appointment is described as permanent, regular, or indefinite. In the OECD the permanent appointment is described as 'un engagement pour une durée indéfinie'.[19]

The discussion of the contrast between permanent employment and that which is not permanent has generally been in terms of ensuring independence of the international civil service and security of tenure, though much emphasis has been placed on the fixed-term contract as a means of attracting efficient national civil servants who are prepared to be seconded rather than resign from their civil services, with a view to securing high levels of experience, efficiency, and geographical representation.[20] The fact that permanent appointments can somewhat less easily be terminated than other kinds of appointments has contributed to their being the foundation of independence as a result of the assurance of security of tenure.[21] Thus, in *Gordon*, which was decided in the early days of the UN, the UNAT said of the permanent appointment:

This type of appointment has been used from the inception of the Secretariat to ensure • the stability of the international civil service and to create a genuine body of international civil servants freely selected by the Secretary-General. In accordance with the regulations established by the General Assembly, permanent appointments cannot be terminated except under staff regulations which enumerate precisely the reasons for and the conditions governing the termination of service.[22]

In *Carson*,[23] for example, the UNAT examined very carefully whether the administration of the UN had fulfilled its obligations in regard to keeping the applicant in service upon the abolition of his post and found in favour of the applicant who had a permanent appointment. The view has been expressed that the permanent contract also ensures stability in the international civil service.[24]

In regard to the Council of Europe the Appeals Board of the Council of

[19] See *d'Espinay Saint-Luc*, Decision No. 44, OECD Appeals Board [1974], Recueil des décisions 1 à 62 (1979) p. 124 at p. 125.

[20] See Barnes, 'Tenure and Independence in the United Nations Civil Service', 14 *Journal of International Law and Politics* (1982) p. 767; Miron, 'Tenure, Fixed-Term Appointments and Secondment in the United Nations', ibid. p. 783; Bowett, 'Tenure, Fixed-Term, Secondment from Governments: The United Nations Civil Service and the European Civil Service Compared' ibid. p. 799.

[21] This is implied in the view that an international civil service must protect the interests of all parts of the world community equitably and dispassionately: see James, 'The Evolving Concept of the International Civil Service', in Jordan (ed.), *International Administration: Its Evolution and Contemporary Applications* (1971) p. 51 at pp. 57–8. See also *de Briey*, CJEC Case 25/80 [1981] ECR p. 637 at p. 647, where the CJEC said that the holder of a contract for an indefinite period did not have the same security of employment as permanent officials.

[22] UNAT Judgment No. 29 [1953], JUNAT Nos. 1–70 p. 120 at p. 123.

[23] UNAT Judgment No. 85 [1962], JUNAT Nos. 71–86 p. 112.

[24] Young, *International Civil Service* (1958) p. 148.

Europe made some pertinent remarks about the nature of the various appointments from the point of view of the law that was applicable, emphasizing the special nature of the permanent appointment which in the Council of Europe, among others, is based on a contract of appointment. It said:

There are three categories of staff in the Council of Europe: permanent staff members, temporary staff members and staff employed on an occasional basis, i.e. on a temporary basis or for a specific task. Whereas permanent staff members are appointed to a permanent post in the Organization in accordance with the procedure laid down by the Regulations on Appointments and are accordingly subject to a statutory system, temporary members of staff and staff recruited on an occasional basis are subject primarily to a contractual relationship.[25]

In *Decision No. 9* the Appeals Board of ELDO made a similar comment on the distinction between contracts of indefinite duration which are permanent and those which are for a fixed term, stating that each kind of contract is subject to a different regime regarding duration, dismissal conditions, and calculation of loss of job indemnity, there being no discrimination between the two classes of contract holders if there were distinctions made between them, the only possibility of discrimination being if distinctions were made within the same class of contract holders.[26]

So important is the permanent appointment in the structure of the international civil service that there has been some significant litigation on the right of a staff member to such an appointment. In *El-Naggar*[27] the applicant more or less contended that he should have had a permenent contract with the UN, whereas he was given a fixed-term contract which was not renewed at the date of its expiry. While the UNAT did not deny that in an appropriate situation a staff member holding a fixed-term contract may have a legitimate expectancy of permanent employment which would then give him a right to have a permanent contract, it found that this was not the situation in the case in hand. On the other hand it said, in regard to another argument of the applicant, that basically it was within the discretion of the Secretary General of the UN to select the type of appointment given to a staff member, the fact that the staff member was more or less doing the work of a permanent employee not being a compelling reason for the award of a permanent contract:

The Applicant argues that although his appointment was in terms a fixed-term

---

[25] *Farcot and Others*, Council of Europe Appeals Board, Appeals Nos. 52–75 [1983], Case-Law Digest (1985) p. 84 at p. 93. The reference to a statutory system in relation to permanent appointments does not contradict the provisions of Article 15 of the Staff Regulations that appointments are made by contract: see Appendix VI *infra*. What the tribunal meant obviously was that those staff members who had permanent contracts became subject almost entirely to the Staff Regulations which embodied statutory provisions. Other staff members were governed more by the special provisions of their contracts of employment.

[26] *Decision No. 9*, ELDO Appeals Board [1973], at p. 7.

[27] UNAT Judgment No. 205 [1975], JUNAT Nos. 167–230 p. 345.

appointment it amounted in law to a permanent one governed by the relevant Staff Regulations and Rules. In support of his claim he relies on two arguments, namely that he was repeatedly recommended for a permanent appointment and that he was turned down on invalid and illegal grounds.

The Tribunal observes that under Article 101 of the Charter the power of appointment rests with the Secretary General. The type of appointment to be offered to a staff member is within the discretion of the Secretary-General. Neither the exceptional competence of a staff member nor favourable recommendations for a particular type of appointment by themselves create an entitlement to such an appointment. Furthermore, the Tribunal holds that its competence does not extend to an examination of the reasons for the issue or refusal of a particular type of appointment to a staff member in the absence of entitlements in this regard.[28]

In *Decision No. 12, ESRO/CR/53*[29] the Appeals Board of ESRO took a similar view. The applicant was appointed on a fixed-term contract to a post of a permanent nature. His contract was not renewed. In reply to his argument that he should have had a permanent appointment because he was employed in a permanent position, the tribunal held that, while in general where the post was of a permanent nature permanent contracts were given, sometimes fixed-term contracts may legitimately be signed with the staff member, the permanence of the functions performed not being in direct relation with the indeterminacy or fixed-term nature of the contract signed with the employee.[30] The Appeals Board of the Council of Europe agreed with this view in *X*,[31] where the applicant contended that, though she had a temporary contract, she was entitled to a permanent appointment. The tribunal held that, even after she had obtained medical clearance, she had no such entitlement.

A somewhat different view has been taken by the OASAT. In *Holtzman*[32] the applicant had received a series of temporary contracts from the OAS, the later of which were contracts whose expiry date was established on a month-to-month basis. The applicant contended that, since he was employed in permanent functions, he should have had a permanent contract. The tribunal said:

An analysis of the rules governing the situation in question shows the following: appointments in the Organization of American States are as follows: permanent, temporary, or fixed-term. Permanent appointments are for an indefinite period. Fixed-term appointments are for services that have specified duration and can have a duration of from one to five years. Temporary appointments are to cover special

---

[28] Ibid. at p. 354.

[29] *Decision No. 12, ESRO/CR/53*, ESRO Appeals Board [1971].

[30] Ibid. at p. 2.

[31] Council of Europe Appeals Board, Appeal No. 2 [1971], Case-Law Digest (1985) p. 9. See also *Tyerman*, Council of Europe Appeals Board, Appeal No. 45 [1978], ibid. p. 66.

[32] OASAT Judgment No. 19 [1976].

programs or projects whose duration is less than one year (Rule (104.2 of the Staff Rules in force for the period of the contract concerned). The so-called 'probationary period' of six months, which may be extended at will by the Secretary General, is provided for permanent contracts and fixed-term contracts.

Consequently, if a person is recruited as a temporary employee which status is recognized by the pleadings of the representative of the Secretary General, he cannot be subject to a probationary period, which is provided solely for permanent contracts and fixed-term contracts. Furthermore, the Tribunal is convinced that the Organization of American States intended interpretation and translation services to be a permanent function of the General Secretariat and that consequently such services should be provided by persons belonging to the international career service, but that, nevertheless, even the routine activities of the Organization may, exceptionally and when it is strictly necessary, be provisionally carried out by persons who received a short-term appointment, the term of which will in no case exceed one year, as follows from Article 16 of the General Standards of the Operation of the General Secretariat, Rule 104.3 (c) of the current Staff Rules, and Resolution AG/RES. 124 (III-0/73) approved by the General Assembly on April 14, 1973.

Consequently, this Tribunal holds that the very fact of signing successive contracts for limited periods of time does not exempt the Organization from the obligation to comply with the above-mentioned rules and that when the duration of such contracts is aggregated they come to constitute, for the purposes of the foregoing rules, a single permanent contract.

This Tribunal holds that the first contract was a temporary contract and that it assimilated that special situation which exceptionally the Secretary General may deal with by means of a temporary contract whose duration does not exceed one year, since Staff Rule 104.2 (e) in force for the period of the contract concerned stipulates that temporary contracts will be used for the carrying out of specific programs or projects or for provisionally filling a vacant post for less than one year, and consequently the situation produced by the above-mentioned contract should have ended in September 1973. However, subsequent to that date the complainant continued to accept contracts that were not permanent contracts and continued to perform the duties of that post as set out in the contracts and to receive the emoluments corresponding to those contracts . . .

Thus, in accordance with what this Tribunal has accepted as an indisputable legal tenet, the post held by the complainant is a permanent post and should be filled by an appointment that is also permanent . . .[33]

Thus, this tribunal has held that there are circumstances in which the staff member who holds a non-permanent contract in the OAS may be entitled to a permanent contract, because he is employed in a permanent post.

As was seen in *El-Naggar*, the UNAT indicated that a staff member who has a fixed-term contract may be entitled to have it converted into a permanent appointment, if he had a legitimate expectancy of such an appointment, though in general the kind of appointment to be given an employee is a

---

[33] OASAT Judgment No. 19 [1976] at pp. 13–14.

matter within the discretion of the administrative authority. Thus, even in the
UN an employee may in certain limited circumstances have a right to a permanent contract. The OASAT seems to have gone further than the UNAT in
holding that in certain circumstances where an employee is employed in a permanent post he may for that reason have a right to have a permanent
contract. The UNAT apparently does not take so broad a view.

Temporary appointments

In broad contrast to permanent appointments are non-permanent or temporary appointments. It has been argued[34] that temporary appointments
have certain advantages over permanent contracts, such as enabling easier
dismissal, giving a better contact with the world outside the organization,
permitting a more rapid turnover of personnel and the possibility of
employing on secondment government officials who preferred appointment
for short periods, and enabling the employment of temporary personnel for
temporary or specialist functions. But to counter these there are many
disadvantages: there are fewer candidates; temporary personnel are less independent; the effort required for recruitment is considerably greater; and new
civil servants need some time to make themselves conversant with their
functions. In practice, however, most of the important organizations appoint
only a minority of their staff on the basis of temporary contracts. Exceptionally, the majority of the staff employed in an organization may be on
temporary contracts.[35]

(a) Temporary indefinite appointments

In regard to temporary contracts, the UNAT had some comments to make
about the temporary indefinite appointment which is used in the UN. In
Howrani the tribunal said:

For the purposes of clarity, the Tribunal would like to point out that the so-called
temporary-indefinite contract utilized by the United Nations is *sui generis*. It has no
counterpart in the contractual arrangements of specialized organizations, and is not
encountered in the field of administrative law generally. The amorphous relationship
which this contract establishes is rather more closely akin to the status relationship of

[34] For the arguments for and against temporary appointments see Schermers, 1 *International
Institutional Law* (1972) pp. 209 ff. See also Kay, 'Secondment in the United Nations
Secretariat: An Alternative View', 20 *International Organization* (1966) p. 63; Reymond, 'The
Staffing of the UN Secretariat', 21 *International Organization* (1967) p. 751.
[35] In NATO most staff members are seconded from their national civil services: Jordan, *The
NATO Staff/Secretariat 1952-57* (1967) p. 116. In the IAEA a temporary fixed-term contract is
the rule: *Meyer*, ILOAT Judgment No. 245 [1974] (IAEA) at pp. 4-5.

a national civil servant employed under a 'statut general des fonctionnaires' or 'civil service law' than to a contractual relationship recognizable at public law.[36]

One consequence of this was that the power of the administration to terminate the appointments of staff members holding temporary indefinite contracts was limited by the written law of the organization and also by general principles of law relevant to the interpretation of that written law.[37] There was consequently no power to terminate the contract without showing cause, as was contended in *Howrani*. While this was true, in *Crawford* the UNAT said: '[T]he holder of a temporary-indefinite contract has a problematical chance of continued employment rather than anything approaching a firm expectancy and cannot impute a certainty with respect to contingencies under such a contract.'[38]

In the Council of Europe where there is a contractual arrangement similar to the temporary indefinite contract used in the UN the Appeals Board of the Council of Europe has held that a staff member holding a temporary indefinite appointment has no right to a transfer into a permanent appointment, even though in certain cases he may have legitimate hopes that the privilege may be granted.[39] In some organizations the Staff Regulations specify that this kind of contract gives no guarantee of permanent employment.[40] Further, some organizations have adopted the policy of offering temporary indefinite contracts to staff members whose fixed-term contracts are due to expire in the event that they are renewed,[41] although there may not be an obligation to do so.[42]

The incidence of the indefinite temporary appointment is much reduced now, it appears. In 1951 56.7 per cent of the staff of the UN held temporary indefinite contracts.[43] By 1966 about 70 per cent of the staff of the UN were permanent employees, only some of the remaining 30 per cent being on temporary indefinite contracts.[44] In 1976 the proportion of permanent staff in the UN secretariat dropped to 65 per cent with an increase in the number of staff members holding fixed-term contracts, the number of holders of temporary indefinite contracts being very low.[45]

---

[36] UNAT Judgment No. 4 [1951], JUNAT Nos. 1–70 p. 8 at p. 10.

[37] *Howrani*, ibid. at p. 21.

[38] UNAT Judgment No. 42 [1953], JUNAT Nos. 1–70 p. 207 at p. 209. See also *Howrani*, UNAT Judgment No. 11 [1951], JUNAT Nos. 1–70 p. 30 at p. 31.

[39] *X*, Council of Europe Appeals Board, Appeal No. 2 [1971], Case-Law Digest (1985) p. 9.

[40] Article 5.22 of the NATO Civilian Personnel Regulations.

[41] See *Waliullah*, ILOAT Judgment No. 190 [1972] (UNESCO); Staff Regulations of ESA, Article 9.

[42] See *Decision No. 63*, NATO Appeals Board [1975], Collections of the Decisions 46 to 73 (1976).

[43] See *Howrani*, UNAT Judgment No. 4 [1951], JUNAT Nos. 1–70 p. 8 at p. 10.

[44] See UN Doc. ICSC/CRP.25/Add.1 (1976) at p. 2.

[45] See UN Doc. A/31/30 (1976).

(b) Short-term appointments

Apart from the temporary indefinite appointment, some organizations employ staff on the basis of temporary contracts. These are distinct from indefinite appointments and provide less guarantee to their holders. They may be described as short-term appointments.

(c) Fixed-term appointments

While the temporary indefinite appointment has been decreasing in importance from the point of view of its usage, the fixed-term contract (which is also a kind of temporary contract) has been increasingly resorted to by international organizations. In some organizations the fixed-term contract is the rule.[46] In other organizations they were granted before the structure of the organizations had stabilized and the Staff Regulations had been adopted.[47]

In the case of the fixed-term contract there is a time limit on the duration of the contract which varies according to the rules of the institution concerned and the functions to be performed. Sometimes, but rarely, the contract may be for a term of less than a year.[48] But generally such contracts are treated differently from the ordinary fixed-term contract, as short-term temporary contracts. The fixed-term appointment is a temporary one.[49]

In the early years of international organization fixed-term contracts were widely in use for professional staff because of uncertainty whether international organizations would continue to exist. Later, when the objectives of such organizations began to appear more urgent and capable of realization, the need for continuity and stability resulted in an increase in the number of permanent professional staff members. With the emergence in the 1960s of new States, fixed-term appointments facilitated the recruitment of nationals from these States. But soon career appointments for professionals became more frequent and the number of fixed-term professional appointments in international organizations diminished for a while, so that in 1972 they constituted only 25 per cent of all professional appointments. More recently, because of the growing need for technical specialists in many fields, the fixed-term appointment has become a more importance type of professional appointment in many international organizations and in 1980 constituted 39 per cent of all professional appointments.[50]

In some organizations, such as the UN, appointments to most of the most

---

[46] e.g. the IAEA: see *Meyer*, ILOAT Judgment No. 245 [1974] (IAEA).

[47] See the European Communities: *Mirossevich*, CJEC Case 10/55 [1954–6] ECR p. 333.

[48] See Ranshofen-Wertheimer, *The International Secretariat: A Great Experiment in International Administration* (1945) p. 300. See also Morgenstern, 'Das Dienstrecht des internationalen Arbeitsamtes', in 4 *Recht und System des öffentlichen Dienstes* (1973) p. 68.

[49] *White*, UNAT Judgment No. 46 [1953], JUNAT Nos. 1–70 p. 224 at p. 227.

[50] See Miron, loc. cit. note 20 *supra*.

senior posts are nearly always for a fixed term. But even apart from these instances the fixed-term contract has been used for specific programmes, for example, in technical assistance,[51] even among administrative personnel,[52] or to meet individual needs and the requirements of the service.[53] Fixed-term contracts are used by the European Communities where the permanent appointment is statutory and in the OECD there exists under the Staff Regulations a fixed-term appointment which is made by a statutory instrument in the same way as a permanent appointment. As will be seen, a special body of law has been developed by international administrative tribunals in regard to the renewal of and conversion into permanent contracts of fixed-term contracts.[54]

It has been held by the UNAT that the duration of fixed-term contracts is a matter within the discretion of the administration.[55] It has also been pointed out that the circumstances of the appointment determine the nature of the contract as being one for a fixed term and also establishes the duration of the contract. In *Vargas* it was said by the ILOAT:

A post is of limited duration if the instrument which creates it or controls its length prescribes for it a fixed period, whether long or short. If there is no such prescription, the post is of indefinite duration, whether it is expected to last a long or a short time. Where a post is attached to a project and the length is not specifically prescribed, its length will be the length of the project; if the project is of limited duration, the post likewise will be of limited duration.[56]

Probationary appointments

Generally there is a probationary period attached to permanent appointments and to some temporary appointments, such as fixed-term appointments. Sometimes the period of probation is covered by a probationary contract. Often the period of probation is a special part of the permanent or temporary appointment, whether it is contractual or not. A probationary period or contract is generally provided for in the Staff Regulations and Staff Rules of the organization but it is possible that, in the absence of explicit provision in the written law and in the absence of provision to the contrary,

[51] *de Olagüe*, UNAT Judgment No. 191 [1974] (IMCO), JUNAT Nos. 167–230 p. 188; *De*, ILOAT Judgment No. 267 [1976] (FAO).

[52] *De Sanctis*, ILOAT Judgment No. 251 [1975] (FAO).

[53] *Makris-Batistatos*, UNAT Judgment No. 121 [1968], JUNAT Nos. 114–166 p. 69; *Godchot*, ILOAT Judgment No. 33 [1958] (UNESCO).

[54] See Ch. 37 *infra*.

[55] *Osman*, UNAT Judgment No. 180 [1973], JUNAT Nos. 167–230 p. 93 at p. 105.

[56] ILOAT Judgment No. 515 [1982] (PAHO) at p. 4.

the administrative authority has a discretion to impose a probationary period, and this may be done even on promotion, where the staff member already has an appointment or contract with the organization.[57] Probationary periods or contracts are generally temporary because they must come to an end, even if they may be extended. They come to an end on the termination of probation either by the staff member's being confirmed in his appointment or by his appointment being terminated.

As will be seen, the probationary period of a contract creates a special relationship between the staff member and the organization.[58] The purpose of probation is to give the staff member a preliminary trial period and train him at the same time. The normal duration of probation is one year, though it may be more or less. In the UN it is normally two years.[59] In the case of the Council of Europe the period is generally two years for the higher category of staff and one year for the others.[60] In the WHO the period is normally one year.[61]

Probation is so important from the point of view of both the organization and the staff member that a special body of law governing it has developed.[62] On the other hand, it has been noted that in regard to certain matters, such as the procedure for the termination of the appointment for unsatisfactory performance, the law governing probationary appointments may be no different from that which applies to permanent appointments.[63] This will depend in general on the written law of the organization concerned, though as a general principle of law the observation may be regarded as appropriate.

---

[57] *Ulliac*, Decision No. 49, OECD Appeals Board [1974], Recueil des décisions 1 à 62 (1979) p. 135.

[58] See Ch. 38 *infra*.

[59] Staff Rule 104.12 (a): see Appendix V *infra*.

[60] Article 18 of Appendix II to the Staff Regulations: see Appendix VI *infra*.

[61] Staff Rule 420.4: see Amerasinghe (ed.), 1 op. cit. (note 1 *supra*) p. 118 at p. 145.

[62] See Ch. 38 *infra*.

[63] See *Châtelain*, UNAT Judgment No. 272 [1981] (ICAO), JUNAT Nos. 231–300 p. 411.

CHAPTER THIRTY-FIVE

Termination of Appointments for Unsatisfactory Service

THE termination of an appointment, particularly a permanent, regular, or indefinite appointment, in an international organization, for unsatisfactory service, can be a matter of serious concern to the staff member affected, as it means that a hoped-for career is brought to an end and in some cases, because of the reasons underlying the termination, the staff member may find it difficult to find alternative employment. On the other hand, the international organization by which such a staff member has been employed would certainly like to have the unfettered power to terminate a staff member's appointment for unsatisfactory service in the interest of the efficient working of the organization. Considering the serious implications of a termination of employment of a permanent nature in an international organization, it is surprising that the total number of cases brought by affected staff members before international administrative tribunals in which staff members of international organizations have complained of unlawful termination of their permanent, regular, or indefinite appointments on the grounds of unsatisfactory service is small. There have also been only a few cases brought before tribunals where other kinds of appointments have been terminated.

Termination of an appointment takes place when, as a result of a deliberate act of the administrative authority, the employment relationship is brought to an end. Termination or non-confirmation of probationary appointments will be considered in a following chapter: non-renewal or non-conversion of fixed-term appointments also requires special treatment and will be dealt with in a subsequent chapter. On the other hand, the termination of short-term or temporary contracts, of fixed-term contracts, and also of consultant's contracts before they expire will be included in this chapter as a matter of convenience, together with the termination of permanent or indefinite appointments. What is being examined here is termination on the grounds basically of unsatisfactory service only. There are other grounds on which appointments may be terminated, such as misconduct or abolition of post. These will be the subject of the next chapter.

The termination of a permanent appointment is undoubtedly a matter of a serious nature. Regular or indefinite appointments are also important from this point of view. These may be assimilated for the purpose of the subject-matter of this chapter to permanent appointments. The termination of a short-term or temporary appointment before it expires and the termination of a consultant's contract before it ends may not be on exactly the same footing, for the very reason that such appointments or contracts do not by their nature have permanence, do not involve security of tenure generally, and do not involve the organization and the employee in the development of a career with the organization. However, the premature termination of such appointments or contracts on the grounds of unsatisfactory service can cause concern to the staff member affected and deserves attention. On the other hand, it may be argued that there are likely to be differences between the treatment of the latter type of contract holders and permanent employees, because of the permanence and security of tenure enjoyed by those who have permanent appointments.

As will be seen,[1] tribunals have noted the fact that there are differences between the rules governing the non-confirmation or termination of probationary appointments and those governing the termination of permanent employment, while at the same time it has been recognized that not all the guarantees afforded permanent employees are denied to probationers. In regard to temporary and fixed-term contract holders or consultants tribunals may conceivably not extend exactly the same protection given to permanent appointees. Thus, for example, there may be differences in regard, particularly, to procedural requirements such as the need for review bodies or appraisal reports. However, tribunals have not generally been very specific in pointing out such differences nor have they readily made general statements distinguishing the two situations. Hence, they may be conveniently treated together with the proviso that not all the protection given permanent employees may always be afforded temporary or fixed-term contract holders or consultants. Conversely, where a certain kind of protection is given to the latter kind of contract holders, it will also *a fortiori* be applicable to permanent employees. As for the differences in treatment, it will not be possible to identify these specifically as the analysis proceeds unless they have been dealt with in the cases. Clearly, for example, in regard to remedies there are bound to be differences in treatment depending on the nature of the appointment.

While tribunals have stated that not all the guarantees applicable to permanent employees are available to probationers and there seems to be some rationale behind this approach, there is no reason to deny to permanent employees or even temporary and fixed-term contract holders and consultants some of the protection afforded probationers. Thus, very often it is possible to extend some of the protection given to probationers to the latter

---

[1] See p. 778 *infra*. The problem of termination for unsatisfactory service of permanent appointments has already received attention in Amerasinghe, 'Termination of Permanent Appointments for Unsatisfactory Service in International Administrative Law', 33 ICLQ (1984) p. 859.

kind of employees. Hence, comparisons may be made and analogies drawn from the treatment by tribunals of probationary appointments.

Basic principles

In dealing with the problem of termination of appointments for unsatisfactory service, international tribunals have not always been explicit as to what is their basic approach to the problem. However, the assumptions have been twofold: firstly, that the organization has discretionary authority to terminate such appointments and secondly, that, while the first proposition is true, that discretion is not an unfettered one and holders of appointments have certain rights in regard to termination of their appointments. Both propositions have been found to flow from written sources of law as well as general principles.

In *Saberi* the WBAT stated: 'The determination whether a staff member's performance is satisfactory is a matter within the Respondent's discretion.'[2] In *Suntharalingam* the same tribunal went further. It was of the view that: 'According to Article V, Section 5(b)[3] of the Bank's Articles of Agreement, the President has the power to dismiss staff members if their services are unsatisfactory. The determination whether a staff member's services are unsatisfactory is a matter within the Respondent's discretion and responsibility'.[4] Both cases concerned the termination of permanent appointments but the statements of principle are applicable to the other kinds of appointments too.

As for the second basic principle, the fact that the organization's discretion is not absolute has been referred to in different ways by various tribunals. UNAT has more than once drawn attention to limitations in a general way. Thus, in *Gordon* the UNAT stated:

This type of appointment has been used from the inception of the Secretariat to ensure the stability of the international service and to create a genuine body of international civil servants freely selected by the Secretary-General. In accordance with the Regulations established by the General Assembly, permanent appointments cannot be terminated, except under Staff Regulations which enumerate precisely the reasons for and the conditions governing the termination of service.[5]

The 'substantial' rights of individuals who hold permanent appointments in

---

[2] WBAT Reports [1982], Decision No. 5 at p. 8.

[3] Article V, Section 5(b) states that: 'Subject to the general control of the Executive Directors, he (the President) shall be responsible for the organization, appointment and dismissal of the officers and staff.'

[4] WBAT Reports [1982], Decision No. 6 at p. 9. See also *Durrant-Bell*, WBAT Reports [1985], Decision No. 24 at pp. 8–9; *Broemser*, WBAT Reports [1985], Decision No. 27 at p. 15.

[5] UNAT Judgment No. 29 [1953], JUNAT Nos. 1–70 p. 120 at p. 123.

the UN were adverted to in *Gillman*.[6] In *Restrepo* the UNAT reaffirmed these principles, specially emphasizing some of the procedural requirements for a decision to terminate a permanent appointment: '[I]t is necessary to indicate the provision on which the termination is based and also to indicate explicitly and specifically the facts which constitute grounds for termination; the reasons for termination must be disclosed to the person concerned in the letter informing him of the decision.'[7] The WBAT also has more than once referred to the limitations on the discretionary power to terminate permanent appointments. In *Saberi*, the administration's appraisal of whether services should be terminated was described as final, 'unless the decision constitutes an abuse of discretion, being arbitrary, discriminatory, improperly motivated or carried out in violation of a fair and reasonable procedure.'[8] Invoking general principles of law, in the absence of express stipulation or exclusion in the Staff Regulations and Staff Rules, the Appeals Board of OECD said: '[L]'existence d'une procédure préalable protectrice des droits des agents doit être présumée incluse dans les règlements relatifs au personnel, sauf si elle était exclude par une disposition formelle contraire'.[9] The limitations on the power of termination of a permanent or indefinite contract may be regarded as flowing from the general principle that the exercise of a discretion by an international organization is not unlimited in international administrative law, which was clearly referred to by the WBAT in *de Merode*.[10] That there are limitations on the power to terminate temporary, fixed-term, or consultants' contracts before they end also appears from the cases. The question is how the limitations apply and have been applied in the practice of tribunals in the case of termination of appointments for unsatisfactory service.

In broad terms, tribunals have looked at the limitations on the discretion to terminate employment for unsatisfactory service from the point of view of defects in substance, irregularity of motive or abuse of purpose, and procedural irregularities, though in every case they may not have categorized the situation in exactly these terms. Thus, the law relating to the subject can be conveniently examined in terms of these categories.

---

[6] UNAT Judgment No. 98 [1966], JUNAT Nos. 87–113 p. 98 at p. 107.

[7] UNAT Judgment No. 131 [1969], JUNAT Nos. 114–166 p. 165 at p. 169.

[8] WBAT Reports [1982], Decision No. 5 at p. 8. See also *Suntharalingam*, WBAT Reports [1982], Decision No. 6 at p. 9 for similar language; *Polak*, WBAT Reports [1984], Decision No. 17 at p. 16; *Durrant-Bell*, WBAT Reports [1985], Decision No. 24 at p. 9; *Broemser*, WBAT Reports [1985], Decision No. 27 at p. 15.

[9] *d'Espinay Saint-Luc*, Decision No. 44, OECD Appeals Board [1974], Recueil des décisions 1 à 62 (1979) p. 124 at p. 126. See also *Larcher*, Decision No. 53, OECD Appeals Board [1975], ibid. p. 145, and *de Briey*, CJEC Case 25/80 [1981] ECR p. 637 at p. 645, where misuse of power was referred to as the basis on which a decision to terminate a temporary indefinite contract for unsatisfactory service would be questioned.

[10] WBAT Reports [1981], Decision No. 1 at p. 21.

Substantive irregularities

There are several aspects to substantive irregularity in relation to termination of appointments on the grounds of unsatisfactory service.

(a) Authority of law

Although no case has specifically dealt with the question whether termination of an appointment for unsatisfactory service should be explicitly authorized by a written regulation or rule or other written source of law, if it is to be relied on by an organization (since in almost all international organizations this situation is provided for in the written law) it would be possible to conclude on the basis of some cases pertaining to related fields that dismissal for unsatisfactory service would be permitted by a general principle of law.

Tribunals have stated, particularly in cases of dismissal from permanent employment, that grounds stated in Staff Regulations are exhaustive,[11] but at the same time there is authority for the view that relations connected with employment in public international organizations are governed by the exigencies of the public interest.[12] Just as dismissal of a permanent appointee for ill health was permitted even in the absence of express stipulation, as in the *Monod Case*, because the principles of public law based on the public interest required it, so dismissal of an employee for unsatisfactory service would probably be permitted in the public interest, even in the absence of express stipulation. In the case of the World Bank, for example, the Personnel Manual Statement did not specifically state that the organization might dismiss staff members for unsatisfactory service (which Principle of Staff Employment 7 and Staff Rule 7.01 now does). However, Article V.5(6) of the Articles of Agreement of the Bank gives the President of the Bank power to dismiss staff members. In *Suntharalingam* the WBAT concluded that the provision, which was not explicit, gave the organization power to dismiss staff members, if their services were unsatisfactory.[13]

(b) Competent authority

It is also a recognized principle in international administrative law, as has been seen, that the decision in question should be taken by the person in the

---

[11] See, e.g., *Gordon* etc., UNAT Judgments Nos. 29–37 [1953], JUNAT Nos. 1–70 pp. 120 ff. at pp. 123 etc.

[12] See the *Monod Case*, League of Nations, Official Journal, 1925, p. 1441; *von Lachmüller*, CJEC Cases 43, 45 & 48/59 [1960] ECR p. 463 at p. 473.

[13] WBAT Reports [1982], Decision No. 6 at p. 9. See also *Durrant-Bell*, WBAT Reports [1985], Decision No. 24 at p. 8.

organization authorized to do so.[14] There are only a few cases concerning termination of employment for unsatisfactory service in which this proposition has been discussed. In *Salle*, for instance, which concerned the non-confirmation of a probationary appointment, the applicant contended that the decision not to confirm him had been taken by the Personnel Officer and not by the Director of Personnel, as was required by the relevant Personnel Manual Statement of the World Bank.[15] The implied principle that the competent authority must take the decision of non-confirmation was not contested by the respondent nor did the WBAT discuss it. The tribunal merely referred to the fact that the final decision which had been taken by certain authorities had been brought to the attention of the applicant,[16] thus accepting the position that the proper person authorized to make the decision should do so. The principle was also implemented by the CJEC in *Vecchioli*.[17] The applicant argued that the competent authority had not taken the decision to terminate his employment. The Court found that the proper members of the European Commission empowered by the Staff Regulations to take the decision had done so. On the other hand, since the applicant had not raised the question whether the proposal to terminate his employment had originated from the proper source in accordance with the law, the Court held that it would not raise the issue *proprio motu*, thus conceding that that issue was of relevance to the general issue of whether the competent authority had taken the decision impugned.

In this connection powers may be validly delegated. The maxim *delegatus non potest delegare* does not apply.[18] In the case of the World Bank, for instance, there was no Personnel Manual Statement which dealt with the question of who had the authority to terminate employment generally. The Articles of Agreement in Article V.5(b) give the President of the Bank the power of dismissal. The power of the President to delegate this authority has never been disputed, as the power of the Vice Presidents to whom he delegates power in turn to delegate this authority has never been questioned.

(c) Evaluation

Of some importance in regard to the substance of a decision to terminate

---

[14] See *supra*, Vol. I Ch. 23 pp. 341 ff.

[15] WBAT Reports [1983, Part I], Decision No. 10 at p. 7.

[16] Ibid. at p. 25. For the same principle see also *Bernardi*, CJEC Case 48/70 [1971] ECR p. 175, which did not involve dismissal but concerned the issue as to which authority was competent to make temporary postings; and *Adler*, UNAT Judgment No. 267 [1980], JUNAT Nos. 231–300 p. 352—a probationary appointment.

[17] CJEC Case 101/79 [1980] ECR p. 3069.

[18] See *Algera*, CJEC Cases 7/56 & 3 to 7/57 [1957] ECR p. 39; *Weiss*, ILOAT Judgment No. 4 [1947] (IIIC). Both these cases did not deal with the power to terminate employment for unsatisfactory service.

employment is the attitude of tribunals to the issue of qualifications and evaluation of performance. In general, in several decisions the UNAT has held that the determination of standards of qualification, whether those standards have been met, and whether or not the services of the applicant have been satisfactory were matters for the administration and not the tribunal. In *Vanhove* the UNAT stated, in a case where the administration's determination that the applicant's services were unsatisfactory was being questioned, that: [T]he determination of standards of qualification of the staff is a matter of administration and not one for the Tribunal. The Tribunal can take into consideration only the decision of the Respondent that an official is below the required standard.'[19] In *Restrepo* the UNAT took a similar view[20] and in *Mila* it reaffirmed the principle that it could not substitute its own judgment for that of the Secretary-General concerning the standard of performance or efficiency of the staff members involved.[21]

In some cases in which the applicants attempted to question the finding by the Bank's management that their services were unsatisfactory the WBAT has stated that the determination whether a staff member's performance was satisfactory was a matter within the respondent's discretion.[22] In *Sherif* the ILOAT was of the view that it was not within its jurisdiction nor was it able to investigate the professional value of the applicant's work and his postings, although the applicant had made every effort to try to persuade the tribunal to make that investigation.[23] It was held that the ILO was within its rights in attempting to make use of the applicant's talents in different postings for almost eight years, even though he was ultimately found to be unsatisfactory.

The CJEC made some refinements of this concept accepted by other tribunals. The Court held in *Prakash* that:

The fact that the applicant's practical abilities were judged against the background of a period marked by considerable genuine difficulties might be evidence that they were judged with some strictness. However the Court cannot, without breaking the rules concerning the separation of judicial and administrative powers, describe that strictness as illegal. Indeed, since value-judgments are within the exclusive jurisdiction of the Institution, it was in principle for the Institution to decide upon the degree of severity or indulgence with which it chose to assess any shortcomings of those concerned.[24]

[19] UNAT Judgment No. 14 [1952], JUNAT Nos. 1–70 p. 37 at p. 41.

[20] UNAT Judgment No. 131 [1969], JUNAT Nos. 114–166 p. 165 at p. 170.

[21] UNAT Judgment No. 184 [1974], JUNAT Nos. 167–230 p. 133 at p. 142. See also *Sandys*, UNAT Judgment No. 225 [1977], JUNAT Nos. 167–230 p. 542 at p. 548.

[22] *Saberi*, WBAT Reports [1982], Decision No. 5 at p. 8; *Suntharalingam*, WBAT Reports [1982], Decision No. 6 at p. 9; *Durrant-Bell*, WBAT Reports [1985], Decision No. 24 at pp. 8–9; *Broemser*, WBAT Reports [1985], Decision No. 27 at p. 15.

[23] ILOAT Judgment No. 29 [1957] (ILO) at p. 6.

[24] CJEC Cases 19 & 65/63 [1965] ECR p. 533 at p. 556; this was a case concerning a probationary appointment.

In *Matta* the WBAT went further in making it quite clear that the characterization or definition of unsatisfactory service was also a matter within the discretion of the management or administration. It said:

> The Tribunal has taken notice of the fact that evaluation of an employee's performance may refer not only to the technical competence of the employee but also to his or her character, personality and conduct generally, insofar as they bear on ability to work harmoniously and to good effect with supervisors and other staff members . . . [25]

Thus, the organization has the discretion to decide on the severity of standards to be applied to the evaluation of performance as well as to define the content of the concept of unsatisfactory service. In line with this view in *Waghorn*[26] the ILOAT held that an organization was entitled to characterize an official's services as unsatisfactory if he was insubordinate or showed a lack of team spirit.[27]

(d) Limitations on the power of definition

However, there are in fact certain limitations on this power to set standards, determine qualifications, and characterize unsatisfactory services. One of these relates to the power to define what is meant by unsatisfactory services (characterization). It has been seen that generally unsatisfactory services can cover more than the technical merit or the quality of work of the staff member. However, it would appear that where the characterization of the concept by the administration exceeds the bounds of reasonableness in the context of the Staff Regulations or Staff Rules etc. concerned, the tribunal will intervene to find it impermissible. Thus, the UNAT held in a series of cases that under the UN Staff Regulations 'unsatisfactory services' would only cover professional conduct and not any outside activities, such as pleading the Fifth Amendment during a Congressional inquiry into political beliefs.[28] Similarly, the ILOAT had held that an official's refusal to appear before a Loyalty Board instituted by his own government does not constitute a lack of the highest standards required of an international civil servant.[29]

---

[25] WBAT Reports [1983, Part I], Decision No. 12 at p. 16.

[26] ILOAT Judgment No. 28 [1957] (ILO).

[27] For other decisions of similar tenor see *Decision No. 12, ESA/CR/24*, ESA Appeals Board [1979], and *Decisions Nos. 8 & 10, ESRO/CR/45*, ESRO Appeals Board [1971]. In the latter case the tribunal implied in finding that the reports on the applicant showed that his services were unsatisfactory that the lack of professional qualifications was a relevant factor to be considered in the evaluation of performance.

[28] *Gordon, Svenchansky*, etc., UNAT Judgments Nos. 29–36 [1953], JUNAT Nos. 1–70 pp. 120 ff. These cases were, however, decided on the basis that the applicants had been dismissed for serious misconduct.

[29] *Froma*, ILOAT Judgment No. 22 [1955] (UNESCO); *Pankey*, ILOAT Judgment No. 23 [1955] (UNESCO); *Van Gelder*, ILOAT Judgment No. 24 [1955] (UNESCO).

The same apparently goes for refusal to obey a court's subpoena.[30] Clearly, if the Regulations and Rules (or the equivalent) of an organization define or lay down standards for the determination of 'unsatisfactory services', a tribunal will not question such definition or standards, unless, perhaps, they are totally unreasonable. It is only where the Regulations and Rules (or the equivalent) are silent that a tribunal will apply the test of reasonableness.

(e) Error of law

Closely connected with the kind of violation discussed in the previous section is the case where the reason given for the termination of service is not permissible in law. This generally occurs as a result of explicit statements in the written law of the organization. In *Gregorio*[31] the applicant alleged that she had been dismissed for failure to respond to the Bank's efforts and that this was not a valid ground for termination of services. The WBAT held that the applicant's failure to respond to the Bank's efforts was merely an aspect of a broader state of affairs which amounted to unsatisfactory service and had not been used *per se* as a ground for dismissal. The tribunal did not deny that, had the applicant been dismissed solely because of her failure to respond to the Bank's efforts, this would have been an inadequate ground for dismissal whether by itself or in relation to unsatisfactory service. There were two rules accepted here by the WBAT. The first is the rule that it would be improper to use as a ground for dismissal a basis which is not permitted in law, in this case by the written law. The second is the rule that it is improper to base a dismissal for unsatisfactory services solely on certain inadequate grounds which in any case would have been an inadequate basis for dismissal. There is no reason why both rules should not be generally accepted.

A different kind of error of law may occur where the respondent fails to take action required of it by the written law or by other applicable principles of law and, hence, not only causes the applicant to perform unsatisfactorily but also characterizes the applicant's performance as unsatisfactory with the result that he is dismissed for unsatisfactory service. The failure of the respondent to fulfil its obligations cannot then be used an an excuse for finding the applicant's services unsatisfactory. In *Polak*[32] the applicant argued that this was what happened in his case. The respondent had chosen to adopt the mechanism of a special programme provided by its Personnel Manual and involving continuous review and evaluation for the purpose of providing advice and guidance with a view to improving the applicant's performance. The applicant contended that no continuous review as envisaged

---

[30] *Leff*, ILOAT Judgment No. 15 [1954] (UNESCO).
[31] WBAT Reports [1983, Part II], Decision No. 14 at p. 14.
[32] WBAT Reports [1984], Decision No. 17: see particularly p. 13.

by the Personnel Manual had been provided. The WBAT did not deny the relevance of the applicant's argument but found that the continuous review had been effectively provided. Firstly, the tribunal did not deny that the commission of the kind of error of law alleged would have affected the legality of the decision to separate the applicant from the respondent's services and secondly, in approaching the issue of the rights of the applicant and the obligations of the respondent it said that the terms of the written law could not be interpreted so literally as to put the respondent in a strait-jacket and deprive it of the right to exercise discretion in the implementation of the requirements of the written law. It is important that what the tribunal required in this respect was a meaningful application of the provisions of the written law with room for the exercise of discretion in the treatment of different cases according to their own circumstances.[33]

In *Decision No. 70*[34] the Appeals Board of NATO held that a decision to terminate the applicant's employment on the ground that his services were unsatisfactory which was based on his failure to acquire new skills when his job description was changed was invalid. It was illegal that acquisition of new skills should have been required upon such a change of job description. There was, thus, an error of law committed.

(f) Mistaken conclusion

In some cases the assessment of performance has not been considered final by the tribunal and it has proceeded to investigate in great detail the facts upon which the assessment of performance by the administration or management had been based.[35] Thus, in *Willame*[36] the CJEC actually examined pieces of the applicant's work in coming to the conclusion that work which only contained paraphrases of extracts from another document, or was largely made up of information supplied by other departments, was not adequate to demonstrate that its author was capable of performing the duties incumbent upon a head of division. In *Prakash*,[37] a case concerning probation, the CJEC said: '[I]t is for the Court to check whether the facts taken into account by the Establishment Board are materially accurate and logically

---

[33] See also *Durrant-Bell*, WBAT Reports [1985], Decision No. 24.

[34] *Decision No. 70*, NATO Appeals Board [1976], Collection of the Decisions 46 to 73 (1976).

[35] See *Mila*, UNAT Judgment No. 184 [1974], JUNAT Nos. 167–230 p. 133; *Prasad*, ILOAT Judgment No. 90 [1965] (FAO); *Prakash* (probation); CJEC Cases 19 & 65/63 [1965] ECR p. 533. In *Durrant-Bell*, WBAT Reports [1985], Decision No. 24, and *Broemser*, WBAT Reports [1985], Decision No. 27, the WBAT examined the assessment made in relation to the conclusion reached in order to show that the conclusion was reasonable, so that it could not be argued that the dismissal was influenced by prejudice.

[36] CJEC Case 12/66 [1967] ECR p. 153.

[37] CJEC Cases 19 & 65/63 [1965] ECR p. 533.

compatible with that judgment (on the plaintiff's services).'[38] The principle that obviously wrong conclusions must not be drawn from the evidence in the dossier was also accepted in *Decision No. 171*[39] by the Appeals Board of NATO, though in that case there was found to be no manifest error in the conclusions reached in regard to the quality of the applicant's service when his permanent appointment was terminated for unsatisfactory service.[40]

In *Wollast*[41] the CJEC dealt with a case concerning the termination of a temporary contractual appointment before it expired. The Court found that the conclusions drawn from the facts that the applicant, a nurse, had been guilty of misconduct were totally erroneous and quashed the decision to terminate her contract. *Weighardt*[42] provided clear evidence of what tribunals can do in limiting the power of the organization to decide on the unsatisfactory nature of services. While the case concerned reclassification, the Court held that earlier assessments which could have made unreasonable the decision that the applicant's services were unsatisfactory were irrelevant in the circumstances of the case. It did not deny that the decision might have been reviewed on the grounds of unreasonableness, if the earlier assessments had been regarded as relevant.[43]

These cases support the proposition that tribunals may determine that a finding by the organization that a staff member's services are unsatisfactory must be upset on the grounds that the decision was unreasonable in relation to the facts on which it was based, that is, where obviously wrong conclusions were drawn from the evidence. Tribunals may make a detailed examination of the facts for this purpose.

There is in addition an initial problem, namely whether the organization or the tribunal may choose or characterize the facts upon which the decision is based. This problem will be discussed below but it is clear that, even where the organization characterizes the facts, the tribunal can determine the reasonableness of the decision that services were unsatisfactory in relation to the facts characterized.

---

[38] Ibid. at pp. 551. The Court held in this case that the administrative authority had not arrived at an erroneous conclusion. In *Vecchioli*, CJEC Case 101/79 [1980] ECR p. 3069, the CJEC found that the administrative authority's conclusions were not erroneous.

[39] *Decision No. 171*, NATO Appeals Board [1984], Collection of the Decisions 135 to 171 (1984).

[40] See also *Polak*, WBAT Reports [1984], Decision No. 17; and *Ido*, ILOAT Judgment No. 588 [1983] (WHO), which concerned a short-term contract.

[41] CJEC Case 18/63 [1964] ECR p. 85.

[42] CJEC Case 11/64 [1965] ECR p. 285. See also *Ghaffar*, ILOAT Judgment No. 320 [1977] (WHO), which was a case concerning the non-confirmation of a probationary appointment.

[43] See the argument of the Advocate General: *Weighardt*, CJEC Case 11/64 [1965] ECR p. 285 at p. 301. See also two cases concerning probationary appointments in which the facts were examined but it was found that the conclusions drawn about the applicant's work were not unreasonable in terms of the facts in the dossier: *Crapon de Caprona*, ILOAT Judgment No. 112 [1967] (WHO); *Kersaudy*, ILOAT Judgment No. 152 [1970] (FAO).

(g) *Irrelevant facts*

In the taking of a decision to terminate employment for unsatisfactory service facts which are related to the decision may be omitted from consideration, they may be considered but be erroneous, or they may be considered but be irrelevant. The power of tribunals to review decisions to terminate employment for unsatisfactory service in the first two cases will be examined further below.

As to the third category, where the administration or management has characterized the facts it is going to consider in taking a decision and has based its decision on those facts, a tribunal may intervene to find that the decision is invalid. The question is whether an administration or management may, especially where the relevant Regulation or Rules are silent, take into account any facts it chooses in taking decisions. In cases of termination of appointments on the ground of unsatisfactory service there may be situations in which a tribunal will hold that the administration or management has taken into consideration facts which it should not have done in deciding that the services of the applicant were unsatisfactory. Apart from the case where facts are wrongly characterized, because the definition of unsatisfactory services is unreasonable, tribunals may, although examples are not easy to find, hold that even though a definition of unsatisfactory services may be reasonable, the facts considered cannot reasonably be regarded as relevant in determining whether the elements of the definition are present. In *de Briey*,[44] a case concerning the termination of a temporary indefinite contract for incompetence or unsatisfactory service, the CJEC held that the entire career of the applicant, including the period before he was given a warning, was relevant to the decision on incompetence, so that it could not be argued that taking into account the applicant's performance before he was warned amounted to a consideration of irrelevant facts.

(h) *Omission of facts*

Tribunals have found that, where facts which a tribunal considers relevant to a decision relating to the quality of service have not been taken into consideration, the decision taken would be tainted. In *Mila*,[45] since the Appointment and Promotion Panel of the UN had to consider the proposal to terminate the applicant's employment without the benefit of a proper investigation and appraisal of the situation by the head of the department, as required by the relevant administrative circular, after the staff member had made a written statement in explanation and rebuttal of a periodic report, the

---

[44] CJEC Case 25/80 [1981] ECR p. 637. See also *Vecchioli*, CJEC Case 101/79 [1980] ECR p. 3069.
[45] UNAT Judgment No. 184 [1974], JUNAT Nos. 167–230 p. 133.

conclusion that the applicant's services were unsatisfactory was based on a report that did not contain all the facts and was an incomplete document and therefore was invalid.[46] In *Polak*[47] the applicant alleged that some favourable assessments of his supervisors had not been taken into account but the WBAT found that this was not the case and that the final evaluation was a balanced appraisal.[48]

In *Willame*[49] the applicant, who had not been retained in employment during the integration procedure because of unsatisfactory service, complained that the evidence of one of his chief supervisors had not been heard when the evidence of others had been taken into account. The CJEC held that this was an irregularity which vitiated the decision taken. Although the defect was referred to as one of procedure, it is strictly one of substance as a result of which facts were omitted. In the same case the applicant had failed, until after the integration procedure had ended, to inform the Establishment Board of the existence of some other pieces of his work which might have influenced its decision. The CJEC rejected the applicant's contention that the decision of the Board was based on incomplete information, as far as this element was concerned. This finding supports the proposition that where the applicant is responsible for the incompleteness of the facts considered, the decision cannot be faulted.

A question which has not been discussed in cases of termination of appointments for unsatisfactory service is whether the incompleteness of the facts must be such that had they been complete the decision would have been different. In a case concerning a probationary appointment, however, it was stated in general terms that 'essential' facts had to be left out of consideration for the decision to be invalid.[50] Since the general principle is that essential facts must be omitted from consideration in order that the decision taken be tainted, there is no reason why that principle should not be applicable to the determination that services are unsatisfactory.

(i) Error of fact

A more common situation than the one discussed above is where facts on which a decision is based are erroneous. There are some decisions in which

---

[46] See also *Ido*, ILOAT Judgment No. 588 [1983] (WHO). This was a case where a short-term appointment was not renewed. In *Sandys*, UNAT Judgment No. 225 [1977], JUNAT Nos. 167–230 p. 542, the principle that inadequate information could result in a tainted decision was admitted but it was found by the tribunal that the Appointment and Promotion Board had all the relevant material for reaching a decision.

[47] WBAT Reports [1984], Decision No. 17 at p. 15.

[48] See also *Vecchioli*, CJEC Case 101/79 [1980] ECR p. 3069.

[49] CJEC Case 12/66 [1967] ECR p. 153.

[50] See *Kersaudy*, ILOAT Judgment No. 152 [1970] (FAO) at p. 5.

appointments have been terminated for unsatisfactory service where the problem of error of fact has been dealt with.

In *Gillman*[51] the UNAT found that the statutory Working Group reached its conclusions on the basis of erroneous information and that the Secretary-General relied on these conclusions when he took the decision to dismiss the applicant. The tribunal found that the Working Group's findings about the applicant's performance were contradicted by documents available to the Working Group and by the oral evidence received by the tribunal. In reviewing the applicant's sick-leave record and subsequent work, the Working Group had not taken into account the effects of an accident in which the applicant had been involved while on official business. The tribunal held that the decision to dismiss was based on erroneous information. In this case facts were not merely unknown to the administration but they had been deliberately ignored by it. In both instances the final decisions would be invalid.[52] In *Decision No. 155*,[53] where a short-term appointment was prematurely terminated for unsatisfactory service, it was held by the Appeals Board of NATO that the decision was vitiated by error of fact.[54]

In the case of error of fact, as has been said in *Gale*, a case concerning probation, the exercise of the power to dismiss for unsatisfactory service must be based on 'materially incorrect facts'.[55] Thus, the facts in respect of which there is error must be material to the decision to terminate.

(j) Irregularities in general

In *Durrant-Bell*[56] the WBAT found that, while the decision that the services of the applicant were unsatisfactory was supported by the facts and was not tainted with prejudice, there were certain inconsistencies and discrepancies in the treatment of her case by the respondent. First, the promotion of the applicant was originally stated to have been based on her improving performance and ability to handle increased responsibilities, while later it was said to have been motivated by the desire to stimulate her performance. Second, though in the performance review for 1981 considerable improvement had been noted in the applicant's performance, soon after there was a sudden change of attitude towards her performance. Third, at first the

---

[51] UNAT Judgment No. 98 [1966], JUNAT Nos. 87–113 p. 98.

[52] In *Decision No. 171*, NATO Appeals Board [1984], Collection of the Decisions 135 to 171 (1984), no error of fact was found. See also *Ido*, ILOAT Judgment No. 588 [1983] (WHO), a case concerning a short-term appointment where no error of fact was found.

[53] *Decision No. 155*, NATO Appeals Board [1983], Collection of the Decisions 135 to 171 (1984).

[54] See also *Luhleich*, CJEC Case 68/63 [1965] ECR p. 581, a case concerning probation, where facts were found to be inaccurate and incomplete.

[55] ILOAT Judgment No. 84 [1965] (UNESCO) at p. 3.

[56] WBAT Reports [1985], Decision No. 24 at pp. 13 ff.

Division Chief of another division did not consider an incident at the print shop as being important or that it should be held against the applicant, while the applicant's Division Chief found in that incident and another incident that took place at the print shop enough reason to have her transferred from his division. These discrepancies and inconsistencies were considered to have left the applicant without the indispensable clarity as to the exact position of the respondent concerning her worthiness, entitlement to promotion on the basis of merit and of performance, and her right accurately to assess the prospects of her career with the respondent. Hence, the applicant was awarded compensation.

The case illustrates that there can be special irregularities. These may not require that the decision be annulled but that only compensation be awarded.

Irregularity of motive

Détournement de pouvoir covers not only malice, ill will, and discrimination but also other irregular motives. Also, as the cases dealing with ill will show, it is not only where the written law expressly prohibits irregular motives[57] that tribunals will intervene but also where such prohibition could be implied in accordance with general principles of law. No doubt the general principles discussed earlier concerning *détournement de pouvoir* apply but there are a few cases on termination for unsatisfactory service.

(a) Détournement de procédure

Détournement de procédure is a special case of *détournement de pouvoir*. In *Miss X*[58] the argument was advanced that the applicant was dismissed for unsatisfactory services, when, if she had been dismissed for reasons of ill health, she could have been subjected to a different procedure and entitled to a disability pension. She could not prove her contention but the UNAT did not reject the argument that *détournement de procédure*, if proved, would have been a valid ground for questioning the termination decision.[59]

However, where there are grounds for taking a decision on either of two bases, there is no *détournement de procédure* where one of those bases is used for the decision rather than the other. In *Decision No. 29*[60] of the

---

[57] See *Lassalle*, CJEC Case 15/63 (1964) ECR p. 31, which did not concern termination for unsatisfactory service, and *supra*, Vol. I Ch. 21 pp. 275 ff.

[58] UNAT Judgement No. 81 [1960], JUNAT Nos. 71–86 p. 67.

[59] See also *Fiddelaar*, CJEC Case 44/59 [1960] ECR p. 535, a case concerning a temporary contractual appointment, where *détournement de procédure* was held not to have been proved.

[60] *Decision No. 29*, OEEC Appeals Board [1957], Recueil des décisions 1 à 62 (1979) p. 80. For a similar decision see *Angelopoulos*, Decision No. 57, OECD Appeals Board [1976], ibid. p. 157. See also *Vecchioli*, CJEC Case 101/79 [1980] ECR p. 3069.

Appeals Board of OEEC it was held that the real reason given for the dismissal, namely unsatisfactory service, was supported by the facts, and that therefore it could not be argued that facts of a disciplinary nature discovered just before the dismissal were the true cause of dismissal.

(b) Extraneous motives

There are cases in which ill will, malice, or extraneous motives have been adduced as a reason for the decision to terminate a permanent appointment for unsatisfactory service, but always the applicant has failed to prove his case. In all these cases the tribunal has made an extensive inquiry into the facts. In *Matta*[61] the WBAT was presented with an allegation of discriminatory treatment based on the applicant's age. The tribunal found that the record did not substantiate the claim and that, on the other hand, the applicant had been given favourable special treatment because of her age, which was not impermissible discrimination.[62] In *Nelson*[63] the UNAT held that it was unable to infer from the fact that the respondent relied on unsatisfactory services instead of an unauthorized outside employment as a ground for termination that the decision was vitiated by extraneous motives. In this case there was evidence of unsatisfactory service as well as of outside employment. In *Sherif*[64] the ILOAT held that the evidence did not show that there was political hostility towards the applicant, so that abuse of authority had not been proved.[65] In *Gregorio*[66] the WBAT found that there was no prejudice or improper motive involved in the dismissal of the applicant for unsatisfactory service. This was so, even though there was a sudden change of attitude on the part of the applicant's immediate supervisor, since there was other evidence to support the conclusion reached.

The general principle that there must be a causal link between the irregular motive and the decision attacked has been applied by tribunals. Thus, in a

---

[61] WBAT Reports [1983, Part I], Decision No. 12.

[62] See also *Suntharalingam*, WBAT Reports [1982], Decision No. 6 at p. 10; *Durrant-Bell*, WBAT Reports [1985], Decision No. 24; *Broemser*, WBAT Reports [1985], Decision No. 27. In all these cases prejudice or ill will was not found.

[63] UNAT Judgment No. 157 [1972], JUNAT Nos. 114–166 p. 348. See also *De Shields*, UNAT Judgment No. 309 [1983], where no prejudice or ill-will was found.

[64] ILOAT Judgment No. 29 [1957] (ILO).

[65] In *Willame*, CJEC Case 12/66 [1967] ECR p. 153, also no abuse of purpose was found.

[66] WBAT Reports [1983, Part II], Decision No. 14. See also *Decision No. 12, ESA/CR/24*, ESA Appeals Board [1979], where the tribunal found that there was no evidence that the applicant's membership of the Staff Association or his health had influenced the decision to terminate his employment for unsatisfactory service; and *Decision Nos. 8 & 10, ESRO/CR/45*, ESRO Appeals Board [1971]. In *Fayemiwo*, UNAT Judgment No. 246 [1979], JUNAT Nos. 231–300 p. 161, the UNAT found that the applicant's Staff Association activities did not influence the decision to terminate his employment and that, therefore, no prejudice or improper motive had been proved.

case involving the termination of a short-term contractual appointment, the UNAT said: 'Even if there had been animosity on the part of this supervisor, the Tribunal considers that no proof has been adduced to show that such animosity could have motivated the termination.'[67] In *Ido*[68] the ILOAT seems to have had some evidence of animosity but to have held that this animosity did not influence the decision to terminate the applicant's short-term appointment.

In regard to the question of proof of *détournement de pouvoir*, while there can be no doubt that the general principles are applicable, very few cases concerning termination of employment for unsatisfactory service have dealt with the issue. In *Suntharalingam* the WBAT held that the applicant had failed to prove prejudice on the part of the administrative authority in terminating his permanent appointment on the ground of unsatisfactory service. It emerged from that case that it was inadequate to show merely that there was irritation and impatience on the part of a supervisor, because this might not necessarily imply harrassment and discrimination.[69]

(c) *Means not related to the objectives*

In *Gregorio*[70] the argument was advanced that termination of a permanent appointment was too severe a measure to be applied in the case of the applicant because what had been characterized as unsatisfactory service in her case was not serious enough to deserve such a penalty. The WBAT held that, while the principle of proportionality should be observed in general, in the applicant's case the discipline of dismissal had not been imposed for a mere failure to respond to the Bank's efforts but because of her prior unsatisfactory service, so that it was not out of proportion to the quality of her service. A similar argument based on the disproportion of the penalty of termination was adduced in *Mila*.[71] The UNAT held that the applicant had not proved his case.

It is difficult to see how the principle of proportionality can be applied to termination for unsatisfactory service. In general when service is unsatisfactory the discipline of termination would be reasonably related to the delinquency. There cannot be degrees of failure to satisfy once the assessment is made that the service is unsatisfactory. It is really the assessment that may be questioned and this could only be done on the ground of substantive irregularity, not *détournement de pouvoir*.

67 *Ball*, UNAT Judgment No. 60 [1955], JUNAT Nos. 1–70 p. 321 at p. 325.
68 ILOAT Judgment No. 588 [1983] (WHO).
69 WBAT Reports [1982], Decision No. 6 at p. 10.
70 WBAT Reports [1983, Part II], Decision No. 14.
71 UNAT Judgment No. 204 [1975], JUNAT Nos. 167–230 p. 333. See also *Angelopoulos*, Decision No. 57, OECD Appeals Board [1976], Recueil des décisions 1 à 62 (1979) p. 157.

In *Angelopoulos*[72] the applicant contended that the rule *non bis in idem* or the rule of double jeopardy had been infringed, because he had first been transferred on account of an unsatisfactory relationship with his supervisor and then dismissed for unsatisfactory services. The Appeals Board of OECD held that he had been dismissed from service because of unsatisfactory relationships with his supervisors both before and after the transfer and that the reasons for the dismissal from service did not result in a violation of the rule against double jeopardy. It is difficult to see how the rule against double jeopardy can be invoked in cases of dismissal for unsatisfactory service.

Procedural irregularity

Generally, where a procedure is specified in the relevant Staff Regulations and Staff Rules, this procedure must be followed. Where the Regulations and Rules are silent, tribunals have had recourse to general principles of law to infer what is required by procedural due process. Thus, in *Gillman*[73] the UNAT found that the Staff Regulations and Staff Rules of the UN did not specify the particular procedure to be followed in terminating a permanent appointment for unsatisfactory service. Nevertheless, the tribunal did examine the question whether a complete and fair procedure had been followed before the action was taken. This was done on the basis of general principles of law. In *Suntharalingam*[74] the applicant contended that the respondent had failed to establish termination procedures, among other things, and therefore deprived him of the procedural fairness to which he was entitled. The tribunal noted that the absence of a formal statement of the procedure to be utilized when terminating employment may have caused some uncertainty on the part of staff members concerning their procedural rights but held that the procedure actually followed by the respondent reflected the basic requirements of due process in termination cases, thus upholding the position that due process is required even in the absence of explicit delineation in the relevant Regulations and Rules. In *Châtelain*[75] the UNAT equated the rules relating to the procedure in ICAO for assessment of performance in cases of appointments such as permanent appointments with the rules relating to the assessment of performance in cases of probationary

[72] Decision No. 57, OECD Appeals Board [1976], ibid.

[73] UNAT Judgment No. 98 [1966], JUNAT Nos. 87–113 p. 98. See also *Sood*, UNAT Judgment No. 195 [1975], JUNAT Nos. 167–230 p. 235, which was a case concerning the premature termination for unsatisfactory service of a fixed-term contract; *Berubé*, UNAT Judgment No. 280 [1981] (ICAO), JUNAT Nos. 231–300 p. 500; and *Angelopoulos*, Decision No. 57, OECD Appeals Board [1976], Recueil des décisions 1 à 62 (1979) p. 157.

[74] WBAT Reports [1982], Decision No. 6 at pp. 7 and 10–11.

[75] UNAT Judgment No. 272 [1981] (ICAO), JUNAT Nos. 231–300 p. 411. See also *Nelson*, UNAT Judgment No. 157 [1972], JUNAT Nos. 114–166 p. 348.

appointments.[76] Though this may not be the case in all organizations, the case showed that there are general principles applicable to the procedure relating to the assessment of performance in general.

Where tribunals have had to implement written rules, the decisions may shed light on how such rules have been interpreted, possibly in terms of general notions of due process. Where the texts are silent, the decisions of tribunals would provide guidance on what general principles of law are applicable. There are many aspects of procedural due process which will be examined below. The governing principle seems to be that the procedure followed must be complete, fair, and reasonable.[77] Tribunals generally insist on a fair and complete procedure or on due process of law, whether the procedure is reflected in the written law or not. In *Gregorio*[78] the WBAT referred to the requirement that there be no arbitrariness in the procedure followed. There the applicant was offered a reassignment option which was subsequently withdrawn before she was dismissed. It was alleged that the procedure followed in the withdrawal of the offer was improper. The tribunal found that delays were caused by the applicant and not by the respondent and therefore the withdrawal of the option in the face of those delays was not arbitrary. This case shows that procedures are important even in matters of detail and even where there is no written law governing them. In *Broemser* the WBAT pointed out:

The Tribunal must observe that the Bank is bound to adhere to established procedures and that in the present case, the procedure followed by the Bank represents not only a clear deviation from the Staff Evaluation Procedure in PMS 4.01 but is also a form of practice which has not been embodied in any staff rule or otherwise made a matter of public record. There is therefore some justification for the Applicant's complaints.[79]

In this case the procedure of the written law had not been followed, thus resulting in a violation of due process.

(a) Appraisal reports

In *Decision No. 171*[80] of the Appeals Board of NATO the question of performance reports was discussed in regard to the dismissal for unsatisfactory service of a permanent appointee. It was held that the written law did not

---

[76] In *Vecchioli*, CJEC Case 101/79 [1980] ECR p. 3069, it was argued that a certain official should not have taken part in the decision taken to dismiss the applicant if the Staff Regulations had been properly followed, the result being that there had been a misuse of powers. The Court rejected the argument, holding that the written law had not been violated.

[77] See *Gillman*, UNAT Judgment No. 98 [1966], JUNAT Nos. 87–113 p. 98 at p. 107.

[78] WBAT Reports [1983, Part II], Decision No. 14 at p. 19.

[79] WBAT Reports [1985], Decision No. 27 at pp. 20–1.

[80] *Decision No. 171*, NATO Appeals Board [1984], Collection of the Decisions 135 to 171 (1984).

prohibit calling for special performance reports in order to assess professional capabilities and that such reports when properly completed would negate the effect of any procedural irregularities connected with earlier reports, because the latter would have ceased to have any bearing on the decision taken. In *Fayemiwo* the UNAT said that an appraisal of the applicant's rebuttal of the final periodic report should have been done, because it was important that justice not only be done but be seen to be done; but that, since the applicant had reduced the possibility by his evasion tactics, the omission was not to be taken into account.[81] Performance and appraisal reports have been considered in connection with cases of non-confirmation of probationary appointments and the view generally expressed in those cases is that these reports must be complete and done, especially if the written rules require them.[82] Where an appraisal report is required in the case of dismissal for unsatisfactory service of an employee, there is no reason why the same principle should not be applicable.

The rule that the proper authority should prepare the appraisal report was adverted to by the Appeals Board of ESRO in *Decisions Nos. 8 & 10, ESRO/CR/45*.[83] While the validity of the rule was implicitly conceded by the tribunal, it held that the report had been prepared by the Director of the organization who was the applicant's direct supervisor and that this was proper. In *Broemser*[84] the WBAT found that the applicant's final evaluation, though performed by the proper officer, did not have the written input from the applicant's other supervisors, as was required by the written law of the organization. This, the tribunal held, was a culpable violation of the law.[85]

(b) Opportunity to defend

The rule that the applicant must have an opportunity to defend himself properly has been applied most frequently in disciplinary cases.[86] However, it has also been applied in cases of termination for non-disciplinary reasons.[87] In *Bertrand*,[88] a case concerning termination of a temporary appointment, but not for unsatisfactory service, a secret letter was not shown to the applicant so that she could not defend herself properly against accusations of

---

[81] UNAT Judgment No. 246 [1979], JUNAT Nos. 231–300 p. 161.

[82] See, e.g., *Buranavanichkit*, WBAT Reports [1982], Decision No. 7; *Luhleich*, CJEC Case 68/63 [1965] ECR p. 581.

[83] *Decisions Nos. 8 & 10, ESRO/CR/45*, ESRO Appeal Board [1971].

[84] WBAT Reports [1985], Decision No. 27.

[85] In *Châtelain*, UNAT Judgment No. 272 [1981] (ICAO), JUNAT Nos. 231–300 p. 414, it was held that the proper procedure relating to appraisal reports had not been followed.

[86] See, e.g., *Alvis*, CJEC Case 32/62 [1963] ECR p. 49.

[87] See, e.g., *Keeney*, UNAT Judgment No. 6 [1951], JUNAT Nos. 1–70 p. 24; *Gale*, ILOAT Judgment No. 84 [1965] (UNESCO).

[88] UNAT Judgment No. 59 [1955], JUNAT Nos. 1–70 p. 312.

wartime collaboration. The UNAT held that at least the gist of the letter should have been revealed to the applicant so that she knew in advance the precise nature of the accusations which she had to meet. In *Suntharalingam* the WBAT clearly thought that the principle was applicable to termination for unsatisfactory service of a permanent appointment when it said: 'As to the possibility of effectively defending himself in the event of termination, the Tribunal notes that when the Applicant exercised his right of appeal he received a complete copy of his AER and thus had full knowledge of the facts necessary to argue his case properly.'[89] The rule implies, as will be seen from the above quotation, that the applicant must be in a position to have full knowledge of the facts. The rule was applied in two cases decided by the Appeals Board of OECD[90] in which the tribunal quashed the decisions to terminate a permanent appointment for unsatisfactory service, because the applicant had not been heard. In *Coll*[91] the UNAT held that a decision prematurely to terminate for unsatisfactory service a fixed-term contract was irregular, because the applicant had not been given an opportunity to be heard. The right of defence was also referred to in *Vecchioli*[92] and *de Briey*,[93] though in both cases the CJEC held that the right had been respected.

In *Châtelain*[94] and *Berubé*[95] the UNAT dealt with the obligation of the organization to give the applicant an opportunity to rebut the appraisal report or reports on which was based the decision that his services were unsatisfactory. In the former case the report was not completed and contained confidential information. It was not transmitted to the applicant. It was held that the applicant's right of defence had been violated, because he had not been given an opportunity of rebutting the information contained in the appraisal report. In the latter case, however, while two reports on the applicant were not shown him, it was clear that he was aware of the facts contained in them from oral communications and other sources. Hence, it was held that there was no procedural irregularity that affected the validity of the decision that his services were unsatisfactory, although the procedural irregularity had to be compensated.

The principle that the applicant must have an opportunity to defend himself has been applied in cases concerning the non-confirmation of probationary appointments.[96] Thus, there is good reason why it should be applied where appointments are terminated for unsatisfactory service.

[89] WBAT Reports [1982], Decision No. 6 at p. 13.
[90] *d'Espinay-Saint-Luc*, Decision No. 44, OECD Appeals Board [1974], Recueil des décisions 1 à 62 (1979) p. 124; *Larcher*, Decision No. 53, OECD Appeals Board [1975], ibid. p. 145.
[91] UNAT Judgment No. 113 [1967] (ICAO), JUNAT Nos. 87–113 p. 276.
[92] CJEC Case 101/79 [1980] ECR p. 3069.
[93] CJEC Case 25/80 [1981] ECR p. 637.
[94] UNAT Judgment No. 272 [1981] (ICAO), JUNAT Nos. 231–300 p. 411.
[95] UNAT Judgment No. 280 [1981] (ICAO), JUNAT Nos. 231–300 p. 500.
[96] See *Buranavanichkit*, WBAT Reports [1982], Decision No. 7; and *Kissaun*, ILOAT Judgment No. 69 [1964] (WHO).

(c) *Review body*

The UNAT has insisted that, even where review by a joint review body is not provided for in regard to the termination of permanent appointments for unsatisfactory service, nevertheless, just as in cases of probationary appointments, such a review must be carried out before the termination decision is taken for the purpose of fulfilling the requirements of a complete, fair, and reasonable procedure. In *Nelson*[97] it was held that a review of the applicant's case should have been carried out by a joint review body with staff participation, as was provided for in the Staff Regulations for cases of termination of probationary appointments, to ensure that the rights of staff members holding permanent appointments were protected prior to the termination of such appointments for unsatisfactory service. The tribunal pointed out that the Joint Appeals Board could not fulfil this function, since it was an appellate body and could only review the decision to terminate after it was taken.

Not only must a review body be presented with the case prior to the taking of the termination decision but there must be a reasonably detailed examination of the case by that body and the administration or management. In *Mila*[98] the UNAT found that the Appointment Panel had failed to investigate in depth why the relations between the team of cleaners and their supervisor had deteriorated and to make a thorough, searching, and balanced review of the applicant's competence before the decision to terminate his permanent appointment for unsatisfactory service was taken. This was held to be a grave irregularity which vitiated the decision taken.[99] It may be noted that in cases involving the non-confirmation of probationary appointments a similar approach has been taken.[100]

In *Angelopoulos*[101] the Appeals Board of OECD held that the presence of a statutory member of the Consultant's Committee when it heard the applicant's appeal did not *per se* vitiate the procedure of review, although that member was the Chief of Personnel, since he did not show any prejudice against the applicant.

Most of these cases involved the UN. It is not known what view other tribunals might take on this subject. The purpose of a review body is to ensure a thorough examination of the facts and case. Even where a review body cannot be insisted on because it is foreign to the system existing in a particular

---

[97] UNAT Judgment No. 157 [1972], JUNAT Nos. 114–166 p. 348.

[98] UNAT Judgment No. 184 [1974], JUNAT Nos. 167–230 p. 133.

[99] See also *Restrepo*, UNAT Judgment No. 131 [1969], JUNAT Nos. 114–166 p. 165, where, however, it was found that the procedure followed was not defective. See also more recently *De Shields*, UNAT Judgment No. 309 [1983].

[100] See, e.g., *de Ungria*, UNAT Judgment No. 71 [1958], JUNAT Nos. 71–86 p. 1; *Peynado*, UNAT Judgment No. 138 [1970], JUNAT Nos. 114–166 p. 221.

[101] Decision No. 57, OECD Appeals Board [1976], Recueil des décisions 1 à 62 (1979) p. 157.

organization, yet tribunals may hold that a thorough examination of the case must be made by the organization. Further, the cases referred to above deal with permanent appointments. It is uncertain whether the same principles applicable to such appointments would be appropriate to short-term and fixed-term appointments which are terminated before they expire. There may be good reason for distinguishing the latter kind of appointments.

(d) Warnings

Generally the Staff Regulations and Staff Rules, or their equivalent, of an organization deal with the question of warnings, formal or written. In *Prasad*,[102] for instance, the decision to terminate a permanent appointment was quashed by the ILOAT on the ground that no written warnings were given the applicant prior to the termination of his employment, as was required by the Staff Manual. Where the written law requires formal or written warnings, the required procedure must be fully followed. In *Mila*[103] it was found that the applicant did not receive any written warnings nor was there a record in his personnel file of any verbal warnings. There was no evidence that any of the verbal warnings that might have been given contained any threat of the action that would be taken if the applicant's performance did not improve. The UNAT held that the respondent's failure to give the applicant due and formal warnings which were recorded in his personnel file was a serious irregularity.[104]

In *Suntharalingam*[105] the WBAT made an extensive examination of the requirements relating to warnings set forth in the written law and found that while the applicant was aware of his immediate supervisor's adverse comments, which was some kind of warning, the adverse comments of his other supervisors had been concealed from the applicant. This was, however, found to be in accordance with the practice of the department in which the applicant was working. Nevertheless, the tribunal concluded that this was a procedural deficiency, but held that it was not such that the staff member was prevented from being aware of the respects in which his performance was unsatisfactory or that the staff member was rendered incapable of effectively defending himself in the event of termination. Hence, no remedy was given the applicant. This decision is in accord with the principle that warnings, written or formal, are normally required in order to put the applicant on notice of his deficiencies and enable him to defend himself. Where this objective had been achieved by other means, the fact that the applicant had

---

102 ILOAT Judgment No. 90 [1965] (FAO).
103 UNAT Judgment No. 184 [1974], JUNAT Nos. 167–230 p. 133.
104 See also *Decision No. 9, ESA/CR/22*, ESA Appeals Board [1979].
105 WBAT Reports [1982], Decision No. 6.

not been formally put on notice that the ultimate consequence could be termination nor was fully aware of all the adverse comments on his work was
not a serious irregularity.[106]

In cases concerning the termination of probationary appointments for
unsatisfactory service it has been held that warnings are necessary prior to the
termination decision so that the staff member has an opportunity to correct
himself.[107] On the other hand, in the same kind of case it has been held that in
exceptional circumstances, such as where it was very unlikely that because of
his age the applicant could correct himself, termination without a warning
was possible.[108]

(e) Transfer or demotion

In *Saberi*[109] the applicant argued that (*a*) since he had been recently promoted,
if his services had been found unsatisfactory, he should have been demoted
before he was dismissed; and (*b*) the failure of the respondent to give him an
opportunity to serve in another department made his dismissal improper.
The tribunal held that he failed on both counts. The WBAT pointed out that
the Personnel Manual Statement dealing with transfer did not not require
transfer before dismissal for unsatisfactory service.[110]

Thus, not only is it clear that the written law of the Bank did not given an
employee a right to be transferred to another department before he was
dismissed for unsatisfactory service and that it did not require that where an
employee has just been promoted and his services were found unsatisfactory
he should have been demoted before he was dismissed, but it would also seem
to be a necessary corollary from these decisions that there are no general
principles of law giving employees such rights. It has also been held that by
proposing the transfer of an employee whose services have been found to be
unsatisfactory, the organization does not forgo the right to dismiss him if he
refuses the transfer.[111]

(f) Statement of reasons

In *Carson* the UNAT made a statement to the effect that it was a matter of

---

[106] See also *Polak*, WBAT Reports [1984], Decision No. 17: *Broemser*, WBAT Reports
[1985], Decision No. 27. In both cases it was held that the requirement of a formal warning had
been in effect fulfilled in one way or another.

[107] See, e.g., *Crapon de Caprona*, ILOAT Judgment No. 112 [1967] (WHO).

[108] See *Heyes*, ILOAT Judgment No. 453 [1981] (WHO).

[109] WBAT Reports [1982], Decision No. 5.

[110] See also *Matta*, WBAT Reports [1983, Part I], Decision No. 12; *Durrant-Bell*, WBAT
Reports [1985], Decision No. 24; *Angelopoulos*, Decision No. 57, OECD Appeals Board
[1976], Recueil des décisions 1 à 62 (1979) p. 157.

[111] *Decisions Nos. 8 & 10, ESRO/CR/45*, ESRO Appeals Board [1971].

some importance to a staff member that the grounds of termination should be communicated to him.[112] In both *Mirza*[113] and *Senghor*,[114] where fixed-term contracts were prematurely terminated, no specific reasons were given for the termination. In the latter case the decision to terminate the appointment referred to a provision of the Staff Regulations which permitted termination for any of the reasons stated in the Regulation. Nevertheless, the UNAT said in both cases that not giving specific reasons for the termination tainted the decisions.

In *Restrepo*,[115] however, the UNAT held that the failure to disclose the reason for termination in the communication of the decision to terminate the applicant's employment for unsatisfactory service was a procedural irregularity but that this irregularity did not justify rescission of the decision in the case, because it was clear on the evidence that the applicant was fully aware of the reason for the termination of her services so that she could make her defence. In *Suntharalingam* the WBAT found that it was a fact that the written confirmation of the decision of termination did not specify the reasons or grounds of the failure to render satisfactory service but held that this irregularity was not importance enough to vitiate the decision contested, because:

It cannot be fairly said that the Applicant was kept unaware of the lack of satisfaction with his service in his department, of the reasons therefor and of the remedial measures which were envisaged . . . He was not deprived of the opportunity to improve his services or rebut the criticism of his performance.[116]

A similar approach is to be detected in *Decision No. 135*[117] of the Appeals Board of NATO.

In the case of the European Communities the Staff Regulations require that the reasons for an administrative act affecting an employee's legal position be given[118] and that the practice be followed. But apart from that, the CJEC has held that it is a general principle of law applicable generally in dismissal cases that normally the specific reasons for the decision should be stated.[119] This was so, even though the contract brought to an end was an

---

112 UNAT Judgment No. 85 [1962], JUNAT Nos.71–86 p. 112 at p. 117. See also *Howrani*, UNAT Judgment No. 4 [1951], JUNAT Nos. 1–70 p. 8 at p. 16.

113 UNAT Judgment No. 149 [1971] (ICAO), JUNAT Nos. 114–166 p. 284.

114 UNAT Judgment No. 169 [1973], JUNAT Nos. 167–230 p. 13.

115 UNAT Judgment No. 131 [1969], JUNAT Nos. 114–166 p. 165.

116 WBAT Reports [1982], Decision No. 6 at p. 13. See also *Gregorio*, WBAT Reports [1983, Part II], Decision No. 14 at p. 15.

117 *Decision No. 135*, NATO Appeals Board [1981], Collection of the Decisions 135 to 171 (1984).

118 Article 25: see Amerasinghe (ed.), 4 *Staff Regulations and Staff Rules of Selected International Organizations* (1983) p. 1 at p. 14.

119 *von Lachmüller*, CJEC Cases 43, 45 & 48/59 [1960] ECR p. 463 at p. 475. In *de Briey*, CJEC Case 25/80 [1981] ECR p. 637, the Court held that, while the argument that reasons for

indefinite one which did not give the applicant security of tenure and there had been circulated before the termination decision was taken a notice referring to the need to reduce staff.

In a case concerning the premature termination of a consultant's contract for unsatisfactory service[120] the WBAT held that the notice of termination should communicate the true reasons for the decision to terminate the contract. The rationale for this was that this was one way to ensure that contracts were not terminated on the basis of inadequate facts or ill-founded justifications and to provide a fair opportunity to the staff member affected to seek rectification of the contested decision, and also to facilitate the presentation of appeals and the resort to other remedies in the Bank's dispute-resolution procedure. The consultant was awarded compensation by the tribunal because the reason given for the termination of his contract at the time it was terminated was not the true reason, the true reason being disclosed to him only four months after his contract was terminated.[121]

It seems to be generally agreed in the case law that in cases of dismissal, at any rate, the true reasons must normally be stated for the action taken. But the rule is to be interpreted in the light of its purpose. It would appear that where the applicant knows from other communications with the respondent the reasons for his impending dismissal so that he can improve or defend himself, the rule need not literally be followed, unless there is a specific written law that makes it an inflexible requirement that the reasons for a termination be stated.

(g) Notification

In *von Lachmüller*[122] the CJEC discussed the importance of giving notice to the employee of the termination of his appointment. The Court was of the view that it was a general principle of law that a reasonable period of notice must be given the employee. In that case it was held that a period of three months for notice was reasonable. Clearly salary may be paid for the period of notice in lieu of notice being actually given. In *Angelopoulos*,[123] where notification of the termination decision was an issue, the Appeals Board of OECD held that the applicant had been put on notice of the decision in time so that he could prepare his defence before the Consultative Committee, a

termination of a contract for an indefinite period should be given was a good one, the facts of the case did not show that the law had been violated in this regard.

[120] *Skandera*, WBAT Reports [1981], Decision No. 2.

[121] In *Vrancheva*, ILOAT Judgment No. 194 [1972] (WHO), the ILOAT held that in the case of a probationer he must be given in advance the exact reasons for the termination of his appointment.

[122] CJEC Cases 43, 45 & 48/59 [1960] ECR p. 463. In *de Briey*, CJEC Case 25/80 [1981] ECR p. 637, it was held that notice according to the terms of the contract was adequate.

[123] Decision No. 57, OECD Appeals Board [1976], Recueil des décisions 1 à 62 (1979) p. 157.

review body, and the Secretary General. This case explains why notification in time of the decision to terminate the employment is necessary.[124]

(h) The essential nature of the procedural requirement

It is now an accepted general principle that procedural irregularities in general should nullify the decision taken only if there was a reasonable possibility that they affected the decision, or, put in a different way, if there was a reasonable possibility that the decision would have been different if there had been no procedural irregularity.[125] There have been very few cases concerning termination of permanent appointments for unsatisfactory service in which the issue has arisen. However, it will be remembered that in some cases concerning such termination in which written warnings and the statement of reasons were in issue, it was held that the technical procedural irregularity did not result in the decision being annulled or even compensation being awarded. In *Suntharalingam*,[126] for instance, the WBAT said that the failure to give clear warnings to the applicant was a procedural deficiency but held that it was not such as prevented him from knowing that his performance was unsatisfactory and from defending himself effectively. These cases would seem to support the principle applied in other cases too that normally the procedural irregularity must be an *essential* one if tribunals are to review decisions.

On the other hand, there have been cases in which the procedural irregularity has been held not to have been such as to have affected the decision, but in which the tribunal has considered it appropriate to award compensation, while allowing the decision to terminate service on account of unsatisfactory service to stand. In *Broemser*[127] the irregularity was failure to follow the proper procedure in regard to the final appraisal of the applicant. In *Berubé*[128] the respondent had failed to communicate two reports to the applicant, although the applicant had become aware of the facts in these reports by other means. In both cases the termination decision was not annulled, though compensation was awarded.

Remedies

In considering remedies ordered by tribunals, among other things it is

---

[124] For notification in the case of termination of probationary appointments see *infra*, Ch. 38 pp. 801 ff.

[125] See *supra*, Vol. I Ch. 24 pp. 387 ff.

[126] WBAT Reports [1982], Decision No. 6.

[127] WBAT Reports [1985], Decision No. 27.

[128] UNAT Judgment No. 280 [1981] (ICAO), JUNAT Nos. 231–300 p. 500.

relevant to bear in mind that whether a short-term appointment or a fixed-term appointment is being prematurely terminated or whether a permanent appointment is being terminated will affect the determination of the remedy to be prescribed.

(a) Reinstatement with or without compensation

In *Prasad*[129] the ILOAT quashed the termination decision and ordered reinstatement, because there had been a procedural irregularity. In a follow-up case[130] the tribunal refused to change its earlier decision and to permit the administrative authority to pay compensation instead of reinstating the applicant. In *Wollast*[131] the CJEC held that the applicant must be regarded as having continued in service. Compensation was additionally awarded. This amounted to the salary payable to the applicant from the date of the termination decision to the date of the judgment less 15 per cent for what he had earned from other employment during that period. The applicant was held to be entitled also to other benefits he would have enjoyed had his appointment not been terminated. In two cases decided by the Appeals Board of OECD[132] where lack of due process was found, the tribunal ordered reinstatement but at the same time assessed compensation at 20 months' and 3 months' salary respectively in the event that the OECD decided not to reinstate the applicants. In *Froma*[133] the ILOAT ordered reinstatement but at the same time assessed compensation in the event that the applicant was not reinstated. Two years' salary was awarded with interest, no deductions being permitted for the 5 months' salary paid as termination indemnity.

(b) Compensation only instead of reinstatement or specific performance

In *Decision No. 155*[134] the Appeals Board of NATO awarded compensation of three months' salary when, because of procedural irregularity, the applicant's contract had been wrongfully terminated before it expired. The tribunal referred, as reasons for the assessment, to the conditions in which the decision to terminate the contract was taken, the fact that the applicant

---

[129] ILOAT Judgment No. 90 [1965] (FAO).

[130] *Prasad*, ILOAT Judgment No. 94 [1966] (FAO).

[131] CJEC Case 18/63 [1964] ECR p. 85.

[132] *d'Espinay-Saint-Luc*, Decision No. 44, OECD Appeals Board [1974], Recueil des décisions 1 à 62 (1979) p. 124; *Larcher*, Decision No. 53, OECD Appeals Board (1975), ibid. p. 145.

[133] ILOAT Judgment No. 22 [1955] (UNESCO). See also *Pankey*, ILOAT Judgment No. 23 (1955) (UNESCO), and *Van Gelder*, ILOAT Judgment No. 24 (1955) (UNESCO), where similar decisions were taken on remedies.

[134] *Decision No. 155*, NATO Appeals Board [1983], Collection of the Decisions 135 to 171 (1984).

was deprived of the chance of having his contract renewed, the injury to reputation and feelings, and the non-payment of salary for about 5 weeks of the original period of his contract as a result of the premature termination. In *Decision No. 70*[135] where the termination decision was vitiated by an error of law the organization objected to reinstatement. The Appeals Board of NATO awarded 10 months' salary as compensation.

In *Châtelain*,[136] where there had been procedural irregularities, the UNAT did not order reinstatement of the permanent employee because of the circumstances. However, the tribunal awarded 8 months' basic salary as compensation, taking into account the fact that the applicant had been unwilling fully to enter into the translation work of the particular branch to which he had been assigned.

In *Skandera*[137] the WBAT awarded 3 months' salary for wrongful termination of a consultant's contract. The injury was described as intangible and it was held that in the circumstances of the case rescission of the decision contested or specific performance of the obligation involved was not a remedy appropriate to the injury done. The applicant's contract had been prematurely terminated without the true reasons being given.

In two cases[138] where the applicants' fixed-term contracts had been prematurely terminated and there was apparently no legitimate expectancy of renewal at the expiry of the terms of the contracts, the UNAT held that the parties could not be restored to the status quo ante. The respondent had objected to reinstatement. Compensation was awarded in lieu of specific performance. The compensation was assessed at the salary of the applicants for the period of the contract which remained to run from the date of the termination of the applicant's employment less any termination indemnities which had been paid.[139]

(c) Remand

In *Willame*,[140] where the CJEC found that there were procedural irregularities, it annulled the termination decision and remanded the case for correction of procedure, since the applicant wished to be reinstated. Damages were awarded on the basis that the applicant remained in the service

---

[135] *Decision No. 70*, NATO Appeals Board [1976], Collection of the Decisions 46 to 73 (1976).

[136] UNAT Judgment No. 272 [1981] (ICAO), JUNAT Nos. 231–300 p. 411.

[137] WBAT Reports [1981], Decision No. 2.

[138] *Coll*, UNAT Judgment No. 113 [1967] (ICAO), JUNAT Nos. 87–113 p. 276; *Mirza*, UNAT Judgment No. 149 [1971] (ICAO), JUNAT Nos. 114–166 p. 284.

[139] See also *Senghor*, UNAT Judgment No. 169 [1973], JUNAT Nos. 167–230 p. 13; *Sood*, UNAT Judgment No. 195 [1975], ibid. p 235; *Decision No. 9, ESA/CR/22*, ESA Appeals Board [1979]. These were also cases in which fixed-term contracts were prematurely terminated.

[140] CJEC Case 110/63 [1965] ECR p. 649.

of the respondent from the date of the impugned decision to the date of the new decision to be taken. Deductions were made for the indemnity paid on dismissal and for any remuneration received from employment outside the European Communities during the period after the dismissal. Non-material damage was held to have been suffered by the applicant which was assessed at BF 20,000. Interest was also assessed on the arrears of remuneration up to the date of the judgment. In *Nelson*,[141] where the termination decision was vitiated because of failure to follow the appropriate procedure, the case was remanded and the maximum compensation permitted by the Statute of the UNAT in such a case of remand was also awarded by the tribunal.

(d) Compensation for non-essential irregularities

Compensation has been awarded for irregularities of a substantive or procedural nature, where the irregularities have been held to be such that they did not affect the decision taken. In *Berubé*,[142] where the irregularity was procedural, $(Can.) 4,000 was awarded as compensation on the ground that the procedural deficiency had to be compensated.[143] In *Durrant-Bell*[144] the irregularities were substantive discrepancies and inconsistencies. Taking into account the generous terms of the respondent's termination offer, the WBAT ordered the payment of 3 months' salary as compensation.

---

[141] UNAT Judgment No. 157 [1972], JUNAT Nos. 114–166 p. 348. *Gillman*, UNAT Judgment No. 98 [1966], JUNAT Nos. 87–113 p. 98, was a similar case with similar results. In addition to the remand of the case three months' salary was awarded. Another similar case was *Mila*, UNAT Judgment No. 184 [1974], JUNAT Nos. 167–230 p. 133, and UNAT Judgment No. 204 [1975], ibid. p. 333.

[142] UNAT Judgment No. 280 [1981] (ICAO), JUNAT Nos. 231–300 p. 500.

[143] See also *Broemser*, WBAT Reports [1985], Decision No. 27.

[144] WBAT Reports [1985], Decision No. 24.

CHAPTER THIRTY-SIX

Termination for Other Reasons than Unsatisfactory Service

TERMINATION of a staff member's appointment may take place for other reasons than unsatisfactory service, whatever the nature of his appointment. Thus, the written law of international organizations provides for termination of appointments for reasons such as abolition or suppression of post (because of a reduction in the size of an organization, for purposes of reorganization, or for other reasons), ill-health or invalidity, disciplinary measures, abandonment of post, or retirement. These are but a few examples of the reasons for termination of appointments which are referred to in the written law of international organizations. International administrative tribunals have not hesitated to control and review the decisions taken by organizations to end the employment relationship in any of these circumstances. Generally, they have sought to apply the written law while interpreting it sometimes in the light of general principles of law and the practice of the organizations. Consequently, it is mainly these interpretations, particularly in the light of such general principles and practices, that are of special interest in connection with the termination of appointments for reasons other than unsatisfactory service.

A preliminary question arises in this connection. Does an international organization have the power to terminate an employment relationship for reasons other than those stated in the written law of the organization? This question has not been extensivley discussed as such by international administrative tribunals, perhaps mainly because most organizations have written laws which are quite comprehensive in this regard, in so far as they refer explicitly to most reasons generally applicable to termination. However, there are a few cases which are relevant to the problem.

In theory the consideration that the staff member has an interest in knowing with certainty the grounds on which he may be dismissed militates against any possibility that the power of an organization to terminate the employment relationship for reasons other than those explicitly stated in the written law of the organization should be recognized. It is arguable for this reason that the organization has the power to legislate in the matter and should assume the risk, if it does not enact explicit rules relating to the reasons for termination of the employment relationship. But this would appear to be too simplistic an approach. The interests of an organization in running a good and efficient administration may require that it have the power to terminate the employment relationship for reasons other than those mentioned in its written law and it is equally arguable that this interest deserves protection. Provided the reason for termination of the employment relationship is recognized by the general principles of law relating to good and efficient administration, there can be no injustice in permitting the organization to terminate appointments for this reason. The staff member's interest in certitude is not genuinely disregarded because, if the reason for termination is recognized by general principles of law, he may be deemed or expected to realize that such a reason is a valid one for the termination of the employment relationship.

This approach sustains some measure of support from what was stated in the *Monod Case* by the Committee of Jurists. The Committee recognized that the employment relationship in the League of Nations was not of a private nature, and, therefore, fell to be considered in the light of the principles of public law and administrative legislation. One of the consequences of this premise was that: 'Relations connected with public employment are always governed by the exigencies of the public interest, to which the private and personal interests of the officials must necessarily give way.'[1] The Committee, therefore, concluded that it was not necessary for organizations to issue regulations confirming the prerogatives that public administrations must have, inasmuch as the existence of those prerogatives was beyond dispute and that, therefore, the Secretary General of the League of Nations could dismiss a permanent official for reasons of ill-health, even though the Staff Regulations of the League of Nations did not explicitly provide for dismissal in such circumstances.

Further, in *von Lachmüller*[2] the CJEC was confronted with a situation in which contracts concluded for a period of unlimited duration were terminated with notice, ostensibly because there was a need to reduce the staff of the services to which the employees belonged. While there were no Staff Regulations in existence at the time the staff members were appointed, they did come into existence later but did not deal with termination of services for the reasons pertinent to this case. The Court stated that the contracts which came under administrative law were subject to the principle of good faith and that:

Consequently the contested decisions of dismissal must, in order to terminate those contracts, be justified on grounds relevant to the interests of the services and there must be nothing arbitrary about them, such, for example, as the need to dispense with the services of an unqualified servant or of one occupying a post which has been abolished in the interests of the service.[3]

---

[1] League of Nations, Official Journal, 1925, p. 1441 at p. 1443.
[2] CJEC Cases 43, 45 & 48/59 [1960] ECR p. 463.
[3] Ibid. at p. 475.

As a consequence, though the Staff Regulations were silent on the question of dismissal in the event that a post was abolished, the administration had the right to dismiss a staff member with an indefinite contract in circumstances in which his post was abolished because of a reorganization that took place. It was found that, though in fact the Staff Regulations were largely silent on the issue of termination of service except for reasons of incompetence or on retirement, and there were no governing Staff Regulations at the time the contracts were entered into, staff recruited before the Staff Regulations came into force could not lay claim to employment in permanent posts. The reasons for this were that the conditions upon which such staff were engaged required, according to the constituent treaty of the organization in which they were employed, that they be given contracts of limited duration and that employment on a permanent basis was inconsistent with the limited nature of any employment relationship created before the entry into force of such Regulations.[4] This meant that such contracts did not give staff members security of tenure. This statement did not purport to deal with the situation generally where Staff Regulations are silent on a particular mode of dismissal, because it laid emphasis on the fact that the contracts came into existence before the Staff Regulations came into force and could not have been permanent contracts. However, it did not purport to contradict the general view expressed in the same case that the termination of employment in the absence of written provision had to be on grounds relevant to the interests of the service. This was tantamount to stating that termination could be for reasons of the public interest as defined by general principles of international administrative law, where the written law was silent.[5]

In *Aragon* the LNT did mention the possibility that *force majeure* could be a relevant factor in deciding whether the period of notice given was sufficient.[6] It held on the facts of the case that *force majeure* did not apply but did not in specific terms deal with the question whether *force majeure* could result in the termination of a contract. *Force majeure* was not mentioned in the Staff Regulations of the League of Nations but in so far as the tribunal proceeded in the case on the basis that the termination of a staff member's contract when the League was dissolved was not impermissible, even though the Staff Regulations did not provide for this eventuality, it did implicitly concede the possibility that *force majeure* on dissolution of the organization could be a valid reason for the termination of employment under a general

---

[4] Ibid. at p. 473.

[5] In the outcome, the Court held that there was an irregularity in that the reason for the termination had not been clearly stated in the letter of dismissal. This does not, however, affect the validity of what the Court implicitly affirmed in its discussion of the issues involved in the case.

[6] LNT Judgment No. 25 [1946] at p. 4.

principle of law even in the absence of express provision for this eventuality in the written law of the organization.[7]

The notion that *force majeure*, even in the absence of specific reference to it in the written law of the organization as a cause for dissolution of the employment relationship, may result in the termination of an appointment was also implicitly referred to by the ILOAT in *Rothbarth*.[8] There the tribunal stated that the facts did not show an attitude on the part of the staff member resulting from a case of *force majeure* which would have entitled the parties to break the fixed-term contract which constituted the contract of employment.[9]

In *Duran (No. 3)* the ILOAT once again expressed views which support the position that the explicit written law is not exclusive in regard to the grounds on which an appointment may be terminated. The statements were made in regard to a contractual appointment. This does not, however, mean that in appropriate circumstances the principle that general principles of administrative law could very well prescribe the conditions in which an appointment may be terminated even in the case of statutory appointments is not valid. The ILOAT stated in that case:

The Tribunal will not enter into the arguments as to which, if any, of the staff rules enumerated in the Organization's letter of 19 December, authorized the termination. It is an elementary principle of the law of contract that if one party clearly and definitely refuses to honour his or her obligations, the other party is entitled to rescind the contract; and it does not matter whether or not any of the rules say so in so many words.[10]

In some early cases the UNAT seems to have expressed a view contradictory to that supported by the cases discussed above. In *Gordon* and several subsequent cases the UNAT stated:

In accordance with the regulations established by the General Assembly, permanent appointments cannot be terminated except under staff regulations which enumerate precisely the reasons for the conditions governing the termination of service.

The Secretary-General thus can act only under a provision of the Staff Regulations. He must indicate the provision upon which he proposes to rely, and must conform with the conditions and procedures laid down in the Staff Regulations.

If he fails to comply with these principles, the Tribunal is entitled to inquire whether the termination of employment is in accordance with the rules in force.[11]

---

[7] *Mayras* and other cases proceeded on the same basis: LNT Judgment No. 24 [1946]; LNT Judgments Nos. 27 to 36 [1946].

[8] ILOAT Judgment No. 6 [1947] (IIIC).

[9] Ibid. at p. 2.

[10] ILOAT Judgment No. 543 [1983] (PAHO) at p. 7.

[11] UNAT Judgment No. 29 [1953], JUNAT Nos. 1–70 p. 120 at p. 123. See also *Svenchansky* etc., UNAT Judgments Nos. 30 to 37 [1953], JUNAT Nos. 1–70 pp. 128, 135, 144, 151, 160, 168, 176, 184.

While the statement appears to be categorical, the case was in fact concerned with a situation which was discussed in the context of a reason for the termination of service which was explicitly referred to in the Staff Regulations. This was unsatisfactory service. Had the immediate cause of the termination of service, namely the resort by the applicant to the Fifth Amendment of the Constitution of the USA before a Senate Subcommittee, been discussed on its own as a grounds for the termination of the applicant's contract, then the question would have arisen whether, in the absence of specific reference to it in the written law, it was a reason for termination of services recognized by general principles of administrative law. This question was not squarely faced or discussed in the case, because the issue had not been raised that, even in the absence of specific reference to a cause for termination of service in the written law of the organization, the organization could resort to the general principles of law in seeking a reason for such termination. On the facts of the case it was apparent that the general principles of law would not have permitted termination of an appointment for the specific reasons given. Hence, the raising of the issue might have been futile. But, as a consequence of this situation, it is equally clear that the tribunal's statement in the form it was made was unnecessary in the circumstances of the case. In any event, if the UNAT's statements in this case (and the other cases with the same facts which were decided about the same time) were not regarded as *obiter dicta*, the only reasonable solution would be to regard the statements as unwarranted and as bad law, particularly because there is much evidence to the contrary and the view taken is not consonant with the best interests of justice.

As already noted, the written law of the many international organizations in fact normally deals extensively with the causes for termination of appointments which explains why there is a considerable dearth of authority on whether general principles of law may permit termination of appointments for reasons other than those specifically referred to in the written law. As a consequence also, most of the decided cases have concerned themselves with the interpretation and application of the written law ostensibly in the light sometimes of general principles of administrative law relating to efficient public administration. What is of interest, therefore, in this connection is not so much the written law which may vary from organization to organization and can in any case be easily verified by reference to that law but the interpretation and application of that law by reference generally and implicitly to the general principles of administrative law.

Abolition or suppression of post

Posts may be abolished for a variety of reasons, but generally such action is resorted to for budgetary reasons or when there is a structural reorganization within the organization. Appointments may be terminated as a result. Generally, the problem of abolition of posts is dealt with in the Staff Regulations or Staff Rules or equivalent legislative provisions of an organization, but it has been stated that posts may be abolished even if the Staff Regulations and Staff Rules do not expressly provide for such a measure. In a situation where certain posts were abolished allegedly for reasons of economy, the rationale and source of authority for such a measure were described by the ILOAT as follows:

> In determining the validity of those claims the Tribunal must consider whether and in what circumstances the abolition of a post is compatible with the rules of the international civil service.
>
> Far from being determined once and for all, the purposes and structure of an organization must move with the times and no institution is immune to change. According to circumstances such change in an organization may entail the abolition of posts. Even if there is no express provision in the Staff Regulations or Staff Rules for such a measure, it is implicit in the principle that no organization is bound to adhere to the purposes and policies which it adopted at any particular time. The complainant is mistaken in contending that abolition of a post is warranted only if the FAO ceases to perform some form of function. The theory is that for a post to exist two conditions must be met: an impersonal one, namely the definition of the functions to be performed, and a personal one, namely the assignment of those functions to a staff member in a particular category. Hence an organization may properly decide to abolish a post in one or the other of two contingencies—either when it ceases to perform certain functions or when it relieves the responsible staff member of those functions and assigns them to one or more other staff members.[12]

This statement does not purport to discuss exhaustively the circumstances which would justify the abolition of posts but it does refer to the process of change as being the ultimate cause underlying post abolition. Secondly, it makes clear that even in the absence of express written provision in the Staff Regulations and Rules posts may be abolished, which is in accord with the position postulated in the previous section. Indeed, as was seen, the LNT did not question the validity of the termination of appointments upon the suppression of posts in the event of the dissolution of the League of Nations, although the Staff Regulations of the institution did not provide for this contingency.[13] Thirdly, it refers to two preliminary conditions one of which should actually obtain if the action taken by the administration of an organization is to be regarded as an abolition or suppression of post. These requirements are important. Positive conditions must be satisfied if the situation is to be regarded as an abolition of post. Where those conditions do not obtain, the situation cannot be treated as an abolition of post. Con-

---

[12] *Gracia de Muñiz*, ILOAT Judgment No. 269 [1976] (FAO) at p. 5.
[13] See *Mayras*, LNT Judgment No. 24 [1946] and the cases following that case, LNT Judgments Nos. 25, 27 to 36 [1946].

versely, where the required conditions are present the situation qualifies to be treated as an abolition of post. In *Getz*[14] the OASAT held that there had been an abolition of post and that the procedure relating to abolition of post should have been followed when the applicant's post was abolished together with his Unit and then the alternative post which was offered him was abolished before he could take up duties.

As might be expected, it has been held that the decision to abolish a post can only be impeached if the applicant can show that it affected his interests in that he was dismissed or was down-graded.[15] This means that it is insufficient that posts have merely been abolished for that action to be questioned, if the applicant has been transferred to or given an equivalent post which he has accepted. The abolition of posts as such cannot be brought into question in the absence of impeachable consequences.

The question whether there had been in fact a proper abolition of post was raised in *Decision No. 21*[16] of the Appeals Board of OEEC. This decision sheds some light on what has to take place, if there has been a genuine abolition of post. The applicant's post had been transferred to another division in the organization and as a consequence the applicant was successively down-graded to several other posts. He was unable to cope with the work in any of these posts because he lacked qualifications. Consequently, his permanent contract was terminated. The tribunal held that there was in reality no suppression of his post as envisaged by the Staff Regulations and that the termination of his service was invalid. The post of the applicant had merely been transferred to another division. In *Decision No. 142*[17] the Appeals Board of NATO rejected the argument that the termination of a permanent appointment was invalid, even though the Personnel Regulations permitted such an action, because the applicant was prevented from serving until her statutory retirement age which was 65. The fact that an appointment is permanent does not prevent the administration from terminating it for the reason that the post has been abolished, if the abolition of post is valid in other respects. In interpreting the Staff Regulations of FAO the ILOAT has held that the reduction of technical assistance staff could legitimately be considered as affecting the whole staff of the organization, as the administration of FAO had done.[18] There was a reduction in the staff of the whole organization as opposed to a reduction only in the technical assistance area,

---

[14] OASAT Judgment No. 26 [1976].

[15] *Hermann*, ILOAT Judgment No. 133 [1969] (UNESCO).

[16] *Decision No. 21*, OEEC Appeals Board [1955], Recueil des décisions 1 à 62 (1979) p. 59. In *Gotschi*, ILOAT Judgment No. 523 [1982] (PAHO), a post was transferred from the Washington office to the Mexico City office of PAHO. The ILOAT held that there had been no abolition of post.

[17] *Decision No. 142*, NATO Appeals Board [1981], Collection of the Decisions 135 to 171 (1984). See also *Decision No. 141*, NATO Appeals Board [1981], ibid.

[18] *Tranter*, ILOAT Judgment No. 14 [1954] (FAO).

which brought into operation the rules relating to the termination of appointments on reduction in staff in the whole organization.

It is also necessary that, where a post is suppressed or abolished, it must be clear on the facts of the case that the staff member holding that post was dismissed from the service directly as a result of that abolition of post and that his services did not terminate for some other reason, if the staff member's services are properly to be regarded as having been terminated on account of the abolition of post. In *Decision No. 7*[19] of the Appeals Board of ELDO the applicant's post was, indeed, abolished when ELDO was reorganized. He was then offered a post in another division. He assumed this post and functioned in it for a little less than six months, when he wrote to the administration stating that the post had no job description and that he, therefore, refused the post. The applicant argued that he was dismissed from the service of ELDO because his post was abolished and that he should be treated accordingly. The tribunal held that he had refused the post too late for his case to be treated as one of termination of service because of abolition of post. It was a simple case of resignation, as the administration had regarded it.

(a) Review of the decision to abolish or suppress posts

The ILOAT has made it clear on more than one occasion that the decision to suppress or abolish a post is a discretionary one and is subject to review in the same way that all discretionary powers are. In *Gracia de Muñiz*[20] the tribunal said:

Although the Director-General enjoys discretionary authority in taking measures which entail abolishing a post, his decision is not wholly free from review by the Tribunal. It may be quashed if it violates a rule of form or procedure, or is based on an error of fact or of law, or if essential facts have not been taken into consideration, or if it is tainted with abuse of authority, or if a clearly mistaken conclusion has been drawn from the facts. In particular the Tribunal will find that there has been abuse of authority where the abolition of a post is motivated, not by relevant and objective considerations, but by a desire to remove a staff member for whose dismissal there are no lawful grounds.[21]

In that case it was held that the applicant's post on a magazine published by FAO had been suppressed and her duties assigned to someone engaged on contract in accordance with the policy of FAO which aimed at reducing editorial expenditure on the magazine without detriment to its purposes, and

---

[19] *Decision No. 7*, ELDO Appeals Board [1973].
[20] ILOAT Judgment No. 269 [1976] (FAO).
[21] Ibid. at p. 5. See also *Hermann*, ILOAT Judgment No. 133 [1969] (UNESCO); *Babbar*, ILOAT Judgment No. 388 [1980] (FAO) at p. 6.

that the proposals of the Director General involving the abolition of the applicant's post was expected to lead to considerable savings. Thus, the abolition of the applicant's post could not be questioned.[22] In *Azola Blanco and Véliz García*,[23] on the other hand, the tribunal found that the relevant Staff Regulation of the ESO did not permit the reduction of posts for economic reasons of a casual or transitory kind but required economic problems of a permanent kind and held that the reduction of posts was improper.

In this connection a disturbing statement appears in *Pibouleau*[24] where a suppression of post by WHO was questioned. The ILOAT said that: 'The Tribunal may neither pass judgment on a policy which falls solely within the competence of the WHO authorities nor review action taken in pursuance of that policy.'[25] Earlier the tribunal had pointed out that the dismissal was not tainted with abuse of authority nor was for extraneous motives and that it was clear that the dismissal was solely because the organization had now to make savings but, nevertheless, it regarded the policy behind the abolition of post as outside its power of review. It is difficult to reconcile these two approaches within the same case and it would, therefore, seem that what the tribunal intended to say was that it would not, in normal circumstances, substitute its own judgment for that of the organization on the policy involved. In any event the above statement, if taken at its face value, would conflict with the cases discussed earlier and would have to be regarded as having been made *per incuriam*.

The UNAT has not found in any case that the policy behind the abolition of posts has been questionable, though it has not hesitated to examine the circumstances in which the abolition of post had taken place. In *Aubert and 14 Others*[26] it found that, while there must be authority to reduce posts which

---

[22] Other cases decided by the ILOAT illustrate the circumstances in which the abolition of post can be proper. In *Savioli*, ILOAT Judgment No. 346 [1978] (WMO), where the suppression of the applicant's post was questioned, it was held that the decision to suppress the post in issue should have been in conformity with Staff Regulation 9.2 of WMO which required that the suppression be for the 'necessities of the service' and that, since the suppression had been for reasons of savings or rationalization, the requirement had been satisfied. In *Hermann*, ILOAT Judgment No. 133 [1969] (UNESCO), it was found that the abolition of post took place in pursuance of the decisions of the Conference of UNESCO which required a reorganization and was, therefore, valid. See also *Chuinard*, ILOAT Judgment No. 139 [1969] (CERN); *Gracia de Muñiz*, ILOAT Judgment No. 269 [1976] (FAO); *Babbar*, ILOAT Judgment No. 388 [1980] (FAO). In all these cases the abolition of posts was questioned but was found to be valid.

[23] ILOAT Judgment No. 507 [1982] (ESO). See also *Acosta Andres*, ILOAT Judgment No. 508 [1982] (ESO). In *Gotschi*, ILOAT Judgment No. 523 [1982] (PAHO), the ILOAT held that, if PAHO had transferred a position from one office to another located in another country, in order to claim that the post had been abolished because the incumbent could in law refuse to be transferred to another locality, this would have been an abuse of discretion.

[24] ILOAT Judgment No. 351 [1978] (WHO).

[25] Ibid. at p. 4.

[26] UNAT Judgment No. 2 [1950], JUNAT Nos. 1-70 p. 3.

may be necessary in order to observe due economy while providing adequately for the service of the UN, the power to reduce posts could not in any way be regarded as affected by provisions of the budget, which must be regarded as conferring authority but not as imposing an obligation to spend the whole of the credit provided in the budget. In *Quémerais*[27] the tribunal held that a change in the field of activity of the organization such as to bring about the complete elimination of a previous activity could, because of the nature of a particular assignment, justify the abolition of a post.[28] These cases implicitly support the view taken by the ILOAT that the decision to abolish posts is subject to review by the tribunal. At the same time the tribunal has not hesitated to state:

The Respondent, however, contends that the savings arising from the conversion of the international post to an area post were substantial and that such substitution would provide opportunity for employment to a local person, which would further the interests of the area and of the Administration.

In view of the well-established jurisprudence of the Tribunal that the Tribunal cannot substitute its judgement for that of the Administration in respect of reorganization of posts or staff in the interest of economy and efficiency, the Tribunal does not enter into the merits of either the abolition of the post of Field Distribution Officer or the substitution of an area staff officer for the international staff officer.[29]

This statement does not in essence conflict with the UNAT's general approach to the question of the validity of a suppression of posts.

The CJEC has also pronounced on the validity of a reduction in posts. It held in *Renckens*[30] that measures taken to suppress certain posts and terminate the appointments of certain individuals when the merger of administrations took place was not a delegation of legislative power but only the implementation of rules laid down in Regulation 259/68. This case shows that it is not impossible to test the validity of a decision to suppress posts before that court. In similar vein the OASAT has noted that the abolition of certain posts was in accordance with the relevant resolutions of the General Asembly of the OAS and its Charter.[31]

The NATO Appeals Board has on occasion made statements to the effect that it will not assess the merits of a reorganization or rule on the advisability of abolishing the post in question.[32] But these statements were made in

---

[27] UNAT Judgment No. 172 [1973], JUNAT Nos. 167–230 p. 31.

[28] See also *Sabillo*, UNAT Judgment No. 164 [1972], JUNAT Nos. 114–166 p. 397, where redundancy was held to be a good reason for the abolition of post.

[29] *van der Valk*, UNAT Judgment No. 117 [1968], JUNAT Nos. 114–166 p. 33 at p. 40.

[30] CJEC Case 27/68 [1969] ECR p. 255.

[31] *Calvimontes*, OASAT Judgment No. 63 [1981].

[32] See *Decision No. 28*, NATO Appeals Board [1971] at p. 2, Collection of the Decisions (1972); *Decision No. 141*, NATO Appeals Board [1981] at p. 2, Collection of the Decisions 135 to 171 (1984); *Decision No. 142*, NATO Appeals Board [1981] at p. 2, ibid.

circumstances where the tribunal was requested virtually to substitute its judgment for that of the organization. They do not necessarily rule out the possibility that in the appropriate circumstances the tribunal would review the decisions to abolish posts in the same way that it would the exercise of any other discretionary power.

Thus, the general trend, as can be seen from the decided cases, is to regard the decision to abolish or suppress posts as being the exercise of a discretionary power which is reviewable on grounds on which the exercise of any discretionary power is reviewable.

As a consequence of the power of tribunals to review the decision to abolish or suppress posts, tribunals have on several occasions examined the questions whether the purpose underlying the suppression or abolition of the post was a proper one or whether there had been a *détournement de pouvoir* in the action taken. The issue whether there has been a *détournement de procédure* has also been examined in this connection. In an early case decided by the Appeals Board of OEEC, *Decision No. 29*,[33] it was found that there was no improper motive or personal dislike underlying the suppression of the applicant's post. Nor was there a *détournement de procédure* in that the suppression of the post was not a disguised reason for dismissing the applicant for disciplinary reasons. In several cases in which the argument that prejudice had motivated the abolition of post was raised the tribunal concerned did not deny that such prejudice could vitiate the decision to abolish the post but found on the facts that such prejudice did not exist.[34] It has been explicitly stated or implied in some cases that the object of removing from a post a staff member for whose dismissal there are no objective grounds would be an abuse of purpose, though in those cases it was found that there was no such motive.[35] In *Chuinard* the ILOAT stated as a general rule that: 'If the Director-General suppresses a post and then re-establishes it soon after, then there is reason to suppose that he was guided by reasons other than the efficiency of the administration, that is to say that he has abused his discretionary powers.'[36] *Russell-Cobb*[37] is an example of a case where no abuse of purpose occurred. The reason given for the reduction in strength was the

[33] *Decision No. 29*, OEEC Appeals Board [1957], Recueil des décisions 1 à 62 (1979) p. 80.

[34] See *Aubert and 14 Others*, UNAT Judgment No. 2 [1950], JUNAT Nos. 1–70 p. 3; *Carson*, UNAT Judgment No. 85 [1962], JUNAT Nos. 71–86 p. 112 *Sabillo*, UNAT Judgment No. 164 [1972], JUNAT Nos. 114–166 p. 397; *Cauro*, Decision No. 34, OEEC Appeals Board [1961], Recueil des décisions 1 à 62 (1972) p. 95; *Gracia de Muñiz*, ILOAT Judgment No. 269 [1976] (FAO).

[35] See *Hermann*, ILOAT Judgment No. 133 [1969] (UNESCO); *Gracia de Muñiz*, ILOAT Judgment No. 269 [1976] (FAO). See also *Gotschi*, ILOAT Judgment No. 523 [1982] (PAHO), where the abuse of discretion found to exist, on a certain hypothesis, would have been a *détournement de pouvoir*, in so far as the purpose would have been to prevent the holder of the post abolished from exercising the right which he legally had of refusing a transfer to another locality.

[36] ILOAT Judgment No. 139 [1969] (CERN) at p. 5.

[37] UNAT Judgment No. 55 [1954], JUNAT Nos. 1–70 p. 274.

existence of budgetary limitations. It was found that this reason was not wrongly stated and that there was no abuse of purpose.[38] In line with the general principles governing *détournement de pouvoir*, where there are more reasons than one for the abolition of a post and one of them is improper, such as the objective of dismissing the staff member for unsatisfactory services, provided the other reason is a lawful one, such as the interests of the organization or financial constraints, it has been held that the abolition of post cannot be questioned on the grounds of *détournement de pouvoir*.[39]

(b) Subsequent action on abolition or suppression of posts

The practice of tribunals shows that even though a post is lawfully abolished, the subsequent action leading to the termination of the staff member's appointment may be reviewed by tribunals, particularly in the exercise of their jurisdiction with regard to the exercise of discretionary power. As was stated by the OASAT in *Calvimontez*, 'the legitimacy of the Secretary General's decision to abolish a post does not prevent the Tribunal from examining compliance with the rules governing the complainant's right, as a member of the Secretariat staff, to job stability and to his career service'.[40] This may take the form of applying the written law or even general principles of law. Generally, there are written provisions which demand application but even in the absence of these tribunals may apply certain general principles in determining whether the affected staff member has been lawfully dismissed or treated.

In *van der Valk*[41] the UNAT made it quite clear that even in the absence of written rules:

> in the case of termination of employees with service ratings of 'satisfactory' or better, there is a presumptive right to consideration for posts elsewhere in the Secretariat for which their qualifications are appropriate, and that an essential of due process is either an affirmative showing that reasonable efforts were made to place such employees in other posts, or a statement of reason why this was not done.[42]

In that case an action was brought in respect of action taken by UNRWA

---

[38] Other cases in which no abuse of purpose was found are *Gracia de Muñiz*, ILOAT Judgment No. 269 [1976] (FAO): where the purpose of the abolition of post was to replace the applicant with a person employed on contract, because this would result in savings, it was held that there was no abuse of purpose; *Renckens*, CJEC Case 27/68 [1969] ECR p. 255; the CJEC held that, while it was within its power to examine whether there had been a genuine rationalization of departments, it was satisfied that this was the case, thus implying that there had been no abuse of purpose.

[39] *Chuinard*, ILOAT Judgment No. 139 [1969] (CERN); *Savioli*, ILOAT Judgment No. 346 [1978] (WMO).

[40] OASAT Judgment No. 63 [1981] at p. 10.

[41] UNAT Judgment No. 117 [1968], JUNAT Nos. 114–166 p. 33.

[42] Ibid. at p. 41.

which did not have any written rules regarding the reassignment of staff members in the event of post abolition. The respondent argued that the obligation to find alternative employment for staff members affected by post abolition should be based on statutory provisions but the tribunal rejected this contention. In *Gracia de Muñiz* the ILOAT also referred to a general principle of law which required that efforts be made to find alternative employment. The tribunal said: 'Moreover, there is a general principle whereby an organization may not terminate the appointment of a staff member whose post has been abolished, at least if he holds an appointment of indeterminate duration, without first taking suitable steps to find him alternative employment.'[43]

It will be noted that the two tribunals do not state the general principle of law in exactly the same way. Particularly, the UNAT restricts the principle to staff members with 'satisfactory' or better ratings, while the ILOAT qualified the principle by reference to those, at least, who hold appointments of indeterminate duration. There is no requirement of satisfactory services for the ILOAT nor is there a requirement that the staff member be an indeterminate contract holder for the UNAT. There may be some differences between the approach by tribunals in detail, but the fact that there is a general principle seems to be established. The NATO Civilian Personnel Regulations are silent on the need for finding alternative employment but this has not deterred the Appeals Board of NATO from taking the view that, while a displaced staff member may not have a right to appointment to an alternative post, the tribunal may examine the procedure followed in not appointing him to vacant posts, particularly whether those posts were filled in an improper manner.[44] In all the relevant cases the tribunal found that the general principles had not been violated. However, it must also be recognized that it is seldom that resort has been had by tribunals to the general principle, because the written law has generally made provision for the requirement that an effort be made to find alternative employment in the organization for the displaced employee.

While the exercise by tribunals of the jurisdiction to review is based broadly on the theory that the power to dismiss an official when a post is abolished is a discretionary power, it emerges clearly from the cases that tribunals have regarded the failure of the administration to make appropriate efforts to give the affected staff member an alternative appointment, when it should have, as the breach of an obligation owed to the staff member. This may be classified broadly as an error of law for the purpose of the law relating

---

43 ILOAT Judgment No. 269 [1976] (FAO) at pp. 5 ff.

44 See *Decision No. 28*, NATO Appeals Board [1971] at p. 3, Collection of the Decisions (1972); *Decision No. 30*, NATO Appeals Board [1971] at p. 2 ibid.

to the exercise of discretionary power. The failure of the administration may be regarded as a breach of an obligation which is a condition for the exercise of discretionary power. It is a substantive irregularity.

As the written law differs from organization to organization, the cases decided only illustrate how tribunals have approached the obligation reflected in the relevant written law by interpreting and applying that law. In the case of the OAS the applicable rule is Rule 110.6 of the Staff Rules. In applying this rule the OASAT has held that an objective justification must be given for the finding that the applicant did not meet the requirements of the other posts available, it being insufficient that a mere statement to this effect is made.[45] In this case the tribunal found that no thorough examination of the applicant's qualifications had been made with a view to offering him an alternative position. In *Hebblethwaite and Others*,[46] it was held that the rule that seniority should be given preference embodied in Rule 110.6 could not be varied retroactively by a resolution of the General Assembly of the OAS. In the same case it was said that the transfer of an affected staff member to a non-existence post could not satisfy the requirement that he be offered alternative employment, if that action had adverse repercussions on him.[47] In *Adib*[48] it was held that decisions of the Inter-American Council for Education, Science, and Culture and a particular Working Group could not alter the obligations of the Secretary General of the OAS under the Staff Rules which he had to follow. Since he had acted in accordance with the latter before dismissing the applicant, the applicant had no case.

The ILOAT has also found that the requirements of the Staff Regulations or Staff Rules of organizations relating to the offer of an alternative post had not been complied with. In *Hermann*[49] the tribunal held that the requirement that efficiency, competence, integrity, and length of service be taken into account, which was contained in the Staff Rules of UNESCO, had not been fulfilled. As a result of this provision, if the applicant was qualified for a vacant post, he should have had priority over all other candidates. Offering the applicant a post in a lower grade was found to be inappropriate in the circumstances, since there were vacancies in the same grade to which the applicant belonged and for which he was qualified.[50]

---

[45] *Calvimontes*, OASAT Judgment No. 63 [1981].

[46] OASAT Judgment No. 30 [1977].

[47] In *Méndez*, OASAT Judgment No. 55 [1980], the tribunal held that, while the applicant had been considered without success for posts in the same grade, the procedure required for finding a position for him in a lower grade which was reflected in Rule 110.6 (i) (ii) had not been followed with the result that the obligation of the OAS had not been carried out. The obligation to offer alternative employment was also found to have been violated in *Getz*, OASAT Judgment No. 26 [1976] and *Chrétien*, OASAT Judgment No. 29 [1977].

[48] OASAT Judgment No. 15 [1975]. In *Mendoza*, OASAT Judgment No. 9 [1974], also the applicant's case was dismissed the Staff Rules had not been violated.

[49] ILOAT Judgment No. 133 [1969] (UNESCO).

[50] In *Savioli*, ILOAT Judgment No. 346 [1978] (WMO), the tribunal, in interpreting the Staff

In *Tranter*,[51] while the ILOAT affirmed that, if an exception based on superior competence were generally made to the rule that permanent staff members should be given priority in reassignment, so that recourse to the exception became a misuse of power, there would be a violation of obligations under the Staff Regulations and Staff Rules of FAO, it found this had not happened in the case of the post abolitions that had taken place involving the applicant. In *Caglar*[52] the ILOAT took the view that, while the fulfilment of the obligation to offer alternative employment under the written law of ITU may be reviewed in a manner similar to that applied to the exercise of discretionary power, in that case (i) there was no procedural flaw, merely because the Secretary General had failed to consult the Joint Advisory Committee a second time; (ii) there was no error of law resulting from the fact that the organization took the view that the reassignment should be subject to a test; (iii) there was no prejudice against the applicant involved in the action taken which would have resulted in an abuse of authority; and (iv) no mistaken conclusions were drawn from the facts, because the Secretary General considered not only the reports on the test but also earlier reports on the applicant's work in coming to the conclusion supported by adequate evidence that the applicant was not qualified for the new post as a result of his earlier shortcomings. There are some other cases decided by the ILOAT in which the tribunal found that the obligations in question had not been violated, because appropriate action had been taken.[53] In one of these cases the tribunal stated that an applicant could not rely on the written provisions of other organizations to substantiate his rights relating to reassignment,[54] while in another it held that though the wrong rules had been referred to in the case, as long as the results of the organization's action fulfilled the requirements of the applicable Regulations and Rules, there had been no violation of the obligation to take adequate steps for reassignment.[55]

Regulations of WMO, found that while the applicant had no right to a hearing as such, even though she had had the opportunity to be heard, the organization had failed in its obligation, because, though there were certain actions it should have performed in the course of finding her a post, it had failed to (i) pursue enquiries within WMO as long as the circumstances required and (ii) suggest to other directors the possibility of appointing her to posts of a different kind from what she had held, even if they belonged to a lower grade. Further, trying to find employment in another organization for the applicant was not a fulfilment of the respondent's obligations. In *Babbar*, ILOAT Judgment No. 388 [1980] (FAO), the ILOAT found that in putting the applicant on the same footing as other employees and not giving weight to his age, seniority, and family circumstances the FAO had not made appropriate efforts to reassign him and therefore failed in its duty under the Staff Regulations and Rules of FAO.

[51] ILOAT Judgment No. 14 [1954] (FAO).

[52] ILOAT Judgment No. 334 [1978] (ITU).

[53] See, e.g., *Chuinard*, ILOAT Judgment No. 139 [1969] (CERN); *Gracia de Muñiz*, ILOAT Judgment No. 269 [1976] (FAO).

[54] *Sauer*, ILOAT Judgment No. 378 [1979] (Eurocontrol).

[55] *Gaydar*, ILOAT Judgment No. 581 [1983] (PAHO). See also *Herrera*, ILOAT Judgment No. 582 [1983] (PAHO); *Montes de Oca*, ILOAT Judgment No. 583 [1983] (PAHO); *Rapoport*, ILOAT Judgment No. 584 [1983] (PAHO).

In some early cases[56] the UNAT found that adequate efforts to find an appropriate assignment for the applicants had not been taken as required by Staff Rule 104, as it was then numbered. These cases turned largely on the facts of each case, hence there was little said in terms of general principle. In a later case, however, in which the tribunal was called upon to apply the present Staff Rule 109.1 (c), the UNAT pointed out that under that Rule the respondent had to prove that (i) the applicant had in fact been considered for available posts and (ii) he was genuinely not found suitable for them.[57] As the respondent could not prove these facts the applicant was held to have been wrongfully dismissed. In *Quémerais*[58] the tribunal found that, although the respondent had the right to test the applicant during a trial period before offering him an alternative post, the procedure it had adopted in evaluating the results of this trial period was bad, because the evaluating committee was not put in a position to be informed of the observations of the applicant as well as the complaints about him. In several cases the tribunal found that the obligation imposed by Staff Rule 9.1 (c) had been carried out by the respondent and that adequate but unsuccessful efforts had been made to find the applicant an attractive assignment.[59]

In *Renckens*[60] the CJEC applied the relevant Staff Regulation. In doing so it stated that the reasons for the failure of the applicant to be reassigned

---

[56] *Aubert and 14 Others*, UNAT Judgment No. 2 [1950], JUNAT Nos. 1–70 p. 3; *Morrow*, UNAT Judgment No. 16 [1952], JUNAT Nos. 1–70 p. 54; *Aglion*, UNAT Judgment No. 56 [1954], JUNAT Nos. 1–70 p. 283.

[57] *Carson*, UNAT Judgment No. 85 [1962], JUNAT Nos. 71–86 p. 112.

[58] UNAT Judgment No. 172 [1973], JUNAT Nos. 167–230 p. 31. In *Decision No. 15*, OEEC Appeals Board [1952], Recueil des décisions 1 à 62 (1979) p. 47 at p. 47, it was said that the tribunal would not examine professional qualifications to verify the propriety of selections made for retention in service on post abolition but this did not mean that the tribunal would not examine the question whether there had been an abuse of discretion in an appropriate case. Thus in the same case the tribunal held that there had been no failure to take into account relevant facts solely because faults committed several years before by two of the employees who had been retained had not been reported to the administrative supervisor. The tribunal conceded that an omission of relevant facts could result in a tainted decision relating to the dismissal of a staff member on the abolition of a post. The tribunal also held that the failure to take into account the above-mentioned facts was not the direct cause of the applicant's not being retained in service. Hence, the tribunal seems to have admitted the principle in regard to the decision to terminate service on abolition of post that a substantive irregularity must be causally connected with the wrong done, if it is to vitiate the decision taken. On the other hand, in *Decision No. 34*, ESRO/CR/89, ESRO Appeals Board [1974], the tribunal held that the applicant had been wronged, because in deciding that his services were to be terminated on post abolition, though the administrative authority had considered the applicant's lack of technical and managerial skills, it had not taken into account the fact that he had had five years' experience. The omission from consideration of this relevant fact vitiated the decision not to retain his services on the abolition of his post.

[59] See *Russell-Cobb*, UNAT Judgment No. 55 [1954], JUNAT Nos. 1–70 p. 274; *Noel*, UNAT Judgment No. 161 [1972], JUNAT Nos. 114–166 p. 382; *van der Valk*, UNAT Judgment No. 117 [1968], ibid. p. 33. In this case the general principle of law was in issue.

[60] CJEC Case 27/68 [1969] ECR p. 255.

should have been clearly and unambiguously stated. Since the decision taken referred to a number of considerations such as age, vocational training, reports on work, and family responsibilities as having been taken into account in not assigning the applicant to a vacant A3 post, the requirement, it was held, had been fulfilled. In *von Lachmüller*[61] it was found that, while the period of notice was reasonable, as was required by a general principle of law, the proper reasons for the termination had not been stated in the letter of dismissal so that they could be challenged, even though there had been a general notification earlier of the impending measures of reducing staff. This was held to have vitiated the procedure of termination for abolition of post. In *Pasetti-Bombardella*[62] it was stated that the merger of administrations was a very special situation to which the normal retirement provisions did not apply. However, the CJEC examined the question whether there had been discrimination between grades in the treatment of staff and found that none existed. In *Mills*,[63] while the general principle that, in the dismissal of staff on reductions being made, single persons and those most recently appointed should in general be dismissed first was admitted, it was held that that principle did not preclude the merits of the staff member from being primarily taken into account.

In two cases decided by the Appeals Board of the OEEC[64] the tribunal found that, while the procedure followed by the respondent was irregular, this defect was inessential and was not the direct cause of the failure of the applicant to be reassigned.

(c) Survival of rights

When posts are abolished or suppressed, the question may arise what rights survive a new regime that may have been brought into existence. This does not happen very often but it has been adverted to in a few cases. In *Decision No. 6(d)*,[65] for example, the contracts of NATO staff members were terminated on the headquarters of NATO being moved and they were given new fixed-term contracts. This situation may be interpreted as a complete suppression of posts and a reorganization of the cadre. A question which arose was whether the right to the termination benefits on reaching the age of retirement and the right to resign which had been accorded to the staff members under their old contracts could be taken away. While the Appeals Board of

[61] CJEC Cases 43, 45 & 48/59 [1960] ECR p. 463.

[62] CJEC Case 20/68 [1969] ECR p. 235. In *Decision No. 15*, OEEC Appeals Board [1952], Recueil des décisions 1 à 62 (1979) p. 47, the tribunal held that there was no discrimination in the treatment of the applicant when he was dismissed on the abolition of his post.

[63] CJEC Case 110/75 [1976] ECR p. 1613.

[64] *Decision No. 15*, OEEC Appeals Board [1952], Recueil des décisions 1 à 62 (1979) p. 47; *Decision No. 29*, OEEC Appeals Board [1957], ibid. p. 80.

[65] *Decision No. 6(d)*, NATO Appeals Board [1967], Collection of the Decisions (1972).

NATO considered that the new regime had not prejudiced the interests of the employees, since they had been allowed to pursue their careers in the normal way, it also held that the rights in issue were acquired rights which survived the new arrangements and could not be taken away. As has already been seen, the retroactive variation of the seniority rule by resolution of the General Assembly of the OAS was disallowed by the OASAT in *Hebblethwaite and Others*.[66] It was held that the rule could not be changed in so far as it applied to the reassignment of staff members whose posts had been abolished.

(d) *Effect of agreement*

Irrespective of the fulfilment of the duties devolving on the organization on the abolition or suppression of posts under general principles of law or under the written law of the organization, if the applicant accepts an offer made by the administration and arrives at a settlement in regard to the termination of his employment and the benefits he is entitled to as a consequence, he cannot resile from that agreement but must accept its terms as being a discharge of the obligations of the organization.[67]

(e) *Indemnities*

While there is apparently no general principle of law entitling a staff member whose service has been terminated upon the abolition of his post to an indemnity, there are written rules prescribing such indemnities in certain organizations. Tribunals have been called upon to interpret these written provisions and to determine the rights of the affected staff member. The details of particular interpretations are unimportant from the point of view of the general law but there have been cases in which tribunals have dealt with certain general principles which are applicable.

Discrimination in the award of indemnities would in principle be forbidden. In three cases decided by the Appeals Board of ELDO, while the principle was not denied, it was held that there was no discrimination, though differences were made between groups, because the differences were not within the same group and they could not be faulted.[68] The tribunal refused to pronounce on the desirability of the distinctions.

It is possible for errors of law to occur in the implementation of the terms of provisions relating to indemnities. Where an error of law is alleged, the tribunal will examine the provisions of the law in order to establish whether it has been properly applied, while it will only take note of a misapplication if it

---

[66] OASAT Judgment No. 30 [1977].

[67] *Zahawi*, ILOAT Judgment No. 633 [1984] (ITU).

[68] *Decision No. 9*, ELDO Appeals Board [1973]; *Decision No. 10*, ELDO Appeals Board [1973]; *Decision No. 11*, ELDO Appeals Board [1973].

has caused loss to the staff member concerned.[69] Tribunals will not hesitate to apply the provisions of municipal law in this connection, if they are the applicable law in the circumstances of the case.[70]

Where the staff member had an option in the choice of indemnities, it has been held that it was sufficient for him to have been genuinely aware of the options through indirect sources such as a Staff Committee or the Head of Administration, even if he had not been informed in writing of the options by the head of the institution.[71] The staff member cannot then claim that he was not informed of the options and decide to change his mind about the option chosen. Where a termination indemnity is payable only if it is claimed within a certain period, the applicant must make his claim in time.[72] If he fails, he cannot in law successfully claim the indemnity before a tribunal, even though equity may be on his side.

The acceptance of an indemnity may in certain circumstances amount to a renunciation of rights against the organization. But it has been held that there are circumstances in which such acceptance may not be an actual renunciation of such rights.[73] This will depend on the circumstances of the case. It is significant that the ILOAT did not in this case say that there was a presumption that the acceptance of an indemnity amounted to a renunciation of rights against the organization, as there might very well be.

(f) Remedies

In most cases in which remedies have been ordered, the dismissal of the applicant has been found to be unlawful because the requirements relating to reassignment had not been fulfilled. In *Desgranges*,[74] on the other hand, four months' leave with pay was found to have been required by the applicable law, before the applicant's appointment was terminated. The ILOAT ordered the payment of four months' salary as compensation because this provision had not been implemented.[75] In one case the Appeals Board of the

---

[69] See *Decision No. 5, ESA/CR/15*, ESA Appeals Board [1977]; *Decision No. 41*, NATO Appeals Board [1972], Collection of the Decisions (1972); *Decision No. 141*, NATO Appeals Board [1981], Collection of the Decisions 135 to 171 (1984); *Decision No. 142*, NATO Appeals Board [1981], ibid.

[70] *Desgranges*, ILOAT Judgment No. 11 [1953] (ILO).

[71] *Decision No. 8*, ELDO Appeals Board [1973].

[72] *Niestlé*, ILOAT Judgment No. 16 [1955] (IIIC); *Sheffey*, ILOAT Judgment No. 601 [1984] (PAHO).

[73] *Gaydar*, ILOAT Judgment No. 581 [1983] (PAHO).

[74] ILOAT Judgment No. 11 [1953] (ILO).

[75] In *Decision No. 141*, NATO Appeals Board [1981], Collection of the Decisions 135 to 171 (1984), the error of law relating to notice was held not to have caused damage which had to be compensated. The decision of the organization was annulled in so far as it related to the notice to be given and to the date of termination. See also *Decision No. 142*, NATO Appeals Board [1981], ibid. In *Decision No. 5, ESA/CR/15*, ESA Appeals Board [1977], the tribunal ordered the payment of the proper indemnity.

OEEC awarded four months' salary as equitable compensation, because, though the termination of the applicant's appointment was in order, he had suffered abnormal prejudice upon the abolition of his post as a result of his long years of service and his age.[76]

In those cases where the dismissal has been found to be wrongful the OASAT has generally ordered reinstatement with compensation of two years' salary as an alternative to reinstatement[77] or reinstatement with compensation of a named figure with or without benefits denied the applicant.[78] It is not clear on what basis the lump sum was calculated but it is possibly a multiple of the applicant's salary. Sometimes but not always the order for reinstatement has been accompanied by the requirement that compensation consisting of the salary due to the applicant between the date of his dismissal and the date of his reinstatement be paid him.[79] It is not clear on what basis in *Calvimontes* the salary payable during this period was not ordered to be paid, if the applicant was reinstated.

In *Hermann*[80] the ILOAT ordered reinstatement within six months together with payment of salary from the date of termination of service to the date of reinstatement, provided the applicant repaid the separation payments made to him, or in the event that the respondent decided not to reinstate the applicant, payment of damages for the whole injury he had suffered including loss of pension rights, equal to five years' salary less the termination indemnity paid him. In *Savioli*[81] and *Babbar*[82] no reinstatement was ordered by the ILOAT, in the former case because of the applicant's relations with some supervisors. Compensation of three years' salary was ordered in *Savioli*, while in *Babbar* the tribunal said that the damages

---

[76] *Cauro*, Decision No. 34, OEEC Appeals Board [1961], Recueil des décisions 1 à 62 (1979) p. 95.

[77] See *Calvimontes*, OASAT Judgment No. 63 [1981].

[78] See *Chrétien*, OASAT Judgment No. 29 [1977]; *Getz*, OASAT Judgment No. 26 [1976]; *Hebblethwaite and Others*, OASAT Judgment No. 30 [1977]; *Méndez*, OASAT Judgment No. 55 [1980].

[79] *Chrétien*, OASAT Judgment No. 29 [1977]; *Getz*, OASAT Judgment No. 26 [1976]; *Hebblethwaite and Others*, OASAT Judgment No. 30 [1977]; *Méndez*, OASAT Judgment No. 55 [1980]. In *Decision No. 21*, OEEC Appeals Board [1955], Recueil des décisions 1 à 62 (1979) p. 59, the tribunal ordered that the wrongful termination decision be annulled with the result that reinstatement alone took place. No compensation was awarded.

[80] ILOAT Judgment No. 133 [1969] (UNESCO).

[81] ILOAT Judgment No. 346 [1978] (WMO). In *Decision No. 34, ESRO/CR/89*, ESRO Appeals Board [1974], where an omission of relevant facts vitiated the decision to terminate the applicant's services, the tribunal did not annul the decision but awarded six months' salary for material damage and no compensation for moral injury, because there was none.

[82] ILOAT Judgment No. 388 [1980] (FAO). In *Gotschi*, ILOAT Judgment No. 523 [1982] (PAHO), where the abolition of post was improper, compensation of $40,000 was awarded for unlawful termination of contract. For awards of compensation (three years' salary) instead of reinstatement, where the decision to abolish a post was unlawful, see *Azola Blanco and Véliz García* ILOAT Judgment No. 507 [1982] (ESO), and *Acosta Andres*, ILOAT Judgment No. 508 [1982] (ESO).

awarded would be modest because of reservations about the applicant and made an *ex aequo et bono* assessment of one year's salary.

The UNAT in *Aglion*,[83] an early case, ordered reinstatement with the payment of salary and benefits between the date of termination of service and the date of reinstatement, or, if reinstatement was not carried out, the payment of the difference in salary and benefits referred to above plus a termination indemnity in accordance with the relevant chapter of the Staff Regulations.[84] In *Morrow*[85] no reinstatement was ordered because the applicant held a temporary indefinite contract and his chances of re-employment were hypothetical; $400 compensation was ordered.[86] In *Aubert and 14 Others*[87] the UNAT ruled that the contracts were still in force without derogation from the right of the administration to follow the proper procedure in regard to reassignment under Staff Rule 104 and to terminate the contracts in the event that the applicants could not be reassigned.

Ill health or invalidity

Employment has been terminated in international organizations for reasons of ill health or 'invalidity', as it is called. In the *Monod Case*[88] the Committee of Jurists appointed by the League of Nations took the position that even in the absence of express stipulation, an organization could dismiss an employee for reasons of ill health, because it was in the public interest that this right should be recognized. It follows that there is a general principle of law permitting termination of employment in international organizations for invalidity. However, in general, international organizations have written provisions governing the termination of service for reasons of health, thus making it unnecessary for them to rely on the general principle of law. As a consequence also of the existence of governing written provisions, tribunals

---

[83] UNAT Judgment No. 56 [1954], JUNAT Nos. 1–70 p. 283. Specific performance in the form of restoration of acquired rights taken away upon suppression of posts and retention in employment thereafter was ordered in *Decision No. 6(d)*, NATO Appeals Board [1967], Collection of the Decisions (1972). The decision to dismiss the applicant was quashed and, as a result, reinstatement took place in *Decision No. 21*, NATO Appeals Board [1970], Collection of the Decisions (1972).

[84] Similar remedies were awarded in *Carson*, UNAT Judgment No. 85 [1962], JUNAT Nos. 71–86 p. 112.

[85] UNAT Judgment No. 16 [1952], JUNAT Nos. 1–70 p. 54.

[86] The remedy was similar in *Quémerais*, UNAT Judgment No. 172 [1973], JUNAT Nos. 167–230 p. 31. In *von Lachmüller*, CJEC Cases 43, 45 & 48/59 [1960] ECR p. 463, the CJEC awarded BF60,000 each to the applicants who had been wrongfully dismissed on the abolition of their posts.

[87] UNAT Judgment No. 2 [1950], JUNAT Nos. 1–70 p. 3.

[88] League of Nations, Official Journal, 1925, p. 1441 at p. 1443.

have not had to deal with the general principle of law, its scope, or the manner of its implementation.

In the application of the written rules relating to termination of service for invalidity, tribunals have been confronted with a variety of issues which they have settled by reference to general principle, generally without mention that they are applying such principle, or by interpretation of the relevant rules. The written rules are generally unambiguously framed so that their application has not caused many serious problems.

A prime cause of concern in some of the decided cases has been whether the finding of invalidity warranting termination was substantiated by the facts; that is, whether the applicant was in fact medically unfit for work, or disabled, or satisfied the requirements of the written law relating to invalidity. In some of these cases the tribunals have not hesitated to examine the evidence themselves in order to establish the true facts. Thus, in *Matta*[89] the WBAT ordered the production of certain evidence on the basis of which it found that the applicant had been properly retired for disability. The tribunal stated:

Examination of the evidence released by the Respondent, on the order of the Tribunal, supporting the decision to terminate the Applicant's employment through recourse to the system of disability retirement, leads the Tribunal to the conclusion that the decision of the Pension Benefits Administration Committee of August 28, 1981 was based on sufficient evidence. The evidence shows that the Applicant's technical skills were not the primary source of complaint by her supervisors and that it was the personality condition confirmed by the medical report that interfered with the Applicant's overall performance, seriously impairing her ability to establish healthy and positive work relationships with colleagues and supervisors.[90]

In *Decision No. 52(a)*[91] and *Decision No. 52(c)*[92] the Appeals Board of NATO took the course of ordering a medical examination in order to determine whether the applicant was medically unfit, because the applicant had, before her employment was terminated, produced a medical certificate stating that she was fit for work, thus raising doubts about the facts. It then decided that the applicant was sick for one year which warranted the termination of her employment under the Staff Regulations pertaining to sickness. A conflicting approach was taken by the CJEC in *Schuerer*[93] where the applicant contended that he was medically unfit and that the finding of the administration that he did not have an occupational disease was mistaken. The Court merely examined the decision of the Invalidity Committee to

---

[89] WBAT Reports [1983, Part I], Decision No. 12.

[90] Ibid. at p. 15.

[91] *Decision No. 52(a)*, NATO Appeals Board [1973], Collection of the Decisions 46 to 73 (1976).

[92] *Decision No. 52(c)*, NATO Appeals Board [1974], ibid.

[93] CJEC Case 107/79 [1980] ECR p. 1845.

ascertain whether the conclusion was clearly and precisely stated that the applicant had an occupational disease. In the absence of such a clear conclusion the Court said that the findings were final and that it could not examine all the facts to establish the proper conclusion, because no new facts had been produced. The explanation of this case may lie in the fact that the finding of the Committee was in favour of the applicant in that it held that he was not medically unfit. In such a case the tribunal will probably not reopen the finding of fact. In the other cases, the findings were that the applicants were medically unfit. On the other hand, a tribunal will not examine medical opinions but will merely satisfy itself that there was enough evidence in such opinions on the facts of the case to support the conclusion of invalidity arrived at by the organization.[94]

In *Decision No. 52(e)*[95] the Appeals Board of NATO indicated that the provisions of the relevant Staff Regulations should be followed and that the applicant was, therefore, entitled to sick leave for 36 months. It was therefore incumbent upon the organization to pay her her salary for this period. Tribunals will also enforce the compensatory provisions of the written rules relating to termination of service upon invalidity.[96] By the same token tribunals will not hesitate to interpret the rules and regulations relating to termination of service for invalidity.[97]

It is conceivable that a *détournement de procédure* might have occurred warranting the quashing of the decision to terminate the applicant's service, where the applicant has been dismissed for reasons other than invalidity when the real reason for the dismissal was the applicant's ill health. This principle was recognized by the ILOAT in *Nowakowski (No. 4)*,[98] although in that case it was found that there was no *détournement de procédure*. There the applicant contended that she was sick and could not work, whereas she was dismissed for unsatisfactory service. The tribunal said that she could not be dismissed for reasons of health unless she was physically or mentally unfit for work which was not the case on the evidence. Thus, there was no reason to conclude that the dismissal for unsatisfactory service was not the true reason for the dismissal.[99]

It is essential that a proper procedure be followed in the termination of an appointment for medical reasons, even if the written law is silent on the matter. In *Miss Y*[100] the applicant's permanent appointment was terminated for reasons of health under Staff Regulation 9.1 (a) of the UN. The basis for

[94] *Miss Y*, UNAT Judgment No. 91 [1964], JUNAT Nos. 87–113 p. 30.
[95] *Decision No. 52(e)*, NATO Appeals Board [1974], Collection of the Decisions 46 to 73 (1976).
[96] *Godinache*, ILOAT Judgment No. 148 [1970] (FAO).
[97] *Beynoussef*, ILOAT Judgment No. 595 [1983] (WHO).
[98] ILOAT Judgment No. 248 [1975] (WMO).
[99] See also *Perinciolo*, CJEC Case 124/75 [1976] ECR p. 1953.
[100] UNAT Judgment No. 83 [1961], JUNAT Nos. 71–86 p. 90.

the termination was the psychiatric factor. An examination four months before the termination of employment did not result in certification by the doctor that the applicant was incapacitated for the service. Subsequently, there was no psychiatric examination before the termination of service. The UNAT held that, while the Staff Regulations and Staff Rules did not specify the exact procedure for termination on the ground of disability, a fair procedure should have been followed. The tribunal drew an analogy from the Staff Rule dealing with sick leave and found that the applicant had been denied due process. On the other hand, where a fair procedure has been followed and the finding is in favour of the applicant, due process does not demand that that procedure be repeated.[101] The applicant's claims that she should have been dismissed on medical grounds and not for disciplinary reasons was, therefore, rejected. Where the procedure is interfered with by the applicant, as where he refused to allow disclosure of his personal medical file, there is no defect in the procedure followed and the organization is permitted to take a decision on the basis of the evidence available to it.[102]

In *Miss Y*[103] the allegation was made that after the case had been remanded there had been prejudice in the determination that the applicant was medically unfit. The tribunal found that there was no proof of such prejudice. It did not deny that prejudice would have vitiated the termination decision.

The remedies ordered in cases where dismissals for invalidity have been found to be improper have not been complicated. They vary with the circumstances of each case. In *Miss Y*,[104] where the termination decision was found to have been predicated upon an unfair procedure, the case was remanded for correction of procedure and the applicant was awarded two months' salary, the tribunal noting that she had been given an *ex gratia* payment in addition to being paid a disability pension. In the subsequent case the applicant failed. In *Godinache*,[105] where the applicant complained that he had been deprived of the proper compensation upon dismissal, the ILOAT ordered payment of compensation according to the relevant Staff Rules. In *Beynoussef*[106] the termination retroactively of the applicant's employment was found to be wrongful. The termination decision was quashed and the case referred back to the WHO for correction of the administrative position prior to termination. The applicant was to be regarded as having been in service till he was properly dismissed and interest at the rate of 10 per cent per

---

[101] *Perinciolo*, CJEC Case 124/75 [1976] ECR p. 1953. It should be noted that the finding of fitness was made by the Disciplinary Board.

[102] *Beynoussef*, ILOAT Judgment No. 595 [1983] (WHO).

[103] UNAT Judgment No. 91 [1964], JUNAT Nos. 87–113 p. 30.

[104] UNAT Judgment No. 83 [1961], JUNAT Nos. 71–86 p. 90.

[105] ILOAT Judgment No. 148 [1970] (FAO).

[106] ILOAT Judgment No. 595 [1983] (WHO).

annum on the sums owing to him was payable in addition to those sums. In *Decisions No. 52(e)*[107] of the Appeals Board of NATO, after the dismissal was found to be valid, the organization was ordered to pay the applicant sick leave benefits for 36 months in accordance with the Staff Regulations.

Disciplinary reasons

Appointments may be terminated for disciplinary reasons. However, such terminations are aspects of disciplinary measures, and will be dealt with below in Chapter 39 on Disciplinary Measures.

Miscellaneous reasons

Any situation in which an appointment is brought to an end and the staff member severs employment connections with the organization may be regarded as a termination of the appointment,[108] whether a decision by the organization to terminate the appointment is involved or not. A termination could result from a variety of factors apart from those already discussed. It may be useful briefly to examine the law relating to termination for these other reasons, although often the points in issue in the cases may have turned on interpretations of the written law.

(a) Retirement

In the OAS the Staff Regulations provide for the extension of the period of service beyond the date of compulsory retirement in certain circumstances. In several cases it has been held that the decision taken by the organization not to extend the period of service of staff members was vitiated because the requirements of the Staff Regulations had not been satisfied.[109] Particularly, it has been pointed out that the applicant's expression of desire to continue in service must be considered, even if it is communicated to the committee considering his case by the applicant and not by the Secretary General,[110] and

---

107 *Decision No. 52(e)*, NATO Appeals Board [1974], Collection of the Decisions 46 to 73 [1976].

108 In *Barrett*, OASAT Judgment No. 2 [1972], the tribunal took the view that compulsory retirement was not a termination of employment as such but a different species of act. However, the decision did not turn on such a definition. The statement could, therefore, be regarded as hair-splitting.

109 See *Barrett*, OASAT Judgment No. 2 [1972], and *Victory*, OASAT Judgment No. 7 [1974].

110 *Vivó*, OASAT Judgment No. 10 [1974]; *Aquino y Padrón*, OASAT Judgment No. 11 [1974].

that it is only a lack of fitness to continue in service that would warrant a refusal of the applicant's request, so that, where no evidencé of a lack of fitness was communicated to the committee, a decision not to grant the applicant's request was improper.[111] On the other hand, it has been held that where the applicant had completed fifteen years of service no conditions were attached, according to the Staff Regulations, to the decision of the organization not to grant an extension of the period of service.[112] In those cases where the decision not to grant the applicant an extension of his period of service was held to be wrongful in effect compensation of twelve months' or nine months' salary was awarded on the basis apparently that a one-year extension was foreseen in the Staff Regulations. In connection with retirement it has been held that a US statute was inapplicable to the case of a US national employed by the OAS in order to enable him to work until he reached the age of 70 years, when the compulsory retirement age in the organization was 65 years.[113].

No significant cases concerning the termination of employment upon retirement have come up for decision before the ILOAT or the UNAT. In *Cunio*,[114] however, the UNAT did hold that in principle the date of birth of an employee warranted in the application for employment settles the date of retirement of that employee, unless there is convincing proof of a change in that date.

The CJEC decided some cases concerning the application of the Staff Regulations which arose after the merger of administrations took place. In *Pasetti-Bombardella*[115] the Court decided that the normal retirement provisions did not apply in the case of staff members whose employment was terminated as a result of the merger. In *Peco*,[116] upon the merger, the applicant was appointed to a post for which he felt he had no qualifications and requested to be compulsorily retired under Article 50 of the Staff Regulations. This was refused by the institution because it felt that he could perform. Later he resigned because of ill health which he alleged was caused by his having to work in his new appointment. He claimed that he had retired in the interests of the service and should be treated as such for the purpose of pecuniary benefits. The Court held that the decision by the institution that the interests of the service did not require the retirement of the applicant on both occasions was not an abuse of discretionary power, because the

---

[111] *Vesprémy Bangha*, OASAT Judgment No. 12 [1975].

[112] *Ramirez Velarde*, OASAT Judgment No. 22 [1976].

[113] *Hernández de Agüero*, OASAT Judgment No. 52 [1980]; *Martínez*, OASAT Judgment No. 54 [1980]; *Zuntz*, OASAT Judgment No. 57 [1981].

[114] UNAT Judgment No. 321 [1984]. See also *Zreikat*, ILOAT Judgment No. 459 [1981] (WHO).

[115] CJEC Case 20/68 [1969] ECR p. 235.

[116] CJEC Case 36/69 [1970] ECR p. 361.

applicant had no right to the retirement systems which he claimed should have been applied.

In *Giry*[117] the applicant who was on leave on personal grounds applied for compulsory retirement under Regulation No. 2530/72 of the organization which dealt with special circumstances where the organization could retire persons in the interests of the service. The organization decided that the provision did not apply to persons on leave on personal grounds and refused to retire the applicant under that provision. The CJEC held that the interpretation given to the Regulation by the organization was not illegal, although it was not obligatory. There was no abuse of discretion in the adoption of that interpretation nor had there been discrimination in the application of the Regulation, because two other persons who had not been on leave on personal grounds had been compulsorily retired under that provision. In *Oslizlok*[118] the applicant was retired in the interests of the service upon the office being reorganized. The applicant contended that the decision was bad for a variety of reasons. The Court found that (i) the decision to reorganize the office was not taken in order to remove the applicant and, therefore, there was no *détournement de pouvoir*, and (ii) the discretionary power to remove the applicant which had to be exercised in a proper fashion had not been abused, in so far as the reasons for the removel were adequately stated and the applicant had been warned of his removal, so that he could make his defence; but in so far as the applicant had not been given an opportunity to be heard in defence of his interests before it was decided not to assign him to another post, the decision to remove him was tainted. The decision not to assign him to another post was, therefore, annulled. In *Belfiore*,[119] however, which concerned another decision to compulsorily retire a staff member, because he had refused a post, it was held that the applicant had not proved that he had not refused the post. The decision was, therefore, good. The reason for compulsory retirement was not questioned by the Court.

(b) Resignation

Resignation is not governed by extensive written rules generally but by general principles of law. It is not questioned that employees with contracts of appointment have the right to resign. The contracts of appointment usually refer to this right. In the case of statutory appointments some question has been raised about this right in the absence of express provision in the written law.[120] Where the resignation must be accepted for it to be valid, as

---

117 CJEC Case 1/74 [1974] ECR p. 1269. See also *Geerlings*, CJEC Case 38/74 [1975] ECR p. 247.

118 CJEC Case 34/77 [1978] ECR p. 1099.

119 CJEC Case 108/79 [1980] ECR p. 1769.

120 See *Aicher*, Decision No. 37, OECD Appeals Board [1964], Recueil des décisions 1 à 62 (1979) p. 102.

in the case of the European Communities, the tribunal will not hesitate to enforce that obligation in the appropriate circumstances.[121]

There have been a few cases in which the validity of resignations have been questioned with the object of having the resignations declared null and void. In some cases it has been alleged that the resignation was not valid on account of duress. In *Akinola Deko*[122] the applicant alleged that his resignation had not been given voluntarily because, there being a possibility of disciplinary proceedings, he had been called up and asked for an explanation before such proceedings were instituted. The ILOAT held that the action taken by the organization was not a violation of the FAO Staff Rules and that the freedom of action of the applicant had not been affected, when he took the decision to resign. In a similar case, where disciplinary proceedings were pending, the Appeals Board of ESA found that the applicant's decision to resign was not the result of duress or pressure but that he was aware of his acts, so that the decision could not be regarded as null and void.[123] It was also said that the resignation did not amount to a waiver of rights in the circumstances of that case and that, therefore, the applicant was entitled upon resignation to the usual indemnity to which he would not have been entitled had he waived his rights.

In *Devdutt*[124] the validity of a resignation was contested by the applicant in a case where he had resigned because neither had he been promoted nor had his position been regraded. It was alleged that there was a procedural defect in the acceptance of his resignation, because the composition and procedure of the Regional Board of Inquiry and Appeal had been irregular and the Director General of ILO had based his decision on the recommendation of the Board. The ILOAT held that in fact the Director General had taken his decision after a recommendation was made by the Headquarters Board of Inquiry and Appeal which differed from that of the other Board and that, therefore, there was no invalidity factor, even if the procedure and composition of the Regional Board had been defective. In the case of a contract of service the subsequent withdrawal of a resignation after it has been made is not effective to negate it and the consent of the organization is not required to make it effective.[125]

In *Reynolds*[126] it was held that a provision in a Staff Manual interpreting a Staff Rule and permitting the FAO to regard a refusal to accept a transfer as a voluntary resignation was bad and should be struck down. Refusal to accept

---

[121] *Campolongo*, CJEC Cases 27 & 39/59 [1960] ECR p. 391.
[122] ILOAT Judgment No. 150 [1970] (FAO).
[123] *Decision No. 18, ESA/CR/38*, ESA Appeals Board [1983]. A resignation, even though chosen as an alternative to termination for unsatisfactory service, is apparently not *per se* made under duress and is, therefore, valid: see *Mr Y*, WBAT Reports [1985], Decision No. 25.
[124] ILOAT Judgment No. 158 [1970] (WHO).
[125] *Hilliar*, LNT Judgment No. 20 [1939] (ILO).
[126] ILOAT Judgment No. 38 [1958] (FAO).

a transfer was not a voluntary resignation but had to be dealt with as a cause for other sanctions. For illegal action the FAO was ordered to pay the applicant his salary from the date of the termination of his service to the date of the judgment and salary in lieu of three months' notice. The organization was also ordered to restore the applicant's right to accumulated leave and to pay him the appropriate termination indemnities.

(c) *Abandonment of post*

Termination of appointments on abandonment of post is generally provided for in Staff Regulations and Staff Rules. In *Dhawan (No. 3)*[127] the ILOAT had to deal with the application of Staff Rule 980 of the WHO which permitted the organization to terminate an appointment on the basis that a staff member had abandoned his post when he had been absent for more than 15 days without a satisfactory explanation. Since the applicant had not been sick and had been away from his job for more than four months without a satisfactory explanation, it was held that the termination decision was valid.

The first question which arises in regard to this ground for dismissal is whether it can be applied where the written law does not provide for it. No decision has clearly stated that there is, indeed, a general principle of law that a staff member may be dismissed because he has abandoned his post *per se*, but in *Dupuy*[128] the UNAT referred to an Annex of the Staff Regulations and the Staff Rules which referred to abandonment of post as confirming a long-standing practice of the UN of regarding unauthorized absence from work in certain circumstances as abandonment of post warranting termination of appointments, although the written law did not specifically state that abandonment of post was a ground for termination of service. It would seem to be reasonable to permit the termination of service for abandonment of post as a general principle of law. It could be regarded as a breach of contract[129] or violation of an implied statutory term.

In *Duran (No. 2)* the ILOAT discussed the meaning of abandonment of post and stated:

If one party to a contract fails or refused to perform his duties under the contract in circumstances which show that he does not intend ever again to resume them, i.e. show in effect that he is abandoning his post, the other party is entitled to treat the contract as at an end; he is not obliged to wait indefinitely in case the first party might change his mind. This is what abandonment means. It contains both a physical and a mental element. A temporary absence from a place does not mean that the place is

---

[127] ILOAT Judgment No. 214 [1973] (WHO).

[128] UNAT Judgment No. 174 [1973], JUNAT Nos. 167–230 p. 49.

[129] See *Duran (No. 2)*, ILOAT Decision No. 392 [1980] (PAHO) at p. 5, where the ILOAT referred to the ordinary principles of contract law as applicable and said that an abandonment of post was a violation of contract entitling the other party to treat the contract as at an end.

abandoned; there must be shown also an intention not to return. So to the physical failure to perform a contractual duty there must be added the intention to abandon future performance. Proof of intention is not always easy, and the object of Rule 980 is to allow the intention to be assumed from the fact of absence without reasonable explanation for fifteen days. The explanation has not got to be one that exonerates the staff member from breach of contract or from other disciplinary measures, but it has to be one which negatives the intention to abandon.[130]

Consequently, while abandonment of place should not be confused with abandonment of duties, there was no requirement that a written explanation had to be submitted in order to avoid the conclusion that the post had been abandoned. The explanation could be oral or in writing or be implied from the circumstances. Thus, where the applicant objected to an order transferring her to Brasilia from headquarters on account of her health, she had made a *bona fide* challenge to the validity of the order which was a satisfactory explanation for not complying with it. In challenging the order in a manner prescribed by the Staff Regulations she was affirming the contract, not abandoning it. Thus, she could not be dismissed on the ground that she had abandoned her post, because she had failed under Staff Rule 980 'to report to duty in excess of 15 days'. However, while the decision to dismiss was quashed, reinstatement or damages were not awarded, because the other decision to reassign her could not be termed invalid. On the other hand, the unauthorized acceptance of alternative employment when sick leave was disallowed was an abandonment of post.[131] Where the behaviour of the parties, especially that of the applicant, clearly indicates a clear abandonment of post, the situation may be regarded as an abandonment of post.[132]

In regard to the procedure to be followed, it has been clearly stated that abandonment of post does not have to be treated by the organization as a breach of discipline requiring the implementation of disciplinary procedures. The organization has the option to treat the situation as involving a breach of discipline but may choose the alternative of regarding it as a plain abandonment of post, in which case disciplinary procedures need not be followed.[133] Thus, the contract of appointment can be simply terminated, though the issue whether there had in fact been an abandonment of post can be contested by the applicant. In *Dhawan* (*No. 3*)[134] it was held that failure to conduct a medical examination immediately prior to termination of the appointment, as generally required by the Staff Rules, did not of itself render invalid the decision to terminate the appointment. In that case the facts showed that

---

[130] Ibid.

[131] *Hilaire*, UNAT Judgment No. 220 [1977], JUNAT Nos. 167–230 p. 503.

[132] *Kennedy*, UNAT Judgment No. 265 [1980], JUNAT Nos. 231–300 p. 330.

[133] See *Dupuy*, UNAT Judgment No. 174 [1973], JUNAT Nos. 167–230 p. 49; *Hilaire*, UNAT Judgment No. 220 [1977], JUNAT Nos. 167–230 p. 503.

[134] ILOAT Judgment No. 214 [1973] (WHO).

the applicant's absence was not caused by sickness or ill health. Hence, the failure to follow the applicable procedure .could not have affected the decision taken. On the other hand, where a post is regarded as abandoned, reasonable notice must be given and a specific date in the future fixed for the termination of the appointment. Retroactive termination cannot be permitted and is unlawful. In circumstances in which the UN had made the termination of employment retroactive, compensation of $2,000 was ordered, because the applicant should have been regarded as having been in service for six months longer than the actual date on which his appointment was terminated.[135]

(d) Expiry of short-term contract

Generally a short-term contract may be allowed to expire as a matter of course. No decision on the part of the organization is entailed. This statement of the law was confirmed by the ILOAT in *Antonaci*.[136] The organization was not under an obligation to grant sick leave in the event of sickness at the time of expiry or pay the applicant's medical expenses. Further, no general principle of law required compensation except that, as in the case of sickness arising out of employment, the written law of the organization may require it.

In two cases the UNAT has implied that, though in general in the case of short-term contracts no expectancy of renewal can be assumed to exist, an expectancy of renewal may be given the staff member by the administration which would create in the staff member a right to the renewal of the contract.[137] In the absence of such expectancy there is no question that the contract merely expires and the employment relationship terminates without it being necessary for the administration to take a decision. Whether the concept of legitimate expectancy pertinent to fixed-term contracts in the law of the UNAT is relevant to short-term contracts is a difficult question. In both the above-mentioned cases the facts showed that the contracts expired at the end of their term. It was therefore unnecessary for any statement to be made relating to a legitimate expectancy.

Where the contract expires as a matter of course, prejudice or extraneous motivation cannot be raised as an objection to the non-renewal of the contract.[138] Those considerations are irrelevant. This is a natural consequence of the fact that in law the contract comes to an end on its expiry and requires no decision as such. Thus, the fact that the vacant post is filled by another person, for whatever reason, cannot constitute an abuse of power.[139]

---

[135] *Kennedy*, UNAT Judgment No. 265 [1980], JUNAT Nos. 231–300 p. 330.

[136] ILOAT Judgment No. 157 [1970] (ILO).

[137] See *Pappas*, UNAT Judgment No. 94 [1965], JUNAT Nos. 87–113 p. 66; *Jazairi*, UNAT Judgment No. 316 [1983].

[138] See *Pappas*, UNAT Judgment No. 94 [1965], JUNAT Nos. 87–113 p. 66.

[139] Ibid.

In a very special case[140] where the applicant had been given a series of temporary contracts and his appointment ended as a result of the expiry of the last temporary contract, the OASAT examined the facts and found that the applicant should have been given a permanent contract and not a series of temporary contracts. The tribunal ordered reinstatement or, in the absence of reinstatement, an indemnity of $16,000, because it held that the termination of the appointment was invalid. The tribunal also stated strangely, that during the period between the termination of his employment and the judgment of the tribunal, the applicant should be regarded as having had no contract, in the event that the order for reinstatement was implemented.

(e) Breach of contract

The ILOAT has dealt with the question whether a contract of service can be terminated for breach of contract. In *Duran (No. 3)*[141] the applicant refused a transfer to a position away from headquarters ostensibly on the ground that she was sick. However, the ill health of the applicant was not proved by her to the administration of the organization and the administration consequently took the course of terminating her appointment, because she had failed to report for her assignment. The letter of dismissal referred to several Staff Regulations and Staff Rules, among them the Regulation and Rules which made the staff subject to assignment by the Director. The ILOAT simply stated:

The Tribunal will not enter into the arguments as to which, if any, of the staff rules enumerated in the Organization's letter of 19 December, authorized the termination. It is an elementary principle of the law of contract that if the party clearly and definitely refuses to honour his or her obligations, the other party is entitled to rescind the contract; and it does not matter whether or not any of the rules say so in so many words.[142]

This appears to be an affirmation that an organization may terminate the appointment of a staff member for breach of contract.

The statement raises a number of questions such as whether any breach of an obligation would warrant termination and what the relationship is between termination for breach of contract and termination for specific reasons such as unsatisfactory service and breach of discipline which require certain specific procedures to be followed and certain conditions to be met.

---

[140] *Holzman*, OASAT Judgment No. 19 [1976].

[141] ILOAT Judgment No. 543 [1983] (PAHO).

[142] Ibid. at p. 7. See also *Verdrager*, ILOAT Judgment No. 325 [1977] (WHO), where a refusal of a transfer was described not only as a violation of the Staff Regulations and Staff Rules but as a grave breach of duty. The termination of contract for this reason was held to be lawful.

Clearly, dismissal should only be possible where the breach of contract is fundamental. It is not likely that the tribunal meant that any minor breach of contract would also warrant dismissal. In *Duran* (*No. 3*) the breach was serious enough: it was a violation of the very important obligation to accept assignment by the Director. Secondly, it would be unreasonable to suppose that an organization can avoid its responsibilities connected with particular methods of termination, such as termination for unsatisfactory service or for disciplinary reasons, by resorting to the principle that it may rescind the contract because of a fundamental breach of contract. If this were not so, an organization might choose to rescind and terminate a contract of employment for unsatisfactory service or breach of discipline, for example, on the ground simply that there had been a fundamental breach of contract, because these misfeasances are also fundamental breaches of contract. In taking this course the organization would avoid the stricter procedures and conditions pertinent to those particular grounds for termination, because there is no special procedure nor are there any special conditions attached to termination in the case of breach of contract. In the case of termination or rescission for breach of contract, the organization simply takes a decision that there has been a breach of contract and terminates the contract, leaving it to the staff member to contest that decision and prove before the administrative tribunal that there was no breach of contract in fact, if he is to succeed in upsetting the decision to terminate the contract of service taken by the organization.

In *Reynolds*[143] also a refusal to accept a transfer on the ground of sickness to another duty station was in issue. There the FAO used an interpretation given in the Staff Manual to regard this act of the staff member as a voluntary resignation. The ILOAT held that this interpretation of the relevant Staff Rule was in conflict with the Staff Rule and could not stand. The refusal by the staff member, the tribunal held, could only result in disciplinary action or termination. Compensation was awarded in a sum equivalent to the staff member's salary from the date of termination to the date of judgment and salary in lieu of three months' notice of dismissal. It was also ordered that termination indemnities be paid and the applicant's right to accumulated leave be restored.

While the decision that the act of the staff member in *Reynolds* was not a resignation cannot be contested, the statements that the refusal to accept a transfer should have been dealt with as a disciplinary breach or as some other act warranting termination gives rise to problems. It would appear that, if *Duran* (*No. 3*) were followed, the staff member's refusal could simply be treated as a fundamental breach of contract warranting rescission of the contract. The problem arises because the tribunal seems to have referred to disciplinary action as a possibility. If termination for disciplinary reasons

---

[143] ILOAT Judgment No. 38 [1958] (FAO).

were an alternative, according to the submissions made above, the organiza-tion should not be allowed to resort to rescission for breach of contract as a means of terminating the contract of service, because particularly, the procedures involved in this latter method of termination are less stringent than in the case of dismissal for disciplinary reasons. It is likely that the *obiter dictum* of the tribunal in this case in which it referred to disciplinary action as a possible alternative was made *per incuriam*, the reference to termination by an act of the organization as being necessary, rather than termination by resignation, being sufficient for the purpose of the *ratio decidendi* of the case. In line with *Duran* (*No. 3*) the case of refusal of a transfer made in good faith for ostensibly plausible reasons may be treated simply as a breach of contract, because it cannot in reality be regarded as amounting to unsatis-factory service or a disciplinary breach warranting termination of the contract of service.

In *Duran* (*No. 3*) the ILOAT referred to the fact that bad faith of the organization was not proven and that it was not bad faith for the organiza-tion not to allow the applicant to veto her place of work. This means that the decision to rescind a contract of service following a breach of contract must be taken in good faith. Absence of good faith would be a ground for nulli-fying the decision.

(*f*) *Violation of highest standards*

In *Froma*[144] the UNESCO terminated an indeterminate appointment under Staff Regulation 9.1 (a) which permitted termination of service, if the staff member did not meet the highest standards required by Article VI(5) of the Constitution of UNESCO and the Staff Regulation 1.4. The ILOAT took the view that it had the power to examine the facts and determine whether the circumstances of the case justified the application of the Staff Regulation concerned. The reason given by the administration for the determination that the Staff Regulation had been violated was that the applicant had failed to appear before a Loyalty Board of his national State. While noting that the organization had been threatened with the withdrawal of a member State for reasons connected with the employment of certain of its nationals, the tribunal stated that the independence of the organization must be safe-guarded and that sight must not be lost of its impartiality which was vital.[145] Hence, the power accorded to the organization under the relevant Staff Regulation had to be exercised only for the good of the service and in the interests of the organization.[146] The tribunal examined the relevant provi-sions of the written law of the organization[147] and concluded that the action

144 ILOAT Judgment No. 22 [1955] (UNESCO).
145 Ibid. at p. 6.
146 Ibid. at p. 9.
147 Ibid. at pp. 12–13.

of the applicant in not appearing before the Loyalty Board did not justify the existence of serious doubts as to the high standards required of an international official. Reinstatement was ordered and as an alternative payment of compensation assessed *ex aequo et bono* at two years' salary.[148] There were two other cases decided at about the same time in which the ILOAT followed its decision in *Froma*.[149]

(g) *Interests of the organization*

In some organizations the written law provides that dismissal may be in the interests of the organization. In *Danjean* (*Nos. 1 and 2*)[150] the ILOAT examined the situation where such a provision was resorted to by CERN in circumstances in which the applicant had failed to co-operate in selecting alternative posts. The ILOAT held that the power to terminate a contract of service under the relevant provision was a discretionary one and its exercise could only be questioned if there was some defect, such as an error of law or fact, which made it possible for a discretionary power to be questioned. The exercise of the power in the case was found to be valid and not in violation of the rules relating to the exercise of discretionary powers.

In *Crawford*[151] the UN terminated a temporary indefinite appointment in the interests of the UN under Staff Regulation 9.1 (c). The main motivation for the decision to terminate the appointment was the fact that the applicant had been a member of the Communist Party for just over one year. Another reason given was the fact that the applicant had invoked the Fifth Amendment of the Constitution before a Senate Subcommittee of the United States. The UNAT had no hesitation in holding that there was freedom of political opinion under Staff Regulation 1.4 and that the action of the applicant in invoking the Fifth Amendment was not wrong. Therefore, the finding that it was in the interests of the organization to terminate the applicant's contract was invalid. Reinstatement was ordered plus the payment of the applicant's full salary from the date of termination of service to the date of reinstatement less the indemnity paid and the amount paid in lieu of notice.

In *Scuppa*[152] the applicant argued that the decision to terminate his appointment in the interests of the service was a disguised disciplinary measure. The CJEC held that this was not the case, because the termination was requested by the applicant and it was made under the relevant Staff Regulation. There was no *détournement de procédure* in short.

---

[148] The tribunal commented adversely on the secrecy of a report of the Special Advisory Board of the UNESCO: ibid. pp. 8–9.

[149] *Pankey*, ILOAT Judgment No. 23 [1955] (UNESCO); *Van Gelder*, ILOAT Judgment No. 24 [1955] (UNESCO).

[150] ILOAT Judgment No. 126 [1968] (CERN).

[151] UNAT Judgment No. 18 [1953], JUNAT Nos. 1–70 p. 65.

[152] CJEC Cases 4 & 30/74 [1975] ECR p. 919.

While the power to terminate employment in the interests of an organization is a discretionary power, the above cases show that tribunals will not
hesitate, where necessary, particularly to impeach the characterization of
facts as being such that the interests of the organization have been en-
dangered, thus warranting termination in the interests of the organization. In
the *Danjean Case* the characterization of facts was found to be good, while in
Crawford it was found to be bad.

(h) Agreement

A contract of service may be terminated by agreement in accordance with
general principles of law. Indeed, the written law of some organizations
specifically refers to this method of termination.[153] This method of termination differs from voluntary resignation in that the termination takes place as
a result of the acts of both parties to the contract of service, while in the case
of voluntary resignation the termination results from the act of the staff
member.

In this case the agreement must be a real one and not tainted by duress or
fraud. This is a general principle of law. In *Sacika*[154] the ILOAT confirmed
the general principle that there must be no fraud in a case where the applicant
claimed that he had been deceived, while holding that the applicant in the case
could not rely on fraud, particularly because he had confirmed the agreement
by continuing to receive payments under the agreement after discovering the
fact which he claimed had been kept from him. This case also supports the
proposition that, if fraud is to invalidate an agreement to terminate a
contract of service, the aggrieved party must take action to rescind the agreement with diligence and must not act in such a way as to give the impression
that he does not intend to rely on the fraud.

A similar situation involving agreement is envisaged where the written law
provides that the organization may take the initiative in terminating a
contract of service in the interests of good administration, provided the staff
member does not contest the action.[155] The termination is based on agreement. In *Bernard*[156] where action of this kind was taken under the UN Staff
Regulations the applicant contended that he had contested the termination of
service, because he had not agreed to it in writing. The UNAT held that no
written agreement was necessary in order to show that the action of the
administration had not been contested. It was sufficient that the evidence
showed that the staff member had consented. Further, the fact that terminal

---

[153] See Article 11.16 of the ILO Staff Regulations: Amerasinghe (ed.), 4 *Staff Regulations and
Staff Rules of Selected International Organizations* (1983) p. 185 at p. 262.
[154] ILOAT Judgment No. 436 [1980] (ILO).
[155] See Staff Regulation 9.1 (a) of the U.N.: see Appendix V *infra*.
[156] UNAT Judgment No. 244 [1979], JUNAT Nos. 231–300 p. 132.

payments had been received without protest supported the conclusion that he had consented. The tribunal also found that no conditions had been attached to the consent, thus taking the view that an agreement must be real in that there must be a meeting of the minds of the parties. Clearly, if a condition had been attached, it would have had to have been accepted by the administration, if the agreement to the termination was to be regarded as being valid.

In *Piracés*[157] the applicant's contract of service was terminated by agreement under Staff Regulations 9.1 (a) of the UN. Later it was said that the applicant's appointment was a regular one and not a permanent one; hence Staff Regulation 9.1 (a) was inapplicable and termination of the contract was ordered under Staff Regulation 9.1 (c) relating to termination in the interests of the service. This was less advantageous to the applicant in that he could not rely on an agreement. The UNAT held that the special agreement terminating the contract of service was binding and should be carried out and respected. The change in the grounds for termination could not, thus, be recognized. Reinstatement was not ordered, because there was an agreement to terminate the contract of service. Compensation was ordered as if that agreement had been carried out, which was the equivalent of the sums paid plus $3,000.

(i) *Expiry under the terms of the contract*

A contract of service may be terminated because of the fulfilment of a term of the contract which provides either explicitly or implicitly for its termination.[158] But in such a case it must be shown that the term of the contract providing for termination had been fulfilled. In *Bulsara*[159] the UNAT found that, while the contract provided for its termination in the event that appointment to a position proved not to be feasible in the near future, the organization was unable to show that the condition had been met. The applicant had in fact been considered for only 1 post when it was claimed that he had been considered for 28 other posts. It was found that the decision that no appointment was feasible had been taken in haste and without due care and consideration. Hence the termination under Staff Regulation 9.1 (b) of the UN which permits termination of appointments of the kind envisaged according to the terms of the contract was declared to be invalid. In regard to compensation, considering that the appointments of technical experts of which the applicant was one were of a temporary nature, the UNAT found that the inside limit of employment was 1 year while the outside limit was the term of the contract, about 3½ years. The tribunal, therefore, concluded that, while

---

[157] UNAT Judgment No. 264 [1980], JUNAT Nos. 231–300 p. 318.
[158] Staff Regulation 9.1 (b) of the UN provides specifically for this eventuality: see Appendix V *infra*.
[159] UNAT Judgment No. 68 [1957], JUNAT Nos. 1–70 p. 398.

the determination of the precise amount of compensation was difficult, the applicant should be paid 1 year's salary less the indemnity paid. This amounted to 9 months' salary.

(j) Force majeure

The LNT referred impliedly in some cases[160] to *force majeure* as a possible ground for not fulfilling in essence a term of a contract of service, such as the requirement that 6 months' notice be given before a contract is terminated, though it held that the condition had not been fulfilled on the facts of those cases. If the principle of *force majeure* is applicable to specific terms of a contract there is no reason why it should not be applicable to the contract as a whole, since it is a general principle of law.

(k) Invalid reasons

In many cases, as has been seen, tribunals have pronounced on the characterization of facts and have decided that certain facts do not warrant characterization as belonging to categories of situations which would justify the termination of appointments. This is the case where, for instance, a tribunal decides that the highest standards of behaviour have not been violated or that the interests of the organization are not jeopardized so as to warrant termination of the contract. Seldom have tribunals been faced with the argument that a particular category of reasons for dismissal was totally invalid and could not be supported in law. In *Decision No. 65(a)*,[161] however, the Appeals Board of NATO held that dismissal because the applicant did not belong to the nationality which the Board of Directors of an organ of the organization had decided should be appointed to his post was insufficient ground for dismissal. The tribunal decided not to reinstate the applicant but to order the payment of compensation. Compensation was awarded of BF 133,000 less the indemnity already paid to the applicant.[162] In *Diaz Acevedo*[163] the ILOAT held that refusal to agree to an amendment of contractual terms, though the applicant's other colleagues were willing to agree, did not warrant dismissal of the applicant. The situation particularly did not amount to 'termination, reduction and functional change in the operational structure of the organization' which under the written law of ESO was a good ground for dismissal.

---

[160] See *Aragon* etc., LNT Judgments Nos. 25 to 36 [1946].

[161] *Decision No. 65(a)*, NATO Appeals Board [1975], Collection of the Decisions 46 to 73 (1976).

[162] *Decision No. 65(b)*, NATO Appeals Board [1979], Collection of the Decisions 65(b), 74 to 99 (1979).

[163] ILOAT Judgment No. 349 [1978] (ESO). The remedy given depended also on the fact that the dismissal of the applicant for disciplinary reasons was improper: see Ch. 39 pp. 821 and 840 *infra*.

Consequences of termination

The action to be taken upon the termination, including payment of indemnities and according of benefits, is generally dealt with in the written law of international organizations. On occasion tribunals have been called upon to interpret these written laws. They have not hesitated to determine the rights of the parties and enforce these laws.[164] This is a matter to be distinguished from remedies for wrongful termination of service. In the former cases the termination decision was justified.

In a case where there was no written law on the matter, it was held that the applicant had no right to reinstatement on the ground that an amnesty had been granted by the President of Italy, after an earlier termination resulting from a criminal sentence imposed on him by the Italian courts had taken place.[165]

Where a settlement, including a release of all claims against the organization, has been concluded, it will be recognized as having effect, unless made under duress and provided duress is proved to have influenced the settlement.[166]

---

[164] See *Campenella*, ILOAT Judgment No. 34 [1958] (UNESCO); *Duncker*, ILOAT Judgment No. 49 [1960] (FAO); *Roy*, UNAT Judgment No. 143 [1971] (ICAO), JUNAT Nos. 114–166 p. 258; *Grasselli*, CJEC Case 32/68 [1969] ECR p. 505; *Richez-Parise and Others*, CJEC Cases 19, 20, 25 & 30/69 [1970] ECR p. 325; *Fiehn*, CJEC Case 23/69 [1970] ECR p. 547; *Gillet*, CJEC Case 28/74 [1975] ECR p. 463; *Newth*, CJEC Case 156/78 [1979] ECR p. 1941; *Decision No. 6(d)*, NATO Appeals Board [1967], Collection of the Decisions (1972); *Decision No. 8*, NATO Appeals Board [1968], ibid.; *Decision No. 9*, NATO Appeals Board [1968], ibid.; *Decision No. 13(b)*, NATO Appeals Board [1969], ibid.; *Ogle*, OASAT Judgment No. 34 [1978].

[165] *Duncker*, ILOAT Judgment No. 49 [1960] (FAO).

[166] *Mr. Y*, WBAT Reports [1985], Decision No. 25.

CHAPTER THIRTY-SEVEN

Fixed-Term Contracts

INTERNATIONAL organizations often resort to the fixed-term appointment as a means of employing personnel. The written law of most organizations has special provisions relating to such appointments. Thus, UN Staff Rule 104.12 (b) states that: 'The fixed-term appointment, having an expiration date specified in the letter of appointment, may be granted for a period not exceeding five years'.[1] In most cases fixed-term appointments are temporary appointments which have a minimum duration of one year and do not exceed five years. Temporary appointments for less than a year are short-term appointments which are usually but not always dealt with differently in the Staff Rules of organizations.[2]

International administrative tribunals very early criticized the excessive use of fixed-term contracts to fill positions which by their nature and purpose were permanent.[3] They recognized that fixed-term contracts were basically intended to be less than permanent and not really a substitute for permanent contracts. However, as a result of the practice of organizations in their incipient years of frequently using the fixed-term contract instead of committing themselves to permanent appointments, tribunals had to face the situation where the fixed-term contract was more often than not not what it appeared to be, namely a contract that came to an end when its term expired. As a consequence of the prevailing practice, the argument was frequently raised before tribunals that the holder of a fixed-term contract had been wronged because his contract had not been renewed. In dealing with this contention, tribunals were not satisfied with applying what in most cases was the explicit written law. They have continuously resorted to interpretation of the written law, to the circumstances of employment, and to other means apparently to circumvent the explicit written law.[4] Different tribunals have,

---

[1] See Appendix V *infra*. See also WHO Staff Rule 420.2: Amerasinghe (ed.), 1 *Staff Regulations and Staff Rules of Selected International Organizations* (1983) p. 118 at p. 145; UNESCO Staff Rule 104.6: Amerasinghe (ed.), 2 ibid. p. 1 at p. 40; and World Bank Personnel Manual Statement No. 2.00, para. 10.

[2] The UN Staff Rules do not treat them differently. See Rule 104.12 (Appendix V *infra*). The WHO, UNESCO, and IAEA Staff Rules deal with them separately: see Amerasinghe (ed.) 1 op. cit. (note 1 *supra*) p. 118 at p. 145; 2 ibid. p. 1 at p. 41 and p. 80 at p. 99. So does the World Bank Personnel Manual: see Personnel Manual Statement No. 2.00, para. 11.

[3] Criticism is implied, for instance, in *Howrani*, UNAT Judgment No. 4 [1951], JUNAT Nos. 1–70 p. 8 at pp. 20–1.

[4] The ICJ also agreed that exclusive importance could not be attached to the letter of the contracts, particularly to the provision according to which in case of non-renewal contracts

however, taken different approaches in solving the problems they have faced.

The special features of the law relating to fixed-term contracts which has developed relate entirely to the problem of non-renewal of such contracts or their non-conversion into permanent appointments. Termination of a fixed-term contract prior to the expiry of the contract is on a different footing. It is properly treated as a termination of appointment, since the termination occurs before the expiry at the end of its term of the contract.

The written law of many international organizations governing fixed-term appointments in general has particularly unambiguous provisions concerning the duration of fixed-term contracts and the possibility of their renewal, while also explicitly denying to the holders of such contracts any expectancy of either a renewal or a conversion to a permanent appointment and stating in effect that the contract shall expire automatically either according to its terms or on the expiration date specified in the letter of appointment.[5] Further, letters of appointment may also refer to the automatic expiration of the contract and the fact that the holder has no expectancy of renewal or conversion of the contract. It is the interpretation of this kind of law that has exercised international administrative tribunals.

Jurisdictional problems

Administrative authorities have in general argued before tribunals that a fixed-term contract comes to an end on the date of expiration, thereby also bringing to an end the relationship between the holder of such a contract and the international organization; that, although there is a separation of the holder of such a contract from the international organization, this separation is not a termination of employment within the meaning of the Staff Regulations and Staff Rules; that, since there is no administrative decision terminating employment taken at the moment the contract ends, there can be

---

expired automatically on the date fixed, and expressed the view that staff members with fixed-term contracts were often treated as being entitled to be considered for continued employment, consistently with the requirements and general good of the organization, in a manner transcending the strict wording of the contracts, so that the practice of renewal was a relevant feature in the interpretation of the contracts, the result being that there was considerable support for the view that there may be circumstances in which non-renewal of a fixed-term contract provides a legitimate ground for complaint: *Judgments of the I.L.O. Administrative Tribunal Case*, ICJ Reports 1956 p. 77 at pp. 90–1. The LNT, on the other hand, clearly stated that an official holding a fixed-term contract was not entitled to any renewal unless there was a promise to that effect included in his terms of appointment: *Garnier*, LNT Judgment No. 23 [1946]. This statement was, however, made *obiter*.

[5] See, e.g., UN Staff Rule 104.12 (b) (Appendix V *infra*); UNESCO Staff Rule 104.6: Amerasinghe (ed.), 2 op. cit. (note 1 *supra*) p. 1 at p. 40; FAO Staff Rules 302.4112 and 302.907: Amerasinghe (ed.), 3 ibid. p. 84 at pp. 113 and 130; IMCO Staff Rules 104.3 (b) and 109.6: Amerasinghe (ed.), 3 ibid. p. 1 at pp. 41 and 75.

no violation of a term or condition of employment; and that, therefore, tribunals have no jurisdiction in cases where the holders of such contracts contest the termination of their contracts. Furthermore, it has been contended that, since the contractual relationship between the holder of a fixed-term contract and the organization ends at the expiration date, the decision whether to give the official another appointment or not is entirely a matter for the organization in respect of which the holder of a fixed-term contract has no claim or right; hence, there can be no violation of rights over which tribunals would have jurisdiction. In addition, it has been argued that, since the fixed-term contract ends on the date of expiry, the holder of such a contract ceases to be a staff member then and a claim in regard to a renewal of the contract or to a conversion of the contract into a different kind of appointment is a claim for a new appointment in respect of which the tribunal should have no jurisdiction because the claimant has no *locus standi*, being only a claimant for an appointment like any other candidate for a new appointment.[6]

As early as 1955 the ILOAT confirmed its jurisdiction to hear complaints brought by officials of UNESCO concerning the validity of decisions not to renew their fixed-term contracts.[7] Staff Rule 104.6 of UNESCO at that time stated that 'a fixed-term appointment shall expire, without notice or indemnity, upon completion of the fixed-term'. The tribunal interpreted this text as dealing only with the duration of the contract and concluded that it in no way barred the tribunal from assuming jurisdiction over a complaint requesting that the legality of the positive or negative decision taken by the administrative authority relating to the renewal of such a contract be examined. The ICJ was called upon to pronounce on the question whether the ILOAT had exceeded its jurisdiction in those cases in which the ILOAT had decided that it had jurisdiction. As was seen in Chapter 16 above,[8] in its advisory opinion the ICJ held that the ILOAT had not exceeded its jurisdiction in declaring those cases admissible, irrespective of its decision on the merits.[9] The reasoning of the ICJ took into account the fact that UNESCO had issued an administrative memorandum which was law-creating and thereby promised to a certain category of staff members the renewal of their fixed-term contracts subject to their fulfilling certain requirements. On the basis of this memorandum the ICJ held that the claim that the fixed-term contracts should have been renewed was more than a mere allegation and gave rise to a genuine dispute of a legal nature based on a contractual offer

---

[6] See, e.g., the 'Exposé de l'UNESCO' in the *Judgments of the I.L.O. Administrative Tribunal of the ILO upon Complaints made against the United Nations Educational, Scientific, and Cultural Organization: Pleadings, Oral Arguments, and Documents* (1956) p. 27, particularly at pp. 103 ff.

[7] *Duberg*, ILOAT Judgment No. 17 [1955] (UNESCO). See also *Leff, Wilcox* and *Bernstein*, ILOAT Judgments Nos. 18, 19 and 21 [1955] (UNESCO).

[8] See *supra*, Vol. I. p. 208.

[9] *Judgments of the I.L.O. Administrative Tribunal Case*, ICJ Reports 1956 p. 77.

and relating to the terms of employment of the staff members. The ICJ also found that the position of a holder of a fixed-term contract who had not had his contract renewed was not the same as that of an applicant for a new appointment in the organization who had no *locus standi* before the tribunal, and hence the tribunal did have jurisdiction over such a person.

The approach taken subsequently by the ILOAT on its jurisdiction in cases involving the non-renewal of fixed-term contracts has been in effect to widen the scope of the ruling given by the ICJ without doing damage to the reasoning of the Court. In a case brought by an official of WHO the ILOAT held that the ruling of the ICJ applied by analogy to the staff of other international organizations in respect of which it had jurisdiction.[10] Although the Staff Rules of EMBL expressly denied its staff members the right to file claims regarding the non-renewal of fixed-term contracts, the ILOAT took the view that it could decide whether it had jursidiction to hear a complaint, since EMBL had unconditionally recognized the jurisdiction of the tribunal, and decided in fact that it did have jurisdiction in the case on the basis that a claim relating to the non-renewal of a fixed-term contract was within its jurisdiction.[11]

The UNAT adopted a somewhat different approach to the issue of its jurisdiction. In an early decision, *Howrani*, the tribunal said that it was difficult to explain how the failure to renew a fixed-term contract upon its expiration date, assuming absence of any irregularities in all other respects, could amount to a non-observance of the terms of appointment of the holder of the contract which had inflicted on him an injury for which he could reasonably claim recovery,[12] since in order that the tribunal might assume jurisdiction, an unlawful act must have been committed and an injury must have been sustained by the claimant. The UNAT seems to have said this, even though at that time the UN Staff Rules pertaining to fixed-term contracts did not exclude an expectancy of renewal or conversion, while providing for termination on the expiration date. None the less, particularly because of the indiscriminate use by the UN of fixed-term contracts, the tribunal considered that there could be cases in which an expectancy for continued employment might arise and that the incorporation of an expiration date in the contract did not destroy that expectancy. On this ground, the UNAT held that it had jurisdiction to examine each case of non-renewal of a fixed-term contract on the merits in order to determine whether the holder of the contract had a legitimate expectancy of continued employment which would have entitled him to relief.

At that time there were numerous complaints by holders of fixed-term contracts that their contracts were not being renewed without reasons being

[10] *Morse*, ILOAT Judgment No. 65 [1962] (WHO).
[11] *Gale*, ILOAT Judgment No. 474 [1982] (EMBL).
[12] UNAT Judgment No. 4 [1951], JUNAT Nos. 1–70 p. 8 at p. 21.

given. In many cases the work connected with the contracts was expected to end on the dates of expiration of the contract. However, in many other cases the work connected with the contracts could have been expected to continue even after the dates of expiration and, indeed, as long as the organization existed. This may have been a reason for the UNAT's coming to the conclusion it did, since it was evident that there was little connection between the expiration date of the contract and the completion of the work performed. Certain fixed-term contract holders could reasonably expect continued employment which justified the assumption of jurisdiction in order to determine whether this was the case.

Subsequent to *Howrani* the UNAT has consistently affirmed its jurisdiction to examine the merits of each case in order to ascertain whether the holder of a fixed-term contract had an expectancy of renewal, while rejecting the respondent's contention that the question whether there was an expectancy of renewal should be examined as a preliminary issue in order to establish the jurisdiction of the tribunal.[13] Similarly, other contentions raised by respondents have been rejected[14] and the UNAT has consistently assumed jurisdiction in cases concerning the non-renewal of fixed-term contracts.

Both tribunals reject the notion that a fixed-term contract terminates automatically on its expiration date, it being necessary that there be an administrative decision not to renew the contract. This was so, according to the ILOAT, in spite of an express statement in the Staff Rules that the contract came to an automatic end on its expiration date.[15] This view enabled the ILOAT to treat the administrative decision as the exercise of a discretionary power over which it had the power of judicial review, while it resulted in the UNAT's assuming jurisdiction over it in order to determine whether a legitimate expectancy had been defeated. Further, both tribunals reject the idea that the termination of a fixed-term contract on its expiration date constitutes a termination in the same sense as dismissal does according to the Staff Regulations and Staff Rules.[16] Thus, both tribunals do not assume jurisdiction on this basis in cases concerning the non-renewal of fixed-term contracts.

Other tribunals[17] which have had to deal with cases concerning the non-renewal of fixed-term contracts have not had their jurisdiction in such cases

[13] See *Yánez*, UNAT Judgment No. 112 [1967] (ICAO), JUNAT Nos. 87–113 p. 264.
[14] *de Pojidaeff*, UNAT Judgment No. 17 [1952], JUNAT Nos. 1–70 p. 61.
[15] *O'Connell*, ILOAT Judgment No. 469 [1982] (PAHO). The case referred to Staff Rule 1040 of WHO: see Amerasinghe (ed.), 1 op. cit. (note 1 *supra*) p. 119 at p. 170.
[16] See, e.g., *Robinson*, UNAT Judgment No. 15 [1952], JUNAT Nos. 1–70 p. 43; *de Pojidaeff*, UNAT Judgment No. 17 [1952], JUNAT Nos. 1–70 p. 61.
[17] See, e.g., the Appeals Board of NATO, *Decision No. 39*, NATO Appeals Board [1972], Collection of the Decisions (1972) at p. 2. For the other tribunals see, e.g., the CJEC (*Kergall*, CJEC Case 1/55 [1954–56] ECR p. 151); the OASAT (*Uehling*, OASAT Judgment No. 8 [1974]); the WBAT (*Mr. X*, WBAT Reports [1984], Decision No. 16).

questioned. Hence, they have assumed jursidiction readily in such cases, while generally not seeking a justification for doing so, though the Appeals Board of NATO has regularly referred to the decision of the ICJ as a justification.

The general nature of non-renewal or non-conversion of a fixed-term contract[18]

On the face of it the expiration date of a fixed-term contract should mark the end of the contractual relationship. It should be for the administrative authority to decide whether the holder of such a contact will be retained in the organization. The UNAT takes the position that this is a discretionary power which, however, may be converted into a legal obligation in certain circumstances. It has consistently followed this reasoning in its interpretation of UN Staff Rule 104.12 (b) and of the terms of fixed-term contracts. Thus, in many cases, after ascertaining that there were no special circumstances, the tribunal rejected claims on the basis of Staff Rule 104.12 (b) and of the terms of the contracts.[19] According to the UNAT, there is at the expiration date or before that a decision not to renew the contract and this decision is to be construed as a decision not to offer a new appointment to the holder of the contract; the administration if free to conclude or not to conclude a new contract;[20] this power flows in the case of the UN from Article 101 of the Charter[21] but international organizations are generally given this power by their constituent instruments; consequently, a challenge of a non-renewal decision is somewhat like an appeal against the refusal to conclude a new contract of appointment.[22] The UNAT has taken the same approach to fixed-term contracts in other organizations over which it has jurisdiction, such as ICAO[23] and IMCO,[24] in so far as it has treated such contracts with these organizations in the same way as such contracts with the UN. In the case of the UNAT what is of significance in its decisions is that it has taken the view that, even though the power to renew or not fixed-term contracts may be discretionary, it can, because of surrounding circumstances, become a legal obligation which has legal consequences. Presumably, other tribunals which

---

[18] The fixed-term contract has been examined in Napoletano, *La cessazione del rapporto di lavoro dei funzionari internazionali* (1980) pp. 24 ff.

[19] See, e.g., *Rajappan*, UNAT Judgment No. 139 [1971], JUNAT Nos. 114–166 p. 236; *Nath*, UNAT Judgment No. 181 [1974], JUNAT Nos. 167–230 p. 106; *Boelen*, UNAT Judgment No. 261 [1980], JUNAT Nos. 231–300 p. 297.

[20] See *Dale*, UNAT Judgment No. 132 [1969] (ICAO), JUNAT Nos. 114–166 p. 172 at p. 180.

[21] See *El-Naggar*, UNAT Judgment No. 205 [1975], JUNAT Nos. 167–230 p. 345 at p. 354.

[22] See *Dale*, UNAT Judgment No. 132 [1969] (ICAO), JUNAT Nos. 114–166 p. 172.

[23] *Yánez*, UNAT Judgment No. 112 [1967] (ICAO), JUNAT Nos. 87–113 p. 264.

[24] *Cipolla*, UNAT Judgment No. 290 [1982] (IMCO), JUNAT Nos. 231–300 p. 567.

appear to follow the UNAT's approach would accept the pith of the UNAT's reasoning.[25]

In *Halliwell* the ILOAT asserted that the discretion to renew or not a fixed-term contract is similar to that exercised when the administration makes a new appointment, though it did not state categorically that the two were identical.[26] In *Corredoira-Filippini* the discretionary authority of the administration was confirmed and the ILOAT stated that after the abolition of the post occupied by the applicant the administration could, at its discretion, either refuse her a new appointment or conclude a new contract with her or someone who had different linguistic skills.[27]

The ICJ, in interpreting the Staff Regulations and Staff Rules of UNESCO, stated[28] that a fixed-term contract was renewable which implied that renewal constituted a further stage of a former contract. Thus, it said, there was established a link between renewal and the original contract and the position on the expiration of his contract of the holder of such a contract was not identical with that of an applicant for a new appointment who had failed to obtain it.

As a consequence of the views expressed by the ICJ which are relevant to the fixed-term contracts of most, if not all, international organizations and not merely those of UNESCO, since the concept underlying fixed-term contracts is similar in most, if not all, Staff Regulations and Staff Rules, and the basic nature of fixed-term contracts remains the same, it would appear that the basic approach originally taken by both the UNAT and the ILOAT required modification, in so far as they both tended to regard the position of the holder of a fixed-term contract which had expired as similar to that of an applicant for a new appointment. The implication is that the holder of a fixed-term contract which has expired is in a special kind of relationship with the organization which places the power to renew or not to renew the contract, discretionary though it may be, in a very special position. In fact both the UNAT and the ILOAT have not hesitated to attach certain specific consequences to this special position, although they have proceeded in different ways.[29]

While it has affirmed that the decision not to renew a fixed-term contract on its expiration did not generally violate any contractual right of the holder of the contract, because the organization had a discretion whether to renew

---

[25] See the OASAT: *Uehling*, OASAT Judgment No. 8 [1974]; the WBAT: *Mr. X*, WBAT Reports [1984], Decision No. 16.

[26] ILOAT Judgment No. 415 [1980] (WHO) at p. 7.

[27] ILOAT Judgment No. 312 [1977] (FAO) at p. 2.

[28] *Judgments of the I.L.O. Administrative Tribunal Case*, ICJ Reports 1956 p. 77 at p. 93.

[29] The Appeals Board of NATO appears to follow the ILOAT very closely in its handling of the non-renewal of fixed-term contracts: see, e.g., *Decision No. 39*, NATO Appeals Board [1972], Collection of the Decisions (1972); *Decision No. 46*, NATO Appeals Board [1973], Collection of the Decisions 46 to 73 (1976).

the contract, or not,[30] the ILOAT has also come to the conclusion that the discretion to renew or not a fixed-term contract is not absolute. As will be seen, in its view there are limitations imposed on the exercise of this power as a result of which the tribunal exercises judicial control over its exercise. Thus, while in the ILOAT's view the holder of a fixed-term contract has no right to expect renewal or conversion of his contract nor the extension of his appointment even for short periods nor to a transfer to a new post,[31] it has, for example, also held that, though the Staff Regulations and Staff Rules may not expressly provide for this, the administrative authority must be given reasons for the decision taken.[32] As a consequence, where the administrative authority has failed to give clear reasons for the non-renewal or non-conversion of the contract, the ILOAT will examine the evidence available and the dossier as a whole in order to enable it to infer the grounds for the decision.[33]

The UNAT, on the other hand, while agreeing that the decision to renew or not a fixed-term contract is a discretionary one,[34] has not drawn the same inference from this premise as the ILOAT. It has taken the view that, though the contract comes to an end when it expires and the administrative authority must take a decision whether to renew it or not, there may be circumstances in which a legitimate expectancy of renewal gives the holder of the contract a right to have the contract renewed.[35] Conversely, unless the holder of the contract can prove a legitimate expectancy of renewal, he will have no rights in respect of renewal of the contract.[36] As a consequence of the view it has taken on the nature of the discretion to renew or not a fixed-term contract, the UNAT has concluded that generally the administrative authority does not have to give the grounds for its decision.[37] On the other hand, it may

[30] See *Halliwell*, ILOAT Judgment No. 415 [1980] (WHO); *Osuna-Sanz*, ILOAT Judgment No. 343 [1978] (ILO); *Chadsey*, ILOAT Judgment No. 122 [1968] (WPU).

[31] *Osuna-Sanz*, ILOAT Judgment No. 343 [1978] (ILO); *Chadsey*, ILOAT Judgment No. 122 [1968] (WPU); *Garcin*, ILOAT Judgment No. 32 [1958] (UNESCO).

[32] *Duberg*, ILOAT Judgment No. 17 [1955] (UNESCO); *Bordeaux*, ILOAT Judgment No. 544 [1983] (CERN).

[33] *Gausi (No. 1)*, ILOAT Judgment No. 223 [1973] (ILO).

[34] *Yánez*, UNAT Judgment No. 112 [1967] (ICAO), JUNAT Nos. 87–113 p. 264.

[35] *Sood*, UNAT Judgment No. 195 [1975], JUNAT Nos. 167–230 p. 235; *Fracyon*, UNAT Judgment No. 199 [1975], JUNAT Nos. 167–230 p. 277; *Sehgal*, UNAT Judgment No. 203 [1975], JUNAT Nos. 167–230 p. 324.

[36] *Pappas*, UNAT Judgment No. 94 [1965], JUNAT Nos. 87–113 p. 66; *Leak*, UNAT Judgment No. 97 [1965], JUNAT Nos. 87–113 p. 90; *Fürst*, UNAT Judgment No. 134 [1969], JUNAT Nos. 114–166 p. 188.

[37] *Yánez*, UNAT Judgment No. 112 [1967] (ICAO), JUNAT Nos. 87–113 p. 264; *Rajappan*, UNAT Judgment No. 139 [1971], JUNAT Nos. 114–166 p. 236; *Fracyon*, UNAT Judgment No. 199 [1975], JUNAT Nos. 167–230 p. 277. In some early decisions the UNAT simply held that there was an obligation for the administrative authority to give reasons for not renewing fixed-term contracts: see *Robinson*, UNAT Judgment No. 15 [1952], JUNAT Nos. 1–70 p. 43. This was required in order to enable the tribunal to decide whether there had been an abuse of purpose or improper motivation behind the non-renewal. There was no specific reference to legitimate

examine the grounds for the decision where there is a legitimate expectancy of renewal of the contract.[38] The purpose of this is to establish whether the decision not to renew the contract was improperly motivated.[39] In many cases, where applications have been rejected because the UNAT found that there was no legitimate expectancy of renewal of the contract, the tribunal has refused to examine the grounds for the decision.[40]

Another aspect of the discretionary power to renew or not fixed-term contracts is the power to decide upon the duration of possible extensions of such contracts. The ILOAT affirmed that the administration had a discretion to decide that a fixed-term contract should be renewed for only one year, though the original contract was for longer than one year, without this decision having the character of a disciplinary measure and consequently without harming the professional reputation of the official concerned.[41] However, the ILOAT has qualified the freedom of the administrative authority to exercise this discretion. For example, it has mentioned the administration's duty to take account of the legitimate interests of the official at the time of recruitment and also subsequently, if an extension is envisaged, without overlooking its own interests.[42]

The UNAT has also agreed that the duration of a renewal of a fixed-term contract is a matter within the discretion of the administration, it being for the applicant to establish his entitlement to an appointment for a specific length of time. Thus, in *Osman*, where the holder of a fixed-term contract who had his contract renewed for a period of time which did not entitle him to claim pension benefits for the total period of his service because the period of his service fell short of the minimum required by a few months, it was held that the applicant had no right to a contract for a specified term as contended by him.[43] However, where the existing fixed-term contract specifies that a renewal, when granted, would be for a certain period of time, if the contract is renewed in circumstances in which it is clear that the holder of the contract

---

expectancy in these cases but it seems to emerge from the decisions that on the facts the tribunal found that there was such an expectancy.

[38] *Yánez*, UNAT Judgment No. 112 [1967] (ICAO), JUNAT Nos. 87–113 p. 264 at p. 274.

[39] *Yánez*, UNAT Judgment No. 112 [1967] (ICAO), ibid.

[40] See, e.g., *Rau*, UNAT Judgment No. 101 [1966], JUNAT Nos. 87–113 p. 133; *Rajappan*, UNAT Judgment No. 139 [1971], JUNAT Nos. 114–166 p. 236; *Harkins*, UNAT Judgment No. 287 [1982], JUNAT Nos. 231–300 p. 542. For an early examination of the approach of tribunals to fixed-term contracts see Akehurst, 'Renewal of Fixed-Term Contracts of Employment in International Organizations', 31 *Revue internationale des sciences administratives* (1965) p. 83. Much has, however, happened since then.

[41] *Hoefnagels*, ILOAT Judgment No. 25 [1957] (WHO).

[42] *Meyer*, ILOAT Judgment No. 245 [1974] (IAEA); *Ronduen*, ILOAT Judgment No. 246 [1974] (UNESCO). In both cases the tribunal held that the administrative authority had acted properly.

[43] UNAT Judgment No. 180 [1973], JUNAT Nos. 167–230 p. 93.

has a legitimate expectancy of renewal, according to the OASAT which follows the approach of the UNAT in cases relating to the non-renewal of fixed-term contracts, the renewal must be for the length of time specified in the existing contract.[44]

The ILOAT, however, is more liberal in its approach to the duration of renewals. The decision on duration is subject to judicial review like the decision not to renew. Thus, in similar circumstances to those prevailing in *Osman* referred to above, the ILOAT held that the decision was impeachable because it was based on mistaken conclusions.[45]

The judgments of other tribunals than the UNAT and the ILOAT do not, apparently, depart from the principles laid down in the cases decided by the one or the other of these tribunals, as far as the general nature of the power to renew or not fixed-term contracts is concerned, and in so far as they do address the issue. It is clear that where the UNAT and the ILOAT differ because of their divergent approaches to the problems of the non-renewal of fixed-term contracts, another tribunal wishing to follow the jurisprudence of these tribunals would have to make a choice.

The situation where the applicant contends that he should have been given a permanent contract by conversion of his fixed-term contract on its termination has come before tribunals more rarely. This situation is similar to the one frequently presented to tribunals where the applicant demands that his contract be renewed. However, there is a difference. The applicant is asking for a permanent contract or appointment. This difference seems to relate to the nature of the new contract or appointment and not to the fact that the applicant should continue in the employment of the organization. The consequence of this difference is that the applicant should have the burden of proving that the circumstances of his case entitle him not merely to a renewal of his fixed-term contract for a period but to a permanent contract or appointment.[46]

---

[44] *Uehling*, OASAT Judgment No. 8 [1974].

[45] *Meyer*, ILOAT Judgment No. 245 [1974] (IAEA). See also *Gale*, ILOAT Judgment No. 474 [1982] (EMBL).

[46] In *El-Naggar*, UNAT Judgment No. 205 [1975], JUNAT Nos. 167–230 p. 345, the applicant contended that his appointment amounted in law to a permanent one. He failed to establish his contention. He did not argue that his fixed-term contract should have been converted into a permanent appointment on its expiration. Hence, the UNAT was not called upon to deal with this point. There are other cases which have concerned decisions not to grant the applicants permanent appointments on the expiry of their fixed-term contracts. However, the issue whether the applicant had a right to a permanent contract rather than a fixed-term contract has apparently not been litigated. The applicant has succeeded or failed on the basis that he proved or did not prove that his right to a permanent appointment had been violated.

The ILOAT approach to the control of the discretion not to renew a fixed-term contract

The ILOAT has consistently held that the administrative authority, notwithstanding its discretionary power to renew a fixed-term contract, is not entirely free to act as it pleases. It exercises control over the exercise of this discretion in a manner similar to that in which it exercises control over discretionary power in general. It has asserted, on the one hand, that: 'Although renewal for a fixed-term is the Director-General's discretion—and the Staff Regulations leave no doubt on that score—the decision is not immune from review.'[47] On the other hand, it has described its power of review in general as being limited and defined it in specific terms. It has said:

The Tribunal may exercise only a limited power of review over such a decision and indeed will quash it only if it was taken without authority, or in breach of a rule of form or of procedure, or if it rested on an error of fact or of law, or if some essential fact was overlooked, or if there was abuse of authority, or if clearly mistaken conclusions were drawn from the evidence.[48]

This is, indeed, a general principle, as understood by the ILOAT, relating to the control of discretionary powers. In applying it to the non-renewal of fixed-term contracts the ILOAT may not have given it as wide a scope as it has done in other areas of the exercise of discretionary power. It would also appear that the application of the principle may vary with the circumstances in which the power is exercised. The law as it was been applied may be classified generally in terms of the recognized categories, namely, substantive irregularities, *détournement de pouvoir*, and procedural irregularities.

It is significant that the Appeals Board of NATO follows the jurisprudence of the ILOAT in respect of the judicial control over the discretion not to renew a fixed-term contract. In virtually every case in which the issue is raised the tribunal makes a general statement of the law as follows: 'whereas it [the tribunal] must accordingly satisfy itself that this refusal emanated from a competent authority in accordance with the proper procedure and that it was not based on errors of fact, error of law, obvious errors of judgment or a misuse of powers.'[49] This statement may be analysed in the same way as the statements of the ILOAT. This tribunal also takes the

---

[47] See *Verron*, ILOAT Judgment No. 607 [1984] (UNESCO) at p. 11.

[48] *Byrne-Sutton*, ILOAT Judgment No. 592 [1983] (ITU) at p. 5. See also *Meyer*, ILOAT Judgment No. 245 [1974] (IAEA) at p. 4; *Verron*, ILOAT Judgment No. 607 [1984] (UNESCO) at p. 11; and *Thadani*, ILOAT Judgment No. 623 [1984] (FAO) at p. 5.

[49] See, for a recent case, *Decision No. 139*, NATO Appeals Board [1981], Collection of the Decisions 135 to 171 (1984) at p. 3. 'Errors of Judgment' probably refer to mistaken conclusions drawn from the evidence in the dossier.

position that holders of fixed-term contracts accept the possibility normally that their contracts will not be renewed.[50]

In some cases, decided when the European Communities entered into contracts of employment, the CJEC readily examined allegations that the non-conversion of fixed-term contracts during the integration procedure, whether because of unsuitability or other reasons, was unlawful because of procedural irregularities, animosity, error of law, error of fact, erroneous conclusions, or violation of the principle *nemo judex in re sua*. The applicants failed to prove their allegations, although the Court did not reject the validity of their legal contentions.[51] In another case the Court examined the question whether the discretion had been properly exercised in terms of the arguments that there had been a *détournement de procédure* and a *détournement de pouvoir* and that irregular procedures had been followed and concluded that none of the allegations had been proved on the facts.[52] It would appear, therefore, that the CJEC was prepared to take the same approach as the ILOAT on the subject of non-renewal of fixed-term contracts.[53]

(a) Substantive irregularities

There are certain substantive defects on the basis of which the ILOAT has found decisions not to renew fixed-term contracts invalid. There have been cases in which principles of law relating to the omission of essential facts, the drawing of mistaken conclusions, and error of law have been applied. While the cases deal only with these three kinds of substantive irregularities, this does not mean that the ILOAT will not find decisions not to renew fixed-term contracts invalid because of other substantive irregularities, such as consideration of irrelevant facts or error of fact. The NATO Appeals Board has specifically considered error of fact as a ground for annulling decisions not to renew fixed-term contracts.

i. Omission of essential facts

Where the substance of the decision not to renew a fixed-term contract is defective because the administrative authority did not take into account

---

[50] *Decision No. 99*, NATO Appeals Board [1979], Collection of the Decisions 65(b), 74 to 99 (1979).

[51] See *Pistoj*, CJEC Case 26/63 [1964] ECR p. 341; *Degreef*, CJEC Case 80/63 [1964] ECR p. 391; *Georges*, CJEC Case 87/63 [1964] ECR p. 469; *Minot*, CJEC Case 93/63 [1964] ECR p. 489.

[52] *Bourgaux*, CJEC Case 1/56 [1954–6] ECR p. 361.

[53] In another case the CJEC seemed ready to follow the approach taken by the UNAT which will be discussed below: see *Kergall*, CJEC Case 1/55 [1954–56] ECR p. 151. This could be regarded as a supplementary solution. It is the only case to be found of this kind decided by the CJEC.

essential facts, the ILOAT has held the decision to be illegal. In these cases the tribunal has questioned the administrative authority's evaluation of the applicant's performance or the assessment of the circumstances of a given situation. The evaluation or assessment is not accepted by the tribunal and the characterization of facts by the administrative authority may also be rejected.

Essential facts may not have been characterized as such or taken into account. In both instances there are grounds for finding the decision invalid. In one case the tribunal will substitute its own characterization of the facts for that of the administrative authority and in the other it will consider the facts overlooked and, thus, control the exercise of discretion. Two cases illustrate adequately the operation of the relevant principles. In *Ballo*[54] the fact that on every occasion on which the Director-General of UNESCO had personally seen the applicant at work the latter had shown himself quite inadequate for his assignments was the essential fact on which he based his decision. However, the ILOAT considered that the favourable evaluation of the applicant's performance made by his immediate supervisors concerning the quality of his day-to-day work was an essential fact which the Director-General had overlooked. The Director-General had based his assessment of the applicant's performance only on a very small part of the applicant's work and, consequently, had failed to take into consideration essential facts. It is significant that, when the Director-General took the decision not to renew the applicant's contract, he was aware of the fact characterized as essential by the tribunal. In *Troncoso*[55] the facts characterized as essential concerned some poor aspects of the applicant's performance and her alleged political activities. The tribunal did not accept the final evaluation of the applicant's performance as given by the administration of PAHO, because essential facts had been omitted. It considered as essential facts (i) the unqualified praise expressed by the applicant's colleagues, and (ii) some earlier favourable appraisals. As to the conflicting evidence concerning some of the applicant's shortcomings in connection with her abilities in the training aspect of her duties, the tribunal noted that, in view of the variety and range of her duties, the applicant could have continued to be assigned to duties which suited her, while being relieved of those for which she was less well suited. In regard to political acitivites, it was observed that the protests from member States concerning the applicant's political activities were never investigated to establish to what extent they were compatible with the interests of the organization. Moreover, some of the member States which allegedly had protested, did subsequently seek the applicant's services. As a result, the ILOAT found the decision not to renew the applicant's contract

[54] ILOAT Judgment No. 191 [1972] (UNESCO).
[55] ILOAT Judgment No. 448 [1981] (PAHO).

invalid because of the failure to take account of essential facts. There were also found to be procedural irregularities in that case which contributed to the illegality of the decision.[56]

ii. *Mistaken conclusions*

The ILOAT will also invalidate a decision not to renew a fixed-term contract, if it is based on conclusions that are clearly erroneous. In this instance too the tribunal does not accept evaluations of performance or assessments of situations made by the administrative authority. The principle may be applied to the duration of extensions of fixed-term contracts. In *Meyer*[57] the ILOAT *proprio motu* considered the question whether the Director-General of IAEA, in refusing to extend a fixed-term contract for a period which would have covered an additional 13 days, drew wrong conclusions from the evidence in the dossier. The refusal to cover that period with the extended contract deprived the applicant of entitlement of his pension benefits, while the inclusion of the 13 days in the contract would not have caused the agency any prejudice. The tribunal found that there was no reason to conclude that the agency's financial interests were at stake, or that employment would have been for more than five years which might have involved regarding the applicant's appointment as permanent, or that a precedent would have been set for claiming employment for periods of five years. Under the circumstances, it was found that by causing the applicant serious loss which was not justified by the need to safeguard any interest of the agency, the Director-General drew from the dossier conclusions which were clearly mistaken.[58]

iii. *Error of fact*

The Appeals Board of NATO has not found in favour of any applicant who claimed that his fixed-term contract was wrongfully not renewed on the ground that there was an error of fact but has held in cases before it that there was no error of fact. Thus, in *Decision No. 46*[59] the NATO Appeals Board held that the facts on which the decision that on his post's being abolished the applicant was not the best qualified for other posts was based were not inaccurate. In *Decision No. 72*,[60] on the other hand, the applicant's

---

[56] See also *Florio*, ILOAT Judgment No. 541 [1982] (FAO). In *Djoehana*, ILOAT Judgment No. 359 [1978] (UNESCO), there were found to be both failure to take account of essential facts and conclusions which were clearly erroneous.

[57] ILOAT Judgment No. 245 [1974] (IAEA).

[58] See also *Gale*, ILOAT Judgment No. 474 [1982] (EMBL). In *Verron*, ILOAT Judgment No. 607 [1984] (UNESCO), and *Thadani*, ILOAT Judgment No. 623 [1984] (FAO), there was found to have been no abuse of authority.

[59] *Decision No. 46*, NATO Appeals Board [1973], Collection of the Decisions 46 to 73 (1976).

[60] *Decision No. 72*, NATO Appeals Board [1976], ibid.

fixed-term contract was not renewed because of the conclusion to which the administrative authority had come that she was unable to adapt to her new duties. It was held that this conclusion was not based on an error of fact or error of judgment.[61]

iv. *Error of law*

Error of law refers to the breach of the written laws of the organization and to any breach of general principles of substantive law. An error of law could occur by application of the wrong Staff Rule. In *Perrone*[62] the applicant's fixed-term contract which came to an end at the same time as her post was abolished was regarded by PAHO as having come to an end under Staff Rule 1040 which provided for the expiration of such a contract and provided no indemnity. The applicant argued that Staff Rule 1050 which dealt with the abolition of post and provided for an indemnity should have applied. The ILOAT conceded that the two provisions appeared to be conflicting but held that for reasons of fairness, because of the applicant's lengthy, loyal, and satisfactory performance for twelve years, Staff Rule 1050 should have been applied, inasmuch as the abolition of the applicant's post was the real reason for her being separated from the organization. Thus, the non-renewal decision was quashed and a termination decision substituted for it. The rationale of the judgment appears to be that, where there is an apparent conflict of rules and where the staff member has performed satisfactorily and loyally for a long period, the administration must apply the rule that is more advantageous to the staff member. If it does not, it commits an error of law.

In *Gale*[63] and *Bordeaux*[64] the ILOAT held that EMBL and CERN respectively had committed errors of law in disclosing neither to the applicant nor to the tribunal the reasons for the non-renewal of the fixed-term contract for the requisite length of time and in believing that they did not need to do so. It would seem that the failure to give reasons was regarded as an error of law in this case and not as a procedural irregularity, because the organization believed it had no obligation to give reasons. There is no good reason why this kind of irregularity should not be treated properly as a procedural irregularity.[65]

---

[61] See also for similar findings *Decision No. 75*, NATO Appeals Board [1976], Collection of the Decisions 65(b), 74 to 99 (1979); *Decision No. 79*, NATO Appeals Board [1977], ibid. 'Error of judgment' must be a reference to mistaken conclusions drawn from the evidence in the dossier.

[62] ILOAT Judgment No. 470 [1982] (PAHO).

[63] ILOAT Judgment No. 474 [1982] (EMBL).

[64] ILOAT Judgment No. 544 [1983] (CERN).

[65] See also *Mofjeld*, ILOAT Judgment No. 260 [1975] (FAO), for another case involving an error of law.

(b) *Détournement de pouvoir*

Détournement de pouvoir is in general a basis resorted to by the ILOAT for finding that decisions not to renew fixed-term contracts are invalid. The tribunal seems to have established that it will quash a decision not to renew a fixed-term contract, if there has been any abuse of purpose or irregular motive. Clearly, once the principle that abuse of purpose is relevant to decisions not to renew fixed-term contracts is admitted, it is not difficult to apply the general principles relevant to the subject to the non-renewal of fixed-term contracts. The cases where abuse of purpose has been discussed in connection with fixed-term contracts merely illustrate these general principles.

First, there are cases where the ILOAT has dealt with the argument that the purpose for which the non-renewal decision was taken was an illegitimate one. In *Duberg*[66] the tribunal held that for UNESCO not to renew a fixed-term contract because the holder had failed to appear before a Loyalty Board of his national State set up to inquire into the political activities of staff members was illegal.[67] In *Chadsey*[68] non-renewal of a fixed-term contract by WPU, because the holder of the contract was *persona non grata* in a member State, was held to be an abuse of purpose.[69]

Secondly, in *Gale*[70] no good reason for the non-renewal of the fixed-term contract emerged, since the EMBL did not allege that the reasons were, for example, to serve the interests of the organization, make structural reforms, or make savings. The ILOAT held that there was no proper purpose for the action taken and that this was an abuse of purpose or *détournement de pouvoir*.

In several recent cases in which the issue was apparently raised, the Appeals Board of NATO held that there had been no abuse of purpose or *détournement de pouvoir* in the decision not to renew the applicant's fixed-term contracts.[71] The purpose of the non-renewal decision was found to be

---

[66] ILOAT Judgment No. 17 [1955] (UNESCO). See also *Leff*, ILOAT Judgment No. 18 [1955] (UNESCO); *Wilcox*, ILOAT Judgment No. 19 [1955] (UNESCO); *Bernstein*, ILOAT Judgment No. 21 [1955] (UNESCO).

[67] See also *Rosescu*, ILOAT Judgment No. 431 [1980] (IAEA).

[68] ILOAT Judgment No. 122 [1968] (WPU).

[69] *Halliwell*, ILOAT Judgment No. 415 [1980] (WHO), was another case where an abuse of purpose was found.

[70] ILOAT Judgment No. 474 [1982] (EMBL). In *Bourgaux*, CJEC Case 1/56 [1954–6] ECR p. 361, where the applicant's post was abolished with the result that his fixed-term contract was not renewed, the Court held that there were no other reasons than the exigencies of the service of the decision and that, therefore, there was no *détournement de pouvoir*.

[71] See *Decision No. 47*, NATO Appeals Board [1973], Collection of the Decisions 46 to 73 (1976); *Decision No. 59(b)*, NATO Appeals Board [1975], ibid.; *Decision No. 63*, NATO Appeals Board [1975], ibid.; *Decision No. 72*, NATO Appeals Board [1976]; ibid.; *Decision No. 75*, NATO Appeals Board [1976], Collection of the Decisions 65(b), 74 to 99 (1979).

proper. In some cases the purpose was achieving a satisfactory turnover, in another the purpose was to get rid of an official who was unable to adapt to new duties, and in yet another the reasons were the applicant's poor ratings and the fact that the post was to be deleted on the expiration of the contract.

Détournement de procédure may also be a reason for annulling a decision not to renew a fixed-term contract. In *Gausi (No. 1)*[72] the real reason for the non-renewal of the contract by ILO was that certain irregularities had been discovered and it was intended to penalize the applicant without following the proper disciplinary procedure. This was held by ILOAT to be improper. In *Bourgaux*[73] the CJEC held that, where the applicant's contract had not been renewed, on the facts a disciplinary procedure was not applicable and that, therefore, there was no *détournement de procédure*.

Some cases have dealt with prejudice or ill will. In *Dicancro*[74] the Director of PAHO did not renew the applicant's fixed-term contract. It was found that the applicant had contested the Director in an election and lost. The Director did not hide his resentment. A charge of misconduct had been raised but this was found to be false, the real reason for the action taken being the Director's prejudice. The decision was quashed.[75] In two cases[76] the ILOAT concluded that prejudice on the part of the administrative authority was the reason for the non-renewal of the fixed-term contracts of the applicants, largely on the basis of the lengthy and good record of satisfactory performance of the applicants, though there were other elements which contributed to this finding. In *Verron*[77] the ILOAT found on the facts that the non-renewal of the applicant's fixed-term contract was not motivated by prejudice.

(c) Procedural irregularities

In other areas of the law, as where probationary appointments are not confirmed or appointments are terminated for unsatisfactory service, international administrative tribunals have held that requirements of due process to be found in the written law or in general principles of law must particularly be followed in the taking of decisions. Where fixed-term contracts are not renewed the situation is different, partly because the expiration of such a contract does not constitute a termination of service. Furthermore, the written law of the majority of international organizations rarely provides for

[72] ILOAT Judgment No. 223 [1973] (ILO).
[73] CJEC Case 1/50 [1954–6] ECR p. 361.
[74] ILOAT Judgment No. 427 [1980] (PAHO).
[75] See also *Olivares Silva*, ILOAT Judgment No. 495 [1982] (PAHO).
[76] *Bâ*, ILOAT Judgment No. 268 [1976] (WHO); and *Chawla*, ILOAT Judgment No. 195 [1972] (WHO).
[77] ILOAT Judgment No. 607 [1984] (UNESCO).

more than a mere notification of the decision not to renew a fixed-term contract. For these reasons judicial control by tribunals over the discretionary decision to renew or not to renew a fixed-term contract was mainly concerned with the substance of or the motives for the administrative decision, while in cases of termination of permanent appointments for unsatisfactory service and of non-confirmation of probationary appointments, judicial control was mainly exercised in respect of the procedure followed. More recently, however, these tribunals seem to have shown a greater interest in matters of procedure.

The procedural requirements concerning fixed-term contracts are generally limited in the written law of international organizations to provisions concerning the notification of the non-renewal decision to the holders of such contracts one to six months before the expiry of the contracts. There are no provisions concerning other procedural requirements to be observed before taking a decision not to renew a fixed-term contract. In these circumstances it is difficult, even if procedural requirements are to be insisted on as necessary, to know what sort of procedures should be required. At best tribunals have dealt with the cases on their merits and have examined procedures in terms of very general principles, where the written law has been silent.

i. *Violation of the written law*
Where there are written provisions on procedure relating to fixed-term contracts, tribunals rquire that they be followed. Sometimes in the absence of specific provisions dealing with such contracts in the written law tribunals will have recourse to provisions in the written law which could be applied to fixed-term contracts by analogy or interpretation. However, this has been done very rarely, because, as has been pointed out, the non-renewal of a fixed-term contract is very different from other forms of termination of appointments.

The written law of some international organizations provides for a formal notification of the decision not to renew a fixed-term contract within a period of one to six months before the expiry of the contract. The purpose of a notification is to protect the holder of a fixed-term contract from a sudden termination and to give him time to make plans for his future. A stipulation concerning notification may be coupled with a provision concerning the automatic termination of the contract upon completion of the agreed period of service in the absence of any offer and acceptance of an extension.[78] The ILOAT's attitude towards this kind of notification provision takes account of its purpose and interprets the provision in terms of its spirit rather than of

---

[78] See WHO Staff 1040 (previously 940): Amerasinghe (ed.), 1 op. cit. (note 1 *supra*) p. 118 at p. 170.

its letter. Thus, in circumstances where no notice was given, the purpose of giving warning and affording protection was found to be fulfilled by extending an official's appointment for 3 months for compassionate reasons because of his health problems, although at the end of the 3-month extension his contract was allowed to terminate without his having been given the 1-month's notice provided for in the WHO Staff Rule.[79] Similarly in *Anciaux*,[80] where a fixed-term contract had been extended by ESO for 6 months in order to remedy the absence of 6 months' notice, it was held that further notice was not necessary.

Failure to give the required notice in accordance with the WHO Staff Rules has been interpreted automatically to renew by implication the fixed-term contract for another term.[81] The ILOAT explained that, had the contract not been considered as renewed automatically because of the failure of the administration to give notice to the applicant on time, a situation would have arisen in which the organization would still have had the right to give one month's notice at any time thereafter, while the automatic termination of the fixed-term contract would also not have taken place. In this case the organization could have chosen between terminating the applicant's appointment under WHO Staff Rule 1040 which carried no indemnity or of abolishing the applicant's post and paying him an indemnity. The tribunal held that the power of renewal under Rule 1040 could not be used to prolong an appointment for a period just long enough to enable PAHO to have the termination coincide with the abolition of the post and avoid paying an indemnity on the ground that the contract had terminated in due course.

There are generally no provisions concerning reports in the written law relating specifically to the termination of fixed-term contracts of international organizations. However, in *Troncoso*[82] ILOAT interpreted a WHO Staff Rule[83] requiring that the evaluation of performance be the basis for decisions concerning the staff member's status and for his retention in the organization as applying to the case of an official whose fixed-term contract was not renewed by PAHO when it expired at the end of its term. The decision not to renew the applicant's appointment was taken without previously obtaining the performance report for the final year of her service. Therefore, it was held that she was deprived of the right to rebut criticisms made of her and the decision was found to be invalid. The ILOAT, further, rejected the organization's contention that the above procedural flaw was rectified during the internal appeals proceedings, since the Board heard both the applicant and witnesses. The tribunal found that the criticisms of the

---

[79] *Segers*, ILOAT Judgment No. 131 [1969] (WHO).
[80] ILOAT Judgment No. 266 [1976] (ESO).
[81] *O'Connell*, ILOAT Judgment No. 469 [1982] (PAHO).
[82] ILOAT Judgment No. 448 [1981] (PAHO).
[83] Staff Rule 530.2: see Amerasinghe (ed.), 1 op. cit. (note 1 *supra*) p. 118 at p. 148.

applicant had not only been challenged but were also open to various inter-pretations with the result that the absence of an evaluation report could not be rectified. The tribunal also held that it was inadequate that the applicant's supervisors informed her orally of her shortcomings, on the ground that a conversation was not a substitute for the report referred to in the Staff Rule which required a report in addition to the normal work review and dis-cussions. As already seen, there were substantive irregularities in this case. Consequently, in this judgment the non-renewal decision was found invalid on both procedural and substantive grounds.[84] In *Decision No. 87*,[85] on the other hand, a report on the applicant's work was conveyed to him before the meeting of the NATO Complaints Committee so that he had a chance to rebut it. Hence, it was held that the Staff Regulations had not been violated, as an adequate procedure had been followed.

There are other possible procedural irregularities which an administrative authority may commit and which may violate the written law. There are not many cases, however, which deal with this kind of defect. In *Decision No. 99*[86] there had been a delay in the internal proceedings which was a technical violation of the Staff Regulations. Since it had no effect on the decision of the NATO Complaints Committee, it was held not to be an injurious irre-gularity. Hence, the decision not to renew the applicant's fixed-term contract was held not to be invalid. In *Anciaux*[87] the ESO had refused to renew the applicant's contract in circumstances in which disciplinary action was warranted. The ILOAT found that, *inter alia*, the right of defence had been respected so that there was no violation of the applicant's rights. This decision may have been the result of the application of the written law by analogy or of general principles of law.

A procedural requirement may also be established as an obligation by appropriate subsidairy legislation. In *Haghou*[88] the ILOAT said that an Information Note circulated by the Director General of ILO was no more than a simple statement of intention without contractual effect in the rela-tionship between the organization and the applicant. The ILOAT implicitly conceded that, if the Note had been intended to establish a rule of law, it would have had to be followed.

ii. *Violation of general principles of law*
Sometimes the tribunal may examine the procedure followed before a

[84] See also *Decision No. 85*, NATO Appeals Board [1977], Collection of the Decisions 65(b), 74 to 99 (1979). In *Decision No. 79*, NATO Appeals Board [1977], ibid., the procedure followed in respect of adverse performance reports was held to be proper.

[85] *Decision No. 87*, NATO Appeals Board [1978], ibid. See also *Decision No. 97*, NATO Appeals Board [1979], ibid., where the appropriate procedure was held to have been followed.

[86] *Decision No. 99*, NATO Appeals Board [1979], ibid.

[87] ILOAT Judgment No. 266 [1976] (ESO).

[88] ILOAT Judgment No. 421 [1980] (ILO).

decision not to renew a fixed-term contract is taken in terms of general principles of law, where the written law is silent, or sometimes in apparent contradiction of the written law. Some Staff Regulations and Staff Rules do not mention the need for notice to be given to the contract holder. Indeed, some of them specifically state that the contract will expire according to its terms without notice or indemnity.[89] In spite of such a provision the ILOAT seems not to have denied the requirement of notice in normal circumstances. In *Kirkbir*[90] the ground for non-renewal of the applicant's contract was the applicant's unsatisfactory performance. The ILOAT noted that the applicant was expressly advised to improve her performance on the occasion of three partial renewals of her contract. Consequently, it was held that the applicant should have expected the administration of UNESCO to decide not to extend her contract, if her performance was still unsatisfactory. This was the answer given to the argument that the applicant had not been notified earlier of this decision. The tribunal did not reject the argument that normally notice should have been given. In an early decision[91] concerning the non-conversion of the fixed-term contract of an UNESCO official into a permanent one the ILOAT confirmed that it could exercise judicial control over the procedure to be followed in the conversion process, even in the absence of any provisions in the internal law of UNESCO concerning the fair consideration of a fixed-term contract holder's candidacy for a permanent appointment. Several procedural irregularities were revealed which constituted violation of due process. *Inter alia*, no periodic reports had been made before the decision of non-conversion had been taken and, consequently, it was held that the applicant had been deprived of the opportunity of having the decision modified. The tribunal rejected the respondent's argument that the written law required no reports. Further, it was found that the procedure followed by the committee entrusted with examining the question of conversion was vitiated by irregularities. While admitting that the administrative authority had the discretionary power to grant or refuse an indeterminate appointment, the tribunal held that the procedural irregularities identified were too serious to be ignored, even though the written law was silent on the matter.[92]

Procedural requirements may be obligatory as a result of a practice of the organization which creates law. In *Sadeghian*[93] the ILOAT held that the practice of the ILO in giving adequate notice of non-renewal of fixed-term contracts to contract holders had created law and had become a term of the

---

[89] See UNESCO Staff Rule 104.6 (b): Amerasinghe (ed.), 2 op. cit. (note 1 *supra*) p. 1 at p. 40.

[90] ILOAT Judgment No. 116 [1968] (UNESCO).

[91] *Garcin*, ILOAT Judgment No. 32 [1958] (UNESCO).

[92] See also *Byrne-Sutton*, ILOAT Judgment No. 592 [1983] (ITU). In *Gale*, ILOAT Judgment No. 474 [1982] (EMBL), an error of law and an abuse of purpose were found but there could also have been a procedural irregularity.

[93] ILOAT Judgment No. 577 [1983] (ILO).

contract. Thus, failure to give adequate notice was a violation of the law which had to be compensated.

Where an administrative authority voluntarily adopts for any reason a procedure which is not obligatory upon it, it may not, in certain circumstances, be bound strictly to follow the details of such procedure. In *Haghou*[94] the Director General of ILO considered action taken by a working party which he had constituted under an Information Note which was held by the ILOAT not to be law-creating, when the working party was not constituted in the way outlined in the Note, because some staff representatives refused to participate. It was held that this was not a procedural irregularity, because the Director General was at liberty to consider the advice given by the body which he had constituted essentially to advise him, even though it was not constituted in exactly the way he had intended it to be constituted. This case may appear to conflict with *Garcin*[95] discussed above. In both cases there were found to be irregularities in regard to bodies constituted by the administrative authority to perform certain functions. It would seem, however, that the procedural irregularities which occurred in *Garcin* were different from the irregularity identified in *Haghou*. In *Haghou* the working party was essentially an advisory body expected mechanically to apply rules established in regard to the non-renewal of contracts, while in *Garcin* the committee was entrusted with the examining, as an investigative arm of the administrative authority, of the cases which came before it. Further, in *Haghou* the alleged defect arose as a result of certain members of the working party voluntarily refusing to participate, which was not attributable to the fault of the administration. Thus, it would seem that *Haghou* can be distinguished on the facts. Even where a procedure is voluntarily adopted by the administrative authority in the absence of a strict or explicit legal obligation to do so, it must act fairly in following that procedure. Exceptionally, however, where the procedure is not of such significance or importance or where the alleged irregularity is not significant, such as was the case in *Haghou*, the procedure need not be followed in the strict details.

In regard to hearings or inquiries it would seem that the ILOAT supports the notion that the administrative authority must conduct an inquiry or the equivalent which will enable it to arrive at an informed decision, though it does not have to follow the strict procedure required of an adversary proceeding. In *Freeman*[96] the Director General of EMBL had before taking a decision consulted eleven scientists on the quality of the applicant's work. It was held that this was sufficient to fulfil the procedural requirement and that the applicant did not have a right to be heard or argue his own case in

[94] ILOAT Judgment No. 421 [1980] (ILO).
[95] ILOAT Judgment No. 32 [1958] (UNESCO).
[96] ILOAT Judgment No. 600 [1984] (EMBL).

person.[97] The decision in *Anciaux*[98] is not very clear. It held that in a case where there were disciplinary reasons for the non-renewal of a fixed-term contract the right of defence had been respected. It does take the view that the right of defence should be respected where disciplinary proceedings are required by the facts of the case but it does not emerge whether this was the result of the application by analogy of the written law or of general principles of law. It is conceivable that the right of defence would be applicable in these circumstances as a result of the impact of general principles of law.[99]

(d) The interests of the organization

It may be asked how far the reason that a fixed-term contract is not being renewed in the interests of the organization is by itself good in law, how far the giving of such a reason precludes tribunals from examining whether the facts support the reason and how far tribunals require that all decisions not to renew fixed-term contracts must in fact be in the interests of the organization.

As some of the cases where *détournement de pouvoir* has been found to invalidate decisions not to renew fixed-term contracts show, it is possible for a tribunal to find that the decision taken was not in the interests of the organization but was for an improper purpose. Thus, in *Duberg*,[100] where the non-renewal of the contract was attributed to the failure of the staff member to appear before a Loyalty Board of the government of his national State, the ILOAT had no hesitation in holding that the interests of the organization could not be identified with the interests of a member State and that the decision taken involved an abuse of purpose. The integrity required by the Staff Regulations of UNESCO could not be so defined as to interfere with the exclusively international character of the responsibilities of UNESCO. This case and cases like it demonstrate that tribunals will examine the motivation behind a decision not to renew a contract to determine whether such motivation is really in the interests of the organization. Similarly, in *Gale*[101] the ILOAT found that the fact that the non-renewal decision taken by EMBL was not supported by any reasons such as structural reforms or that keeping the applicant on the staff would have been contrary to the interests of EMBL had resulted in an abuse of purpose. This case shows that non-

---

[97] See also *Lingham*, ILOAT Judgment No. 628 [1984] (ILO).

[98] ILOAT Judgment No. 266 [1976] (ESO).

[99] In *Goyal*, ILOAT Judgment No. 136 [1969] (UNESCO), the ILOAT found that the applicant had been condemned before the accusations against him had been judged and held that this was an irregularity. There was here a violation of a general principle of law relating to procedure.

[100] ILOAT Judgment No. 17 [1955] (UNESCO). See also *Chadsey*, ILOAT Judgment No. 122 [1968] (WPU); *Rosescu*, ILOAT Judgment No. 431 [1980] (IAEA); *Troncoso*, ILOAT Judgment No. 448 [1981] (PAHO).

[101] ILOAT Judgment No. 474 [1982] (EMBL).

renewal decisions must always be in the interests of the organization, although, as the other cases referred to earlier show, the mere fact that the purpose appears to satisfy the interests of the organization or that it is alleged that the purpose is consistent with the interests of the organization does not prevent the tribunal from establishing whether the purpose is in fact consistent with the interests of the organization.

A non-renewal decision which is taken after the conclusion has been reached that it is in the interests of the organization may be declared not to be so . because the conclusion is erroneous and results in a substantive irregularity. Thus, where the holder of a fixed-term contract was deprived of an extension of 13 days which would, in terms of time, have enabled him to qualify for pension benefits, it was held that the IAEA had come to the mistaken conclusion on the facts that the extension would have caused prejudice to the organization and that it was in its interests not to grant it.[102]

(e) Grounds for the non-renewal of fixed-term contracts

The administrative decision not to renew a fixed-term contract being a discretionary one, it is important to understand how far the ILOAT will examine the grounds for the non-renewal of such contracts. Reasons given have been generally that the applicant's performance was not satisfactory, the applicant was not suitable, he was guilty of unsatisfactory conduct, or that his post was abolished. In each of these cases the ILOAT has not substituted its own judgments for those of administrative authorities but has only exercised judicial control over the discretionary power vested in such authorities. On the other hand, the above reasons have been readily accepted as good grounds for non-renewal of fixed-term contracts. The ILOAT also seems implicitly to take the view that the grounds for such non-renewal must be acceptable and that administrative authorities do not have unfettered discretion in this regard.

The assessment made by the administrative authority that the applicant's performance was unsatisfactory will normally be accepted by the ILOAT as a good ground for non-renewal of a contract. Thus, a personal assessment of a supervisor in the ILO that an official was not the type of person who could work within a team was not questioned by the ILOAT, although it did state that the assessment could have been right or wrong.[103] It found that there was no improper motive nor was there any other ground warranting its intervention. Where the applicant's work was found to be unsatisfactory, because his report-writing in English was poor and he had stated in his curriculum

[102] *Meyer*, ILOAT Judgment No. 245 [1974] (IAEA).

[103] *Steele*, ILOAT Judgment No. 310 [1977] (ILO). See also *Zimmer*, ILOAT Judgment No. 327 [1977] (UNESCO), where the applicant's performance was found to be unsatisfactory.

vitae submitted to the ILO that he had a sound knowledge of English, the administrative decision was held to be unimpeachable.[104] Unsatisfactory working relations can by themselves be a valid ground for non-renewal of a contract in spite of the applicant's professional competence and devotion to duty.[105] The ILOAT has refused to interfere with the judgment of fact made by the Director General of ILO concerning the consequences of the applicant's unsatisfactory working relations.[106] The applicant's strained working relations were a valid ground for a decision not to renew a contract,[107] as was the applicant's unsatisfactory performance coupled with difficult working relationships.[108] The ILOAT will not generally interfere with such decisions. It may make an examination of assessments of unsatisfactory performance but this will be solely for the purpose of establishing that there were substantive irregularities or an abuse of purpose in order to enable it to exercise judicial control.

Another issue related to evaluation of performance which also belongs to the domain of discretion is the suitability of an official. Suitability is a broader term which encompasses performance, qualifications, skills, conduct, personality, and fitness for a given post. At the time of the renewal of a contract suitability might be critical and it is always in issue when an official is a candidate for the conversion of his fixed-term contract to a permanent contract. In both situations suitability must be based on relevant facts properly disclosed by the record, while it is possible for references to be made to the official's conduct in previous years in order to support an evaluation of work and conduct during the reporting period, in so far as it is related to subsequent events.[109] To the applicant's contention that the non-renewal decision was tainted because the Director General of UNESCO omitted to consider some essential facts, such as his satisfactory performance and qualifications, the ILOAT replied that performance and qualifications were only two among several other factors to be considered, especially in the case of a highly graded official who was directly associated with the achievement of the goals of the organization.[110] In *Hoefer*[111] and *Chadsey*[112] too suitability was in issue. The ILOAT did not question the findings of the administrative authority. In all these cases the purpose of the tribunal's examining the facts was not to substitute its own judgment for that of the administrative

---

[104] *Osuna-Sanz*, ILOAT Judgment No. 343 [1978] (ILO).

[105] *Rebeck*, ILOAT Judgment No. 77 [1964] (WHO).

[106] *Fraser*, ILOAT Judgment No. 337 [1978] (ILO).

[107] *Agarwala*, ILOAT Judgment No. 121 [1968] (FAO).

[108] *Hrdina*, ILOAT Judgment No. 229 [1974] (ILO).

[109] *Morse*, ILOAT Judgment No. 65 [1962] (WHO).

[110] *Nieto-Alvarez-Uria*, ILOAT Judgment No. 516 [1982] (UNESCO).

[111] ILOAT Judgment No. 406 [1980] (FAO).

[112] ILOAT Judgment No. 122 [1968] (WPU).

authority but to ascertain whether any irregularities had been perpetrated which would have entitled it to intervene.

The question of unsatisfactory conduct is closely related to that of unsuitability. The most important case[113] is an early decision by the ILOAT concerning an official of WHO whose fixed-term contract was not renewed on the grounds that his conduct was in breach of WHO Staff Regulation Articles 1.5 and 1.6 requiring reserve, tact, and discretion of international civil servants. The tribunal was particularly cautious in the examination of this case, inasmuch as the non-renewal decision was based on a single unfavourable report after twelve years of satisfactory service. It stated that the decision would be valid, only if the report disclosed serious deficiencies in the work or conduct of the applicant, which it did.[114]

In *Anciaux*[115] the applicant's misconduct was not followed by any disciplinary action. His contract was not renewed. The tribunal noted that the Director General of ESO could either have taken disciplinary action against him or could have refused to renew his contract. Cases, such as *Anciaux*, show that misconduct may be an appropriate ground for not renewing a fixed-term contract, even though the full disciplinary procedure is not followed. The requirement in such a case is that the right of defence be respected which was done in these cases. There is no *détournement de procédure* as long as this is done. If this safeguard is not provided, the tribunal would hold, as it did in *Gausi (No. 1)*,[116] that the proper procedure had not been followed, that is, that there had been a *détournement de procédure*. The full disciplinary procedure did not have to be followed, if the right of defence has been respected.

Another common ground for the non-renewal of a fixed-term contract is the abolition of the post occupied by the holder of such contract. Post abolition for financial reasons or reorganization is a discretionary power. Thus, the Director General of FAO could validly abolish a Spanish-language position occupied by the applicant and replace it with an English-language position.[117] Posts may be abolished for budgetary reasons.[118] Post abolition can also be coupled with unsatisfactory performance as a reason for non-renewal of a contract. In this case it is to be expected that those whose performance was unsatisfactory will be denied the renewal of their contracts.[119]

---

[113] *Morse*, ILOAT Judgment No. 65 [1962] (WHO).

[114] See also *Finkelstein*, ILOAT Judgment No. 291 [1977] (UNESCO).

[115] ILOAT Judgment No. 266 [1976] (ESO). See also *Magassouba*, ILOAT Judgment No. 324 [1977] (WHO).

[116] ILOAT Judgment No. 223 [1973] (ILO).

[117] *Corredoira-Filippini*, ILOAT Judgment No. 312 [1977] (FAO).

[118] See *Bidoli*, ILOAT Judgment No. 166 [1970] (FAO); *De Sanctis*, ILOAT Judgment No. 251 [1975] (FAO); *Johnson*, ILOAT Judgment No. 414 [1980] (ILO).

[119] *de Villegas*, ILOAT Judgment No. 404 [1980] (ILO).

Theoretically, a decision not to renew a contract because the post the holder of the contract occupied had been abolished will be subject to review like any other exercise of discretionary power because of substantive irregularities, procedural irregularities, or *détournement de pouvoir*.[120] The question whether the holder of a fixed-term contract is entitled to a transfer before his post is abolished and when he should be so transferred seems to be dealt with by the ILOAT entirely by reference to the written law or practice of the organization concerned.

(f) The right to be transferred

As in the case of post abolition referred to above, the ILOAT does not acknowledge a general right to be transferred for fixed-term contract holders before a decision is taken not to renew their contracts. Such a right would depend entirely on the written law or practice of the organization. Nor is the matter to be resolved by reference to whether the contract holder had a legitimate expectancy of renewal or conversion of his fixed-term contract.

Only one case has been found in which an administrative decision was held to be a violation of the Staff Regulations of the organization.[121] In that case the decision not to renew the applicant's contract was found to be tainted, because, *inter alia*, there was a violation of WHO Staff Regulation 4.4[122] which stated that preference should be given to candidates already in service when vacancies occurred. At the time the applicant's contract came up for renewal there were two vacant positions and neither of them was offered to the applicant because of her nationality, which was not in accordance with the Staff Regulations. On the other hand, in a case concerning a UNESCO official[123] the fact that the applicant was unsuccessful in applying for many vacancies was not sufficient to show that the organization had not tried to keep him on its staff, since he had been granted several short extensions. The applicant's high grade was an additional factor which explained his lack of success. The ILOAT, while noting that the organization had made efforts to place the applicant, stopped short of saying that the organization had an obligation to transfer him to a vacant post. In *Loroch*[124] also the ILOAT made no statement that the applicant had a right to a transfer, although it examined why she had not been transferred.[125] In some cases concerning the

---

120 See the cases cited in note 118 *supra*. In none of these cases were defects found.
121 *Halliwell*, ILOAT Judgment No. 415 [1980] (WHO).
122 See Amerasinghe (ed.), 1 op. cit. (note 1 *supra*) p. 118 at p. 144.
123 *Rajan*, ILOAT Judgment No. 321 [1977] (UNESCO).
124 ILOAT Judgment No. 297 [1977] (FAO).
125 See also *Corredoira-Filippini*, ILOAT Judgment No. 312 [1977] (FAO).

officials of ILO the ILOAT explicitly stated that the holder of a fixed-term contract had no right to a transfer before he was refused a renewal.[126]

(g) *Legitimate expectancy; promise of renewal*

In some early decisions the ILOAT referred to legitimate expectancy of a renewal or of continued employment as entitling holders of fixed-term contracts to be given further employment with the international organizations for which they worked. Thus, in *Duberg*[127] the ILOAT considered that the applicant, who fulfilled all necessary conditions, had the right to be offered a new contract. The conditions to be fulfilled in this case were found in an administrative memorandum promising renewal to holders of fixed-term contracts who had achieved the required standards of efficiency, competence, and integrity and whose services were needed. The rights created by the expectancy depended on the written law of the organization. In this case and those like it there seems to have been more than an expectancy. There seems to have been some kind of promise that employment would be continued on the fulfilment of certain conditions. There is a distinction between a promise and an expectancy, a promise being the result, *inter alia* of some positive act on the part of the organization which involves a legal undertaking. Furthermore, in these cases the tribunal found that in any case there had been a *détournement de pouvoir* which made the non-renewal of the contracts illegal. In *Garcin*[128] the ILOAT considered the applicant's lengthy service and satisfactory performance as more or less entitling him legitimately to expect to make a career with UNESCO but in this case the decision not to renew the contract was quashed because of procedural irregularities.

Generally in cases in which the applicants' expectancy of continued employment is referred to, administrative decisions have been quashed because of substantive irregularities, procedural irregularities, or *détournement de pouvoir*.[129] The ILOAT has in principle adopted the approach that an expectancy of any kind is not relevant to the question whether an administrative decision not to renew a fixed-term contract is invalid or a violation of law. It does not create a right in the holder to have his contract renewed. The tribunal examines other features of the administrative decision in order to establish whether there has been an illegality. Illegality depends on whether there has been a substantive irregularity, a *détournement*

---

[126] *Osuna-Sanz*, ILOAT Judgment No. 343 [1978] (ILO); *de Villegas*, ILOAT Judgment No. 404 [1980] (ILO).

[127] ILOAT Judgment No. 17 [1955] (UNESCO). See also *Leff*, *Wilcox*, and *Bernstein*, ILOAT Judgments Nos. 18, 19, and 21 [1955] (UNESCO).

[128] ILOAT Judgment No. 32 [1958] (UNESCO).

[129] See, e.g., *Hoefer*, ILOAT Judgment No. 406 [1980] (FAO); *Gale*, ILOAT Judgment No. 474 [1982] (EMBL); *Djoehana*, ILOAT Judgment No. 359 [1978] (UNESCO).

de pouvoir, or a procedural irregularity. However, the issue of expectancy has been raised mainly in cases in which the tribunal not only found that there was no expectancy but also found that irregularities which would have, according to its jurisprudence, entitled it to quash the administrative decision were absent.[130] In *Meyer*,[131] on the other hand, the ILOAT found that there was no legitimate expectancy of continued employment but, nevertheless, held that the administrative decision was invalid because of an abuse of authority. There have been some cases in which the tribunal found that there were no irregularities such as would have entitled it to invalidate the administrative decision and in which the applicants argued that they had a legitimate expectancy of continued employment but in which the tribunal pointed out that the applicants had not received a commitment or a promise carrying legal force.[132] This kind of conclusion indicates that the ILOAT does not consider that an expectancy, however, legitimate, is adequate to give a holder of a fixed-term contract a right to renewal, in so far as the tribunal refused really to determine whether there was such an expectancy and to concede that it was relevant to the question of the illegality of the administrative decision not to renew the contract.

On the other hand, it is clear that the tribunal in the above cases did regard a commitment or a promise carrying legal force as capable of giving the holder of a fixed-term contract the right to renewal. It has been explained that the commitment must be such as to amount to a promise or to make a renewal a matter of good faith.[133] Not doing so would then be contrary to the general principles of the law of contract. The ILOAT however, unlike the UNAT, has denied the character of a binding rule to the general practice of an organization of renewing fixed-term contracts in certain circumstances. Thus, in *Rosescu*,[134] for example, the ILOAT refused to accept administrative practice as a source of law but instead found the administrative decision invalid for *détournement de pouvoir*.

The ILOAT has taken the concept of expectancy into consideration in connection with remedies, where it has found the administrative decision unlawful for other reasons. This is, perhaps, the only circumstance in which the ILOAT has regarded expectancy as a relevant consideration.

---

[130] See *Kaushiva*, ILOAT Judgment No. 155 [1970] (UNESCO); *Hrdina*, ILOAT Judgment No. 229 [1974] (ILO); *De Sanctis*, ILOAT Judgment No. 251 [1975] (FAO); *Fraser*, ILOAT Judgment No. 337 [1978] (ILO). In all such cases some good reason for non-renewal, such as post abolition, was found to exist.

[131] ILOAT Judgment No. 245 [1974] (IAEA).

[132] See *Rebeck*, ILOAT Judgment No. 77 [1964] (WHO); *Rajan*, ILOAT Judgment No. 321 [1977] (UNESCO); *de Villegas*, ILOAT Judgment No. 404 [1980] (ILO).

[133] *Agarwala*, ILOAT Judgment No. 121 [1968] (FAO).

[134] ILOAT Judgment No. 431 [1980] (IAEA). See also *Anciaux*, ILOAT Judgment No. 266 [1976] (ESO).

The UNAT approach to the non-renewal of a fixed-term contract

The UNAT's approach to the issue of the renewal or non-renewal of fixed-term contracts has been practically unique. It seems to have developed a totally new technique of dealing with this problem.

(a) The concept of expectancy

The UNAT has created a concept of expectancy which does not appear to have a counterpart in national administrative legal systems nor to be based on an interpretation of the written law of organizations or of the fixed-term contracts involved. The UNAT has had recourse to this concept in order to render eligible for judicial redress the holders of fixed-term contracts whose contracts were not renewed at the expiration date. The expectancy derives from an examination by the tribunal of the history of the contractual relationship between the holder of the contract and the organization. It is based on the circumstances of employment as a source of law with the consequence that terms and conditions of employment which are not expressed may be gathered from correspondence, surrounding facts, and specific circumstances.[135] The tribunal proceeds to investigate the history of the contractual relationship and of particular circumstances and surrounding facts in order to establish whether they have created in the mind of the holder of the contract an expectancy that his contract would be renewed at the expiration date. An expectancy is a state of mind which has been created by positive action taken by the holder of a contract coupled with specific behaviour on the part of the administrative authority.

The concept of expectancy has been created in spite of the fact that in general the written law of organizations explicitly excludes any expectancy of continued employment for holders of fixed-term contracts. Hence, as a result of the creation of the concept of expectancy, the written law prevails only in the absence of any countervailing circumstances, surrounding facts, or behaviour on the part of the administrative authority which could have created in the mind of the holder of the contract an expectancy of continued employment. Where the required expectancy can be shown to exist, the holder of the contract has certain rights in respect of the renewal or conversion of his contract resulting from such expectancy *per se*.

(b) The nature of the expectancy required

What is required to impose an obligation on the administrative authority in

---

[135] See *Sikand*, UNAT Judgment No. 95 [1965], JUNAT Nos. 87–113 p. 70; *Bhattacharyya*, UNAT Judgment No. 142 [1971], JUNAT Nos. 114–166 p. 248; *El-Naggar*, UNAT Judgment No. 205 [1975], JUNAT Nos. 167–230 p. 345.

respect of renewal or conversion of a fixed-term contract is that a 'legitimate' expectancy of continued employment must be created in the mind of the contract holder. A simple hope for continued employment does not constitute a legitimate expectancy. It is only the latter that can create an obligation binding on the administrative authority.[136] Any holder of a fixed-term contract can reasonably nourish a mere hope or expectancy for continued employment, if he performs satisfactorily. The above distinction was made particularly clear in *Seraphides*.[137] The applicant who was on a fixed-term contract successfully took part in a competition for promotion and her name was placed on the roster for assignment. However, her contract expired and the applicant ceased to be a staff member prior to the date on which a vacancy occurred. The UNAT stated that the applicant could have expected to remain in the service of the organization beyond the date of expiry of her contract. None the less, this was in the circumstances of the case a mere expectation which did not give rise to any commitment on the part of the administrative authority. It is the behaviour of the administrative authority in the special of circumstances of each case that creates a legitimate expectancy.[138] The behaviour of the administrative authority and the special circumstances might occur before, during, or after the conclusion of the initial fixed-term contract or its subsequent extensions.

A fixed-term contract holder must normally contribute to the creation of a legitimate expectancy by fulfilling conditions such as excellent performance. Such performance may be a factor in the creation of a legitimate expectancy but, as is to be seen from the many cases in which a legitimate expectancy was denied, it is usually not the only requirement for the creation of a legitimate expectancy. Sometimes, however, the tribunal has given special weight to this kind of condition. In *Levcik*,[139] for example, the applicant's legitimate expectancy was exclusivley based on his outstanding qualifications, special competence, his supervisors' recommendations that he be retained, and the fact that he was kept completely informed of all the above. It should be noted that in this case the respondent had accepted a recommendation of the Joint Appeals Board of the UN that the decision of non-renewal was improper and that compensation be paid. Consequently, what was in issue was the question of compensation. The tribunal did not have to decide *ab initio* whether there were adequate grounds for determining that there had been a legitimate

---

[136] See *Fürst*, UNAT Judgment No. 134 [1969], JUNAT Nos. 114–166 p. 188; *Bhattacharyya*, UNAT Judgment No. 142 [1971], ibid. p. 248.

[137] UNAT Judgment No. 140 [1971], ibid. p. 240. In *Flad*, UNAT Judgment No. 318 [1983] at p. 8, a distinction was made between a mere expectation and a confirmed expectancy. There the applicant's unsuitability destroyed any possibility that he could have had a legitimate expectancy.

[138] *de Olagüe*, UNAT Judgment No. 191 [1974] (IMCO), JUNAT Nos. 167–230 p. 188.

[139] JUNAT Judgment No. 192 [1974], ibid. p. 204.

expectancy. In any event it is only in exceptional cases that a legitimate expectancy is created solely by the holder's positive action and in the absence of any specific behaviour on the part of the administrative authority.

(c) Constitutive elements of a legitimate expectancy

The constitutive elements of a legitimate expectancy of renewal or conversion of a fixed-term contract are varied. It is not possible to identify them in the abstract. Each case has to be considered on its merits. It is only possible to indicate how the UNAT has proceeded in taking into account various factors.

In an early decision of the UNAT, *Robinson*,[140] some constitutive elements were referred to as having positively contributed to the creation in the mind of the applicant of a legitimate expectancy for continued employment. These were: (i) the applicant's excellent performance, (ii) the fact that there were very few candidates in his field of specialization, (iii) the fact that he occupied an established post, (iv) the fact that his division was understaffed, and (v) the fact that he was aware of the favourable opinion of his supervisors and their recommendations for the conversion of his fixed-term contract into a permanent one. Furthermore, it was the administrative authority that had taken the initiative in offering him his original appointment for the reason that he was well known in his field.

In other cases special circumstances prior to the conclusion of the initial fixed-term contract and during its subsequent extensions have been identified as being particularly relevant in creating a legitimate expectancy in the mind of the holder of a fixed-term contract. For example, in one case[141] in a letter sent to the applicant before the conclusion of the initial contract, it was stated that the contract was renewable, subject to satisfactory performance and mutual consent. Because of the reference to mutual consent the administrative authority contended that it could refuse to renew the contract. However, the UNAT decided otherwise for two reasons: (i) the normal practice of the agency was to renew contracts of field experts such as the applicant, and (ii) the respondent at the expiration of the applicant's contract had offered him a two-month contract as an interim arrangement pending final determination in respect of a longer extension. The UNAT regarded the interim contract as part of a plan that the respondent had for a more durable solution. Therefore, both the interim contract and the administrative practice gave rise to a legitimate expectancy. The interim contract seems to have been a significant factor in the creation of the expectancy. Further, the

---

[140] UNAT Judgment No. 15 [1952], JUNAT Nos. 1–70 p. 43.

[141] *Dale*, UNAT Judgment No. 132 [1969] (ICAO), JUNAT Nos. 114–166 p. 172. In *Rajappan*, UNAT Judgment No. 139 [1971], ibid. p. 236, the tribunal found no additional circumstances which could support a legitimate expectancy.

applicant's performance was not at issue. In a similar case,[142] the applicant's legitimate expectancy directly derived from his satisfactory performance and a letter sent to the applicant a few months before the conclusion of the intial fixed-term contract in which it was mentioned that at the expiration of his contract there would be opportunities for regular appointment and for senior posts, depending upon qualifications and satisfactory performance. Therefore, the satisfactory performance and the terms of the above letter were the basis for the legitimate expectancy of renewal of the applicant's contract. This was so in spite of his letter of appointment which reproduced verbatim the UN Staff Rule denying any expectancy of continued employment.

A legitimate expectancy can also arise as a result solely of the behaviour of the administrative authority while the fixed-term contract is in force. Written assurances given to holders of fixed-term contracts by the competent administrative authorities that efforts will be made to secure them further assignments or to convert their contracts to permanent ones constitute formal commitments creating binding obligations on the part of the organization.[143] The fact that the holder of a contract was informed that his supervisors had sent to headquarters a memorandum recommending the extension of his contract for 2 years, as well as the fact that he was authorized to remove his household goods, created in his mind a legitimate expectancy creating a binding obligation on the organization.[144]

Whether the expectancy is for one contractual term or for more will depend on the circumstances of each case.[145] The period for which the applicant can expect his contract to be renewed will depend on the rules in force and not merely on the statements of the respondent. Thus, when the rules in force referred only to a 6-month renewal, even though the respondent had given assurances of renewal for the same period as that of the existing fixed-term contract which was 2 years, the UNAT held that the legitimate expectancy was for a 6-month renewal.[146] In *Cipolla*[147] the applicant had worked for 10 years on fixed-term contracts with IMCO on a project which had not been completed when he was informed that his contract would not be renewed. He had continued to work after the date of expiry of his contract and it was some time after that date that he was informed that his contract would not be renewed beyond 3 months. The UNAT held that the respondent had been

---

[142] *Bhattacharyya*, UNAT Judgment No. 142 [1971], ibid. p. 248.

[143] *Fasla*, UNAT Judgment No. 158 [1972], JUNAT Nos. 114–166 p. 355.

[144] *Klee,* UNAT Judgment No. 242 [1979], JUNAT Nos. 231–300 p. 113. A legitimate expectancy of renewal was also found to exist in *Surina*, UNAT Judgment No. 178 [1973], JUNAT Nos. 167–230 p. 82.

[145] See *Sehgal*, UNAT Judgment No. 203 [1975], JUNAT Nos. 167–230 p. 324, and compare this case with *Perucho*, UNAT Judgment No. 285 [1982], JUNAT Nos. 231–300 p. 527.

[146] *Paveskovic*, UNAT Judgment No. 341 [1984].

[147] UNAT Judgment No. 290 [1982] (IMCO), JUNAT Nos. 231–300 p. 567.

negligent and remiss in not informing the applicant in time of the fact that his contract would not be renewed for 1 year, as had been done in the previous 2 years, and found that he had a legitimate expectancy that the contract would be renewed for 1 year.

In several cases the UNAT found that there was no legitimate expectancy, especially when the alleged behaviour of the administration did not create a binding obligation because it was not initiated by a competent authority. For example,[148] an offer of extension made to the holder of a fixed-term contract by a Deputy Resident Representative could not creat a contractual obligation because the Deputy Resident Representative was not the competent agent to make such an offer. Furthermore, neither the fact that the applicant was authorized to take home leave less than six months before the expiration of his contract nor governmental approval of continuation of the project for which he was hired was sufficient to create a legitimate expectancy.[149] In *Perucho*,[150] however, the seniority of a competent officer, a Director, was a determinant factor in creating in the mind of the applicant, a production foreman, a reasonable expectancy for continued exployment which was held to be a legitimate expectancy.

Written assurances given to holders of contracts have often been rejected by the UNAT as being merely statements of intention which could not create binding obligations on the part of the administration.[151]

The behaviour of fixed-term contract holders has sometimes been held to have been such as to prevent them from claiming a legitimate expectancy. Thus, in *Nath*[152] an applicant who accepted without protest a one-year extension of his contract and later contended that his legitimate expectancy was based on oral assurances given to him was told that his behaviour belied his claims.[153]

The facts of *El-Naggar*[154] were somewhat complex and in a way special. At the time of his appointment, the applicant received a fixed-term contract for 5 years because problems of geographical distribution of which he was aware did not permit the choice of a permanent appointment. In view of this the tribunal found that he could not subsequently claim that he virtually held a permanent appointment. The UNAT also referred to an article in the UN

---

[148] *Al-Abed*, UNAT Judgment No. 128 [1969], JUNAT Nos. 114–166 p. 136.

[149] See also *Fort*, UNAT Judgment No. 102 [1966], JUNAT Nos. 87–113 p. 142; *Touhami*, UNAT Judgment No. 135 [1970], JUNAT Nos. 114–166 p. 196; *Irani*, UNAT Judgment No. 150 [1971], ibid. p. 292.

[150] UNAT Judgment No. 285 [1982], JUNAT Nos. 231–300 p. 527.

[151] See *Fürst*, UNAT Judgment No. 134 [1969], JUNAT Nos. 114–166 p. 188; *Rajappan*, UNAT Judgment No. 139 [1971], JUNAT Nos. 114–166 p. 236; *Nath*, UNAT Judgment No. 181 [1974], JUNAT Nos. 167–230 p. 106.

[152] UNAT Judgment No. 181 [1974], JUNAT Nos. 167–230 p. 106.

[153] See also *Boelen*, UNAT Judgment No. 261 [1980], JUNAT Nos. 231–300 p. 297.

[154] UNAT Judgment No. 205 [1975], JUNAT Nos. 167–230 p. 345.

Press Release in which it was stated that the applicant would be getting a new assignment with the UN which would be announced shortly and noted that this statement was made too early—more than a year before the expiration of his five-year contract—to be considered as a promise of continued employment. Similarly, a memorandum recommending the applicant for a career appointment was considered to be only a proposal. Finally, the UNAT pointed out that the letter offering him employment contained no promise for continued employment upon satisfactory performance, as was the case in *Bhattacharyya*, and rejected the applicant's contention that he could legitimately expect to remain in the organization.

An offer of renewal may be conditional. If the condition is not fulfilled there is no obligation to renew or convert the fixed-term contract.[155]

(d) Consequences of the existence of a legitimate expectancy

The decisions in which the UNAT has decided that the applicant had a legitimate expectancy that his fixed-term contract would be renewed show a confused canvas in regard to the legal consequences which flow from the existence of such an expectancy. In most cases the tribunal has not concluded that there was an unqualified obligation to renew the contract, the failure to discharge which resulted in injury to the applicant. Instead, it has inquired whether the respondent had made bona-fide efforts to find an alternative post for the applicant before concluding that the obligation of the respondent had not been fulfilled. In these cases it has found that the respondent had not made the efforts required of it. This was the case, for example, in *Dale*[156] and *Perucho*.[157]

While the UNAT has not decided in any case that, though there was a legitimate expectancy of renewal of the fixed-term contract, the respondent had not violated its legal obligations, because it had made a bona-fide effort to find a suitable alternative position for the contract holder and had failed to find such a position, the tribunal has raised questions about the nature of the respondent's obligations in cases where there is a legitimate expectancy of renewal of the contract by virtue of the manner in which it has proceeded in the cases in which it has found that there was such a legitimate expectancy and that the applicant's rights had been infringed. In investigating the question whether the respondent had made reasonable bona-fide efforts to find the applicant suitable alternative employment, even though there was a legitimate expectancy of renewal, the tribunal has conveyed the impression

---

[155] *Rau*, UNAT Judgment No. 339 [1984].

[156] UNAT Judgment No. 132 [1969] (ICAO), JUNAT Nos. 114–166 p. 172.

[157] UNAT Judgment No. 285 [1982], JUNAT Nos. 231–300 p. 527. See also *Bhattacharyya*, UNAT Judgment No. 142 [1971], JUNAT Nos. 114–166 p. 248; *Délano de Stuven*, UNAT Judgment No. 298 [1982], JUNAT Nos. 231–300 p. 640.

that in its view the existence of such an expectancy does not place upon the respondent an absolute obligation to renew the fixed-term contract but only imposes upon it an obligation to make reasonable bona-fide efforts to find the holder of the contract a suitable alternative position. This may, indeed, be the tribunal's view, though it does not emerge clearly from these decisions.

On the other hand, in *Paveskovic*,[158] where it was held that there was a legitimate expectancy that the fixed-term contract would be renewed for 6 months but that the respondent had violated its obligations because it had not renewed the contract for more that 2 months, the UNAT did not inquire whether the respondent had made bona-fide efforts to find the applicant a position for the remaining 4 months. It is not clear whether it was regarded as obvious that the respondent had not made such efforts.

(e) Substantive irregularities

There have been cases in which the UNAT has found that the respondent has been guilty of substantive irregularities in connection with the non-renewal of fixed-term contracts. There are two significant features connected with this kind of defect in the UNAT decisions. Firstly, the tribunal has not interested itself in or found any such defect in the cases brought before it except in the form of what may amount to an error of law, including a breach of a term of the contract of employment. Secondly, the tribunal has generally not found any such defect to exist except in cases where there has also been an infringement of a legitimate expectancy; that is to say, the tribunal uses such a defect as a reason for finding that the applicant's rights have been violated only as an additional ground to the infringement of a legitimate expectancy. However, there is one instance, as will be seen, in which the tribunal will hold the error of law, which in this case is also a breach of contract, to be by itself a violation of the applicant's rights, irrespective of the existence of a legitimate expectancy. This is where the respondent has accepted a recommendation of its internal Appeals Board and has failed to carry it out. But for this exception, it would seem that always the tribunal has found a legitimate expectancy to exist before it was prepared to hold that a substantive irregularity resulted in a violation of law entitling the applicant to redress. However, there is no reason why an error of law, including a breach of contract, cannot by itself amount to unlawful conduct on the part of the administrative authority in a case where a fixed-term contract is not renewed, even though there is no legitimate expectancy of renewal. On the other hand,

---

158 UNAT Judgment No. 341 [1984]. In *Pattillo*, UNAT Judgment No. 294 [1982], JUNAT Nos. 231–300 p. 593, the respondent conceded that, because of a legitimate expectancy, the applicant's contract should have been renewed for a 2-year period. The issue before the tribunal was, therefore, what compensation should be paid the applicant.

it is very rarely that such an error of law would occur in the absence of such an expectancy. In view of the tribunal's approach to the whole question of renewal of fixed-term contracts, the same argument may not have as much cogency for other substantive irregularities, such as error of fact or erroneous conclusions, with which the tribunal has apparently not been confronted.

In *Levcik*[159] an error of law arose because the UN characterized the applicant's contractual relationship with the UN as a secondment by his national State's government whereas it was a fixed-term contract. There was found to be a legitimate expectancy of renewal in this case.[160] In *Bulsara*[161] the UN failed satisfactorily to justify that the applicant's assignment was not feasible in the near future as required by his initial contract of employment. Such errors of law as occurred in these cases only served to aggravate the illegality of the decision not to renew the contract, as they clearly showed what actions the respondent institution should have taken in connection with the renewal of the contract. There are two ways in which the law in respect of which there has been an error relates to the issue of legitimate expectancy. Firstly, in most cases it contributes positively to the finding that there was a legitimate expectancy and secondly, it could limit or define more specifically the content of the legitimate expectancy by specifying what the respondent institution must do to satisfy that expectancy.

In two cases the UNAT found that the acceptance by the UN of the recommendations of its Joint Appeals Board which included a finding that the applicant had a legitimate expectancy of a renewal of his contract placed an obligation upon the UN, failure to carry out which amounted to an error of law and a breach of contract. In *El-Naggar*,[162] while the UNAT found that the applicant did not have a legitimate expectancy of renewal, nevertheless, it also found that the UN had accepted the recommendation of the Joint Appeals Board which was that the applicant should be kept on the staff of the UN because he had a legitimate expectancy of continued employment. This imposed an obligation upon the UN to make bona-fide efforts to keep the applicant on the staff which it had not fulfilled. It is significant that the UNAT held that the UN owed the applicant a specific obligation which according to its own findings the UN did not owe the applicant before the recommendations of the internal board were accepted by the UN. In *Klee*[163] the decision of the UNAT was similar to the above decision, the only diffe-

---

[159] UNAT Judgment No. 192 [1974], JUNAT Nos. 167–230 p. 204.

[160] See also *Bhattacharyya*, UNAT Judgment No. 142 [1971], JUNAT Nos. 114–166 p. 248.

[161] UNAT Judgment No. 68 [1957], JUNAT Nos. 1–70 p. 398.

[162] UNAT Judgment No. 205 [1975], JUNAT Nos. 167–230 p. 345.

[163] UNAT Judgment No. 242 [1979], JUNAT Nos. 231–300 p. 113. In *Délano de Stuven*, UNAT Judgment No. 298 [1982], ibid. p. 640, also the tribunal found that the UN had violated the obligation it had assumed by accepting a recommendation of its Joint Appeals Board of making renewed efforts to find the applicant a position.

rence being that the UNAT found that the applicant in *Klee* did in fact have a legitimate expectancy that his contract would be renewed. In both these cases the error of law was associated with the acceptance of an internal recommendation by the administrative authority which amounted to an undertaking.

(*f*) *Détournement de pouvoir*

There are a few cases in which the UNAT has investigated the question of abuse of purpose or improper motive. However, the tribunal has found that improper motive has caused injury to the applicant as an unlawful element in the decision not to renew a fixed-term contract, only when there has also been found to be a legitimate expectancy that the contract would be renewed. In *Fasla*,[164] for instance, the UNAT found a performance report tainted by personal prejudice and declared the decision not to renew the applicant's contract invalid. There was also in this case a legitimate expectancy of renewal. In addition there were found to be certain procedural irregularities.[165]

It would seem that abuse of purpose or improper motive was originally examined by the UNAT in circumstances in which it was clear that the applicant had a legitimate expectancy of renewal of his fixed-term contract. Thus, it appears that it was an additional reason for finding the decision not to renew unlawful. There is no authority for the view that in the absence of a legitimate expectancy of renewal, the tribunal may hold, as the ILOAT has done, that the decision not to renew the contract is vitiated by a *détournement de pouvoir* which will entitle the applicant to a remedy. There is no reason to suppose also that in the absence of a vitiating element, such as a *détournement de pouvoir*, the tribunal would not have, in the cases it has decided, found in favour of the applicant after he had succeeded in establishing that a legitimate expectancy of renewal of his contract had not been met. In *Boelen*[166] the tribunal, after finding that there was no legitimate expectancy of renewal, proceeded to examine the question of prejudice, but in this case it did not find that there was prejudice. On the other hand, it may be asked why the tribunal did examine the question whether there was prejudice if it became moot, once it was established that there was no legitimate expectancy of renewal. It must be conceded that it is an exceptional and unsettling case, although it seems to be the precursor of a different approach on the part of the tribunal. The procedure adopted in this case has been followed in many subsequent cases, although in none was there found to be a *détournement de*

---

164 UNAT Judgment No. 158 [1972], JUNAT Nos. 114–166 p. 355.
165 A similar case was *Robinson*, UNAT Judgment No. 15 [1952], JUNAT Nos. 1–70 p. 43. See also *Levcik*, UNAT Judgment No. 192 [1974], JUNAT Nos. 167–230 p. 204.
166 UNAT Judgment No. 261 [1980], JUNAT Nos. 231–300 p. 297.

pouvoir.[167] Further, sometimes it has been explicitly stated, after it had been established that there was no legitimate expectancy, that the decision not to renew the contract must be exercised in the proper manner.[168] These cases work in favour of the view that a different approach is developing.

(g) *Procedural irregularities*

There are cases in which the UNAT has found the existence of procedural irregularities in the decisions not to renew fixed-term contracts. In some cases the applicant's right to be duly considered for the renewal of his contract was violated because of an invalid performance report. Thus, in *Fasla*[169] the fact sheet which the respondent circulated to different UN agencies was found incomplete and misleading because it had been drawn up on the basis of performance reports tainted by several irregularities in violation of UN Staff Rule 112.6[170] and Administrative Instruction ST/AI/115.[171]

There are other kinds of procedural irregularities which have surfaced. In *Sehgal*[172] the UNAT held that the applicant was denied due process because the respondent showed a lack of objectivity in dealing with the issue of the renewal of the applicant's contract in connection with the rebuttal of his periodic report. In *Robinson*[173] there was a finding that the respondent had failed to give reasons for the non-renewal of the contract, although this was not characterized specially as a procedural irregularity, while the tribunal used the absence of reasons as evidence of improper motivation.

In all the above cases there was also a finding that the applicant had a legitimate expectancy that his contract would be renewed. In several cases in which it was not found that there was a legitimate expectancy of renewal, the UNAT has found that there were no effective procedural irregularities, because the Secretary General of the UN was aware of the irregularities when he decided not to renew the contracts of the applicants.[174] In some cases the

---

[167] *Harkins*, UNAT Judgment No. 287 [1982], ibid. p. 542; *Panis*, UNAT Judgment No. 297 [1982], ibid. p. 625; *Gakuu*, UNAT Judgment No. 306 [1983]; *Mensa-Bonsu*, UNAT Judgment No. 307 [1983]; *Flad*, UNAT Judgment No. 318 [1983]; *Jekhine*, UNAT Judgment No. 319 [1983]; *Ridler*, UNAT Judgment No. 327 [1984]; *Large*, UNAT Judgment No. 331 [1984]; *Yakimetz*, UNAT Judgment No. 333 [1984].

[168] See *Harkins*, UNAT Judgment No. 287 [1982], JUNAT Nos. 231–300 p. 542 at p. 549; and *Jekhine*, UNAT Judgment No. 319 [1983] at p. 7.

[169] UNAT Judgment No. 158 [1972], JUNAT Nos. 114–166 p. 355.

[170] See Appendix V *infra*.

[171] See also *Fracyon*, UNAT Judgment No. 199 [1975], JUNAT Nos. 167–230 p. 277.

[172] UNAT Judgment No. 203 [1975], ibid. p. 324.

[173] UNAT Judgment No. 15 [1952], JUNAT Nos. 1–70 p. 43.

[174] See *Rau*, UNAT Judgment No. 101 [1966], JUNAT Nos. 87–113, p. 133; *White*, UNAT Judgment No. 46 [1953], JUNAT Nos. 1–70 p. 224; *Carter*, UNAT Judgment No. 47 [1953], ibid. p. 229; *Zimmet*, UNAT Judgment No. 52 [1954], ibid. p. 251. In *Mensa-Bonsu*, UNAT Judgment No. 307 [1983], no procedural violation was found after it was established that there was no legitimate expectancy of renewal.

procedural irregularities were regarded as minor and as not serious enough to affect the non-renewal decision. Thus, in *Boelen*[175] a periodic report was not accompanied by clear instructions regarding its rebuttal, there was no record of an appraisal of the applicant's formal complaints relating to its contents, nor was a special report prepared and given to the applicant, all of which were in violation of the Administrative Instruction ST/AI/115. The UNAT held that these omissions did not carry such weight as would have required it to find the decision not to renew the applicant's contract illegal. In this last case the UNAT investigated the question of procedural irregularities even after it had established that the applicant had no legitimate expectancy of renewal of her contract. This case and others in which no effective procedural irregularities were found to exist, even after it was established that there was no legitimate expectancy of renewal of the contract, already raised some serious questions concerning the relevance of procedural irregularities to the issue of non-renewal of fixed-term contracts. It would have been tempting to regard them only as relevant where the existence of a legitimate expectancy of renewal is established, as seems to be the case in general with substantive irregularities. On the other hand, the above cases do show that the tribunal is prepared to examine the question whether an effective procedural irregularity exists, even in the absence of such a legitimate expectancy.

Some subsequent cases seem to indicate that this new approach is likely to be followed. Two cases may be cited as examples. In *Jabbour*,[176] while it was found that there was no legitimate expectancy of renewal and therefore reinstatement was not ordered, the UNAT found that the UN had been negligent as an employer in not treating the applicant fairly and justly, although he had served the UN for a long time, and that the 4½-years' delay caused by the respondent's conduct in handling the internal appeals procedure was an unwarranted irregularity. The applicant was awarded compensation. In *Jekhine*[177] it was also found that there was no legitimate expectancy of renewal, though the applicant may have had some kind of expectation of renewal. However, the UNAT held that the respondent had been remiss in inquiring into the facts and that the decision not to renew the applicant's contract could have been more accurate with the result that substantial injury had been caused warranting the award of compensation. This was a case of procedural irregularity.[178]

While in these cases, the tribunal did not find that the procedural irregularities which had occurred vitiated the non-renewal decision, it did examine the question whether there had been any such irregularities after holding that

---

[175] UNAT Judgment No. 261 [1980], JUNAT Nos. 231–300 p. 297. See also *Gakuu*, UNAT Judgment No. 306 [1983]; and *Nuhbegovich*, UNAT Judgment No. 338 [1984].

[176] UNAT Judgment No. 305 [1983].

[177] UNAT Judgment No. 319 [1983].

[178] See also *Large*, UNAT Judgment No. 331 [1984].

there was no legitimate expectancy of renewal of the contract, with a view apparently to establishing whether such irregularities did exist or could have vitiated the decision and only incidentally found that the irregularities committed did not vitiate the decision, while they did cause sufficient damage or injury as required compensating. As in the case of *détournement de pouvoir*, it is not entirely clear what this approach by the tribunal signifies. It is a very strong indication that the tribunal will, as the ILOAT does, be prepared to hold a non-renewal decision invalid because of a procedural irregularity, even where there is no legitimate expectancy of renewal.

(h) The question of the dependency of substantive and procedural irregularities and détournement de pouvoir on legitimate expectancy

As seen in the analysis above of procedural irregularities and *détournement de pouvoir* particularly, there is a measure of doubt whether the UNAT will subject the discretionary power of not renewing a fixed-term contract to its control by reference to the various kinds of irregularity, in the absence of a finding that the contract holder had a legitimate expectancy of renewal. At this stage of the development of the jurisprudence of the UNAT there is an indication of the direction in which the tribunal will move. There is more than a hint that the tribunal might well move in the direction of applying these controls even in the absence of a finding that there was a legitimate expectancy of renewal, because of some cases, starting with *Boelen*, where the tribunal has seriously examined the allegations that there were prejudice and procedural irregularities, after definitely establishing that there was no legitimate expectancy of renewal, and even found the existence of certain procedural irregularities, even though they were minor ones. If the tribunal was not so inclined, there is little reason for it to have examined these allegations after making such a finding, as it would have had to dismiss them anyway because once the finding was made, it would have had no basis for controlling the exercise of the discretion. In short, after finding that there was no legitimate expectancy, it would properly have had to dismiss all other allegations as being irrelevant to the case.

Cases such as *Robinson* which were decided in the early years of the UNAT's existence seem to indicate that the tribunal regarded the existence of a legitimate expectancy as the only basis for the exercise of its control, other factors being subsidiary. But there would be no contradiction between such decisions as *Robinson* and its application of controls even in the absence of legitimate expectancy in the way the ILOAT does, if the UNAT were to adopt such an approach. If the tribunal does clearly adopt the technique of exercising control even in the absence of a legitimate expectancy, it would be basically accepting the approach of the ILOAT. The difference between the approaches of the two tribunals would then be that in the case of the ILOAT approach there is no additional ground for redress where there is a legitimate expectancy of renewal of the contract but there are no irregularities such as would entitle the ILOAT now to interfere with the exercise of the discretionary power. There would be an additional ground on which the UNAT could find that there was a violation of the contract holder's rights, namely failure to renew the contract in a situation where the contract holder had a legitimate expectancy of such renewal.

In the circumstance that the UNAT does clearly adopt the alternative of more extensive control of the discretion not to renew fixed-term contracts, there is no reason to make any distinctions between substantive irregularities, procedural defects, and *détournement de pouvoir*. They would all be valid concepts by reference to which the UNAT could exercise control. Furthermore, there would be no particular restrictions on the kind of irregularity that could arise within each of these categories of defects.

(i) *The right to be transferred*

In the cases decided by the UNAT the rights of the holder of a fixed-term contract in respect of transfer on the expiration of the contract depends on the existence of a legitimate expectancy for continued employment as well as on the written law of the organization and especially on provisions concerning preferential rights for inside candidates in the filling of vacancies.

When a legitimate expectancy is established, then the administrative authority must carry out the obligation it assumed in regard to keeping the holder of the contract on its staff. The UNAT has been particularly strict in examining the efforts made by the administrative authority in this regard. It had recourse to the general principle of good faith when it examined the efforts made by the administrative authorities to find a suitable post for the holder of a fixed-term contract whose contract was about to expire and ruled that a bona-fide search for an alternative post should have taken place. Thus, in *Dale*[179] the tribunal examined the procedure followed by ICAO in the filling of vacancies, as well as in recruitment during the relevant period during which the applicant's candidacy should have been taken into consideration, and found that he had been considered for only one post. Therefore, it was held that the organization had failed to execute the obligation which it had to keep the applicant on its staff and which derived directly from the existence of a legitimate expectancy of renewal of his contract. In *Bhattacharyya*[180] the obligation of the respondent to make a *bona fide* search for an alternative post was not only based on the applicant's legitimate expectancy but also on UN Staff Rule 109.1 (c),[181] since the applicant's post

[179] UNAT Judgment No. 132 [1969] (ICAO), JUNAT Nos. 114–166 p. 172.
[180] UNAT Judgment No. 142 [1971], ibid. p. 248.
[181] See Appendix V. *infra*.

had been abolished and the respondent failed to consider his seniority. Moreover, at the time UNICEF was expanding its activities and the applicant was replaced by an internally recruited junior professional. Also there existed several vacancies for which the applicant was both suitable and qualified.[182]

In the absence of a legitimate expectancy there is no obligation on the administrative authority to transfer the contract holder in an effort to keep him on its staff. Thus, in *Nath*[183] no expectancy was established and it was held that the efforts made to find alternative exployment were outside the scope of the contractual obligation of UNICEF towards the applicant.[184]

In *Bulsara*[185] the source for the respondent's obligation to find alternative employment for the applicant was a stipulation in the initial contract in which it was spelled out that the only ground for termination was 'if an assignment proved not to be feasible in the near future'. The UNAT ruled, after a thorough examination of the respondent's efforts, that it had failed to prove that the reappointment of the applicant was not feasible.

Finally, the respondent's obligation to keep the applicant on the staff may arise out of its acceptance of the recommendations of the Joint Appeals Board. Thus, in *El-Naggar*[186] the Board had concluded that the applicant had no legitimate expectancy for continued employment and stated that the non-renewal decision would have been valid. However, it was held that the respondent had failed to fulfil the obligation it had assumed when it accepted the Board's recommendation that the applicant should be kept on the staff and offered a new contract on the expiry of his contract. The respondent's efforts were found to have been insufficient and of short duration, and particularly the applicant's refusal to accept a technical assistance position did not discharge the respondent of its obligation to make fair and objective efforts to find him an alternative position.

The approach taken by other tribunals

Not many cases concerning the renewal or conversion of fixed-term contracts have been decided by other tribunals, with the exception, perhaps, of the Appeals Board of NATO. As has been seen, the Appeals Board of NATO appears to follow closely the approach taken by the ILOAT in dealing with the renewal of fixed-term contracts.

---

[182] See also *Fasla*, UNAT Judgment No. 158 [1972], ibid. p. 355; *Perucho*, UNAT Judgment No. 285 [1982], JUNAT Nos. 231–300 p. 527.
[183] UNAT Judgment No. 181 [1974], JUNAT Nos. 167–230 p. 106.
[184] See also *Surina*, UNAT Judgment No. 178 [1973], ibid. p. 82.
[185] UNAT Judgment No. 68 [1957], JUNAT Nos. 1–70 p. 398.
[186] UNAT Judgment No. 205 [1975], JUNAT Nos. 167–230 p. 345.

The CJEC apparently has not dealt with fixed-term contracts since the early years of its existence. As was seen, that Court at that time seems to have accepted the approach of the ILOAT. On the other hand, in *Kergall*[187] the Court appears to have applied the concept of expectancy to arrive at the conclusion that the applicant's contract should have been renewed. The Court referred to the circumstances of employment, the contemplation of the parties, and the intent of the European Community in deciding that stability in employment relations was not excluded and that the applicant could expect to have his contract renewed. As a consequence, though the Court did not use the language of expectancy, it held that the respondent should have offered him an alternative post and continued his employment. It was not an adequate reason to justify the non-renewal of his contract that the post which he held had been abolished. The applicant was awarded compensation. This case, however, concerned a special situation in which fixed-term contracts were used before the Staff Regulations of the European Communities came into force. It cannot be regarded as reflecting the law relating to such contracts now, although in that case the Court seems to have been ready to apply the concept of legitimate expectancy as an additional ground for reviewing decisions not to renew fixed-term contracts, while exercising the same kind of control exercised by the ILOAT.

The OASAT has also not had to decide many cases dealing with the non-renewal or non-conversion of fixed-term contracts. In the one case in which it was faced with that issue[188] the tribunal referred to the concept of 'expectation'. It took the view that simply because the contract stated that it could be renewed each year, it did not mean that the holder of the contract could have an expectation that it would be renewed. This language seems similar to the language of legitimate expectancy employed by the UNAT. It may be safe to conclude, therefore, that the OASAT would, at least, follow the approach taken by the UNAT.

The WBAT has had to decide only one case concerned with the non-renewal or non-conversion of a fixed-term contract. In *Mr. X* the tribunal stated: 'The possibility exists also that there may be something in the surrounding circumstances which creates a right to the conversion of a fixed-term appointment to a permanent one.'[189] The tribunal found that a statement made by the respondent gave such a hope but that this hope was conditional and concluded that the applicant had not met the conditions which included satisfactory performance. The WBAT seems in this case to have taken the UNAT approach that a legitimate expectancy can give the holder of a fixed-term contract a right to its conversion or renewal. In

---

[187] CJEC Case 1/55 [1954–56] ECR p. 151.
[188] *Uehling*, OASAT Judgment No. 8 [1974].
[189] WBAT Reports [1984], Decision No. 16 at p. 14.

determining whether the applicant had fulfilled the condition of satisfactory performance the respondent, it was held, exercised a discretionary power which was subject to review by the tribunal as the exercise of discretionary powers in general were. Whether the tribunal will regard control of the exercise of the discretion not to renew or convert a fixed-term contract through the concept of legitimate expectancy as additional to control of the exercise of that discretion in the way the ILOAT does or whether it will restrict itself to the concept of legitimate expectancy remains to be seen.

The Appeals Boards of OEEC and OECD have considered some cases concerning the non-renewal or non-conversion of fixed-term appointments. It is of importance that the regular type of appointment with the OECD is not contractual but statutory. The general approach taken by this tribunal is to regard the decision not to renew or convert a fixed-term appointment as a discretionary one over which the tribunal may exercise control.[190] The Appeals Board has clearly stated that the holder of a fixed-term appointment has no right to have it renewed or converted and that it expires without notice on the date of expiration.[191] The tribunal has not shown any inclination to apply a concept of legitimate expectancy, particularly in view of its recognition that there is absolutely no right to renewal or conversion. Thus, it is unlikely that it would follow the jurisprudence of the UNAT on this point.

In *Pfalzgraf*[192] the tribunal applied the concept of *détournement de pouvoir* to the exercise of the discretionary power not to renew the applicant's appointment and found that there had been no such *détournement de pouvoir*. The Tribunal has examined in one case the issue of *détournement de procédure* and found none.[193] In one case it found that procedural defects involving performance reports were negligible[194] and in another that there was no procedural irregularity.[195] In *Pfalzgraf*[196] the tribunal found that the administrative authority did not give reasons for the termination of the fixed-term appointment and for not considering the applicant as a candidate for a permanent appointment when his post could only be occupied by a staff member who was permanent. This was held to be a violation of the rules of procedure and the decision terminating the applicant's employment was annulled. The tribunal has also found in one

---

[190] See *Bessoles*, Decision No. 56, OECD Appeals Board [1976], Recueil des décisions 1 à 62 (1979) p. 154; *Mondot*, Decision No. 94, OECD Appeals Board [1982], Recueil des décisions 83 à 102 (1983) p. 35 at p. 36.

[191] See *Dame X*, Decision No. 4, OEEC Appeals Board [1950], Recueil des décisions 1 à 62 (1979) p. 11; *Bessoles*, Decision No. 56, OECD Appeals Board [1976], ibid. p. 154; *Mondot*, Decision No. 94, OECD Appeals Board [1982], Recueil des décisions 83 à 102 [1983] p. 35.

[192] Decision No. 55, OECD Appeals Board [1975], Recueil des décisions 1 à 62 (1979) p. 150.

[193] *Carr-Hill*, Decision No. 62, OECD Appeals Board [1978], ibid. p. 174.

[194] *Bessoles*, Decision No. 56, OECD Appeals Board [1976], ibid. p. 154.

[195] *Carr-Hill*, Decision No. 62, OECD Appeals Board [1978], ibid. p. 174.

[196] Decision No. 55, OECD Appeals Board [1975], ibid. p. 150.

case that the administrative authority had not violated the law in strictly applying the provisions of the Statut du Personnel to the renewal or conversion of a fixed-term appointment and interpreting so as not to conflict with the Statut du Personnel a decision of the Council of OECD, which allowed him to renew or convert the appointments of long-term consultants, depending on the duration of their initial consultant-assignment with OECD, but did not provide a sufficient number of positions in the budget to implement that decision.[197] The Council's decision, it said, did not give the consultants any right to have their appointments renewed or converted. In *Ferguson-Syrimis*,[198] however, the tribunal held that the administrative authority had violated the Statut du Personnel in transferring the applicant to a position which was a permanent one and not converting her appointment at the same time into a permanent one, but retaining her only till her fixed-term appointment ended. It annulled the decision of the administrative authority. Both these cases deal with error of law apparently, one holding that there was no such error and the other that there was.

The approach taken by the Appeals Boards of OEEC and OECD seems to indicate a preference for the ILOAT solution to the problem of the fixed-term appointment. Control is exercised over the decision not to renew or convert the appointment solely by reference to the principles relating to the abuse of discretion, although there has been no general statement to this effect made by the tribunal.[199] There does not seem to be any tendency to apply a concept of legitimate expectancy, as the UNAT has done.

The Appeals Board of the Council of Europe apparently has not had to deal with questions relating to non-renewal or non-conversion of fixed-term appointments.

---

[197] *Martin*, Decision No. 60, OECD Appeals Board [1978], ibid. p. 167.

[198] Decision No. 52, OECD Appeals Board [1974], ibid. p. 142. In *Decision No. 17, ESRO/CR/54* [1971], ESRO Appeals Board, the Appeals Board of ESRO found that there was no error of law in the non-renewal of a fixed-term contract, although it was alleged that there was one. The Appeals Board of ESRO seemed ready to follow the ILOAT approach. In the same case it was also found that there was no improper motivation in the non-renewal of the contract which resulted from an abolition of post.

[199] In *Seletti*, Decision No. 103, OECD Appeals Board [1984], the Appeals Board came close to making such a general statement but did not make itself explicit. The Appeals Board of ESRO and the Appeals Board of ESA have apparently followed the ILOAT approach: see *Decision No. 1, ESRO/CR/4*, ESRO Appeals Board [1966]; *Decision No. 5, ESRO/CR/23*, ibid. [1969]; *Decision No. 12, ESRO/CR/53*, ibid. [1971]; *Decision No. 14, ESRO/CR/51*, ibid. [1971]; *Decision No. 17, ESRO/CR/54*, ibid. [1971]; *Decision No. 22, ESRO/CR/63*, ibid. [1972]; *Decision No. 23, ESRO/CR/64*, ibid. [1972]; *Decision No. 24, ESRO/CR/63*, ibid. [1972]; *Decision No. 37, ESRO/CR/97*, ibid. [1975]; *Decision No. 2, ESA/CR/5*, ESA Appeals Board [1976]; *Decision No. 11, ESA/CR/26*, ibid. [1979]; *Decision No. 12, ESA/CR/24*, ibid. [1979]; *Decision No. 14, ESA/CR/30*, ibid. [1980]; *Decision No. 20, ESA/CR/37*, ibid. [1983]

Remedies

In so far as there is a difference in the jurisprudence of the ILOAT and the UNAT as regards the manner in which the non-renewal or non-conversion of fixed-term contracts has been treated, there is a difference in the approach to remedies. Further, the differences in the Statutes of the two tribunals have influenced the issue of remedies. There is not much of significance in the cases decided by other tribunals on the question of remedies but what there is can be dealt with conveniently under one of the two approaches, the ILOAT or the UNAT approach.

(a) The ILOAT approach to remedies

As the Statute of the ILOAT gives the tribunal the power to order reinstatement or compensation without giving the administrative authority the power to choose between the two, there are several alternatives that the ILOAT has been able to adopt. Further, in the exercise of its inherent jurisdiction the ILOAT has awarded compensation, even where it has not found the non-renewal or non-conversion decision invalid and has also taken other measures. The decisions of the Appeals Boards of NATO, the OECD, ESRO, and ESA will be considered together with those of the ILOAT.

i. *Reinstatement or specific performance*
Reinstatement is not a remedy often ordered by the ILOAT, because of the nature of fixed-term contracts and the difficulty for various reasons of restoring the status quo ante. If it were ordered, it would mean that the fixed-term contract would have to be renewed. In one case the ILOAT did order the administrative authority to extend the applicant's fixed-term contract by 13 days, so as to enable him to qualify for pension benefits.[200] In another case, where the applicant's contract was not converted into a permanent contract, the tribunal ordered the administrative authority to renew the applicant's candidacy for permanent appointment, taking into account all the relevant circumstances of the case,[201] thus ordering specific performance. The tribunal did not, however, order that a permanent appointment be granted the applicant. In *O'Connell*,[202] where the applicant claimed an indemnity for post abolition, it was held that she could not claim reinstatement because it was contradictory to the claim for an indemnity but the respondent was ordered to pay the indemnity which was a form of specific performance.

In *Ferguson-Syrimis*,[203] where the issue was whether the applicant should

---

[200] *Meyer*, ILOAT Judgment No. 245 [1974] (IAEA).

[201] *Chadsey*, ILOAT Judgment No. 122 [1968] (WPU).

[202] ILOAT Judgment No. 469 [1982] (PAHO).

[203] Decision No. 52, OECD Appeals Board [1974], Recueil des décisions 1 à 62 (1979) p. 142.

have been given a permanent appointment, the Appeals Board of OECD ordered specific performance by requiring that the applicant's appointment be converted into a permanent one from the date of her transfer to the position she was holding.

ii. Decision quashed

In one case the ILOAT merely quashed the decision not to renew the applicant's contract without ordering any further remedies. In *Mofjeld* [204] in which the decision was found illegal for error of law, the only remedy requested by the applicant was the quashing of the impugned decision. The tribunal did this, no additional relief being granted, since the applicant stated that his complaint related to his future career and good name.

iii. Choice between reinstatement and compensation

In *Duberg*,[205] where the decision not to renew the contract was found invalid because of *détournement de pouvoir*, the tribunal decided that the decision had to be rescinded but also assessed compensation. The tribunal awarded 1 year's salary for not having the contract renewed and an additional year's salary for moral prejudice, caused by the publicity given in the press by the organization to the Director General's loss of confidence in the applicant, and particularly for the difficulty the applicant would encounter in finding new employment.[206] In *Pfalzgraf*[207] the Appeals Board of OECD ordered compensation if the administrative authority chose not to reinstate the applicant. Compensation was fixed at 30 months' salary.

iv. Compensation only awarded

On one occasion the ILOAT found that it was impossible to restore the status quo ante and ordered compensation to be paid without annulling the decision not to convert the contract into a permanent appointment. In *Garcin*[208] the tribunal found that procedural irregularities had vitiated the decision not to convert the contract. That decision was not annulled but the applicant was granted compensation for the material and moral injury he had suffered in the amount of $12,000.

In most cases reinstatement is either explicitly refused by the tribunal, because it would be inappropriate or inadvisable, or not considered by the

---

[204] ILOAT Judgment No. 260 [1975] (FAO). See also *Decision No. 23, ESRO/CR/64*, ESRO Appeals Board [1972].

[205] ILOAT Judgment No. 17 [1955] (UNESCO). See also *Leff, Wilcox*, and *Bernstein*, ILOAT Judgments Nos. 18, 19, and 21 [1955] (UNESCO).

[206] See also *Ballo*, ILOAT Judgment No. 191 [1972] (UNESCO); *Goyal*, ILOAT Judgment No. 136 [1969] (UNESCO).

[207] Decision No. 55, OECD Appeals Board [1975], Recueil des décisions 1 à 62 (1979) p. 150.

[208] ILOAT Judgment No. 32 [1958] (UNESCO).

tribunal presumably for the same reason, and compensation alone is awarded. Very rarely the applicant may not request reinstatement. In *Djoehana*[209] reinstatement was refused, because UNESCO could not make use of the applicant's services. In *Dicancro*[210] the tribunal found that reinstatement was not in the interests of the organization, PAHO. The tribunal has also held that reinstatement would be inadvisable and refused it.[211] In all such cases compensation was awarded.

In several cases the ILOAT has not considered the alternative of reinstatement but simply ordered that compensation be paid.[212] In *Halliwell* [213] the applicant did not claim reinstatement, wherefore the tribunal only awarded compensation.

Where compensation has been ordered, in addition to that awarded for the material injury the ILOAT has sometimes considered the question of moral injury or prejudice. In *Dicancro*[214] the tribunal stated that damages for moral prejudice were justified, because the non-renewal of the applicant's contract took the appearance of a summary dismissal and because of the attitude of the administrative authority concerning the withdrawal of the charge of misconduct of which he was found guilty. The applicant was awarded $20,000 as compensation specially for moral prejudice. In *Perone* [215] the tribunal rejected the applicant's claim for damages for moral prejudice, because the mere fact of a tainted decision did not entitle the victim to such compensation. In *Gausi* (*No. 1*)[216] and *Chawla*[217] the tribunal simply awarded damages for both material and moral damages without any discussion of the issue of moral damages. In the latter case prejudice had tainted the decision.

In some cases the expectancy of continued employment was mentioned as a factor to be considered in the assessment of damages.[218] The tribunal has in most of these cases taken into account the expectancy while not stating that

---

[209] ILOAT Judgment No. 359 [1978] (UNESCO).

[210] ILOAT Judgment No. 427 [1980] (PAHO).

[211] *Rosescu*, ILOAT Judgment No. 431 [1980] (IAEA). There are other cases in which reinstatement has been refused because it was inappropriate or inadvisable for a variety of reasons: *Troncoso*, ILOAT Judgment No. 448 [1981] (PAHO); *Perrone*, ILOAT Judgment No. 470 [1982] (PAHO); *Gale*, ILOAT Judgment No. 474 [1982] (EMBL); *Bordeaux*, ILOAT Judgment No. 544 [1983] (CERN). See also *Bâ*, ILOAT Judgment No. 268 [1976] (WHO); and *Florio*, ILOAT Judgment No. 541 [1982] (FAO). In *Chawla*, ILOAT Judgment No. 195 [1972] (WHO), reinstatement was considered to be difficult.

[212] See *Gausi* (*No. 1*), ILOAT Judgment No. 223 [1973] (ILO); *Olivares Silva*, ILOAT Judgment No. 495 [1982] (PAHO); *Sadeghian*, ILOAT Judgment No. 577 [1983] (ILO).

[213] ILOAT Judgment No. 415 [1980] (WHO).

[214] ILOAT Judgment No. 427 [1980] (PAHO).

[215] ILOAT Judgment No. 470 [1982] (PAHO).

[216] ILOAT Judgment No. 223 [1973] (ILO).

[217] ILOAT Judgment No. 195 [1972] (WHO).

[218] See *Halliwell*, ILOAT Judgment No. 415 [1980] (WHO); *Dicancro*, ILOAT Judgment No. 427 [1980] (PAHO); *Rosescu*, ILOAT Judgment No. 431 [1980] (IAEA).

the applicants had been deprived of contractual rights to renewal or conversion of their contracts.

In a number of cases where compensation was ordered for material injury alone the tribunal has awarded a lump sum. In *Rosescu*,[219] for example, the tribunal disallowed the applicant's full claim because the organization could not be held responsible for his difficulties in finding other employment, if he had chosen not to return to his national Sate because of disagreements on tax matters with the authorities in the State, while at the same time it awarded him compensation amounting to $50,000.[220]

In some cases the tribunal explained the heads of damages or the reason for the amount. In *Djoehana*,[221] for example, the tribunal mentioned the facts that a letter sent to the applicant by the administrative authority should have warned him that his position in UNESCO was precarious and that, since the extensions granted him in 1975 and 1976 were so short, he should have realized that he was going to lose his job in a few months and had to look for employment outside UNESCO. It awarded the applicant one year's salary.[222] In some other cases, however, the tribunal has simply named a figure.[223]

In one case against PAHO,[224] where the respondent had committed an error of law in not treating the applicant as if his post had been abolished under the Staff Rules, the organization was ordered to pay compensation in accordance with Staff rule 1050.4 which provided for an indemnity in the case of post abolition.

v. *Remand*

In *Decision No. 85*[225] the Appeals Board of NATO stated that annulment did not mean that a new contract must be offered but only that the proper

---

219 ILOAT Judgment No. 431 [1980] (IAEA).

220 In *Troncoso*, ILOAT Judgment No. 448 [1981] (PAHO), the applicant was awarded $12,000. In *Florio*, ILOAT Judgment No. 541 [1982] (FAO). $12,000 compensation was awarded *ex aequo et bono*. In *Bordeaux*, ILOAT Judgment No. 544 [1983] (CERN), the amount awarded *ex aequo et bono* was SF 20,000. The Appeals Board of NATO awarded compensation of 12 months' salary on the basis of a fair assessment: *Decision No. 85*, NATO Appeals Board [1977], Collection of the Decisions 65(b), 74 to 99 (1979).

221 ILOAT Judgment No. 359 [1978] (UNESCO).

222 See also *Gale*, ILOAT Judgment No. 474 [1982] (EMBL), where reasons for the award of DM 10,000 were given. In *Bâ*, ILOAT Judgment No. 268 [1976] (WHO), the tribunal took into account the applicant's length of service and satisfactory performance and awarded 12 months' salary.

223 See *Halliwell*, ILOAT Judgment No. 415 [1980] (WHO), SF 8,000 with interest; *Olivares Silva*, ILOAT Judgment No. 495 [1982] (PAHO), $15,000: in this case it was mentioned that compensation could not be large because the prospects of employment for the applicant were uncertain; *Sadeghian*, ILOAT Judgment No. 577 [1983] (ILO), SF 6,000.

224 *Perrone*, ILOAT Judgment No. 470 [1982] (PAHO).

225 *Decision No. 85*, NATO Appeals Board [1977], Collection of the Decisions 65(b), 74 to 99 (1979).

procedure must be followed and a decision taken. Reinstatement was said to be impossible, because it would have given rise to substantial difficulties. In one case, in which a procedural irregularity was found, the Appeals Board of ESA merely invited the ESA to follow the appropriate procedure before deciding whether to renew or not to renew the contract.[226]

(b) The UNAT approach to remedies

Following the provisions of its Statute the UNAT has in the appropriate case left to the respondent the choice between specific performance (or reinstatement) and compensation,[227] except where it has ordered only compensation.

Where the status quo ante cannot be restored, the UNAT has, in accordance with its usual practice,[228] merely awarded compensation without ordering reinstatement or specific performance. Thus, where there was a lapse of time and there was no available post similar to the one the applicant had occupied, no reinstatement was ordered.[229] However, there have been cases where specific performance in certain respects has been ordered,[230] though this was not reinstatement.

Generally the tribunal calculates the compensation taking into account all relevant factors, though sometimes it merely indicates guidelines to be observed by the respondent. The relevant factors considered in the calculation of compensation generally depend on the circumstances of each case.

i. General approach

In some cases, when a contract has not been renewed at the expiration date and the decision has been found invalid the UNAT has referred to Annex III, paragraph (b) of the UN Staff Regulations[231] in order to determine compensation. Thus, if the holder of a fixed-term contract could have anticipated a renewal for 1 year but the original contract was not renewed, it is as if the contract had been terminated 12 months before its expiration date, with the consequence that the holder of such a contract would be entitled to a termination indemnity of 1 week's salary for each of the 12 months of uncompleted

---

[226] Decision No. 14, ESA/CR/30, ESA Appeals Board [1980].

[227] See El-Naggar, UNAT Judgment No. 205 [1975], JUNAT Nos. 167–230 p. 345; Cipolla, UNAT Judgment No. 290 [1982] (IMCO), JUNAT Nos. 231–300 p. 567.

[228] See, e.g., Sood, UNAT Judgment No. 195 [1975], JUNAT Nos. 167–230 p. 235.

[229] Fracyon, UNAT Judgment No. 199 [1975], JUNAT Nos. 167–230 p. 277. See also Bulsara, UNAT Judgment No. 68 [1957], JUNAT Nos. 1–70 p. 398.

[230] The removal of a memorandum from the applicant's personnel file: Perucho, UNAT Judgment No. 285 [1982], JUNAT Nos. 231–300 p. 527.

[231] See Appendix V infra.

service.[232] However, it has been conceded that this formula is not always an adequate method of calculating compensation. Due consideration must also be given to the circumstances under which the failure to fulfil a legitimate expectancy of extension had occurred.[233]

Sometimes, there could be extenuating circumstances favouring the respondent.[234] On the other hand, there could be aggravating circumstances warranting the award of more compensation in addition to that derived from the formula. Thus, where the respondent had, in not converting the applicant's contract into a permanent one, disregarded the principle of good faith, the applicant was awarded compensation in the amount of 6 months' salary.[235] In *Levcik*[236] the respondent was guilty of an error of law which led to the non-renewal of the applicant's contract. As a consequence the applicant was awarded 1 year's salary as compensation.[237] In *Perucho*[238] there was fault on both sides and an award of four months' salary was considered adequate. In *Délano de Stuven*[239] the amount of compensation was reduced because the applicant had refused to serve outside Chile. In these two cases there were extenuating circumstances. The award of compensation by the UNAT in cases where fixed-term contracts have not been renewed or converted into permanent contracts has, however, not been done on a very exact basis.[240]

The subsequent effects of the decision not to renew the contract may also sometimes be relevant to the question of compensation, if they are directly

[232] See *Dale*, UNAT Judgment No. 132 [1969] (ICAO), JUNAT Nos. 114–166 p. 172; *Bhattacharyya*, UNAT Judgment No. 142 [1971], ibid. p. 248; *Surina*, UNAT Judgment No. 178 [1973], JUNAT Nos. 167–230 p. 82.
[233] See *Fracyon*, UNAT Judgment No. 199 [1975], ibid. p. 277; *Levcik*, UNAT Judgment No. 192 [1974], ibid. p. 204.
[234] See *Dale*, UNAT Judgment No. 132 [1969] (ICAO), JUNAT Nos. 114–166 p. 172; *Surina*, UNAT Judgment No. 178 [1973], JUNAT Nos. 167–230 p. 82.
[235] *Fracyon*, UNAT Judgment No. 199 [1975], ibid. p. 277.
[236] UNAT Judgment No. 192 [1974], ibid. p. 204. Similar to this case is *Kergall*, CJEC Case 1/55 [1954–56] ECR p. 151, where an error of law had occurred, because the applicant's contract was not renewed when his post was abolished. The applicant was awarded 1 year's salary as compensation. In *Uehling*, OASAT Judgment No. 8 [1974], there was also an error of law, in so far as the applicant's contract had not been renewed for 2 years, as it should have been, but for a lesser period. The applicant was compensated with 4 months' salary which was the salary for the period he had not worked.
[237] For cases where the circumstances of the non-renewal favoured applicants see *Klee*, UNAT Judgment No. 242 [1979], JUNAT Nos. 231–300 p. 113; *Pattillo*, UNAT Judgment No. 286 [1982], ibid. p. 536.
[238] UNAT Judgment No. 285 [1982], ibid. p. 527.
[239] UNAT Judgment No. 298 [1982], ibid. p. 640.
[240] In *Fasla*, UNAT Judgment No. 158 [1972], JUNAT Nos. 114–166 p. 355, a sum of 6 months' salary was awarded. In *El-Naggar*, UNAT Judgment No. 205 [1975], JUNAT Nos. 167–230 p. 345, a sum of 6 months' salary was awarded for failure to carry out the recommendation of the Joint Appeals Board which was accepted by the respondent and which was that an effort be made to keep the applicant on the respondent's staff, and 3 months' salary was awarded for failure to keep him on the staff, as undertaken, till a suitable position was found.

related to that decision. Thus, in *Paveskovic*[241] certain effects on his health of the decision not to renew the applicant's contract were taken into account in assessing his compensation at $4,000 in circumstances in which his contract had not been extended for six months but only for two months.

ii. *Expectancy*

Expectancy, as has been seen, is taken into consideration in determining compensation. In *Lawrence*,[242] for instance, when the applicant's contract was unlawfully terminated before it expired (not strictly a case of non-renewal), it was held that in calculating the compensation payable, he should be treated not only as if he had not been separated from service for the period of his existing contract but, because he had a legitimate expectancy of renewal, as if he had received the appointment he had sought and then been separated from service by termination. Generally the applicant is treated as if he would have been given the appointment which he had a legitimate expectancy of receiving. As a result, there is no reason to distinguish between decisions concerning compensation for non-renewal from decisions in which the issue was conversion of a contract into a permanent one. It would also seem to be irrelevant whether the reason for the existence of a legitimate expectancy was countervailing circumstances or rights created by administrative documents, since the consequences seem to be identical in both cases.[243]

Once the UNAT has established that there were countervailing circumstances which created in the mind of the holder of a fixed-term contract a legitimate expectancy of continued employment, the duration of the expected renewal becomes relevant to the calculation of compensation. The UNAT accepts the normal practice of the organization for this purpose; that is, the expectancy is limited to a period of time equal to the initial contract or to its last extension.[244] Clearly, it would make a difference, then, whether the applicant could expect a renewal or a conversion into a permanent appointment of his contract.

iii. *Material injury*

Although the cases do not always discuss very clearly the methods used in arriving at the particular compensation awarded, there are some cases in which some indications have been given of relevant criteria in connection with material injury, where fixed-term contracts have not have renewed or converted into permanent ones. In *Levcik*,[245] for example, the applicant

[241] UNAT Judgment No. 341 [1984].

[242] UNAT Judgment No. 185 [1974], JUNAT Nos. 167–230 p. 146.

[243] Compare *Levcik*, UNAT Judgment No. 192 [1974], ibid. p. 204; *Sood*, UNAT Judgment No. 195 [1975], ibid. p. 235.

[244] See *Fracyon*, UNAT Judgment No. 199 [1975], ibid. p. 277; *Perucho*, UNAT Judgment No. 285 [1982], JUNAT Nos. 231–300 p. 527.

[245] UNAT Judgment No. 192 [1974], JUNAT Nos. 167–230 p. 204.

remained unemployed for 10 months and when he found a position his salary was lower than the one he had with the UN. This fact led the UNAT to award the applicant 1 year's net base salary as compensation. In *Lawrence*[246] which was a case in which the applicant's fixed-term contract was terminated before it expired and which has already been adverted to the applicant was treated as if he should have had his contract renewed at the end of its term. The findings in this case relating to material injury are pertinent to the situation where a fixed-term contract holder's contract is unlawfully not renewed at the end of its term. There the measure of the material injury caused to the applicant was determined by the fact that his age and the orientation of his career during twelve years with UNDP made it particularly difficult for him to find a similar position elsewhere. The UNAT has always rejected claims relating to pension benefits on the basis that the damage compensated should not be too remote or indirect.

The UNAT directly and specifically dealt with the issue of compensation for loss of earnings as early as 1952 in *Robinson*.[247] There it took the view that because of the high qualifications possessed by the applicant and the shortage of persons of his knowledge and experience, the applicant would have been able to secure a new appointment in his country, had he returned to it. For this reason he was awarded only $2,000.

iv. *Moral injury*

The UNAT has had to address the issue of moral injury in dealing with compensation for non-renewal or non-conversion of fixed-term contracts. Generally, if a request for compensation for moral injury is not justified by precise evidence, it is rejected. This was held to be the case in *Senghor*[248] which concerned the termination of a fixed-term contract before its expiration. There is no reason why the same principle should not be applicable to non-renewal or non-conversion of fixed-term contracts. On the other hand, moral injury will be compensated, if it is proved. Thus, in *Al-Abed*[249] the applicant was held to have sustained a moral injury because of an improper notification of the non-renewal of his contract, which gave the impression that disciplinary action was being taken against him. The compensation awarded for that injury lay in the reference in the judgment to the fact that the respondent had disregarded the principle of good faith.[250]

246 UNAT Judgment No. 185 [1974], ibid. p. 146.
247 UNAT Judgment No. 15 [1952], JUNAT Nos. 1–70 p. 43.
248 UNAT Judgment No. 169 [1973], JUNAT Nos. 167–230 p. 13.
249 UNAT Judgment No. 128 [1969], JUNAT Nos. 114–166 p. 136.
250 See also *Lawrence*, UNAT Judgment No. 185 [1974], JUNAT Nos. 167–230 p. 146, which concerned the termination of a fixed-term contract before it expired.

v. *Procedural irregularities*

As already noted, the UNAT has held in certain cases that the applicant had been injured by procedural irregularities, although there had been no unlawful decision not to renew his fixed-term contract. In these cases, though the decision impugned was held not to be invalid, the applicant was awarded some compensation for the injury suffered. A procedural irregularity concerning the rebuttal of periodic reports was held insufficient to render the non-renewal decision illegal in one case[251] but the UNAT awarded compensation in the amount of 2 months' net base salary as being adequate for the violation of the procedural rules concerned. In *Irani*,[252] in which the applicant failed to establish a legitimate expectancy for continued employment, he was, nevertheless, granted compensation in the amount of 3 months' net base salary because of the respondent's negligence in not promptly informing the applicant of its opposition to an extension of his contract.[253]

vi. *Specific performance*

Apart from the cases where reinstatement has been ordered as a possible alternative to compensation, the UNAT ordered another form of specific performance in *Fasla*.[254] A report which was tainted with prejudice was declared to be invalid and it was ordered that it be treated as such for all purposes.

---

[251] *Boelen*, UNAT Judgment No. 261 [1980], JUNAT Nos. 231–300 p. 297.

[252] UNAT Judgment No. 150 [1971], JUNAT Nos. 114–166 p. 292.

[253] Other cases in which compensation was awarded for procedural irregularities, although the decisions not to renew the contracts were not invalid, were *Touhami*, UNAT Judgment No. 135 [1970], ibid. p. 196; *Jabbour*, UNAT Judgment No. 305 [1983]; *Jekhine*, UNAT Judgment No. 319 [1983]; *Ridler*, UNAT Judgment No. 327 [1984]; *Large*, UNAT Judgment No. 331 [1984]. For compensation awarded for procedural and other irregularities in the absence of a finding that the decision of non-renewal was not invalid see also *Sehgal*, UNAT Judgment No. 203 [1975], JUNAT Nos. 167–230 p. 324; and *Jabbour*, UNAT Judgment No. 305 [1983].

[254] UNAT Judgment No. 158 [1972], JUNAT Nos. 114–166 p. 355. See also *Fracyon*, UNAT Judgment No. 199 [1975], JUNAT Nos. 167–230 p. 277, where it was ordered that a defective performance report be excluded from the applicant's file.

CHAPTER THIRTY–EIGHT

Probationary Appointments

A PROBATIONARY period is generally required by the Staff Regulations and Staff Rules of international organizations for almost all of the different kinds of appointments, whether they are, for example, permanent, regular, or fixed-term. Thus, the Staff Rules of WHO make any appointment of one year or more subject to a period of probation, irrespective of the type of appointment.[1] The Staff Regulations of the EEC state that officials other than those in Grades A1 and A2 must serve a probationary period before they can be established.[2]

Probationary appointments may be confirmed or not confirmed and, therefore, terminated during the initial or extension of the period of probation, or at the end of such period. Further, at the end of or during the period of probation, whether extended or not, a further probationary period may be added as a result of transfer or promotion. It will depend on the Staff Regulations or Staff Rules of the organization concerned or their interpretation whether a further probationary period may be imposed on transfer or promotion in these circumstances. Sometimes, depending on the Staff Regulations and Staff Rules of an organization, a probationary period may be imposed on promotion of a staff member who has already been confirmed in service. Thus, in *Ulliac*[3] the OECD Appeals Board held that according to the Staff Regulations in force at the time the Secretary General of the OECD had the power to impose a probationary period of three months on an applicant who was promoted to a higher grade from a position within the service of the OECD. Such a situation may be implied, even if not explicitly referred to in the Staff Regulations or Staff Rules of the organization. In any case, where a probationary appointment is not confirmed, whether because of transfer, promotion, extension, or separation from service, questions may arise relating to the legality of the action taken. Most decided cases deal with situations where a probationer has been separated from service at the end of

---

[1] Rule 420.4: see Amerasinghe (ed.), 1 *Staff Regulations and Staff Rules of Selected International Organizations* (1983) p. 119 at p. 145. The subject of probationary appointments has been examined before in Amerasinghe and Bellinger, 'Non-Confirmation of Probationary Appointments', 54 BYIL (1983) p. 167.

[2] Article 34.1: see Amerasinghe (ed.), 4 op. cit. (note 1 *supra*) (1983) p. 1 at p. 16. See also Staff Rule 104.12 of the UN: Appendix V *infra*; Article 17 of the Staff Regulations of the Council of Europe and Article 17 and 18 of Appendix II to those Staff Regulations: Appendix VI *infra*.

[3] Decision No. 49, OECD Appeals Board [1974], Recueil des décisions 1 à 62 (1979) p. 135.

or during the probationary period. Several decided cases deal also with the extension of probation and problems connected therewith. Further, irrespective of whether a probationary appointment is confirmed or not, certain rights which a probationer enjoys *vis-à-vis* the organization during the probationary period may be violated with the result that he is entitled to a remedy, although generally the violation of such rights would only become an issue, if the probationer were not confirmed in his appointment.

Similarities exist in the Staff Regulations and Staff Rules of international organizations which govern probation. Generally in interpreting and applying these Regulations and Rules the different international administrative tribunals have pronounced decisions which are not in conflict with each other. This makes it possible to deduce underlying general principles relating to probation. On the other hand, there may be some decisions which depend on the specific content of the relevant Staff Regulations and Staff Rules of the particular organizations. International administrative tribunals have reviewed the legality of decisions taken in relation to probationary appointments by reference to the written law of organizations and in the light of other principles and rules derived from the applicable sources of law.

The general nature of probation

In general the approach taken by tribunals is to recognize that international organizations have considerable discretionary authority in dealing with probationary appointments. Tribunals have in practice merely reviewed and controlled the exercise of this discretionary power. On the other hand, where the organization owes certain specific duties to the probationer, tribunals have not hesitated to hold that these must be performed.

The reason for according to organizations an extensive discretion in dealing with probationary appointments seems to be that probation primarily serves the interests of international organizations. The main purpose of probation is really to enable the organization to find out whether the probationer is suitable for employment. In *Mirossevich*[4] the Advocate General of the CJEC stated that a probationary period was required in the interests of the administration which, before committing itself, legitimately wished to be assured that the probationer was suitable for employment. In *Salle*[5] the WBAT stated that it was of the essence of probation that the organization be vested with the power to define its own needs, requirements, and interests and to decide whether, judging by the staff member's

---

[4] CJEC Case 10/55 [1954–6] ECR p. 333 at p. 351. See also *de Bruyn*, CJEC Case 25/60 [1962] ECR p. 21 at p. 30.
[5] WBAT Reports [1983, Part I], Decision No. 10 at p. 10.

performance during the probationary period, he did or did not qualify for employment with the organization; and that the administrative authority during the probationary period tested not only the probationer's professional ability but also whether he could adjust to the specific requirements of the organization. In *Molina*[6] the ILOAT stated that the most important object of probation was to enable the administration to ascertain whether the probationer fitted in with the organization, and that this purpose was paramount: with the result that when evidence in the probationer's personnel file containing information concerning the probationer's suitability was not conclusive in this regard, the Director General had the power additionally to evaluate the probationer's personality, and the administrative authority could further assess the probationer's intellectual and moral qualities in determining whether he was suitable for his assigned post.

Conversely, however, it cannot be denied that the probationer has an interest, which has been considered and cannot be ignored, in being definitively employed. Thus, in *Mirossevich*[7] the Advocate General of the CJEC stated that probation was also in the interests of the probationer, who had an 'interest' in being definitively employed and could not be deprived arbitrarily of this interest, if he had satisfied the obligations required of him. In general as a result of this interest certain rights accrue to the probationer throughout the period of his probationary appointment. For example, he can legitimately expect guidance and training in order to qualify for employment, his duties must be well-defined, and he should be given a fair chance to demonstrate his suitability. In *Johnson* the UNAT clearly referred to these requirements arising from the contract of employment.[8]

One of the features of probation is the provisional status conferred upon the probationer during the probationary period. During this period, it appears, the administration has many discretionary powers, such as deciding on the duration of probation, establishing the standard of performance, defining the interests of the organization, and laying down the procedural rules applicable. As has been stated above, tribunals intervene in order to review the exercise of this discretionary power. They will, apart from protecting any specific rights the probationer may have, review the legality of the procedure followed, prevent any abuse of motive (*détournement de pouvoir*), and ensure the substantive legality of administrative decisions. Tribunals are especially cautious in reviewing decisions relating to probationary appointments, because they want to ensure that probation serves its

---

6 ILOAT Judgment No. 440 [1980] (WHO) at p. 9. See also *Decision No. 1*, ELDO Appeals Board [1966], at p. 3.

7 CJEC Case 10/55 [1954–6] ECR p. 333 at p. 351.

8 UNAT Judgment No. 213 [1976], JUNAT Nos. 167–230 p. 429 at pp. 440 ff. See also *Mirossevich*, CJEC Case 10/55 [1954–6] ECR p. 333 at pp. 342 ff.

purpose as a trial period. This was particularly emphasized recently by the
ILOAT in *Molina*.[9]

Tribunals have expressly affirmed the provisional status of probation
which derives from the nature and purpose of probation with the result that,
in their interpretation of Staff Regulations and Staff Rules, they have often
denied probationers many of the guarantees available to confirmed staff
members. Thus, in *Schawalder-Vrancheva* (*No. 2*) the ILOAT stated that
probationers could not enjoy the same guarantees as staff members who were
confirmed in fixed-term or permanent contracts and that their appointments
could be terminated whenever it was decided that they were unsuitable.[10] In
Kersaudy[11] the ILOAT made a similar statement and added that in the case
of FAO its Staff Regulations and Staff Rules permitted the termination of a
probationer's service during the probationary period to be attributed simply
to the interests of the organization.[12]

It would seem, however, that the guarantees granted to confirmed staff
members are not always denied to probationers. Thus, in *Eskenasy*[13] the
point at issue was the establishment of the quality of the probationer's work
and the determination of the degree of his efficiency. The OASAT noted
that, while the purpose of the determination was not the same, the nature of
the determination was essentially the same for probationers as for confirmed
staff members. The tribunal referred in this regard to Staff Rule 104.5 (b) (i)
of the OAS which provided that probationers enjoy all the benefits granted
to permanent staff members. The approach taken by the OASAT enhances
the rights of probationers. It does not deny that probationers enjoy a
provisional status but it goes considerably further than the ILOAT decisions
in protecting the rights of probationers. While it is true that probationers in
most organizations do enjoy some of the rights accorded to permanent staff
members, the extreme position taken by the OASAT resulted from the
specific provisions of the Staff Rules of the OAS.

The duration and extension of probation

The duration of probationary appointments varies from one organization to
another. Generally, Staff Regulations and Staff Rules provide, at least, for a
maximum probationary period. Although probation is primarily in the

9 ILOAT Judgment No. 440 [1980] (WHO) at p. 7.
10 ILOAT Judgment No. 226 [1974] (WHO) at p. 5.
11 ILOAT Judgment No. 152 [1970] (FAO) at p. 5.
12 In *Joyet*, ILOAT Judgment No. 318 [1977] (WHO) at p. 3, the ILOAT referred to the provisional status of probation.
13 OASAT Judgment No. 40 [1979] at p. 16. See also *Châtelain*, UNAT Judgment No. 272 [1981] (ICAO), JUNAT Nos. 231–300 p. 411.

interests of the international organization concerned, probationers certainly have an interest in reducing to a minimum the period during which they are kept in a state of uncertainty. If a maximum period is prescribed in the Regulations and Rules, it must not be exceeded. In *Lane*[14] the UNAT found that the applicant irregularly remained 22 months in service beyond the expiration of his extended probationary period in violation of Staff Rule 104.12 of the UN Staff Rules, which provided that the normal probationary period was 2 years with the possibility of extension for no more than an additional year. It is important that the tribunal stated that there could be no automatic conversion of a probationary appointment into a permanent one either by efflux of time or because of an omission of the administration. That the prescribed maximum period of probation was exceeded must be clearly established, if a violation of rights is to be proved.[15]

There is no minimum period of probation nor is there a specific date for its termination except that it must come to an end at the latest when the maximum stated period comes to an end, as has been seen above. In *Mariaffy*[16] The applicant contended that he was on sick leave for 5 of the 21 months during which he was on probation with the result presumably that the period of probation was not long enough. The UNAT held that a probationary appointment had no specific expiration date and that the administrative authority had a wide margin of discretion in determining when the probationary period should end. In *Sternfield*[17] the applicant complained that only 5 months after the beginning of his probation he was informed that he would not be confirmed. The ILOAT held that there was no minimum period of probation required either by the Staff Rules of WHO or by any general principle of law and that consequently a probationer's appointment could be terminated at any time after his unsuitability for the assigned post had been established.[18]

Whether the period of probation should be extended lies within the discretion of the administrative authority.[19] However, it appears that generally probationers must be informed of the decision to extend their probation. On the other hand, tribunals have regarded tacit extensions as regular inasmuch as such extensions do not prejudice the interests of probationers who could refuse them. The UNAT took this view in *Lane* and the ILOAT in *Molina*.[20] However, it is established that a probationer cannot

---

[14] UNAT Judgment No. 198 [1975], JUNAT Nos. 167–230 p. 267.

[15] See *Mange*, ILOAT Judgment No. 8 [1951] (WHO).

[16] UNAT Judgment No. 168 [1973], JUNAT Nos. 167–230 p. 7.

[17] ILOAT Judgment No. 197 [1972] (WHO).

[18] See also *de Roy*, CJEC Case 92/75 [1976] ECR p. 343.

[19] See *Decision No. 2*, ELDO Appeals Board [1968], at p. 4. But the discretion may be abused: see *Decision No. 4, ESRO/CR/22*, ESRO Appeals Board [1969], at p. 7.

[20] UNAT Judgment No. 198 [1975], JUNAT Nos. 167–230 p. 267; ILOAT Judgment No. 440 [1980] (WHO).

be tacitly confirmed nor can a probationary apointment be automatically converted into a permanent one as a result of the administration's failure to take positive action at the end of a probationary period.[21]

An extension of probation is normally granted, if the performance of the probationer is not quite satisfactory,[22] or if the probationer experiences difficulties in adjusting to the requirements of the service.[23] In *Nagels*[24] the probationary appointment was extended twice for the above reason. The fact that the probationary period is extended certainly does not imply that the probationer will or must ultimately be confirmed.[25]

Decisions extending the period of probation have been contested by probationers whose performance had been rated satisfactory in their performance reports. In *Peynado*[26] the probationary period was extended in spite of two entirely favourable reports and the approval of the Secretary General of the UN of the deicision confirming the applicant's appointment. The UNAT did not explicitly hold that the extension of the applicant's probation for an additional year was *per se* irregular, but it said that it was disturbed by a number of unsatisfactory features of the case, namely, *inter alia*, (a) the retroactive appraisal of earlier performance properly evaluated in two period reports one of which was signed by the same officer who subsequently changed his mind; and (b) the fact that, notwithstanding the Secretary General's approval, the case was referred back to the Appointment and Promotion Board under Staff Rule 104.13 (c) (iii), which provides for such reference in the absence of an agreed favourable recommendation. The tribunal, therefore, awarded compensation for procedural defects. Thus, where a probationary period is extended, especially where performance has been satisfactory, the appropriate procedures must be followed. The UNAT took a similar view in *Johnson*.[27] In a very early decision of the ILOAT[28] the applicant's performance has been qualified as satisfactory and her supervisor had recommended her for permanent appointment but the review body had extended the probationary period. The ILOAT found that the extension had been improperly imposed upon the applicant but held against her, because she had not appealed against the decision and, therefore, could not question it before the tribunal. Thus, a decision to extend probation must be appealed in time, if it is to be questioned later as having been irregular, even where the

21 See *Lane*, UNAT Judgment No. 198 [1975], JUNAT Nos. 167–230 p. 267.
22 See *de Ungria*, UNAT Judgment No. 71 [1958], JUNAT Nos. 71–86 p. 1; *Kersaudy*, ILOAT Judgment No. 152 [1970] (FAO); *Ghaffar*, ILOAT Judgment No. 320 [1977] (WHO); *Salle*, WBAT Reports [1983, Part I], Decision No. 10.
23 See *Vrancheva*, ILOAT Judgment No. 194 [1972] (WHO).
24 CJEC Case 52/70 [1971] ECR p. 365.
25 See *Salle*, WBAT Reports [1983, Part I], Decision No. 10 at p. 10.
26 UNAT Judgment No. 138 [1970], JUNAT Nos. 114–166 p. 221.
27 UNAT Judgment No. 213 [1976], JUNAT Nos. 167–230 p. 429.
28 *Marsh*, ILOAT Judgment No. 10 [1951] (ILO).

probationer's work has been rated as satisfactory. This last case would seem to support the proposition that where a probationer's work is satisfactory, the period of probation may not normally be extended. In this respect it conflicts with what is implied in *Peynado* and *Johnson*, namely that in theory even where a probationer's work is satisfactory, the period of probation may be extended, provided the proper procedures are followed.

There are situations in which the respondent organization may justifiably refuse to extend the period of probation and refuse to confirm a probationer. In *Mariaffy*,[29] even though the applicant's supervisor had recommended extension of the probationary period on the grounds that the applicant's performance, although satisfactory, had not shown that he had actually contributed to the work of the department, because of the five months' sick leave which he had taken, the UNAT held that the respondent had no legal obligation to extend the probationary period in order to compensate for the sick leave the applicant had taken. The shortening of the period of probation was attributable to the applicant, not to the respondent's fault. In *Crapon de Caprona*[30] the ILOAT stated that the respondent could refuse to extend the probationary period, if it appeared that the probationer's performance could not possibly improve with an extension. The tribunal considered that the extension granted to the applicant at his request, in order to avoid having to move during the winter, was outside the scope of WHO Staff Rule 440 (now Staff Rule 540) pertaining to the end of probation and therefore was not really a regular extension of probation which could justifiably have been refused in the case.

Tacit extensions of probationary periods have also been contested before tribunals. In *Loomba*[31] the ILOAT said that failure to notify the applicant of the decision extending the probationary period would normally amount to an irregularity. However, the tribunal concluded in that case that the applicant should have inferred that his probationary period had been tacitly extended because of the special circumstances of his case, namely, that at his own request an investigation had been ordered, with the result that the probationary period had been extended pending the results of that investigation. The tribunal conceded that a tacit extension of probation was possible in appropriate circumstances. It also stated that the probationer must prove that he had suffered damage from any uncertainty in which he was kept as a result of an inappropriate tacit extension, if he was to qualify for compensation. In *di Pillo*[32] the CJEC recognized that a tacit extension was as a rule irregular in a case in which it was found that the probation report was drawn

29 UNAT Judgment No. 168 [1973], JUNAT Nos. 167–230 p. 7.
30 ILOAT Judgment No. 112 [1967] (WHO).
31 ILOAT Judgment No. 169 [1970] (FAO).
32 CJEC Cases 10 & 47/72 [1973] ECR p. 763.

up after a delay of three months in violation of Staff Regulation 34 of the European Communities. The Court, therefore, awarded compensation to the applicant for being kept in a state of uncertainty. The purpose of ensuring that the probationer is aware of the extension of his probationary period is to give him a chance to defend himself.[33]

Rights of the organization in respect of termination

In dealing with the termination of probationary appointments tribunals have accorded to the administrations or managements of international organizations certain rights or powers in regard to the assessment of the probationer's performance. As will be seen later, however, tribunals do exercise some control over the exercise of these powers.

(a). The standard of satisfaction required

Tribunals have recognized the discretionary power of administrations or managements to determine the professional qualifications of their staff members. The discretionary power of the administrative authority in probationary cases is generally broader than usual as a result of probation. The administrative authority further has the discretion to establish the standards of performance which the probationer should satisfy before the appointment is confirmed. Tribunals do not evaluate these standards. However, *inter alia*, they exercise some control over the legality of the administrative act applying these standards to the probationer's performance by reference to the facts which the administrative authority may select in reaching the relevant conclusion. The administrative authority has the discretion to evaluate not only the professional capabilities of the probationer but also his moral and psychological fitness for the specific requirements of the service and on this basis to take the decision to confirm or not to confirm his appointment. The Staff Regulations and Staff Rules of several international organizations confer this discretion on the administration or management and tribunals have consistently reaffirmed the power of administrative authorities to exercise this discretionary power.

It would seem that seldom has a probationary appointment been terminated for unsatisfactory service in the narrow sense of that term. On the contrary, in the majority of cases probationers have failed to adjust to the special requirements of the given international organization. The cases demonstrate how tribunals have approached challenges to determinations made by administrative authorities in regard to performance. In

---

[33] See *Kersaudy*, ILOAT Judgment No. 152 [1970] (FAO).

Cooperman[34] the UNAT stated that the applicant's record was a mixed one and that it did not have the power to pronounce upon the ratings given by various officers from time to time. In several cases the ILOAT stated that it would not substitute its own opinion for that of the Director General of WHO as regards the suitability of a probationer whether it be in respect of his performance or his conduct.[35] In *Buranavanichkit*[36] the WBAT stated that the concept of unsatisfactory performance could be defined by the administrative authority to include the probationer's character, personality, and conduct generally in so far as they bore on ability to work harmoniously and to good effect with superiors and other staff members, and that the tribunal would not review the merits of a decision taken by the administration as to unsatisfactory performance as thus defined except for the purpose of satisfying itself that there had not been an abuse of discretion.

Conversely, satisfactory performance in the narrowest sense of the term alone, evidenced in successive periodic reports during the probationary period, does not confer a right to permanent tenure. In *de Ungria*[37] the applicant's appointment was terminated in the interests of the organization because he failed to meet the standards required for permanent appointment. The UNAT agreed that, though the applicant's performance was entirely satisfactory, his unauthorized outside activities could be taken into account in order to disqualify him from permanent appointment.[38] In *Adler*[39] the applicant's performance was rated as satisfactory in three successive periodic reports. However, his appointment was terminated in the interests of the organization, because he had failed to demonstrate his suitability as an international civil servant. The tribunal did not question this action. In the same decision the UNAT held that, though the applicant's supervisor recognized some of his qualities and requested only his transfer and not the termination of his appointment, the administrative authority had the discretion to decide whether or not the applicant should be given a permanent appointment.[40] In *Milous*[41] the applicant's unsatisfactory conduct (he

---

[34] UNAT Judgment No. 93 [1965], JUNAT Nos. 87–113 p. 55. The same principle was reaffirmed in *Peynado*, UNAT Judgment No. 138 [1970], JUNAT Nos. 114–166 p. 221, and *Adler*, UNAT Judgment No. 267 [1980], JUNAT Nos. 231–300 p. 352.

[35] See *Kissaun*, ILOAT Judgment No. 69 [1964] (WHO); *Crapon de Caprona*, ILOAT Judgment No. 112 [1967] (WHO); *Joyet*, ILOAT Judgment No. 318 [1977] (WHO); *Heyes*, ILOAT Judgment No. 453 [1981] (WHO).

[36] WBAT Reports [1982], Decision No. 7 at p. 10.

[37] UNAT Judgment No. 71 [1958], JUNAT Nos. 71–86 p. 1.

[38] See also *Chiacchia*, UNAT Judgment No. 90 [1963], JUNAT Nos. 87–113 p. 25, where insubordination and lack of punctuality were held to be valid grounds for disqualification from permanent appointment.

[39] UNAT Judgment No. 267 [1980], JUNAT Nos. 231–300 p. 352.

[40] See also *Mange*, ILOAT Judgment No. 8 [1951] (WHO).

[41] ILOAT Judgment No. 42 [1960] (WHO).

communicated to the King of Jordan his supervisor's alleged hostility towards the king) was held by the ILOAT to have made him unsuitable for international service.[42]

(b) Professional qualifications in relation to unsatisfactory performance

There are cases in which the professional qualifications of probationers have not been questioned but, none the less, their performance has been described as unsatisfactory, either because they failed to adjust to the specific requirements of the organization or because they failed to perform some of their duties satisfactorily. Tribunals in such cases seem to be more cautious in accepting the standard of performance laid down by the administration as well as the choice of relevant facts by the administration. Thus, on occasions tribunals have themselves examined pieces of the probationer's work in order to ascertain whether the evaluation of performance by the administrative authority was proper. Nevertheless, they have not been generally inclined to interfere with the choice of standards or facts.

In *Crapon de Caprona*[43] the ILOAT did state that, as a rule, the administrative authority might set *reasonable* standards. While the same principle was reaffirmed in *Kersaudy*,[44] the ILOAT also held that the standard set by FAO was only one among many factors to be considered in the evaluation of the probationer's performance. The other factors were identified as being the difficulty of the work as well as the circumstances in which the work was performed. In the former case, the applicant had some fifteen years of experience as a translator. His appointment was, however, terminated on the grounds of unsatisfactory performance. The case was one in which the applicant's professional qualifications were never questioned. The tribunal, instead of relying on the evaluation of the applicant's performance by the administration, proceeded to examine his translations and found that in fact some of the corrections were disputable and possibly unjustified but that most of them were pertinent. Ultimately the tribunal concurred with the opinion of the reviewers that the applicant's work was below the average standard required. It appears that the ILOAT will not interfere with an evaluation given by the administration in these circumstances, unless it is abundantly clear that the applicant's work had in fact met the standards set by the organization. Further, in the same case the tribunal embarked on an examination of the applicant's translations and concluded that there were some doubts about the importance or value of the criticisms made of the

---

[42] See also *Kissaun*, ILOAT Judgment No. 69 [1964] (WHO); and *Loomba*, ILOAT Judgment No. 169 [1970] (FAO), to the same effect on the matter of unsuitability for the service.
[43] ILOAT Judgment No. 112 [1967] (WHO).
[44] ILOAT Judgment No. 152 [1970] (FAO).

quality of the translations. However, it took into consideration the applicant's insufficient work output (number of words translated) and held that his low work output was one of the elements of his unsatisfactory performance. Thus, it appears that when there is an objective factor, such as an easily measured work output, the ILOAT is more reluctant to question the administrative authority's evaluation of performance. The existence of such an objective factor makes it possible to confirm the assessment of the quality of the probationer's work made by the administration.[45]

(c) Professional qualifications in relation to unsuitability

In many cases the ILOAT has upheld the termination of probationary appointments for unsuitability, although the professional skills and general performance of applicants have not been in question. In *Kraicsovits*[46] the applicant failed to adjust to the conditions in which his work had to be done in that he disliked field work. The non-confirmation of his appointment was upheld.[47] In *Al-Zand*[48] the applicant lacked practical experience and was, therefore, found to be unsuitable for the post to which he was assigned. The ILOAT said in this case that 'unsuitable' meant 'unsatisfactory' and that the applicant's appointment was rightly terminated in the interests of the organization in accordance with the FAO Staff Regulations.[49]

Irrespective of professional qualifications the ILOAT has held that a probationer's appointment may be terminated because he is unsuitable for medical reasons, provided the reasons are properly established,[50] and that defaulting in financial obligations and incurring debts beyond the capacity of the probationer to repay within a normal period makes the probationer unsuitable for service, because such conduct is incompatible with the standards of conduct required of an international civil servant and is likely to bring the organization and its officials into public disrepute.[51]

(d) The timing of the decision to terminate a probationary appointment

The Staff Regulations and Staff Rules of international organizations generally provide that the administrative authority may terminate a probationary appointment at any time during the maximum period of probation.

---

[45] See also *Sternfield*, ILOAT Judgment No. 197 [1972] (WHO), for a similar decision.

[46] ILOAT Judgment No. 140 [1969] (FAO).

[47] See also *Schawalder-Vrancheva (No. 2)*, ILOAT Judgment No. 226 [1974] (WHO).

[48] ILOAT Judgment No. 389 [1980] (FAO).

[49] For another FAO case of a similar character see *Guisset*, ILOAT Judgment No. 396 [1980] (FAO). Unsuitability was found to exist also in *Heyes*, ILOAT Judgment No. 453 [1981] (WHO), and *Molina*, ILOAT Judgment No. 440 [1980] (WHO).

[50] *Baracco*, ILOAT Judgment No. 192 [1972] (WHO).

[51] *Wakley*, ILOAT Judgment No. 53 [1961] (WHO).

Tribunals in their interpretation of some Staff Regulations and Staff Rules recognize that on the timing of the termination decision, which is left to the discretion of the administration, may depend certain rights of the probationer. In this connection, a distinction has been made between termination at the end of the probationary period and termination during probation. Timing is also important when the appointment is terminated in the interests of the organization. The importance of the timing of the decision to terminate a probationary appointment has been discussed in cases dealing with the Staff Regulations and Staff Rules of the UN, the OAS, and FAO.

Timing was first considered important by the UNAT in *Cooperman*,[52] in which the tribunal in interpreting the Staff Regulations of the UN[53] said that, when a probationary appointment was terminated at the end of the probationary period, the employee's suitability for permanent appointment had to be reviewed in accordance with a well-defined procedure by a review body, namely, the Appointment and Promotion Board. This meant that a probationer whose employment was terminated at the end of his probationary period enjoyed an element of protection which was denied to those whose employment was terminated during probation. The applicant's employment was terminated during probation without reference to this Board. The tribunal held that the termination decision was valid, and that the appointment could be terminated during probation in the interests of the organization on the basis of Staff Regulation 9.1 (c), which permitted such termination. In addition, it was said that the Secretary General could unilaterally define the interests of the UN. The tribunal could only examine the bona fides of the administrative authority in this situation.[54]

At the end of the probationary period, however, an appointment could only be validly terminated even pursuant to Staff Regulation 9.1 (c) and Staff Rule 104.13 (a) (i) which could also be applied before the end of that period, in accordance with the procedure specified in Staff Rule 104.13 (c) (i) and (iii),[55] which deal with reference to the Appointment and Promotion Board in the absence of an agreed favourable recommendation.[56] In *Peynado*[57] the UNAT held that, because the applicant's employment was terminated at the end of his period of probation, though in the interests of the organization, he

[52] UNAT Judgment No. 93 [1965], JUNAT Nos. 87–113 p. 55.

[53] See Staff Regulation 9.1 (c) and Staff Rules 104.12 (a) and 104.13 (c) (iii): Appendix V *infra*.

[54] In *Mariaffy*, UNAT Judgment No. 168 [1973], JUNAT Nos. 167–230 p. 7, medical advice was the basis for the termination under Staff Rule 104.13 (a) (i) (see Appendix V *infra*) of employment during probation. The termination was held to be valid.

[55] See Appendix V *infra*.

[56] See *de Ungria*, UNAT Judgment No. 71 [1958], JUNAT Nos. 71–86 p. 1; *Chiacchia*, UNAT Judgment No. 90 [1963], JUNAT Nos. 87–113 p. 25; *Johnson*, UNAT Judgment No. 213 [1976], JUNAT Nos. 167–230 p. 429.

[57] UNAT Judgment No. 138 [1970], JUNAT Nos. 114–166 p. 221.

was entitled to a fair and reasonable procedure before the Appointment and Promotion Board which examined his suitability for permanent employment. It was also said that the applicant was entitled to all the guarantees provided in the Staff Rules and Administrative Instruction ST/AI/115, para. 13 which gave the probationer a right to make a written statement in response to a report and required an investigation thereafter by the Head of the Department. The tribunal pointed out that the fact that the decision not to confirm the probationer had been reviewed by the review body (the Appointment and Promotion Board) did not necessarily guarantee the validity of that decision. The tribunal awarded compensation to the applicant for the injury caused by defects in the procedure followed in the process of terminating his probationary appointment.[58]

In *Eskenasy*[59] the OASAT made the same distinction as had been made in the UNAT cases between termination of a probationary appointment during probation and termination at the end of such period. The tribunal held that, if a probationary appointment had not been terminated in the interests of the General Secretariat during the probationary period or its extension, then the probationer should have been duly evaluated in the last month of his probation and given the opportunity to present his comments, in accordance with the Staff Rules.[60] The tribunal concluded that a probationary appointment could not be terminated at the end of the probationary period summarily and simply in the interests of the General Secretariat.

All the ILOAT decisions rendered on this issue were the result of actions brought by staff members of the FAO. The tribunal's general view was that the Director General could unilaterally define the interests of the organization and that judicial control would be exercised only in the case of misuse of power. The following ILOAT decisions show that the administrative authority possesses a wide discretion in defining the interests of the organization.

In interpreting the FAO Staff Regulations and Staff Rules as well as the FAO Administrative Manual the ILOAT has concluded that a probationer's appointment could be terminated at any time during or at the end of his probationary period on the grounds of *unsatisfactory service*. However, in *McIntire*[61] the tribunal held that in that event the reasons for the termination should be specific enough and should be communicated to the staff member. On the other hand, it was recognized that the Director General of FAO could

[58] In *Lane*, UNAT Judgment No. 198 [1975], JUNAT Nos. 167–230 p. 267, where the applicant had been dismissed at the end of his probation, the UNAT reaffirmed the principle stated in *Cooperman* and *Peynado*.

[59] OASAT Judgment No. 40 [1979].

[60] The relevant Staff Rules were 104.5 (f) and (h): see Amerasinghe (ed.), 3 op. cit. (note 1 *supra*) p. 214 at p. 241.

[61] ILOAT Judgment No. 13 [1954] (FAO).

terminate the appointment of a probationer at any time by invoking *the interests of the organization* in accordance with the Staff Regulations.[62] In *Loomba*[63] the applicant's appointment was terminated in the interests of the organization under the above provisions, because of his character and his psychological unsuitability for international service which, moreover, was verified by the tribunal itself from the content and tone of his correspondence. The tribunal held that the respondent did not have to provide the applicant with a written statement of reasons, inasmuch as he was given a warning and was informed of his supervisor's intention to dismiss him. Consequently, he was sufficiently informed of the grounds of his termination. It was also said that in any case under the relevant provisions, because the termination was in the interests of the organization, this procedure was not required to be followed.[64]

The decided cases warrant the conclusion that the timing of the decision to terminate the probationary appointment could affect the powers of the organization. In the case of the organizations referred to in the judgments, where the decision to terminate the appointment is taken before the end of the period of probation, the discretionary powers of the organization are subject to less control by tribunals, because of the manner in which the Staff Regulations and Staff Rules of certain organizations have been drafted and interpreted by the tribunals. When the decision to terminate the probationary appointment is taken at the end of the period of probation, the conditions to be observed are more stringent. This seems to be so in the case of the UN and the OAS, where the Staff Regulations and Staff Rules permit termination of a probationary appointment in the interests of the organization. However, in the case of FAO the ILOAT has apparently decided that termination in the interests of the organization at any time demands less severe requirements of the organization than in other situations. This appears to be because the Staff Regulations of FAO are drafted in such a manner that no overriding distinction is made between dismissal at the end of the probationary period and dismissal during the probationary period. In some organizations, such as the EEC and WHO, no provision is made for the termination of a probationary appointment in the interests of the organization. Similarly, in some organizations the Staff Regulations and Staff Rules make no distinction between termination of a probationary appointment during probation and dismissal at the end of the probationary period. In those instances, it is doubtful whether the timing of the decision to terminate a probationary appointment would make a difference or whether reference to the interests of the organi-

---

[62] Article IX, Section 301.0913 of the FAO Staff Regulations: see Amerasinghe (ed.), 3 op. cit. (note 1 *supra*) p. 84 at p. 89. See also *Kersaudy*, ILOAT Judgment No. 152 [1970] (FAO).
[63] ILOAT Judgment No. 169 [1970] (FAO).
[64] Similar cases were *Guisset*, ILOAT Judgment No. 396 [1980] (FAO); *Al-Zand*, ILOAT Judgment No. 389 [1980] (FAO); *Pini*, ILOAT Judgment No. 455 [1981] (FAO).

zation would release the organizations from their usual obligations under the Staff Regulations and Staff Rules.

Substantive rights of the probationer during probation

While international administrative tribunals recognize that the administrative authority has discretionary power during the probationary period, they also have acknowledged that probationers have certain substantive rights. Probation is based on the contract of employment or arises from the act of appointment and creates rights and obligations for both parties. Some of these rights and obligations derive from the nature of probation. Furthermore, most of the Staff Regulations and Staff Rules of international organizations provide for some of the rights which the probationer has against the administrative authority, such as the right to training and guidance. However, tribunals have, in the absence of explicit provision, had recourse to general principles of law in determining the rights of probationers and the obligations of the administrative authority.

In many decisions tribunals have expressly referred to the obligations of the administrative authority.[65] In *Eskenasy*,[66] for example, the OASAT referred to some of the duties the administrative authority had to perform in order to give the probationer a fair evaluation to which the probationer had a right. Some of the necessary elements of the evaluation system which the administrative authority was under an obligation to provide were identified as effective communications between supervisor and probationer, definition of the probationer's duties and responsibilities as derived from his job description, and specification of the manner in which such duties should be carried out. The CJEC has stated that there is an obligation which arose from the contract of exmployment to give the probationer an opportunity to prove his ability.[67]

(a) Right to fair conditions for performance

In *Chiacchia*[68] the applicant contended that she had the right to work during her probationary period under favourable conditions. Although it did not

[65] See, e.g., *Johnson*, UNAT Judgment No. 213 [1976], JUNAT Nos. 167–230 p. 429; *Ghaffar*, ILOAT Judgment No. 320 [1977] (WHO); *Heyes*, ILOAT Judgment No. 453 [1981] (WHO); *Eskenasy*, OASAT Judgment No. 40 [1979]; *Salle*, WBAT Reports [1983, Part I], Decision No. 10.

[66] OASAT Judgment No. 40 [1979].

[67] See *Mirrosevich*, CJEC Case 10/55 [1954–6] ECR p. 333; *Nagels*, CJEC Case 52/70 [1971] ECR p. 365.

[68] UNAT Judgment No. 90 [1963], JUNAT Nos. 87–113 p. 25.

explicitly deny this right, the UNAT said that, if the unfavourable conditions under which the applicant had worked during her probationary period had been known to the Secretary General of the UN when he evaluated her and took the decision to terminate her appointment, her rights would not have been infringed. Thus, the UNAT seems to be of the view that the knowledge of the situation by the authority responsible for taking the decision to terminate the appointment would result in the authority not having strictly to fulfil this particular obligation. In *Ghaffar*[69] the ILOAT found that, when he took his decision to terminate the applicant's appointment, the Director General of WHO had overlooked the difficult conditions under which the applicant had worked during his probation, inasmuch as the duties assigned to him were not in accord with his job description, and found fault with this omission. These two cases, though difficult in their reasoning, would seem to support the proposition that there is normally an obligation to provide favourable conditions of work but where these are not provided, if true and proper weight is given to the omission in arriving at the decision to terminate the appointment, the failure to provide the required conditions of work ceases to be a culpable omission.

(b) *Right to have functions within the scope of the job description*

In *Johnson*[70] the UNAT noted that in many instances the respondent had failed to carry out its obligations towards the applicant. For example, at the end of her second year of probation the complete reorganization of the department to which she had been assigned as well as the change of her supervisor resulted in a new job description for her. However, the administrative authority failed officially to inform her of these changes and, consequently, her new supervisor was unable to make her understand what he expected of her in the new situation. The tribunal found fault with this omission.[71] In *Nagels*,[72] on the other hand, where the applicant argued that there was a discrepancy between the nature of the duties assigned to his post as described in the notice for the vacancy for which he had applied and the actual duties with which he was entrusted, the CJEC found that the applicant had failed to perform satisfactorily the administrative aspects of his duties, which in fact were very closely linked to the subject-matter as described in the vacancy notice. Furthermore, the Court noted that, although a misunderstanding might have occurred because of the wording of the notice in Dutch (the applicant's mother tongue), discussions

---

[69] ILOAT Judgment No. 320 [1977] (WHO).

[70] UNAT Judgment No. 213 [1976], JUNAT Nos. 167–230 p. 429.

[71] See also *Ghaffar*, ILOAT Judgment No. 320 [1977] (WHO).

[72] CJEC Case 52/70 [1971] ECR p. 365.

which took place with his department prior to his recruitment as to the nature of the position as well as his curriculum vitae in which it was mentioned that he had administrative experience, indicated adequately that the applicant himself contributed to such misunderstanding. The Court held against the applicant.

(c) Right to guidance and training

The obligations of the administration to provide guidance and training are generally found in the Staff Regulations and Staff Rules of the several organizations. In *Heyes*[73] the ILOAT stated that the WHO Staff Rules[74] required that the respondent should provide the applicant with guidance and instruction which included suggestions for improvement, if performance were unsatisfactory. This was, therefore, an obligation which the respondent had to fulfil. Tribunals have taken into consideration the circumstances of the case whenever the enforcement of such obligations has been in issue. Thus, in *Crapon de Caprona*,[75] where the applicant contended that he did not receive adequate training during his probationary period, the ILOAT held that he had had fifteen years' experience as a translator and consequently did not need any special training.[76] In *Salle*[77] the WBAT pointed out that the relevant Personnel Manual Statement required that the probationer be provided adequate supervision and guidance and also, in certain circumstances, adequate language training but held that the administration had, in the circumstances of the case, discharged the obligation placed upon it.

(d) Right to be warned about shortcomings

In *Crapon de Caprona*[78] the ILOAT stated that a probationer should be informed of his shortcomings. Similarly, in *Heyes*,[79] in interpreting WHO Staff Rule 1060,[80] the same tribunal stated that only in a very exceptional case was it possible to terminate a probationer's appointment under the Staff Rule without previously giving him an opportunity to correct himself.

---

73 ILOAT Judgment No. 453 [1981] (WHO) at p. 6.
74 Staff Rule 530: see Amerasinghe (ed.), 1 op. cit. (note 1 *supra*) p. 118 at p. 148.
75 ILOAT Judgment No. 112 [1967] (WHO). See also *Kersaudy*, ILOAT Judgment No. 152 [1970] (FAO). In *Vrancheva*, ILOAT Judgment No. 194 [1972] (WHO), where the decision to terminate the appointment was quashed on the grounds of procedural irregularity, the tribunal did not explicitly deal with the contention that the applicant had not received guidance.
76 See also *Sternfield*, ILOAT Judgment No. 197 [1972] (WHO).
77 WBAT Reports [1983, Part I], Decision No. 10.
78 ILOAT Judgment No. 112 [1967] (WHO).
79 ILOAT Judgment No. 453 [1981] (WHO) at p. 6.
80 See Amerasinghe (ed.), 1 op. cit. (note 1 *supra*) p. 118 at p. 171.

(e) Right to assistance and protection

In *Guisset*,[81] where the applicant contended that he had been persecuted and the victim of a plot, the ILOAT clearly stated that the administration had the duty, even in the absence of express provision, to respect the staff member's dignity and reputation, even when he was on probation. The tribunal held, however, that the applicant's professional position had not been damaged, although it was not entirely clear whether his dignity and reputation had not, because the applicant had been reinstated in his country's foreign service.

(f) Right to be transferred

It is not clearly established that the administration has a duty to transfer a probationer during probation in order to give him an opportunity to prove himself. However, probationers have often referred to it. It would appear that the general approach taken was to recognize that the discretion to transfer a probationer during his probationary period lay exclusively with the administrative authority, which could decide when and whether to take such action. If the administrative authority decided to transfer the probationer, then the decision accrued to his benefit. However, there now seems to be a difference of opinion on this subject. The UNAT does not seem to recognize a right to transfer. The ILOAT in a recent decision took a somewhat different approach.

In *Adler*[82] the UNAT found that the applicant's supervisor had clearly stated that the applicant had several talents but was unsuitable for the post to which he was assigned. Therefore, his probationary period was extended with a view to finding him a suitable position in another department. However, these efforts were fruitless. The tribunal held that the administration had no obligation to transfer him. In an early UNAT decision, *Chiacchia*,[83] the tribunal affirmed that the probationer did not have the right to be given another chance by transfer when unsuccessful.

In *Al-Zand*[84] the ILOAT held that the applicant whose performance was unsatisfactory had no right to ask FAO for a transfer to another post. However, in a subsequent decision, *Guisset*,[85] also an action brought by an FAO staff member, the ILOAT clearly stated the principle, also mentioned in passing in *Al-Zand*, that generally before dismissing a staff member thought should be given to transferring him to some other post on trial, especially if he was junior in rank. But, in this particular case, the tribunal

---

[81] ILOAT Judgment No. 396 [1980] (FAO) at p. 6.
[82] UNAT Judgment No. 267 [1980], JUNAT Nos. 231–300 p. 352.
[83] UNAT Judgment No. 90 [1963], JUNAT Nos. 87–113 p. 25.
[84] ILOAT Judgment No. 389 [1980] (FAO).
[85] ILOAT Judgment No. 396 [1980] (FAO).

excluded the possibility of transfer, since the applicant was hired for a specific post (Special Assistant to the Director General) because of the friendship between himself and the Director General. Consequently, the ILOAT noted that when the applicant lost the Director General's confidence he could no longer render to the organization the special services for which he had been hired and there was no reason to keep him any longer in the organization. In the two above-mentioned decisions there was no reference to FAO Staff Regulations or Staff Rules as such in the discussion on the right to a transfer. In both cases that right was mentioned but on the facts of each case the right was found not to exist. In *Al-Zand* the applicant was considered to be lacking pragmatism which in effect rendered him 'unsatisfactory'. In *Guisset*, the applicant was found unsuitable because of the incompatibility of temperament between himself and the Director General, his dismissal being in the interests of the organization under the relevant FAO Staff Rules.[86] However, because of the personal nature of his appointment, the right to a transfer was inapplicable. It could be, therefore, that, depending upon the circumstances, a probationer might have, in an appropriate case, a right to transfer. In considering whether such a right exists in a given case the tribunal would take into account the nature of the applicant's deficiency and even the nature of the appointment. In *Molina*[87] the ILOAT again considered the issue whether an unsuccessful probationer had a right to be transferred. In this case the applicant, a WHO staff member, contended that he should have been transferred for the remaining 11 months of his 2-year contract. The tribunal held that there was no reasonable possibility of transferring him to another unit because he had specialized in computer science and could only work in the Data Processing Department. The applicant's appointment was terminated under WHO Staff Rule 1060[88] for unsuitability, because he was incompatible in the group to which he had been assigned.[89]

In the decided cases, although the existence of a right to a transfer before a probationer is dismissed has apparently been acknowledged by the ILOAT provided the appropriate circumstances are present, in no case has it been held that the applicant had a right to be transferred before his probationary appointment was terminated. Hence, it is difficult to anticipate how the principle will be applied in favour of applicants.

In *Johnson*[90] where the applicant was transferred during her probation the

---

[86] Staff Rule 301.0913: see Amerasinghe (ed.), 3 op. cit. (note 1 *supra*) p. 84 at p. 89.

[87] ILOAT Judgment No. 440 [1980] (WHO).

[88] See Amerasinghe (ed.), 1 op. cit. (note 1 *supra*) p. 118 at p. 171.

[89] In *Gale*, ILOAT Judgment No. 84 [1965] (UNESCO), transfer was recommended by the Appeals Board as a remedy for which compensation was an alternative. The ILOAT confirmed the decision of the Appeals Board. There were procedural and substantive irregularities in the case. This was not a case where the right to transfer before dismissal was discussed.

[90] UNAT Judgment No. 213 [1976], JUNAT Nos. 167–230 p. 429. The power of the organization to make a transfer during probation may be limited, presumably if it amounts to an abuse

UNAT held that the periodic report covering the period after the applicant's transfer should have been considered when her assignment was reviewed for the purpose of granting her a permanent appointment. The omission to take into consideration the periodic report covering the period of probation after the transfer was declared irregular. Thus, where the applicant is in fact transferred, he must have the full benefit of the transfer. It should be noted that this case did not deal with the right to be transferred. It is not clear from the case whether there were provisions in the Staff Regulations and Staff Rules of the organization requiring transfer nor whether the tribunal would have regarded the applicant's rights as having been violated, if he had not been transferred.

Judicial control of administrative decisions

International administrative tribunals exercise a certain amount of judicial control over administrative decisions terminating probationary appointments. The Staff Regulations and Staff Rules of international organizations contain provisions relating to the termination of probationary appointments. In the interpretation of these written instruments and when the texts are silent, tribunals have also had recourse to general principles of law and such sources of the law in controlling the exercise of discretionary powers. Tribunals have been particularly concerned as to whether the probationer was given a fair trial. Therefore, tribunals exercise tight controls over the procedures pertaining to the termination of probationary appointments whether laid down in the Staff Regulations and Staff Rules of the organization or not. Although tribunals exercise some control over matters of substance, judicial control over procedures is in most cases ultimately the main protection available to the probationer. To some extent also the power of the administration to choose the relevant facts in certain situations may limit judicial control. Abuse of motive (*détournement de pouvoir*) is also a ground for the exercise of judicial control. The record shows that in the majority of cases, while they have not hesitated to investigate how discretionary powers have been exercised, tribunals have often found that the decision was substantively correct or that the decision was not tainted by abuse of motive or by procedural irregularities.

There are many general statements which have been made by tribunals concerning their power of review, but some of these were not meant to be comprehensive. However, they do give some idea of the approach taken by

---

of discretion, as by being a violation of the written law: see *Decision No. 4, ESRO/CR/22*, ESRO Appeals Board [1969], at p. 6.

tribunals and the relevant bases on which decisions may be reviewed. The NATO Appeals Board in *Decision No. 90*[91] held that the termination of a probationary appointment should be based on 'adequate' grounds and that it was for the tribunal to determine whether the grounds adduced justified the termination decision. The CJEC in a very early case, *Mirossevich*,[92] stated that the administrative authority could at its discretion evaluate the capacities of probationers to carry out their duties and the Court would review only the 'ways and means' which may have led to such evaluation. In *Adler*[93] the UNAT declared that it would review a decision if there were evidence that it was motivated by prejudice or based on extraneous factors. In *Kersaudy* the ILOAT made a statement of general principle relating to the judicial power to review administrative decisions:

The Tribunal is competent to review any decision of the Director-General to terminate the appointment of a staff member during or on the expiry of the probationary period if it is taken without authority, is in irregular form or tainted by procedural irregularities, or is taken on illegal grounds or based on incorrect facts, or if essential facts have not been taken into consideration or where there has been a misuse of authority, or if conclusions which are clearly false have been drawn from the documents in the dossier. But the Tribunal may not substitute its own judgment for that of the Director-General concerning the work or conduct of the person concerned or his qualifications for employment as an international official.[94]

This statement adequately summarizes the grounds on which tribunals may exercise their power of review.

(a) Procedural matters

The most common procedural irregularity encountered in connection with decisions to terminate probationary appointments is the infringement of what may be broadly called the probationer's right to due process. The most important procedural irregularities so far identified relate to periodic reports, the time limit for the submission of such reports, completeness of such reports, the opportunity to rebut such reports, reference of the case to a review body, absence or nature of warnings given to the probationer, the statement of reasons in the termination decision, and notification of decisions. Generally, the procedural requirements from which these irregularities flowed were mentioned in the various Staff Regulations and Staff Rules of the international organizations concerned. But tribunals have

---

91 *Decision No. 90*, NATO Appeals Board [1978] at p. 3, Collection of the Decisions 65(b), 74 to 99 (1979).
92 CJEC Case 10/55 [1954–6] ECR p. 333 at p. 342.
93 UNAT Judgment No. 267 [1980], JUNAT Nos. 231–300 p. 352 at p. 380.
94 ILOAT Judgment No. 152 [1970] (FAO) at p. 5.

explicitly or implicitly had recourse to the general principles of law by way of interpretation and filling in lacunae in ascertaining whether a fundamental right had been infringed.

i. *Periodic reports*

The objective of periodic reports or appraisal reports is to inform the probationer about the quality and quantity of his work and to point out his shortcomings and how he may improve. They are prepared periodically during the probationary period. Tribunals do not usually order the rectification of these reports but may apply sanctions as a result of errors contained in them. In *Molina*[95] the report of a first-level supervisor was annulled but in this case prejudice in the drawing up of the report was inferred from the whole dossier. Thus, it was a reason connected with abuse of motive that led to the annulment of the report and not a procedural irregularity. As will be seen, reports have been annulled by the CJEC.

Tribunals do attach importance to appraisal reports and have had to pronounce on the procedure relating to them. In a very early decision of the ILOAT, *Marsh*,[96] the tribunal noted a serious procedural irregularity, namely, that one of the applicant's supervisors had failed to evaluate her. Consequently, the tribunal considered the report to be an incomplete document which had undeniably exercised a determining influence on the whole of the subsequent procedure, including the decision of the Director General of ILO, and quashed the termination decision. The tribunal further said that the time-limits for the submission of reports evaluating the probationer, as stated in the Staff Regulations, were conceived with a view to enabling the probationer to be informed of the contents of such reports on time and eventually to defend himself against criticism *before* the administration's decision to terminate his appointment was made. However, if a report were favourable to the applicant, then the disregard of the time-limit was not prejudicial to the probationer. The tribunal found in the case that the second report was 3 months late and covered only 2 months of the 6 months' extended probation and that this was irregular.[97] In *Buranavanichkit*[98] the WBAT held that the fact that the evaluation report did not include, as required by the Personnel Manual Statement, the comments of two of the

[95] ILOAT Judgment No. 440 [1980] (WHO).

[96] ILOAT Judgment No. 10 [1951] (ILO).

[97] Similar cases were *Adler*, UNAT Judgment No. 267 [1980], JUNAT Nos. 231–300 p. 352; *Johnson*, UNAT Judgment No. 213 [1976], JUNAT Nos. 167–230 p. 429; *Lane*, UNAT Judgment No. 198 [1975], ibid. p. 267; and *Châtelain*, UNAT Judgment No. 272 [1981] (ICAO), JUNAT Nos. 231–300 p. 411, where the UNAT found in a case against ICAO that a confidential report had not been completed and held in favour of the applicant. Also in this case the prescribed rules relating to such reports had not been followed in that the applicant had not been interviewed after she had made her observations.

[98] WBAT Reports [1982], Decision No. 7.

supervisors who had worked with the applicant for 11 and 7 months respectively constituted a culpable procedural irregularity.

The CJEC has also had to address the issue of periodic reports. In *Luhleich*[99] the applicant's probation report was drawn up after a delay of one year. The Court held that this delay constituted a procedural irregularity, inasmuch as it emerged from the evidence that a report prepared on time would have been favourable to the applicant. On the other hand, in *Prakash*[100] the Court held that the delay in the preparation of the probationer's report, although an irregularity *per se*, was not a vitiating element because his superior had intentionally delayed the drawing up of the report in order to give him a second chance. Therefore, a report prepared on time would not have been more favourable to the applicant.[101]

In *Luhleich*[102] the Court found that two important sources of information had not been made available through the appraisal report to the Establishment Board (the review body). The first was the testimony of one of the applicant's supervisors and the second was the report prepared by the Consolo Committee which had made an investigation into the working conditions in the applicant's Department. The Court held that the appraisal report was an incomplete document because it was based upon inaccurate or incomplete facts. In *Tither*,[103] though the applicant was late in sending in his medical certificates connected with his absence, they did arrive, so that, according to the CJEC, they should have been taken into account in the report on his probation. Because they had not been, the report was annulled as was the decision not to confirm the applicant. In the same case the applicant complained that a second unfavourable report was drawn up concerning his probation soon after the first one which was favourable to him had been completed, because of his absence from the office. This in itself, in the view of the CJEC, was not excluded in the circumstances by the Staff Regulations, although they referred only to one appraisal report to be drawn up one month before the expiration of the probationary period.[104] This was, therefore, not a procedural irregularity.[105]

In *Eskenasy*,[106] where the OASAT had to decide whether a memorandum could formally be considered an appraisal report, the tribunal held that this

---

99 CJEC Case 68/63 [1965] ECR p. 581.

100 CJEC Cases 19 & 65/63 [1965] ECR p. 533.

101 See also *di Pillo*, CJEC Cases 10 & 47/72 [1973] ECR p. 763; *Tither*, CJEC Case 175/80 [1981] ECR p. 2345; *Munk*, CJEC Case 98/81 [1982] ECR p. 1155.

102 CJEC Case 68/63 [1965] ECR p. 581.

103 CJEC Case 175/80 [1981] ECR p. 2345.

104 Article 34 (2) of the Regulations: Amerasinghe (ed.), 4 op. cit. (note 1 *supra*) p. 1 at p. 16.

105 In *Alvarez*, CJEC Case 206/81 [1982] ECR p. 3369, a report was annulled because facts had been omitted from it. The court pointed out that the applicant had not had an opportunity to rebut the omitted facts.

106 OASAT Judgment No. 40 [1979].

memorandum addressed by the applicant's supervisor to the Personnel Department and merely stating that the applicant's performance was unsatisfactory and that therefore he should not be confirmed did not constitute an evaluation of performance in accordance with the Staff Rules.[107] The tribunal held that this procedural irregularity was serious enough to entail the annulment of the termination decision and the reinstatement of the probationer.

From the decisions examined above it appears that the ommission to cover in a report even a part of the probationary period always constitutes a serious procedural irregularity. However, the disregard of time limits concerning appraisal reports may or may not constitute a serious procedural irregularity depending upon the circumstances. Further, it is necessary that the comments of all the required supervisors and all the relevant facts and documents should be included in these reports. It is also necessary that the report be a genuine evaluation.

ii. *Competence to prepare reports*

The Staff Regulations and Staff Rules of international organizations seldom specify the official who is competent to prepare the appraisal report. However, in *Sternfield*[108] the ILOAT was of the view that in international organizations the appraisal report should normally be drawn up by the immediate supervisor of the staff member. In the same decision the tribunal made an exception to this principle where the unit by its nature excluded a hierarchical line organization. This was the case of the Division of Public Information to which the applicant had been assigned. The tribunal stated that in these circumstances the Director himself had authority to draw up the applicant's appraisal report instead of the Assistant Director, his immediate supervisor. In *de Bruyn*[109] the respondent contended that the favourable report drawn up by the Director of the department did not constitute the appraisal report, that the real report could only be made by the Secretary General, and that, since the Secretary General could not address a report to himself, the termination decision taken by the Secretary General was the probationary report. The CJEC held that the report should have been made by the Director of the department, the supervisor in the case. Consequently, the report submitted by the Director of the department constituted the probationary report.[110] In *Adler*[111] the UNAT found that, among other procedural irregularities, the periodic reports were signed by unauthorized officers in violation of administrative practices. This was held to be a deficiency for which compensation was payable.

[107] Staff Rule 104.5 (h): Amerasinghe (ed.), 3 op. cit. (note 1 *supra*) p. 214 at p. 241.
[108] ILOAT Judgment No. 197 [1972] (WHO).
[109] CJEC Case 25/60 [1962] ECR p. 21.
[110] See also *D'Auria*, CJEC Case 99/77 [1978] ECR p. 1267.
[111] UNAT Judgment No. 267 [1980], JUNAT Nos. 231–300 p. 352.

The cases support the proposition that the appraisal report must be drawn up by the competent officer, but that, unless the Staff Regulations and Staff Rules are explicit, the most appropriate officer in the circumstances will be regarded as the competent officer. Tribunals have not hesitated to determine who the competent officer is in a given case.

iii. *Review body*

The UNAT in its interpretation of Staff Regulation 9.1 (c) and Staff Rules 104.12, 104.13, and 104.14[112] of the UN recognized that probationers whose employment was terminated at the end of the probationary period had some rights which were denied to those whose employment was terminated during probation. For example, as already pointed out, when a probationer's appointment is terminated at the end of the probationary period, the administration must refer the case to a review body, that is, the Appointment and Promotion Board. Where the review body examines the suitability of the probationer and follows the appropriate procedure, the rights of due process of the probationer are respected.[113] In *Peynado*,[114] however, the tribunal held that the mere review of the applicant's appointment by the Appointment and Promotion Board did not mean that the procedure followed in terminating his appointment was necessarily valid. The Board had relied on a periodic report in regard to which the applicable procedure had not been followed. Hence, its recommendation was tainted, as was the subsequent decision of the Secretary General to terminate the applicant's appointment. In *Cooperman*[115] the UNAT held that a probationer whose employment had been terminated in the interests of the organization during his probationary period under Staff Regulation 9.1 (c), was not entitled to have his suitability reviewed by the special review body provided for in Staff Rule 104.14.

Thus, where review by a review body is required by the Staff Regulations and Staff Rules reference must be made to this body but, if prior to this reference the procedure has been tainted, the mere reference to the review body will not cure that defect. It is also clear that not always is reference to a review body required. All the decided cases concerning review bodies are judgments of the UNAT relating to the UN.

iv. *Rebuttal of the appraisal report*

The right to rebut the appraisal report is an important element of the right to due process. In *Peynado*,[116] as already pointed out, the UNAT held that the

---

112 See Appendix V *infra*.
113 *de Ungria*, UNAT Judgment No. 71 [1958], JUNAT Nos. 71–86 p. 1.
114 UNAT Judgment No. 138 [1970], JUNAT Nos. 114–166 p. 221.
115 UNAT Judgment No. 93 [1965], JUNAT Nos. 87–113 p. 55.
116 UNAT Judgment No. 138 [1970], JUNAT Nos. 114–166 p. 221. See also *Johnson*, UNAT Judgment No. 213 [1976], JUNAT Nos. 167–230 p. 429.

review of the applicant's appointment by the Appointment and Promotion Board did not constitute a guarantee that the procedure followed in terminating his appointment was valid. The tribunal found that the applicant's right had been infringed because the Appointment and Promotion Board had based its recommendation to the Secretary General on an incomplete document. The document was incomplete because the applicant's rebuttal of the third period report had not been duly investigated nor had the head of the Department, in accordance with the relevant Aministrative Instruction,[117] recorded an appraisal in writing of this rebuttal. The tribunal awarded compensation for procedural defects. In *Buranavanichkit*[118] the WBAT found that reliance was placed in terminating a probationary appointment on problems relating to the applicant's employment by the Bank on a previous occasion. This information was not communicated to nor was available to the applicant. The tribunal held that reliance on it was irregular and contrary to the principle of due process, since she did not have an opportunity to answer it. The same principle was affirmed by the ILOAT in *Kissaun*.[119] In that case the tribunal stated that the right to be heard existed even in the absence of special provisions in the Staff Regulations and Staff Rules of the organization.[120]

It is sufficient that the probationer was given the opportunity to explain his case either orally or in writing,[121] though there is no obligation to hear him personally.[122] The administrative authority is under no obligation to give the probationer a chance to make a second rebuttal.[123]

Tribunals are generally agreed on the main principle that the probationer must be given a genuine opportunity to rebut the appraisal report and anything which appears in it or has been used to support it. In this connection, the proper procedure must, of course, be followed, although there are no rigid rules relating to such procedure.

v. *Warnings*

In *Crapon de Caprona*[124] the ILOAT did not deny and by implication

---

[117] No. ST/A1/115, para. 13.

[118] WBAT Reports [1982], Decision No. 7. In *Alvarez*, CJEC Case 206/81 [1982] ECR p. 3369, the CJEC annulled the non-confirmation of probation because the appraisal report did not contain facts recorded in certain relevant memoranda which were, therefore, not communicated to the applicant who did not have an opportunity to rebut them.

[119] ILOAT Judgment No. 69 [1964] (WHO).

[120] The right of rebuttal was held not to have been respected in *Vrancheva*, ILOAT Judgment No. 194 [1972] (WHO). See also *Molina*, ILOAT Judgment No. 440 [1980] (WHO).

[121] See *Milous*, ILOAT Judgment No. 42 [1960] (WHO); and *Terrain*, ILOAT Judgment No. 109 [1967] (WHO).

[122] See *Sternfield*, ILOAT Judgment No. 197 [1972] (WHO); and *Prakash*, CJEC Cases 19 & 65/63 [1965] ECR p. 533.

[123] *di Pillo*, CJEC Cases 10 & 47/72 [1973] ECR p. 763.

[124] ILOAT Judgment No. 112 [1967] (WHO) at p. 4.

acknowledged that the decision to terminate a probationer's appointment could not be taken without previously giving him a warning and an opportunity to correct himself. In *Heyes*[125] the ILOAT was more explicit in holding that a probationer's appointment could not be terminated without warning except in a very exceptional case. It considered that the case of the applicant could be classified as an exceptional one; his faults were of manner, and given his age (in his 30s), it was very unlikely that he could correct them. Consequently, the tribunal endorsed the opinion of the applicant's supervisor who believed that the applicant's shortcomings were not curable. Generally the probationer must be warned about his faults so that he has an opportunity to correct himself. Exceptionally, however, such warnings may not be a requirement.

vi. *Statement of reasons*

In *Vrancheva*[126] the ILOAT stated that the omission to inform the applicant in advance of the exact reasons for her termination was an irregularity and an infringement of her rights justifying the quashing of the termination decision.[127] In *Kersaudy*[128] the ILOAT found that, though what had happened before the case went to the Appeals Committee was not clear, the applicant had been informed of the ground of his termination before the Appeals Committee and had therefore been given the opportunity to present his comments. This was held to satisfy the requirement that reasons for the termination be stated.

It would seem to be the general rule that reasons for the non-confirmation of probation must be stated, the purpose being to give the probationer an opportunity to comment. However, if the reasons are not given before the termination decision is taken, it is sufficient that they are disclosed to the probationer during the proceedings before an appellate body, so that he has this opportunity to comment.

vii. *Notification of decisions*

The probationer must be notified in good time of the decision terminating a probationary appointment and of decisions extending the period of probation. In *Loomba*[129] the ILOAT found that the omission of the administration explicitly to inform the applicant of the two successive extensions of his probation constituted a procedural irregularity.

---

[125] ILOAT Judgment No. 453 [1981] (WHO) at p. 6.

[126] ILOAT Judgment No. 194 [1972] (WHO).

[127] See also *de Bruyn*, CJEC Case 25/60 [1962] ECR p. 21. The Appeals Board of ELDO took a different view, namely that reasons did not have to be stated: *Decision No. 1*, ELDO Appeals Board [1966]; *Decision No. 2*, ELDO Appeals Board [1968].

[128] ILOAT Judgment No. 152 [1970] (FAO).

[129] ILOAT Judgment No. 169 [1970] (FAO).

The time-limit for notification of the termination decision is a matter that has been dealt with only by the CJEC. The Court noted that Article 34 of the Staff Regulations[130] of the European Communities did not provide for a time-limit. However, the Court endeavoured to define what would constitute a reasonable period of time between the date of the drawing up of the probation report and of the notification to the probationer of the initial decision to terminate the appointment, on the one hand, and the final decision to terminate the appointment, on the other. In *Nagels*[131] 16 days were held to be a reasonable period of time; in *di Pillo*[132] 7 weeks; in *de Roy*[133] 6 days; and in *D'Auria*[134] 8 weeks. All that can be said is that there is a time-limit for the notification of decisions. The period of time which elapses must in all the circumstances of the case be reasonable but there is no fixed period as such for any purpose.

In *Munk*[135] the CJEC held that the time between the notification of the initial decision not to confirm the applicant and the final decision not to confirm him after he had responded to the initial decision was not too short. There was adequate time for him to send his reply. Hence, the procedure could not be faulted on the ground that the time given was not reasonable.

(b) Abuse of purpose

Tribunals have intervened where there is evidence that a discretionary power connected with probation was exercised for reasons extraneous to the interests of the service. In most of the decided cases arguments relating to abuse of purpose have been concerned with prejudice or ill will. Tribunals have seldom found administrative decisions tainted with prejudice or improper motive. It is significant that in *McIntire*[136] the ILOAT was prepared to quash an administrative decision connected with probation on the grounds of prejudice when it could also have quashed it on the basis of procedural irregularity.

In *McIntire*[137] the ILOAT held that the administrative authority misused its power because the decision not to confirm the applicant was not based on the applicant's unsatisfactory services but on personal considerations which had nothing to do with his performance. There was clear evidence that the termination decision was due to an extraneous factor, since the applicant had

---

[130] See Amerasinghe (ed.), 4 op. cit. (note 1 *supra*) p. 1 at p. 16.
[131] CJEC Case 52/70 [1971] ECR p. 365.
[132] CJEC Cases 10 & 47/72 [1973] ECR p. 763.
[133] CJEC Case 92/75 [1976] ECR p. 343.
[134] CJEC Case 99/77 [1978] ECR p. 1267.
[135] CJEC Case 98/81 [1982] ECR p. 1155.
[136] ILOAT Judgment No. 13 [1954] (FAO).
[137] Ibid.

one week prior to the termination of his probation received the title of Chief of Section. The extraneous factor was identified to be a letter sent to the organization by the US Government concerning the applicant.[138] In *de Bruyn*[139] also the decision was apparently based on improper motive. The decision not to confirm the applicant failed to specify any reason for the termination. The CJEC held that the decision was based on grounds not valid in law and was in open contradiction to a positive appraisal report drawn up by the applicant's supervisor. The Court awarded the applicant compensation for non-material damage. The Court did not refer to improper motive, but this would seem to be the grounds for the decision.

In the majority of cases, tribunals have on the facts rejected the allegations of misuse of power based on improper motive. In *Chiacchia*,[140] for instance, the Appeals Board of the UN had found elements of *a priori* unfavourable attitudes toward the appellant on the part of her supervisors. However, the Appeals Board did not find sufficient evidence of prejudice but recommended to the Secretary General that he consider giving the appellant a second chance. The Secretary General did not change his decision. The UNAT held that the applicant had failed to establish improper motive and rejected her application. In *Molina*[141] the applicant contended that the termination decision not to confirm him was taken for reasons not connected with his performance and based on the prejudice of his supervisor. The ILOAT, however, held that the decision was not tainted with prejudice, that the Director General of WHO did not draw wrong conclusions from the evidence submitted and that he took into consideration the applicant's difficult working relations not only with his supervisor but also with other colleagues. None the less, the ILOAT found the appraisal report written by the supervisor to be tainted with prejudice and ordered that the report be annulled and removed from the files of the organization. In this case, it would seem that, while the primary appraisal report was illegal because of prejudice, the final decision was not based on this report and therefore the prejudice was not the cause of that decision. This was clearly a case in which the element of bias or prejudice did not have a causal connection with the impugned decision.[142]

---

[138] In *Ghaffar*, ILOAT Judgment No. 320 [1977] (WHO), the decision was quashed, among other things, on the ground of prejudice.

[139] CJEC Case 25/60 [1962] ECR p. 21.

[140] UNAT Judgment No. 90 [1963], JUNAT Nos. 87–113 p. 25.

[141] ILOAT Judgment No. 440 [1980] (WHO).

[142] See also *Schawalder-Vrancheva (No. 2)*, ILOAT Judgment No. 226 [1974] (WHO). For other decisions where no abuse of motive was found, see *Kraicsovits*, ILOAT Judgment No. 140 [1969] (FAO); *Kersaudy*, ILOAT Judgment No. 152 [1970] (FAO); *Mirrosevich*, CJEC Case 10/55 [1954–6] ECR p. 333; *Prakash*, CJEC Cases 19 & 65/63 [1965] ECR p. 533; *D'Auria*, CJEC Case 99/77 [1978] ECR p. 1267; *Munk*, CJEC Case 98/81 [1982] ECR p. 1155; *Decision No. 2*, ELDO Appeals Board [1968].

(c) *Matters substantive to the decision to terminate*

Judicial control over the substantive content of administrative decisions terminating probationary appointments is generally very limited. Tribunals recognize the wide discretion of the administrative authority in this regard and have been very cautious in interfering with the actions of the administration. Tribunals have intervened in probation cases only where there is some evidence that there was an error in regard to the facts on which the decision was based or that clearly wrong conclusions were drawn from the facts. Other grounds for quashing decisions relating to probation on the ground of substantive irregularity have apparently not been tested, though in some cases general statements have been made.

In *Adler*[143] the UNAT stated that it would intervene only if the decision was based on erroneous information or was motivated by prejudice. In *Maier*[144] the ILOAT defined its power of review in respect of substantive defects *per se* by limiting it to verifying whether:

(a) the decision of the administrative authority was tainted with illegality;
(b) the decision was based on incorrect facts;
(c) the administrative authority had failed to take account of essential facts; or
(d) the administrative authority had drawn from the evidence conclusions that were 'clearly false' or 'manifestly unfounded'.

These are grounds for review of the exercise of discretionary powers in general and are, therefore, applicable to decisions taken in regard to probation. Frequently, in probation cases, an irregularity as to the substance of the decision has been coupled with procedural irregularity.[145]

i. *Mistaken conclusions*

Though tribunals have admitted that in probation cases the drawing from the facts of conclusions which are clearly false and manifestly unfounded is a ground for review,[146] there are not many cases which have held that a termination decision has been vitiated by such a fault. In *Crapon de Caprona*[147] the ILOAT reviewed the applicant's translations and found that some of the

---

[143] UNAT Judgment No. 267 [1980], JUNAT Nos. 231–300 p. 352 at p. 380.

[144] ILOAT Judgment No. 503 [1982] (EPO) at p. 4. See also *Crapon de Caprona*, ILOAT Judgment No. 112 [1967] (WHO) at p. 3; *Sternfield*, ILOAT Judgment No. 197 [1972] (WHO) at p. 5; *Joyet*, ILOAT Judgment No. 318 [1977] (WHO) at p. 3.

[145] See *Johnson* UNAT Judgment No. 213 [1976], JUNAT Nos. 167–230 p. 429; *Vrancheva*, ILOAT Judgment No. 194 [1972] (WHO); *Mirossevich*, CJEC Case 10/55 [1954–6] ECR p. 333; *Luhleich*, CJEC Case 68/63 [1965] ECR p. 581.

[146] See, e.g., *Crapon de Caprona*, ILOAT Judgment No. 112 [1967] (WHO); *Sternfield*, ILOAT Judgment No. 197 [1972] (WHO).

[147] ILOAT Judgment No. 112 [1967] (WHO).

corrections were 'debatable' and 'possibly unjustified' but most of them were pertinent. The tribunal also held that his linguistic skills were beyond doubt, but that it was not unreasonable to consider his work as unsatisfactory and that, therefore, the conclusions drawn by the Director General of WHO were not manifestly unfounded.[148]

In *Maier*[149] the ILOAT held that the conclusion drawn that personal incompatibility made the work of the team of which the applicant was a member impossible was a mistaken conclusion drawn from the facts. The tribunal found that the disagreements between his chief and the applicant were trivial and no more serious than the ordinary frictions of everyday life and that there was no evidence of any factor likely to impair the unit's efficiency. The applicant was awarded damages for having been wrongfully not confirmed, because the final decision was manifestly unfounded.

ii. *Error of fact*
Error of fact is a ground for review. This is where the evidence does not support a fact or facts on which a relevant conclusion is based. In two very similar decisions in which the applicants complained of error of fact the CJEC reached opposite conclusions. In *Luhleich*[150] the Court held that the most important criticisms made of the applicant were based on inaccurate or incomplete facts. The Court reached its conclusion after a thorough examination of the facts, and after considering the harsh attitude of the applicant's superior as well as the many organizational difficulties prevailing at the time in the ISPRA Centre. The Court said that neither the finding that the applicant's conduct was inappropriate nor the finding that he had failed to adjust to the necessities of the service was well founded. In *Prakash*[151] the applicant contended that the decision to terminate his probationary appointment was based on erroneous facts. The issue for the CJEC was whether the defendant's findings that the applicant had a tendency towards excess in preparing programmes and in calculating resources was accurate. The Court held that it could not substitute its own assessment of the applicant's contribution for that of the defendant, nor could it decide whether or not a particular apparatus was sufficient for undertaking a given piece of research. Nevertheless, the Court held itself competent to carry out a thorough examination of the facts leading to the defendant's finding. The Court mainly relied upon the testimony of the Director who basically confirmed the accusation of the first-in-line supervisor. The testimony of the Director was

---

[148] See also *Kersaudy*, ILOAT Judgment No. 152 [1970] (WHO); *Sternfield*, ILOAT Judgment No. 197 [1972] (WHO); *Munk*, CJEC Case 98/81 [1982] ECR p. 1155.

[149] ILOAT Judgment No. 503 [1982] (EPO).

[150] CJEC Case 68/63 [1965] ECR p. 581.

[151] CJEC Cases 19 & 65/63 [1965] ECR p. 533. See also *Decision No. 158*, NATO Appeals Board [1983], Collection of the Decisions 135 to 171 (1984), for a similar decision.

deemed acceptable to the Court, although the latter was not familiar with the applicant's work, because the Director was perfectly aware of the harsh attitude of the first-in-line supervisor towards his subordinates. Furthermore, the Court relied upon the information supplied by the applicant's former employer confirming some of the applicant's shortcomings. Finally, the Court held that the witnesses heard did not corroborate the applicant's allegation nor was the applicant able to prove that he did not have enough resources and sufficient apparatus for the short-term project. Consequently, the Court held that the applicant did have a propensity towards excess and that there could be no serious doubts about the accuracy of the facts leading to the defendant's finding.

iii. *Standards of judgment*
Tribunals will not substitute their own standards of judgment for those of the administration. Standards, unlike the establishment of facts, are solely within the discretion of the administrative authority. Thus in *Prakash*[152] the CJEC stated that in regard to performance the applicant might have been judged rather strictly. However, the Court said that, should it describe that strictness as illegal, it would be violating the rule of separation of the judicial and administrative powers. It was the administrative authority that had exclusive jurisdiction to decide upon the degree of severity chosen in assessing its employees.

iv. *Competent authority*
There is a dearth of cases dealing with the question of the competent authority in regard to probation. However, in *Chiacchia*[153] the applicant complained that the decision not to confirm her appointment was not taken by the Secretary General who was the competent authority and who had died when the Director of Personnel had communicated to her that decision. The UNAT held that the relevant decision had been taken by the Secretary General before he died and that the Director of Personnel merely communicated the decision to her. Similarly, the complaint that the Director of Personnel took a decision confirming the first decision when he was not the competent authority was dismissed on the ground that the new Secretary General, the competent authority, had taken the relevant decision which the Director of Personnel merely communicated to the applicant. This judgment clearly assumed that decisions relating to probation must be taken by the competent authority.[154]

---

[152] CJEC Cases 19 & 65/63 [1965] ECR p. 533.
[153] UNAT Judgment No. 90 [1963], JUNAT Nos. 87–113 p. 25.
[154] See also *Salle*, WBAT Reports [1983, Part I], Decision No. 10 at p. 25; and *Decision No. 2*, ELDO Appeals Board [1968], where it was held that the competent authority took the decision impugned.

Remedies

As has been seen, in probation cases the discretionary power of the administration is wide and judicial control is sparingly exercised. In regard to remedies, however, tribunals have retained the right to choose among the different remedies available to them. When tribunals quantify the amount of compensation, they seem to take into consideration the kind of appointment for which the probationer was hired. Thus, the distinction between a fixed-term and a permanent appointment has become relevant.[155] Also, tribunals have addressed the issue of awarding compensation irrespective of whether the termination decision itself was illegal and was required to be quashed.

Tribunals have delineated several options in regard to the selection of the most adequate remedy. They may decide (a) to quash the decision and order reinstatement with or without compensation, (b) to leave the choice between reinstatement and compensation to the administrative authority, (c) if the decision is found invalid but is not annulled, to award compensation for the irregularities, (d) to remand the case, (e) if the decision were tainted with some inessential procedural irregularities, to award compensation for the damage suffered, or (f) although the decision is valid, to order specific performance in some respects or award costs only on account of some defects.

(a) The tribunal may choose to quash the termination decision and order reinstatement with or without awarding damages. In *Marsh*[156] the ILOAT annulled the termination decision because the appraisal report was based on incomplete information and the Director General of ILO had relied upon it when he took the termination decision. The ILOAT ordered the reinstatement of the applicant as a probationer for a period of 6 months.[157] In *Mirrosevich*[158] the CJEC annulled a termination decision on the grounds that the probation was not properly conducted and ordered the reinstatement of the applicant so that she could enter on a new probationary period of 6 months according to the new Staff Regulations in force. However, the applicant's claim for compensation was rejected on the grounds that the outcome of the probation would have been uncertain, even if the probation had been conducted properly. In addition, the applicant's claim for non-material damages was rejected on the ground that she was offered a new post with

---

[155] See *Kissaun*, ILOAT Judgment No. 69 [1964] (WHO); *Loomba*, ILOAT Judgment No. 169 [1970] (FAO); and *Johnson*, UNAT Judgment No. 213 [1976], JUNAT Nos. 167–230 p. 429.

[156] ILOAT Judgment No. 10 [1951] (ILO).

[157] In *Ghaffar*, ILOAT Judgment No. 320 [1977] (WHO), also reinstatement was ordered together with compensation from the date of dismissal to reinstatement.

[158] CJEC Case 10/55 [1954–6] ECR p. 333. See also *Tither*, CJEC Case 175/80 [1981] ECR p. 2345, where a defective report was annulled as was the decision to dismiss the applicant. This amounted to reinstatement.

possibilities of a promotion and this offer was similar to compensation.[159]

(b) The tribunal may annul the decision but leave the administration the choice of either reinstating or paying compensation to the probationer. In *McIntire*[160] the ILOAT rescinded the termination decision. However the administration was given the choice of either reinstating the applicant or paying him (i) compensation equal to 15 months' salary with interest at 4 per cent from the date at which the probationary period should normally have ended and until the actual payment of the claim; and (ii) $3,000 for the material and moral damage he had suffered from the date of the termination of his appointment to the date of the judgment. In *Eskenasy*[161] the OASAT found that the termination decision was invalid and ordered the retroactive reinstatement of the applicant and the reopening of the case. However, in accordance with Article VII.2 of its Statute, the tribunal fixed compensation in the amount of one year's basic salary, should the administration decide not to reinstate the applicant. Where the Statute of the tribunal so states, the tribunal will have to give the administration the option to pay compensation, if it decides not to reinstate the applicant, even though the tribunal may consider that the applicant should be reinstated.[162]

(c) Compensation may be awarded in lieu of specific performance, since, though the termination decision is found invalid, it is not annulled either because the applicant does not want reinstatement or reinstatement is not possible, since considerable changes have taken place in the organization. In *Johnson*[163] the UNAT found the termination decision invalid as a result of several procedural irregularities, and that the applicant had been deprived of permanent appointment by the fault of the respondent. However, because of the considerable structural changes which had taken place in the department to which the applicant had been assigned, it was impossible to require a new evaluation of the applicant's suitability. Consequently, the tribunal awarded the applicant compensation in lieu of specific performance. The tribunal noted that the applicant could have expected to remain in service until superannuation, that is, till September 1983, seven years from the date of the judgment. Therefore, the applicant was awarded the maximum, namely the equivalent of 2 years' net base salary. In *de Bruyn*[164] the applicant

[159] In *Alvarez*, CJEC Case 206/81 [1982] ECR p. 3369, also reinstatement was ordered but not additional compensation which was claimed.

[160] ILOAT Judgment No. 13 [1954] (FAO).

[161] OASAT Judgment No. 40 [1979].

[162] See, e.g. Article XII.1 of the Statute of the WBAT, and Article 9.1 of the Statute of the UNAT: Appendices III and I *infra*.

[163] UNAT Judgment No. 213 [1976], JUNAT Nos. 167–230 p. 429. See also *Châtelain*, UNAT Judgment No. 272 [1981] (ICAO), JUNAT Nos. 231–300 p. 411, where the tribunal did not order reinstatement but awarded compensation equivalent to 8 months' net base salary. This was a case involving procedural irregularities perpetrated in the taking of a decision to terminate an appointment for unsatisfactory service.

[164] CJEC Case 25/60 [1962] ECR p. 21.

claimed only damages for breach of contract. The CJEC found the termination decision to be illegal and awarded the applicant damages of BF 40,000 for the non-material damage caused her.[165] In *Buranavanichkit*[166] the WBAT found that there were certain procedural irregularities but that rescission of the contested decision and reinstatement was not an appropriate remedy in the circumstances. It awarded a sum equivalent to 1 year's net base salary as compensation for the damage done. In *Maier*[167] the applicant did not claim reinstatement. The ILOAT awarded as compensation DM 4,000 plus interest at 10 per cent per annum from the date of the filing of the application. The tribunal did not consider reinstatement.

(*d*) The tribunal may find the termination decision unlawful and remand the case. In *Vrancheva*[168] the non-confirmation decision was quashed and the respondent was invited to reopen the case, investigate the facts, hear the applicant, and decide if her probation could be terminated under WHO Staff Rule 960. The ILOAT deferred the ruling on the request for compensation. In the follow-up case[169] after the remand the termination of the probationary appointment was found lawful. Consequently, the applicant's request for compensation was rejected.[170]

(*e*) The decision may be tainted with some procedural irregularities which in reality could not have had a material bearing on the substance of the decision. The tribunal may then simply award compensation for the damage suffered because of the procedural irregularities, the decision being in reality regarded as lawful. In *Peynado*[171] the UNAT found that the periodic report was an incomplete document. The respondent did not request the remand of the case for correction of procedure and the tribunal awarded the applicant compensation in lieu of specific performance for the injury caused by the procedural defects in the amount of 3 months' net base salary. This was probably a case where the correction of the irregularity would not have changed the decision.[172] In *Loomba*[173] the applicant had not been officially notified of the two successive extensions of his probation and the ILOAT confirmed that the compensation recommended by the Appeals Committee and granted by the Director General of FAO was more than adequate to

---

[165] See also *Luhleich*, CJEC Case 68/63 [1965] ECR p. 581.

[166] WBAT Reports [1982], Decision No. 7.

[167] ILOAT Judgment No. 503 [1982] (EPO).

[168] ILOAT Judgment No. 194 [1972] (WHO). The relevant Staff Rule referred to in the case is now Rule 1060: see Amerasinghe (ed.), 1 op. cit. (note 1 *supra*) p. 118 at p. 171.

[169] *Schawalder-Vrancheva (No. 2)*, ILOAT Judgment No. 226 [1974] (WHO).

[170] See also *Kissaun*, ILOAT Judgment No. 69 [1964] (WHO), where the case was remanded and compensation was assessed at the same time for the prejudice suffered.

[171] UNAT Judgment No. 138 [1970], JUNAT Nos. 114–166 p. 221.

[172] See also *Lane*, UNAT Judgment No. 198 [1975], JUNAT Nos. 167–230 p. 267; *Adler*, UNAT Judgment No. 267 [1980], JUNAT Nos. 231–300 p. 352.

[173] ILOAT Judgment No. 169 [1970] (FAO).

compensate the applicant for the damage suffered because he had been kept in a state of uncertainty. He was compensated as if his appointment had been confirmed and then terminated. The amount of compensation was 6 months' salary. The applicant was the holder of a 1-year fixed-term contract with a 6-month probation period. In *di Pillo*[174] where the dismissal decision was found lawful, the CJEC awarded the applicant compensation for the procedural irregularity which resulted from the lateness in the drawing up of the probation report. The Court noted that the applicant had suffered damage, because after the expiry of his probation he had been kept in a state of uncertainty as to his future in general. It fixed the amount of compensation at BF 200,000, taking into consideration the post he had occupied. There are some other cases in which the same principle has been discussed and confirmed, although damages have not been awarded.[175]

(*f*) The termination decision may be found lawful, but the tribunal may, nevertheless, order specific performance in some respects or award costs only. There are only two cases in which this has happened. In *Molina*[176] the non-confirmation of the applicant was found lawful and consequently he was denied reinstatement and compensation. However, the ILOAT ordered that the appraisal report written by the first-in-line supervisor be annulled and removed from the files of the organization, because it was tainted with prejudice. In *Nagels*[177] the application was dismissed as unfounded. The CJEC, however, awarded the applicant half his costs on the ground that the misunderstanding about the nature of his duties, which occurred at the time of his recruitment, had not been due entirely to his fault and had given rise to the proceedings.

[174] CJEC Cases 10 & 47/72 [1973] ECR p. 763.
[175] See *Prakash*, CJEC Cases 19 & 65/63 [1965] ECR p. 533; *Guisset*, ILOAT Judgment No. 396 [1980] (FAO).
[176] ILOAT Judgment No. 440 [1980] (WHO).
[177] CJEC Case No. 52/70 [1971] ECR p. 365.

CHAPTER THIRTY-NINE

Disciplinary Measures

INTERNATIONAL organizations are generally empowered by their written law to take disciplinary measures against staff members in case of misconduct. Most Staff Regulations and Staff Rules have fairly detailed provisions relating to such measures. The Staff Regulations of the UN provide in Article X that:

Regulation 10.1: The Secretary General may establish administrative machinery with staff participation which will be available to advise him on disciplinary cases.
Regulation 10.2: The Secretary General may impose disciplinary measures on staff members whose conduct is unsatisfactory.
   He may summarily dismiss a member of the staff for serious misconduct.[1]

The Staff Rules in Chapter X[2] provide for a Joint Disciplinary Committee (Rule 110.1), specifying its composition (Rule 110.2) and its procedures (Rule 110.5), while Rule 110.3 states that:

(a) Except in cases of summary dismissal, no staff member serving at any duty station where a Joint Disciplinary Committee has been established shall be subject to disciplinary measures until the matter has been referred for advice to the Joint Disciplinary Committee, provided that referral to the Joint Disciplinary Committee may be waived by mutual agreement of the staff member concerned and the Secretary General.
(b) Disciplinary measures under the first paragraph of staff regulation 10.2 shall consist of written censure, suspension without pay, demotion or dismissal for misconduct, provided that suspension pending investigation under rule 110.4 shall not be considered a disciplinary measure.
(c) Written censure shall be authorized by the Secretary General and shall be distinguished from reprimand of a staff member by a supervisory official. Such reprimand shall not be deemed to be a disciplinary measure within the meaning of this rule.

and Rule 110.4 states that:

If a charge of misconduct is made against a staff member and the Secretary General so decides, the staff member may be suspended from duty, with or without pay, pending investigation, the suspension being without prejudice to the rights of the staff member.

   Disciplinary measures and procedures are dealt with in Part VI of the Staff

---

[1] See Appendix V *infra*. For a general description of disciplinary measures in some organizations see Plantey, *The International Civil Service: Law and Management* (1981) pp. 226 ff.
[2] See Appendix V *infra*.

Regulations of the Council of Europe.[3] Provision is made in Article 55 for a Disciplinary Board and in Article 57 for suspension, while Article 54 provides:

1. Any failure by a staff member to comply with his obligations under the Staff Regulations, and other regulations, whether intentionally or through negligence on his part, may lead to the institution of disciplinary proceedings and possibly disciplinary action.
2. Disciplinary measures shall take one of the following forms:
   a. written warning;
   b. reprimand;
   c. deferment of advancement to a higher step;
   d. relegation in step;
   e. downgrading;
   f. removal from post.
3. A single offense shall not give rise to more than one disciplinary measure.

Article 56 states that:

1. Disciplinary proceedings shall be instituted by the Secretary General after a hearing of the staff member concerned.
2. Disciplinary measures shall be ordered by the Secretary General after completion of the disciplinary proceedings provided for in Appendix X to these Regulations.

Appendix X to the Staff Regulations[4] contains more detailed provisions on disciplinary proceedings.

   Chapter 8 of the Principles of Staff Employment of the World Bank states the general principles relating to disciplinary measures.[5] It provides:

8.1 A staff member who fails to observe the standards of conduct established pursuant to these Principles, who engages in misconduct, or who neglects to perform assigned tasks without reasonable excuse, may be subject to disciplinary measures. Depending on the seriousness of the offense and other relevant factors, the disciplinary measures taken in a particular case may be censure, suspension from duty with or without pay or with reduced pay, demotion, reduction in pay, or separation of the staff member from the service of the Organizations as provided in Chapter 7 above. A staff member may also be suspended from duty with pay, without prejudice, pending investigation of a charge under this paragraph.
8.2 Staff members have the right to be notified in writing of the grounds for disciplinary action.

Staff Rule 8.01 expanding on the implementation of these measures has not been issued. The Staff Regulations and Staff Rules of many other organizations have at least some provisions on disciplinary measures.[6]

---

[3] See Appendix VI *infra.*
[4] See Appendix VI *infra.*
[5] See Appendix VII *infra.*
[6] See, e.g., Article X of the Staff Regulations and Staff Rules 1110 and 1130 of the WHO:

The fact that the written law of so many international institutions has fairly extensive provisions on disciplinary measures testifies at the same time to the importance attached to such measures in the administration of such institutions and also to the need to have well-defined rules relating to such measures, particularly for the protection of staff members. In spite of the solicitude reflected in the extensive nature of the provisions of the written law of organizations on the subject, international administrative tribunals have often been asked to interpret and apply these provisions, because they do not always provide the answers to problems that have arisen. Though, because of the explicitness of the written law, tribunals have less often than in other fields had to invoke general principles of law in the application of the law relating to disciplinary measures, they have certainly had to apply such general principles where the written law has had lacunae, they have interpreted the written law in light of such general principles, and they have had to ensure that the written law has been properly followed. Tribunals have generally shown a special concern for the protection of the rights of staff members in this area, because it touches a very important and sensitive aspect of the lives and careers of staff members in international organizations. What is of importance is that tribunals have not been reluctant to afford remedies where there is the slightest hint of a violation of the law.

The basic approach

So important a place does the issue of taking disciplinary measures occupy in the law of the international civil service that tribunals have generally tended to take a special basic approach to it. Whereas most decisions taken by the administration of international organizations in relation to the service of staff members are generally regarded as taken in the course of exercising discretionary powers, with certain definite consequences, decisions taken in regard to disciplinary measures have not generally been regarded in exactly the same way with the same consequences. Thus, for example, the decision taken by the administrative authority to terminate permanent employment for unsatisfactory service or to transfer or promote a staff member is treated as the exercise of a discretionary power with the consequence that a tribunal has a limited power of review over the exercise of that power. On the other hand, while the decision to impose disciplinary measures appears to be

---

Amerasinghe (ed.), 1 *Staff Regulations and Staff Rules of Selected International Organizations* (1983) p. 118 at p. 173 ff.; Chapter X of the Staff Regulations and Staff Rules of UNESCO: Amerasinghe (ed.) 2 ibid. p. 2 at pp. 70 ff.; Article XI of the Staff Regulations and Staff Rules of IAEA: Amerasinghe (ed.), 2 ibid. p. 80 at pp. 156 ff.; Articles 86–9 of the Staff Regulations of the European Communities: Amerasinghe (ed.), 4 ibid. p. 1 at pp. 26 ff.; Chapter XI of the Staff Rules of the OAS: Amerasinghe (ed.), 3 ibid. p. 215 at pp. 267 ff.

similar to a decision to terminate employment for unsatisfactory service or to transfer or promote a staff member in that it involves the exercise of a discretion to take a certain kind of action, the tendency has been to treat the decision to impose disciplinary measures as one which is taken in the exercise of a quasi-judicial power to impose sanctions or penalties for offences as opposed to the exercise of executive discretion, with the result that the consequences for the exercise of control by tribunals are different.

In a case concerning two reprimands which under the Staff Regulations and Staff Rules of FAO were not included among the disciplinary measures available and were, therefore, less than disciplinary measures the ILOAT said:

A warning or reprimand must be based on unsatisfactory conduct since what it is saying in effect is that if the conduct is repeated a disciplinary measure may be taken. But whereas in the case of censure which is of a disciplinary nature the Tribunal exercises full power of review as to the facts and the law because of the protection which staff members of the organization should enjoy, when the measure takes the form of a reprimand which is not of a disciplinary nature the Tribunal will exercise a limited power of review. That is to say, the Tribunal will not interfere unless the measure was taken without authority, or violates a rule of form or procedure, or is based on an error of fact or of law, or if essential facts have not been taken into consideration, or if it is tainted with abuse of authority, or if a clearly mistaken conclusion has been drawn from the facts.[7]

This statement makes a clear distinction between censure which is a disciplinary measure and reprimand which is less than a disciplinary measure. What was said of censure, as a disciplinary measure, would certainly be applicable to all disciplinary measures, particularly because censure was under the written law of the FAO the least of the disciplinary measures. Thus, it emerges that the ILOAT was of the view that in the case of disciplinary measures it had a full power of review over both facts and law. In other words it did not act merely as a tribunal of limited review. Had the imposition of disciplinary measures been regarded as the exercise of just another discretionary power, the tribunal would have had the power only to review the exercise of that power in the event that there had been an abuse of discretion, that is, in the limited situations referred to by the ILOAT.

In a more restricted exercise the Appeals Board of NATO said that, because the Personnel Regulations of NATO provided that dismissal was a disciplinary measure taken in the case of serious misconduct by a staff

---

[7] *Connolly-Battisti (No. 2)*, ILOAT Judgment No. 274 [1976] (FAO). A different view of the powers of tribunals to review decisions relating to disciplinary measures is implied in Akehurst, *The Law Governing Employment in International Organizations* (1967) pp. 141 ff., and de Vuyst, 'The Use of Discretionary Authority by International Organizations in their Relations with International Civil Servants', 12 *Denver Journal of International Law and Policy* (1983) p. 237 at pp. 246 ff.

member, the tribunal could judge whether the disciplinary action taken against the applicant in the case was founded in fact on serious misconduct.[8] While this statement deals with serious misconduct and dismissal which are the most heinous cffence and the most serious penalty and refers only to the establishment of the charge involved, it does not regard the decision as to whether there is serious misconduct as taken in the exercise of a discretionary power, as in the case, for instance, with the decision whether services are unsatisfactory or whether a promotion or transfer is appropriate. Thus, the Appeals Board of NATO did not regard its powers in respect of the establishment of the charges as being merely those of a court of limited review. This is in keeping with the view that in disciplinary matters an international administrative tribunal may fully review the administrative decision and not merely review in a limited manner what may be regarded as the exercise of a discretionary power. While the tribunal did not pronounce on the nature of its powers in regard to disciplinary decisions in general, its approach would warrant the conclusion that it had similar judicial powers in dealing with these to those it had in dealing with the determination that there had been serious misconduct. In other cases[9] its actions have supported this conclusion and there is nothing, on the other hand, in its decisions to contradict it. Indeed, in one case it held that the penalty imposed was not warranted by the offence committed.[10]

The readiness of tribunals to substitute their own judgments for those of administrative authorities in disciplinary cases instead of treating them as instances of the exercise of discretionary power has been demonstrated by the methodology followed in decisions taken by several tribunals, apart from the ILOAT and the Appeals Board of NATO. In *Gordon* the UNAT examined fully the conduct of the applicant as a result of which he had been summarily dismissed and found that:

Whatever view may be held as to the conduct of the Applicant, that conduct could not be described as serious misconduct which alone under Article 10.2 of the Staff Regulations and the pertinent Rules justifies the Secretary General in dismissing a staff member summarily without the safeguard afforded by the disciplinary procedure.[11]

The tribunal also expressed a judgment on how the penalty of summary dismissal should be inflicted without referring to any element of discretion

---

[8] *Decision No. 4*, NATO Appeals Board [1967], Collections of the Decisions (1972) at pp. 3–4.

[9] See *Decision No. 10*, NATO Appeals Board [1968], Collection of the Decisions (1972); *Decision No. 29*, NATO Appeals Board [1971], ibid.; *Decision No. 31*, NATO Appeals Board [1971], ibid.; *Decision No. 71*, NATO Appeals Board [1976], Collection of the Decisions 46 to 73 (1976).

[10] *Decision No. 31*, NATO Appeals Board [1971], Collection of the Decisions (1972).

[11] UNAT Judgment No. 29 [1953], JUNAT Nos. 1–70 p. 120 at p. 126.

when it said: 'Except in cases of agreement between the person concerned and the administration, the disciplinary procedure should be dispensed with only in those cases were the misconduct is patent and where the interest of the service requires immediate and final separation.[12] In a later case the UNAT referred to serious misconduct as being misconduct committed in the exercise of a staff member's professional duties or acts committed outside his professional activities but prohibited by provisions creating general obligations for staff members and held that it was called upon to consider whether the allegations made constituted serious misconduct justifying his summary dismissal without reference to the Joint Disciplinary Committee.[13] The case concerned the use of official channels to circulate a private document in such a way that it appeared to be an official document. The tribunal made a lengthy examination of the facts and came to the conclusion on its own that the conduct of the applicant warranted summary dismissal.[14]

In *Alvis*[15] the CJEC found that there was a procedural defect in the application of disciplinary measures involving dismissal but examined the facts and held that the charges brought against the applicant were supported by the facts so that the dismissal could not be questioned, thus confirming the action taken by the administration because it was justified on the facts of the case, even though there had been a procedural defect.[16]

The Appeals Boards of the OEEC[17] and the ESA[18] have also followed the methodology referred to above.

The ILOAT has adopted the procedure of arriving at its own determination of the case both on the facts and the law in several other cases. In *Giannini*[19] the tribunal examined the facts and found that the applicant was under the Staff Regulations and Staff Rules of FAO guilty of such serious misconduct as to warrant summary dismissal. In *Diaz de Borsody*[20] the applicant raised only the issue of procedural irregularity on which she failed but the tribunal went out of its way to hold that, although the applicant had not argued the merits of the case, the written censure which was given her by FAO on the ground of insubordination was justified on the facts of the case, as they had been established.[21]

---

[12] Ibid. For other cases in which *Gordon* was followed see *Svenchansky, Harris, Eldridge, Glassman, Older, Bancroft, Elveson,* and *Reed*, UNAT Judgments Nos. 30 to 37 [1953], JUNAT Nos. 1–70 pp. 128, 135, 144, 151, 160, 168, 176, 184.

[13] *Gillead*, UNAT Judgment No. 104 [1967], JUNAT Nos. 87–113 p. 176 at p. 186.

[14] See also *Wallach*, UNAT Judgment No. 53 [1954], JUNAT Nos. 1–70 p. 260.

[15] CJEC Case 32/62 [1963] ECR p. 49.

[16] See also *Fonzi*, CJEC Cases 27 & 30/64 [1965] ECR p. 481; *Gutmann*, CJEC Cases 18 & 35/65 [1966] ECR p. 103.

[17] *Decision No. 27*, OEEC Appeals Board [1957], Recueil des décisions 1 à 62 [1979] p. 76.

[18] *Decision No. 13*, *ESA/CR/32*, ESA Appeals Board [1980].

[19] ILOAT Judgment No. 79 [1964] (FAO).

[20] ILOAT Judgment No. 511 [1982] (FAO).

[21] See also *Amonfio*, ILOAT Judgment No. 539 [1982] (WHO); *Hickel*, ILOAT Judgment

There have, however, been a few cases (decided by the UNAT principally) in which a different view than that taken above has been adopted. For a tribunal to take the view that, where a measure which is less than a disciplinary measure according to the written law of the organization is in issue, it will treat that measure as the exercise of a discretionary power pure and simple[22] creates no problem. But there have been cases involving misconduct resulting in disciplinary sanctions in which the tribunal appears to have concluded that the power to take disciplinary action was a discretionary one subject only to limited review. In *Roy* that UNAT said that the power to determine whether there had been misconduct was a wide discretionary one.[23] This view was supported in *Reid* where the tribunal stated:

The Tribunal observes that the reports of the Joint Disciplinary Committee and of the Joint Appeals Board are advisory and that the Respondent is entitled to reach a different conclusion from that of those bodies on a consideration of all the facts and circumstances of the case. However, the Tribunal is competent to review the Respondent's decision if such decision is based on a mistake of facts or is arbitrary or is motivated by prejudice or by other extraneous considerations.[24]

In *Archibald*[25] the tribunal held that a decision summarily to dismiss the applicant for serious misconduct was within the discretion of the administration and would only be reviewed if it was arbitrary, based on a mistake of facts, or improperly motivated.[26]

In *Roy* it was found that there had been a procedural defect which vitiated the decision to impose disciplinary sanctions, so that the view taken of the tribunal's power of review would not have made a difference to the outcome of the case. But in the other three cases the tribunal applied the law relating to discretionary powers and found that the applicant had no case. If the view that a total review of the exercise of the power to impose disciplinary sanctions had been adopted in these cases, it is not clear how they would have been decided.

In a recent case, *Lakey*,[27] the ILOAT also stated that, while absence

---

No. 5 [1947] (IIIC); *Andreski*, ILOAT Judgment No. 63 [1962] (UNESCO); *Di Giuliomaria*, ILOAT Judgment No. 87 [1965] (FAO); *Jurado (No. 17)*, ILOAT Judgment No. 96 [1966] (ILO); *Jurado (Nos. 12 & 13)*, ILOAT Judgment No. 111 [1967] (ILO); *Nair*, ILOAT Judgment No. 170 [1970] (FAO); *Flad*, ILOAT Judgment No. 172 [1971] (WHO); *George*, ILOAT Judgment No. 237 [1974] (FAO); *Diaz Acevedo*, ILOAT Judgment No. 349 [1978] (ESO); *Hagan*, ILOAT Judgment No. 540 [1982] (WHO). In all these cases the tribunal pronounced on the whole case *de novo*.

[22] See *Connolly-Battisti (No. 2)*, ILOAT Judgment No. 274 [1976] (FAO); *Connolly-Battisti (No. 6)*, ILOAT Judgment No. 420 [1980] (FAO). Both cases concerned reprimands.

[23] UNAT Judgment No. 123 [1968] (ICAO), JUNAT Nos. 114–166 p. 89 at p. 102.

[24] UNAT Judgment No. 210 [1976], JUNAT Nos. 167–230 p. 396 at p. 407.

[25] UNAT Judgment No. 222 [1977], ibid. p. 522.

[26] See also *Hecquet*, UNAT Judgment No. 322 [1984] at p. 8, which also concerned a case of serious misconduct and where a similar view of the law was taken.

[27] ILOAT Judgment No. 475 [1982] (CIPEC) at p. 5.

without justification was an offence subject to disciplinary sanctions which included, among others, dismissal from the service, the written law contained imprecise terms which resulted in the administration's having a discretion to interpret those terms. This discretion would be reviewed by the tribunal in the usual way, if the discretion were abused.

It should be noted that *Lakey* concerned a disciplinary sanction for misconduct and not serious misconduct. Thus, it seems to be settled that in cases of serious misconduct involving summary dismissal, at least, the ILOAT and the other tribunals, except the UNAT, are likely to regard the exercise of the power to take disciplinary measures as the exercise of a quasi-judicial power which is totally subject to review by the tribunal and not merely as the exercise of a discretionary power. Even in the case of misconduct which is not treated as serious misconduct resulting in summary dismissal the approach that has better support in the decisions, except in those of the UNAT, would regard the power to impose disciplinary sanctions as a quasi-judicial power which is subject to total review by the tribunal, *Lakey* being the only case which contradicts this approach. It is difficult to distinguish *Lakey* from the other cases on the basis that the written law contained imprecise terms, as this is a general problem that could arise in connection with applying the law relating to disciplinary measures, since, indeed, the exercise of the power to take disciplinary measures would involve the application of rules which may contain vague and general terms requiring a choice on the part of the administration.

While it is possible to say that in the case of tribunals other than the UNAT there is, in spite of *Lakey*, sufficiently strong authority to support the view that they would generally exercise full judicial control over the power of administrations to take disciplinary measures and not treat such powers merely as discretionary powers, the position of the UNAT is less clear. It is not possible for the purpose to make a distinction on the basis of the cases decided by the UNAT between serious misconduct involving summary dismissal and misconduct, since the more recent cases which treat the power to impose disciplinary sanctions as simply a discretionary power deal with both. On the other hand, the cases decided by the UNAT which treat the power as subject to full control are, first, early cases and, second, deal entirely with cases of serious misconduct involving summary dismissal. It may be possible to distinguish between those cases which deal with misconduct and those concerning serious misconduct involving summary dismissal. Thus, it would be possible to say that the position of the UNAT in regard to cases concerning misconduct, as opposed to serious misconduct involving summary dismissal, is to regard the power as purely a discretionary power the exercise of which is subject to limited review by the UNAT. The conflict that exists in the cases decided by the UNAT relates, therefore, to the situation where serious misconduct involving summary dismissal is in issue.

The early cases tend to regard cases of serious misconduct resulting in summary dismissal as subject to total judicial review, while the later cases treat them as subject only to limited review by the tribunal. Thus, the position of the UNAT can be described as doubtful in regard to cases involving serious misconduct resulting in summary dismissal, while in regard to cases of simple misconduct it seems to be established that the UNAT will treat the power to take disciplinary measures as a discretionary power the exercise of which is subject to limited review by the tribunal. The UNAT is in a minority of one among the tribunals which have had to deal with disciplinary issues but its position has to be recognized. It is a significant departure from what seems to be the norm.

Serious misconduct involving summary dismissal or other penalties

The definition of serious misconduct will depend to a large extent on the written law of the organization. Even where the written law does not specifically define serious misconduct, it will depend on other provisions of the written law whether there has been conduct on the part of the staff member, such as breach of his obligations, which can be characterized as serious misconduct. In any case the decision whether there has been serious misconduct may involve judgment and a discretionary element. In most cases tribunals have examined the written law and the exercise of judgment and decided whether in the given cases there had been serious misconduct. It is only in *Archibald*[28] that the UNAT treated the decision as to the existence of serious misconduct as involving the exercise of discretionary power which the tribunal would review in a limited way. In this event the decision that there has been serious misconduct will only be upset if there has been an abuse of discretion: which in *Archibald* was not proved, since the applicant had not even pleaded an abuse of discretion.

In *Andreski* the ILOAT stated that, while the Staff Regulations and Staff Rules of UNESCO provided for summary dismissal, this did not mean termination of service without notice but a termination of service which had not been preceded by a recommendation made by an administrative organ in which the staff was represented.[29] Since the administration had ordered the dismissal after consulting a special committee which was not a joint disciplinary committee provided for in the written law for cases of misconduct, the dismissal was summary and could only be for serious misconduct. Thus, it is the nature of the procedure—that is, the fact that the procedure is not the one required for the imposition of disciplinary sanctions for ordinary

---

[28] UNAT Judgment No. 222 [1977], JUNAT Nos. 167–230 p. 522.
[29] ILOAT Judgment No. 63 [1962] (UNESCO) at p. 3.

misconduct—that determines whether there has been action taken; such as a summary dismissal, which can only be taken in cases of serious misconduct. This is the situation in regard to the written law of most organizations.

In the same case the ILOAT defined serious misconduct in the following terms:

As this is the heaviest penalty which can be inflicted, and can be applied without prior consultation with a joint body, this provision must not be given a broad interpretation. It applies to an official who, in the first place, fails in his duty and, in the second place, thereby commits serious misconduct.[30]

The tribunal then stated: 'It is, therefore, necessary to consider whether the conditions on which the validity of such an action depends were complied with, i.e., whether complianant failed in his duty and was thus guilty of serious misconduct.[31] Finally, it came to the conclusion that:

Complainant's approaches to national authorities, institutions and persons suffice on their own to justify the penalty he incurred. On the one hand, he failed to comply with several of his obligations under the Staff Regulations and Staff Rules: by accusing one of his colleagues of incapacity and subversion in statements directed to persons and agencies outside the Organization, he brought the international civil service into disrepute, contrary to Regulation No. 1.4; by communicating to third parties information on official matters which had not been publicised in any way, he acted contrary to the duty of discretion defined by Regulation No. 1.5; and on the other hand, by letting it be supposed that U.N.E.S.C.O. had employed and was maintaining in its employment an expert devoid of the necessary qualifications and guilty of acting in a manner incompatible with his position, he harmed the interests of the Organization contrary to the solemn undertaking to which he had subscribed in accordance with Regulation No. 1.9 when he accepted appointment.[32]

Sometimes the Staff Regulations and Staff Rules themselves give an explanation of serious misconduct which must then be satisfied, in order that the conduct may lawfully be treated as serious misconduct. Thus, the FAO Administrative Manual required that the conduct be so serious that it had jeopardized or was likely to jeopardize the reputation of the organization and its staff.[33]

In several other cases the ILOAT has examined the facts and come to the conclusion that there had been serious misconduct on the part of the applicant which justified summary dismissal. In *Gianini*[34] the applicant, an accountant in the FAO, had taken funds from his colleagues for the purpose

[30] Ibid.
[31] Ibid.
[32] Ibid. at p. 4.
[33] Article 330.251. This provision does not exist in this form in the current Staff Rules of FAO. The provision was also applied in *Di Giuliomaria*, ILOAT Judgment No. 87 [1965] (FAO).
[34] ILOAT Judgment No. 79 [1964] (FAO).

of transferring them abroad and converting them into foreign exchange and had failed to do so, had misappropriated petrol coupons, and had induced a colleague to lend him a large sum of money without disclosing his true financial situation and that the debt could really not be repaid within the promised time. The ILOAT held that this conduct which also showed that his management of his personal affairs was bad and which had been established to the satisfaction of the tribunal was serious misconduct warranting summary dismissal. Trafficking in foreign currency through the diplomatic pouch has been held to be serious misconduct of this nature.[35]

There are some cases in which the ILOAT has found that the conduct of the applicant was not serious misconduct warranting dismissal and found for the applicant. In *Di Giuliomaria*,[36] for example, the applicant who was a member of the Staff Association and its representative on a Special Salary Committee had drafted and circulated to members of the General Assembly of FAO a statement which was critical of actions of the Director General of FAO and of the Staff Council. His language was moderate. This was held not to be serious misconduct warranting summary dismissal.[37]

Other tribunals have also adverted to the issue of serious misconduct and applied the law to the facts to find that there was or was not serious misconduct warranting summary dismissal. In *Gordon* and some other cases decided at the same time the UNAT said:

Misconduct punishable under article 10 could also be either misconduct committed in the exercise of a staff member's professional duties or acts committed outside his professional activities but prohibited by provisions creating general obligations for staff members. . . . Except in cases of agreement between the person concerned and the administration, the disciplinary procedure should be dispensed with only in those cases where the misconduct is patent and where the interest of the service required immediate and final separation.[38]

In these cases the UNAT ruled that refusal by pleading the Fifth Amendment to the Constitution to give evidence before a Senate Subcommittee of the US

---

[35] *Bhandari*, ILOAT Judgment No. 159 [1970] (WHO). See also *Sood*, ILOAT Judgment No. 160 [1970] (WHO); *Sethi*, ILOAT Judgment No. 161 [1970] (WHO); *Raj Kumar*, ILOAT Judgment No. 162 [1970] (WHO). Other cases decided by the ILOAT in which serious misconduct has been found to exist are *Nair*, ILOAT Judgment No. 170 [1970] (FAO); *Amonfio*, ILOAT Judgment No. 539 [1982] (WHO); *Jurado (No. 17)*, ILOAT Judgment No. 96 [1966] (ILO); *Jurado (Nos. 12 & 13)*, ILOAT Judgment No. 111 [1967] (ILO).

[36] ILOAT Judgment No. 87 [1965] (FAO).

[37] See also *Diaz Acevedo*, ILOAT Judgment No. 349 [1978] (ESO).

[38] *Gordon*, UNAT Judgment No. 29 [1953], JUNAT Nos. 1–70 p. 120 at pp. 125–6. See also *Svenchansky*, *Harris*, *Eldridge*, *Glassman*, *Older*, *Bancroft*, *Elveson*, and *Reed*, UNAT Judgments Nos. 30 to 37 [1953], JUNAT Nos. 1–70 p. 128 at pp. 133–4, p. 135 at p. 141, p. 144 at pp. 149–50, p. 151 at p. 157, p. 160 at pp. 165–6, p. 168 at p. 174, p. 176 at pp. 181–2, p. 184 at pp. 189–90. See also *Gillead*, UNAT Judgment No. 104 [1967], JUNAT Nos. 87–113 p. 176 at p. 186, which was decided later.

by a US national was not serious misconduct warranting summary dismissal.[39]

In *Decision No. 4*[40] a staff member was dismissed for disclosing information in a note which he typed. The Appeals Board of NATO held that it could determine whether there was serious misconduct warranting dismissal and found that the breach of confidence was not serious enough to justify the dismissal. In *Decision No. 10*,[41] on the other hand, the Appeals Board of NATO found that the facts established showed that there was misconduct serious enough to warrant dismissal.

In *Gutmann*[42] the CJEC was confronted not with summary dismissal but with a suspension which could only be ordered for serious misconduct. The Court made it quite clear that the administration must state its complaints properly in order to allow the Court to carry out its review, in particular as regards the seriousness of the misconduct, thus confirming that it took the view that it could examine the facts and establish on its own whether the charge of serious misconduct had been proved. The Court found that the complaints, as stated, did not show any such conduct as could have been characterized as serious misconduct.

Where the UNAT has taken the approach of treating the decision to impose disciplinary sanctions purely as an exercise of discretionary power, it has, nevertheless, made statements similar to those it made earlier in *Gordon* relating to the nature of the conduct to be characterized as serious misconduct,[43] although it has refused to examine the facts and substitute its own judgment for the decision of the administration on the issue. It found in the case in question, *Archibald*, that there was no plea by the applicant of abuse of discretion so that an examination of the case was precluded.

Where tribunals have had to decide whether the conduct of applicants had been properly found to amount to serious misconduct, they have either applied the provisions of the written law relating to the definition of serious misconduct or made an assessment themselves of whether the finding was appropriate by reference to general principles of law. No clear definition of serious misconduct emerges in the absence of provision in the written law.

---

[39] In *Wallach*, UNAT Judgment No. 53 [1954], JUNAT Nos. 1–70 p. 260, serious misconduct was found to lie in a failure by the applicant to answer questions relating to his application for employment, although the applicant argued that his failure to give evidence before a Senate Subcommittee of the US, as the applicant had done in *Gordon*, was not serious misconduct.

[40] *Decision No. 4*, NATO Appeals Board [1967], Collection of the Decisions (1972).

[41] *Decision No. 10*, NATO Appeals Board [1968], Collection of the Decisions (1972).

[42] CJEC Cases 18 & 35/65 [1966] ECR p. 103 at p. 116.

[43] *Archibald*, UNAT Judgment No. 222 [1977], JUNAT Nos. 167–230 p. 522 at p. 527.

Review of disciplinary measures for misconduct

In reviewing the decision to impose disciplinary sanctions for misconduct, whether the tribunal concerned takes the view that the decision is subject to total review by the tribunal or it favours the approach that the decision was taken in the exercise of a discretionary power which is subject to limited review by the tribunal, it has been the practice to examine the cases in terms of concepts which have been developed largely in relation to the exercise of discretionary powers. This is partly because cases have been pleaded in those terms and for reasons of convenience. Suffice it to say that, where appropriate, a tribunal which follows the procedure of total review of the decision taken will theoretically not hesitate to substitute its own judgment for that of the administration, when it deems it necessary to do so, in order to carry out its function of totally reviewing the decision. In any case it would only be necessary to do this where the tribunal finds that the applicant has not succeeded in showing that the defects relevant to the control of the exercise of discretionary powers exist and the tribunal, nevertheless, thinks that the decision was wrong in substance. Further, where the case is pleaded in terms of the concepts relevant to the control of the exercise of discretionary powers, it appears that tribunals will not, when they find for the respondent in general, necessarily examine the case on its merits. They limit themselves to the pleas. Sometimes, the nature of the plea makes it unnecessary to examine the merits, but if the applicant wants his case examined on the merits, he must make the appropriate plea. This seems to be an important limitation, imposed by the approach taken by tribunals, on the powers of tribunals to review totally a decision on disciplinary sanctions.

In one of the few cases in which the decision to take disciplinary measures has been treated as the exercise of a discretionary power the tribunal has referred to abuse of discretion as the ground for upsetting the decision. Thus, in *Lakey*[44] the ILOAT, in examining the case, referred to the fact that there had been no abuse of discretion. In *Reid*, as already seen, the UNAT explained that the competence of the tribunal was limited to reviewing the decision of the respondent, if it was based on a mistake of facts, or was arbitrary, or was motivated by prejudice or by other extraneous considerations.[45] In the three cases in which the tribunals took the view that they could only make a limited review of the decision to impose disciplinary measures for misconduct as such and found that there had been no abuse of discretion, there is no way to conjecture how the cases might have turned out, had the tribunals carried out a total review of the decision. In *Reid* the UNAT held that there had been no abuse of discretion, because due process had been

---

[44] ILOAT Judgment No. 475 [1982] (CIPEC).
[45] UNAT Judgment No. 210 [1976], JUNAT Nos. 167–230 p. 396 at p. 407.

accorded the applicant. In *Hecquet*[46] also it was found that there had been no absence of due process, but it was further said that there was no error of fact or any other flaw. In *Lakey* the ILOAT found that the competent authority had made the decision, there was no irregular procedure, no error of fact, no error of law, no omission of essential facts, no mistaken conclusions, and no improper motive or discrimination.

It would be appropriate to examine the various heads under which the facts of cases brought before tribunals have been considered.

Détournement de pouvoir

It is possible that disciplinary measures be found unlawful by reason of *détournement de pouvoir* but, although the issue has been raised in several cases, there are few in which tribunals have found the existence of *détournement de pouvoir*.

(a) Improper motive or prejudice

In *Lakey* the applicant argued that, while she had been dismissed from service for being absent from office without excuse, the real reason for her dismissal was that she had complained about the difference between her salary and that of one of her colleagues. The applicant failed because on the facts it was apparent that her dismissal had been the result of her being absent from office or that there had been no improper motive.[47]

(b) Discrimination and inequality of treatment

The argument of inequality of treatment has been raised in connection with disciplinary sanctions but without success. In *Khelifati*[48] the applicant argued that, while he had been dismissed from service for being drunk on duty, several other staff members who had also been drunk on duty had not been punished. The ILOAT held that this would not result in inequality of treatment, even if it were proved, because the rule of equal treatment may not be properly applicable to staff members against whom disciplinary action has been taken or may be taken for different reasons and in different circumstances.[49]

---

[46] UNAT Judgment No. 322 [1984].

[47] See also *Sheye*, UNAT Judgment No. 300 [1982], JUNAT Nos. 231–300 p. 655.

[48] ILOAT Judgment No. 207 [1973] (UNESCO).

[49] See also *Lakey*, ILOAT Judgment No. 475 [1982] (CIPEC), where the argument of discrimination failed.

(c) *Proportionality*

The question of proportionality has been adverted to in an earlier chapter[50] where cases concerning disciplinary proceedings have been discussed. While it has generally been conceded that tribunals will entertain the issue whether the disciplinary sanction imposed is proportionate to the offence committed and declare invalid the decision taken to impose the sanction, if the sanction is, in the opinion of the tribunal concerned, out of proportion to the offence committed,[51] the Appeals Board of ESA did in one case say that the tribunal would not substitute its judgment for that of the administration in regard to the question whether the sanction imposed was proportionate to the offence committed.[52] The Appeals Board of the ESA appears to be the only tribunal that takes this view. The opposite view is better supported by the authorities and is in keeping with the principle that the means must be appropriate to the objective to be achieved.

There are some other cases than those discussed in the earlier chapter worth mentioning in which the ILOAT has held that the disciplinary sanction imposed was out of proportion to the offence committed. In *Diaz Acevedo*[53] the applicant was accused of disrespect. The tribunal held that the degree of disrespect, if proved, was not sufficient to warrant summary dismissal for serious misconduct, a reprimand being completely adequate. This was a case concerning summary dismissal for serious misconduct.

In *George*,[54] on the other hand, the ILOAT held that, where the administration had found the applicant guilty of two charges and it was clear that there was no basis for one charge, the other charge of taking an official car for private use and returning it damaged was sufficient to justify the penalty of dismissal.[55]

The imposition of a mild penalty, such as a reprimand, for a serious infringement of official duties cannot be questioned on the ground that it was not in proportion to the offence committed, since such action may be warranted for various reasons, including the fact that it was the first time that the applicant had committed an offence.[56]

[50] See *supra*, Vol. I Ch. 21 pp. 292 ff.
[51] See also *Diabasana*, ILOAT Judgment No. 345 [1978] (WHO); *van Eick*, CJEC Case 13/69 [1970] ECR p. 3.
[52] *Decision No. 8, ESA/CR/20*, ESA Appeals Board [1978].
[53] ILOAT Judgment No. 349 [1978] (ESO). In *Connolly-Battisti (No. 7)*, ILOAT Judgment No. 403 [1980] (FAO), a formal warning of severe disciplinary measures was in issue. The tribunal held that a warning of this nature was not a disciplinary measure and could be given at the discretion of the Director General of FAO, but subject to the principle of proportionality. Even if the offence of using official stationery for Staff-Association activities had been established, the tribunal held that such a formal warning was out of proportion to the offence committed.
[54] ILOAT Judgment No. 237 [1974] (FAO).
[55] See also *Hagan*, ILOAT Judgment No. 540 [1982] (WHO).
[56] *Fonzi*, CJEC Cases 27 & 30/64 [1965] ECR p. 481.

(d) Non bis in idem

The rule *non bis in idem* has also been applied to disciplinary measures, as was seen in the earlier chapter referred to above. There are a few more cases which may be considered. In *Gutmann*,[57] after a suspension had been quashed by the CJEC in an earlier judgment, the administrative authority issued the applicant a reprimand and instituted fresh proceedings. The tribunal found that the complaints in the second proceedings were very general and that the facts were not so clearly defined as to distinguish them from the grounds of complaint which formed the basis for the earlier suspension. Thus, it was held that the rule *non bis in idem* had been violated and the decision to institute the fresh proceedings was tainted. On the other hand, where a charge had been brought by the administration of ESA and the dispute had been settled by the conclusion of an agreement between the applicant and the administration which the applicant later refused to honour, it was held by the Appeals Board of ESA that the revival of the proceedings against the applicant on the same charge was not a violation of the rule that there should not be double jeopardy.[58]

(e) Détournement de procédure

In *van Eick*[59] the applicant contended that he had been dismissed for disciplinary reasons in circumstances in which the real reason for the dismissal was a reduction in force, in respect of which the proper procedures had, therefore, not been followed. The CJEC found that the taking of disciplinary measures in the circumstances of the case was justified, so that there was no *détournement de procédure*.[60] There have been numerous cases, whether involving dismissal or transfer or some other administrative action, in which the applicant has unsuccessfully argued that there had been a *détournement de procédure*, because the situation required that disciplinary proceedings should have been taken rather than that the procedure actually followed be followed.[61] In these cases the facts showed that the procedure followed was lawfully chosen by the administrative authority.

In a few cases the applicant has succeeded in showing that a disciplinary procedure should have been instituted in connection with the action taken. In

[57] CJEC Cases 18 & 35/65 [1967] ECR p. 61.
[58] *Decision No. 8, ESA/CR/20*, ESA Appeals Board [1978].
[59] CJEC Case 13/69 [1970] ECR p. 3.
[60] See also *Perinciolo*, CJEC Case 124/75 [1976] ECR p. 1953.
[61] See *supra*, Vol. I Ch. 21 pp. 277 ff. and in particular *Cuenca*, OASAT Judgment No. 53 [1980]; *Reynolds*, ILOAT Judgment No. 38 [1958] (FAO); *Nowakowski (No. 4)*, ILOAT Judgment No. 248 [1975] (WMO); *Scuppa*, CJEC Cases 4 & 30/74 [1975] ECR p. 919; *Mills*, CJEC Case 110/75 [1976] ECR p. 1613.

Gutmann,[62] for instance, the CJEC found that the real reason for a transfer appeared to be a disciplinary one so that disciplinary proceedings should have been instituted before the action was taken.[63]

In *Vecchioli*[64] the CJEC held that where there was incompetence, the official might be dismissed or downgraded for incompetence without disciplinary proceedings being taken, even if the attitude of the official on the facts would have led to disciplinary proceedings. The decision is in keeping with the principle that where there are two procedures available on the facts of the case, either one may be chosen by the administrative authority.[65]

Substantive irregularities

There are several cases in which contentions relating to substantive irregularities in the taking of the decision to impose disciplinary sanctions have been raised, sometimes successfully and sometimes unsuccessfully.

(a) Competent authority

In two cases it was unsuccessfully argued that the official who had signed the order imposing the sanction was not the authority competent to take the decision to impose the sanction. Where the Deputy Director General of FAO and not the Director General had signed the order, the ILOAT held that, while it was desirable that the Director General sign the order, it was in order for the Deputy Director General to sign it, as in this case he probably initiated the action to issue the reprimand.[66] In this case it was clear that the reprimand was not a disciplinary sanction according to the written law of FAO but the principle would probably remain valid for disciplinary sanctions. In *Lakey*[67] it was required by the written law of CIPEC that the disciplinary sanction be imposed by the Executive Director of CIPEC and not by the Secretary General. The Secretary General had signed the order imposing the sanction of dismissal from the service. The ILOAT held that, since the Secretary General had acted as the Executive Director in making the order of dismissal, there was no incompetence on his part to make the order.

---

62 CJEC Cases 18 & 35/65 [1966] ECR p. 103.
63 See also *Guillot*, CJEC Case 53/72 [1974] ECR p. 791.
64 CJEC Case 101/79 [1980] ECR p. 3069.
65 See *supra*, Vol. I Ch. 21 pp. 281 ff.
66 *Connolly-Battisti (No. 6)*, ILOAT Judgment No. 420 [1980] (FAO).
67 ILOAT Judgment No. 475 [1982] (CIPEC).

(b) Error of Law

In *Lakey*[68] it was held by the ILOAT that, where dismissal from the service had been chosen as a sanction for the absence of the applicant from office, the administrative authority of CIPEC had not committed an error of law in so doing, because the written law permitted in such a case the free choice of one of four possible sanctions, including dismissal from the service.[69]

(c) Error of fact

In several cases tribunals have held that administrative authorities have in conducting disciplinary proceedings committed errors of fact which have vitiated the decision taken. In *Pollicino*[70] the applicant was accused of behaving indiscreetly by disclosing to the press information about her case which was being investigated. She denied having done this. The ILOAT held that the burden shifted to the respondent to prove its allegation and that, while absolute proof was not required, a set of precise and concurring presumptions being adequate, the respondent had failed to make out its case and, therefore, its conclusion was unwarranted. In *Campitelli*[71] the ILOAT was confronted with an allegation that the applicant was guilty of a theft of chains. There were arguments in favour of the finding and arguments against it, which, however, in the view of the tribunal, cancelled out each other. Therefore, it was held that there was no proof of the allegation and that the decision to impose a disciplinary sanction was vitiated by an error of fact.[72]

In some cases the argument that an error of fact had been committed has been rejected. In *Khelifati*,[73] for instance, the ILOAT held that, while it was not for the accused to prove the falsity of the charges against him that he was drunk on duty, there was no evidence to disprove the two witnesses on whom the administration of UNESCO had relied, so that there was no error of fact.[74]

[68] Ibid.

[69] See also *Decision No. 71*, NATO Appeals Board [1976], Collection of the Decisions 46 to 73 (1976), where there was found to be an error of law which vitiated the decision to impose a disciplinary sanction.

[70] ILOAT Judgment No. 635 [1984] (FAO).

[71] ILOAT Judgment No. 640 [1984] (FAO).

[72] See also *Flad*, ILOAT Judgment No. 172 [1971] (WHO); *Zang-Atangana*, UNAT Judgment No. 130 [1969], JUNAT Nos. 114–166 p. 155; *Connolly-Battisti (No. 7)*, ILOAT Judgment No. 403 [1980] (FAO).

[73] ILOAT Judgment No. 207 [1973] (UNESCO).

[74] See also *Hecquet*, UNAT Judgment No. 322 [1984]; *Lakey*, ILOAT Judgment No. 475 [1982] (CIPEC); *Sheye*, UNAT Judgment No. 300 [1982], JUNAT Nos. 231–300 p. 655.

(d) Omission of facts

In *Schofield (No. 3)*[75] the ILOAT held that, where the applicant was alleged to have entered unannounced the Regional Director's office and behaved rudely, the Director General of WHO did not base his decision to reprimand the applicant on a consideration of all the relevant facts, because he had not considered any explanation or excuse the applicant had to give. This was so, although the Director General had taken into account the applicant's statement to the Personnel Department concerning the incident and the version given by the Regional Director. He should also have considered the applicant's explanation subsequent to that. Thus, the decision was vitiated.[76]

(e) Consideration of irrelevant facts

There are no cases to be found in which a tribunal has pronounced a disciplinary decision tainted because the administrative authority had taken into consideration irrelevant facts. However, in X[77] the CJEC found that, where the applicant was absent from office because of her own behaviour which resulted in disciplinary proceedings, the administrative authority was not wrong to take into account in the proceedings facts which had been brought to its attention in earlier proceedings which did not result in disciplinary sanctions. This was not a case of double jeopardy which would have been prohibited but only a situation in which facts which were the basis of earlier proceedings were taken into account.

(f) Erroneous conclusions

In several cases tribunals have found that erroneous conclusions reached by the administrative authority in the disciplinary proceedings had vitiated the final decision to impose a disciplinary sanction. In *Connolly-Battisti (No. 7)*,[78] for example, the ILOAT found that on the facts the FAO had come to a mistaken conclusion that the applicant had disobeyed her superior in regard to the issue of the time she should spend on activities of the Non-Local Staff Association of which she was Chairperson.[79]

In some cases tribunals have merely observed or held that the administrative authority in taking the decision to impose disciplinary sanctions had not reached any mistaken conclusions on the basis of the facts.[80]

[75] ILOAT Judgment No. 410 [1980] (WHO).

[76] In *Lakey*, ILOAT Judgment No. 475 [1982] (CIPEC), also it was held that the administrative authority had not failed to consider all the relevant facts.

[77] CJEC Case 12/68 [1969] ECR p. 109.

[78] ILOAT Judgment No. 403 [1980] (FAO).

[79] See also *X*, CJEC Case 12/68 [1969] ECR p. 109; *Decision No. 71*, NATO Appeals Board [1976], Collection of the Decisions 46 to 73 [1976].

[80] See *Lakey*, ILOAT Judgment No. 475 [1982] (CIPEC); *Sheye*, UNAT Judgment No. 300 [1982], JUNAT Nos. 231–300 p. 655; *van Eick*, CJEC Case 35/67 [1968] ECR p. 329.

Procedural irregularities

There have been issues raised in cases relating to disciplinary proceedings concerning irregularities of a procedural nature.

(a) Composition of the disciplinary body

In *Decision No. 167*[81] it was found that the Disciplinary Board set up under the Civilian Personnel Regulations of NATO to recommend the penalty had been wrongly constituted. Since it could not be said that the Secretary General's decision would have been the same, if the composition of the Board had been different, the Appeals Board of NATO held that the decision to impose disciplinary sanctions was invalid.

In *Gyamfi*[82] the WBAT applied an important general principle of law relating to due process. The tribunal stated that: 'it is a fundamental rule of both judicial and quasi-judicial procedures that whoever is invited to pass judgment on another must assume his responsibility free from any possible prejudice developed through previous involvement in the case.'[83] This principle is an aspect of the principle *nemo iudex in re sua* (no one should be judge in his own cause). In *Gyamfi* the tribunal held that it was improper for a personnel officer and a legal officer who had already been involved in the investigation of other aspects of the applicant's conduct or case to sit on the committee investigating the disciplinary charges against the applicant.

(b) Right of defence

The ILOAT has held that the applicant must be informed in clear and precise terms of the grave charges against him and must be allowed to defend himself before the competent authority before the latter takes its decision.[84] The UNAT has also emphasized the need to respect the right of defence[85] and has held that, where formal charges had never been made and the applicant had not been given an opportunity to rebut the charges, there was a procedural irregularity.[86]

---

[81] *Decision No. 167*, NATO Appeals Board [1984], Collection of the Decisions 135 to 171 [1984].

[82] WBAT Reports [1986], Decision No. 28.

[83] Ibid. at p. 25.

[84] *Hickel*, ILOAT Judgment No. 5 [1947] (IIIC). See also *Gutmann*, CJEC Cases 18 & 35/65 [1966] ECR p. 103, where the need for the precise indication of the charges was emphasized.

[85] *Zang-Atangana*, UNAT Judgment No. 130 [1969], JUNAT Nos. 114–166 p. 155. The Appeals Board of the Council of Europe and NATO have also emphasized the right of defence: *Pagani*, Council of Europe Appeals Board, Appeal No. 78 [1982], Case-Law Digest (1985) p. 113; *Decision No. 58*, NATO Appeals Board [1975], Collection of the Decisions 46 to 73 (1976).

[86] *Lindblad*, UNAT Judgment No. 183 [1974], JUNAT Nos. 167–230 p. 126. See also

Further, a proper inquiry must be held. Thus, in a case where the applicant was disciplined for attempted theft from a shop, only the shop manager and three of his employees were heard in evidence. Only one of them had witnessed the alleged theft. This was held to be an inadequate inquiry.[87] On the other hand, the ILOAT has not committed itself to the view that an oral hearing is always necessary, in so far as it assumed in *Schofield (No. 3)* that the case could have been decided on the written record alone.[88] It is also clear that in any case the written record must be complete. The position seems to be that in appropriate circumstances the administration may be required to hold an oral inquiry, if this is necessary for the completeness of the record.

In *Larcher*[89] the Appeals Board of OECD held that, even if the Staff Regulations were silent, provided they did not state the opposite, the applicant was entitled to the right to defend himself. In that case a supervisor's report of a specific incident was sent to the Personnel Department and the applicant was informed that the supervisor would have to let the Chief of Personnel know that the applicant had committed a fault but the applicant was not informed that disciplinary sanctions would be imposed nor was any attempt made to make him aware of the charges. It was held that this was a procedural irregularity. From this case it also emerges that the fact that the applicant was given a hearing by the Advisory Committee after the decision to terminate his employment had been taken did not cure the defect that existed. Further, where the written law contains provisions concerning submissions and replies and the right of defence, these must be followed.[90]

In *Alvis*[91] the CJEC had a difficult case. While holding that, according to a general principle of law, the right of defence and the opportunity to reply must be respected, which had not been done in this case, the Court, nevertheless, held that this defect was not sufficient to vitiate the decision to impose disciplinary sanctions. The Court examined the facts and found that two charges brought against the applicant were established, so that the procedural irregularity did not have an adverse effect on the legality of the decision taken. This case is theoretically in accord with the methodology of

---

d'Espinay-Saint-Luc, Decision No. 44, OECD Appeals Board [1974], Recueil des décisions 1 à 62 (1979) p. 124. In *Gyamfi*, WBAT Reports [1986], Decision No. 28 at p. 24, it was held that the right of defence had not been respected, because of repeated failures to inform the applicant of the accusation against him and to hear his side of the case.

[87] *Flad*, ILOAT Judgment No. 172 [1971] (WHO). See also *Roy*, UNAT Judgment No. 123 [1968] (ICAO), JUNAT Nos. 114–166 p. 89.

[88] ILOAT Judgment No. 410 [1980] (WHO) at p. 6.

[89] Decision No. 53, OECD Appeals Board [1975], Recueil des décisions 1 à 62 (1979) p. 145. On the right of defence see also *Pagani*, Council of Europe Appeals Board, Appeal No. 78 [1982], Case-Law Digest (1985) p. 113.

[90] *van Eick*, CJEC Case 35/67 [1968] ECR p. 329, where it was held that the written law had been followed.

[91] CJEC Case 32/62 [1963] ECR p. 49.

establishing whether the decision taken by the administrative authority was sound on the merits. It would seem that tribunals will only examine the merits of the case, if they feel that a procedural irregularity of this nature could definitely have had no effect on the decision of the administration.[92]

Where the applicant has made a confession, it is not required that there be formal notification of the charges against him, if the confession relates to the charges which form the basis of the disciplinary action; and this is so, even if the written law requires a formal notification of charges.[93] Where the applicant fails to avail himself of the opportunity to reply, there is no infringement of the rule that a right to reply must be afforded.[94] Where the applicant should, in the circumstances of his case, have known what the detailed accusations were, it is not a vitiating flaw that the administrative authority had given him a general notification of the charges which did not contain much detail.[95]

Clearly the requirement that a right to be heard be afforded does not always apply in the case where the written law of the organization permits summary action, generally in the case of serious misconduct. Even in this situation, though, the written law may recognize such a right.[96] However, in the case of serious misconduct permitting summary action, it would be required that the formal charges be communicated to the accused staff member in writing. This emerges from the decision in *Amonfio*,[97] where it was not denied that normally a detailed notification of formal charges should be made. The case concerned a written regulation which required a notification of charges but it is likely that there is a general principle of law to this effect.

The applicant must be heard by the appropriate authority. Thus, according to the written law of the European Communities the Commission had to hear the applicant before a disciplinary decision to terminate his appointment was taken. It was held by the CJEC in *van Eick*[98] that this power could not be delegated to an official of the insititution.

It is improper for the administration to interfere with or act in a way which might prejudice the fair conduct of proceedings in an inquiry or appeals

---

[92] See also *Amonfio*, ILOAT Judgment No. 539 [1982] (WHO).

[93] *Bhandari*, ILOAT Judgment No. 159 [1970] (WHO); *Sood*, ILOAT Judgment No. 160 [1970] (WHO); *Sethi*, ILOAT Judgment No. 161 [1970] (WHO); *Raj Kumar*, ILOAT Judgment No. 162 [1970] (WHO).

[94] *Diaz de Borsody*, ILOAT Judgment No. 511 [1982] (FAO); *Hecquet*, UNAT Judgment No. 322 [1984]; *X*, CJEC Case 12/68 [1969] ECR p. 109.

[95] *Amonfio*, ILOAT Judgment No. 539 [1982] (WHO).

[96] See *Bhandari*, ILOAT Judgment No. 159 [1970] (WHO); *Sood*, ILOAT Judgment No. 160 [1970] (WHO); *Sethi*, ILOAT Judgment No. 161 [1970] (WHO); *Raj Kumar*, ILOAT Judgment No. 162 [1970] (WHO).

[97] ILOAT Judgment No. 539 [1982] (WHO).

[98] CJEC Case 35/67 [1968] ECR p. 329.

procedure. Thus, where the management of the organization had assembled before the proceedings of the appeals committee witnesses chosen to testify before it, it was held by the WBAT that the practice cast doubt upon the credibility of the testimony of the witnesses, even though the alleged intention of the organization was to familiarize the witnesses with procedures and liberate them from any possible inhibitions.[99] This conduct was, therefore, inconsistent with the fundamental principles of due process of law.

(c) Investigation, witnesses, and evidence

The applicant must be allowed to participate in the examination of the evidence,[100] especially where witnesses are examined. Thus, where the applicant had not been given a chance of questioning the witnesses examined[101] or where witnesses had been examined in his absence,[102] this procedural rule was held to have been violated. Where, however, the applicant fails to press his claim to the right to question witnesses, when they are being examined, he cannot contend that his right to a fair procedure has been infringed.[103]

The applicant is normally entitled to consult documents connected with his case which are in the exclusive possession of the administration. These must be related to the facts on which the decision to take disciplinary action is based.[104] While the right exists even in the absence of provision in the written law, as it is required by equity and justice, the applicant does not have a right to a roving examination of all documents available but may 'see only those documents which are relevant to his case.[105] The question of relevance will have to be decided when it is raised by a body such as the Joint Disciplinary Committee of the UN where such a body has functions in relation to disciplinary issues.[106] Where there is a confession and there is corroboration of

---

[99] *Gyamfi*, WBAT Reports [1986], Decision No. 28.

[100] See *Lindblad*, UNAT Judgment No. 183 [1974], JUNAT Nos. 167–230 p. 126; *Lebaga*, UNAT Judgment No. 340 [1984] (IMO).

[101] *Ferrecchia*, ILOAT Judgment No. 203 [1973] (ILO). Failure to reveal the names of accusers and to communicate in due time the exact nature of the allegations against the applicant and the denial of the right to cross-examine witnesses have been held by the WBAT to be an infringement of the right to due process: *Gyamfi*, WBAT Reports [1986], Decision No. 28.

[102] *Lebaga*, UNAT Judgment No. 340 [1984] (IMO).

[103] See *van Eick*, CJEC Case 35/67 [1968] ECR p. 329.

[104] See *Bhandari*, ILOAT Judgment No. 159 [1970] (WHO); *Sood*, ILOAT Judgment No. 160 [1970] (WHO); *Sethi*, ILOAT Judgement No. 161 [1970] (WHO); *Raj Kumar*, ILOAT Judgment No. 162 [1970] (WHO). On the question of documents to which the applicant is entitled, see also *Pagani*, Council of Europe Appeals Board, Appeal No. 78 [1982], Case-Law Digest (1985) p. 113.

[105] *Bang-Jensen*, UNAT Judgment No. 74 [1958], JUNAT Nos. 71–86 p. 15.

[106] Ibid.

that confession, it is not necessary that the applicant be allowed access even to documents that may be relevant.[107]

Since the disciplinary action is being taken by the organization concerned, even though it is an interested party in the taking of the action, it is appropriate that the investigation of the offence be made by its officials or its bodies, there being no requirement that an external authority make the investigation, particularly where the offence is a violation also of the laws of a State.[108] The CJEC has held that a senior official of the organization rather than the appointing authority may ordinarily hear the staff member in order to satisfy the requirement that an investigation be held.[109]

(d) Representation

The issue whether a staff member has a right to be represented by counsel in proceedings before a board or committee entrusted by the organization with investigating such staff member's case has been raised before the UNAT. In *Bang-Jensen*[110] the applicant's contention that he should have been allowed to have legal counsel represent him before the Joint Disciplinary Board was rejected because it was held that the Staff Rules of the UN permitted a staff member to be represented in such proceedings only by another staff member and this right had not been denied him. It was noted that the applicant had not contested the Staff Rule in terms of general principles of law, in so far as it did not permit legal representation, and that, therefore, he was bound by it. In *Lebaga*,[111] however, the UNAT applied a general principle of law. The Staff Regulations and Staff Rules of the IMO were silent on the issue of representation before the Disciplinary Board. The UNAT in effect held that the applicant was entitled to representation at least to the same extent as was guaranteed by the Staff Rules of the UN and that, since he was not so represented nor was informed of his right to be so represented, there had been a procedural defect. The fact that the applicant had been assisted by counsel before the Joint Appeals Board, when he had recourse to the internal appeals procedure after the decision to discipline him had been taken, did not erase the defect. The UNAT pointed out that, while the written law of the IMO had not been violated in this case, because it was silent on the right to

---

[107] *Bhandari*, ILOAT Judgment No. 159 [1970] (WHO); *Sood*, ILOAT Judgment No. 160 [1970] (WHO); *Sethi*, ILOAT Judgment No. 161 [1970] (WHO); *Raj Kumar*, ILOAT Judgment No. 162 [1970] (WHO).

[108] *Bhandari*, ILOAT Judgment No. 159 [1970] (WHO); *Sood*, ILOAT Judgment No. 160 [1970] (WHO); *Sethi*, ILOAT Judgment No. 161 [1970] (WHO); *Raj Kumar*, ILOAT Judgment No. 162 [1970] (WHO).

[109] See *Fonzi*, CJEC Cases 27 & 30/64 [1965] ECR p. 481.

[110] UNAT Judgment No. 74 [1958], JUNAT Nos. 71–86 p. 15.

[111] UNAT Judgment No. 340 [1984] (IMO).

representation, the defects in procedure were fundamental and amounted to a denial of due process of law.[112]

(e) Statement of reasons

It seems not to be contested that reasons must be given for the disciplinary action taken. In *Zang-Atangana* the UNAT said:

The Tribunal considers that for a disciplinary measure to be valid the reasons for it must be stated with a reasonable degree of precision and with due regard for the facts of the case as evidenced by the file. This requirement is particularly important in the case of a staff member who under the Staff Rules is not assured of the guarantees provided by referral to a Joint Disciplinary Committee.[113]

(f) Right of appeal

Unless the written law gives a staff member a right of appeal to the same body that takes the disciplinary decision, there is no such right accorded to a staff member by general principles of law. This is so even where the decision is taken in default of his appearance. Thus, in *X* the CJEC stated in regard to such a right of appeal:

Such a remedy is not provided for by the Staff Regulations which have secured the legal protection of officials in disciplinary matters by the institution of an appeal to the Court of Justice.
There does not exist, further, any general principle of law from which it would be possible to infer the existence of the type of remedy to which the applicant refers.[114]

(g) Fixed-term contracts

Where a fixed-term contract is not renewed for disciplinary reasons, the ILOAT has impliedly held that such non-renewal is valid provided there are no procedural flaws and the right of defence has been respected in the taking of the decision. Thus, in *Anciaux* the ILOAT stated: 'It appears from the documents in the dossier that the impugned decision is not tainted with any formal or procedural flaw; . . . and that it respected the right of defence.'[115]

(h) Due process in general

A failure of due process in the taking of a disciplinary decision, particularly

---

112 For the right to representation see also *Pagani*, Council of Europe Appeals Board, Appeal No. 78 [1982], Case-Law Digest (1985) p. 113.
113 UNAT Judgment No. 130 [1969], JUNAT Nos. 114–166 p. 155 at p. 164.
114 CJEC Case 12/68 [1969] ECR p. 109 at p. 116.
115 ILOAT Judgment No. 266 [1976] (ESO).

before a committee or body investigating the offence, would attract the jurisdiction of tribunals to review such a decision.[116] Basically, of course, a disciplinary procedure must be pursued where a sanction which is of a disciplinary
nature in all the circumstances of the case is imposed.[117] Not to follow such a
procedure would be a failure in due process. Where summary dismissal for
serious misconduct is permitted, the full procedure required for imposing
sanctions for misconduct that is not serious need not be followed, provided
there is no other procedural irregularity.[118]

    There are, on the other hand, certain omissions or actions which have not
been characterized as such procedural defects as would lead to an absence of
due process. Where a Staff Regulation requires consultation with a head of
division, consultation with the Chief of Personnel has been held to be
adequate, it not being necessary that there be consultation with the head of
the applicant's division.[119] Where a procedure available under the written law
is dispensed with at the formal request of the applicant[120] or where a statutory
committee, for the purpose of having access to the annexes to a report for
evidence or for advisory purposes, decides to use the report prepared by
another committee by which the statutory committee does not consider itself
bound,[121] there is no absence of due process. The Appeals Board of the ESA
has held that delays in procedure caused by the administrative authority in
order to protect the rights of the applicant are not impeachable as failures in
due process.[122]

---

[116] See *Reid*, UNAT Judgment No. 210 [1976], JUNAT Nos. 167–230 p. 396 at p. 407; *Sheye*,
UNAT Judgment No. 300 [1982], JUNAT Nos. 231–300 p. 655. In *Gyamfi*, WBAT Reports
[1986], Decision No. 28 at pp. 23–4, it was held that the manner of implementing an order of
suspension was an abuse of due process.

[117] See *Goyal*, ILOAT Judgment No. 136 [1969] (UNESCO); *Pagani*, Council of Europe
Appeals Board, Appeal No. 78 [1982], Case-Law Digest (1985) p. 113; *Larcher*, Decision No.
53, OECD Appeals Board [1975], Recueil des décisions 1 à 62 (1979) p. 145; *Decision No. 33*,
NATO Appeals Board [1971], Collection of the Decisions (1972).

[118] See *Bhandari*, ILOAT Judgment No. 159 [1970] (WHO); *Sood*, ILOAT Judgment No.
160 [1970] (WHO); *Sethi*, ILOAT Judgment No. 161 [1970] (WHO); *Raj Kumar* ILOAT
Judgment No. 162 [1970] (WHO).

[119] *Lakey*, ILOAT Judgment No. 475 [1982] (CIPEC).

[120] *Jurado (No. 17)*, ILOAT Judgment No. 96 [1966] (ILO).

[121] *Bang-Jensen*, UNAT Judgment No. 74 [1958], JUNAT Nos. 71–86 p. 15.

[122] *Decision No. 8*, ESA/CR/20, ESA Appeals Board [1978]. The CJEC has held that in
issuing a reprimand the administrative authority was not required by the written law to consult
the Disciplinary Board: *Fonzi*, CJEC Cases 27 & 30/64 [1965] ECR p. 481, and that, where there
was a technical defect in the procedure, because one of the members of a committee was absent
and did not sign a finding of a medical nature which was favourable to the applicant, the
procedure did not have to be repeated, in order to satisfy the requirements of due process, since
there had been no failure of due process: *Perinciolo*, CJEC Case 124/75 [1976] ECR p 1953. The
CJEC has also held that, while the time-limit for terminating disciplinary proceedings under the
written law should be observed, it is not mandatory, with the result that, though its non-
observance may render the organization liable for the damage caused, such non-observance does
not render the decision a nullity: *van Eick*, CJEC Case 13/69 [1970] ECR p. 3. No damages were
awarded for the defect in this case. Minor formal flaws, such as the absence of the title of the

An irregularity in the procedure before an internal appellate body, such as an Appeals Board, may be considered by the tribunal as vitiating the decision taken only to the extent that it might, particularly by reason of the gravity of the irregularity, have affected the final decision of the administrative authority.[123] In the case in question the Appeals Board had heard the parties and did not commit any procedural irregularity. On the other hand, the observance of due process by the internal appellate body, such as the Joint Appeals Board of the UN, will not cure the absence of due process at an earlier stage, as where the right of defence had been ignored.[124]

Miscellaneous matters

When a staff member has resigned, because he had been informed or was aware that disciplinary proceedings were being contemplated against him, the resignation is valid, unless it can be shown that there had been duress or fraud.[125] In *Akinola Deko*[126] it was held by the ILOAT that calling up the applicant and asking him for an explanation before disciplinary proceedings were begun was not a violation of the written law of FAO on the part of the administration and that such conduct did not affect the freedom of action of the applicant in choosing to resign.

Where an applicant had been dismissed earlier because of a criminal sentence imposed by the Italian judiciary, the ILOAT has held that the applicant had no right to reinstatement after he was granted an amnesty by the President of Italy.[127]

Sometimes a warning or a reprimand or some other form of disapproval may not be a disciplinary sanction governed by the law relating to disciplinary sanctions. This will depend on the written law of the organization. In such a case the decision taken will be subject to the general law relating to the exercise of discretionary power.[128] On the other hand, a note expressing dissatisfaction with progress in particular work which may not be a disciplinary

---

official signing the order, do not vitiate the decision taken: *Decision No. 4*, NATO Appeals Board [1967], Collection of the Decisions (1972).

123 *Andreski*, ILOAT Judgment No. 63 [1962] (UNESCO).

124 *Roy*, UNAT Judgment No. 123 [1968] (ICAO), JUNAT Nos. 114–166 p. 89.

125 See *Barakat*, ILOAT Judgment No. 89 [1965] (ILO); *Akinola Deko*, ILOAT Judgment No. 150 [1970] (FAO); *Decision No. 18, ESA/CR/38*, ESA Appeals Board [1983].

126 ILOAT Judgment No. 150 [1970] (FAO).

127 *Duncker*, ILOAT Judgment No. 49 [1960] (FAO).

128 See *Connolly-Battisti*, (*No. 2*) ILOAT Judgment No. 274 [1976] (FAO); *Connolly-Battisti* (*No. 7*), ILOAT Judgment No. 403 [1980] (FAO); *Connolly-Battisti (No. 6)*, ILOAT Judgement No. 420 [1980] (FAO); *Decision No. 33*, NATO Appeals Board [1971], Collection of the Decisions (1972); *Labeyrie*, CJEC Case 16/67 [1968] ECR p. 293.

sanction in itself could become one, if it is placed in the applicant's personnel file. In this case the proper disciplinary procedure must be followed.[129]

Remedies

(a) Reinstatement with or without compensation

Tribunals have in some cases ordered reinstatement, where a staff member's employment had been terminated wrongfully as a result of a disciplinary decision. In *Pollicino*[130], where there had been an error of fact which vitiated the disciplinary decision to terminate the applicant's appointment, reinstatement was ordered by the ILOAT.[131]

In *Cuenca*,[132] where the wrong procedure had been followed, so that there was a *détournement de procédure* in not instituting disciplinary proceedings, the OASAT ordered in addition to reinstatement the payment to the applicant of his salary from the date of his dismissal to the date of his reinstatement. If the respondent chose not to reinstate the applicant, the payment of 3 years' salary was ordered. The Appeals Board of OECD has also ordered reinstatement in a case where there had been a *détournement de procédure*, with the alternative of paying 3 months' salary, if the organization chose not to reinstate the applicant.[133]

In *Mendis*,[134] where the penalty of termination of service was held to be disproportionate to the offence committed, the ILOAT ordered the decision to dismiss the applicant to be quashed which meant reinstatement and allowed him to keep the 3 months' salary plus allowances which he had been paid as an indemnity on being dismissed.[135]

---

[129] *Decision No. 33*, NATO Appeals Board [1971], Collection of the Decisions (1972).

[130] ILOAT Judgment No. 635 [1984] (FAO).

[131] Reinstatement was ordered in several other cases where there had been procedural irregularities: *Decision No. 58*, NATO Appeals Board [1975], Collection of the Decisions 46 to 73 (1976); *van Eick*, CJEC Case 35/67 (1968) ECR p. 329—no additional damages, material or moral, were awarded; *Lebaga*, UNAT Judgment No. 340 [1984] (IMO)—compensation assessed at 6 months' salary as an alternative to reinstatement; *Gyamfi*, WBAT Reports [1986], Decision No. 28—compensation of 1 year's salary assessed as an alternative to reinstatement and in addition in any event the payment of 1 year's salary ordered as damages; *Decision No. 167*, NATO Appeals Board [1984], Collection of the Decisions 135 to 171 (1984)—additional compensation of 3 months' salary awarded. See also *d'Espinay-Saint-Luc*, Decision No. 44, OECD Appeals Board (1974), Recueil des décisions 1 à 62 (1979) p. 124.

[132] OASAT Judgment No. 53 [1980].

[133] *Larcher*, Decision No. 53, OECD Appeals Board [1975], Recueil des décisions 1 à 62 (1979) p. 145.

[134] ILOAT Judgment No. 210 [1973] (WHO).

[135] In *Habash*, UNRWA Special Panel of Adjudicators, Case No. 3 [1985], the tribunal ordered reinstatement on finding that the penalty of dismissal was disproportionate, and, if reinstatement were not made, 22 months' salary as compensation.

In *Svenchansky*[136] and *Eldridge*[137] the applicants requested reinstatement in cases where they had been wrongfully dismissed for serious misconduct. Reinstatement was ordered. Further, payment of salary up to the date of judgment less the termination indemnity paid and the amount paid in lieu of notice was ordered.

(b) Specific performance

Specific performance of some kind has also been ordered in disciplinary cases. In *Schofield (No. 3)*[138] which involved a written reprimand in circumstances in which the ILOAT found that there had been a failure to consider all the relevant facts, the decision to issue the reprimand was quashed which meant that the reprimand had to be erased from the records. No compensation was awarded, because there had been an element of impropriety in the conduct of the applicant. In *Pagani*[139] the Appeals Board of the Council of Europe annulled a decision to withdraw an incremental step in salary to which the applicant was entitled, because there had been a *détournement de procédure*. The increment had, therefore, to be restored to the applicant.[140] The CJEC annulled, because of *détournement de procédure*, a decision ordering suspension of the applicant, since the reasons for the decision were not properly stated, and a decision to transfer the applicant, thus restoring the *status quo ante*.[141] In a second case brought by the same applicant the Court annulled on the ground that the principle *non bis in idem* had been violated a decision to continue and suspend disciplinary proceedings in respect of the charges involved in the previous case.[142]

(c) Compensation

In many cases compensation has been awarded without reinstatement or specific performance. These cases have involved decisions to terminate the applicant's employment. In most cases the decision concerned has not been quashed or annulled. In only a few cases have damages been awarded for moral injury.

[136] UNAT Judgment No. 30 [1953], JUNAT Nos. 1–70 p. 128.
[137] UNAT Judgment No. 32 [1953], ibid. p. 144.
[138] ILOAT Judgment No. 410 [1980] (WHO).
[139] Council of Europe Appeals Board, Appeal No. 78 [1982], Case-Law Digest (1985) p. 113.
[140] See also *Decision No. 31*, NATO Appeals Board [1971], Collection of the Decisions (1972); *Decision No. 33*, NATO Appeals Board [1971], ibid. In *Connolly-Battisti (No. 7)*, ILOAT Judgment No. 403 [1980] (FAO), a warning which was not a disciplinary sanction was ordered quashed, because it was based on an error of fact.
[141] *Gutmann*, CJEC Cases 18 & 35/65 [1966] ECR p. 103.
[142] *Gutmann*, CJEC Cases 18 & 35/65 [1967] ECR p. 61. See also *Guillot*, CJEC Case 53/72 [1974] ECR p. 791, for another case in which specific performance was ordered where there had been a *détournement de procédure*.

i. *Material damage*

In *Reynolds*,[143] where the applicant had been treated by the FAO as if he had resigned voluntarily, because he had refused to accept a transfer, and the ILOAT held that the proper procedure had not been followed, since the act of the applicant could not lawfully be treated as a resignation, the FAO was ordered to pay the applicant his salary from the date of the termination of his employment to the date of the judgment and the termination indemnities he would have been entitled to under the Staff Regulations, if his employment had been terminated lawfully. His right to accumulated leave was also restored. In *Ferrecchia*,[144] where the termination decision was found to be out of proportion to the offence committed, the decision was not annulled but the ILOAT ordered the payment of 1,000,000 lire, considering the seriousness of the applicant's misbehaviour, the length of his service, the amount of his salary, and the termination benefits given him.[145]

Where the decision to terminate the applicant's employment was based on an error of fact and involved a procedural irregularity, the UNAT did not order reinstatement, on the ground that the applicant may not have retained his post till his contract expired, but, in view of the payment of termination indemnities, awarded compensation of $3,000.[146]

In *Decision No. 4*[147] the Appeals Board of NATO reviewed a decision to terminate the applicant's employment for serious misconduct, because the misconduct was not serious enough for dismissal, and quashed the decision taken. The tribunal did not, however, order reinstatement but awarded an indemnity of 12 months' salary less the 2 months' salary paid in lieu of notice. In several early cases, where dismissal on the basis of serious misconduct had been wrongful, the UNAT awarded substantial compensation in varying amounts in lieu of reinstatement, because reinstatement was not requested.[148]

---

[143] ILOAT Judgment No. 38 [1958] (FAO).

[144] ILOAT Judgment No. 203 [1973] (ILO).

[145] The ILOAT awarded compensation also in *Diaz Acevedo*, ILOAT Judgment No. 349 [1978] (ESO); *Campitelli*, ILOAT Judgment No. 640 [1984] (FAO); and *Di Giuliomaria*, ILOAT Judgment No. 87 [1965] (FAO). In two cases decided by the UNRWA Special Panel of Adjudicators (*Rida*, UNRWA Special Panel of Adjudicators, Case No. 1 [1984], and *Nahhal*, UNRWA Special Panel of Adjudicators, Case No. 2 [1984]) where the penalty of dismissal was found disproportionate, reinstatement was not ordered but compensation of 1 year's salary was ordered.

[146] *Zang-Atangana*, UNAT Judgment No. 130 [1969], JUNAT Nos. 114–166 p. 155. See also *Lindblad*, UNAT Judgment No. 183 [1974], JUNAT Nos. 167–230 p. 126, where 30 days' pay was awarded in a case involving procedural irregularity.

[147] *Decision No. 4*, NATO Appeals Board [1967], Collection of the Decisions (1972).

[148] *Harris, Glassman, Older, Bancroft*, and *Elveson*, UNAT Judgments Nos. 31, 33–6 [1953], JUNAT Nos. 1–70 pp. 135, 151, 160, 168, 176. In *Reed*, UNAT Judgment No. 37 [1953], ibid. p. 184, the UNAT awarded $10,000 to cover the period till the date of retirement of the applicant and the payment of a pension from that date. The applicant was due to retire shortly.

ii. *Moral injury*

Damages for moral injury have been awarded in some cases decided by the ILOAT. In *Hickel*,[149] where the tribunal reviewed the decision taken by the administration and found that the applicant had not been guilty of misconduct, the tribunal ordered the applicant's salary up to the end of his contract and the contributions of the organization to the pension fund be paid. In addition 200,000 fr. were awarded *ex aequo et bono*. The award was said to have account of both the material injury and the moral injury. Where the applicant had virtually been suspended without the proper disciplinary procedure being followed, the ILOAT said that, while the applicant did not suffer material damage, because his salary had been paid, he suffered moral prejudice, since his reputation and prospects of finding other employment had been damaged.[150] Consequently, the tribunal ordered the payment of equitable compensation. In the follow-up case resulting from the inability of the parties to agree on the compensation the ILOAT ordered 6 months' salary ($7,000) to be paid.[151]

(d) Other action

In *Roy*,[152] where a procedural irregularity was found, the UNAT remanded the case for correction of procedure and in addition awarded 2 months' salary as compensation.

In *X*[153] the CJEC concluded that, while the evidence had not been misinterpreted in the case, the question of the imputability of the impugned conduct should be investigated further because of the fact that the applicant had been mentally disturbed. Hence, an expert's report on this matter was requested by the Court. This was a case where employment had been terminated as a consequence of disciplinary proceedings.

In *de Compte*[154] the CJEC issued an interlocutory order suspending the decision to institute disciplinary proceedings pending the disposal by the Court of the application to annul that decision.

---

[149] ILOAT Judgment No. 5 [1947] (IIIC).

[150] *Goyal*, ILOAT Judgment No. 136 [1969] (UNESCO).

[151] *Goyal* (2), ILOAT Judgment No. 176 [1971] (UNESCO). See also *Flad*, ILOAT Judgment No. 172 [1971] (WHO), where material and moral damages were awarded. The additional damages of $60,000 awarded by the WBAT in any event in *Gyamfi*, WBAT Reports [1986], Decision No. 28, were apparently for the moral injury caused.

[152] UNAT Judgment No. 123 [1968] (ICAO), JUNAT Nos. 114–166 p. 89.

[153] CJEC Case 12/68 [1969] ECR p. 109.

[154] CJEC Case 293/82R [1982] ECR p. 4001.

(e) No remedy

In *Alvis*[155] the CJEC found that there had been a procedural irregularity in the disciplinary proceedings taken against the applicant which resulted in his dismissal. He had not been heard in his defence. However, the Court examined the merits of the case and found that in spite of this defect, the allegations against the applicant were fully supported by the evidence and that, therefore, he should have no remedy, the case being dismissed.

[155] CJEC Case 32/62 [1963] ECR p. 49.

CHAPTER FORTY

Classification and Grading of Posts

I N almost all international organizations, posts are assigned certain grades or classified, primarily in order to ensure that officials with comparable powers and performing comparable duties are paid comparable salaries or are placed in the same salary range or bracket. As was stated by the management of the World Bank in a circular to staff members, one of the main objectives of the job grading programme recently initiated by the World Bank was 'to assure all positions are graded properly and fairly so as to ensure equal pay for work of equal value and fair salary differential between work of different values.'[1] In the process, which may vary widely from organization to organization, generally posts are assigned a grade or classification according to the content of the job done which depends on a description, express or implied, of the duties and powers associated with a particular post, sometimes called a 'job description'. Since the primary objective of the grading or classification of posts is equitable salary administration which is achieved by the grouping of posts in categories or grades, the whole process of grading or classification of posts can be a very sensitive issue and a very difficult one for organizations to administer.

In general, the Staff Regulations of institutions have provisions on grading or classification of posts but these provisions differ widely. Some of the most extensive basic provisions are to be found in the Staff Regulations of the European Communities. While indicating that classification should be according to the nature and importance of the duties of posts and on the basis of a definition of duties and powers of each post, the Regulations lay down the total structure of the classification system. The principal provisions are contained in Article 5 of the current Staff Regulations which states:

1. The posts covered by these Staff Regulations shall be classified, according to the nature and importance of the duties to which they relate, in four categories A, B, C and D, in descending order of rank.

Category A shall comprise eight grades, divided into career brackets ordinarily containing two grades each for staff engaged in administrative and advisory duties which require university education or equivalent professional experience.

Category B shall comprise five grades, divided into career brackets ordinarily containing two grades each for staff engaged in executive duties which require an

---

[1] 'Job Grading Update No. 4', dated 5 April, 1985, para. 3. The OASAT has referred to the principle of equal pay for equal work as a general principle of labour law applicable to the international civil service: see *Reeve*, OASAT Judgment No. 59 [1981] at p. 8.

advanced level of secondary education or equivalent professional experience.

Category C shall comprise five grades, divided into career brackets ordinarily containing two grades each for staff engaged in clerical duties which require secondary education or equivalent professional experience.

Category D shall comprise four grades, divided into career brackets ordinarily containing, two grades each for staff engaged in manual or service duties which require primary education, if necessary supplemented by some technical training.

By way of derogation from the preceding provisions, however, posts coming within the same specialized professional field may, in accordance with the procedure for revision of these Staff Regulations, be formed into services embracing a number of grades of one or more of the foregoing categories.

2. Posts of translators and interpreters shall be grouped in a Language Service designated by the letters L/A, comprising six grades equivalent to Grades 3 to 8 of Category A and divided into career brackets ordinarily containing two grades each.

3. Identical conditions of recruitment and service career shall apply to all officials belonging to the same category or the same service.

4. A table showing basic posts and corresponding career brackets is given in Annex I.

By reference to this table each institution shall, after consulting the Staff Regulations Committee referred to in Article 10, define the duties and powers attaching to each basic post.[2]

Annex I[3] referred to in Article 5.4 of the Staff Regulations identifies the titles of the grades reflected in Article 5.1 for each category. Article 92[4] and Annex IB[5] of the Staff Regulations contain some special provisions relating to officials in the scientific or technical services of the European Communities.

The provisions of the Staff Rules of the OAS are as or more extensive in dealing with grading and classification of posts.[6] Rule 102.1 specifically states that classification shall be related to the nature of duties, the level of responsibility, and the qualifications required, while Rule 102.3 assigns responsibility for ensuring that the nature of duties and the level of responsibility required of a staff member are compatible with the classification standards applicable to the grade of his post. Rule 102.3 and Rule 102.4 also detail procedures for review of classifications.

Not all the Staff Regulations of organizations have detailed provisions relating to grading or classification. Thus, Regulation 2.1 of the UN merely states: 'In conformity with principles laid down by the General Assembly, the Secretary-General shall make appropriate provision for the classification of posts and staff according to the nature of the duties and responsibilities required.'[7] There are no Staff Rules dealing with the subject. While the

---

[2] See Amerasinghe (ed.), 4 *Staff Regulations and Staff Rules of Selected International Organizations* (1983) p. 1 at p. 9.

[3] See Amerasinghe (ed.), 4 ibid. p. 1 at p. 32.

[4] Amerasinghe (ed.), 4 ibid. p. 1 at p. 28.

[5] Amerasinghe (ed.), 4 ibid. p. 1 at p. 33.

[6] See Rules 102.1–4: Amerasinghe (ed.), 3 ibid. p. 214 at pp. 221 ff.

[7] See Appendix V *infra*.

relationship between the nature of duties and responsibilities of posts and their classification is referred to, no other details are specified. The administration is left to make the necessary arrangements regarding details of the classification system and procedures. Similarly Article 2.2 of the ILO Staff Regulations refers to the relationship between duties and responsibilities of posts and their classification and details the scheme of classification but goes no further:

Posts shall be classified in categories and grades, in accordance with the duties and responsibilities attaching to them, as follows:
(1) Director-General,
    Deputy Director-General,
    Assistant Director-General,
    Treasurer and Financial Comptroller.
(2) Director and Principal Officer category, comprising the grades of D.2 and D.1, and assimilated special posts.
(3) Professional category, comprising the grades of P.5, P.4, P.3, P.2 and P.1, and assimilated special posts.
(4) General Service category, comprising all other grades.[8]

The Personnel Manual Statements of the World Bank Group do not contain any provisions relating to grading and classification of posts. It has been left to the management to make *ad hoc* provision for the system of grading and classification which, however, has been done in circulars to the staff. While in the World Bank Group there has as yet been no permanent formulation of the responsibility of management for grading and classification of posts and of the rights of staff members in this regard, the functions of grading and classification of posts have been assumed by the management and have been carried out, pursuant to certain written instructions communicated to the staff, by the management itself.

While the Staff Regulations or Staff Rules of most organizations do not make an explicit connection between salaries paid staff members and the grade assigned to their posts, as is made in the statement made by the management of the World Bank cited above, it is implied in these Staff Regulations and Staff Rules that there is such a basic connection, because the grading system itself is in fact concerned with the allocation of salaries to the grades to which the posts are assigned. On the other hand, the relationship between grades or classification and the nature of duties, responsibilities, and powers of posts is clearly recognized in the Staff Regulations and Staff Rules which deal with grading and classification.

International administrative tribunals have been called upon to implement Staff Regulations and Staff Rules dealing with grading and classification of

---

[8] See Amerasinghe (ed.), 4 op. cit. (note 2 *supra*) p. 185 at p. 198.

posts, where disputes have arisen in regard to their application. They have interpreted and applied these regulations in the course of settling these disputes. Their main concern in these disputes has been with the actual exercise of grading posts, because in most cases it is the assignment of a grade to a post that has been questioned, though sometimes there are other matters relating to the rights of staff members that have been in issue. In applying the Regulations and Rules tribunals have interpreted them in light of general principles of admnistrative law where it has been necessary to do so.

Basic principles

There are certain very basic principles applicable to grading and classification of posts, irrespective of the express provisions of Staff Regulations and Staff Rules. They are so basic that there is no instance where the Staff Regulations or Staff Rules of an institution expressly or implicitly rejects them. These principles have been explicitly reiterated or implicitly recognized on several occasions and by more than one tribunal and with little or no reference to the language of the Staff Regulations and Staff Rules of the relevant institutions. Some Staff Regulations and Staff Rules may expressly incorporate them.

(a) Post must correspond to grade

The first basic principle is that of correspondence of grade and post. This means that an official is entitled to be assigned to a post which corresponds to his grade.[9] A corollary to this principle is that an official must also be given work or duties and responsibilities appropriate to his grade.[10] In *Klaer*[11] the applicant who held a position in grade A1 in the European Communities was assigned to advise another official in the same grade. The CJEC found that staff members in grade A1 had to be directly respousible to the High Authority. Therefore, giving the applicant the duties and responsibilities of an unclassified adviser with responsibility to another officer in the same grade and without responsibility to the High Authority was improper. In *Vera*[12] the applicant who had a P5 grade in the OAS was transferred from a P5-graded post to a lower post in the P4 grade, though he retained his grade at P5. The OASAT held that a lateral transfer must be to a post of the same grade, the qualifications of the applicant not being a justifying factor for

[9] See *Peco*, CJEC Case 36/69 [1970] ECR p. 361; *Macevicius*, CJEC Case 66/75 [1976] ECR p. 593; *Kruse*, CJEC Case 218/80 [1981] ECR p. 2417; *Vera*, OASAT Judgment No. 33 [1977].
[10] See *Schofield* (*No. 4*), ILOAT Judgment No. 411 [1980] (WHO); *Puel*, ILOAT Judgment No. 526 [1982] (WMO); *Rudin* (*No. 3*), ILOAT Judgment No. 630 [1984] (ILO).
[11] CJEC Case 15/65 [1965] ECR p. 1045.
[12] OASAT Judgment No. 33 [1977].

transfer to a lower-graded post. A similar conclusion was reached by the ILOAT in *Schofield (No. 4)*[13] where an officer who was promoted to grade P6 in WHO was assigned to a P5 post. It was stated that a staff member was entitled to be given work and responsibility appropriate to his grade[14] and the decision impugned was quashed. On the other hand, the applicant, it was said, was not entitled to a job which was equal in status to a promotion to grade D1 of which he felt he had been deprived.[15]

Tribunals have applied the principle with negative results in so far as they have found that in a given situation the applicant, while relying on this principle, had not proved that the duties or post assigned to him did not match his grade.[16] Where, on the reorganization of a department, the responsibilities of the applicant were reduced, the CJEC took the view that there was no such reduction of duties as to result in a downgrading of the applicant, because not merely must the measure being questioned bring about a reduction of responsibilities but it was necessary that, taken together, the remaining responsibilities must fall clearly short of those corresponding to. the applicant's grade and post, considering their character, importance, and scope.[17] Negatively also, tribunals have stated in the application of this principle that, where the principle is satisfied in substance, it is not a good argument that a professional was assigned to perform 'essentially executive' duties entailing a reduction in status,[18] and that the tribunal could not order the head of an institution to place the applicant in a position suited to his qualifications and experience,[19] presumably because this was a factor irrelevant to the issue of matching a grade with a post.

There are some qualfications to this principle. In *Rosani and Others*[20] it was said by the CJEC that the principle of equivalence between grade and posts does not apply to posts within the same grade, though duties and powers must normally correspond to the grade. What this means is that the principle cannot be invoked to enable a staff member to claim one post rather than another within the same grade on the ground that the post does not correspond to the grade, provided in fact the duties and powers of both posts do correspond to the grade in question. Where the applicant freely accepts a lower-graded position[21] or his contract states that he should perform work in

---

[13] ILOAT Judgment No. 411 [1980] (WHO).
[14] Ibid. at p. 5.
[15] See also *Rudin (No. 3)*, ILOAT Judgment No. 630 [1984] (ILO).
[16] See *Walther*, ILOAT Judgment No. 106 [1967] (BIRPI); *Rémont*, ILOAT Judgment No. 228 [1974] (FAO); *Puel*, ILOAT Judgment No. 526 [1982] (WMO).
[17] *Macevicius*, CJEC Case 66/75 [1976] ECR p. 593.
[18] *Peco*, CJEC Case 36/69 [1970] ECR p. 361.
[19] *Puel*, ILOAT Judgment No. 526 [1982] (WMO).
[20] CJEC Cases 193 to 198/82 [1983] ECR p. 2841.
[21] *Walther*, ILOAT Judgment No. 106 [1967] (BIRPI). For acquiescence see also *Decision No. 4, ESA/CR/13*, ESA Appeals Board [1977].

a lower grade,[22] he cannot invoke the principle. Further, in *Danjean* (*Nos. 1 and 2*) the ILOAT stated:

Moreover, while as a general rule employees in a given grade must be assigned to work normally done by members of that grade, it is within the discretion of the Director General, provided that there is no change in the grade or reduction in salary, nor any lowering of the dignity of the persons concerned, to assign them to work done by lower-grade employees if the needs of the service so require, for instance, if the Administration needs more or higher grade employees to perform such work, or if a staff member in a given grade proves to be unfitted for the work normally assigned to that grade. In the case at issue it appears from the evidence that the Director General did not outstep the limits of his authority as defined above . . . [23]

It would seem that the principle, while basic, is not absolute in every sense. There are some exceptional circumstances in which exact correspondence between grade and duties cannot be required. This may be so especially when the assignment of lower-grade duties is on a temporary basis.

The requirement that post and services correspond to grade is strictly construed. Thus, where the applicant, a secretary, had been doing translations in her position, though these were not part of her secretarial duties, and subsequently was assigned to a proper secretarial post where she did not have translation work to do, it was held that she could not successfully protest the denial of the translation functions because the Staff Regulations of the European Communities only guaranteed the right of the staff member to have duties corresponding to his or her post and grade.[24] The principle in issue could work against a staff member in such circumstances as the above where a claim is made to functions which are not necessarily part of the functions corresponding to grade and post.

The principle must also be interpreted reasonably. Thus, in determining what duties correspond to a grade, a comparison is to be made, not between the present and past duties of the post but between the present duties of the post and duties assigned at present to the grade. In *Kuhner*,[25] when a department was reorganized and the applicant was reassigned, he contended that he had been downgraded because his duties did not correspond to his grade. The CJEC applied the above rule to the change in the content of the applicant's job and found that under the new arrangements his post did correspond to his grade.

(*b*) *Salary is related to grade*

A second basic principle is that remuneration is dependent on grade and post

---

[22] *Danjean* (*Nos. 1 and 2*), ILOAT Judgment No. 126 [1968] (CERN).
[23] Ibid. at p. 7.
[24] *Kruse*, CJEC Case 218/80 [1981] ECR p. 2417.
[25] CJEC Cases 33 & 75/79 [1980] ECR p. 1677.

and not the converse.[26] Hence, a staff member cannot claim a particular grade or post on the basis of the salary paid him. On the other hand, he is entitled to a salary corresponding to the grade he holds. Apart from the case of temporary assignment of functions belonging to a higher grade, a consequence of the principle is that where a staff member is assigned to a post the duties and powers of which belong to a higher grade than the one he holds, promotion must be effected with due promptitude, so that he can be paid a salary appropriate to his grade. Where there was undue delay in processing a promotion in spite of the fact that the recommendation of the Chief of Personnel was made early, the ILOAT held that the promotion should be given effect retroactively from the proper date on which it should reasonably have been made with the result that the applicant was entitled to payment of a higher salary from that date.[27] This was held to be so, even though the Staff Regulations of PAHO specifically stated that a salary increase should become effective on the first of the month nearest to the final date of approval of promotion to the new grade.

(c) Non-reduction of salary

A third principle is that there cannot be a reduction in salary on a change of grade. The principle was implicitly conceded in *Conley and Zambrana*[28] where the OASAT held that, while the basic salary of the staff member was reduced on reclassification, the total salary received was higher than the total salary received before reclassification, because the amount of the post-adjustment allowance was higher after the reclassification than before, with the result that the principle referred to above had not been violated. What is total salary for the purpose of this principle may be a difficult question. While a post-adjustment allowance is included in the concept, it may be debated what other elements of earnings are to be included. In this connection it may be relevant to refer to the decision of the ILOAT in *Azola Blanco and Véliz García (No. 3)*[29] where it was held that emoluments received for overtime were to be included in the 'gross remuneration' received by a staff member for the purposes of calculating the compensation due to such staff member for wrongful dismissal which was set by the tribunal at a sum equal to 3 times the total gross remuneration paid to him in respect of a specified period of 1 year.[30]

[26] *Besnard and Others*, CJEC Cases 55 to 76, 86, 87 & 95/71 [1972] ECR p. 543.

[27] *Gatmaytan*, ILOAT Judgment No. 424 [1980] (PAHO).

[28] OASAT Judgment No. 32 [1977]. See also *Dadivas*, ILOAT Judgment No. 60 [1962] (WHO).

[29] ILOAT Judgment No. 643 [1984] (ESO).

[30] The argument that 'gross remuneration' for the purposes of compensation may be different from total salary for the purposes of reclassification or regrading has not been raised before any tribunal as yet. The definition of salary in general has been discussed in considerable detail in Chapter 42: see pp. 947 ff. *infra*.

(d) Grade must correspond to duties and powers

The fourth basic principle is the converse of the principle that staff members must be assigned to posts corresponding to their grade. It is that officials are entitled to be assigned a grade corresponding to their duties and powers. The aim of this principle is:

[O]n the one hand to avoid inequality of treatment between officials to whom duties of a comparable nature have been validly assigned, and on the other hand to ensure that no official is required to give services which do not fall within the definition of the duties attaching to his post.[31]

This is the principle implicitly conceded in all those cases where tribunals have examined claims for reclassification or upgrading, whether the decision has resulted in the reclassification being ordered or not. In *Jamet*,[32] for instance, the applicant who was a draughtsman was assigned to a post of designer but in fact did not perform the functions of designer. His claim to be upgraded was rejected by the CJEC because he could not show that the duties he performed and the powers he enjoyed corresponded to those of positions in the higher grade.[33]

In *Champoury*[34] the UNAT stated that: 'staff members in the Professional category in posts carrying similar duties and responsibilities should have the same grading, irrespective of the place where they are serving.'[35] This principle was seen as flowing from Staff Regulation 2.1 of the UN. It was further stated that, while under that same Regulation the General Assembly had the power conceivably to qualify in certain circumstances the principle that the grade given a post should always correspond to the duties and responsibilities of the post, provided it laid down a principle to be followed, it had not done so. It would seem that the tribunal was not ready lightly to concede a derogation from the general principle, even though Staff Regulation 2.1 did say that classification of posts should proceed in accordance with principles laid down by the General Assembly. In that case a decision of the General Assembly approving a budget which classified the applicant as a P1 was held not to amount to the establishment of a principle relating to classification which qualified the general principle stated above. The tribunal consequently applied the general principle and ordered that the applicant be reclassified as a P2. It is unlikely in any case that Staff Regulation 2.1 can be interpreted in such a way as to permit the General

---

[31] *Boursin*, CJEC Case 102/63 [1964] ECR p. 691 at p. 708.

[32] CJEC Case 37/71 [1972] ECR p. 483.

[33] See also *Rémont*, ILOAT Judgment No. 228 [1974] (FAO). In *de Bruin, Derbal and Keller*, ILOAT Judgment No. 425 [1980] (EPO), the ILOAT said that the Staff Regulations of EPO gave officials a right to a grade corresponding to their duties.

[34] UNAT Judgment No. 76 [1959], JUNAT Nos. 71–86 p. 35.

[35] Ibid. at p. 44.

Assembly totally to erode the general principle that posts should be classified according to the duties and responsibilities attaching to them.

Very early in the history of the CJEC, the Court adverted to and applied the general principle that a staff member was entitled to have his post classified according to the principle that the grade assigned to the position he held should correspond to the duties he performed. In *Maudet*[36] the Court found that the conversion of the applicant's grade after the Staff Regulations came into force was done in accordance with the provisions of the Staff Regulations but, nevertheless, held that at any time a staff member had a right also under the Staff Regulations to request that his position be reclassified according to the principle of correspondence of grade and duties. As a result the Court held that the applicant's claim for reclassification was good and that the decision not to reclassify him should be annulled.

There is a difficult case in which the CJEC appears to have qualified the principle discussed above. In *Prelle*[37] the applicant argued that he normally carried out duties and responsibilities which were those assigned to a higher grade, A3, so that his grade should have been changed from A4 to A3. While the Court did not deny this fact which came to light because the applicant was asked temporarily to perform functions assigned to a staff member in the same department who was in the higher grade, it stated:

Nevertheless, the fact that an official carries out tasks which also belong to a post in a higher career bracket, although it may be a factor to be taken into account in respect of his possible promotion, cannot of itself suffice to justify a reclassification of his post.

This is particularly so in departments such as the one to which the applicant belongs where the duties assigned to servants in different grades are of a comparable nature and are for this reason interchangeable.

Therefore the assignment of the duties in question to the post occupied by the applicant cannot have the effect of upgrading the post and making it necessary to classify it in a higher grade.[38]

The apparent qualification of the principle discussed above seems to be relevant in two circumstances. First, the duties and responsibilities assigned to the different grades must be of a comparable nature and, for this reason, be interchangeable. This may be a very special situation in the grading system of international institutions. But, where it prevails, the apparent qualification to the principle that grade must correspond to duties and responsibilities would be applicable for the reason that it is possible to assign the staff member to either of two grades. In this situation the administration may

---

36 CJEC Cases 20 & 21/63 [1964] ECR p. 113. See also *Reynier and Erba*, CJEC Cases 79 & 82/63 [1964] ECR p. 259.

37 CJEC Case 77/70 [1971] ECR p. 561.

38 Ibid. at pp. 566–7.

choose the grade to be assigned. The second circumstance is that the staff member affected must be in the lower grade. He cannot then claim to be upgraded. It would seem reasonable that the apparent qualification could not be applied by the administration arbitrarily to downgrade a staff member from a higher grade to a lower one.

It may also be noted that the Court did mention that the apparent qualification was applicable particularly where the department was such that duties assigned to officials in different grades were similar and therefore interchangeable. This observation not only serves to emphasize the exceptional nature of the situation in which the apparent qualification applies but it may signify that the similarity of duties and responsibilities assigned to different grades must be in the nature of a phenomenon prevailing in general and across the board rather than in individual instances, albeit in a particular department.

In a different situation the Appeal Board of the OECD has held that in the case of temporary staff the rule of correspondence of grade and duties applies less strictly, though, if the grade has been systematically maintained at an inadequate level, the tribunal would interfere with the discretion of the administration on the ground of manifest error.[39] In the case concerned the tribunal held that there had been no violation of the law, because, although the applicant had been recruited at a low level he had been rapidly promoted to a higher level and ultimately, after a short delay which was not unwarranted, had been promoted to his present grade.

Where a staff member by contract or agreement accepts a particular grade, though his duties belong to a higher grade, he is bound to such agreement or contract and cannot claim to be upgraded. In *Beelen*[40] a staff member of the EPO agreed by contract to be graded B4, until he was age 30, although his post was normally graded B5. It was the policy of the EPO not to place staff members in grade B5 before they reached the age of 30. The ILOAT held that the applicant was bound by his contract, could not question his grade until he was 30, and must carry out his contract in good faith.[41]

The assignment of grades

In very general terms, it may be said that there have been two divergent

---

[39] *Doronzo*, Decision No. 35, OECD Appeals Board [1963], Recueil des décisions 1 à 62 (1979) p. 98. In *Van Lamoen*, Council of Europe Appeals Board, Appeal No. 100 [1984], Case-Law Digest (1985) p. 137, it was held that the grading system and principles did not apply to temporary staff.

[40] ILOAT Judgment No. 545 [1983] (EPO). See also *Decision No. 34*, NATO Appeals Board [1971], Collection of the Decisions (1972), and *Decision No. 94*, NATO Appeals Board [1978], Collection of the Decisions 65(b), 74 to 99 (1979).

[41] See also *Decision No. 5*, OEEC Appeals Board [1950], Recueil des décisions 1 à 62 (1979) p. 14.

approaches to disputes relating to the grading or classification of posts, especially in regard to disputes challenging the decision to assign a particular grade to a post. The CJEC has spearheaded one approach, while the ILOAT has been the protagonist in respect of the alternative approach. The object of both approaches has, however, been the same, namely the determination of the question whether the decision to classify the post in a certain way or not to reclassify the post as requested is valid.

(a) The approach of the CJEC

The CJEC has always conducted a thorough examination of the facts of cases brought before it in which reclassification has been requested as a result of the refusal of the administration to assign a particular grade to a particular post. The object of this examination has been to establish whether in fact the applicant's post involves duties and responsibilities corresponding to the grade claimed. As early as 1964 the Court ordered reclassification of the staff member as requested by him after examining the duties and responsibilities of his position, on finding that the administration had wrongfully refused to reclassify him, because it considered that it had acted legally under the Staff Regulations in keeping him in his existing grade after the Staff Regulations came into force.[42]

In *Müller*[43] the applicant contended that his post, which was that of a financial comptroller, involved duties and responsibilities which should have been classified as belonging to a grade in the A category rather than as belonging to the grade B1. The Court, in order to resolve the problem presented to it, considered in detail 'the nature of the duties in dispute'[44] and came to the conclusion that, though the applicant exercised some supervisory activities, the quality and nature of the supervision carried out was not indicative of a high grade, that his duties did not necessarily require knowledge of a university level or equivalent professional experience, that the independence enjoyed by him which was characteristic of a financial comptroller and the fact that he reported directly to the Director General were not decisive, and that for all these reasons 'it does not appear that the duties exercised by the applicant necessarily correspond to administrative and advisory duties as defined in the second subparagraph of Article 5(1) of the Staff Regulations.'[45] In *Mulders*,[46] a later case, the Court examined the facts in order to determine whether the applicant, who was an accounting officer, had the same duties and responsibilities as a financial comptroller

---

[42] *Maudet*, CJEC Cases 20 & 21/63 [1964] ECR p. 113.
[43] CJEC Case 28/64 [1965] ECR p. 237.
[44] Ibid. at p. 250.
[45] Ibid. at p. 251.
[46] CJEC Case 8/69 [1969] ECR p. 561.

which would have required that he be placed in the same grade as a financial comptroller. The Court held that the facts showed that assigning the applicant the same grade as a financial comptroller was not warranted.[47] These were cases in which the CJEC examined the facts and found that the claim for reclassification was not justified.

It is very rarely that the CJEC has examined the facts in cases where reclassification was claimed and found that the request for reclassification was justified. In *Maudet*,[48] as has already been seen, the Court found that the applicant's claim was good and ordered the decision not to reclassify him to be quashed.

In examining claims for reclassification or grading the CJEC has held that, where the terms of a definition of duties do not correspond to clearly distinct concepts, their application is to a certain extent within the discretion of the administration and that the fact that the application of such terms may be open to criticism is not of itself sufficient to make the decision taken relating to classification improper.[49] The meanings given to the terms 'sector of activity' and 'administrative unit' in determining whether a subdivision of the institution came within those concepts were questioned in *Jullien*[50] but were found to be unimpeachable on the basis of the above principle.

The Court has also examined whether a grading committee which was entrusted with recommending grades for new recruits on the basis of established criteria had applied those criteria fairly in the case of the applicant in recommending the grade to which he was to be assigned.[51] It accepted the criteria in this case in examining the question whether the grade assigned was proper. In finding that the criteria had been applied fairly the Court presumably meant that the grading decision was on the facts of the case a proper one.

The Court will apparently declare a grading decision tainted, if it finds that the procedure invoked and the steps taken in establishing a classification are not in accord with what is required by the Staff Regulations or other applicable law.[52] The cases in which the Court examined the procedure followed concerned the re-establishment of staff, but there is no reason why the principle should not be applicable generally. The Court has found in two

[47] See also *Krawczynski*, CJEC Case 83/63 [1965] p. 623. For other cases in which the CJEC examined the facts and came to the conclusion that the classification of the applicants was not unlawful, see *Müller*, CJEC Cases 109/63 & 13/64 [1964] ECR p. 663; *Jullien*, CJEC Case 10/64 [1965] ECR p. 69; *Brus*, CJEC Cases 48/64 & 1/65 [1965] ECR p. 351; *Stipperger*, CJEC Case 49/64 [1965] ECR p. 521; *Jamet*, CJEC Case 37/71 [1972] ECR p. 483.

[48] CJEC Cases 20 & 21/63 [1964] ECR p. 113.

[49] *Jullien*, CJEC Case 10/64 [1965] ECR p. 69. See also *Brus*, CJEC Cases 48/64 & 1/65 [1965] ECR p. 351.

[50] CJEC Case 10/64 [1965] ECR p. 69.

[51] *Petersen*, CJEC Case 102/75 [1976] ECR p. 1777.

[52] See *Collotti*, CJEC Case 70/63 [1964] ECR p. 435. See also *Maudet*, CJEC Cases 20 & 21/63 [1964] ECR p. 113.

cases it has decided that there was in effect no violation of the procedures required by the Staff Regulations, but in so far as it said that it had power, in the exercise of its jurisdiction, to re-establish the classification in question, it seems to have believed that it had the power to examine a classification decision where the proper procedures had not been followed.[53] In one case the Court found that, while the procedure prescribed had been violated, since the impugned decision had been withdrawn within a reasonable time, there was no illegal decision that could be quashed.[54]

Discrimination or inequality of treatment is recognized by the CJEC as a ground for annulling a decision not to reclassify a staff member. Where the principle of equality of treatment was violated as between new recruits and those in service reclassification was ordered.[55]

The OASAT follows the practice of the CJEC in so far as it has itself examined in detail the facts of cases in which applicants have claimed that they should be reclassified, in order to determine whether the applicants should be given the grades they claimed. In *Brocos*,[56] for instance, the tribunal held that the expert testimony, the evidence submitted, and the standard embodied in the Staff Regulation required that the applicant be reclassified upwards from grade G5 to G7.[57] In another case[58] the applicant claimed that he should have been graded in grade P5 rather than grade P4 four years before the date of his application because he had been performing the duties of a P5 officer during that time. Just before the claim was made the applicant's title was taken away and his duties were distributed among several other officers in the same grade. While the tribunal held that it could not order the restoration to the applicant of a post that did not exist, because it had never been included in the budget, it also examined the claim that the applicant should have been in grade P5 for the four previous years. It examined in detail the duties formerly assigned to the applicant and found that on the facts the claim for reclassification was not justified.[59]

The UNAT has not had occasion to deal with complaints about grading very often. When it has done so it has examined the substance of the grading decision. It has investigated the facts in order to establish whether the claim to be assigned a particular grade was justified. In *Champoury*,[60] the only case

[53] See *Collotti*, CJEC Case 70/63 [1964] ECR p. 435; *Maudet*, CJEC Cases 20 & 21/63 [1964] ECR p. 113.

[54] *Algera*, CJEC Cases 7/56 & 3 to 7/57 [1957] ECR p. 39.

[55] *Williams*, CJEC Case 9/81 [1982] ECR p. 3301. In *Micheli*, CJEC Cases 198 to 202/81 [1982] ECR p. 4145, no discrimination was found because objective differences existed between the classes of staff members concerned.

[56] OASAT Judgment No. 39 [1979].

[57] See also *Boita*, OASAT Judgment No. 36 [1978]; *Saravia*, OASAT Judgment No. 47 [1979].

[58] *Galván*, OASAT Judgment No. 46 [1979].

[59] See also *García and Others*, OASAT Judgment No. 6 [1974].

[60] UNAT Judgment No. 76 [1959], JUNAT Nos. 71–86 p. 35.

to be found on the subject, the applicant claimed that instead of the grade P1 he should have had, as a proof-reader, the grade P2. The UNAT found that elsewhere in the UN officials who held posts which had attached to them the functions and duties carried out by the applicant were graded P2. It, therefore, ordered the applicant to be classified in the P2 grade. This decision is consistent with the other approach taken by other tribunals than the CJEC and the OASAT which will be discussed below, since it ordered specific performance ostensibly on the basis that the decision of the Secretary General not to reclassify the applicant which could be regarded as the exercise of a discretionary power resulted in inequality of treatment; but to the extent that the UNAT did examine *per se* the content of the duties and functions of the applicant in order to determine whether they matched those of the grade he claimed, it seems to have followed the approach taken by the CJEC and the OASAT.

(b) The approach of the ILOAT

The idea that a decision taken in regard to classification or grading could only be questioned, if it had been taken arbitrarily or in bad faith was mooted by the ILOAT as early as 1958 in *Cardena*[61] where it was found that the decision of the ITU to reclassify the applicant was not tainted with any irregularity and was, therefore, good. However, something like the general formula used in relation to the limited power of review of discretionary powers appears first to have been referred to in *Walther*.[62] The tribunal stated:

[T]he Director is free to exercise his discretion in carrying out the responsibilities assigned to him. It follows that the Administrative Tribunal must confine itself to determining whether the decisions taken are tainted by errors in law or based on materially incorrect facts, or whether essential facts have not been taken into consideration, or again whether conclusions which are manifestly incorrect have been drawn from the evidence in the dossier of the person concerned.[63]

More recently in *Mahadev* the tribunal used more comprehensive language appropriate to describing its power of review in classification cases on the basis that the power of classification was discretionary, when it said:

[T]he Administrative Tribunal will not quash a post classification unless the decision was taken without authority, or violated a rule of form or procedure, or was based on a mistake of fact or of law, or essential facts were overlooked, or there was misuse of authority, or clearly mistaken conclusions were drawn from the facts.[64]

---

61 ILOAT Judgment No. 39 [1958] (ITU) at p. 4.
62 ILOAT Judgment No. 106 [1967] (BIRPI).
63 Ibid. at p. 5.
64 ILOAT Judgment No. 530 [1982] (WHO) at p. 5. For general statements see also *Rudin*, ILOAT Judgment No. 377 [1979] (ILO) at p. 4; *Robinson*, ILOAT Judgment No. 428 [1980]

The tribunal will not substitute its own judgment for that of the administration[65] but will merely review the exercise of the discretion. However, where the tribunal has found that the discretionary power has been improperly exercised, it has not hesitated to examine the facts and come to its own conclusion as to the proper grade to be assigned to the applicant. In *Price (No. 2)*[66] the tribunal held that the decision not to upgrade the applicant from grade P3 to grade P4 was vitiated by errors of fact or was based on the consideration of irrelevant matters or was tainted by irregularity of procedure. Then it said that according to its own reading of the facts which was endorsed by the recommendation of the Appeals Board, the applicant should be reclassified in grade P4.[67] On the other hand, in *García*,[68] where it was found that the discretion to grade was improperly exercised because of a defect of procedure in a situation where the applicant was graded P4 when he claimed the higher grade P5, the case was remanded for correction of procedure.

It would seem that the general practice of the tribunal supports the view that in cases where it finds that the discretion to grade has been exercised improperly for reasons other than procedural irregularities it will carry out the grading exercise itself by examining the facts and assigning the appropriate grade. Where the exercise of the discretion is vitiated because of procedural irregularity the tribunal will order a reassessment of the grading decision according to the proper procedure.

In an early case, the tribunal followed a different procedure from that described above. In *Dadivas*[69] it did not confine itself to determining whether the discretion to assign a grade had been improperly exercised. Instead, it examined the duties of the applicant who contended that, as an official who performed the duties of a budget clerk with the same title, he should be graded M5, as all budget clerks were graded, and not M4, a lower grade. It also found upon an examination of the facts that during a later period when budget clerks were reclassified as M4 the classification as an M4 was proper. While the results of this case may not have been different if the technique used in other cases had been used, the procedure followed was unusual. In fact the finding that the later classification was valid could have been made also by concluding that the discretion had been properly exercised and the

---

(ITU) at pp. 3–4; *Ayyangar*, ILOAT Judgment No. 529 [1982] (WHO); *Polacchi*, ILOAT Judgment No. 606 [1984] (FAO) at p. 5.

[65] See *Walther*, ILOAT Judgment No. 106 [1967] (BIRPI) at p. 6; *García*, ILOAT Judgment No. 591 [1983] (PAHO) at p. 4. See also *Polacchi*, ILOAT Judgment No. 606 [1984] (FAO).

[66] ILOAT Judgment No. 342 [1978] (PAHO).

[67] See also *de Bruin, Derbal and Keller*, ILOAT Judgment No. 425 [1980] (EPO).

[68] ILOAT Judgment No. 591 [1983] (PAHO). See also *Cuvillier*, ILOAT Judgment No. 333 [1978] (ILO).

[69] ILOAT Judgment No. 60 [1962] (WHO).

decision that the earlier refusal to reclassify the applicant as an M5 was unlawful might very well have been reached by examining the exercise of the discretion and finding that it had been improperly exercised. In reclassifying the applicant thereafter as an M5 the tribunal might have had to examine the facts as it did in *Price* (*No. 2*) and the result would have been the same. The technique adopted in *Dadivas* has not been followed in later cases, as it happens.

In reviewing the exercise of the discretionary power to grade or classify the ILOAT has generally referred to categories of vitiating elements which are normally relevant to reviewing the exercise of discretionary powers and applied the law relating to these categories. There appears to be nothing of special significance emerging from the application of the law relating to discretionary powers to the exercise of the power to regrade.

i. *Error of law*

In *Hakin* (*No. 3*) the issue arose whether the Staff Regulations had been correctly applied in regard to the classification of staff members 'on the basis of the scale of equivalence of seniority, grade and step approved by the Administrative Council'.[70] The tribunal found that even by the applicant's own admission the Director General of IPI had correctly applied the Staff Regulations in assessing the seniority of the applicant, with due regard to the situation created at the time his appointment had earlier been confirmed. In *Joshi* the applicant alleged that the Director General of UPU had exceeded his authority in successively applying two different systems of grading which was a claim that he erred in law. The tribunal found that:

In so far as the Regulations confer certain powers on the Director General in respect of grading, they do not determine the substance of the measures to be taken. In particular, they do not forbid the successive adoption of different systems. Consequently in applying different standards in 1971 from those which had been applicable in 1968 the Director General did not exceed his authority. In fact, the complainant is confusing two different questions: authority and the use made of authority. In order to invalidate the plea of lack of authority, it is enough to confirm that the Director General did not overstep the limits of his powers, and it is not necessary to consider how he exercised those powers.[71]

It is possible that acquired rights be violated by a grading decision which

---

[70] ILOAT Judgment No. 218 [1973] (IPI) at p. 4. There are other cases in which it has been alleged that Staff Regulations or other regulations had been wrongly applied. The decision has always been that there has been no error of law in the application of governing rules by the administration: see *Boyle*, ILOAT Judgment No. 178 [1971] (ITU); *Hakin* (*No. 2*), ILOAT Judgment No. 217 [1973] (IPI). In *Polacchi*, ILOAT Judgment No. 606 [1984] (FAO) at p. 5, reference was made to the application of a 'wrong principle' as being an abuse of discretion. This was a reference to an error of law.

[71] ILOAT Judgment No. 208 [1973] (UPU) at pp. 4–5.

would amount to an error of law by the administration. In *Biggio* (*No. 3*) *et al.*,[72] however, the tribunal found that acquired rights relating to the level of salary had not been violated by the amalgamation of two grades which had existed under the old system of grading, the applicant having been assigned to an appropriate grade under the new system which also did not result in his being assigned to a lower grade.[73]

ii. *Error of fact*

In some cases, while applicants have not specifically argued that there had been an error of fact in the taking of the grading decision, the tribunal has specifically pointed out that an error of fact had not been proved by the applicant.[74] There was an implicit assumption in these cases that an error of fact would have vitiated the decision and would have resulted in an abuse of discretion.

iii. *Omission of facts and consideration of irrelevant facts*

In several cases the tribunal has adverted to the principle that essential facts must not be overlooked or omitted from consideration in the taking of the grading decision, in so far as it has held that essential facts had not been omitted from consideration and, thus, the decision was not vitiated by this substantive irregularity.[75] In *Walther*[76] the applicant argued that in the case of his reclassification request the *ad hoc* committee which had considered his case was not in possession of all the information required for an informed consideration of his case. The tribunal held that the applicant had not proved this allegation. The applicant further contended that the Director of BIRPI had ignored the fact that as far back as 1955 the Swiss Federal Council had recognized that the duties assigned to the applicant at that time were those of a Counsellor. The tribunal held that this was only one factor among others which had to be taken into account under the Staff Regulations and that the Director had not in fact ignored it.[77]

A decision may be vitiated because irrelevant facts have been taken into consideration. In *Price* (*No. 2*)[78] the tribunal gave as one reason for the illegality of the grading decision the fact that irrelevant matters had been

---

[72] ILOAT Judgment No. 366 [1978] (IPI/EPO).

[73] See also *Robinson*, ILOAT Judgment No. 428 [1980] (ITU). In *Mollard*, ILOAT Judgment No. 299 [1977] (ILO), it was held that taking into account responsibility and technical knowledge in addition to the duties materially described was in accordance with the Staff Regulations of the ILO.

[74] See *Boyle*, ILOAT Judgment No. 178 [1971] (ITU); *Mollard*, ILOAT Judgment No. 299 [1977] (ILO): *Price* (*No. 2*), ILOAT Judgment No. 342 [1978] (PAHO).

[75] See *Arnold*, ILOAT Judgment No. 397 [1980] (ITU); *Mahadev*, ILOAT Judgment No. 530 [1982] (WHO); *Michl*, ILOAT Judgment No. 585 [1983] (EPO).

[76] ILOAT Judgment No. 106 [1967] (BIRPI).

[77] See also *Cardena*, ILOAT Judgment No. 39 [1958] (ITU).

[78] ILOAT Judgment No. 342 [1978] (PAHO).

taken into consideration. In *Mollard*[79] the tribunal found to the contrary that irrelevant matters had not been taken into consideration in so far as the level of responsibility and technical knowledge had been considered in addition to the description of the duties of the post.

iv. *Erroneous conclusions*

In *Robinson*[80] the applicant argued that, since the affirmation by nine other officials that he performed the duties of a P4-grade official should have warranted the conclusion that he did so, the failure of the administration to grade him accordingly was an abuse of discretion. The tribunal held that there was no mistaken conclusion drawn from the facts, in so far as the administration came to the conclusion that he did not perform the functions of a P4-grade official, because there were other facts such as the opinions of the experts in post description which warranted the conclusion reached.[81] There are some other cases in which the tribunal decided that mistaken conclusions had not been reached and that the grading decision was, therefore, not vitiated.[82] In some cases reference is made to the absence of a mistaken assessment which might have vitiated the grading decision.[83] This is probably similar to the notion that there had been no mistaken conclusions drawn from the facts. *Price (No. 2)*[84] seems to be the only case in which the tribunal has held that the conclusion reached was mistaken. In regard to a claim for regrading from P3 to P4 after an audit of duties was done the conclusion reached that the applicant should not be regraded was held to have no proper basis in fact as was also shown clearly by the findings of the Appeal Board. The result was that the decision was vitiated.

Similar to the defect of mistaken conclusions seems to be the adoption of a mistaken approach. In *Dadivas and Callanta*[85] reclassification to a higher grade was requested because of an increase of duties, among other things. The tribunal held that the assessment to be made of whether the increase in duties should be reflected in a reclassification was a technical one and that the administration had not taken a mistaken approach to the question. The decision not to regrade was, therefore, not an abuse of discretion.[86]

---

[79] ILOAT Judgment No. 299 [1977] (ILO).

[80] ILOAT Judgment No. 428 [1980] (ITU).

[81] See also *Michl*, ILOAT Judgment No. 585 [1983] (EPO).

[82] See *Boyle*, ILOAT Judgment No. 178 [1971] (ITU); *Rudin*, ILOAT Judgment No. 377 [1979] (ILO); *Arnold*, ILOAT Judgment No. 397 [1980] (ITU); *Mahadev*, ILOAT Judgment No. 530 [1982] (WHO).

[83] See *Sarna*, ILOAT Judgment No. 594 [1983] (WHO).

[84] ILOAT Judgment No. 342 [1978] (PAHO).

[85] ILOAT Judgment No. 153 [1970] (WHO).

[86] See also *Espínola*, ILOAT Judgment No. 446 [1981] (PAHO).

v. *Inequality of treatment*

The principle of equality of treatment has been referred to in connection with the regrading of posts and the awarding of bonuses to those in the same grade. In *Joshi* the applicant argued that the principle had been violated because of the application of different grading standards to new recruits. The tribunal explained the facts and the law as applied to the case as follows:

> The complainant's main contention is that as a result of the adoption of new classification standards he has been put at a disadvantage in relation to officials appointed later. Not only can the latter officials be appointed at the outset to a higher grade than that to which the complainant was originally appointed; they are entitled to a full retirement pension at the age of 60, or five years earlier than the complainant himself. The complainant is therefore basing his plea on the principle of equality, although he has not expressly said so.
>
> According to this principle, which is applicable in international organisations as a general rule of law even if not embodied in any specific text, persons who find themselves in a similar factual and legal position should be put on the same legal footing. At the time of his appointment the complainant was subject to the old grading standards. His position was therefore different from that of staff members recruited in accordance with the new standards. Thus, since he was not in the same position as those staff members, the complainant did not suffer any discrimination in relation to them.
>
> Moreover, the principle of equality must be applied within the limits imposed by efficient administration. If any amendment of grading standards were to entail a review of the position of staff members already appointed, complications would inevitably arise which might discourage the organisations from making necessary adjustments and thus compromise their efficient operation. In particular, it would be generally difficult and sometimes impossible to put serving officials on the same footing as newly-appointed officials. Further, it would not always be possible for the organisations to meet the additional financial responsibilities consequent on the regrading of all their staff members. It would therefore be unreasonable to require an organisation to review the terms of appointment of all its staff in the light of the principle of equality as a result of changes in standards of recruitment.[87]

It was held that the principle of equality had not been violated. In *Hakin (No. 2)*[88] the allocation of bonuses to different grades of staff was held not to result in inequality of treatment. While these two cases decided that the principle of equality of treatment had not been violated on their facts, there is no reason to doubt that the principle of equality of treatment is relevant to the exercise of the discretion to assign a grade and that in the appropriate circumstances it may be held that the principle has been violated. It can safely be assumed that both the principles of non-discrimination and equality of treatment are

---

[87] ILOAT Judgment No. 208 [1973] (UPU) at p. 6.
[88] ILOAT Judgment No. 217 [1973] (IPI).

applicable to the subject of grading and classification provided the proper circumstances obtain.

vi. *Prejudice or ill will*

In *Sarna* the applicant contended that he had not been classified as a profess-ional because of personal prejudice and bias against him on the part of the Regional Director, the Chief of Administration and Finance, and the Personnel Officer in WHO. In regard to the facts of the case, it was stated:

> The complainant refers to the rapid promotion of another staff member, Mr. Sethi, from a post under the complainant's supervision to one of equal status. He also mentions the reimbursement to Mr. Sethi of the cost of his visit to headquarters in July 1974 and his subsequent promotion. As can be seen in the letter dated 23 July 1974 annexed to the rejoinder the reimbursement to Mr. Sethi was entirely justified, and his promotion was the result of his outstanding work. The matters cited by the complainant as showing prejudice and bias fall far short of establishing any abuse of authority on the part of the WHO and the allegation of personal prejudice and bias must be dismissed as groundless.[89]

In *Ayyangar*[90] it was held that the protracted nature of the reclassification process was not evidence of prejudice.

While a grading or classification decision has not been declared vitiated by reason of prejudice or bias, the ILOAT has clearly acted on the under-standing that prejudice or bias is a good reason for faulting the exercise of the discretion to grade or classify.

vii. *Procedural irregularities*

There are several cases in which the ILOAT has found that procedural irregularities vitiated the decision not to regrade the applicant. In *Price (No. 2)*[91] it was held that the consultation of an outsider and the conduct of a procedure by the Chief of Division without the applicant's being given an opportunity also to reopen his case were procedural irregularities. The decision not to regrade was found defective for other reasons of a substantive nature as well and, as a consequence, not only was it quashed but the tribunal examined the facts and ordered reclassification.[92] In *García*[93] the Director of PAHO acted upon a recommendation of the Board of Inquiry and Appeal of PAHO which had been made in the context of an unsafe and obscure system

---

[89] ILOAT Judgment No. 594 [1983] (WHO) at p. 5.

[90] ILOAT Judgment No. 529 [1982] (WHO). For other cases in which it was held that the personal prejudice had not been proved see *Dadivas and Callanta*, ILOAT Judgment No. 153 [1970] (WHO); *Rémont*, ILOAT Judgment No. 228 [1974] (FAO); *Dobosch*, ILOAT Judgment No. 451 [1981] (PAHO).

[91] ILOAT Judgment No. 342 [1978] (PAHO).

[92] See also *Cuvillier*, ILOAT Judgment No. 333 [1978] (ILO).

[93] ILOAT Judgment No. 591 [1983] (PAHO).

of classification which it virtually ignored in proceeding on the basis of its best judgment and general principles of administration. The tribunal held that the defectiveness of the system in force did not warrant anyone proceeding unsystematically and that the original decision taken by the Classification Unit which went to the Board of Inquiry and Appeal should have been reconsidered. The procedure which should have been followed was that '[t]he Director should have remitted the request to the Unit for reconsideration after he had provided it with clear and intelligible parameters and criteria.'[94]

In several cases the procedure followed was found to have been fair and proper. In *Boyle*[95] the tribunal held that there was no need for the administration to consult the staff on the qualifications required for a particular post and that the procedure followed on appeal was fair because both sides had been given an opportunity to be heard.[96] Reference back to a grading committee by the Director General of ILO on a complaint being made by the applicant, was not an abuse of procedure.[97] Where there was a reorganization with the result that the number of posts was reduced, new posts were created, and posts were redefined and reclassified, it was held that there was no general requirement that the new posts be advertised before the reclassification was done.[98] The right to be heard before a review committee does not require that the complainant be heard in person.[99]

It has been recognized apparently that adequate reasons must be given for the decision taken in regard to grading or reclassification, in so far as it has been held in *Arnold*[100] that adequate reasons for the decision taken had been given in the case so that there was no violation of a procedural principle.

The principle that, if the procedural irregularity is to vitiate the decision taken, it must be such that it had an adverse influence on the decision taken has also been recognized. In *Espínola*[101] it was conceded that according to the Staff Regulations the Director of PAHO should have established a plan for the reclassification of all posts, which had not been done. However, it was held that, even if there was no such plan, the Board of Inquiry and Appeal had not been hampered by the absence of such a plan. Therefore, the non-observance of the procedural requirement did not vitiate the decision.

---

[94] Ibid. at p. 5.
[95] ILOAT Judgment No. 178 [1971] (ITU).
[96] See also *Joshi*, ILOAT Judgment No. 208 [1973] (UPU).
[97] *Rudin*, ILOAT Judgment No. 377 [1979] (ILO).
[98] *Arnold*, ILOAT Judgment No. 397 [1980] (ITU).
[99] *Robinson*, ILOAT Judgment No. 428 [1980] (ITU). In *Danjean* (*Nos. 1 and 2*), ILOAT Judgment No. 126 [1968] (CERN), it was found that the procedure before the Joint Appeals Board was not defective.
[100] ILOAT Judgment No. 397 [1980] (ITU).
[101] ILOAT Judgment No. 446 [1981] (PAHO).

viii. *Other irregularities*

While the decided cases do not cover all the possible irregularities, whether substantive or procedural or connected with abuse of authority, which may vitiate the grading decision, there is no reason why the same principles as apply to the exercise of discretionary powers in general should not apply to the exercise of the discretion to grade or classify. Thus, it is possible that abuse of purpose (*détournement de pouvoir*) in a broad sense or other substantive and procedural irregularities than those referred to above could vitiate the decision to assign a grade.

(c) *Other tribunals*

There seems to be some general indication that the Appeals Board of ESRO would have followed the approach to grading decisions taken by the ILOAT. That tribunal took the view that it could not examine the merits of the different grades that the organization attributes to the functions performed by the staff nor of the qualifications necessary for each grade.[102] In conceding that these decisions could not be examined on the merits the tribunal was asserting that it would not substitute its own judgment on the matters involved for that of the administration. It would follow from this that the tribunal would probably have regarded the decision to grade as a discretionary decision to be controlled and reviewed by the tribunal in the same way as the ILOAT does.

In *Doronzo* the Appeals Board of the OECD said that it would interfere with the discretion exercised by the Secretary General in grading temporary staff, if there were a manifest error.[103] The language used is that relating to the exercise of discretionary powers. It is, thus, likely that the OECD regards the decision to assign a grade as a discretionary power, as the ILOAT does.

In *Decision No. 95* the Appeals Board of NATO stated in regard to a decision not to recommend the upgrading of the applicant's post in the budget for lack of sufficient justification: 'whereas, however, it must satisfy itself that the relevant decisions have been taken by a competent authority in accordance with the proper procedure and that they were not based on errors of fact, errors of law, obvious errors of judgment or a misuse of powers.'[104] The decision in the case was found not to be an improper one. The tribunal appears to have taken the same approach as the ILOAT.[105]

---

[102] *Decision No. 3 (2nd Appeal)*, *ESRO/CR/21*, ESRO Appeals Board [1969], at p. 4.

[103] Decision No. 35, OECD Appeals Board [1963], Recueil des décisions 1 à 62 [1979] p. 98 at p. 100.

[104] *Decision No. 95*, NATO Appeals Board [1978] at p. 3, Collection of the Decisions 65(b), 74 to 99 (1979).

[105] The same approach seems to have been endorsed in *Decision No. 94*, NATO Appeals Board [1978], Collection of the Decisions 65(b), 74 to 99 (1979), and *Decision No. 145*, NATO Appeals Board [1981], Collection of the Decisions 135 to 171 (1984).

Specific rules applied by tribunals

The problems relating to grading that have come before tribunals have varied from tribunal to tribunal. In dealing with them, apart from the principles and law discussed in the previous section, tribunals have enunciated certain rules which may be of value in dealing with problems of a similar or analogous nature which arise before other tribunals. These rules relate to various aspects of grading or classification.

(a) Substantive obligations

In connection with a grading decision or in dealing with the functions to be assigned to a post belonging to a certain grade, the administration must carry out the substantive obligations imposed upon it by the relevant laws. In *Walther*[106] the ILOAT found that under Article 2 of the Staff Regulations of BIRPI the Director, in determining the grade of each post, had the twofold obligation of hearing the opinion of an *ad hoc* committee and of basing himself on the standards used by other international organizations. The ILOAT held that the Director had not violated either of these obligations. In particular in adapting the standards used by other organizations to the specific nature and specific characteristics of BIRPI he had not misinterpreted the Regulation.

In most cases the violation of such obligations imposed on administrations would result in an error of law or in a procedural irregularity which under either of the two approaches to the problem of grading described above would amount to a vitiating element in the grading process. However, the rule would apply even where the obligations do not relate specifically to the substance of the decision or the procedure connected with it, such as where the obligation is a condition of the exercise of the decision to assign a grade. In connection with the reorganization of four departments which were converted into two departments in ITU, posts were redefined in such a way that the applicant was assigned to a P2 post after certain duties were taken away from the post he previously held and another officer was assigned to a P3 (higher) grade which was given those duties that had been taken away. This officer had the qualifications but was allegedly less experienced than the applicant. The ILOAT found that in making the appointment the administration had not violated any of the obligations applicable also to the reorganization of departments and contained in Staff Regulation 1.2 which required that staff members were to be assigned to duties in accordance with their qualifications.[107]

106 ILOAT Judgment No. 106 [1967] (BIRPI).
107 *Arnold*, ILOAT Judgment No. 397 [1980] (ITU).

However, the obligations must be clear and definite. Thus, in *Decision No. 17*[108] the Financial Regulations of NATO required that certain duties relating to the signing of contracts be performed by an official who had a particular A2 post with a certain title. When these duties and the title were taken away from this official, the Appeals Board of NATO held that the administration was in violation of a clear obligation under the applicable law and ordered that the duties and title be restored to the officer concerned. On the other hand, in *Espínola*[109] the ILOAT referred to the obligations allegedly violated and contained in the Administrative Manual of PAHO and said that they merely gave directions in general terms. The tribunal implied that no specific obligations could be identified which had been violated and that the allegation made amounted to a contention that the classification was incorrect.

(b) Temporary assignments

i. The temporary assignment to a staff member of duties belonging to a higher grade than that of such staff member does not of itself bind the organization to assign such staff member the higher grade, especially if the facts show that the appointing authority never intended the staff member to perform such duties. In *Boursin* the CJEC stated:

In the present case, whatever the nature of the duties the applicant might have been asked to perform by his Director General, it is clear that the defendant never authorized the applicant to be directly attached to the latter. On the contrary, it showed evidence of the opposite intention on several occasions.[110]

In *Grosz*[111] the principle was restated that the appointing authority must agree to the staff member performing duties attached to a higher grade, even if they are temporary. In the absence of such agreement, the mere fact of performing such duties does not give the staff member a right to the higher grade. Even if there is such agreement, if it is clear that the agreement was that the duties belonging to the higher grade be performed on a temporary basis, this does not give the staff member a right to be upgraded.[112]

ii. The general rule seems to be that, in accordance with the general principle of labour law that there should be equal pay for equal work, particularly where the law of the organization provides for the payment of a

---

[108] *Decision No. 17*, NATO Appeals Board [1969], Collection of the Decisions (1972).
[109] ILOAT Judgment No. 446 [1981] (PAHO).
[110] CJEC Case 102/63 [1964] ECR p. 691 at p. 708.
[111] CJEC Case 35/69 [1970] ECR p. 609.
[112] See *Tontodonati*, CJEC Case 28/72 [1973] ECR p. 779. See also *Van Reenen*, CJEC Case 189/73 [1975] ECR p. 445. In *Plug*, CJEC Case 191/81 [1982] ECR p. 4229, a temporary posting by agreement was held not to give the staff member a right to a change of grade or description of duties.

temporary allowance, if a staff member performs duties assigned to a post belonging to a higher grade, he is entitled to be paid the due temporary allowance for the period during which those duties were performed.[113] There are some qualifications to this, however. First, the staff member must prove that his duties did belong to a higher grade.[114] Secondly, there must be nothing in the law of the organization which does not permit the payment of a temporary allowance and it must be evident that the arrangements made for temporary service were not made under the general powers of any administration in respect of the organization of its departments to institute a system for the temporary replacement of absent officers which may be exercised outside the terms of the rules of the organization for the payment of temporary allowances.[115] In a situation where the above general powers are utilized there is no unlawful act and the principle of unjust enrichment does not apply, because it cannot be shown that there was such enrichment.[116] Thirdly, it must be clear that the appointing authority (as the organ competent to represent the organization in the situation) agreed to have the staff member perform the temporary duties. Where this cannot be shown, there is no right to the temporary allowance.[117]

iii. Where, because of special circumstances, such as a merger of institutions, officials accept a lower grade voluntarily on a temporary basis, pursuant to the provisions of the Staff Regulations, the temporary measure is justified on a short-term basis and cannot be prolonged to the detriment of the officials concerned. As a consequence these officials should have strict guarantees concerning their right of priority to posts in the same grade as they hold when the assignment of such posts is done. This requires that the suitability for vacant posts of candidates having this priority should be considered independently of any reference to the possible merits of those not having such rights.[118]

(c) Post descriptions

There is some jurisprudence on the subject of job descriptions.

i. Under Article 16 of the Staff Regulations of the ILO job descriptions are required to be done but no time-limit is mentioned. In *Lamming*[119] the ILOAT held that in the absence of a specific time-limit, it could not be

---

[113] *Decision No. 94*, NATO Appeals Board [1978], Collection of the Decisions 65(b), 74 to 99 (1979); *Reeve*, OASAT Judgment No. 59 [1981].

[114] *Elz*, CJEC Cases 22 & 23/60 [1960] ECR p. 181.

[115] *Danvin*, CJEC Case 26/67 [1968] ECR p. 315.

[116] Ibid.

[117] *Grosz*, CJEC Case 35/69 [1970] ECR p. 609; *Micheli*, CJEC Cases 198 to 202/81 [1982] ECR p. 4145.

[118] These principles were established in *Wonnerth*, CJEC Case 12/69 [1969] ECR p. 577.

[119] ILOAT Judgment No. 40 [1960] (ILO).

concluded that there was no time-limit but the Director General was bound to give effect to the Articles within a reasonable time. Where the Staff Regulations are explicit, the administration must prepare the job descriptions or have them prepared for the purpose of grading posts.[120] Generally, a tribunal will not question the description of a post.[121] However, this rule would probably be varied where the description patently does not reflect the duties performed by the holder of the post.

ii. Each institution is responsible for defining the duties and powers of each basic post in such institution. There is no requirement that the definitions used in other institutions or organizations should be followed, even in the case of different institutions within a homogeneous group such as the institutions in the European Communities.[122]

iii. While post descriptions may generally be changed by the administration in the process of carrying out its administrative functions, the Appeals Board of ESRO has held that a staff member must agree to a change in the nature of the functions he performs.[123] In *Decision No. 70*[124] the Appeals Board of NATO held that the applicant's duties could not be changed and the applicant could not be required to acquire skills of a different nature to those called for in the description of his budget post. It would seem that the job description is crucial to the issue of classification and grading and that by virtue of this, not only must a proper description be done, as stated earlier, but changes in the description must be made in such a way that the administration does not act *ultra vires*. The consent of the staff member to changes in his job description is a matter to be considered as normally relevant.

iv. There is no right to a title,[125] unless the law of the institution requires that a title go with a certain post.[126] In the same way a titular classification, such as international staff as opposed to administrative staff, does not accompany the grading of a post.[127] This type of decision is not relevant to the grading exercise.

---

[120] See *de Bruin, Derbal and Keller*, ILOAT Judgment No. 425 [1980] (EPO).
[121] *Decision No. 145*, NATO Appeals Board [1981], Collection of the Decisions 135 to 171 (1984).
[122] *Micheli*, CJEC Cases 198 to 202/81 [1982] ECR p. 4145; *Rosani and Others*, CJEC Cases 193 to 198/82 [1983] ECR p. 2841.
[123] *Decision No. 4, ESRO/CR/22*, ESRO Appeals Board [1969].
[124] *Decision No. 70*, NATO Appeals Board [1976], Collection of the Decisions 46 to 73 (1976).
[125] *Decision No. 29, ESRO/CR/78*, ESRO Appeals Board [1972]. However, where a title has been given to a staff member as a reward, withdrawing it without good reason would be wrongful: see *Sharma*, ILOAT Judgment No. 30 [1957] (ILO).
[126] See *Decision No. 17*, NATO Appeals Board [1969], Collection of the Decisions (1972).
[127] *Rufo*, Decision No. 41, OECD Appeals Board [1970], Recueil des décisions 1 à 62 (1979) p. 116.

(d) Requirements for and effect of reclassification

i. There is no general principle that requires that grade depend on the number and status of subordinates.[128]

ii. The concept of a provisional reclassification of posts will generally not be acceptable, especially where the Staff Regulations state that officials are entitled to a grade corresponding to their duties. In *de Bruin, Derbal and Keller*[129] the ILOAT rejected the argument that the reclassification done after the transfer of staff from IPI to EPO was provisional, in a situation in which the Staff Regulations stated that the officials of EPO were entitled to grades corresponding to their duties. However, it was also held that the administration could thereafter change the post descriptions attached to each post in the course of managing the institution provided it did not act *ultra vires*.

iii. Where a reclassification is obligatory according to the facts and the law, the reclassification must take place from the appropriate date, even if it must be given effect to retroactively. Thus, in *Steijn et al.*[130] the ILOAT ordered that the reclassification take effect retroactively on the date of the appointment of the applicants or on the date the Staff Regulations which entitled them to reclassification came into force, whichever was later. The appropriate date will depend on the circumstances of each case.[131]

The impact of this rule on salary administration can be significant. There is no jurisprudence on this aspect of the question except for the decision in *Gatmaytan*.[132] This decision warrants the conclusion that, even in the face of explicit written rules to the contrary, there may be reason to require that the applicant's salary be adjusted retroactively so as to ensure that he is treated fairly in all the circumstances of the case. In this context the general principle of labour law that there should be equal pay for equal work which was referred to by the OASAT in *Reeve*[133] is relevant, while its application in specific circumstances may be a matter for future judicial determination.

iv. Staff members must co-operate in any reclassification exercise, if they are to be able to claim any rights flowing therefrom.[134]

v. In the case of the European Communities problems have arisen concerning the step in the new grade at which the reclassified staff member should be placed. In *Collotti*[135] the issue arose as a result of the reclassification done

128 See *Loebisch*, CJEC Case 14/79 [1979] p. 3679.
129 ILOAT Judgment No. 425 [1980] (EPO).
130 ILOAT Judgment No. 275 [1976] (IPI).
131 See *Gatmaytan*, ILOAT Judgment No. 424 [1980] (PAHO); *Saravia*, OASAT Judgment No. 47 [1979]; *Williams*, CJEC Case 9/81 [1982] ECR p. 3301.
132 ILOAT Judgment No. 424 [1980] (PAHO).
133 OASAT Judgment No. 59 [1981].
134 *Moore*, ILOAT Judgment No. 393 [1980] (PAHO).
135 CJEC Case 70/63 [1964] ECR p. 435.

subsequent to the enactment of the new Staff Regulations. The Staff
Regulations were silent on the matter. The court held that the analogy of
promotion was not relevant in this situation. According to the rules applied
on promotion the applicant would have been placed at a step appreciably
lower than the one he had in his former grade because he would have been
assigned the next step above closest to the salary point he had reached. Since
this would have resulted in discrimination between staff members in service
and those who had been recruited newly, a different rule had to be applied.
The applicable rule was that the staff member should be classified in his new
grade at the same step as that which he occupied in his former grade. In
Moreau[136] a different situation obtained. After the unification of the institutions the applicant contended that he should be given the same step as he had
as a contractual servant in his previous grade. Because this solution would
have resulted in discrimination between classes of officials who were
comparable, it was not accepted by the CJEC. Here the analogy of
promotion was accepted and the rule applied was that the step assigned in the
new grade should take account of the salary attained previously, as was
required by the Staff Regulation dealing with promotion.

The two cases are clearly distinguishable on the facts. They may also be
explained by reference to the principle that there should be no discrimination between classes between which a distinction is not objectively
justified.

vi. In the European Communities the problem has arisen of upgrading
posts when the budget makes provision for the conversion of fewer posts than
are required to be converted. The CJEC has held that in these circumstances
the general principles of public service require that, while each institution has
a wide discretion as to its internal organization and the assessment of posts:

it is the importance of the different branches or posts as well as of the duties and
responsibilities incumbent upon them which must be the principal criterion by virtue
of which it is appropriate to decide whether a given branch must be directed by—or
whether a given post must be assigned to—an official in a grade corresponding to a
post of head of division rather than a post of principal administrator.[137]

As a consequence the merits of the incumbents could only be considered after
the needs of the different branches and posts had been assessed. Since the
record in *Dautzenberg* did not show that the needs of the different branches
had first been considered before the merits of the staff members holding the
posts had been taken into account, in making the decision to upgrade one
post belonging to a particular branch, as permitted by the budget, in that case
the decision to upgrade such post was annulled.

---

[136] CJEC Cases 15/64 & 60/65 [1966] ECR p. 459.
[137] *Dautzenberg*, CJEC Case 2/80 [1980] ECR p. 3107 at p. 3117.

(e) Effect of assurances

The effect of assurances of reclassification given to the staff members has been considered by the ILOAT. In *Boyle*[138] the tribunal held that mere promises or proposals made by a superior that the applicant would be upgraded do not bind the institution. A similar conclusion was reached in *Rémont*[139] on slightly different facts. In *Pinto de Magalhaes (No. 2)*[140] assurances were given in good faith by the applicant's supervisor that the applicant would be upgraded because her supervisor believed that the new post to which she was assigned should be graded G7, the applicant being in grade G5. The new post was ultimately graded G5 even after the appeals procedures had been followed. The ILOAT held: 'The commitments did not confer on the complainant any right to the upgrading of her post to G.7. The ILO was not in breach of any obligation, has caused the complainant no injury on that account, and is not liable.'[141] These cases lead to certain definite conclusions. The nature of the assurance is a very relevant consideration. It may very well be that the assurance is less than a promise to upgrade. In case the assurance appears to be that the applicant would be reclassified, the nature of the situation, including the procedures involved in reclassification, may indicate that the official who gave the assurance could do no more than promise that the procedure for reclassification would be initiated and followed rather than give an assurance of a particular result. In any event, the authority of the official making the promises or giving the asssurances in relation to such assurances or promises would be a relevant factor to be considered. In the cases referred to above, it would appear that the assurances were either that the regrading procedure would be initiated and followed or that they were given by officials who really had no authority to promise reclassification as such, even if it were possible for any official in the organizations to promise such reclassification.

The indication given by the administrative authority in a budget request that it was going to consider the position of a staff member as in a higher grade than such official holds does not bind the administration to upgrade the position.[142] A budget request is only an internal document aimed at persuading the budget authority. An indication of this kind is of even less value than an assurance or a promise.

---

[138] ILOAT Judgment No. 178 [1971] (ITU).
[139] ILOAT Judgment No. 228 [1974] (FAO).
[140] ILOAT Judgment No. 589 [1983] (ILO).
[141] Ibid. at p. 5.
[142] *Brus*, CJEC Cases 48/64 & 1/65 [1965] ECR p. 351.

(ƒ) *Right to a post*

In an organization where the career of an official progresses on the basis of a system of categories and consecutive grades commencing with the grade in which he was recruited and the administration assigns posts according to grade, a special situation may arise where a post is reassessed upon a reorganization and is consequently upgraded. The CJEC has held that in such a case the staff member holding the post subsequently upgraded has no right to the post, especially because the duties of the post have changed, but is liable to be reassigned to a post in his own grade.[143] This rule is applicable, obviously, in very exceptional situations such as obtained in *Huybrechts*. If it were applied generally without any qualifications as to the nature of the reassessment which in the decided case was upon an increase of duties as a result of a reclassification, or as to the nature of the duties performed in the past by the staff member who held the post, and in circumstances in which the system of grades is flexible, not rigid, it would undermine the principle that an appropriate grade must be assigned to a staff member according to the duties and responsibilities he has, which has been conceded even by the CJEC.

(g) *Delays*

Delays in the process of regrading are not by themselves a violation of the law. In *Liotti*[144] the ILOAT found on the facts that the administration of FAO had justifiable misgivings, had to make an audit, and had to follow an elaborate procedure laid down by the Manual. These factors accounted adequately for the delay which could not therefore be impeached. On the other hand, where the delay in upgrading is unreasonably long, it can affect the date on which the reclassification takes effect.[145]

(h) *Withdrawal of classification decision*

While a decision relating to classification which is invalid because of procedural irregularity could legally be withdrawn within a reasonable time after the decision is made without a violation of the rights of the staff member concerned, a decision relating to classification which has been validly taken cannot be withdrawn.[146] It would seem to be a requirement for this rule to operate that the decision must be a final one.

---

[143] *Huybrechts*, CJEC Case 21/68 [1969] ECR p. 85.
[144] ILOAT Judgment No. 149 [1970] (FAO).
[145] See *Gatmaytan*, ILOAT Judgment No. 424 [1980] (PAHO).
[146] *Algera*, CJEC Cases 7/56 & 3 to 7/57 [1957] ECR p. 39.

Remedies

(a) The CJEC

In the cases decided by the CJEC in which the decision not to reclassify the applicant as requested was held to be unlawful or the decision relating to grading has been found to be invalidly taken, the CJEC has ordered some form of specific performance. In *Maudet*,[147] where the reclassification claimed by the applicant after the enactment of the Staff Regulations was found to be appropriate, the decision not to reclassify him was annulled. This meant that the applicant had to be reclassified.[148] In *Klaer*[149] a decision to appoint the applicant who was in grade A1 to a post with duties not corresponding to his grade was annulled. The implication of this decision was that the applicant had to be appointed to a grade-A1 post.[150] In *Algera*,[151] when a valid decision to bring the applicants within the Staff Regulations after they were enacted was illegally withdrawn, the decision was annulled and the applicants were awarded damages for non-material damage. Damages were set at 100 EPU units of account for each applicant.

(b) The ILOAT

In two cases, where the refusal to reclassify the applicants was found to be wrongful on substantive grounds particularly, the ILOAT ordered the reclassification to be made.[152] In one of these cases the respondent was ordered to increase the salary of the applicant from the date on which she should have been upgraded.[153] In *Gatmaytan*[154] the ILOAT ordered payment of the difference in salary from the proper date on which the applicant should have been reclassified to the date on which he was actually reclassified and ordered that the reclassification take effect from the proper date. In two cases in which the failure to reclassify was tainted by procedural defects the decisions not to reclassify were quashed but the cases were remanded for

---

[147] CJEC Cases 20 & 21/63 [1964] ECR p. 113.

[148] See also *Williams*, CJEC Case 9/81 [1982] ECR p. 3301.

[149] CJEC Case 15/65 [1965] ECR p. 1045.

[150] Some form of specific performance was ordered also in *Dautzenberg*, CJEC Case 2/80 [1980] ECR p. 3107; *Wonnerth*, CJEC Case 12/69 [1969] ECR p. 577; *Collotti*, CJEC Case 70/63 [1964] ECR p. 435.

[151] CJEC Cases 7/56 & 3 to 7/57 [1957] ECR p. 39.

[152] *Dadivas*, ILOAT Judgment No. 60 [1962] (WHO); *Price (No. 2)*, ILOAT Judgment No. 342 [1978] (PAHO). In *Sharma*, ILOAT Judgment No. 30 [1957] (ILO), where a title was wrongfully withdrawn, restoration of the title was ordered.

[153] *Dadivas*, ILOAT Judgment No. 60 [1962] (WHO). In *Steijn et al.*, ILOAT Judgment No. 275 [1976] (IPI), the ILOAT ordered regrading retroactively from the appropriate date. Appropriate classification on a permanent basis was ordered in *de Bruin, Derbal and Keller*, ILOAT Judgment No. 425 [1980] (EPO).

[154] ILOAT Judgment No. 424 [1980] (PAHO).

correction of procedure.[155] No damages were requested as such, although in one case the applicant had requested any other relief as was fair. No damages were awarded in either case.

In *Rudin* (*No. 3*),[156] where the applicant was kept idle without any duties to perform, compensation of $25,000 was ordered for the moral injury, it being found also that there was no injury to reputation.[157]

(c) The Appeals Board of NATO

In *Decision No. 17*,[158] where the Appeals Board of NATO found that the applicant had been ilegally deprived of certain duties and his title, the tribunal ordered specific performance in the form of restoration of the duties and title. In *Decision No. 70*,[159] where the applicant's dismissal was found to be illegal, because his job description had been changed without his consent and he had been asked to acquire new skills, the decision to dismiss him was quashed. However, since the respondent stated that reinstatement would be difficult in the prevailing situation, the applicant was awarded compensation of 10 months' salary.

(d) The UNAT

In *Champoury*,[160] where the refusal to upgrade the applicant was found to be illegal, the decision not to upgrade was quashed and the UNAT ordered specific performance in the form of upgrading.

(e) The OASAT

In *Vera*,[161] where the applicant had wrongfully not been assigned to a post corresponding to his grade, specific performance was ordered by the OASAT—the respondent was ordered to give the applicant a post corresponding to his grade. In four cases where the refusal to reclassify was found to be illegal, the OASAT ordered the reclassification to be done by the respondent.[162] In *Brocos*[163] the tribunal further ordered that a job description be done. In *Brocos* and *Saravia*[164] retroactive reclassification was ordered,

---

[155] *Cuvillier*, ILOAT Judgment No. 333 [1978] (ILO); *García*, ILOAT Judgment No. 591 [1983] (PAHO).

[156] ILOAT Judgment No. 630 [1984] (ILO).

[157] Compensation only was awarded also in *Schofield* (*No. 4*), ILOAT Judgment No. 411 [1980] (WHO).

[158] *Decision No. 17*, NATO Appeals Board [1969], Collection of the Decisions (1972).

[159] *Decision No. 70*, NATO Appeals Board [1976], Collection of the Decisions 46 to 73 (1976).

[160] UNAT Judgment No. 76 [1959], JUNAT Nos. 71–86 p. 35.

[161] OASAT Judgment No. 33 [1977].

[162] *García and Others*, OASAT Judgment No. 6 [1974]; *Boita*, OASAT Judgment No. 36 [1978]; *Brocos*, OASAT Judgment No. 39 [1979]; *Saravia*, OASAT Judgment No. 47 [1979].

[163] OASAT Judgment No. 39 [1979].

[164] OASAT Judgment No. 47 [1979].

with the necessary consequences. In *Reeve*,[165] where the applicant was held to have been entitled for temporary services to the payment of differential salary between the G5 and G7 levels, the OASAT ordered the payment of such salary during the appropriate period.

---

[165] OASAT Judgment No. 59 [1981].

CHAPTER FORTY-ONE

Transfer and Reassignment

PROVISION is generally made for the transfer or reassignment of staff members in the Staff Regulations and Staff Rules of international organizations. However, these vary in detail and specificity. Thus, the UN Staff Regulations provide in very general terms that: 'Staff members are subject to the authority of the Secretary-General and to assignment by him to any of the activities or offices of the United Nations.'[1] The Staff Rules[2] do not elaborate significantly on the rules governing assignment which is referred to in this Regulation. In the case of the Council of Europe the Staff Regulations are also very general and merely state that the Secretary General 'shall assign each staff member, in the interests of the service, to a post in his category corresponding to his grade.'[3] The Staff Regulations of the European Communities are somewhat more elaborate but only marginally so. These provide principally in Article 7(1) that: 'The appointing authority shall, acting solely in the interest of the service and without regard to nationality, assign each official by appointment or transfer to a post in his category or service which corresponds to his grade.'[4] The provisions dealing with transfers and reassignment of the Staff Regulations and Staff Rules of most international organizations are as general as these. Exceptionally there may be detailed rules relating to certain kinds of transfers or even transfers in general. Staff Rule 5.06 of the World Bank deals in considerable detail with assignments to lower-level positions which involve assignments to a position graded at a lower level than the current job held by the staff member.

Where the provisions dealing with transfers and reassignments of Staff Regulations and Staff Rules are fairly general, as in the case of the UN or the Council of Europe, it is likely that problems and questions could arise in their interpretation and application. Even where the Regulations and Rules are fairly detailed and specific, questions of interpretation and general principle may very well arise, although in a narrower area. Of course, where the provisions of Regulations and Rules are too general or too vague to afford

---

[1] Regulation 1.2: see Appendix V *infra*.

[2] See Rule 101.4: Appendix V *infra*.

[3] Article 11: see Appendix VI *infra*. Article 20 deals with secondment to the organization from outside the organization but not secondment within or from the organization: see Appendix VI *infra*.

[4] See Amerasinghe (ed.), 4 *Staff Regulations and Staff Rules of Selected International Organizations* (1983) p. 1 at p. 11. Articles 4 and 29 of the Staff Regulations also deal with transfers: ibid. at pp. 11, 15.

effective protection to the staff member or define clearly the rights of the organization the room for interpretation and judicial intervention may be wider. In any event, international administrative tribunals have been called upon to decide cases contesting transfers and reassignments and involving the rights of staff members and the powers of organizations. These decisions have not only given judicial interpretations of the literal texts of Regulations and Rules but also applied general principles of law in determining the rights and obligations of the parties. Much general principle has to do with the control of the exercise of discretionary powers in the classical manner, but there are some special respects in which tribunals have applied certain general principles in interpreting Regulations and Rules which have resulted sometimes in the imposition of broader controls and sometimes in the rejection of limitations and strictures on the powers of organizations to transfer and reassign staff members.

Definitions

It may be necessary both for the purposes of implementing the Staff Regulations or Staff Rules and written law of an organization and for the purposes of applying the general law relating to the treatment of staff to define or distinguish between the various forms that the assignment of staff members may take. Tribunals have adverted to these distinctions in circumstances in which they have had a bearing on the law to be applied, whether it be general principles or texts of Staff Regulations and Staff Rules.

An important distinction has been made between transfer and reassignment or assignment. In *Kahale*[5] the applicant was reassigned in the same department from the position of Chief, Social Defence Section, to Senior Officer for Special Assignments, both assignments being at the same grade level. No transfer order was issued by the Director of Personnel, the Director of the applicant's division having made the new assignment. For the purposes of the administrative requirement that a transfer order be issued on transfer the UNAT held that the action taken was not a 'transfer' but that it was a reassignment which was, nevertheless, covered by Staff Regulation 1.2. In those circumstances it was unnecessary for the Director of Personnel to issue a transfer order and it did not matter that he had withheld the transfer order.[6]

---

[5] UNAT Judgment No. 165 [1972], JUNAT Nos. 114–166 p. 406.

[6] In *Rodriguez*, UNAT Judgment No. 167 [1973], JUNAT Nos. 167–230 p. 1, the UNAT was faced with the problem whether the reassignment of the applicant was in the circumstances of the case a transfer, or an assignment with the result that Staff Regulation 1.2 was applicable, or whether it was *sui generis*. In the event that the action taken had been covered by Regulation 1.2, the UNAT was of the view that the discretion of the Secretary General would have been narrower than if it had not, though in the latter case the discretion would also have been subject to some

In several cases the CJEC has distinguished between reassignment and transfer. In the view of the Court the latter is governed not only by Article 7 (1) of the Staff Regulations of the European Communities but also by Articles 4 and 29, while the former is covered only by Article 7 (1). It decided for this purpose that, where an assignment was made to a vacant post of a staff member holding another post, there was a transfer but, where the incumbent and the post were both moved, there was only a reassignment. As a result, while the latter was only subject to the requirements of Article 7 (1) relating to the interests of the service and the correspondence of grade and post, the former was subject not only to those requirements but also to the provisions of Articles 4 and 29 which related in general to procedures.[7]

The OASAT has also adverted to the issue of definitions or descriptions in relation to the Staff Rules of the OAS. In *Getz*[8] the physical transfer of the applicant from the Follow-up and Review Unit to the Special Advisory Services Unit was arranged, when the functions in the former Unit were redistributed. Before the transfer actually took place the post contemplated for the applicant was eliminated from the budget by the committee on the budget. Before the 'transfer' was finalized the applicant was removed from his former post. The tribunal held that there was no transfer to the post in the Special Advisory Services Unit, because there could not be a transfer to a non-existent post. The result was that the organization could not rely on this 'transfer' to satisfy the requirements of the Staff Rules and General Standards relating to the abolition of posts. In *Vera*[9] the applicant was transferred from the position to Chief of Unit which was a P5 post to that of Principal Specialist which was a P4 post, though he retained his grade and salary. The transfer was without his consent. The OASAT held that since Staff Rule 105.2 (a) defined a transfer as 'a change of post, without change in grade or salary', a transfer, to fall within that Rule, must be to a post with the same grade, so that the transfer in issue could not be made without the consent of the staff member. Had the transfer been to a post in the same grade, the consent of the staff member would not have been required.[10]

kind of control. The applicant, the Latin American Institute for Economic and Social Planning, and the Economic Commission for Latin America had come to an agreement that the appointment of the applicant with the former Institute would be terminated and that he would apply to the latter Commission for an assignment. In the outcome the Secretary General assigned the applicant to a position with which the latter was dissatisfied. The UNAT held that because of the agreement between the parties the assignment by the Secretary General was not a transfer or assignment covered by Regulation 1.2 but had to be treated as an act coming within the broad discretion of the Secretary General which was, nevertheless, subject to controls, though not to the same controls as applied under Regulation 1.2.

[7] *Carbognani and Coda Zabetta*, CJEC Cases 161 & 162/80 [1981] ECR p. 543; *Kindermann*, CJEC Case 60/80 [1981] ECR p. 1329; *Nebe*, CJEC Case 176/82 [1983] ECR p. 2475.
[8] OASAT Judgment No. 26 [1976].
[9] OASAT Judgment No. 33 [1977].
[10] In *Korter*, CJEC Case 148/79 [1981] ECR p. 615, the CJEC held that a transfer to a

In *Gotschi*[11] the ILOAT had to decide whether in the situation presented to it there had been a transfer or an abolition of post. If the latter had taken place, the refusal of the applicant to accept the new position could have been regarded as a good reason for terminating his employment on the abolition of the post, while, if the former was the case, under the Staff Rules of PAHO relating to transfers of officials in the General Service category, since the transfer was from the place of recruitment of the official to another location, it could only have been effected with the consent of the official and the applicant would have been justified in refusing the transfer so that he could not have been dismissed. In the case the applicant's post of Visual Aids Technician which was located in Washington was, in the process of decentralization, 'abolished' in Washington and recreated in a unit of PAHO in Mexico City. When the applicant refused to take up the position in Mexico City the organization argued that the post in Washington had been abolished. The ILOAT held that the rules relating to transfer could not be circumvented by the subterfuge of abolition of post and that in reality the applicant had been transferred from Washington to Mexico City, with the result that he could lawfully refuse the transfer.

In *Pagani*[12] the Appeals Board of the Council of Europe held that a secondment was to be distinguished from a transfer, the latter being dealt with in detail in the Staff Regulations, while the former was not. Thus, where the applicant had been 'seconded' to the Directorate of Legal Affairs from his original service to fill a specific temporary post which was later made permanent, the termination of his secondment could only be dealt with under the general provisions of the Staff Regulations and under the general principles of law and could not be treated as a transfer under the Staff Regulations. While the change of assignment in the case of secondment had to be in the interests of the service and could be terminated in the interests of the service, which involved wide discretionary powers, secondment was not covered by the Staff Regulations which did not, therefore, apply to it. On the other hand, the tribunal did take the view that the discretion, even though not covered by the Staff Regulations, was subject to controls emanating from general principles of law.

The cases show that distinctions have been made between transfer and other forms of assignment or treatment of staff principally for the purposes

---

temporary posting was not a transfer for the purposes of the relevant provisions of the Staff Regulations of the European Communities. It said that in order to be able to invoke those provisions of the Staff Regulations the applicant had to show that the assignment was to a permanent posting which as such had a direct bearing on his career prospects.

[11] ILOAT Judgment No. 523 [1982] (PAHO).

[12] Council of Europe Appeals Board, Appeal No. 76 [1982], Case-Law Digest (1985) p. 96. For secondment from one organization to another, see *Higgins*, UNAT Judgment No. 92 [1964] (IMCO), JUNAT Nos. 87–113 p. 41. Such secondment is different from transfer within an organization.

of the written law of organizations. These dinstinctions have had some material influence on the outcome of cases. However, there is no way in which they can be systematized as they turn on the specific facts of cases and on the provisions of the written·law being invoked. They do illustrate that the various forms of assignment may have to be distinguished for the purposes of certain rules applicable to the treatment of international officials.

Intrinsic defects

Closely related to the question whether an assignment can be described as a transfer for the purpose of the law to be applied is the issue whether a transfer can be ruled intrinsically defective and, therefore, invalid because it does not meet some basic requirements. The cases in which this issue has arisen have been decided against applicants so that it cannot be said that tribunals recognize intrinsic defects arising from the nature of transfers. In *Nowakowska*[13] the ILOAT considered the transfer of a staff member to a temporary post in the library of the WMO. The fact that the transfer was to a temporary post was considered not to be a relevant factor. It was held that the relevant Staff Regulation covered assignments to temporary as well as permanent posts. It followed that assignments to temporary posts by way of transfer could not be regarded as outside the purview of that Staff Regulation. Thus, it was only if that Regulation had been violated that the transfer could be questioned. In the case the tribunal found that the law had not been violated, particularly by an abuse of discretion.[14]

Transfer as a priority

In applying the written law of international organizations tribunals have had to face the question whether staff members have a priority right to a transfer where the organization resorts to other forms of filling vacant posts, such as promotion or appointment, and conversely whether a staff member can claim that a method other than transfer has priority over transfer. Tribunals have in the interpretation of the written law generally taken the view that the administrations of organizations have a fairly wide discretion in the choice of the method they will use to fill vacancies.

In *García*[15] the applicant argued that a P5 post of Deputy Director of a

[13] ILOAT Judgment No. 115 [1967] (WMO).
[14] In *Bosmans*, CJEC Case 189/81 [1982] ECR p. 2681, it was held by the CJEC that a transfer in a personal capacity to a post in the applicant's grade did not violate the law by adversely affecting the applicant.
[15] OASAT Judgment No. 56 [1980].

particular office in the OAS should have been filled by competition so that he, who held a P4 post, could apply. The post had been filled by the transfer of the holder of another P5 post. The OASAT held that under Staff Rule 105.2[16] of the OAS appointment and promotion were not the only means of filling vacancies and that transfer was possible. Competition had no priority over transfer. The filling of the vacancy by transfer was a valid exercise of discretion under the Staff Rules of the OAS. The Rules did not provide for any priorities.

In several cases the CJEC has held that it was open to the organization to fill a vacant position by promotion from a lower grade rather than by transfer of an official in the same grade, there being no priority as such between these forms of filling vacancies.[17] The Court found that Article 4 of the Staff Regulations which implied that a vacancy could be filled by transfer, promotion, or an internal competition[18] did not indicate any priorities as among the forms of appointment referred to therein, though it required that these be given priority over external competition. Conversely, where a post had been moved to another Directorate together with the incumbent, the Court held that the applicant could not claim that a vacancy notice should have been posted so that the post in the new Directorate could have been filled by transfer, instead of the incumbent being reassigned.[19] Reorganization of Directorates was within the discretion of the organization so that it could choose between transfer and reassignment as methods of filling posts. Likewise it has been held that simply for the reason that an internal competition had been held, this method of appointment did not have priority over internal transfer as a means of filling a vacant post.[20]

Right to a transfer

The question may be asked what rights staff members have in respect of claims they may make for transfers and what are the obligations of administrations in this regard. This issue was in effect raised in *Dobosch*.[21] The applicant failed to find favour with his supervisors and for that reason claimed that he should be transferred. Since there was no suitable post available at the time, the administration of PAHO temporized. There was no complete inaction, though. Ultimately an alternative post was offered which

---

[16] Amerasinghe (ed.) 3 op. cit. (note 4 *supra*) p. 214 at p. 243.

[17] See *Rittweger*, CJEC Case 21/70 [1971] ECR p. 7; *Reinarz*, CJEC Case 55/70 [1971] ECR p. 379.

[18] Amerasinghe (ed.), 4 op. cit. (note 4 *supra*) p. 1 at p. 11.

[19] *Vistosi*, CJEC Case 61/70 [1971] ECR p. 535.

[20] *Gilbeau*, CJEC Case 157/77 [1979] ECR p. 1505.

[21] ILOAT Judgment No. 451 [1981] (PAHO).

the applicant found unacceptable. The ILOAT held that the mere fact that the administration had in effect failed to give a positive response did not result in an abuse of power. The case would seem to warrant the conclusion that when a transfer is requested or is a possible solution to a problem, the administration must in good faith consider the possibility of transfer and refuse it only after efforts are made to accommodate the possibility, particularly when there are good reasons prompting the staff member to make the request. The staff member clearly has no right in general to a transfer but at the same time the administration has certain obligations in regard to requests for transfers or in situations which render transfers a possible solution. The administration has a discretion to refuse or to make a transfer but must not commit an abuse of power in taking action in the situation. Clearly, for instance, at one extreme, mere inaction on the part of the administration would amount to such an abuse of power, as is implied in *Dobosch*. On the other hand, there are other failures which may, nevertheless, amount to an abuse of power. For example, apart from discrimination or prejudice in dealing with a staff member's request in the situation, there may be substantive irregularities committed in the handling of his case which would result in the action taken in the situation being an abuse of power. In *Angelopoulos*[22] the Appeals Board of the OECD also took the approach of recognizing merely that there was an obligation placed on the administration not to abuse its discretion to refuse a transfer, while refusing implicitly to recognize that the staff member had a right to a transfer.

In general, the ILOAT has held that an applicant cannot normally claim to be transferred to any post having the same grade as his post. He can only make a claim to be transferred to a particular post for which he may have competed.[23] In short, there is no right to have a request merely for a transfer out of a post normally considered by the administrative authority. But in the same case the ILOAT hinted that after long service a staff member may be justified in expecting a claim for a transfer out of a post to be considered.

As has been seen in an earlier chapter,[24] staff members on probation may have a qualified right to a transfer before their probationary appointments are terminated, even in the absence of explicit provision in the written law. This right, if it exists, is really a right to have the alternative of transfer seriously considered, as it would appear from the cases discussed in that chapter. The right is not an absolute right. In the case of probationary appointments the situation may be regarded as similar to the general situation discussed above, where a transfer is requested or the circumstances make transfer a feasible alternative. While the staff member may have the right to

---

[22] Decision No. 57, OECD Appeals Board [1976], Recueil des décisions 1 à 62 (1979) p. 157.

[23] See *Tewfik*, ILOAT Judgment No. 196 [1972] (UNESCO).

[24] See *supra*, Ch. 38 pp. 792 ff.

be considered for a transfer, the administration must not abuse its discretion to refuse a transfer.

In a previous chapter[25] it was found that there was no general principle of law requiring the administration to transfer a staff member, in order that he he may have another chance, before terminating his appointment for unsatisfactory services. This rule would apply where it has become clear that the services of the staff member are unsatisfactory. It would be reasonable to suppose that where this is not clear, the rule established in *Dobosch* and *Angelopoulos* would be applicable. While the staff member may have no right to a transfer or to be considered for one, where his services are unsatisfactory, the administration is not precluded from offering the staff member a transfer, even where his services are unsatisfactory, in order to give him another chance. In this situation the offer of a transfer which is refused does not deprive the administration of the right to terminate the staff member's services for unsatisfactory service.[26] The offer of a transfer does not operate as an estoppel in relation to the action the administration may take based on the finding that the services of the staff member were unsatisfactory.

Further, as has been seen in a previous chapter,[27] over and above the provisions of the written law, there is a duty placed upon the administration to make all reasonable efforts in good faith to transfer to another post a staff member whose post is abolished before terminating his services on the ground that his post was abolished. This obligation is a special one, as has been described, and goes beyond the mere obligation to consider a staff member for a transfer in a situation where he asks for one or a transfer is advisable, as there are definite priorities involved.[28]

Restrictions on transfer

Apart from any particular restrictions on the right of the administration to transfer a staff member in the statutory written law, there may be other restrictions imposed by general principles of law, provided clearly that the written law does not countermand them.

The ILOAT has stated in several cases, in the process of establishing that a transfer was validly carried out, that there was no reduction in salary involved in the transfer. This element was mentioned in those cases, clearly because the tribunal thought that, if there had been a reduction in salary, the transfer would have been proscribed. Thus, in a case where the applicant was

---

[25] See Ch. 35 p. 674 *supra*.
[26] See *Decisions Nos. 8 & 10, ESRO/CR/45*, ESRO Appeals Board [1971].
[27] See Ch. 36 pp. 692 ff. *supra*.
[28] See, e.g., *Wonnerth*, CJEC Case 12/69 [1969] ECR p. 577.

transferred from one section of the service to which he was recruited to another, the tribunal specifically referred to the fact that there had been no reduction in salary involved in the transfer in finding that, therefore, the transfer could not be questioned.[29] In *Tarrab* (*No. 9*) a transfer was made in circumstances in which the ILO was experiencing severe budgetary problems because of the withdrawal from membership of the USA. The ILOAT explicitly stated that the administration could not, of its own accord, 'reduce the applicant's salary, lower his grade or injure his dignity in making the transfer.'[30] Thus, these are clear limitations on the power of transfer.

In *Detière*[31] the UNAT dealt with the proposition that, because the contract of employment of the applicant stated that he was hired for a particular position, he could not be transferred therefrom. The applicant was hired as the Secretary of the European Civil Aviation Conference to be stationed in the regional office of ICAO in Paris. He was later transferred to the headquarters of ICAO in Canada. At the very outset the tribunal stated that the contract of employment of the applicant did not show that he was hired specifically and exclusively for the position he held in the Paris office, since it clearly indicated that he was appointed to the staff of ICAO and that, therefore, he could not rely on the contract to question the transfer as being unlawful.[32] By implication the tribunal recognized that transfers could be validly prohibited or restricted by the contract of employment of staff members, even though the statutory law of the organization may make general provisions for transfers of staff members. Undoubtedly, whether there is a special contractual commitment will depend on the terms of the contract and how they are interpreted. Further, there would seem to be no legal impediment to a special commitment of a contractual nature relating to transfer being given a staff member even after his contract of employment has been entered into and while he is already in service.

In *Decision No. 4, ESRO/CR/22*[33] the Appeals Board of ESRO made some interesting statements of law about transfers made during probation. Clearly the view taken of general principles in that case will apply only where the written law does not contradict or qualify such general principles. The tribunal said of a transfer made during the probationary period that it should satisfy two conditions: first, the new duties must be comparable to those for which the staff member on probation was hired; second, the transfer must be temporary. In that case, while the transfer was on a permanent basis which would have made it invalid, the transfer had been withdrawn so that the

---

[29] *Jurado* (*No. 7*), ILOAT Judgment No. 100 [1967] (ILO) at p. 4. See also *Nowakowska*, ILOAT Judgment No. 115 [1967] (WMO); *Tarrab*, ILOAT Judgment No. 132 [1969] (ILO).

[30] ILOAT Judgment No. 534 [1982] (ILO) at p. 3.

[31] UNAT Judgment No. 136 [1970] (ICAO), JUNAT Nos. 114–166 p. 205.

[32] Ibid. at pp. 212–13.

[33] *Decision No. 4, ESRO/CR/22*, ESRO Appeals Board [1969].

illegality became moot. While this statement of the law may be unimpeachable in general, the general principles could, of course, be modified where the staff member on probation consents to a transfer that does not fulfil these conditions.

There may be other general principles which limit the right of an organization to make transfers, such as the requirement that the post assigned must correspond to the grade of the incumbent.[34] This principle would demand that a transfer be to a post of equivalent grade. However, issues relating to such general principles have not been raised in the cases.

It is also clear that the written statutory law can normally modify any applicable general principles, just as such law can impose restrictions on the right to transfer. Thus, Staff Rule 5.06 of the World Bank which gives the management of the World Bank power to assign staff members in certain circumstances to a lower grade without their consent may be regarded as a statutory provision of this kind.[35] Restrictions imposed by statutory law may, for example, take the form of preventing the unilateral transfer by the administration in certain circumstances of a staff member confirmed in his appointment, as was the case in ESRO, though examples of such restrictions of substance are not numerous. A good example of a case in which a tribunal recognized a stricture on the right to transfer imposed by the statutory law is *Vera*.[36] A transfer was made by the OAS of a staff member who was Chief of Unit and held a P5 position to the position of Principal Specialist which was a P4 post, though he retained his P5 grade and salary. The OASAT held that Rule 105.2 (a)[37] of the OAS required that a lateral transfer made without the consent of the staff member concerned must be to a post in the same grade. Hence the transfer violated the statutory law and was invalid.

The discretion to transfer

Apart from the restrictions discussed above it is generally accepted that the administration of an international organization has the power to make transfers of staff members when and how it wills even when the statutory law does not explicitly confer that power on it.[38] At the same time, the cases have

[34] See Ch. 40 pp. 846 ff. *supra* and *Danjean* (*Nos. 1 & 2*), ILOAT Judgment No. 126 [1968] (CERN); *Schofield* (*No. 4*), ILOAT Judgment No. 411 [1980] (WHO); *Quiñones*, ILOAT Judgment No. 447 [1981] (PAHO); *Tarrab* (*No. 9*), ILOAT Judgment No. 534 [1982] (ILO); *Go*, ILOAT Judgment No. 631 [1984] (WHO); *Macevicius*, CJEC Case 66/75 [1976] ECR p. 593.

[35] See also *Decisions Nos. 8 & 10*, *ESRO/CR/45*, ESRO Appeals Board [1971].

[36] OASAT Judgment No. 33 [1977].

[37] See Amerasinghe (ed.), 3 op. cit. (note 4 *supra*) p. 214 at p. 243.

[38] See also Akehurst, *The Law Governing Employment in International Organizations* (1967) p. 134. There is a general principle of law supporting the position taken in the text. In de Vuyst, 'The Use of Discretionary Authority by International Organizations in their Relations with

referred to the concept of abuse of discretion as being a reason for finding that a transfer is invalid. Tribunals have often said that there has been no 'abuse of discretion' in the making of a transfer and that, therefore, it could not be questioned. In *Bauta*,[39] for instance, the applicant was transferred by the OAS to a 'position of trust' from the international career service in which he held a P5 post. His grade did not change. His P5 grade was retained and he would have returned to the international career civil service at the end of this assignment at the P5 level. While there were no provisions governing transfers to positions of trust in the Staff Rules of the OAS, the OASAT did not hold that the transfer could not be made but examined the facts and came to the conclusion that there had been no abuse of discretion and that, therefore, the transfer was valid.

The idea that there must not be an abuse of discretion in the exercise of the powers to transfer implies that the power to transfer is a discretionary one which should, therefore, be subject to the usual controls to which the exercise of discretionary powers are subject. The concept of the power to transfer as an inherent discretionary power has been recognized in the decisions of tribunals. Thus, the Appeals Board of the Council of Europe,[40] the Appeals Board of the OECD,[41] and the WBAT,[42] and the ILOAT[43] have in various ways either explicitly described the power to transfer as discretionary or assumed that it was discretionary.

In most decided cases the discretionary power to transfer is vested in the administrative authority under the Staff Regulations or Staff Rules. However, there can be no doubt that this discretion is available to international organizations as a matter of general principle, even when the statutory law is silent on the subject. This was implied, for instance, in *Bauta*, discussed above.

International Civil Servants', 12 *Denver Journal of International Law and Policy* (1983) p. 237 at p. 252, the view was expressed that transfer is within the discretion of the administrative authority of an international organization.

[39] OASAT Judgment No. 48 [1979]. See also *Rodriguez*, UNAT Judgment No. 167 [1973], JUNAT Nos. 167–230 p. 1; *Ho*, UNAT Judgment No. 189 [1974], JUNAT Nos. 167–230 p. 170; *Zamudio*, ILOAT Judgment No. 212 [1973] (WHO); *Tarrab (No. 9)*, ILOAT Judgment No. 534 [1982] (ILO); *Einthoven*, WBAT Reports [1985], Decision No. 23.

[40] *Pagani*, Council of Europe Appeals Board, Appeal No. 76 [1982], Case-Law Digest (1985) p. 96 at p. 101.

[41] *Angelopoulos*, Decision No. 57, OECD Appeals Board [1976], Recueil des décisions 1 à 62 (1979) p. 157 at p. 159.

[42] *Einthoven*, WBAT Reports [1985], Decision No. 23 at p. 14. See also *Gyamfi*, WBAT Reports [1986], Decision No. 28 at p. 23.

[43] *Quiñones*, ILOAT Judgment No. 447 [1981] (PAHO) at p. 6. See also, e.g., *Frank (Nos. 1 & 2)*, ILOAT Judgment No. 154 [1970] (ILO) at p. 4; *Arnold*, ILOAT Judgment No. 397 [1980] (ITU) at p. 5.

Control of the discretion to transfer

While the discretionary nature of the power to transfer is not disputed, it is also evident that the decisions have taken the view that this discretionary power is subject to control and review by international administrative tribunals. Much of the control exercised by tribunals emanates from general principles of law, particularly in so far as the written law does not specifically refer to the limitations imposed on the exercise of the discretion.

Tribunals have often stated the general principles upon which they exercise control over the decision to transfer. These principles are not different from those that apply to the control of discretionary power in general. The nature of the control exercised was expressed in classical terms by the ILOAT in several cases. Thus, in a case involving the transfer of an officer from one office to another in PAHO under specific Staff Rules the tribunal, after recognizing that the power of the Director of PAHO under the Staff Rules was discretionary, stated:

It will therefore set aside the impugned decision only if it was taken without authority, or violated a rule of form or procedure, or was based on an error of fact or of law, or if essential facts were overlooked, or if there was misuse of authority, or if mistaken conclusions were drawn from the facts. The Tribunal will allow the complaint if it finds any of these flaws.[44]

The earliest case in which the ILOAT stated in general terms the principles governing the control of the discretionary power to transfer staff members was *Nowakowska*.[45] Substantially the tribunal has repeated its basic ideas in other cases concerning transfers.[46] In both *Pagani*[47] and *Vangeenberghe*[48], which concerned reassignments or transfers of staff members within the organization, the Appeals Board of the Council of Europe took a general view similar to that taken by the ILOAT in the above cases.

In *Méndez*, a case which involved the transfer of a staff member from one department to another in the OAS, the OASAT stated in general terms that the legitimacy of the exercise of the discretionary power to redistribute personnel among the units of the secretariat of the OAS and, therefore, to transfer the applicant:

---

[44] *Quiñones*, ILOAT Judgment No. 447 [1981] (PAHO) at p. 6.

[45] ILOAT Judgment No. 115 [1967] (WMO) at p. 7.

[46] See *Frank* (*Nos. 1 & 2*), ILOAT Judgment No. 154 [1970] (ILO) at p. 4; *Arnold* ILOAT Judgment No. 397 [1980] (ITU) at pp. 5–6; *Glorioso*, ILOAT Judgment No. 450 [1981] (PAHO) at p. 7.

[47] Council of Europe Appeals Board, Appeal No. 76 [1982], Case-Law Digest (1985) p. 96 at p. 101.

[48] Council of Europe Appeals Board, Appeal No. 77 [1982], Case-Law Digest (1985) p. 104 at p. 110.

must be subject, among other aspects, to the fact that circumstances do not intervene *de facto* that change its nature or‚that are not in accord with its basic objectives; that it is not contrary to the rules in force and that it does not impair the legal rights of the staff member affected by the decision.[49]

This statement is capable of subsuming under it all the detailed elements contained in the statements of the ILOAT referred to above, although it is not as specific as the statements of the ILOAT.

In *Einthoven*, after referring to the discretionary nature of the power of the World Bank to establish a policy relating to transfer and apply it, the WBAT described the controls it would apply over the exercise of the power in the following terms:

It therefore becomes necessary to determine whether the Respondent has violated some mandatory Bank policy or procedure, or whether it has otherwise abused its discretion by taking action that was 'arbitrary, discriminatory, improperly motivated or carried out in violation of a fair and reasonable procedure'.[50]

Other tribunals have generally not been as exhaustive in the general statement of the manner in which they will control the exercise of the discretionary power to make transfers.[51] However, they have acted in a way which supports the general statements made by the tribunals referred to in the preceding paragraphs.

A significant corollary to the general approach described above is the refusal of tribunals to substitute their own judgments for those of the administration in respect of the transfers in issue. Thus, in *Nowakowska* the ILOAT made it quite clear that 'the Tribunal may not substitute its own judgment for that of the Secretary-General in regard to the work or conduct or qualifications of the person concerned.'[52] This rule is applicable clearly where there is no defect entitling the tribunal to quash the decision of the administrative authority, as was pointed out in *Douwes*.[53] Where the law has been violated and the decision taken is unlawful, because it amounts to an abuse of discretion, the tribunal will quash the decision or award compensation for the irregularity. This would amount normally to a finding that the decision should not have been taken. What the tribunal does not do is to evaluate the decision to make the transfer purely on its own merits.

---

[49] OASAT Judgment No. 21 [1976] at p. 5.

[50] WBAT Reports [1985], Decision No. 23 at p. 14. See also *Gyamfi*, WBAT Reports [1986], Decision No. 28 at p. 23.

[51] See, e.g., *Angelopoulos*, Decision no. 57, OECD Appeals Board [1976], Recueil des décisions 1 à 62 (1979) p. 157 at p. 159.

[52] ILOAT Judgment No. 115 [1967] (WMO) at p. 7. In *Angelopoulos*, Decision No. 57, OECD Appeals Board [1976], Recueil des décisions 1 à 62 (1979) p. 157 at p. 159, the tribunal said that it will not evaluate the professional aptitude of the applicant for the vacant post.

[53] ILOAT Judgment No. 129 [1969] (FAO) at p. 2.

(a) Détournement de pouvoir

Tribunals have expressly or implicitly accepted *détournement de pouvoir* as a ground for finding a decision to transfer invalid.[54] In many cases the question whether there had been a misuse of authority or an abuse of purpose has been examined, although it is only in a few that an abuse of purpose or misuse of authority has been found to exist.

i. *The interests of the service*

Often it has been assumed or stated that the transfer must be in the interests of the service of the organization. In the case of the European Communities Article 7 of the Staff Regulations specifically refers to the requirement that assignment must be solely in the interests of the service. The CJEC has referred to this requirement in finding that the transfer in question has not been for reasons alien to the interests of the service.[55] It follows that the CJEC will be prepared to invalidate a transfer, if it can be shown that it was not in the interests of the service.

The ILOAT has made it clear that it regards the power of transfer as being exercisable only in the interests of the service of the organization. In *Jurado (No. 7)*[56] the tribunal stated, in concluding that the transfer could not be questioned, that a transfer from one section of a service in the ILO to another was in keeping with the interests of the service. In one case the fact that the transfer was made because the applicant could not work harmoniously with his colleagues and establish satisfactory relations with the government was said to render the transfer in the interests of the organization.[57] In *Go*,[58] on the other hand, while pointing out that the Staff Rules of the WHO permitted transfer in the interests of the organization, the ILOAT found that on the facts the interests of the organization demanded the opposite of the transfer made, because the applicant was a good manager and was doing a good job at

---

[54] See, e.g., *Angelopoulos*, Decision No. 57, OECD Appeals Board [1976], Recueil des décisions 1 à 62 (1979) p. 157 at p. 159; *Pagani*, Council of Europe Appeals Board, Appeal No. 76 [1982], Case-Law Digest (1985) p. 96; *Méndez*, OASAT Judgment No. 21 [1976]; *Panis*, UNAT Judgment No. 297 [1982], JUNAT Nos. 231–300 p. 625; *Frank (Nos. 1 & 2)*, ILOAT Judgment No. 154 [1970] (ILO); *Gutmann*, CJEC Cases 18 & 35/65 [1966] ECR p. 103; *Einthoven*, WBAT Reports [1985], Decision No. 23.

[55] *Ditterich*, CJEC Case 86/77 [1978] ECR p. 1855; *Kindermann*, CJEC Case 60/80 [1981] ECR p. 1329.

[56] ILOAT Judgment No. 100 [1967] (ILO). See also *Nowakowska*, ILOAT Judgment No. 115 [1967] (WMO); *Douwes*, ILOAT Judgment No. 129 [1969] (FAO). In *Ditterich*, CJEC Case 86/77 [1978] ECR p. 1855, the CJEC found that the reasons given were not alien to the interests of the service. See also *Nebe*, CJEC Case 176/82 [1983] ECR p. 2475.

[57] *Douwes*, ILOAT Judgment No. 129 [1969] (FAO).

[58] ILOAT Judgment No. 631 [1984] (WHO). In *Silow*, ILOAT Judgment No. 151 [1970] (FAO), the tribunal found that the circumstances did not warrant overturning the decision to transfer on the ground that it was not in the interests of the organization, although the applicant produced some evidence to show that the transfer was not in the interests of the organization.

the position he held. The tribunal did state also that, while the administration was the best judge of the interests of the organization, the circumstances of the case showed that there was a complete misapprehension of the facts, because no unprejudiced person could have concluded that the removal of an efficient Director without his being replaced, especially when his achievement had not been questioned even by his critics, was in the interests of the organization. This case illustrates how the principle that a transfer must be in the interests of the organization will be implemented by the ILOAT. In general the tribunal leaves it to the administrative authority to decide what is in the interests of the organization. The presumption, therefore, that a transfer is in the interests of the organization will only be upset if in the circumstances of the case it is evident that the conclusion that the transfer was in the interests of the organization was completely mistaken.[59]

Conversely, the ILOAT has affirmed as a general principle that the interests of the organization are paramount and that transfer may take place in the interests of the organization to the detriment of other interests, including the interests of the individual or individuals affected. This is the conclusion to be drawn from the case in which the tribunal held that the texts of the Staff Rules of the WHO which specifically refer to the interests of the organization as a basis for transfers were in keeping with the general principles of the international public service which recognize the priority of the general interest over individual interests.[60]

The UNAT has also had occasion to refer to the interests of the service as the governing object of the exercise of the power to make transfers.[61] Other tribunals such as the WBAT and the CJEC have taken a similar view.[62] Basically the view taken by the ILOAT seems to be generally accepted.

ii. *The interests of the staff member*
As already pointed out, the interests of the organization are paramount. It follows that the interests of the staff member are secondary, to say the least. Some Staff Regulations and Staff Rules require that consideration be given to the staff member's interests but generally this is only to the extent possible, the principal consideration being the interests of the organization.[63]

In several cases the ILOAT found that the interests of the staff member need not have been accommodated, because the interests of the organization required that action be taken in disregard of them. Thus, in *Tarrab*[64] the fact

[59] See also *Douwes*, ILOAT Judgment No. 129 [1969] (FAO).
[60] *Verdrager*, ILOAT Judgment No. 325 [1977] (WHO).
[61] *Fürst*, UNAT Judgment No. 241 [1979], JUNAT Nos. 231–300 p. 93. See also *Kahale*, UNAT Judgment No. 165 [1972], JUNAT Nos. 114–166 p. 406.
[62] *Einthoven*, WBAT Reports [1985], Decision No. 23 at p. 17. See also *Demont*, CJEC Case 791/79 [1981] ECR p. 3105 at pp. 3115–6.
[63] See Staff Rule 510.1 of PAHO.
[64] ILOAT Judgment No. 132 [1969] (ILO). See also *Geist*, CJEC Case 61/76 [1977] ECR p. 1419.

that the measure taken affected the applicant personally and entailed a major change of residence for him did not affect the validity of the transfer.[65] In *Glorioso*[66] the ILOAT pointed out that the Staff Rules of PAHO required that the particular interests of the staff member be considered only to the extent possible and did not give those interests any priority as such. Clearly, even under the general principle of law, the interests of the staff member are relevant to the question of transfer but they do not take precedence over those of the organization.

The UNAT[67] and the WBAT[68] have also taken the view that while the relevant Regulations and Rules, as interpreted by them, required that the staff member's interests be considered, he cannot always expect to have them honoured, because the interests of the organization must prevail.

The ILOAT has, however, indicated that when the staff member's interests can be accommodated without detriment to the interests of the organization, they must be respected. This means that, while a transfer must be in the interests of the organization as a priority, it must also accommodate the particular interests of the staff member as a secondary requirement, if this can be done, while, nevertheless, fulfilling the requirement that the transfer be in the interests of the organization. In short the interests of the staff member cannot be ignored completely. If they are, there would be a *détournement de pouvoir*. Thus, in *Quiñones*[69] the ILOAT concluded on the facts that PAHO should have made sure that there was no other fit staff member, particularly because of the age, seniority, and outstanding work record of the applicant, and should even have held a competition, before transferring the applicant. Since no attempt had been made to safeguard the staff member's interests, the transfer was found to be wrongful. In this case clearly the particular interests of the staff member were compatible with the interests of the organization. The interests of the organization could have been protected while safeguarding the interests of the staff member. It was not a case where the staff member's interests conflicted with the interests of the organization and could only have been respected at the expense of the interests of the organization.

It is likely in a case where the interests of the staff member appear not to be compatible with the interests of the organization that a tribunal will not interfere with the conclusion reached by the administrative authority, unless the conclusion is manifestly wrong. Although this was not expressly stated in *Quiñones*, the facts showed that the decision taken by the administrative authority in that case was open to the criticism that it was manifestly wrong.

---

[65] See also *Silow*, ILOAT Judgment No. 151 [1970] (FAO).

[66] ILOAT Judgment No. 450 [1981] (PAHO).

[67] *Fürst*, UNAT Judgment No. 241 [1979], JUNAT Nos. 231–300 p. 93.

[68] *Einthoven*, WBAT Reports [1985], Decision No. 23 at p. 17.

[69] ILOAT Judgment No. 447 [1981] (PAHO). See also *Demont*, CJEC Case 791/79 [1981] ECR p. 3105 at p. 3116.

This position would be in accord with the view expressed in *Go*,[70] discussed above, that a decision that a transfer is in the interests of the organization will generally not be upset unless it is manifestly mistaken. If such a decision must be manifestly wrong, if it is to be upset, it seems reasonable that a decision that the particular interests of the staff member cannot be accommodated within the interests of the organization must also be subject to the same test.

iii. *Improper purpose or motive*

A decision to transfer a staff member may be vitiated by an improper motive or purpose. As already pointed out, a decision to transfer will not be upset because it is not in the interests of the organization or, where relevant, of the staff member, unless it is manifestly wrong. The cases dealing with improper motive or purpose, therefore, merely establish what purposes are clearly not in the interests of the organization (or the staff member) and which ones cannot be regarded as being outside the interests of the organization (or the staff member).

Ensuring good working relations and taking measures to restore calm or ensuring full understanding between officials have been held by the Appeals Board of the Council of Europe to be good motives for a transfer.[71] The OASAT has found that achieving more efficient services or the better execution of programmes is a good object in redistributing personnel.[72] Putting an end to friction between colleagues and the inability to establish satisfactory relations with government officials have been found to be a good reason for a transfer.[73] The ILOAT has also found that the following reasons for transfers were acceptable and showed legitimate objectives: the fact that the applicant had had differences of opinion with his supervisors and had circulated within the two organizations for which he worked his criticism of their activities;[74] the fact that the applicant's work was not entirely satisfactory;[75] strained relations of the applicant with her supervisor;[76] and the work requirements of the organization.[77] Making a transfer to a vacant post was not tainted by abuse of motive, according to the CJEC, even when the decision was taken in advance, because it was apparent that the comparative merits and qualifications of the applicant had been taken into considera-

---

[70] ILOAT Judgment No. 631 [1984] (WHO).

[71] *Pagani*, Council of Europe Appeals Board, Appeal No. 76 [1982], Case-Law Digest (1985) p. 96; *Vangeenberghe*, Council of Europe Appeals Board, Appeal No. 77 [1982], Case-Law Digest (1985) p. 104.

[72] *Méndez*, OASAT Judgment No. 21 [1976].

[73] *Douwes*, ILOAT Judgment No. 129 [1969] (FAO). See also *Frank (Nos. 1 & 2)*, ILOAT Judgment No. 154 [1970] (ILO).

[74] *Silow*, ILOAT Judgment No. 142 [1969] (IAEA).

[75] *Pessus (No. 2)*, ILOAT Judgment No. 282 [1976] (Eurocontrol).

[76] *Glorioso*, ILOAT Judgment No. 450 [1981] (PAHO).

[77] *de Groot*, ILOAT Judgment No. 576 [1983] (ITU).

tion.[78] The lack of interest in administrative duties on the part of the applicant, his disagreements with his Director, the flouting of authority, and the attitude of the applicant to the reorganization being carried out have been held to be good motives for transfer.[79]

It is possible to deduce, by implication sometimes, from some cases what might be an abuse of purpose. A transfer made to a position where the duties are such as to render the staff member unqualified to perform them reveals bad faith and amounts to an abuse of purpose.[80] If a transfer is made because of the applicant's association with the Staff Association of the organization,[81] or if the purpose of the transfer is to get rid of a single officer of a staff committee which as a body had antagonized the head of the institution,[82] the transfers are tainted, because these objectives interfere with the right of association of staff members and are unlawful. Similarly, to transfer a staff member, because he has been appointed to a staff committee to appear before the International Civil Service Commission, would be an abuse of purpose.[83] Where it could not be proved that the applicant had poor relationships with his subordinates and managed his department improperly, particularly because immediately prior reports described him as having good relations with his staff and fulfilling his duties appropriately, there was no good reason for transferring the applicant and the absence of such reason was proof that the transfer was not in the interests of the service which amounted to an abuse of purpose.[84]

When there are two reasons for a transfer and only one of them is a proper one, the existence of the other does not *per se* result in a *détournement de pouvoir*. This is in accord with the general principle of law. Thus, when the transfer was made not only because of the policy of exchanging staff between the central administration of the European Communities and the office in Rome, but also with the intention of reducing the staff in the Rome office, though the latter objective may have been an improper reason for a routine transfer, the presence of the former objective which was a lawful one made the transfer valid.[85] It was found that the principal reason for the transfer was the rotation of staff.

iv. *Discrimination, prejudice, and ill will*
It has been accepted, in accordance with general principles, that

[78] *Reinarz*, CJEC Case 55/70 [1971] ECR p. 379.
[79] *Kley*, CJEC Case 35/72 [1973] ECR p. 679.
[80] See *Rodriguez*, UNAT Judgment No. 167 [1973], JUNAT Nos. 167–230 p. 1.
[81] *Glorioso*, ILOAT Judgment No. 450 [1981] (PAHO).
[82] *Beaudry-Darismé*, ILOAT Judgment No. 494 [1982] (PAHO).
[83] *de Groot*, ILOAT Judgment No. 576 [1983] (ITU).
[84] *Gutmann*, CJEC Cases 18 & 35/65 [1966] ECR p. 103.
[85] *Carbognani and Coda Zabetta*, CJEC Cases 161 & 162/80 [1981] ECR p. 543; *Demont*, CJEC Case 791/79 [1981] ECR p. 3105.

discrimination could vitiate a transfer, though discrimination has not been found to exist in any case. In *Einthoven*[86] the WBAT found that there was no evidence of discriminatory treatment of the applicant in reassigning him from the Operations Evaluation Department of the Bank to an operational department, because the procedures for reassignment after their tour of duty of members of the former department had been properly applied.[87]

In numerous cases it has been held that the applicant had failed to prove the existence of prejudice or ill will which would have vitiated the decision to transfer the applicant.[88] For example, the request for a medical examination based on the behaviour of the applicant at conferences which resulted in his transfer has been held not to be *per se* evidence of personal prejudice or improper motivation.[89] On the other hand, where the applicant was transferred from the job he was doing, although he had performed satisfactorily, because a person hired from outside the WHO was introduced into the post he had held, when a new Director was appointed in the department in which the applicant worked, it was found that there was a personal prejudice in favour of the officer hired resulting in bias against the applicant which vitiated the transfer.[90] In *Quiñones*[91] it was held that the lack of consideration in transferring the applicant to a post which did not suit her could only be explained on the basis of prejudice against her.

v. *Détournement de procédure*

In a few cases applicants have contended that their transfers have been disguised disciplinary sanctions and that, therefore, the transfer decision involved a *détournement de procédure*, because the disciplinary procedure had not been followed.[92] In none of these cases did the applicants succeed in showing that the transfer was a disciplinary measure. In *Vangeenberghe*[93] the Appeals Board of the Council of Europe held that ensuring through a transfer good working relations by preventing bad relations was not a disciplinary measure requiring a disciplinary procedure.[94]

[86] WBAT Reports [1985], Decision No. 23.
[87] See also *Pagani*, Council of Europe Appeals Board, Appeal No. 76 [1982], Case-Law Digest (1985) p. 96, where no discrimination was found.
[88] See *Kahale*, UNAT Judgment No. 165 [1972], JUNAT Nos. 114–166 p. 406; *Fürst*, UNAT Judgment No. 241 [1979], JUNAT Nos. 231–300 p. 93; *Karlik*, UNAT Judgment No. 308 [1983]; *Go*, ILOAT Judgment No. 631 [1984] (WHO); *Scuppa*, CJEC Cases 4 & 30/74 [1975] ECR p. 919; *Geist*, CJEC Case 61/76 [1977] ECR p. 1419.
[89] *Borsody*, ILOAT Judgment No. 476 [1982] (FAO).
[90] *Sita Ram*, ILOAT Judgment No. 367 [1978] (WHO).
[91] ILOAT Judgment No. 447 [1981] (PAHO).
[92] See, e.g., *Angelopoulos*, Decision No. 57, OECD Appeals Board [1976], Recueil des décisions 1 à 62 (1979) p. 157; *Panis*, UNAT Judgment No. 297 [1982], JUNAT Nos. 231–300 p. 625; *Quiñones*, ILOAT Judgment No. 447 [1981] (PAHO); *Demont*, CJEC Case 791/79 [1981] ECR p. 3105. See also *Tarrab*, ILOAT Judgment No. 132 [1969] (ILO).
[93] Council of Europe Appeals Board, Appeal No. 77 [1982], Case-Law Digest (1985) p. 104.
[94] See also *Pessus (No. 2)*, ILOAT Judgment No. 282 [1976] (Eurocontrol).

In *Pagani*[95] the refusal to type an urgent text in Italian, though capable of being punished by disciplinary proceedings, was held also to be capable of being dealt with by transfer in order to maintain good working relations, with the result that the choice of transfer as a solution to the problem was not an abuse of procedure, since two alternative procedures were available.[96]

vi. *Non bis in idem*
The rule that there cannot be double jeopardy was referred to in *Angelo-poulos*.[97] In that case the applicant was transferred, because he had a difficult relationship with his supervisor, and then, because he could not get on with his second supervisor, he was dismissed. He contended that this was a violation of the rule *non bis in idem*, since he was penalized twice for the same fault of not having good working relations with his supervisor. The tribunal had no hesitation in concluding that there was no question of double jeopardy in the case. The decision is understandable, since there were two different faults upon which different actions were taken.

(b) *Substantive irregularities*

Substantive irregularities which could render a transfer invalid have been considered in several cases.

i. *Arbitrariness*
In *Turner*[98] the CJEC was faced with the argument that the transfer of the applicant resulted in her being in a post which was inappropriate to her training and previous record. The applicant was a doctor who practised in a specialized medical field. On a reorganization of the medical department she was assigned to a position of an administrative nature which the Court found was manifestly inappropriate to her training and previous record. The Court held that the transfer was arbitrary and could not stand. This case supports the view that a transfer could be found unlawful, if the tribunal considers that the action taken by the administrative authority can be characterized by it not merely as unreasonable or improper, but as arbitrary. Arbitrariness would have to be decided upon on the basis of the facts of each case.

In *Einthoven*,[99] on the other hand, the WBAT found that the policy of transferring staff members from the Operations Evaluation Department of the Bank to operational departments through the normal reassignment

---

[95] Council of Europe Appeals Board, Appeal No. 76 [1982], Case-Law Digest (1985) p. 96. See also *Demont*, CJEC Case 791/79 [1981] ECR p. 3105.

[96] See also *Kley*, CJEC Case 35/72 [1973] ECR p. 679.

[97] Decision No. 57, OECD Appeals Board [1976], Recueil des décisions 1 à 62 (1979) p. 157.

[98] CJEC Cases 59 & 129/80 [1981] ECR p. 1883.

[99] WBAT Reports [1985], Decision No. 23.

channels was not arbitrary. Likewise it found that the Transportation Sector Reassignment Panel of the respondent which had taken the decision in execution of the policy of the Bank to assign the applicant to the Western Africa Region, albeit in the transportation sector, in which he had been working in the Operations Evaluation Department, had not acted arbitrarily by so assigning him, because it had acted reasonably in all the circumstances of the case. Clearly in the view of the tribunal the facts showed that there was no room for a finding of arbitrariness. It is significant that the tribunal examined in detail the facts connected with the decision of the administrative authority before concluding that there was no arbitrariness. This case also shows that the tribunal considered that the issue of arbitrariness should be settled on the basis of all the particular circumstances of the case before it.

ii. *Error of law*

Error of law has been held to be a substantive irregularity which would entail a finding that the decision to transfer was tainted. Some of the strictures on transfer discussed earlier may be regarded as relevant to this form of substantive irregularity but they were so fundamental that it was considered advisable to deal with them separately.

There are many cases in which tribunals have found that there has been no error of law in the making of the decision to transfer. Suffice it to give two examples. In *Frank (Nos. 1 and 2)*[100] the ILOAT held that transferring the applicant without his consent was not illegal, because the consent of the staff member was not a legal requirement for the validity of a transfer. It was pointed out that the requirement of consent for the transfer laid down in Article 1.9 (b) of the Staff Regulations of the ILO applied only to transfers for temporary duty outside the office which was not the situation in the case in hand. It was also held that the applicant's terms of appointment did not require that his initial assignment be for a certain length of time so that his immediate transfer was not an illegality.[101] In *Duran*[102] it was decided by the ILOAT that a transfer should not involve a diminution of responsibilities as measured by a detailed comparison of the two post descriptions involved, though in that case there was no proof that this was so. Transfers to a less important and desirable position was not an abuse of power, even if the responsibilities must be comparable. Thus, transfer from the position of Deputy Chief of Personnel at the headquarters of PAHO to that of Senior Administrative Officer to the regional office of PAHO in Brasilia could not

---

[100] ILOAT Judgment No. 154 [1970] (ILO).

[101] *Bergin*, ILOAT Judgment No. 193 [1972] (FAO), was a case in which it was said that the existence of fraud or deceit could cause an error of law.

[102] ILOAT Judgment No. 375 [1979] (PAHO).

be questioned.[103] To take into account efficiency, competence, and integrity in deciding not to transfer is not an error of law.[104]

In *Detière*[105] the UNAT held that there had been an error of law. The applicant contended that the Service Code of ICAO required that the respondent should ascertain that the posts were comparable and pay regard to the personal interests of the staff member being transferred and that, since the administrative authority had not met these requirements, the decision to make the transfer was improper. The UNAT held that, since the job description of the post to which the transfer was made was not done until after the transfer was made, the administrative authority could not have made a fair comparison of the posts and further that, since the applicant had not been informed of the possibility of a transfer, his interests could not have been consulted. Hence, there was a violation of the substantive legal requirements of the Service Code and the transfer was tainted.

In most cases the written law of the organization lays down the substantive requirements the non-fulfilment of which would result in an error of law. However, some of the substantive limits to the exercise of the power to transfer may also be found in the general principles of law. Where the written law is relied on, it must be clear that there is a law which limits the discretion of the administrative authority. Thus, where Instructions stated that assignments away from ILO headquarters should normally be for a minimum of 3 years, the ILOAT held that the instrument did not lay down a mandatory rule, so that the applicant could be transferred after 15 months.[106]

iii. *Error of fact*

In *Glorioso*[107] the applicant argued that the assessments made by the administrative authority in ordering the transfer being contested were not accurate because they were based on errors of fact. The tribunal held that no errors of fact had been found. In *Duran (No. 3)*[108] it was argued that the transfer was to a post that required the knowledge of Spanish of which the applicant had an inadequate knowledge. The tribunal found that the conclusion that the applicant's knowledge of Spanish was not inadequate was not wrong and that therefore the administrative authority's decision to transfer her was not based on a factual error which would have vitiated the transfer decision.[109]

---

103 See also *Arnold*, ILOAT Judgment No. 397 [1980] (ITU).

104 *Glorioso*, ILOAT Judgment No. 450 [1981] (PAHO). No errors of law were said to exist also in *Tarrab*, ILOAT Judgment No. 132 [1969] (ILO), and in *Angelopoulos*, Decision No. 57, OECD Appeals Board [1976], Recueil des décisions 1 à 62 [1979] p. 157.

105 UNAT Judgment No. 136 [1970] (ICAO), JUNAT Nos. 114–166 p. 205.

106 *Tarrab*, ILOAT Judgment No. 132 [1969] (ILO).

107 ILOAT Judgment No. 450 [1981] (PAHO).

108 ILOAT Judgment No. 543 [1983] (PAHO).

109 See also *Angelopoulos*, Decision No. 57, OECD Appeals Board [1976], Recueil des décisions 1 à 62 (1979) p. 157, where no error of fact was found in the decision contested; and *Gyamfi*, WBAT Reports [1986], Decision No. 28.

iv. *Consideration of irrelevant facts*

In *Pagani*[110] the decision to terminate the applicant's secondment and transfer her was alleged to have been taken partly because she had refused to type an urgent document in Italian when it was not a requirement of her assignment that she should type in Italian. It was found that the head of a Service could make such a request, there being no general restriction, because of the linguistic needs of the institution, with the result that taking her refusal into consideration in deciding on the transfer did not amount to taking into account irrelevant facts. The principle that irrelevant facts should not be considered was accepted, although it was found that the principle had not been violated.[111]

v. *Omission of facts*

In *Quiñones*[112] the ILOAT found that the Staff Regulations and Staff Rules of PAHO required that the organization consider competence and integrity in the assignment of staff. However, the tribunal held that the written law had not been violated by an omission of fact, because the administrative authority had not disregarded these factors in arriving at the transfer decision. In *Frank (Nos. 1 and 2)*[113] and *Arnold*[114] also it was held by the ILOAT that no essential facts had not been taken into consideration, so that the transfer decisions were sustained.

In *Sita Ram*,[115] on the other hand, where the applicant was transferred out of an office so that a candidate from outside the WHO could be appointed to a post in the office, it was held by the ILOAT that all the relevant facts surrounding the posting and performance of the applicant in the office concerned had not been considered. This was an element which vitiated the transfer decision.

vi. *Erroneous conclusions*

In *Pinto de Magalhaes*[116] the administrative authority came to the conclusion that the applicant had created a relationship of close dependence between him and another staff member belonging to the same group of financial staff, such a relationship being inadmissible between officials applying financial controls, with the result that his transfer was ordered. The applicant had proposed that the salary of the other staff member be paid into a joint

---

[110] Council of Europe Appeals Board, Appeal No. 76 [1982], Case-Law Digest (1985) p. 96.
[111] In *Einthoven*, WBAT Reports [1985], Decision No. 23 at p. 20, also it was held that no irrelevant facts had been considered.
[112] ILOAT Judgment No. 447 [1981] (PAHO).
[113] ILOAT Judgment No. 154 [1970] (ILO).
[114] ILOAT Judgment No. 397 [1980] (ITU).
[115] ILOAT Judgment No. 367 [1978] (WHO).
[116] ILOAT Judgment No. 311 [1977] (ILO).

account to be held by him and the other staff member. The applicant had asked the opinion of his superiors and dropped the matter when they expressed disapproval. The ILOAT held that on the facts the applicant had merely made a proposal which had never matured, so that it was a clearly mistaken conclusion that there was financial dependence of one staff member on another. The transfer decision was, therefore, found tainted.

In *Duran*,[117] on the other hand, the ILOAT found that the evidence relating to the sickness of the applicant was not at all conclusive in favour of the finding that the applicant was too sick to go to Brasilia and that, therefore, PAHO had not drawn an erroneous conclusion that the health of the applicant was not such that she could not transfer to Brasilia. There are some other cases in which the ILOAT has held that the conclusions reached by the administrative authority were not clearly erroneous so that the transfer decision based on those conclusions could not be impeached.[118]

(c) *Procedural irregularities*

A violation of procedural requirements, whether stated in the written law[119] or emanating from general principles of law, could affect the validity of a decision to transfer but it must be established that the procedure was required by the law and was not merely optional or desirable. Thus, the issuance of a vacancy notice which was referred to in a section of the Administrative Manual of PAHO was held by the ILOAT not to be required by a rule of law, since the provision in question was not in itself a Staff Rule but only purported to establish a policy to implement the Staff Rules,[120] the result being that the applicant could not rely on it to argue that there had been a procedural irregularity in the decision to transfer her. Further, the non-observance of the procedure required must cause the applicant prejudice, if it is to be operative as a vitiating element. Thus, where a post description was not done for six months after the applicant's transfer to a post, the ILOAT held that, since her supervisor was able to make a fair appraisal of her work in spite of the absence of a post description, she could not rely on the procedural failure.[121] Insignificant errors cannot, by the same token, affect the transfer decision, particularly where the applicant has no doubt concerning the effects of the decision.[122]

117 ILOAT Judgment No. 375 [1979] (PAHO).

118 See *Frank* (*Nos. 1 & 2*), ILOAT Judgment No. 154 [1970] (ILO); *Arnold*, ILOAT Judgment No. 397 [1980] (ITU); *Borsody*, ILOAT Judgment No. 476 [1982] (FAO). In all these cases it was held that erroneous conclusions had not been reached.

119 See, e.g. *van Gent*, WBAT Reports [1983, Part I], Decision No. 11.

120 *Duran*, ILOAT Judgment No. 375 [1979] (PAHO). See also *Arnold*, ILOAT Judgment No. 397 [1980] (ITU); *Frank* (*Nos. 1 & 2*), ILOAT Judgment No. 154 [1970] (ILO); *Kahale*, UNAT Judgment No. 165 [1972], JUNAT Nos. 114–166 p. 406.

121 *Glorioso*, ILOAT Judgment No. 450 [1981] (PAHO).

122 *Oberthür*, CJEC Case 105/81 [1982] ECR p. 3781. See also *Vangeenberghe*, Council of

Making a transfer order without a formal administrative decision is a procedural error which affects the validity of the transfer decision. In *Decision No 1, ESA/CR/6*[123] the Appeals Board of the ESA was faced with this situation. There the transfer order was withdrawn, when the applicant complained to the Director General of ESA. The tribunal assumed that the order was invalid, because it considered whether any damage had been caused by the transfer of the applicant being carried out, although it found that in fact there had been no prejudice to the applicant.

i. *Statement of reasons*

There must be a communication of the reasons for the decision to transfer, clearly in order to enable the affected staff member to complain, if he is dissatisfied, or to defend himself.[124] A failure to do this results in the decision to transfer being unlawful. Some Staff Regulations or Staff Rules make this a requirement, but even apart from that it seems to be a requirement of the general law. However, it may not be always necessary for the reasons to be stated explicitly in the notice of transfer, if it was possible for the staff member clearly to gather them from such documentation as memoranda communicated to him, from interviews with administrative officials and supervisors, or from other relevant surrounding circumstances, the object to be achieved being that the staff member transferred should genuinely have the opportunity of getting to know the real reasons for his transfer.[125] By the same token there does not have to be an exhaustive statement of reasons but they should be sufficiently clear to enable the staff member to deduce the real reasons from all the circumstances of the case.[126]

A defect caused by the failure to give reasons in the notice of transfer, as where a summary notice of transfer is issued, may be cured if the reasons are given later,[127] obviously within a reasonable time, so that the staff member

Europe Appeals Board, Appeal No. 77 [1982], Case-Law Digest (1985) p. 104, where the omission of the date of transfer was held to be a clerical error which could not affect the validity of the decision to transfer the applicant.

[123] *Decision No. 1, ESA/CR/6*, ESA Appeals Board [1976].

[124] *Go*, ILOAT Judgment No. 631 [1984] (WHO). In this case the Staff Rules of WHO required that the reasons be given, but a general principle of law would appear to require this: see *Vangeenberghe*, Council of Europe Appeals Board, Appeal No. 77 [1982], Case-Law Digest (1985) p. 104, where the Staff Regulations were silent on the matter and it was held that reasons must be given.

[125] See *Frank (Nos. 1 & 2)*, ILOAT Judgment No. 154 [1970] (ILO); *Vangeenberghe*, Council of Europe Appeals Board, Appeal No. 77 [1982], Case-Law Digest (1985) p. 104; *Kley*, CJEC Case 35/72 [1973] ECR p. 679; *Geist*, CJEC Case 61/76 [1977] ECR p. 1419; *Ditterich*, CJEC Case 86/77 [1978] ECR p. 1855; *Kuhner*, CJEC Cases 33 & 75/79 [1980] ECR p. 1677; *Carbognani and Coda Zabetta*, CJEC Cases 161 & 162/80 [1981] ECR p. 543; *Arning*, CJEC Case 125/80 [1981] ECR p. 2539; *Demont*, CJEC Case 791/79 [1981] ECR p. 3105; *Nebe*, CJEC Case 176/82 [1983] ECR p. 2475.

[126] *Kley*, CJEC Case 35/72 [1973] ECR p. 679.

[127] *Arnold*, ILOAT Judgment No. 397 [1980] (ITU).

has an opportunity to object. The reasons given must be accurate. Stating the wrong reasons will vitiate the transfer decision, because it is an effective procedural irregularity.[128]

ii. *Opportunity to reply*

It would appear that the affected staff member is entitled to have an opportunity to reply, if he objects to the decision to transfer him.[129]

iii. *Notification of decision*

There must be timely notification of the decision to the staff member affected. A mere publication of positions with their incumbents is inadequate. A communication in writing would normally be required. A delay in notification could affect the rights of a staff member but he must show that he had been prejudiced and caused damage. The delay does not, in any case, *per se* affect the substantive validity of the decision.[130]

iv. *Consultation*

Where the written law requires consultation with the staff member being transferred, failure to consult with him will result in a procedural irregularity. In *Vangeenberghe*[131] the Appeals Board of the Council of Europe pointed out that the Staff Regulations required that the official in question be approached for his views before he was transferred. The duty to consult may be implied in the written law, although it is not explicitly imposed by the written law. Thus, in *Detière*[132] the UNAT held that, since the Staff Regulations of ICAO required that due regard be paid to the personal interests of the staff member concerned, there was a duty to inform the staff member of the planned transfer and give him an opportunity of apprising the administrative authority of his personal interests.

In the absence of a specific requirement that the staff member concerned be consulted, it is not clear whether there is a duty to consult such staff member. In *Frank (Nos. 1 & 2)*,[133] in so far as the ILOAT stated that, there being no opportunity to consult the staff member before he arrived in Geneva, it could not be said that the administrative authority had not consulted him, because he had been consulted after he arrived in Geneva, the tribunal seems to have assumed that there was a duty to consult the staff

---

[128] *Turner*, CJEC Cases 59 & 129/80 [1981] ECR p. 1883. See also *Geist*, CJEC Case 61/76 [1977] ECR p. 1419.

[129] See *Go*, ILOAT Judgment No. 631 [1984] (WHO).

[130] See *Arning*, CJEC Case 125/80 [1981] ECR p. 2539. In this case the Staff Regulations (Article 25) of the European Communities required notification but the requirement of notice is in keeping with general principles of law.

[131] Council of Europe Appeals Board, Appeal No. 77 [1982], Case-Law Digest (1985) p. 104.

[132] UNAT Judgment No. 136 [1970] (ICAO), JUNAT Nos. 114–166 p. 205.

[133] ILOAT Judgment No. 154 [1970] (ILO).

member concerned. However, in *Méndez*[134] the OASAT refused to recognize a duty to consult the staff member concerned in the absence of reference to such a duty in the written law. In *Arning*[135] the CJEC took a similar view in holding that, since transfer did not involve the right of defence, there was no legal obligation of consultation before the decision was taken in the absence of a specific requirement in the written law, though general principles of good administration, good faith, and mutual confidence might have required that the affected staff member be allowed to make known his point of view and for that reason be consulted.

While the CJEC and the OASAT take the view that there is no obligation under any general principle of law to consult the staff member concerned before the decision to transfer is made, this view creates problems with the rule discussed earlier that, where the interest of the staff member and the organization are compatible, the interest of the staff member must be recognized and respected. For, if there is no duty to consult the staff member concerned, it may be argued that the observance of the rule relating to respect for the interests of the staff member cannot be facilitated and ensured. This is, indeed, a problem. However, the rule relating to the interests of the staff member is a substantive rule and it is possible to accept a situation where the organization is left to observe it by following any procedures, including consultation, it may think fit. This position is, then, compatible with the non-existence of a definite and rigid procedural rule that the staff member concerned must in all circumstances be consulted before the decision to transfer is made.

v. *Due process*

In accordance with general principles due process must be observed at every stage of the procedure in arriving at and finalizing the decision to transfer. This includes the internal appeals procedure where such a process is relevant. In *Bergin*[136] it was found that, where the views of officials in Iran became relevant to the taking of the transfer decision, they had been inquired into and confirmed by the Chief of the Operations Office of the Applicant's Division, after he had heard what the applicant had to say, the inquiry having been regularly conducted, so that there had been no absence of due process. In *Einthoven*[137] and *Duran (No. 3)*[138] the WBAT and the ILOAT respectively found upon examination that there was no absence of due process in the internal appeals procedure.

---

[134] OASAT Judgment No. 21 [1976].
[135] CJEC Case 125/80 [1981] ECR p. 2539.
[136] ILOAT Judgment No. 193 [1972] (FAO).
[137] WBAT Reports [1985], Decision No. 23.
[138] ILOAT Judgment No. 543 [1983] (PAHO).

Consent of the transferee

As was stated by the CJEC, there is no general requirement that the staff member transferred consent to the transfer, since, if there were, this would be an intolerable restriction on the ability of the administrative authority to organize its services and to adapt to changing requirements.[139] The administrative authority is generally at liberty to organize its offices to suit the tasks entrusted to it and to assign its staff in the light of such tasks.[140] However, where the written law of the organization or a general principle of law requires the consent of the staff member to a transfer, his consent must be obtained. Thus, in the case of post abolition, it is likely that even general principles of law require that the staff member must consent to his transfer.[141] The written law may also require consent in certain organizations in certain cases, such as temporary transfers,[142] or where the staff member belongs to the General Service category and is transferred from the place of his recruitment,[143] or where a transfer is to a lower-grade post,[144] or where the staff member is a fixed-term contract holder.[145]

Where the transfer is consented to initially and not objected to the staff member is, as a general rule, estopped from withdrawing his consent.[146]

Refusal of a transfer

Where a transfer which is validly made is refused by the staff member, the ILOAT has held that this is a grave breach of duty which may be visited with termination of service.[147] In *Zang-Atangana*[148] the UNAT held that a refusal to comply with a transfer order renders the staff member subject to disciplinary measures entailing the institution of disciplinary proceedings.

Where the holder of a fixed-term contract refuses a transfer at the time his contract is about to expire, this is a good ground for not renewing his contract and it is not necessary that such a refusal be treated as a disciplinary issue.[149]

---

[139] *Carbognani and Coda Zabetta*, CJEC Cases 161 & 162/80 [1981] ECR p. 543 at p. 563. See also *Frank (Nos. 1 & 2)*, ILOAT Judgment No. 154 [1970] (ILO); *Pessus (No. 2)*, ILOAT Judgment No. 282 [1976] (Eurocontrol).

[140] See *Labeyrie*, CJEC Case 16/67 [1968] ECR p. 293; *Vistosi*, CJEC Case 61/70 [1971] ECR p. 535; *Geist*, CJEC Case 61/76 [1977] ECR p. 1419.

[141] See *Decision No. 4, ESRO/CR/22*, ESRO Appeals Board [1969].

[142] *Frank (Nos. 1 & 2)*, ILOAT Judgment No. 154 [1970] (ILO).

[143] *Gotschi*, ILOAT Judgment No. 523 [1982] (PAHO).

[144] *Vera*, OASAT Judgment No. 33 [1977].

[145] *Decision No. 20, ESA/CR/37*, ESA Appeals Board [1983].

[146] *Bergin*, ILOAT Judgment No. 193 [1972] (FAO).

[147] *Verdrager*, ILOAT Judgment No. 325 [1977] (WHO).

[148] UNAT Judgment No. 130 [1969], JUNAT Nos. 114–166 p. 155.

[149] See *Panis*, UNAT Judgment No. 297 [1982], JUNAT Nos. 231–300 p. 625; *Hoefnagels*, ILOAT Judgment No. 25 [1957] (WHO).

By offering a staff member whose services are unsatisfactory a transfer the administrative authority does not forgo its right to terminate the staff member's services on the ground of unsatisfactory service.[150] The refusal of a transfer cannot normally be treated *per se* as a case of abandonment of post entailing automatic termination.[151] It is also not a basis for summary dismissal for serious misconduct.[152] Where a termination is lawfully refused, the subterfuge of abolition of post cannot be used to terminate the services of the staff member.[153] The refusal of a transfer cannot *per se* be treated as a resignation, even though a subsidiary rule of the organization may permit this, when the Staff Regulations provide otherwise.[154]

Transfer and the right of association

The right of association is normally guaranteed staff members of international organizations by the written law of these organizations. It has been held, as already seen, that the exercise of this right of association cannot be used as a reason for transferring a staff member, as this would result in a misuse of authority or *détournement de pouvoir*. This was conceded in *Glorioso*,[155] where, however, it was not proved that the reason for the transfer was the applicant's association with the Staff Association of PAHO.[156]

Remedies

There are several cases in which transfers were held to have been vitiated by illegalities. In these cases the remedies ordered have varied. There are some cases in which damages for moral injury have been discussed, even where there had been no violation of the law. On the other hand, there are also cases in which procedural irregularities have been found to be too trivial to warrant the granting of a remedy.

(a) Reinstatement or specific performance

Reinstatement or specific performance with or without compensation has

---

[150] *Decisions Nos. 8 & 10, ESRO/CR/45*, ESRO Appeals Board [1971].
[151] *Duran (No. 2)*, ILOAT Judgment No. 392 [1980] (PAHO).
[152] *Reynolds*, ILOAT Judgment No. 38 [1958] (FAO).
[153] *Gotschi*, ILOAT Judgment No. 523 [1982] (PAHO).
[154] *Reynolds*, ILOAT Judgment No. 38 [1958] (FAO).
[155] ILOAT Judgment No. 450 [1981] (PAHO).
[156] See also *de Groot*, ILOAT Judgment No. 576 [1983] (ITU).

been ordered in several cases where it has been possible in circumstances in which improper transfer decisions had been taken. Whether reinstatement is ordered or what form specific performance will take will depend naturally on the circumstances of the case. Suffice it to describe a few decisions as examples. In *Vera*,[157] where the transfer was held to be invalid because it was contrary to the written law, the OASAT ordered that the applicant be reinstated in his previous post but refused an additional claim for damages.[158] In *Duran (No. 2)*[159] the ILOAT quashed a decision to terminate a staff member's appointment on the ground of abandonment of post, because a transfer was refused in the bona-fide belief that the transfer was improper, but refused the applicant's additional request for compensation on the ground that damages could only be awarded, if she could have shown that the transfer order was invalid, which she had not done.[160] In *Turner*,[161] where the transfer of the applicant was found to be unlawful on the ground of arbitrariness, the transfer order was annulled and the organization was ordered to make a future posting in accordance with the principles laid down in the judgment for the proper exercise of the power to transfer the applicant. No damages were awarded in addition or as an alternative to specific performance.

In *Quiñones*[162] rescission was not requested, where there had been a *détournement de pouvoir*. Specific performance was ordered in that the organization was directed to prefer the applicant to equally well-qualified candidates, if she applied for a position comparable to the one she held before the date of the transfer order. In addition moral damages of $8,000 were awarded.[163]

In *Sita Ram*[164] the impugned transfer decision was quashed on the ground of prejudice and moral damages of $12,000 were ordered. On the other hand, claims by the applicant to be restored to the duties he had before the transfer order was made, to be given retroactively the grade given to the officer appointed to perform those duties as a result of whose appointment he was

---

[157] OASAT Judgment No. 33 [1977].

[158] In *Gutmann*, CJEC Cases 18 & 35/65 [1966] ECR p. 103, reinstatement was ordered but no additional damages were awarded. In *Detière*, UNAT Judgment No. 136 [1970] (ICAO), JUNAT Nos. 114–166 p. 205, reinstatement with the alternative of compensation was ordered. In addition damages were awarded.

[159] ILOAT Judgment No. 392 [1980] (PAHO).

[160] See also *Getz*, OASAT Judgment No. 26 [1976], and *Reynolds*, ILOAT Judgment No. 38 [1958] (FAO), which were cases in which remedies similar to those ordered in *Duran (No. 2)* were ordered. In *Getz* additional compensation was awarded and an indemnity was assessed as an alternative to reinstatement. In *Reynolds* additional compensation was awarded.

[161] CJEC Cases 59 & 129/80 [1981] ECR p. 1883.

[162] ILOAT Judgment No. 447 [1981] (PAHO).

[163] See also *Gatmaytan*, ILOAT Judgment No. 424 [1980] (PAHO), where specific performance was ordered.

[164] ILOAT Judgment No. 367 [1978] (WHO).

transferred, or as an alternative to be paid the difference between the salary he would have received, had he been given the position to which the other officer had been appointed and the grade belonging to that position, and his present salary were refused on the ground that the recognition of such claims were outside the tribunal's competence.[165]

Where reinstatement is not requested or the status quo ante cannot be restored, specific performance will not be ordered, but the award of damages will be considered.[166] But this has happened rarely.

(b) Compensation

Apart from those cases discussed above where damages have been awarded in addition to or as an alternative to specific performance, some cases where the claims of the applicants have been held to be well-founded have taken the course of awarding damages whether material or moral.

i. Material damages

In *Decision No. 34, ESRO/CR/89*[167] the Appeals Board of ESRO awarded 6 months' salary, where a transfer had illegally not been made when the applicant's post was abolished and his appointment terminated. No specific performance was ordered.[168] In another case,[169] where a post was abolished and the WBAT held that the applicant had been transferred to a lower-grade position in violation of the procedural rules governing transfers in the specific situation, the tribunal did not award specific material damages or order specific performance but ordered that the Bank pay the applicant compensation equivalent to 2 years' salary, rather than the 18 months' salary offered by the Bank, if the applicant chose the option of resigning from the service of the Bank.

Where a transfer is illegal, pure and simple, it is in general unusual for the impugned decision not to be quashed and for material damages to be awarded in lieu of reinstatement. But in *Schofield (No. 4)*[170] the WHO had failed to make adequate efforts to find a P6 officer a P6 job but had transferred him to a P5 position. The ILOAT quashed the transfer decision but,

---

[165] Rescission of the decision was ordered and moral damages were awarded also in *Pinto de Magalhaes*, ILOAT Judgment No. 311 [1977] (ILO). See also *Go*, ILOAT Judgment No. 631 [1984] (WHO).

[166] See *Rodriguez*, UNAT Judgment No. 167 [1973], JUNAT Nos. 167–230 p. 1.

[167] *Decision No. 34, ESRO/CR/89*, ESRO Appeals Board [1974].

[168] In *Gotschi*, ILOAT Judgment No. 523 [1982] (PAHO), where a post was unlawfully abolished and the applicant's appointment was terminated because he had refused a transfer, no reinstatement was ordered but material damages of $40,000 were awarded for unlawful termination of service.

[169] *van Gent*, WBAT Reports [1983, Part I], Decision No. 11.

[170] ILOAT Judgment No. 411 [1980] (WHO).

since the applicant had left the service of the WHO, ordered payment of only SF 3,000 in damages, on the ground that, although P6 jobs were difficult to find, the applicant had refused some after an effort was made to find one and the obligation was not to guarantee a P6 job but not to delay or fail to look for one in good faith.

The issue of awarding material damages even where a transfer decision is legal has been adverted to by the ILOAT but in the case in question it was found that there had been no material damage so that the issue was moot.[171] In case of insignificant procedural errors which do not affect the validity of the transfer decision,[172] where the procedural error does not cause the applicant prejudice,[173] or where the illegal decision is subsequently withdrawn and the applicant is restored to his former position in circumstances where no prejudice can be proved to have been caused the applicant during the period of his transfer,[174] no material damages have been awarded.

ii. *Moral damages*

The question of moral damages in the case of transfer, whether illegal or legal, is somewhat complicated.

In several cases, where the action taken involving transfers has been found to be illegal, moral damages, though claimed, have not been awarded on the ground generally that there was no serious injury to reputation or to dignity or that the applicant's professional standing had not been affected.[175] In some cases, where moral damages have been claimed on account of illegal transfers, it has been stated that the judgment in the case was sufficient vindication of the applicant's honour or that the annulment of the impugned decisions made good the non-material damage or that no symbolic damages would be awarded in addition to the substance of the judgment ordering reinstatement and restoring the applicant's honour.[176]

There have been cases in which the transfer decision has been quashed or specific performance has been ordered where also moral damages have been awarded. Where for instance, there had been a *détournement de pouvoir* in ordering the transfer, the ILOAT awarded moral damages amounting to $25,000, in addition to quashing the transfer decision on the ground that,

---

[171] *Pessus (No. 2)*, ILOAT Judgment No. 282 [1976] (Eurocontrol).

[172] *Oberthür*, CJEC Case 105/81 [1982] ECR p. 3781. See also *Vangeenberghe*, Council of Europe Appeals Board, Appeal No. 77 [1982], Case-Law Digest (1985) p. 104.

[173] *Glorioso*, ILOAT Judgment No. 450 [1981] (PAHO).

[174] *Decision No. 1, ESA/CR/6*, ESA Appeals Board [1976].

[175] *Rodriguez*, UNAT Judgment No. 167 [1973], JUNAT Nos. 167–230 p. 1, *Decision No. 34, ESRO/CR/89*, ESRO Appeals Board [1974]; *Decision No. 1, ESA/CR/6*, ESA Appeals Board [1976].

[176] See *Turner*, CJEC Cases 59 & 129/80 [1981] ECR p. 1883; *Gutmann*, CJEC Cases 18 & 35/65 [1966] ECR p. 103; *Detière*, UNAT Judgment No. 136 [1970] (ICAO), JUNAT Nos. 114–166 p. 205.

while the applicant had not suffered in reputation, he had, among other things, been denied the opportunity of continuing to work on a job of high interest and responsibility and been relegated to a position of lower responsibility.[177]

Where transfers or action involving transfers have been found not to be illegal, tribunals have, nevertheless, considered whether to award moral damages. In all the cases, however, it has been held that moral damages were not payable. While sometimes the tribunal has merely stated that moral damages would not be awarded,[178] on occasion the tribunal has considered with negative results whether the professional standing and reputation of the applicant had been impaired by the action taken.[179] In one case the ILOAT said that it was not necessary to consider whether the moral prejudice was serious enough to warrant the award of damages, because the applicant had been responsible partly for the prejudice caused and PAHO had mitigated any prejudice caused by giving the applicant new duties which could bring her promotion.[180]

[177] *Go*, ILOAT Judgment No. 631 [1984] (WHO). See also *Pinto de Magalhaes*, ILOAT Judgment No. 311 [1977] (ILO)—SF 10,000; *Sita Ram*, ILOAT Judgment No. 367 [1978] (WHO)—$12,000; *Quiñones*, ILOAT Judgment No. 447 [1981] (PAHO)—$8,000.

[178] See *Méndez*, OASAT Judgment No. 21 [1976]; *Pessus (No. 2)*, ILOAT Judgment No. 282 [1976] (Eurocontrol).

[179] See *Borsody*, ILOAT Judgment No. 476 [1982] (FAO); *Arning*, CJEC Case 125/80 [1981] ECR p. 2539.

[180] *Glorioso*, ILOAT Judgment No. 450 [1981] (PAHO).

CHAPTER FORTY-TWO

Promotion

THE Staff Regulations and Staff Rules of most organizations contain provisions on promotion of staff members after they have joined the service of the organizations. Some organizations have fairly detailed provisions, while other have less detailed provisions. In the case of the UN Staff Regulation 4.2 states: 'The paramount consideration in the appointment, transfer or promotion of the staff shall be the necessity for securing the highest standards of efficiency, competence and integrity.'[1]

Staff Rule 104.14 in implementing this provision deals with the Appointment and Promotion Board and its functions as an advisory body and incidentally establishes some substantive requirements to be considered by the Board in giving advice on promotions.[2] In the case of the Council of Europe Article 21 of the Staff Regulations states:

1. Promotion consists in the appointment of a staff member to a post in a higher grade. It shall take place after a vacant or regraded post has been thrown open to competition.
2. The Secretary General shall decide on promotions in accordance with the conditions laid down by the regulations on appointments.[3]

Appendix II to the Staff Regulations which concerns appointments elaborates on the procedure for promotion, particularly in Articles 14–16.[4] There is little stated about substantive requirements for promotion in this Appendix. The Staff Regulations of the European Communities refer to promotion as a means of filling vacant posts in Article 29, deal with some procedures for promotion in Articles 30 and 31, and elaborate further on the decisions relating to promotion in Articles 45 and 46.[5] The provisions of Articles 45 and 46 are perhaps the most detailed on promotion as far as Staff Regulations go. They deal with some substantive requirements connected with promotions and state:

Article 45. 1. Promotion shall be by decision of the appointing authority. It shall be effected by appointment of the official to the next higher grade in the category or service to which he belongs. Promotion shall be exclusively by selection from among

---

[1] See Appendix V *infra*.
[2] See Appendix V *infra*.
[3] See Appendix VI *infra*.
[4] See Appendix VI *infra*.
[5] See Amerasinghe (ed.), 4 *Staff Regulations and Staff Rules of Selected International Organizations* (1983) p. 1 at pp. 13, 18, 19.

officials who have completed a minimum period in their grade, after consideration of the comparative merits of the officials eligible for promotion and of the reports on them.

For officials appointed to the starting grade in their service or category, this period shall be six months from the date of their establishment; for other officials it shall be two years.

2. An official may be transferred from one service to another or promoted from one category to another only on the basis of a competition.

Article 46. An official appointed to a higher grade shall, in his new grade, have the seniority corresponding to the notional step equal to or next above the notional step reached in his former grade, plus the amount of the two-yearly increment for his new grade.

For the purpose of this provision, each grade shall be divided into notional steps corresponding to months of service and notional salaries on rising by one twenty-fourth of the two-yearly increment for that grade throughout the span of the actual steps. An official appointed to a higher grade shall in no case receive a basic salary lower than that which he would have received in his former grade.

An official appointed to a higher grade shall be classified not lower than the initial step for that grade.[6]

However detailed or fragmentary the written law of an organization may be, international administrative tribunals may have to decide cases involving not only the interpretation and implementation of that written law, but also the application of general principles of law to decisions taken in regard to promotion. Generally, the written law does not contain all the rules relevant to a decision on promotion, apart from the fact that tribunals may sometimes have to interpret the written law and see that it is properly applied. Consequently, tribunals have had to deal in the bulk of the cases decided by them with the application of general principles of law governing decisions on promotion. It may be noted that tribunals have not hesitated to apply general principles of law to decisions on promotion where such principles are appropriately applicable.

The right to a promotion

The written law of organizations is not in general formulated in such a way that it specifically confers on a staff member who fulfils certain requirements a right to promotion. Tribunals have frequently pointed this out, while also speaking in terms which indicate that there is no right to a promotion as such even under the general principles of law. Thus, in *Küster*[7], where the

6 Ibid. at pp. 18, 19.
7 CJEC Case 123/75 [1976] ECR p. 1701. In *Grosz*, CJEC Case 35/69 [1970] ECR p. 609, the CJEC held that even the fact that the applicant held a higher-grade post on a temporary basis did not give him a right to be promoted.

applicant complained that the administration had decided on an internal competition under the Staff Regulations instead of promoting him, when he had satisfied all the eligibility requirements for promotion, the CJEC held that, even though the applicant had fulfilled all the conditions for promotion, including the eligibility requirements, he had no right to a promotion and the choice between an internal competition and promotion was entirely at the discretion of the administration.

The ILOAT has held that quality assessments of his work did not entitle the applicant to a promotion, promotion not being mandatory for the organization, even if it had been warranted.[8] In *Puel*[9] the ILOAT found that the applicant had many years of worthy service and was well qualified for a promotion to the next grade but, nevertheless, concluded in effect that, while her work showed her not to be unworthy of the grade to which she aspired, she did not have a right to be promoted. The tribunal said:

An official is as a rule entitled to expect promotion by steady career advancement in the international civil service as prescribed in the Staff Regulations and Rules of the organization. The fulfilment of this reasonable expectation depends not only on the official's seniority, qualifications and skills but also on the organization's administrative structure and the state of its finances.[10]

The tribunal did not alter this view, although it went out of its way to point out that it was something of an anomaly that an official with the applicant's qualifications and skills had not been promoted for thirteen years and that her reasonable expectations had not been fulfilled.[11] In *Sharma*[12] the ILOAT rejected a claim that the applicant should have been promoted on the ground that he had no right to a promotion.

The Appeals Board of the OEEC also took the view that staff members do not have a right to a promotion. Where a staff member who had a contract for auxiliary services in an assistant-level position claimed that she should have been promoted, the tribunal held that neither the nature of the functions she performed nor the fact that she had passed a test for the position of reviser of stencils could confer on her the right to obtain a specific grade.[13]

That there is no right to a promotion is so clearly established that the CJEC has held that, even where the procedure for filling a vacant post by promotion has been begun, the administration is under no obligation to fill the post, because staff members can claim no right to be promoted.[14]

---

[8] *Peltre*, ILOAT Judgment No. 330 [1977] (IPI).
[9] ILOAT Judgment No. 526 [1982] (WMO).
[10] Ibid. at p. 5.
[11] Ibid.
[12] ILOAT Judgment No. 30 [1957] (ILO).
[13] *Decision No. 5*, OEEC Appeals Board [1950], Recueil des décisions 1 à 62 (1979) p. 14.
[14] *Morina*, CJEC Case 18/83 [1983] ECR p. 4051.

While the general position that staff members have no right to be promoted, whatever the circumstances, is clear, it would also seem to be implied in the reasoning of certain decisions that the statutory law of an organization or a contract of service can extend to a staff member the right to be promoted. Thus, where it was alleged that an internal document covering the field offices of UNDP entitled a Deputy Resident Representative to be promoted to the grade of P4 from the grade of P3, the UNAT held that a proper construction of the document did not confer this right upon that official,[15] thus implying that an internal document which is a valid source of law could create such a right for a particular official, if it clearly purports to do so. In *Karlik*[16] it was held that there was no contractual commitment to secure for the applicant on secondment a promotion to the P5 grade from the P4 level. The good intentions and hopes of the Director of the relevant body did not not create a legal obligation. Underlying this decision is the assumption that in the proper circumstances there could be a contractual commitment to promote a staff member which would give him a right to promotion.

The ILOAT also has examined an administrative circular of CERN in order to establish whether it gave the applicant a right to promotion and found that it did not,[17] implying again that such an internal legislative instrument could confer upon a staff member the right to be promoted, if it expressly so stated. The CJEC has examined a decision of the Commission of the European Communities in order to establish whether the staff member was entitled to promotion three months after he was reinstated in his position after secondment to another service and found that, according to its proper interpretation, it did not do so.[18]

It would seem that, while there can be contractual commitments which create a right to promotion or legislative instruments which confer such a right, tribunals will not easily construe documents or situations as giving rise to such a right, especially since the general presumption is that there is no right to promotion as such. This presumption is so overwhelming that a clear intention to the contrary on the part of the administration needs to be established, whether in contractual terms or through the medium of the law creating statutory instruments, such as regulations or administrative decisions.

As already seen, an expectation of promotion does not give rise to a right to promotion and in any case, even if a legitimate expectancy of promotion

---

[15] *Fürst*, UNAT Judgment No. 134 [1969], JUNAT Nos. 114–166 p. 188.

[16] UNAT Judgment No. 308 [1983]. In *Decision No. 5*, OEEC Appeals Board [1950], Recueil des décisions 1 à 62 (1979) p. 14, the Appeals Board of the OEEC said that the contract of service for auxiliary staff governed the position of the applicant, it being implied that that contract, though it could have, did not confer upon her the right to be promoted.

[17] *Danjean (Nos. 1 and 2)*, ILOAT Judgment No. 126 [1968] (CERN).

[18] *Steinfort*, CJEC Case 299/82 [1983] ECR p. 3141.

could be converted into a right, the UNAT has held that qualifications, experience, favourable performance reports, and seniority cannot be considered by staff members as giving rise to such an expectancy.[19] While the UNAT may have referred to an expectancy as a possible source of a right, it did not indicate how such an expectancy could positively be created. Thus, it may be inferred, following the case law of other tribunals, that the UNAT did not intend to contradict the assumption that a right could only be created by a contractual commitment or by the statutory law of the organization. By using the concept of expectancy the UNAT did not purport to introduce another possible source for the right to promotion than contractual commitment or statutory law. Expectancy could, in short, be created only by such means and not by anything short of contractual commitment or the statutory law.

The discretion to promote

In the absence of a specific legal obligation creating a corresponding right to promotion, the administrative authority exercises a discretionary power to promote staff members.[20] In many cases it has been said that the Secretary General or Director General of the organization or the administrative authority had, under the Staff Regulations and Staff Rules, a discretion in regard to the promotion of staff members.[21] It has also been conceded that even where the Staff Regulations do not specifically deal with the power to promote, the administration of the organization has under the general principles of law a discretionary authority in regard to promotion. Thus, where the principles applicable to promotion of staff members such as the applicants were laid down only in a decision of the Administrative Council of the IPI, the ILOAT said that the decision not to promote the applicants from their present grade to the next grade fell within the Director General's discretionary authority.[22] It may be assumed that even in the absence of a written

---

[19] See *Roberts*, UNAT Judgment No. 312 [1983] at p. 10.

[20] See *Vassiliou*, UNAT Judgment No. 275 [1981], JUNAT Nos. 231–300 p. 457. See also Akehurst, *The Law Governing Employment in International Organizations* (1967) p. 119, and de Vuyst, 'The Use of Discretionary Authority by International Organizations in their Relations with International Civil Servants', 12 *Denver Journal of International Law and Policy* (1983) p. 237 at pp. 251 ff.

[21] See *Vassiliou*, UNAT Judgment No. 275 [1981], JUNAT Nos. 231–300 p. 457; *Roberts*, UNAT Judgment No. 312 [1983]; *Lee*, ILOAT Judgment No. 199 [1973] (FAO); *Lamadie*, ILOAT Judgment No. 262 [1975] (IPI); *Peltre*, ILOAT Judgment No. 330 [1977] (IPI); *d'Aloya*, CJEC Case 280/80 [1981] ECR p. 2887; *de Hoe*, CJEC Case 151/80 [1981] ECR p. 3161; *Ragusa*, CJEC Case 282/81 [1983] ECR p. 1245; *Øhrgaard and Delvaux*, CJEC Case 9/82 [1983] ECR p. 2379; *Meunier*, Council of Europe Appeals Board, Appeal No. 51 [1980], Case-Law Digest (1985) p. 79; *Decision No. 11, ESRO/CR/65*, ESRO Appeals Board [1972].

[22] *Ledrut and Biggio*, ILOAT Judgment No. 300 [1977] (IPI) at p. 3.

law on promotion the administrative authority would enjoy a discretion whether to promote or not to promote staff members.

The discretion whether to promote is not an absolute one, however. Tribunals exercise control over the exercise of this discretion in the same way as they control any other discretionary power. In *Peltre* the ILOAT stated:

A decision on promotion is generally discretionary, and as a rule the Tribunal may quash it only if it was taken without authority or violated a rule of form or of procedure, or was based on a mistake of fact or of law, or if essential facts were not taken into account, or if the decision is tainted with abuse of authority, or if clearly mistaken conclusions were drawn from the facts.[23]

The CJEC, while using different language, has observed that it does have control over the exercise of the discretionary power to promote, though it is limited. It has generally emphasized the limited nature of the control. Thus, in connection with the evaluation of the interests of the service and the merits of the applicant for the purpose of promotion, as required by Article 45 of the Staff Regulations of the European Communities, the Court stated:

As the case concerns a decision to promote an official, it should first be emphasized that in order to evaluate the interests of the service together with the merits which must be taken into account in the context of the decision provided for by Article 45 of the Staff Regulations, the appointing authority has a wide margin of discretion and that, in that sphere, the Court must restrict itself to the question whether, regard being had to the methods and means which may have led to the assessment made by the administration, the latter remained within bounds which are not open to criticism and did not use its power in a manifestly incorrect manner.[24]

In *de Hoe* the Court said that in assessing whether the conditions of eligibility required in the vacancy notice had been satisfied the administration enjoyed a wide discretion the exercise of which could only be questioned in case of manifest error.[25] The CJEC has not, as the ILOAT has done, made exhaustive statements with regard to the extent of its control over the discretion to promote, whether in respect of the areas to which the control applies or with respect to the manner in which the control will be exercised, but there is no reason to doubt that it did not intend to limit the exercise of its controlling authority in any way. In fact it has examined a wide range of decisions connected with promotions in exercising its control and also applied its

---

[23] ILOAT Judgment No. 330 [1977] (IPI) at p. 4. See also *Lamadie*, ILOAT Judgment No. 262 [1975] (IPI); *Ledrut and Biggio*, ILOAT Judgment No. 300 [1977] (IPI); *Biggio (No. 2)*, *Van Moer, Ramboer, Hoornaert, Bogaert, Descamps and Dekeirel*, ILOAT Judgment No. 340 [1978] (IPI).

[24] *Colussi*, CJEC Case 298/81 [1983] ECR p. 1131 at p. 1142. See also *d'Aloya*, CJEC Case 280/80 [1981] ECR p. 2887 at p. 2900; *Ragusa*, CJEC Case 282/81 [1983] ECR p. 1245 at pp. 1256–7; *Øhrgaard and Delvaux*, CJEC Case 9/82 [1983] ECR p. 2379 at p. 2390.

[25] CJEC Case 151/80 [1981] ECR p. 3161 at p. 3173.

controls through mechanisms and concepts similar to those used by the ILOAT. Other tribunals should not have difficulty in following the example of the ILOAT and the CJEC when called upon to exercise control over the discretionary power to make promotions.

Tribunals have not limited themselves with respect to the nature of the decisions taken in connection with promotion over which they will exercise control. These decisions have individually been described as discretionary and tribunals have examined them in order to find out whether there has been an abuse of discretion, even though generally the outcome of the investigation has revealed that the discretion had not been abused. Thus, in the area of the policy governing promotions, the ILOAT has taken the view that the administrative authority has a discretion to make the rules to be applied in regard to promotion, which discretion is subject to control by the tribunal, though once the rules have been made, they must be followed.[26] In *d'Aloya*[27] the CJEC held that in deciding that for the purposes of promotion the shorthand speed of the candidate in English should be taken into account to the exclusion of his or her shorthand skills in his or her mother tongue, the administrative authority had not abused its discretion, even though no provision was made for compensatory skills. The Court implicitly conceded that policy decisions in regard to promotion were subject to control like any other discretionary decisions. In *Decision No. 11, ESRO/CR/65*,[28] however, the Appeals Board of ESRO made the categorical statement that, while it would ensure that rules were correctly interpreted and applied and thus exercise control over the exercise of discretion by the administrative authority, it had no right to adjudicate on matters of policy. This view is different from that taken by the ILOAT and the CJEC. There is no reason why the limitation imposed by the Appeals Board of ESRO should be allowed to stand. It is submitted that the view taken by the other two tribunals is the better view.

The decision as to what method of selection should be used is also a discretionary one which will not be upset, unless there has been an abuse of discretion. Thus, where there were several methods of selection available to the administrative authority and it decided not to resort to direct selection as a means of filling a P5 post, the ILOAT held that the administrative authority enjoyed discretionary authority as regards the method of selection and that it could either choose or not choose direct selection for the filling of vacant posts. Hence, the decision not to promote the applicant to the P5 grade in order to fill the post was within the discretion of the administrative authority.

---

[26] *Lamadie*, ILOAT Judgment No. 262 [1975] (IPI).
[27] CJEC Case 280/80 [1981] ECR p. 2887.
[28] *Decision No. 11, ESRO/CR/65*, ESRO Appeals Board [1972].

Since there were no flaws in that decision, it could not be attacked.[29] Particularly where the law of the organization permits a choice of methods, a tribunal will control the exercise of discretion to choose the method of filling a vacancy only where there has been a manifest abuse of discretion.

The point of time at which a promotion will be made is a matter within the discretionary authority of the administrative authority. Thus, where the applicant would have been in a more advantageous position financially, if her promotion had been delayed, it was held that she could not argue that she should have had the benefit of the delayed promotion, because the decision as to when to promote the applicant was within the discretion of the administration.[30]

Where, after the applicant took part in a competition, the Secretary General of the Council of Europe decided to cancel the competitive examination, the Appeals Board of the Council of Europe conceded that the Secretary General had a discretionary power to cancel the competition procedure but that this was not an absolute discretion.[31] In that case the tribunal held that the discretion had been abused. It is also a matter within the discretion of the administrative authority, where a probationary period may be required on promotion under the law of the organization, to decide whether such a period should be required and what that period should be. This decision is clearly subject to the requirement that the discretion should not be abused. In *Ulliac*[32] the applicant was put on probation upon being promoted but failed to achieve confirmation. The decision to put him on probation after he was promoted was held to have been properly taken.

The above analysis reveals that there are many decisions connected within promotion, apart from the decision to promote a staff member or not promote him, which are discretionary. These are all subject to control by tribunals in the event that the discretionary authority is abused.

In their approach to the control of discretionary powers connected with promotion, tribunals have made it clear that they will not as a rule and in the absence of any proven abuse of discretion substitute their own judgments for those of the adminstrative authority in deciding whether a decision connected with promotion is legal or not. In *Decision No. 34*[33] the Appeals Board of

---

[29] *Tarrab (No. 4)*, ILOAT Judgment No. 395 [1980] (ILO). See also *Mogensen and Others*, CJEC Case 10/82 [1983] ECR p. 2397; *Colussi*, CJEC Case 298/81 [1983] ECR p. 1131. In the former case it was held that it was within the discretionary authority of the administration to choose transfer as a method of filling a vacancy rather than promotion. The Court could only control the exercise of that discretion in the event that there had been a manifest error in its exercise.

[30] *Lee*, ILOAT Judgment No. 199 [1973] (FAO).

[31] *Meunier*, Council of Europe Appeals Board, Appeal No. 51 [1980], Case-Law Digest (1985) p. 79.

[32] Decision No. 49, OECD Appeals Board [1974], Recueil des décisions 1 à 62 (1979) p. 135.

[33] *Decision No. 34*, NATO Appeals Board [1971], Collection of the Decisions (1972).

NATO held that it would not rule on the relative suitability of the applicant and other applicants for the post in issue. In *Vassiliou*[34] the UNAT held that, since promotion was a subject within the discretion of the Secretary General of the UN, in the absence of a legal obligation to promote the applicant it would not enter into the merits of the applicant's claim.[35] In *d'Aloya*[36] the CJEC held that it would not substitute its own assessment of criteria laid down for promotion for that of the administrative authority.[37]

Abuse of discretion

Tribunals have accepted abuse of discretion as a general ground for attacking successfully decisions connected with promotion. There are specific irregularities which have been mentioned in this connection but apart from these tribunals have referred generally to the fact that the discretion to promote or not to promote can be abused. In none of the decided cases has any tribunal found that there had been an abuse of discretion which did not fit into one of the specific categories, such as error of law or *détournement de pouvoir*. On the other hand, tribunals have pointed out in many cases that on the facts the administration had not abused its discretion.

The ILOAT has held that, although the applicant satisfied all the conditions for promotion in regard to seniority and the marks obtained, the Director General of the IPI could, without abusing his discretion, for financial reasons and from a desire to keep a hierarchy of staff members within a category, promote fewer than deserved to be promoted.[38] In *Léger and Peeters*[39] the ILOAT found that the President of the EPO had not abused his discretion in deciding how seniority should be calculated and applying his definition after an advisory committee had made its recommendations.[40]

In *Guglielmi*[41] the applicant argued that the subject for an essay in a

---

[34] UNAT Judgment No. 275 [1981], JUNAT Nos. 231–300 p. 457 at p. 475. See also *Fürst*, UNAT Judgment No. 134 [1969], JUNAT Nos. 114–166 p. 188.

[35] See also *Fonzi*, CJEC Cases 27 & 30/64 [1965] ECR p. 481.

[36] CJEC Case 280/80 [1981] ECR p. 2887.

[37] See also *Giannini*, CJEC Case 265/81 [1982] ECR p. 3865; *Ragusa*, CJEC Case 282/81 [1983] ECR p. 1245; *Guglielmi*, CJEC Case 268/80 [1981] ECR p. 2295. See also *Decision No. 35, ESRO/CR/93*, ESRO Appeals Board [1974], where it was said that in the absence of *détournement de pouvoir* or an abuse of powers it would not substitute its own judgment of qualifications and functions for that of the organs of the organization.

[38] *Brisson, Demeter, Van de Vloet and Verdelman*, ILOAT Judgment No. 303 [1977] (IPI).

[39] ILOAT Judgment No. 457 [1981] (EPO).

[40] See also *Carbo*, ILOAT Judgment No. 519 [1982] (PAHO); *Biggio (No. 2), Van Moer, Ramboer, Hoornaert, Descamps and Dekeirel*, ILOAT Judgment No. 340 [1978] (IPI). In the latter case it was said that there was no flaw in the exercise of the discretion not to promote the applicant.

[41] CJEC Case 268/80 [1981] ECR p. 2295.

competition organized to decide on promotions was too difficult but the CJEC held that, although in fact this was not so, the administrative authority had not manifestly abused its discretion in choosing the particular essay subject. In *Giannini*[42] and *Mogensen and Others*[43] also the Court found that an abuse of discretion had not been committed so that it would not interfere with the administration's exercise of discretion in making a promotion.

In *Decision No. 11, ESRO/CR/65*[44] the Appeals Board of ESRO found that the Director General of ESRO had taken into account his consultations and the opinions of his advisers in coming to his decision and that there was no evidence to show that he had wrongly appreciated the functions of the applicant, his decision having been founded basically on an evaluation of the applicant's post and functions, so that it could not be said that there had been an abuse of discretion. Where the Secretary General of OECD recommended promotion but ultimately followed the decision of the Council not to create a post in the higher category and, therefore, not to promote the applicant, the Appeals Board found that, although originally the Secretary General had recommended promotion, there was no fault on his part in following the decision of the Council.[45]

Though abuse of discretion may be a very general and broad ground for finding defective a decision relating to promotion, generally tribunals have referred to established categories such as the accepted substantive irregularities, procedural irregularities, or *détournement de pouvoir* as grounds for controlling such decisions.

Détournement de pouvoir

Misuse of authority or abuse of purpose has been often referred to as a ground for upsetting a decision related to promotion. In *Decision No. 35, ESRO/CR/93*,[46] for example, the Appeals Board of ESRO held that it would not examine the qualifications and functions of the applicants and substitute its own judgment on such matters for that of the administration in the absence of a *détournement de pouvoir* or an abuse of powers. In most cases it has been found that there was no abuse of purpose or *détournement de pouvoir*.

[42] CJEC Case 265/81 [1982] ECR p. 3865.
[43] CJEC Case 10/82 [1983] ECR p. 2397.
[44] *Decision No. 11, ESRO/CR/65*, ESRO Appeals Board [1972].
[45] *Wolfson*, Decision No. 75, OECD Appeals Board [1979], Recueil des décisions 63 à 82 (1980) p. 39. See also *Krug*, Decision No. 87, OECD Appeals Board [1981], Recueil des décisions 83 à 102 (1983) p. 11; *Lancy*, Decision No. 88, OECD Appeals Board [1981], ibid. p. 15; *Bernot*, Decision No. 89, OECD Appeals Board [1981], ibid. p. 19.
[46] *Decision No. 35, ESRO/CR/93*, ESRO Appeals Board [1974].

(a) Improper purpose

In *Giuffrida*[47] it was found that the sole purpose of the competition organized for the purpose of promotion was to enable an official with an anomalous administrative status to be appointed to the position advertised and, thus, to be promoted. This was held by the CJEC to be an improper purpose.

In *Grosz*[48] the post held by the applicant on a temporary basis was transferred to another directorate and another person was promoted to fill the position instead of the applicant's being promoted. The CJEC found that there was no indication that the actions taken were for reasons other than the interests of the service so that all was in order and no improper purpose had been proved.[49] In *Campogrande and Others*[50] the allegation was made that the object behind the decisions taken was to promote certain selected candidates and restrict the number of promotions so that an external competition could be held and external candidates appointed. The CJEC held that this had not been proved, so that there was no improper purpose.[51] Where it could not be proved that the applicant's trade-union activity was the reason for his not being promoted[52] or that geographical distribution had been wrongfully used as a reason for not promoting the applicant,[53] the CJEC has held that there had been no *détournement de pouvoir*. There are other cases decided by the CJEC in which an improper purpose has not been successfully proved.[54] In some cases the Court has held that there was no other reason for the decision taken in regard to promotion than the interests of the service which was an appropriate purpose, thus disproving the existence of an improper purpose.[55]

In *Decision No. 34*[56] the Appeals Board of NATO was confronted with the argument that undue pressure was exercised on behalf of the candidate appointed with the result that he was chosen and the applicant was not promoted. The tribunal found that, though the appointee had fewer qualifications than the applicant, the Selection Board had decided that the most

---

[47] CJEC Case 105/75 [1976] ECR p. 1395.

[48] CJEC Case 35/69 [1970] ECR p. 609.

[49] See also *Huybrechts*, CJEC Case 21/68 [1969] ECR p. 85, where it was held that it had not been proved that there had been haste in promoting another candiate which would have indicated an improper purpose.

[50] CJEC Cases 112, 144 & 145/73 [1974] ECR p. 957.

[51] See also *Guglielmi*, CJEC Case 268/80 [1981] ECR p. 2295.

[52] *Cowood*, CJEC Case 60/82 [1982] ECR p. 4625.

[53] *Ragusa*, CJEC Case 282/81 [1983] ECR p. 1245.

[54] See *Küster*, CJEC Case 123/75 [1976] ECR p. 1701; *Mulcahy*, CJEC Case 110/77 [1978] ECR p. 1287; *Hoffman*, CJEC Case 280/81 [1983] ECR p. 889.

[55] See *Ganzini*, CJEC Case 101/77 [1978] ECR p. 915; *De Roubaix*, CJEC Case 25/77 [1978] ECR p. 1081; *de Hoe*, CJEC Case 151/80 [1981] ECR p. 3161.

[56] *Decision No. 34*, NATO Appeals Board [1971], Collection of the Decisions (1972).

important qualification was the ability of the candidate to control staff, which the appointee had; and that, even though the Selection Board may have been approached on behalf of certain candidates, this fact had not materially affected the decision taken, so that there had been no *détour-nement de pouvoir*.[57]

(b) Prejudice or ill will

In all the cases discovered in which the allegation of prejudice or ill will has been raised as the reason for the decision not to promote the applicant, tribunals have held that the existence of prejudice or ill will had not been proved. In *Gluecksmann*[58] the applicant failed to prove that there had been prejudice resulting from the fact that he was active in staff matters.[59] In *Ali Khan*[60] there was held to be no prejudice against the applicant because, though he was thoroughly trained and had seniority, the person appointed did have actual socio-economic research experience which the applicant did not have and which was a requirement for the position to which the applicant claimed he should have been appointed with a promotion. In some other cases tribunals have held that on the facts no prejudice had been proved.[61]

(c) Discrimination and inequality of treatment

The ILOAT has been confronted with the argument that there had been discrimination or inequality of treatment in the decision relating to promotion but has held in favour of the applicant only in one case. As already seen in a previous chapter, the ILOAT found in *Wenzel*[62] that there was discriminatory treatment in the criteria applied by EPO for promotion. In all the other cases the ILOAT has held that there was no discrimination or inequality of treatment in the decisions taken relating to promotion by which the applicants argued they had been prejudiced. In addition to the cases referred to in the earlier chapter[63] in which the ILOAT has found that there

---

[57] See also *Decision No. 11, ESRO/CR/65*, ESRO Appeals Board [1972]; *Decision No. 29, ESRO/CR/78*, ibid. [1972]; *Decision No. 35, ESRO/CR/93*, ibid. [1974]. In *Decision No. 34*, NATO Appeals Board [1971], Collection of the Decisions (1972), in respect of a second decision not to promote the applicant and appoint another candidate the tribunal found that there had been no abuse of purpose.

[58] ILOAT Judgment No. 520 [1982] (PAHO).

[59] In *Burgos*, ILOAT Judgment No. 527 [1982] (PAHO), abolition of post as a reason for the failure to promote the applicant was held to dispel any inference of prejudice.

[60] ILOAT Judgment No. 564 [1983] (ILO).

[61] See *Karlik*, UNAT Judgment No. 308 [1983]; *Roberts*, UNAT Judgment No. 312 [1983]; *Brisson, Demeter, Van de Vloet and Verdelman*, ILOAT Judgment No. 303 [1977] (IPI); *Sehgal*, ILOAT Judgment No. 531 [1982] (WHO); *Bernardi*, CJEC Case 90/71 [1972] ECR p. 603.

[62] See Vol. I p. 326 *supra*.

[63] See *supra*, Vol. I Ch. 22 pp. 326 ff.

was no discrimination or inequality of treatment in the decisions taken, the ILOAT has held that the IPI did not treat the applicant unequally by following the promotion roster of its Careers Committee,[64] and that there was no discrimination by the IPI in not promoting the applicant when a more senior staff member with the same qualifications and three other staff members who had exceptional merit had been promoted.[65]

The CJEC has decided in favour of the applicant only one case involving discrimination or inequality of treatment in promotion. As seen in an earlier chapter, this case concerned the requirements that for promotion candidates shall have a perfect knowledge of Italian which was held to be discriminatory on the basis of nationality.[66] There were some other cases also discussed in the earlier chapter[67] in which the CJEC found that the distinctions made were not discriminatory or did not result in inequality of treatment. Apart from these cases, the CJEC has held that requiring that the appointee to a position in the Legal Department have knowlege and experience of a given national legal system does not amount to discrimination on the basis of nationality.[68]

Substantive irregularities

Tribunals have considered various substantive irregularities as grounds for finding illegal the exercise of the discretion to promote. In several cases they have declared the decision tainted because of the presence of such an irregularity.

(a) Error of law

In a few cases tribunals have held that an error of law vitiated the decision taken with regard to promotion. The UNAT has held that the reservation of a post for a francophone African with the result that the applicant's application for promotion to the post was not even considered, because he was not a francophone African, while the post was filled by a lateral transfer, was a violation of Staff Regulation 4.4 of the UN which required that the fullest regard be had to the requisite qualifications and experience of persons already in service.[69] It was not an excuse in this case that lateral transfer had

---

[64] *Ledrut and Biggio*, ILOAT Judgment No. 300 [1977] (IPI).

[65] *Peltre*, ILOAT Judgment No. 330 [1977] (IPI). See also *Dauksch (No. 2)*, ILOAT Judgment No. 348 [1978] (IPI).

[66] *Lassalle*: see *supra*, Vol. I Ch. 22 p. 323.

[67] See *supra*, Vol. I Ch. 22 p. 326.

[68] *Kurrer*, CJEC Case 33/67 [1968] ECR p. 127. See also *Küster*, CJEC Case 79/74 [1975] ECR p. 725; *Küster*, CJEC Case 23/74 [1975] ECR p. 353.

[69] *Estabial*, UNAT Judgment No. 310 [1983].

been chosen as a means to filling the vacancy, because this choice was the result of the illegal restriction made. In *Lamadie*[70] the ILOAT held that, while the administration could choose between two provisions relating to promotion on the basis of what was more suitable for the administration, once the choice had been made, it should observe the terms of that provision, so that the promotion of the applicant should have taken place as from 1 January 1974 and not as from 1 September 1974, as was permissible under the alternative provision.[71]

The Appeals Board of NATO was called upon in several cases to consider whether Article 57.1 of the NATO Civilian Personnel Regulations had been violated. The Regulation stated that before initiating recruitment outside the staff, the administrative authority should consider the qualifications of serving members of the staff in relation to vacant posts in the establishment. In *Decision No. 148*[72] the administrative authority informed the applicant who had applied for a promotion to a vacant post of Senior Secretary in grade B4 that it preferred to appoint another external candidate but that if she wished to be considered, she would be nominated to the vacant position. Confronted with the choice of maintaining her application for the promotion in the face of the preference expressed or of withdrawing it, the applicant decided to withdraw her application. The tribunal held that the Regulation had been violated, because it was required under it that she should have been appointed as the superior internal candidate.

With *Decision No. 148* may be compared some cases decided by the Appeals Board of NATO in which the same Regulation was in issue. In *Decision No. 34*[73] the tribunal held that the Regulation did not require that the qualifications of external candidates be considered only if there was no qualified staff member to fill the vacant post, it being possible to consider both categories of candidates at the same session, provided the qualifications of staff members were considered before it was decided to select and appoint an external candidate. While, if the administrative authority considers one or more internal candidates suitable, it cannot legally recruit outsiders, the Regulation did not require that vacancy notices should not be circulated and

[70] ILOAT Judgment No. 262 [1975] (IPI).

[71] In *Grassi*, CJEC Case 188/73 [1974] ECR p. 1099, the CJEC held that the requirement of the vacancy notice that the candidate for promotion should have a command of his mother tongue together with a thorough knowledge of the other three languages of the European Communities must be satisfied by the person appointed, so that, where the appointee had a thorough knowledge only of French and an imperfect knowledge of the other two requisite languages, the official should not have been appointed to the vacant position. There was in this case a clear violation of the legal requirements.

[72] *Decision No. 148*, NATO Appeals Board [1982], Collection of the Decisions 135 to 171 (1984).

[73] *Decision No. 34*, NATO Appeals Board [1971], Collection of the Decisions (1972).

that the existence of the vacancy should not be made known outside the institution.[74]

The ILOAT has held that a Staff Regulation which provided that those on the staff should be preferred to external candidates did not require that those with long service be preferred to new recruits, so that it was not an error of law for the administration to promote an officer with 15 months' service over a staff member with 25 years' service.[75] In *Brisson, Demeter, Van der Vloet and Verdelman*[76] the ILOAT held that it was not an error of law for the administration of IPI not to consider the roster of normal career patterns in deciding on a promotion, because, first, the declaration of the Administrative Council of IPI referring to the roster of normal career patterns was made before the Staff Regulations came into force, the applicant having joined IPI after the Regulations came into force, and second, the roster existed for guidance and did not impose a binding rule.[77] In *Grassi*[78] the CJEC held that it was not an error of law for the administrative authority to ignore continued absences for duty on the Staff Committee which resulted in others acting as head of unit for the staff member promoted, in determining that the staff member had several years of experience as head of a unit for the purposes of the requirements of the vacancy notice.[79]

In *Sehgal*[80] the ILOAT found that there had been a technical violation of the law in that the post descriptions for the positions being filled had not been done, but held that, since the Selection Committee merely screened the candidates for upgraded posts and the applicant was eliminated on the preliminary screening, the violation of the law did not affect the conclusions of the committee and, therefore, did not prejudice the applicant, so that he could not complain. This decision is in accord with the general law.

[74] *Decision No. 96*, NATO Appeals Board [1978], Collection of the Decisions 65(b), 74 to 99 (1979). See also *Decision No. 100*, NATO Appeals Board [1979], Collection of the Decisions 100 to 134 (1981); *Decision No. 101*, NATO Appeals Board [1979], ibid.

[75] *Carbo*, ILOAT Judgment No. 519 [1982] (PAHO).

[76] ILOAT Judgment No. 303 [1977] (IPI). See also *Karskens*, ILOAT Judgment No. 304 [1977] (IPI); *Peltre*, ILOAT Judgment No. 330 [1977] (IPI).

[77] For other cases decided by the ILOAT in which there was found to be no error of law, see *Ali Khan*, ILOAT Judgment No. 564 [1983] (ILO); *Ledrut and Biggio*, ILOAT Judgment No. 300 [1977] (IPI); *Schmitter*, ILOAT Judgment No. 301 [1977] (IPI); *Beerten*, ILOAT Judgment No. 313 [1977] (IPI).

[78] CJEC Case 188/73 [1974] ECR p. 1099.

[79] Other cases in which the CJEC held that there was no error of law are *de Wind*, CJEC Case 62/75 [1976] ECR p. 1167; *Giannini*, CJEC Case 265/81 [1982] ECR p. 3865; *Øhrgaard and Delvaux*, CJEC Case 9/82 [1983] ECR p. 2379; *Steinfort*, CJEC Case 299/82 [1983] ECR p. 3141. In this last case the written law was interpreted and it was found that there had been no violation of the law.

[80] ILOAT Judgment No. 531 [1982] (WHO).

(b) Error of fact

The CJEC held in *Grassi*[81] that there had been an error of fact in the assessment made of the person promoted instead of the applicant. Where a thorough knowledge of two languages of the European Communities was required and the rating given the candidate promoted on one of them was 'fair', the Court concluded that on the evidence of witnesses the candidate's rating did not reveal a thorough knowledge of that language so that the conclusion reached that he had a thorough knowledge of the language was based on a factual error.[82] In *Karskens*[83] the ILOAT found that there was no evidence that the merits of the persons promoted failed to meet the requirements of grade-step and seniority laid down for the positions, so that there was no error of fact.[84]

(c) Consideration of irrelevant facts

In the cases in which it has been alleged that irrelevant facts had been taken into consideration, the applicants have not been successful in contesting a decision to promote other candidates. In *Colussi*[85] the CJEC held that in connection with promotion it was not irrelevant to consider age and seniority, as these could constitute decisive factors where other qualifications and merits were equal, and that it was not irrelevant to consider competence and efficiency.[86]

(d) Omission of facts

The question whether essential facts had been ignored has been adverted to in several cases. In some cases it has been found that essential facts had not been considered. In *Raponi*[87] the *curriculum vitae* of the applicant submitted to the appointing authority by the administrative service of the organization did not

---

[81] CJEC Case 188/73 [1974] ECR p. 1099.

[82] See also *Mulcahy*, CJEC Case 110/77 [1978] ECR p. 1287.

[83] ILOAT Judgment No. 304 [1977] (IPI).

[84] No error of fact, as alleged, was found to exist in *Ledrut and Biggio*, ILOAT Judgment No. 300 [1977] (IPI), or in *Decision No. 96*, NATO Appeals Board [1978], Collection of the Decisions 65(b), 74 to 99 (1979), *Decision No. 100*, NATO Appeals Board [1979], Collection of the Decisions 100 to 134 (1981), or *Decision No. 101*, NATO Appeals Board [1979], ibid.

[85] CJEC Case 298/81 [1983] ECR p. 1131.

[86] In *Hoffman*, CJEC Case 280/81 [1983] ECR p. 889, the CJEC held that, while a comparison of qualifications may be of significance for recruitment and certain other purposes, for promotion other factors, in particular the general quality of work performed in the execution of duties, were relevant and could be considered. See also *Roberts*, UNAT Judgment No. 312 [1983] at p. 10, where it was said that a decision to promote could be challenged on the ground that extraneous factors had been taken into consideration.

[87] CJEC Case 27/63 [1964] ECR p. 129. See also *Bernusset*, CJEC Cases 94 & 96/63 [1964] ECR p. 297.

correspond either to the *curriculum vitae* which appeared in the personal file of the applicant nor to that attached to his request for promotion. As a result the appointing authority may well have been insufficiently informed about the applicant's career and there would not have been an examination of his linguistic proficiency as required by implication in the vacancy notice, particularly because there was no evidence that the appointing authority had consulted the applicant's personal file. For this reason the CJEC held that essential factors had been insufficiently considered. In *de Pascale*,[88] where the appointing authority had examined only the proposal of one of its members which contained the qualifications of only one official and vague allusions to the possible merits of other candidates, the Court pointed out that there had been no verification by reference to the personal files of the candidates in which, in particular, the opinion of their superiors were reflected, so that the decision to promote another candidate than the applicant was vitiated, because there had not been a full consideration of the facts.[89] In *Gratreau*, where it was held that essential facts had not been considered, the CJEC said:

Although it is true that in exceptional circumstances the absence of periodic reports may be compensated for by the existence of other information on an official's merits, such is not, however, the case with a report irregularly included in a personal file after it has been challenged by the official. Moreover, the mere existence of a proposal for promotion, even in eulogistic terms, and a list of the official's publications, drawn up by him and containing no objective assessment of their scientific value, cannot make up for the absence of a proper periodic report.[90]

In *Roberts*[91] the UNAT held that, since the comparative merits of the candidates had been appraised freely by the administrative authority, the decisions on promotion could not be challenged on the ground that performance and length of service had been inadequately considered or on any other similar ground.[92] In *Sehgal*[93] the ILOAT held that the fact that the applicant was not given special consideration could not be regarded as an incomplete consideration of facts.[94]

Further, where the fact not considered could not have had an effect on the decision taken, it is not a vitiating element that it has not been considered, as where the most recent periodic report which was not considered could only

[88] CJEC Case 97/63 [1964] ECR p. 515.

[89] See also *de Dapper*, CJEC Case 29/74 [1975] ECR p. 35; *Oberthür*, CJEC Case 24/79 [1980] ECR p. 1743.

[90] CJEC Cases 156/79 & 51/80 [1980] ECR p. 3943 at p. 3955.

[91] UNAT Judgment No. 312 [1983].

[92] See also *Schmitter*, ILOAT Judgment No. 301 [1977] (IPI).

[93] ILOAT Judgment No. 531 [1982] (WHO).

[94] See also *Huybrechts*, CJEC Case 21/68 [1969] ECR p. 85; *Bernardi*, CJEC Case 90/71 [1972] ECR p. 603; *de Hoe*, CJEC Case 151/80 [1981] ECR p. 3161.

have confirmed the excellent assessments of the applicant made earlier, so that the omission was not detrimental to her.[95]

(e) Erroneous conclusions

No case has been found in which a tribunal has decided that mistaken conclusions had been reached by the administrative authority in taking the decision to make the promotion contested or in not promoting the applicant, although such a ground for finding a decision on promotion tainted has not been rejected by tribunals and there have been cases in which tribunals have considered whether mistaken conclusions had been reached. In *Brisson, Demeter, Van der Vloet and Verdelman*[96] the ILOAT found on examination of the dossier that the administrative authority of IPI had not reached an erroneous conclusion. Although the facts showed that the applicant had satisfied all the conditions for promotion in respect of marks obtained and seniority, the administration had not reached a mistaken conclusion in not promoting her for other reasons, since promotion was not mandatory, even if warranted. In *Rittweger*[97] the CJEC held that the conclusions reached by the administration on qualifications showed no discrepancy between the qualifications required by the vacancy notice and the qualifications of the official appointed to the vacant position, so that it could not be said that mistaken conclusions about the suitability of the appointed candidate had been reached.[98]

Procedural irregularities

It is conceivable that a decision taken with regard to promotion may be tainted because of procedural irregularity. There have been several cases in which tribunals have held that a promotion decision was tainted, because there was a procedural irregularity, but there have also been many cases in which a procedural irregularity was found not to exist.

---

[95] *De Roubaix*, CJEC Case 25/77 [1978] ECR p. 1081. Some other cases in which it was found that there had been no omission of relevant facts were: *Dauksch (No. 2)*, ILOAT Judgment No. 348 [1978] (IPI); *Rittweger*, CJEC Case 21/70 [1971] ECR p. 7; *Küster*, CJEC Case 123/75 [1976] ECR p. 1701; *d'Aloya*, CJEC Case 280/80 [1981] ECR p. 2887.

[96] ILOAT Judgment No. 303 [1977] (IPI). See also *Peltre*, ILOAT Judgment No. 330 [1977] (IPI).

[97] CJEC Case 21/70 [1971] ECR p. 7.

[98] Other cases in which conclusions reached on promotion were held not to be mistaken are *Mulcahy*, CJEC Case 110/77 [1978] ECR p. 1287; *Dauksch (No. 2)*, ILOAT Judgment No. 348 [1978] (IPI); *Decision No. 96*, NATO Appeals Board [1978], Collection of the Decisions 65(b), 74 to 99 (1979); *Decision No. 100*, NATO Appeals Board [1979], Collection of the Decisions 100 to 134 (1981); *Decision No. 101*, NATO Appeals Board [1979], ibid.

In *Moore*[99] the applicant successfully contested the selection procedures adopted by the administration of PAHO which the respondent acknowledged had been irregular. The respondent offered to regrade her post so that she could be promoted. The ILOAT, while finding that an illegality had been committed, also recognized that she had been offered substantial redress. On the other hand, in *Kurrer*[100] the CJEC held that a very narrow statement in the vacancy notice of the qualifications and experience required did not restrict the area of jurisdiction of and the significance of consultation by the appointing authority with the Promotion Committee and the Joint Committee of the institution, so that the procedure followed had not been impaired.

There are, besides, many aspects of procedural irregularity which have been considered by tribunals.

(a) Violation of written law in general

In *Nayyar*[101] the UNAT held that there had been a violation of the written law requiring written presentations before the Appointment and Promotion Panel of the UN which flawed the work of that body. The CJEC has held that for promotion from one category to another within the European Communities the written law of the organization required that a competition be held and that, where this had not been done, the promotion process was vitiated.[102] These are instances of cases where a tribunal has found that the written law relating to the procedures had been violated.

On the other hand, there are cases in which the tribunal has examined the written law in relation to the facts and decided that the written law had not been violated. Thus, in *Raponi*[103] the Staff Regulations required that there be a post description for any post to be filled. The applicant contended that a proper description of the post had not been given in the vacancy notice. The CJEC held that, considering the requirements of the service, the complexity of the task of describing various posts, and the actual description given in the vacancy notice, such description was adequate.

The provision involved must be a legal measure. Thus, implementing provisions of a general nature may not be on the same level as Staff

---

[99] ILOAT Judgment No. 393 [1980] (PAHO).

[100] CJEC Case 33/67 [1968] ECR p. 127. In some cases the tribunal merely stated that no procedural irregularity could be found: see *Decision No. 34*, NATO Appeals Board [1971], Collection of the Decisions (1972); *Decision No. 96*, NATO Appeals Board [1978], Collection of the Decisions 65(b), 74 to 99 (1979); *Decision No. 35*, ESRO/CR/93, ESRO Appeals Board [1974].

[101] UNAT Judgment No. 293 [1982], JUNAT Nos. 231–300 p. 586.

[102] *Van Belle*, CJEC Case 176/73 [1974] ECR p. 1361.

[103] CJEC Case 27/63 [1964] ECR p. 129. See also *de Pascale*, CJEC Case 97/63 [1964] ECR p. 515; *Bernusset*, CJEC Cases 94 & 96/63 [1964] ECR p. 297.

Regulations. They may be only internal measures which are not strict law
and, therefore, are not legally binding. A departure from them in order to
take account of an exceptional situation would not then be an infringement
of a procedural requirement such as to justify annulment or the award of
damages.[104]

(b) Reports

Whether reports are necessary for the procedure of promotion will depend
largely on the internal written law of the organization. Thus, where during a
transitional period there were no general provisions in the Staff Regulations
of the European Communities relating to periodic reports, it was held that
there was no obligation for the administrative authority to make use of such
reports and that in the absence of such periodic reports there was no requirement that *ad hoc* reports be made use of in assessing the candidates for
promotion.[105]

Where, however, there are reports which are used in evaluation, the candidate must be given a chance of rebutting them. This is so, apparently,
irrespective of whether the written law makes an opportunity of rebuttal a
requirement or not. Thus, in *Roberts*[106] favourable reports on the applicant
were subsequently retracted by his superiors. The UNAT held that appraisals
differing from the official reports entailed responsibility on the part of the
administration. The reason for this was that the applicant had had no opportunity of rebutting them or even being made aware of such negative
appraisals which could have influenced the decisions on promotion in a negative way. Hence, such a practice was an irregularity.[107]

(c) Delay

When there is undue delay in taking a decision relating to a promotion, the
delay will be a vitiating factor, where the decision is unfavourable to the
applicant.[108] What is undue delay will obviously depend on the facts of each
case.

(d) Absence of due process

There may be some flaws arising in the procedure followed under the general
head of absence of due process which render the decision taken illegal but

---

[104] See *Geeraerd*, CJEC Case 782/79 [1980] ECR p. 3651.

[105] *Raponi*, CJEC Case 27/63 [1964] ECR p. 129.

[106] UNAT Judgment No. 312 [1983].

[107] See also *Tomiak*, UNAT Judgment No. 314 [1983]; *Rittweger*, CJEC Case 21/70 [1971]
ECR p. 7.

[108] *Estabial*, UNAT Judgment No. 310 [1983].

applicants have generally not been very successful in establishing a failure in due process. It has been held by the CJEC in *Ragusa*[109] that, if the administration by internal decision voluntarily institutes a compulsory consultative procedure, it is under an obligation to follow that procedure. This is in keeping with the maxim *legem patere quem fecisti*. However, in that case it was held that the institution had followed the requisite procedure.

In connection with due process, the argument that a board or committee had not been properly constituted may have to be considered. In *Ragusa*[110] the applicant argued that there was a procedural irregularity because an *ad hoc* committee appointed to advise the Director General concerned did not have the composition required by Article 3 of Annex III of the Staff Regulations of the European Communities.[111] The CJEC, however, held that since the committee was an *ad hoc* committee, that provision of the Staff Regulations did not apply to it, so that there was no absence of due process in the manner in which it had been constituted. In *Brisson, Demeter, Van der Vloet and Verdelman*[112] the ILOAT held that the fact that the Chief of the Personnel Service of IPI both determined the performance mark of the applicants and sat on the committee recommending promotion was not a procedural flaw, because the two functions were compatible and the official was expected to be impartial in both capacities, the situation being quite a normal one.[113]

In *Morina*[114] the CJEC was of the view that once the procedure for filling a vacancy had been begun there was no absolute obligation upon the administration to fill the vacancy. It was not a breach of due process, as such, to terminate the procedure, provided other relevant safeguards were observed. In *Küster*[115] the delegation of power to appoint members of a Selection Board was questioned, because allegedly it had not been publicized as required by the Staff Regulations. The CJEC found that the delegation had been brought to the attention of various concerned members of the administration and also of the Staff Committee established under the Staff Regulations, so that the requirement of publicity was satisfied. It was noted that the Staff Regulations did not specify how such a provision was to be brought to the attention of the staff. In some cases it has been simply noted that there had been no absence of due process, because a Selection Board had been properly constituted, or in general.[116]

---

109 CJEC Case 282/81 [1983] ECR p. 1245.
110 Ibid.
111 See Amerasinghe (ed.), 4 op. cit. (note 5 *supra*) p. 1 at p. 36.
112 ILOAT Judgment No. 303 [1977] (IPI).
113 See also *Ali Khan*, ILOAT Judgment No. 564 [1983] (ILO).
114 CJEC Case 18/83 [1983] ECR p. 4051.
115 CJEC Case 123/75 [1976] ECR p. 1701.
116 See *Karlik*, UNAT Judgment No. 308 [1983]; *Decision No. 34*, NATO Appeals Board [1971], Collection of the Decisions (1972).

In one case it was found that there had been an infringement of the right of defence. In *Decision No. 100*[117] the applicant argued that he had not been heard orally by the Complaints Committee or by the head of the NATO body taking the decision before the decision was finally taken. The Appeals Board of NATO held that, while the Staff Regulations of NATO did not require that the Complaints Committee hold an oral hearing, they did require that the applicant be heard by the head of the NATO body concerned before a final decision was taken. Hence, the applicant's right to due process had been infringed.

(e) Reasons

Where a decision is taken adverse to the applicant, normally it is a requirement that reasons be given for the decision. In *Meunier*[118] the Council of Europe held a competition for a vacant post and then cancelled the competitive examination, even though the applicant had obtained good marks. No reason was given for the cancellation of the examination, the applicant having been informed orally of the cancellation. The Appeals Board of the Council of Europe held that, while it was within the discretion of the administration to cancel the examination, since the legitimate interests of the applicant could have been injured, because she had taken the written examination and had an interest in the completion of the procedure, the reasons for that action should have been given her. The failure to give reasons was a procedural irregularity which vitiated the decision.

Reasons given do not have to be detailed, provided that they have significant meaning and can be interpreted appropriately in the light of other available documents. In *Decision No. 96*[119] the applicant was told that he had no shortcomings in qualifications but that other candidates were bettter qualified. The Appeals Board of NATO examined the report of the Selection Board and found that this was so, because the applicant had had no experience in electronics and engineering which requirements had been emphasized, while the other candidates had had such experience. The communication to the applicant was interpreted in the light of the report of the Selection Board.[120] The detail required in the reasons given depends on the circumstances of the case. It is related to the margin of discretion. Thus,

---

[117] *Decision No. 100*, NATO Appeals Board [1979], Collection of the Decisions 100 to 134 (1981). See also *Decision No. 101*, NATO Appeals Board [1979], ibid.

[118] Council of Europe Appeals Board, Appeal No. 51 [1980], Case-Law Digest (1985) p. 79.

[119] *Decision No. 96*, NATO Appeals Board [1978], Collection of the Decisions 65(b), 74 to 99 (1979). See also *Decision No. 100*, NATO Appeals Board [1979], Collection of the Decisions 100 to 134 (1981); *Decision No. 101*, NATO Appeals Board [1979], ibid.

[120] See also *Küster*, CJEC Case 123/75 [1976] ECR p. 1701.

where a procedure for filling a vacant post was begun and then cancelled, it was adequate to give as a reason that the post had been transferred in the interests of the service for reasons unconnected with the applicant's application for promotion.[121]

The CJEC has also held that, where an applicant has been refused promotion, it is generally not necessary to state the reasons for the rejection of the applicant in the decision to make the appointment.[122] The factors on which the assessment was based cover not only efficiency and vocational aptitude but also character, behaviour, and general personality which are not suited for inclusion in the reasons given for the appointment, since if they were stated, they might prove prejudicial to the interests of unsuccessful candidates. *A fortiori* it was not necessary to give reasons for a candidate's not being included in a preliminary promotion list.[123] It has also been stated that there is no requirement that an explanation be given of the use made of the information available to the administration in the assessment of the comparative merits of officials.[124]

On the other hand, it has been held that, when a complaint relating to his rejection for promotion is made by the applicant, the Staff Regulations of the European Communities require that he be given the reasons for his rejection.[125] These reasons would relate to the fulfilment of the legal conditions upon which the validity of the promotion made depends. In the case in question it was stated by the administration that the decision was taken after the comparative merits of the officials eligible for promotion had been considered and after all assessments of their ability, work, and conduct in the department, as they appeared in the periodic reports rendered, had been taken into account. This statement of reasons, although concise, was held to be adequate.

(f) Nature of the procedural irregularity

It has been held on occasion that, though there had been a technical violation of procedural law, no damage had been done the applicant, or the violation was unimportant or trivial. In *Thorgevsky*[126] the UNAT found that there had been procedural delays in the taking of the decisions which were unfavourable to the applicant but that, while such delays were not in keeping with the

---

[121] *Morina*, CJEC Case 18/83 [1983] ECR p. 4051.

[122] *Raponi*, CJEC Case 27/63 [1964] ECR p. 129. See also *Bernusset*, CJEC Cases 94 & 96/63 [1964] ECR p. 297; *Huybrechts*, CJEC Case 21/68 [1969] ECR p. 85; *Bernardi*, CJEC Case 90/71 [1972] ECR p. 603; *Ganzini*, CJEC Case 101/77 [1978] ECR p. 915.

[123] *Fonzi*, CJEC Cases 27 & 30/64 [1965] ECR p. 481.

[124] *Hoffman*, CJEC Case 280/81 [1983] ECR p. 889.

[125] *Grassi*, CJEC Case 188/73 [1974] ECR p. 1099. See also *de Hoe*, CJEC Case 151/80 [1981] ECR p. 3161.

[126] UNAT Judgment No. 262 [1980], JUNAT Nos. 231–300 p. 305.

Staff Rules or the proper administration of justice, no injury had been caused the applicant. In *Küster*[127] fictitious marks were awarded to two candidates who had not been appointed to the vacant position. It was held by the CJEC that the irregularity did not affect the applicant adversely and, therefore, could not be contested.[128]

Acquired rights

The UNAT has held that, though a staff member may not have an acquired right to promotion, he may have an acquired right to a procedure to be applied to the promotion process. In *Capio*[129] the procedure for promotion had been changed by a resolution of the General Assembly of the UN in 1979. At the time the change was introduced by the administration, the procedure for the promotion of the applicant had been initiated by her chief of service and her department had already formulated its recommendations. The tribunal, therefore, held that the applicant had an acquired right to have the former procedure applied to her promotion. The right had become acquired because the procedure had been begun. Subsequent to this case the administration of the UN took steps to protect the acquired rights of staff members in situations similar to that of the applicant in *Capio*. In *Sue-Ting-Len*[130] the UNAT held that on the facts the applicant did not fall within the provisions intended to protect staff members with acquired rights and, therefore, did not have an acquired right, while in *Sun*,[131] it was held that the applicant was covered by those provisions and was entitled to have those provisions applied to him. The UNAT was of the view that the provisions introduced by the UN were adequate to protect those who had acquired rights and their acquired rights and it was merely a question of interpreting those provisions in order to ascertain whether the applicant in each case was covered or not. It should be noted that in these cases what was in issue was the acquired right to a procedure for promotion not to the right to promotion or to a substantive requirement connected with promotion.

In *Chamentowski* the ILOAT stated clearly that a staff member of the EPO had no acquired right to the conditions for promotion which were subject to amendment and which staff members could expect to be

---

[127] CJEC Case 23/74 [1975] ECR p. 353.

[128] For trivial defects of procedure held to be ineffective see also *Ali Khan*, ILOAT Judgment No. 564 [1983] (ILO); *Ragusa*, CJEC Case 282/81 [1983] ECR p. 1245.

[129] UNAT Judgment No. 266 [1980], JUNAT Nos. 231–300 p. 340.

[130] UNAT Judgment No. 295 [1982], ibid. p. 596. See also *Schurz*, UNAT Judgment No. 311 [1983].

[131] UNAT Judgment No. 296 [1982], JUNAT Nos. 231–300 p. 611.

amended.[132] In *Lamadie (No. 2) and Kraanen*[133] the issue of acquired rights arose when IPI merged with EPO. According to the Staff Regulations of IPI a staff member was entitled to a biennial step increment in his new grade on promotion, while under the Staff Regulations of EPO he was entitled as a rule only to one 12-month step increment in the grade held before promotion. According to the Integration Agreement governing the merger of IPI with EPO no salary increase was to be granted on promotion. The ILOAT held that a staff member had no acquired right to the conditions of promotion prevailing under the regime of the IPI as such. The only acquired right granted by the rules of IPI on promotion was the prospect of advancement because this would have been the basis for the acceptance of his appointment by a staff member. Similarly, a staff member cannot claim an acquired right to promotion on the basis of seniority conferred at the time of appointment.[134] Such seniority gave him a benefit at the time of appointment in the form of a higher salary and he could not claim any rights on the basis of seniority again in respect of promotion.

Policy on promotion

It is a matter within the discretion of the administrative authority to make rules and determine the policy relating to promotion, but this discretion may not be abused.[135] The mere rejection or amendment of a recommendation of a Careers Committee whose function it is to advise on policy does not amount to an abuse of discretion, nor the fact that it is decided that those who resign will not be entitled to promotion, where promotion is made retroactive.[136] Where requirements for promotion have been established by the administration, they will only be declared improper if it can be shown that the administration acted *ultra vires* or abused its discretion in some other way.[137]

It is also an established rule that, where a policy is decided upon by the administration, it must be adhered to in the implementation of the promotion system. Thus, where the administration established two alternative procedures for promotion and attached different dates to them for the effectiveness of promotions, it was held by the ILOAT that the dates were not interchangeable and that the promotion must be made from the date attached to

---

[132] ILOAT Judgment No. 596 [1984] (EPO).

[133] ILOAT Judgment No. 365 [1978] (IPI/EPO). See also *Biggio (No. 3), Van Moer (No. 2) and Fournier,* ILOAT Judgment No. 366 [1978] (IPI/EPO).

[134] *Ledrut and Biggio,* ILOAT Judgment No. 300 [1977] (IPI).

[135] *Andary,* ILOAT Judgment No. 263 [1975] (IPI). See also *Lamadie,* ILOAT Judgment No. 262 [1975] (IPI).

[136] *Andary,* ILOAT Judgment No. 263 [1975] (IPI).

[137] *Carbo,* ILOAT Judgment No. 519 [1982] (PAHO).

the provision applied.[138] It is a matter left to the discretion of the administration to impose a period of probation as a condition of promotion,[139] of course, provided the written law of the organization does not preclude this.

Choice of promotion

According to the written law of an organization the free choice between transfer, promotion, or such other means of filling a vacancy as internal competition, may be permitted. In these circumstances the choice is at the discretion of the administrative authority. Both the OASAT and the CJEC have asserted this.[140] It does not seem to be unreasonable that the same choice would be available in the absence of express provision in the written law. The discretion is, however, subject to control by tribunals on the basis of abuse of discretion, such abuse being determined in light of the written law as well as general principles. Thus, among other things, where the written law required that the highest standard of ability, efficiency, and integrity be maintained, the exercise of the discretion to choose the method for filling vacant positions could be tested in terms of this requirement.[141] At the same time it has been said by the CJEC that no statement of reasons need be given for the choice actually made.[142]

Classification and promotion

It would appear that, if a staff member is transferred from a lower position to a position in a higher grade, he is entitled to be promoted to the grade of the latter position. This proposition emerges from *Thevenet*,[143] where the applicant claimed that he had been transferred to a post with a P5 classification and should, therefore, have been promoted from grade P4 which he held to grade P5. The OASAT held that, since he could not prove that the post to which he had been transferred was a P5 post, his claim failed. Had he been able to prove that the post was a P5 post, no doubt the tribunal would have held that he was entitled to be promoted to the higher grade.

---

[138] *Lamadie*, ILOAT Judgment No. 262 [1975] (IPI).

[139] *Ulliac*, Decision No. 49, OECD Appeals Board [1974], Recueil des décisions 1 à 62 (1979) p. 135.

[140] *García*, OASAT Judgment No. 56 [1980]; *Ley*, CJEC Cases 12 & 29/64 [1965] ECR p. 107; *Rittweger*, CJEC Case 21/70 [1971] ECR p. 7; *Küster*, CJEC Case 23/74 [1975] ECR p. 353; *Küster*, CJEC Case 123/75 [1976] ECR p. 1701; *Colussi*, CJEC Case 298/81 [1983] ECR p. 1131; *Mogensen and Others*, CJEC Case 10/82 [1983] ECR p. 2397.

[141] *Mogensen and Others*, CJEC Case 10/82 [1983] ECR p. 2397.

[142] *Ley*, CJEC Cases 12 & 29/64 [1965] ECR p. 107.

[143] OASAT Judgment No. 43 [1979].

Abolition of post

Where a staff member seeks promotion and the post to which he seeks to be promoted is thereafter abolished, this is a good reason for not promoting him.[144] While it cannot be doubted that the abolition of a post, even after promotion is sought, is within the discretion of the administrative authority, and that the abolition of post is not in itself evidence of prejudice,[145] it is reasonable to suppose that the discretion to abolish the post, especially in these circumstances, is subject to the rules applicable to abuse of discretion.

Temporary staff

Temporary staff members do not have a right to the posts they hold or to promotion so that they can occupy the positions they hold. Those positions can be filled at any time by transfer or promotion of other staff members without prejudicing the rights of the temporary staff member.[146]

Right to associate

Especially where the written law of the organization permits Staff-Association or Staff-Union activities and state that such duties are to be deemed part of normal service, absences from duty caused by such activities may be ignored in assessing whether the requirement of service for the purposes of promotion have been satisfied. Thus, where there was a requirement of several years' experience as head of an administrative unit and the person promoted would not have satisfied this requirement, if his continued absences from duty because of business on the staff committee which resulted in others acting for him were taken into account as not being appropriate service as head of a unit, the CJEC held that it was proper to regard the absences as being appropriate service for the purpose of the promotion requirements.[147]

Salary on promotion

It has been stated by tribunals that salaries may not be reduced on promotion

---

[144] *Burgos*, ILOAT Judgment No. 527 [1982] (PAHO).
[145] *Burgos*, ILOAT Judgment No. 527 [1982] (PAHO).
[146] See *Grosz*, CJEC Case 35/69 [1970] ECR p. 609; *Küster*, CJEC Case 23/74 [1975] ECR p. 353; *Van Reenen*, CJEC Case 189/73 [1975] ECR p. 445.
[147] *Grassi*, CJEC Case 188/73 [1974] ECR p. 1099.

and that Staff Regulations are generally formulated so as to prevent this.[148] As a consequence it has been held that Staff Regulations must be so interpreted as to achieve this end and that, where Staff Regulations are implemented in such a way that the staff member suffers a decrease in salary, their interpretation cannot be correct.[149] A special application of the above principles occurred in *Grafström*.[150] The applicant was promoted from the G category in FAO to the P category with an increase in pensionable remuneration. But soon after, the scales of the G category were changed with the result that she would have been better off financially, had she remained in the G category. It was held that the decision to promote her in the manner adopted was improper as regards her salary. This case is different from *Thorgevsky*,[151] where the UNAT held that a subsequent decrease in pensionable remuneration was not actionable. In this case in which the applicant was also promoted from the G category to the P category, though her pensionable remuneration initially turned out not to be lower than her former pensionable remuneration, subsequently it turned out to be lower than it would have been had she remained in the G category. The comparative decrease was not due to any action taken subsequently by the administration of the organization, as was the case in *Grafström*, which accounts for the difference in the conclusions reached by the two tribunals.

The definition of salary for the purposes of the rule that salaries should not be reduced on promotion is likely to be similar to that relevant to the general rule that salaries may not be reduced when structural salary changes are made. This rule will be discussed in a subsequent chapter.[152]

Tribunals will scrupulously see to it that the provisions of the written law relating to the increase of salaries on promotion are observed, especially when called upon to settle a disputed interpretation of those provisions.[153] However, a staff member generally has no right to a delay in promotion in order to secure an added financial advantage, as the time of promotion is within the discretion of the administrative authority.[154]

It also seems to be the law that a staff member cannot necessarily expect to have an increase in salary on promotion, since, even if he does not have an immediate salary increase, his position is not the same as before. Not only

---

[148] See *Conley and Zambrana*, OASAT Judgment No. 32 [1977]; *Alonso*, ILOAT Judgment No. 233 [1974] (PAHO).

[149] See *Garnett*, UNAT Judgment No. 175 [1973], JUNAT Nos. 167–230 p. 64; *Alonso*, ILOAT Judgment No. 233 [1974] (PAHO); *Brembati*, CJEC Cases 59 & 71/69 [1970] ECR p. 623; *Besnard and Others*, CJEC Cases 55 to 76, 86, 87 & 95/71 [1972] ECR p. 543.

[150] ILOAT Judgment No. 257 [1975] (FAO).

[151] UNAT Judgment No. 262 [1980], JUNAT Nos. 231–300 p. 305.

[152] See Ch. 43 pp. 947 ff. *infra*. See also *Rombach*, ILOAT Judgment No. 460 [1981] (EPO).

[153] *Garnett*, UNAT Judgment No. 156 [1972], JUNAT Nos. 114–166 p. 344; *Brembati*, CJEC Cases 59 & 71/69 [1970] ECR p. 623.

[154] *Lee*, ILOAT Judgment No. 199 [1973] (FAO).

may he be given more satisfying work but he will be better placed for further promotion which will eventually bring an increase in salary.[155]

There can be no discrimination in the administration of salaries on promotion.[156]

Remedies

While generally specific performance in the form of an applicant's promotion has not been ordered by tribunals, particularly because staff members have no right to promotion and it is usually not clear that, if the decision relating to promotion had been taken legally, the applicant would have been promoted, tribunals have ordered a variety of remedies in connection with decisions taken with regard to promotion.

(a) Annulment

The CJEC has most often simply annulled the decision to promote someone other than the applicant which means that the promotion decision will have to be taken again, if the position is to be filled. No damages have generally been awarded in these cases.

The decision to promote has been annulled where there were substantive irregularities, such as the failure to consider facts[157] or errors of fact.[158] Decisions to promote have also been annulled where there have been procedural irregularities, such as the failure to give the applicant a right to comment on an appraisal[159] or the following of a wrong procedure.[160] Furthermore, the CJEC has annulled a decision to promote another candidate where it found that there had been a *détournement de pouvoir* in the taking of the decision.[161]

In *Lassalle*[162] the CJEC quashed a vacancy notice, which amounted to an annulment, because the action was brought before the decision to promote could be taken. The vacancy notice was found to contain discriminatory

---

[155] *Lamadie (No. 2) and Kraanen*, ILOAT Judgment No. 365 [1978] (IPI/EPO); *Biggio (No. 3), Van Moer (No. 2) and Fournier*, ILOAT Judgment No. 366 [1978] (IPI/EPO).

[156] See *de Gregori*, ILOAT Judgment No. 409 [1980] (FAO). In *de Gregori*, the distinctions made were held not to be discriminatory.

[157] *Raponi*, CJEC Case 27/63 [1964] ECR p. 129; *de Pascale*, CJEC Case 97/63 [1964] ECR p. 515; *Bernusset*, CJEC Cases 94 & 96/63 [1964] ECR p. 297; *de Dapper*, CJEC Case 29/74 [1975] ECR p. 35.

[158] *Grassi*, CJEC Case 188/73 [1974] ECR p. 1099.

[159] *Rittweger*, CJEC Case 21/70 [1971] ECR p. 7.

[160] *Van Belle*, CJEC Case 176/73 [1974] ECR p. 1361.

[161] *Giuffrida*, CJEC Case 105/75 [1976] ECR p. 1395.

[162] CJEC Case 15/63 [1964] ECR p. 31.

provisions. Also the Court has annulled a decision to place an applicant at a particular point in the salary scale on promotion, because it found that the written law had been wrongly interpreted.[163] The result was that the decision would have had to be taken again and properly.

In one case in which the applicant suffered a financial disadvantage because of a change made, soon after the applicant's promotion, for the benefit of staff members in the grade and category from which the applicant had been promoted, the ILOAT quashed the decision relating to the salary of the applicant and remitted the case so that special arrangements could be made by the administration of FAO to ensure that the applicant's rights were respected.[164]

(b) Damages in addition to annulment

In *Meunier*[165] the Appeals Board of the Council of Europe awarded damages of 15,000 fr. in addition to annulling a decision to cancel without giving reasons to the applicant, who had sat the competitive examination and had been told that she had obtained a good result, a competition for a vacant post after the competitive examination had been held.

(c) Specific performance

In *Capio*[166] and *Sun*[167] the UNAT ordered specific performance. Where the acquired rights of the applicants to have a certain procedure for promotion applied to them had not been respected, the UN was ordered to apply the appropriate procedure. No additional damages were awarded nor were damages assessed in the event the respondent decided not to carry out the order of specific performance.

Where the applicant wrongfully suffered a decrease in salary on promotion because a Staff Regulation of PAHO was misconstrued, the ILOAT ordered that the proper salary increase be given the applicant.[168]

In a case[169] in which the rules relating to promotion were discriminatory against the applicant, because experience gained in national patent offices before candidates for promotion joined the staff of the EPO was placed at a premium for promotion, the ILOAT ordered that the applicant be promoted retroactively. This is an unusual case in which promotion was ordered. No

---

[163] *Brembati*, CJEC Cases 59 & 71/69 [1970] ECR p. 623.

[164] *Grafström*, ILOAT Judgment No. 257 [1975] (FAO).

[165] Council of Europe Appeals Board, Appeal No. 51 [1980], Case-Law Digest (1985) p. 79.

[166] UNAT Judgment No. 266 [1980], JUNAT Nos. 231–300 p. 340.

[167] UNAT Judgment No. 296 [1982], ibid. p. 611.

[168] *Alonso*, ILOAT Judgment No. 233 [1974] (PAHO).

[169] *Wenzel*, ILOAT Judgment No. 572 [1983] (EPO).

additional compensation or compensation in lieu of specific performance was awarded.

(d) Damages without annulment or specific performance

In *Decision No. 148*[170] where the administration of NATO had committed a substantive error of law as a result of which the applicant had not been promoted, although the applicant requested promotion as a possible alternative, the Appeals Board of NATO only awarded compensation of 1 year's salary without annulling the decision to appoint another person to the position to which the applicant aspired and without ordering the promotion of the applicant. The reason given was that the applicant would have been on one year's probation, even if she had been promoted, and would have had no guarantee of permanency. In *Estabial*[171] a substantive error of law and a procedural irregularity had been committed as a result of which another candidate was appointed to the position to which the applicant aspired. The UNAT stated that the applicant had no right to promotion and awarded compensation of 2 months' net base salary for both illegalities. The decision to appoint the other candidate was not annulled, nor was promotion of the applicant ordered. In *Oberthür*[172] a failure to consider relevant facts resulted in other candidates than the applicant being promoted. Since forty other persons had been promoted, in the circumstances the CJEC held that to annul the promotions would have been an excessive penalty and that no one promotion could have been properly annulled. It, therefore, awarded BF 20,000 as compensation. The Court said that the applicant would be able to take part in the next promotion procedure.

The other cases in which compensation has been awarded without annulment or specific performance involve irregularities of a procedural nature which resulted in the illegality of the decision taken. In *Nayyar*[173] the UNAT awarded $1,000 as compensation for the material damage but said that, since deterioration in the applicant's health could not be shown to have been the result of his not being promoted, no damages were being awarded on that count.[174] In *Tomiak*[175] the decision contested was the refusal to include the applicant's name in the promotion register of a previous year. The UNAT did not order promotion, because promotion was discretionary, nor did it

---

[170] *Decision No. 148*, NATO Appeals Board [1982], Collection of the Decisions 135 to 171 (1984).

[171] UNAT Judgment No. 310 [1983].

[172] CJEC Case 24/79 [1980] ECR p. 1743.

[173] UNAT Judgment No. 293 [1982], JUNAT Nos. 231–300 p. 586.

[174] See also *Roberts*, UNAT Judgment No. 312 [1983], a case similar to *Nayyar* in regard to remedies. Three months' salary was awarded for the injury.

[175] UNAT Judgment No. 314 [1983].

order that the applicant's name be included in the promotion register for the year in question, because the register was no longer in effect. Instead, it ordered compensation of $7,500 for the procedural irregularity, whether the applicant's possibilities of promotion had or had not suffered.

The ILOAT awarded compensation of $2,000 for a procedural irregularity which the administration of PAHO admitted.[176] PAHO had also agreed to regrade the applicant's post so that she would be promoted. The compensation was in addition to this offer of redress.

(e) Extra judicial settlement

In one case the CJEC ordered the parties to reach an extra judicial settlement and report back to the Court in circumstances in which there had been a failure to consider all the relevant facts which led to the applicant's being prejudiced.[177] It was said that, since seventy-five officials had been promoted, the Court would not annul the decisions to promote those officials.

(f) Compensation in absence of illegality

The Appeals Board of the OECD has awarded compensation even where the administrative authority had not committed an illegality in not promoting the applicant.[178] The tribunal gave as reasons the facts that the applicant had performed duties appropriate to the higher grade for some time and that he had been given precise hopes of promotion by responsible managers.

(g) Moral and consequential damages

In a case in which there had been an error of law in the promotions procedure which, however, did not affect the applicant adversely, since he was eliminated in a screening process, the ILOAT stated that it would not award damages for injury to reputation, humiliation, harassment, damage to career prospects, and injury to health.[179] Moral damages have not been awarded in any case in which the decision not to promote the applicant has been found tainted.

---

[176] *Moore*, ILOAT Judgment No. 393 [1980] (PAHO).

[177] *Gratreau*, CJEC Cases 156/79 & 51/80 [1980] ECR p. 3943.

[178] *Wolfson*, Decision No. 75, OECD Appeals Board [1979], Recueil des décisions 63 à 82 (1980) p. 39.

[179] *Sehgal*, ILOAT Judgment No. 531 [1982] (WHO).

(*h*) *No remedy because of the nature of the procedural irregularity*

As already seen, in *Thorgevsky*[180] the UNAT held that no remedy would be given, because the procedural irregularity did not cause the applicant any injury; and in *Küster*[181] the CJEC took a similar position, because the irregularity was too trivial or unimportant.

---

[180] UNAT Judgment No. 262 [1980], JUNAT Nos. 231–300 p. 305.

[181] CJEC Case 23/74 [1975] ECR p. 353. In *Decision No. 100*, NATO Appeals Board [1979], Collection of the Decisions 100 to 134 (1981), the applicant was not awarded compensation because he did not request compensation for the procedural irregularity committed. See also *Decision No. 101*, NATO Appeals Board [1979], ibid.

CHAPTER FORTY-THREE

Structural Salary Adjustments and Salary Scales

SALARIES may be adjusted structurally by international organizations. The reasons for such adjustments are generally changes in the cost of living, competitiveness, and such factors. Adjustments for such reasons are different from increases for merit or for satisfactory performance and are generally treated separately by institutions. The establishment or change of salary scales is a related subject. International administrative tribunals have had to deal with disputes relating to both these subjects. Much of the case law has concerned the interpretation of Staff Regulations but there has been a good deal which has discussed certain applicable general principles.

The Staff Regulations of many organizations have provisions which embody the prevailing salary scales.[1] However, few of them have explicit provisions about the methods of changing them or adjusting salaries for cost of living and other reasons. In the Staff Regulations of the UN adjustment for cost of living is taken care of by a system of post adjustments which are set out in Annex I to those Regulations[2] but there is no indication in the Staff Regulations how the post adjustments should be applied in a given case. The Staff Rules, however, refer to the International Civil Service Commission as being the authority to determine the classifications for the purpose of applying the post adjustments.[3] Many international organizations have a similar system of salary scales set forth in the Staff Regulations, coupled with a system of post adjustments.[4]

In the case of the European Communities the Staff Regulations contain the following provisions dealing with general adjustments of salaries and of salary scales on the basis of cost of living and other factors:

1. The Council shall each year review the remunerations of the officials and other servants of the Communities. This review shall take place in September in the light of a joint report by the Commission based on a joint index prepared by the Statistical

---

[1] See Annex I of the UN Staff Regulations: Appendix V *infra*; Article 3.1.1 of the ILO Staff Regulations: Amerasinghe (ed.), 4 *Staff Regulations and Staff Rules of Selected International Organizations* (1983) p. 185 at p. 201; Article 66 of the Staff Regulations of the European Communities: Amerasinghe (ed.), ibid. p. 1 at p. 22.

[2] See Appendix V *infra*.

[3] Staff Rules 103.7 (c); see Appendix V *infra*.

[4] See Article 3.9 of the ILO Staff Regulations: Amerasinghe (ed.), 4 op. cit. (note 1 *supra*) p. 185 at pp. 210 ff.

Office of the European Communities in agreement with the national statistical offices of the Member States; the index shall reflect the situation as at 1 July in each of the countries of the Communities.

During this review the Council shall consider whether, as part of economic and social policy of the Communities, remuneration should be adjusted. Particular account shall be taken of any increases in salaries in the public service and the needs of recruitment.

2. In the event of a substantial change in the cost of living, the Council shall decide, within two months what adjustments should be made to the weightings and if appropriate to apply them retrospectively.[5]

In addition the Regulations provided for adjustments according to the place of work as follows:

An official's remuneration expressed in Belgian francs shall, after the compulsory deductions set out in these Staff Regulations or in any implementing regulations have been made, be weighted at a rate above, below or equal to 100%, depending on living conditions in the various places of employment.[6]

The CJEC has, among other things, been concerned with applying these provisions.

There are instances of organizations which have no regulatory provisions relating to the adjustment of salaries for cost of living and other factors. Thus, the Staff and Personnel Manuals of the World Bank are silent on the matter, although the Principles of Staff Employment state in general terms in Section 6.2 (a) that the World Bank shall establish and periodically review the general levels of staff compensation and adjust such levels, as appropriate.[7] The WBAT has, thus, had to decide cases entirely on the basis of general principles of law and practice. The absence of governing provisions in the Staff Rules and Personnel Manual Statements does not mean that there are no rules governing the exercise of the power to adjust salaries for cost of living and other factors or to change salary scales. What it does mean is that the tribunal has to look to other sources than Staff Regulations and Staff Rules in order to establish controlling principles and rules. As will be seen, the WBAT has, even in the absence of specific provisions in the written law of the organization, been able to do this and exercise some control over the power to adjust salaries for cost of living and other factors.

Basic Principles

There seems to be a general basic principle conceded that on an adjustment of

---

[5] Article 65: Amerasinghe (ed.), 4 op. cit. (note 1 *supra*) p. 1 at p. 22.

[6] Article 64: Amerasinghe (ed.), ibid.

[7] See Appendix VII *infra*.

salaries or a change in salary scales there cannot be a reduction in salary. The principle has been most consistently asserted by the OASAT. In *Alaniz and Others* the Tribunal stated: 'The principle of Labor Law is known whereby not even the will of the parties is sufficient to change the contract to the point of reducing the salary of workers.'[8] In *Chisman and Others* the tribunal reiterated this principle and explained it further in a case which involved a reduction of salary as a result of a change being introduced into the system of salary administration:

In *Alaniz* (Judgment No. 13), this Tribunal has cited the well-known principle of labor law that, normally, not even the will of the parties is sufficient to change the contract to the point of reducing workers' wages. A reduction in salaries, when made unilaterally by the employer as in the present case, without the consent of the employees, constitutes a manifest disregard for the proper balance of the employment relationship, which cannot be justified in even the most difficult situations, since the General Secretariat has the possibility in such cases of using other legal means for dealing with them.[9]

In *Kaplan* the UNAT very early in its history made a distinction between contractual and statutory elements in the relations between the UN and staff members and stated that the contractual elements could not be changed without the agreement of the parties but that statutory elements might always be changed at any time through regulations established by the organization's General Assembly, such changes being binding on the staff.[10] Among contractual matters which could not be changed without the agreement of the two parties was included the staff member's salary. While the inclusion of salary among contractual elements which could not be changed without the agreement of the parties was not discussed or explained in any detail, it is clear that the UNAT intended to subscribe to the principle referred to above that salary could not be reduced.[11]

Where the UNAT differs from the OASAT is in that it did not state in *Kaplan* that salary could not be reduced even with the consent of the staff member but implied rather that salaries could be changed or reduced by agreement. The difference in approach is noteworthy, although in practical terms it may not be significant, as it is very rarely that salaries will be reduced by agreement. On the other hand, it is important that the OASAT referred to the principle it stated as a general principle of labour law.

A significant case that arose in this connection was decided by the ILOAT.

---

[8] OASAT Judgment No. 13 [1975] at p. 11.

[9] OASAT Judgment No. 64 [1982] at pp. 27 ff. See also *Fernández and Others*, OASAT Judgment No. 65 [1982] at p. 7.

[10] UNAT Judgment No. 19 [1953], JUNAT Nos. 1–70 p. 71 at p. 74. See also *Middleton* etc., Judgments Nos. 20 to 25 and 27 [1953], ibid. pp. 76, 80, 86, 91, 95, 101, 110.

[11] In *Puvrez*, UNAT Judgment No. 82 [1961] (ICAO), JUNAT Nos. 71–86 p. 78, the UNAT seems again to have accepted the broad principle that there could be no reduction in salary.

In *de Los Cobos and Wenger*[12] the ILO deducted over a period of 6 months an amount equivalent to 2.2 per cent of the net salary, as increased or reduced by post adjustment, of officials in the professional and higher categories. This amount was the net salary corresponding to 4 days of compulsory leave, which were to be unpaid, ordered by the organization because of the financial crisis faced by the organization upon the withdrawal of the United States from membership which might have resulted in some staff having to be dismissed unless the salaries of all were reduced. In reply to the argument that the acquired rights of the applicants had been impaired, the tribunal pointed out that: the right to payment of salary was a contractual right with the result that, if it was to be regarded as an acquired right which was inviolate, it should have arisen under an express provision of the contract and both parties should have intended that it be inviolate; not all rights relating to remuneration were acquired rights (for example, while there may be an acquired right to the payment of an allowance, there may not be such a right to the method of calculation or, in other words, to the amount of the allowance); and, if the parties had had in mind the circumstances in which the ILO had been led to take the decision to reduce salaries, it was unlikely that they would have had in mind that the amount of remuneration should be inviolate.[13] Thus, it would seem that the ILOAT was of the view that the principle that salaries could not be reduced was not absolute.

It is important, however, that the tribunal did state that 'the complainants still received during the peirod of the reduction a sum higher than that of their basic salary.[14] This is an important qualification. The reduction of salary in effect was a deduction from the increase in the allowance paid by way of post adjustment which left the basic salary intact. While the tribunal did say that, particularly because it was evident that most of the staff members were in favour of the reduction, they would not have treated the agreed salary as inviolate but would have consented to its slight and temporary reduction,[15] the crux of its reasoning was the emphasis it placed on the fact that the basic salary of the applicants had not been reduced.

This case could, therefore, be viewed as having acknowledged that there is a principle that salaries should not be reduced, in the view of the tribunal, because the right to the payment of salaries is an acquired right, but that what this means is that it is only the basic salary that should not be reduced and not the basic salary increased by allowances such as the post adjustment allowance which exists in the UN system of organizations. This is, perhaps, the only rational way to reconcile this case with the cases decided by the OASAT and the UNAT and discussed earlier.

12 ILOAT Judgment No. 391 [1980] (ILO).
13 Ibid. at pp. 8, 9.
14 Ibid. at p. 8.
15 Ibid. at p. 9.

It is significant that the tribunal did not place much emphasis on the agreement of the majority of the staff as being an element of consent to the reduction of salary resulting in a lawful renunciation of acquired rights. It preferred to regard such agreement as evidence of the fact that the acquired right did not pertain to the total remuneration of the staff members, thus permitting slight and temporary reductions. While, on the one hand, it did specifically state that the fact that basic salaries had not been reduced was of importance, on the other hand, it did not deny, by implication, that even these may be reduced by agreement of the parties, since it merely regarded the right to the basic salary as an acquired right and not as subject to the general principle that salaries could not be reduced even with the agreement of the staff members. In this respect the ILOAT's view is closer to that of the UNAT rather than that of the OASAT.

It is also of significance that in *de Los Cobos and Wenger* the ILOAT did not concede clearly that the basic salary taken together with the post adjustment could be reduced in the general course of administration, because the right to such emoluments was not an acquired right. There was no explicit acknowledgement that the right to such remuneration was not an acquired right. On the contrary, the tribunal seems to have implied that this amount of remuneration was normally inviolate but was not intended to be sacrosanct in exceptional circumstances such as those in the case in hand. This seems to emerge from the following passage:

At the time when the complainants' basic salary was determined, and later when it was adjusted, the parties are unlikely to have had in mind the circumstances in which the ILO was led to take the impugned decision. But, had they done so, would they ordinarily have intended that the amount of remuneration should be inviolate?[16]

The tribunal was careful to point out that the reduction, while it did not result in the applicants' receiving less that their basic salaries, was also slight and short-lived.[17] Thus, it could very well be that the tribunal was not prepared to commit itself to the view that the total amount of salary was as a rule reducible, provided it was not reduced below the level of the basic salary. Reduction of the salary to which a staff member can be shown to have a right, if not an acquired right, could only take place not only in very exceptional circumstances, such as prevailed in *de Los Cobos and Wenger*, but also provided generally the reduction was slight and temporary. Even if it cannot be concluded that the tribunal intended to restrict the scope of the power to reduce the emoluments as described to the particular exceptional circumstances which prevailed in that case and to slight and temporary reductions, equally it cannot be inferred that it intended to give the organization a wide

16 Ibid. at p. 8.
17 Ibid.

discretion to reduce salaries in the course of administration, provided the reduction did not result in staff members receiving less than their basic salaries. Rather would it appear that the tribunal would have supported a very limited power to reduce the salaries as described, provided the circumstances were exceptional and special, the general rule applicable being that such salaries may not be reduced.

In this context, the Report of the Committee of Jurists to the chairman of the First Committee of the Assembly of the League of Nations on the power of the Assembly to reduce the salaries of officials, which was given in 1932,[18] is noteworthy. On the basis that officials had an acquired right to the maintenance of their salaries because they were incorporated in their contracts and, therefore, the right to them was contractual, the committee concluded that the League Assembly did not have a right to reduce the salaries of officials even in the exercise of its budgetary authority. There was an obligation placed upon the organization to make appropriate provision in its budget for the payment of salaries to which the staff members had an. acquired right. Interference with this right was said to be possible only with the consent of the official concerned. The view taken by this committee is similar to the one impliedly adopted by the UNAT which has been adverted to earlier.

The definition of salary in relation to the basic principles

For the purpose of the application of the rule that salaries may not be reduced, especially when changes in salary are made or when salary scales are altered, it is necessary to determine what exactly is included in the concept of 'salary' which may not be reduced.

The term 'salary' has been defined in a variety of ways for different purposes. It may be useful to refer to some of the definitions given.

In *Lhoest*[19] the question was what was included in the applicant's salary for the purposes of calculating a termination indemnity, where the relevant Staff Regulation of the League of Nations required payment of one year's salary as indemnity. The applicant claimed that a cost-of-living allowance granted by the League was included in the salary payable. The allowance had been granted for one financial year only. The ILOAT held that this allowance was a temporary supplement to salary which had been voluntarily granted and, therefore, could not be included in the salary payable as termination indemnity. In *Jacquemart*,[20] where the issue also was what the content of

---

18 League of Nations Official Journal, Special Supplement No. 107 (1932), p. 206.
19 ILOAT Judgment No. 1 [1947] (LN).
20 CJEC Case 114/77 ECR p. 1697. This decision is similar to that in *Benassi*, CJEC Case

basic salary was for the purposes of calculating a severance grant, the CJEC held that the question related to the interpretation of Article 12 of Annex VIII of the Staff Regulations which referred to a grant calculated on the basis of the last 'basic salary' before deductions. The Court came to the conclusion that the concept of 'basic salary' for the purpose of the severance grant comprised not only the amounts included in the table of salaries which was established after the annual review of salaries but also the amounts to which those salaries were subject, where appropriate, as a result of the weighting for the provisional seats established by the Council as a result of that same review. The reason for the difference in approach between the decision of the ILOAT and that of the CJEC lies in the fact that in the former case the cost of living allowance was a temporary one granted for one financial year, while the weighting done by the European Communities for the provisional seats results in salaries for officials which are as composite salaries regarded as basic for the period during which the weighting applies. The weighting procedure is a continuing one which requires that the additional amounts resulting at any given time from the weighting be taken into account in the calculation of the salary upon which the severance grant is based. Nevertheless, the difference between the two cases demonstrates that there can be variations as between tribunals in the definition of salary, even for the same purpose.

In *Pugsley*[21] the issue was whether a 15 per cent increase in salary awarded as a cost-of-living increase was to be applied to a settling-in allowance which had been granted to the applicant under the Staff Regulations. The Appeals Board of the Council of Europe held that the Staff Regulations provided for the application of the increase for cost of living only to certain components of remuneration in which the settling-in allowance was not included. While the decision was specifically based on the interpretation of the Staff Regulations, it would seem that it would have been justified even in the absence of a reference, implied or otherwise, in the Staff Regulations, to the components of remuneration to which the increase for the cost of living was to be applied, since the allowance in question was a single payment which could not really be regarded as part of the staff member's salary.

In *Djoehana (No. 2)*[22] salary for the purpose of compensation ordered by the ILOAT in an earlier case was held to be net salary plus salary adjustment. Net salary is the salary payable after the staff assessment is deducted and the salary adjustment is the allowance paid in consideration of certain factors taken into account depending on the country or city in which the staff

---

194/80 [1981] ECR p. 2815, which concerned the identification of basic salary for the purposes of pensionable service.

[21] Council of Europe Appeals Board, Appeal No. 6 [1971], Case-Law Digest (1985) p. 30.

[22] ILOAT Judgment No. 538 [1982] (UNESCO).

member works. It did not include dependent's allowances or temporary personal allowances. In *Azola Blanco and Véliz García (No. 3)*[23] the ILOAT held that in calculating the compensation to be paid to the applicants for wrongful dismissal, which was set at a sum equal to three times the gross remuneration paid to the applicants in respect of a specific period of one year, payments for overtime work done during that period had to be included. In *Harris and Others*[24] the UNAT had ordered compensation to be paid to the applicants in earlier judgments, which compensation was based, among other things, on the salary paid to each applicant. It was held that the UN was not under an obligation to pay the applicants the taxes that would be levied by their national states on the compensation received. While this decision does not deal with the concept of salary directly, it may indirectly be authority for the proposition that taxes payable on salary are not included in salary for the purposes of compensation ordered by the UNAT.

In *Rombach*[25] the ILOAT was called upon to interpret Article 49 (13) of the EPO Staff Regulations which stated that: 'In no case may the obtaining of a higher grade by a permanent employee result in a reduction in his total net remuneration'. The question at issue was what was included in the concept of 'total net remuneration' for the purpose of determining whether a staff member's compensation had been reduced on the assignment of a higher grade on promotion. It was found that Article 64 of the Staff Regulations, though it did not give a formal definition of 'total net remuneration', suggested that the term should be taken to mean basic salary and such allowances and benefits as are payable after the deduction of internal tax. The tribunal, however, stated that the balance of the arrangements for equitable remuneration, which also aimed at preventing unwarranted discrimination in favour of or against any staff member, would be upset, if 'total net remuneration' for the purposes of Article 49 were taken to include all benefits and allowances, without distinction as to their nature and purpose and the terms on which they were payable. It further stated:

The purpose of the safeguard in article 49, paragraph 13, is to preserve mutual trust. The staff member should be in a position to know what remuneration he may expect over the long term. The list of benefits and allowances in article 67, paragraph 1, is not exhaustive. Other provisions of the Staff Regulations confer entitlement to benefits and allowances in other circumstances. They appear to fall into two groups:
(a) benefits and allowances which are permanent or at least payable over a fairly lengthy period, such as the residence allowance, allowance for dependents, education benefit, expatriation allowance and language allowance;
(b) temporary benefits and allowances, payable for a limited period, such as the installation benefit, overtime pay (article 57) and pay for shift work (article 58).

---

23 ILOAT Judgment No. 643 [1984] (ESO).
24 UNAT Judgment No. 67 [1956], JUNAT Nos. 1–70 p. 388.
25 ILOAT Judgment No. 460 [1981] (EPO).

The preservation of mutual trust and, consequently, the safeguard provided in article 49, paragraph 13, are applicable only to allowances which are permanent or payable over a certain period of time. To depart from that principle would be to create unacceptable anomalies in the structure of remuneration at the EPO. The duty allowance is a temporary one. The staff member who receives it knows that he will continue to do so only as long as he is performing duties pertaining to a higher grade. If, like the complainant, he is assigned the duties of a higher grade because of promotion, there are no grounds for payment of the duty allowance and there is no legal basis for it in article 49, paragraph 13.[26]

For the purpose of the rules relating to promotion, or even grading, in the EPO, it would seem that benefits and allowances which are permanent or payable at least over a lengthy period are included in the concept of 'total net remuneration', while temporary benefits and allowances such as overtime payments and duty allowances are not.

The elements to be taken into account in arriving at the meaning of the term 'salary' or 'remuneration' may vary, depending on the purpose for which a definition is sought. As has been seen, overtime payments may be included in the remuneration which forms the basis of the calculation of compensation to be paid to an applicant as a result of a decision of a tribunal, while they may be excluded in the determination of salary for the purpose of the rule that total net remuneration shall not be reduced upon promotion to a higher grade. Further, in *Puvrez*, as seen earlier, the UNAT seems to have assumed that in the case of a change of grade, a dependency allowance was relevant to the calculation of total emoluments but had to be set off against the post-adjustment allowance, with the result that an increase in the latter could offset the withdrawal of the former, while in *de Los Cobos and Wenger* the ILOAT took the view that, though as a minimum limit, 'basic salary' (that is, the salary paid less all allowances and other benefits) could never be reduced, salary comprising the basic salary together with the post-adjustment allowance could not be reduced except in exceptional circumstances.

The uncertainty reflected in the decisions as to what comprises salary and as to what it is that cannot be reduced, though there is some element of earnings that cannot be reduced, leads to the conclusion that in any event the definition of salary must depend on the purpose for which the definition is being adopted. Even Staff Regulations may define 'salary' differently for different purposes. In regard to salary adjustments for cost of living and other factors and the establishment of salary scales the problem of determining below what level remuneration being paid at any given time must not fall is complicated by the fact that different organizations have different systems for dealing with salary adjustments based on the cost of living and other factors. Further, the question of the relationship of allowances, such as

---

[26] Ibid. at pp. 5–6.

dependency allowances and benefits, to the issue of salary adjustments for reasons of cost of living and other factors is not an easy one to answer.

It would seem reasonable that, in line with the decision in *de Los Cobos and Wenger*, what can absolutely not be reduced is basic salary. The basic salary of a staff member will be determined by the system adopted by the particular organization for which he works. Where the basic salary is a total figure including the structural increases for cost of living and other factors already awarded (which is the case with, for instance, the salaries of staff members of the World Bank and the European Communities), this will be the remuneration to be considered for the purposes of the rule that salary cannot be reduced in any circumstances. Where the basic salary does not include elements which are kept separate and which cover allowances for cost of living and other factors (which is the case with, for instance, the salaries of staff members of the UN and ILO), the rule that salary cannot be reduced in any circumstances will apply only to the salary excluding those elements. This would seem to be the logical implication of *de Los Cobos and Wenger*.

In *de Los Cobos and Wenger* it was also decided by implication that there was over and above basic salary an element of remuneration which could not be decreased except in very exceptional circumstances. This was the element comprising the post-adjustment allowance or the allowance based on cost of living and other factors. Clearly, the definition of salary for this subsidiary rule becomes relevant only in the case of those organizations where the allowance based on cost of living and other factors is not made part of the basic salary structure and only to the extent that such allowance is not built into that salary structure, as is the case in the UN and most of the specialized agencies. The definition and the rule itself does not appertain to those organizations, such as the World Bank and the European Communities, which systematically build previous increases for cost of living and other factors into the structure of their basic salaries. The rule that this definition pertains to is also clearly subject to the variations in the allowance which are naturally consequent upon the changes in the cost of living and other relevant factors which may have the effect of decreasing at any given time the allowance for post adjustment or its equivalent. In the UN system it will be noted that the post-adjustment allowance not only varies from station to station with the result that a staff member may suffer a decrease in salary on transfer, but also may change from month to month in the same station with the result that the remuneration of a staff member in a given station may fluctuate. Thus, it seems reasonable that the subsidiary rule implied in *de Los Cobos and Wenger* cannot guarantee that the allowance based on cost of living and other factors will not fluctuate and, perhaps, be reduced on the basis of the very reasons on which the allowance is postulated. What the rule means appears to be that, given the definition of salary for the purposes of the rule, that element of the salary as defined which represents the adjustment for cost of living and other factors may not be reduced, except in very exceptional circumstances, unless the reduction is due to the operation of factors inherent in the existence of that element of the salary itself.

While the definition of salary for the purpose of the two rules referred to may be established satisfactorily on the lines indicated above, some difficulties may be encountered with the decisions in *Puvrez* and *Rombach*. *Puvrez*, it will be remembered, dealt with the withdrawal of a dependency allowance, while *Rombach* stated in detail what was meant by 'total remuneration' for the purpose of a written law of the EPO forbidding the reduction of salary on promotion.

The decision in *Puvrez* was that the applicant's salary had not been reduced, because, though he had lost his dependency allowance as a result of a change in the definition of 'dependent', the increase in his post-adjustment allowance was sufficiently large to offset that loss. In fact in that case the applicant's salary, comprising his basic salary plus the post-adjustment allowance, had not been reduced. Hence, the second rule as explained above was apparently not violated. But the decision seems to imply that the applicant had some kind of entitlement to the dependency allowance which resulted in its being considered part of the remuneration which could not be reduced. On the other hand, in so far as the tribunal did not consider the post-adjustment allowance sacrosanct, there being no exceptional circumstances such as obtained in *de Los Cobos and Wenger*, but regarded it as capable of being set off against the lost dependency allowance, it seems to have taken the view that the post-adjustment allowance was reducible in the absence of exceptional circumstances even for other reasons than those inherent in the existence of the allowance. It is important to note that the tribunal did not say that the reason for the increase in the post-adjustment allowance was the withdrawal of the dependency allowance. If that had been the view taken, the tribunal could not be understood to have implied that the post-adjustment allowance could be reduced for reasons other than those which were its *raison d'être*. In view of the conclusion reached by the tribunal, there is no alternative but to regard the decision as conflicting with the view that, except in very exceptional circumstances, the post-adjustment allowance or allowance based on cost of living and other factors, in circumstances in which it is considered an element of salary over and above basic salary, cannot generally be reduced for reasons other than those germane to its existence.

The real issue in the case was whether the dependency allowance was irreducible. This depended on other factors than whether it was part of the salary of a staff member which could not ordinarily be reduced. In so far as the tribunal inclined to the view that it could have been abolished in the circumstances of the case, provided the abolition was not retroactive, there was no reason for the tribunal to establish a set-off between the dependency allowance taken away and the increase in the post-adjustment allowance which was a separate operation altogether.

There is another possible approach to the analysis of this case. The tribunal may have been of the view that the staff member was not entitled as of right to the increase in the post-adjustment allowance, and that, therefore, the increase awarded could be regarded as a replacement for the dependency allowance to which he was entitled and of which he had been deprived. An increase in a post-adjustment allowance is different from an amount of such allowance already granted and may be regarded as discretionary. This explanation would reconcile the view of 'salary' taken in *Puvrez* with the definition of 'salary' for the second rule demanding irreducibility. However, this explanation is not satisfactory. In the UN system of salary adjustment for cost of living and other factors it would seem that the staff member is entitled to legitimate increases in his post-adjustment allowance as long as the system of adjustment of the allowance remains in force, because that is an established system under the Staff Regulations and Staff Rules. A staff member would cease to have a right to such increases only if the system is changed officially. Thus, it is difficult to infer that in *Puvrez* the tribunal would have assumed that the applicant was not entitled as of right to the increase in the post-adjustment allowance, although it does not appear from the decision in what circumstances the allowance was increased. It would, therefore, seem that the tribunal, while not denying that the applicant was entitled to the increase in the post-adjustment allowance, nevertheless concluded that it could be set off against the loss of a dependency allowance to which it did not clearly say that the applicant was entitled. The resulting implication is, however, that the applicant was entitled to the dependency allowance but could have his salary reduced to the extent of the increase in the post-adjustment allowance. Thus, in any event the decision must be regarded as being in conflict with the second principle implied in *de Los Cobos and Wenger*. If the tribunal genuinely considered irreducible the salary of the applicant including the increase in the post-adjustment allowance, it would have dealt with the question of the dependency allowance separately and not confused it with the increase in the post-adjustment allowance. Questions relating to allowances such as dependency allowances are individually related to the doctrine of acquired rights and are strictly not dependent on the rule relating to the maintenance of salary level. The issue in *Puvrez* should strictly have been dealt with on this basis.

In *Rombach* the ILOAT implied that there were certain allowances of a permanent nature which were included in the concept of 'total net remuneration' for the purpose of the rule expressed in the written law that total net remuneration may not be reduced on the assignment of a higher grade. These were allowances other than allowances granted on account of the cost of living and other factors, such as dependency and education allowances. This view would seem to extend the definition of salary for the purposes of the rule that salary may not be reduced, particularly in the course of salary administration based on changes in the cost of living and other factors and where salary scales are changed, in so far as it includes more than basic salary and adjustments for cost of living and other factors in such definition. It could be that the concept of 'total net remuneration' for the purposes of the rule of the written law applied in *Rombach* must be distinguished from the concept of 'salary' that may not be reduced in any circumstances or only in very exceptional circumstances. Further, it should be noted that it was unnecessary for the decision in that case for the tribunal to define 'total remuneration' in the way it did. The issue was whether a duty allowance was part of the remuneration which could not be reduced. Thus, whether 'total net remuneration' was defined in the way the tribunal defined salary in *de Los Cobos and Wenger* or in the way it was defined in *Rombach*, the result in the case would have been the same. Nevertheless, the definition outlined in *Rombach* is in conflict with the definition of salary in *de Los Cobos and Wenger*.

It would seem that the definition in *Rombach* fails to make a proper distinction between 'salary' which may not be reduced and those items of remuneration to which staff members are entitled, because they have an acquired right or an essential right to them, if that definition is to be regarded as serviceable for the rule that salary may not be reduced when adjustments are made on the basis of cost of living and other factors or on the change of salary scales. The total issue of whether a staff member has a right, which cannot be taken away without his consent, to an allowance or a benefit and to how much of that allowance or benefit he is entitled, is really separate from the question of what constitutes the salary of a staff member which cannot be reduced. There may be a right, which cannot be taken away without consent, to an allowance or benefit or even to non-reduction of an allowance or benefit, but this right is best regarded as separate from the right that a staff member has to have his salary not reduced, especially when salary is adjusted for cost of living and other factors or changes are made in salary scales. It would be improper to regard such allowances as a total package included in salary or to treat them as interchangeable with salary, as this would lead to undesirable and unforeseeable results.

Adjustments in salary

Staff members may question a decision to adjust their salaries on the basis of cost of living and other factors, because they consider the decision a violation of their terms or conditions of employment. The main issue in this connection is whether staff members have any rights in regard to increases in their salaries on the basis of cost of living and other factors. Subsidiary issues may also arise in regard to the nature of the decision attacked and the powers of the various organs of an organization in respect of such a decision.

(a) Decision impugned

Decisions relating to increases for cost of living and other factors are often taken by the legislative or policy-making body of the institution concerned. The question then is whether an international administrative tribunal can amend or order rescission of such a decision. As has been seen, most Statutes of tribunals or the Staff Regulations of the institutions concerned give tribunals jurisdiction expressly or by implication over the decisions of the administrative or executive organ of the institution concerned. In some cases the Statutes of tribunals refer to the violation of the contract or terms of employment.

In spite of the fact that tribunals may not be given explicit jurisdiction over the acts of legislative or policy-making bodies of international organizations, they have had no difficulty in indirectly pronouncing on the validity of such acts in connection with the adjustment of salaries. In *Stevens and Others*,[27] when a resolution of the Committee of Ministers of the Council of Europe imposing a levy on the structural increase of salaries on the basis of cost of living and other factors was in effect the subject of the litigation, the Appeals Board of the Council of Europe, while noting the argument that the disputes system of the institution provided only for appeals against the Secretary General of the institution who had merely executed the decision taken by the decision-taking organ of the institution, held that the Appeals Board was called upon to deal with objections raised against individual decisions taken by the Secretary-General, in application of the decision of the Committee of Ministers, relating to the levy on staff salaries. Pronouncing on individual administrative decisions making the necessary deduction from the salary increase was clearly within the jurisdiction of the Appeals Board. Ultimately, while holding that the administration could not unilaterally alter the position of the applicants by imposing the levy, the Appeals Board was able to conclude that the levy introduced by the resolution of the Committee of Ministers disregarded the rights of the applicants to the payment of the remuneration provided for in the salary scales for the relevant period under consideration and was consequently illegal. In effect, as a result, the Appeals Board, though specifically annulling the imposition of the levy by the Secretary General of the Council of Europe, was able indirectly to pronounce on the validity of the resolution of the Committee of Ministers without actually annulling that resolution.

[27] Council of Europe Appeals Board, Appeals Nos. 101–113 [1985], Case-Law Digest (1985) p. 144.

In *Decision No. 169(b)*[28] and *Decisions Nos. 174–180, 182, 184–186, 188–195*[29] the Appeals Board of NATO was even more explicit. In both cases the tribunal held that it had no jurisdiction to annul the decisions of the Council of NATO which was the policy-making body taking the decisions relating to the salary increases in issue. On the other hand, it found that it could pronounce on the application of the decisions to the individuals concerned by the head of the NATO body who was responsible for implementing the decisions of the Council, even though such head was implementing decisions of the policy-making body. In these cases also an international tribunal was indirectly able virtually to decide on the legality of decisions of a policy-making body, although it took the view that it could not annul such decisions.

In *de Merode*[30] the WBAT was faced with claims for the rescission of certain administrative decisions relating to salary increases which merely gave effect to resolutions of the Executive Directors of the World Bank, who constitute the policy-making organ of the institution. While the tribunal said that the competence of the tribunal to pass judgment upon the claims was not disputed, it had no hesitation in holding that, since the applications alleged non-observance of the contracts of employment or terms of appointment of the applicants, the tribunal had competence to determine the issues raised. In that case the decisions contested were administrative decisions of the management of the institution, though those decisions merely gave effect to resolutions made by the Executive Directors. The tribunal did not have to decide the issue whether a decision of the policy-making body could be annulled by it but it clearly held that it could decide whether a decision of the administrative organ was illegal, even though it merely gave effect to such a decision of the policy-making body.

(b) Powers of organs

There have been occasions on which tribunals have, in the course of deciding whether a decision relating to a structural salary increase was valid, pronounced on the question what powers particular organs of the institution had in relation to the determination of structural salary increases. In *Lanner*[31] the Appeals Board of the OEEC examined the provisions of the OEEC Convention and the Staff Regulations of the OEEC in this connection. It found that according to the Convention the Council had the power to make all decisions and that the Secretary General was placed under the authority of

---

[28] *Decision No. 169 (b)*, NATO Appeals Board [1984], Collection of the Decisions 135 to 171 (1984).
[29] *Decisions Nos. 174–180, 182, 184–186, 188–195*, NATO Appeals Board [1985].
[30] WBAT Reports [1981], Decision No. 1.
[31] Decision No. 31, OEEC Appeals Board [1960], Recueil des décisions 1 à 62 (1979) p. 85.

the Council, while the Staff Regulations stated that staff members would receive remuneration in accordance with regulations adopted by the Secretary General in conformity with the provision of the Convention which placed him under the authority of the Council and that, if such regulations entailed expenses which were not authorized by the Council, they must be submitted for approval to the Council. As a result, the tribunal held that the Secretary General could only implement with a regulation a decision of the Council, since he did not have any authority of his own to adjust salaries and, therefore, was right in considering that he could not on his own adjust the salary of the applicant for the cost of living. It was also clear that the intention of the Council was that the Secretary General should not adjust salaries without prior consideration by the Council on each occasion. Thus, while the adjustment of salaries for cost of living in the OEEC was achieved by a regulation promulgated by the Secretary General, the substantive decision to adjust salaries on account of the cost of living was the province of the Council. The case not only established that there was a certain competence vested in certain organs of the OEEC in regard to the adjustment of salaries but also showed clearly that the Appeals Board of the OEEC would examine the relevant instruments, including the constituent instrument of the organization, in order to establish the competence of the various organs.[32]

The WBAT assumed in *de Merode*[33] that the Executive Directors of the World Bank had the necessary authority to determine the adjustment of salaries for cost of living and other factors and that decisions taken by the Executive Directors in regard to the adjustment of salaries for cost of living and other factors were taken by the proper organ of the World Bank, though they were given effect to by an administrative decision taken by the administrative organ of the World Bank. In *Chisman and Others*[34] the OASAT held that the General Assembly of the OAS had power to pass resolutions relating to salary scales which took precedence over the Staff Regulations which were established by the General Assembly.

In *Buyl and Others*[35] the CJEC examined the procedure followed by the Commission of the European Communities in amending a Staff Regulation pertaining to exchange rates for salaries. The Commission had submitted the

---

[32] In *Connolly-Battisti* (*No. 5*), ILOAT Judgment No. 323 [1977] (FAO) at pp. 4–5, the ILOAT found upon investigation that the Director General of FAO had power to act on his own in regard to salary administration but was in any event under the supervision of the Council which had the power to instruct the Director General to take action. Hence, action taken in these circumstances was not *ultra vires*.

[33] WBAT Reports [1981], Decision No. 1.

[34] OASAT Judgment No. 64 [1982]. The OASAT not only did not hesitate to examine the authority of the policy-making body of the OAS to make decisions altering the Staff Regulations governing the rights of staff members in regard to salaries but held that the General Assembly could do so by a resolution rather than by a formal alteration of the Regulations.

[35] CJEC Case 817/79 [1982] ECR p. 245.

proposal concerned to the European Parliament for advice, as was required by the Merger Treaty, but then changed some of the details before adopting the proposal. The CJEC, while holding that consultation was an essential feature of the institutional balance sought by the Treaties which made it essential that the European Parliament be consulted before a Regulation was adopted amending the Staff Regulations, if such Regulation was to be valid, yet concluded that the requirement of consultation may be regarded as having been met when the Regulation finally adopted conformed to the proposal submitted to the European Parliament, so long as changes made after the submission to the Parliament were of method rather than of substance. Thus, where updated exchange rates were substituted for the European Unit of Account and certain transitional provisions were accepted as a result of comments made by the Parliament, the CJEC held that the substitution made was a change of method rather than of substance and that the transitional provisions were broadly an acceptance of the wishes of the Parliament. The first change was not a substantive one, the second was a change which resulted from the advice of the Parliament. Thus, neither change was a violation of the rule requiring consultation.

Buyl and Others shows that a tribunal can, if it wishes, examine the procedure adopted by an organ, including the policy-making body, of the institution in making adjustments relating to salary in order to ensure that such procedure conforms to the law. It would seem to make no difference for this purpose that the CJEC has general jurisdiction over the European Communities in all matters concerning the Communities, including matters other than employment relations, while international administrative tribunals in general have a limited jurisdiction over employment relations.

(c) The content of the increase

The Staff Regulations of some organizations have written provisions relating to structural salary increases. Where these exist, tribunals will interpret them, monitor the fulfilment of obligations created for the organizations by them, and control the exercise of any discretion permitted by them. In this connection the CJEC has had to decide cases contesting the implementation of Article 65[36] of the Staff Regulations of the European Communities. In *Commission of the European Communities* v. *Council of the European Communities*[37] the Court held that, when the Council exercised its discretion under that Regulation in making the annual review of the level of remuneration, it had to include any increase in salaries in the public service as one of all the factors to be taken into consideration. While the Regulation did not

---

[36] See pp. 942 ff. *supra*.
[37] CJEC Case 59/81 [1982] ECR p. 3329.

require the Council to take account exclusively of changes in the salaries of national civil servants when adjusting the salaries of staff members of the European Communities, the requirement meant that the Council could not, by reason of the fact that it took other criteria into consideration, omit to take account of one of the two criteria expressly referred to in the Regulation. Hence, a decision taken by the Council on the basis of factors which excluded the salaries of national civil servants could not be upheld. In interpreting Article 65 (2) of the Staff Regulations the Court held in the same case that the discretion of the Council in relation to the adjustment of remuneration to take account of a considerable increase in the cost of living was less wide than in relation to the annual adjustment of salaries. Under that provision, when the cost of living rose substantially, the Council was under an obligation to take steps to adjust the weightings, particularly in view of the fact that that provision was intended to guarantee the maintenance of equal purchasing power for all officials regardless of their place of employment. Therefore, the power available to the Council was not to determine whether weightings should be adjusted at intervals of six months or quarterly, but at intervals of two months to decide whether or not there had been a substantial increase in the cost of living and, if there had been such an increase, to draw the appropriate conclusions. Where the Council had not acted in conformity with this interpretation of the provision in question, the decision of the Council was declared improperly taken.[38]

In another case the interpretation of Article 64[39] of the Staff Regulations was contested. That regulation required that salaries be weighted, depending on the hiring conditions in the various places of employment. The CJEC held that this provision required that not only the capitals of the member states but the exact places where the duties of a sufficiently large number of staff members of the organization were performed had to be considered, with the result that in cases in which the cost of living in such a place of employment underwent fluctuations greater than those occurring in the capital of the state in question, the organization had to determine separate weightings.[40]

In the absence of written provisions there does not seem to be a general principle of law imposing an obligation on organizations to make structural adjustments to salaries. There is a discretionary power given to the organization to do so. Where there is a discretionary power, whether under the written law or not, vested in the organization relating to structural adjustments to salary, tribunals will exercise control over the exercise of that discretion. It has never been conceded that the exercise of this discretion in regard to salary

---

[38] See also *Roumengous*, CJEC Case 158/79 [1982] ECR p. 4379; *Birke*, CJEC Case 543/79 [1982] ECR p. 4425; *Battaglia*, CJEC Case 737/79 [1982] ECR p. 4497.

[39] See p. 943 *supra*.

[40] *Roumengous*, CJEC Case 158/79 [1982] ECR p. 4379. See also *Birke*, CJEC Case 543/79 [1982] ECR p. 4425, and *Battaglia*, CJEC Case 737/79 [1982] ECR p. 4497.

increases is unfettered. Undoubtedly, it is an arbitrary exercise of power that a tribunal will question but tribunals have not often been called upon to exercise control over the exercise of the discretion to increase salaries. No doubt the general principles applicable to the control of the exercise of discretionary powers are applicable. In *Lanner*[41] the Appeals Board of the OEEC referred to the possibility that a delay in procedure could result in a tainted decision.

Most of the cases in which the discretion to increase salaries for structural reasons has been examined by tribunals have been concerned with situations in which under the written law there was an obligation to adjust salaries structurally, the discretion being as to how the amount of the adjustment was to be established. There are no cases in which the law, whether written or otherwise, has not required an adjustment to be made in salaries and in which the discretionary element in the carrying out of that obligation has been reviewed.

i. *Error of law*

In *Connolly-Battisti (No. 5)*[42] the ILOAT was faced with the argument that the FAO had committed an error of law in interpreting and applying a set of guiding principles relating to the increase of salaries for cost of living. The tribunal, while stating that in such circumstances, since the texts were a set of principles and not precise requirements, they would be considered broadly and not in such a way as to put the discretion of the administration into a legal strait-jacket, found that the reduction of the increase from 5 per cent to 1 per cent was arbitrary or desgned to serve some undisclosed purpose and was, therefore, in violation of the guiding principles. The tribunal explained its conclusion as follows:

Under the Guiding Principles the calculation of an interim adjustment is very simple: for every 5 per cent by which the wage index rises, there is a corresponding increase of 5 per cent in the official's salary. When therefore the increase in the complainant's salary is reduced to 1 per cent, some explanation is clearly called for. It has not been forthcoming . . .

It is not for the complainant nor for the Tribunal to construct a case which the Organization does not wish to put forward. The Tribunal has nevertheless examined the documents exhibited by the complainant to see whether they suggest any explanation of the reduction from 5 per cent to 1 per cent which could serve to bring the Director General's decision within the spirit, if not the letter, of the Guiding Principles. Some reduction of the 5 per cent could almost certainly be justified by reference to the progressive increase of Italian income tax; paragraph 49 of the Guiding Principles appears to comtemplate that this would be a factor to be taken into account.

---

[41] Decision No. 31, OEEC Appeals Board [1960], Recueil des décisions 1 à 62 (1979) p. 85 at p. 87.
[42] ILOAT Judgment No. 323 [1977] (FAO).

Paragraph 50 on the other hand indicates that fringe benefits should be left out of account. Commissary savings, if they are to be taken into account at all, can be taken into account only as a fringe benefit. If, contrary to what is suggested in paragraph 50, they are to be taken into account as a fringe benefit in the interim adjustment, they must surely comply with paragraph 30, that is to say, as an inside benefit they must be shown to exceed corresponding outside benefits. There is no indication in the dossier that any such comparison was made for the purposes of the interim adjustment. Nor is there any calculation to be found showing what part of the reduction is attributable to the incidence of Italian taxation.

Indeed, the only conclusion that can be drawn from the material in the dossier is that the reduction of the 5 per cent was either arbitary or designed to serve some purpose of which the Tribunal is ignorant.[43]

In *Macchino Farías*[44] the ILOAT detected a different error of law. The Staff Regulations of ESO stated that the salary scales of local staff members, which in Chile were linked to the official consumer price index, 'may' be changed, 'if necessary', by the administration every month. The administration altered the incidence of changes to a quarterly system from a monthly system, contending that there was absolutely no obligation to change salaries at all. The tribunal held that the word 'may' did not give the administration a discretion to change salaries but imposed an obligation on it to change salaries to take account of the cost of living. The discretionary element lay in being able to choose between a monthly change or a quarterly change. Since the administration had acted under the impression that it had no duty to change salaries at all, it had acted under a mistaken interpretation of the law and committed an error of law which rendered the decision tainted.

ii. *Disregard of essential fact and error of fact*
In *Commission of the European Communities* v. *Council of the European Communities*[45] an increase in salary which was admittedly based on the joint consideration of two indices was in issue. In 1972/3 the indices were 3.6 per cent and 3.9 per cent. The Council chose a figure for the increase of 3.65 per cent. In 1973/4 the indices were 7.3 per cent and 3.2 per cent. The Council chose 3.3 per cent for the increase. Two allegations were made. One was that the higher index for 1972/3 was erroneous and should have been much higher. The second allegation was that in choosing the figures it did the Council abused its power.

The first allegation was in effect that there had been an error of fact in the exercise of the power. This was rejected by the Court on the ground that there was no proof that a mistake had been made.

---

[43] Ibid. at pp. 13–14.
[44] ILOAT Judgment No. 608 [1984] (ESO).
[45] CJEC Case 70/74 [1975] ECR p. 795.

The second contention was rejected on the ground that there had been no disregard of an essential factor. The Court said:

> If in a permanent system of adjustment of salaries in which the measure of the variation in national salaries is considered as resulting from the joint consideration of two indices, the Council systematically and without valid reason adopts the lower index, it would be disregarding an essential factor in the system to which it had intended to commit itself.[46]

However, since the Council had adopted the lower index only for a limited period and in the context of a system of appraisal adopted on a trial basis, there was no disregard of an essential factor.

iii. *Duty to follow established rules*

It would seem that in connection with structural salary increases, the organs of institutions must follow the maxim *legem patere quem ipse fecisti*. This requires that where an organ establishes a system in accordance with which it will exercise its discretion to increase salaries structurally, it is bound to follow that system until it changes that system. There is no restriction on the power of the organ to change the system (provided, presumably, it does not act arbitrarily, as this would be an abuse of discretion); but as long as it does not change the system, replace it, or abolish it, it must observe the requirements of the system. The ILOAT explained this rule very clearly in *Connolly-Battisti (No. 5)* where it dealt with a system established by FAO under the Staff Regulations of FAO:

> This raises a large question which, since it has not been fully argued, the Tribunal will not now completely decide. It will assume that the argument that the Organization is not bound to adopt the method prescribed by the Guiding Principles, and that it did so in 1964 solely by its own choice, is correct. It does not however follow that it may thereafter vary the system at any time. Many of the obligations put upon the Organization by the Regulations are in general terms, leaving the Organization free to choose its own method of discharging them. The method chosen may be announced in an administrative circular or similar document or it may become established by practice. Once it is settled, it becomes, until it is altered, part of the obligation. By giving reasonable notice the Organization may change the method, provided of course that the new method complies with the general terms of the obligation. But until the change is made, an official is entitled to have the obligation discharged in the manner selected by the Organization itself, and to complain if it is not. The method proposed in the Guiding Principles and adopted by the Organization has never been changed. On the contrary it has been followed for a decade.[47]

In contrast to the above, the Appeals Board of the OEEC decided a case where it held that it was apparent that a decision concerning a salary increase

---

[46] Ibid. at p. 810.
[47] ILOAT Judgment No. 323 [1977] (FAO) at pp. 9–10.

taken by the Council of OEEC did not violate any rigid system but was within the flexibility implicit in the principle of salary adjustment adopted earlier.[48] The principle *legem patere quem ipse fecisti* was, however, not denied as the tribunal did not say that there were any rigid principles established.

In *Commission of the European Communities* v. *Council of the European Communities*[49] the Council of the European Communities had adopted in 1972 for a period of three years a particular system of adjusting remuneration under Article 65 of the Staff Regulations. According to the system, in the first two years decisions would be taken by the Council in the light of two indices which were adopted. The automatic application of the arithmetical mean between the two indices was rejected. For 1972/3 the two indices disclosed an increase in the purchasing power of national salaries of 3.6 per cent and 3.9 per cent. The Commission of the European Communities proposed an increase in salaries amounting to 3.75 per cent. The Council established the increase at 2.5 per cent, which was below the lower index. The CJEC held that the Council had assumed obligations which it had bound itself to observe for the period it had defined. The Court said:

The circumstances that Article 65 by endowing the Council with a wide power of appraisal with regard to the economic and social policy of the Communities, requires it to take account of all possible relevant factors, does not prevent it from pre-determining, under certain circumstances and conditions, in a first stage and for a limited time, the framework of, and the factors to be taken into account in, its decision.[50]

The decision taken by the Council was, therefore, found to be invalid because in effect it violated the principle *legem patere quem ipse fecisti*.

iv. *Détournement de pouvoir*

In *Abrias and Others*[51] the decision of the Council of the European Communities to impose a small levy on increases in salaries for several years by amending the Staff Regulations to provide for the levy was contested. One of the grounds on which the decision was attacked was that there was a *détournement de pouvoir*, because it ignored the principle of parallelism enshrined in Article 65 of the Staff Regulations which required that the increase in the salaries in the public sectors in member States be taken into account and that the purchasing power of the salaries of staff members should not be reduced in comparison to the salaries of public servants in member States and also because the levy was motivated by reasons other than

---

[48] *Lanner*, Decision No. 31, OEEC Appeals Board [1960], Recueil des décisions 1 à 62 (1979) p. 85 at p. 88.
[49] CJEC Case 81/72 [1973] ECR p. 575.
[50] Ibid. at p. 584.
[51] CJEC Case 3/83 [1985].

those specified in the Staff Regulations. The CJEC did not deny the relevance of the principle of *détournement de pouvoir* to the exercise of the power to increase salaries for structural reasons but held that, since the decision was taken not under the Staff Regulations as they originally stood but by way of revision of the Staff Regulations under the power vested in the Council by the constituent treaty, the legality of the modification of the Staff Regulations could not be questioned by arguments based on other provisions of those Regulations which had been modified by the decision.

In *Connolly-Battisti (No. 5)*[52] it was held that the reduction of a salary increase from 5 per cent to 1 per cent was designed to serve some undisclosed purpose. Although the tribunal did not specifically state that there had been a *détournement de pouvoir*, it is clear that it was implied that the purpose behind the action taken was improper, thus, tainting the decision taken.

In *Abrias and Others* the applicants contested the decision imposing a levy also by reference to the argument that the amendment to the Staff Regulations imposing a levy was a *détournement de procédure*, since it had not been passed according to the procedure required for the imposition of a tax but by an amendment to the Staff Regulations. The CJEC held that the levy was not a tax of the same nature as those governed by the provisions relating to taxes but was essentially a levy of a temporary nature, so that it did not have to be introduced by a different procedure than was adopted. The Court did not deny that the principle of *détournement de procédure* could be applied to structural salary increases but found that on the facts of the case the principle had not been violated.

v. *Statement of reasons*

In *Abrias and Others,*[53] in dealing with the requirement of the EEC Treaty that reasons should be stated for any act, the CJEC said that the obligation, even in relation to structural salary increases, depended on the nature of the act involved. Where the act was of general application as a regulation, it was sufficient that the statement of reasons indicated the general situation behind the measure and the goals to be reached. The case did not deal with the situation where the written law is silent on the requirement of reasons.

(d) *Practice*

In the absence of binding obligations imposed by the written law of an organization, there may be an obligation to adjust salaries for cost of living or other factors created by the practice of the organization. In *de Merode*[54]

---

[52] ILOAT Judgment No. 323 [1977] (FAO).
[53] CJEC Case 3/83 [1985].
[54] WBAT Reports [1981], Decision No. 1.

the WBAT held that, while neither a statement of policy by the President of the World Bank nor a decision of the Executive Directors of the World Bank which did not state a general policy which they intended to follow in the future could create rights for the staff of the World Bank, the fact that the Bank had made periodic adjustments of salaries out of the conviction that it was legally obliged to do so had established a practice of making periodic adjustments in the salaries of staff members reflecting changes in the cost of living and other factors. This practice had become part of such conditions of employment of staff members as were fundamental and essential and could not be changed unilaterally by the Bank.

The WBAT did not spell out in detail the content of the obligation. It did say that the Bank was obliged to carry out periodic reviews of salaries taking into account various relevant factors, including the rises in the cost of living in a period of inflation, but that it retained a measure of discretion in this regard. Negatively it pointed out that the Bank was under no duty to adjust salaries automatically to increases in the cost of living, though those increases had to be considered by it in taking its decisions.[55] It is also clear from the judgment in *de Merode* that the tribunal did not come to a conclusion on whether the Bank had established a binding practice as to how it would ascertain the content of the obligation to grant structural increases in salary, since it was not called upon to do so.

In *Lanner*[56] the Appeals Board of the OEEC found that a principle of salary adjustment based on indexation had been adopted by the OEEC Council in 1958 but that the Council had not bound itself to any rigid system. Hence the flexibility it intended to retain enabled it in exceptional circumstances to introduce a limitation to the principle of indexation. In this case a practice which had become a legal obligation was not established.

(e) *Acquired rights*

The principle of acquired rights has been raised either expressly or by implication in connection with structural salary adjustments. It has been argued that staff members have in the appropriate circumstances an acquired right to a particular system of salary adjustment which could not be altered or taken away unilaterally by the organization. But generally this argument has not met with much success. The argument is different from that which the WBAT discussed in *de Merode* and was based on practice, though the effect is for all practical purposes the same. In both cases the consequence of the argument is that a right to certain salary adjustments which cannot unilaterally be taken away or altered is sought to be established.

---

55 Ibid. at p. 56.
56 Decision No. 31, OEEC Appeals Board [1960], Recueil des décisions 1 à 62 (1979) p. 85.

In *Lamadie (No. 2) and Kraanen*[57] the applicants argued that the staff members of the EPO who had been in the IPI had an acquired right to the salary system, which included the system of salary adjustment of the European Communities, because the Staff Regulations of the IPI incorporated that system. The ILOAT held that the written law of the IPI did not give staff members a continuing right to the salary system of the European Communities but only established the IPI salary system on the same basis as that of the European Communities when the Staff Regulations of the IPI came into force on 1 January 1972. It was a one-time equivalence. Thus, this argument based on acquired rights had to fail.

The applicants also argued that the former staff members of IPI had an acquired right to the system of salary adjustment practised in the IPI, even after they became part of the EPO. The ILOAT stated that the applicants had no acquired right to the methods of salary adjustment practised in the IPI. No detailed explanation of why this was so was given, although it cannot perhaps be doubted that in the circumstances of the case the tribunal's conclusion was correct.

In *Decision No. 93*[58] for the year 1975/6 NATO decided on a salary increase equivalent to 80 per cent of the rise in the cost-of-living index. For the first half of the calendar year 1976 a change was made and the increase was paid at the equivalent of two-thirds of the rise in the cost-of-living index. The applicant claimed 100 per cent of the rise in the cost-of-living index for the whole fiscal year. He contended that his acquired rights had been taken away and that the second decision was retroactive and, therefore, illegal. The Appeals Board of NATO held that there was no acquired right to an increase equivalent to 100 per cent of the rise in the cost-of-living index, since the right to a salary increase was not an individual one but was contained in the Staff Regulations which could be modified. The distinction made was between individual and statutory rights, the latter not being subject to acquisition. The decision was also found not to be retroactive.

While this decision held that there was no acquired right to a salary increase in the case, it did not deny that the principle of retroactivity was relevant to salary adjustments for cost of living and other reasons. Further, it held that, even if the action taken did not interfere with an acquired right, it should not in any way upset the balance of the contract of employment, which it did not do. The above requirement was additional. It was not dependent on nor related to the doctrine of acquired rights, in the understanding of the tribunal.

[57] ILOAT Judgment No. 365 [1978] (IPI/EPO). See also *Biggio (No. 3) et al.*, ILOAT Judgment No. 366 [1978] (IPI/EPO); *Mertens (No. 2)*, ILOAT Judgment No. 371 [1979] (EPO).
[58] *Decision No. 93*, NATO Appeals Board [1978], Collection of the Decisions 65(b), 74 to 99 (1979).

In *Decisions Nos. 174–180, 182, 184–186, 188–195*[59] the Appeals Board of NATO was confronted with the same situation which was found to exist in *Abrias and Others*,[60] which was decided by the CJEC at about the same time. A levy had been imposed on salary increases for a specific period by a decision of the NATO Council. The tribunal held that the imposition of the levy was not retroactive nor upset the balance of the contract and, therefore, could not be questioned. The provisions dealing with structural salary increases did not create acquired rights and could be unilaterally changed. Further, although they did not create acquired rights, they could be changed, only if the amendment or modification did not upset the balance of the contract and was non-retroactive. What the NATO Council had done in imposing the levy also did not upset the balance of the contract nor was retroactive, and therefore could not be questioned. In *Abrias and Others*[61] the CJEC faced a similar argument ostensibly based on acquired rights. The applicants argued that the principle of parallelism in Article 65 of the Staff Regulations of the European Communities could not be modified unilaterally because it was a fundamental element in the contract of employment. This argument was rejected by the CJEC. First, it was stated that there was no violation of the legitimate expectancy of officials, because already in 1980 the Council of the European Communities had expressed an intention to modify the system established in 1976 and the staff unions had been closely associated in the establishment of the levy. Second, the system established in 1976 contained a caveat that the Council was entitled to determine whether that system could be corrected for eventual distortions or improved. For both reasons, the CJEC concluded that the applicants could not claim that their acquired rights had been violated, because the right to a structural salary increase was such that it could be modified by the Council in the circumstances in which the modification was made. In *Amos et al.*[62] the Appeals Board of OECD, confronted with a similar situation as the CJEC was in *Abrias and Others*, held that acquired rights had not been violated by the imposition of the levy, because it had not interfered with such a condition of employment as would have induced staff members to accept employment in the OECD and also did not upset the balance of the employment contract. The tribunal also held that the rule against retroactivity had not been violated.

The CJEC and the Appeals Boards of NATO and the OECD gave different reasons for finding that an acquired right had not been violated and that the terms of employment had not been breached. However, they were agreed

[59] *Decisions Nos. 174–180, 182, 184–186, 188–195*, NATO Appeals Board [1985].

[60] CJEC Case 3/83 [1985].

[61] Ibid.

[62] Decision No. 105, OECD Appeals Board [1985]. See also *Gouin and Strub*, Decision No. 106, ibid.

that acquired rights had not been violated by the imposition of a small levy on salary increases.

A similar levy as that imposed on salary increases in NATO, OECD, and the European Communities was imposed by the Council of Europe. In *Stevens and Others*[63] the Appeals Board of the Council of Europe took a different view from that of the Appeals Board of NATO and the CJEC. The tribunal held that the staff had an individual right to the salary scales established as a result of the decision to increase salaries and that the increase given could not be reduced unilaterally by the imposition of a levy. The tribunal stated:

The alteration which was decided unilaterally had, as a result, reduced the remuneration to which the staff were entitled. Now, in this case, the legal position of the appellants as members of the staff of the Council of Europe, could not be unilaterally altered by the Administration.

Such an alteration reducing the remuneration of the staff adversely affects their individual rights in the conditions in which it was carried out; it could only be decided after and in agreement with the staff of the Organization. This does not affect the power of the Committee of Ministers to impose wage restraint, even during the period covered by the fixed scales, if they should be justified by exceptionally serious and urgent circumstances, which is not the case here.[64]

It is not clear whether the tribunal regarded the situation as one involving a reduction of salary or of reduction of a salary increase. However, it is significant that, while it regarded the imposition of the levy in the circumstances as a violation of acquired rights, it did say that in exceptionally serious and urgent circumstances wage restraints may be exercised which could result in the reduction of salary increases.

There is a basic conflict between the cases which take the view that there is no acquired right to a structural salary increase because it is not an individual right which cannot be unilaterally modified by the institution but is a statutory right relating to the organizational structure of the institution, which can be modified unilaterally by the institution, at least in certain circumstances, and *Stevens and Others* which concludes that the right to a salary increase is an acquired right which cannot be unilaterally modified by the institution. *Stevens and Others* clearly dealt with a situation involving the reduction of a salary increase. It cannot truly be regarded as a case dealing with reductions in salary which are generally not permitted, as has been seen.

The conflict cannot be resolved by reference to the particular written laws and legal systems of the different organizations concerned, particularly because there does not seem to be any material difference in those laws or

---

[63] Council of Europe Appeals Board [1985], Appeals Nos. 101–113, Case-Law Digest (1985) p. 144.
[64] Ibid. at p. 153.

systems. It would appear, therefore, that one of these views is preferable to the other. The weight of authority is in favour of the view that the right to salary increases is not by itself an acquired right, as long as it flows from the statutory law of the organization.

A significant qualification was made by the Appeals Board of NATO when it said that the action taken in reducing the salary increase or abolishing it altogether must not upset the balance of the contract. Further, the fact that staff members may not have an acquired right as such to structural salary adjustments does not affect the possibility, discussed earlier, that they may have a right, which cannot be unilaterally modified by the institution, to such adjustments as a result of the practice of the institution.

(f) Discrimination and inequality of treatment

The principles of non-discrimination and equality of treatment have been considered relevant to the issue of salary adjustments for cost of living and other factors. The European Communities had, pursuant to the provisions of the Staff Regulations, weighted the salaries of officials, their remuneration being determined at each place of employment, taking into account the local practice, and set aside sums in the budget for specific local establishments for increases in salary occurring under these provisions. Staff members who were not working in these various local establishments contended that they were discriminated against by this measure. The CJEC, while not denying that the principle of non-discrimination was relevant to structural salary adjustments, held that there was no discrimination involved in the provision of the Staff Regulations and that, as long as they were followed, there could be no claim that the setting aside of the sums in the budget for increases in salaries of staff members at specific local establishments was illegal.[65] In *de Los Cobos and Wenger*[66] it was held that some categories of officials may be exempted from reductions in remuneration while others are not, if there is good reason for the distinction between categories. Thus, experts who were paid out of funds obtained from outside the ILO, General Service Category staff in the field offices whose remuneration was lower or who were in a special social situation, and those who voluntarily helped to ease the financial burden of the organization could legally be exempted from reduction in salary while others were not.[67]

---

[65] *Asmussen and Others*, CJEC Case 50/74 [1975] ECR p. 1003.

[66] ILOAT Judgment No. 391 [1980] (ILO).

[67] See also *Van Lamoen*, Council of Europe Appeals Board, Appeal No. 100 [1984], Case-Law Digest (1985) p. 137. In this case also it was held that a distinction made in salary administration was legitimate. The difference made was between temporary staff members and permanent staff members. The former were not given the same allowances for cost of living and expatriation as the latter.

There have been no instances where a tribunal has held that salary adjust-ments on the basis of cost of living and other factors have been implemented in a discriminatory manner in such a way as to result in inequality of treatment.

(g) *Temporary staff*

In *Van Lamoen*[68] the Appeals Board of the Council of Europe has held that temporary staff may not be entitled to the same allowances based on the cost of living as permanent staff members.

Salary scales

There does not seem to be a general rule that salary scales cannot be changed. In several cases decided by the OASAT it was held that the introduction of new scales by the OAS on the adoption of a system of parity in salaries with the UN was not illegal.[69] According to these decisions staff must accept the new scales. In *Alaniz and Others* the tribunal explained the change as a nova-tion of contractual terms but undoubtedly the same principle would be applicable where the employment relationship is not based on contract. Where the system of parity with the UN was subsequently abandoned and new salary scales were introduced, the OASAT again held that the change could not be questioned.[70]

While some difficult questions, such as whether the maximum of a range in a salary scale may be reduced by the introduction of a new scale, have not been presented to international administrative tribunals, there is some juris-prudence on the implementation and application of changes in salary scales.

In *Belchamber*[71] the UNAT held that, whether by practice or under the Staff Regulations, the UN had a duty to consult with the staff representatives before altering the salary scales of General Service category staff in Geneva. However, the tribunal found that the obligation had not been violated, purely because the staff had not consulted a second time with the ICSC and with the administration after the ICSC made its recommendations. The staff had failed to avail itself of that opportunity so that the fault was not that of

[68] Council of Europe Appeals Board, Appeal No. 100 [1984], ibid.

[69] See *Alaniz and Others*, OASAT Judgment No. 13 [1975], and *Buchholz and Others*, OASAT Judgment No. 37 [1978].

[70] *Chisman and Others*, OASAT Judgment No. 64 [1982]. In *Decision No. 77*, NATO Appeals Board [1977], Collection of the Decisions 65(b), 74 to 99 (1979), the Appeals Board of NATO affirmed that, while new salary scales might be introduced, salaries could not be reduced.

[71] UNAT Judgment No. 236 [1978], JUNAT Nos. 231–300 p. 39. For a detailed discussion of this case and the cases that follow on consultation with staff, see Ch. 44 pp. 995 ff. *infra*.

the administration. In *Bénard and Coffino*[72] the issue was whether the proper procedure had been followed by the administration of ICITO-GATT before new salary scales were adopted for the General Service category staff. The applicants argued that there was an agreement to negotiate with the staff prior to the adoption of the new scales. The ILOAT held that, even if there had been such an agreement with the Staff Association, it must become a part of the Staff Regulations or become part of the practice of the organization, if it was to obligate the administration. In the absence of such incorporation or practice the applicants could only rely on the Staff Regulations which required consultation with the Staff Committee on matters of policy including salaries. Consultation did not necessarily mean negotiation or collective bargaining. Hence, since the Staff Regulations had not been ignored, the organization had not violated the rights of the applicants. There was no general principle of law which gave the staff a right to bargain collectively or negotiate with the administration before a change in salary scales was made.[73]

In *Alaniz and Others*[74] the OASAT held that, where there was a change of salary scale, the appropriate standards set by the OAS had to be followed in the implementation of the new scales. Where this was not done, the applicants were given a remedy. In *Chilot et al.*[75] the Appeals Board of the OECD held that, upon the establishment of a new system for fixing the salaries of auxiliary staff, which was more favourable than the previous criteria used, the applicants had no right to retroactive application of the new system of fixing salaries. They had been treated according to their contracts of employment and, therefore, had no reason to complain.

Inequality of treatment in the application of a new scale is actionable. This means, among other things, that those in different situations must be treated differently. In *Connolly-Battisti (No. 4)*[76] the applicant, who had stagnated at a certain incremental step for seven years because of the budgetary policy of the FAO, received only one increment when this policy was changed and new salary scales were introduced, as did others who had been at the same incremental step as her for a much shorter period of time. It was possible to

[72] ILOAT Judgment No. 380 [1979] (ICITO-GATT). See also *Domon and Lhoest*, ILOAT Judgment No. 381 [1979] (WHO); *Hatt and Leuba*, ILOAT Judgment No. 382 [1979] (WMO).
[73] In *Hatt and Leuba*, ILOAT Judgment No. 382 [1979] (WMO), the Staff Regulations of the WMO referred to the equivalent scales of the office of the United Nations in Geneva as being the criterion for the salary scales of the staff in the WMO. This provision, it was held, permitted the salary scales adopted on the basis of equivalence with the scales of the UN to be questioned, if the Secretary General of the UN had not followed the proper procedure before establishing them. The tribunal found on the basis of a decision of the UNAT which dealt with the legality of those salary scales established by the UN that the Secretary General of the UN had not violated any legal requirements.
[74] OASAT Judgment No. 13 [1975].
[75] Decision No. 93, OECD Appeals Board [1982], Recueil des décisions 83 à 102 [1983] p. 32.
[76] ILOAT Judgment No. 294 [1977] (FAO).

grant her more than one such increment. It was held by the ILOAT that this resulted in inequality of treatment. In the interpretation and application of the regulations of the FAO the administration had to act in such a way as to avoid causing such inequality of treatment. Subsequently, in a case concerning the execution of the judgment in the above case, the ILOAT held that, where there was a choice between the increase in salary (10 per cent) implicit in the judgment of the tribunal and new salary scales, the applicant could not choose some elements of the old system and some of the new to suit her purpose.[77] In *Comolli*[78] the OASAT held that in the case of the holder of a fixed-term contract for two years the contract governed his salary which could not be changed by the adoption of a new salary scale for permanent employees. The situation of the applicant was held to be different from that of a permanent employee.

As the decisions on procedure and inequality of treatment discussed above show, while the establishment or change of salary scales is a matter for the administration of an organization, it seems likely that tribunals will review the decisions taken in this regard in certain circumstances. It would seem to be reasonable that such review will be based on the treatment of the decisions as decisions taken in the exercise of a discretionary power in a very general sense.[79]

Remedies

(a) Reduction of salaries

In *Chisman and Others*, where the OASAT found that the salaries of certain applicants had been reduced, it made an order for specific performance in the following terms:

[T]hat in cases where there was a reduction in salary, the Secretary General is obliged to pay the complainants the differences between the salary they received in the month of December 1978, counting in the payment authorized by resolution AG/RES. 499 (X-0/80), and the salary they received beginning on January 1, 1979.[80]

(b) Salary adjustments

Where the ILOAT found that a decision structurally to increase salaries was tainted because it was arbitrary, a 10 per cent interim adjustment being called

---

[77] *Connolly-Battisti (No. 8)*, ILOAT Judgment No. 401 [1980] (FAO).

[78] OASAT Judgment No. 17 [1975].

[79] In *Cardena*, ILOAT Judgment No. 39 [1958] (ITU) at p. 4, it was said that the salary scales adopted must not result in arbitrary or unjustifiable treatment of officials.

[80] OASAT Judgment No. 64 [1982] at p. 29.

for when a 2 per cent adjustment had been awarded, the ILOAT ordered that the decision of the Director General of FAO ordering a 2 per cent adjustment be quashed and 'that the pensionable salary payment made to the complainant on 28 May 1975 be recalculated on the basis that there should have been a 10 per cent interim adjustment instead of a 2 per cent, and that payment be made accordingly'.[81] In *Macchino Farías*,[82] where the decision to make quarterly adjustments to salaries was made as a result of an error of law, the ILOAT remitted the case to the Director General of ESO to take a new decision on the correct basis. In *Stevens and Others,*[83] where the Appeals Board of the Council of Europe found that the levies on salary increases could not be legally imposed, the tribunal ordered the decisions to impose such levies annulled and the reimbursement of the sums wrongfully levied.

In *Commission of the European Communities* v. *Council of the European Communities*[84] the CJEC found that the salary increase in question had not been taken in accordance with the system adopted by the respondent. It ordered that the increase be declared void and in effect that the decision to increase salaries be taken in accordance with its judgment. Pursuant to the EEC Treaty the increase already ordered was allowed to have effect till the new decisions were taken. Similarly where the Court found that the weightings of salary increases had not been properly done, it ordered that the decisions be annulled and the same action be taken as was ordered in the case cited above.[85] In *Roumengous*, where the weighting of salaries had also not been properly done, the Court stated that it:

[A]nnuls that applicant's salary statement for January 1979, in so far as it is restricted to giving effect to Council Regulation No. 3087/78, both as to the amount of the adjustment of the weighting and as to the retroactive effect of that adjustment, together with the decisions rejecting the applicant's complaints; declares Regulation No. 3087/78 not applicable to the applicant in so far as it takes no account of the cost of living in Varese and limits the retroactive effect of the adjustment of the weighting to 1 January 1978 . . .[86]

It then ordered the respondent to report back to the Court before a certain date on the measures taken to compensate the applicant.

---

[81] *Connolly-Battisti (No. 5)*, ILOAT Judgment No. 323 [1977] (FAO) at p. 15.

[82] ILOAT Judgment No. 608 [1984] (ESO).

[83] Council of Europe Appeals Board, Appeals Nos. 101–113 [1985], Case-Law Digest (1985) p. 144.

[84] CJEC Case 81/72 [1973] ECR p. 575.

[85] *Commission of the European Communities* v. *Council of the European Communities*, CJEC Case 59/81 [1982] ECR p. 3329.

[86] CJEC Case 158/79 [1982] ECR p. 4379 at p. 4403.

(c) Salary scales

In *Connolly-Battisti* (*No. 4*) the ILOAT found that the treatment of the applicant on the introduction of new salary scales had resulted in inequality of treatment, because she had been placed at step XII of grade G6 instead of step XIV. The tribunal ordered that the decision of the respondent placing her at step XII be quashed and that the respondent take steps necessary to ensure that '[t]he complainant is treated as if on 1 February 1975 she had been at step XIV in grade G.6 for a period of five months.'[87]

In *Alaniz and Others*[88] the OASAT found that standards adopted by the OAS had not been fully applied in the implementation of new salary scales. The tribunal ordered specific performance as if the standards had been applied in the following terms:

[C]onsequently, complainants are entitled to receive the following differences covering the period July 1, 1970–April 1973;

A. The difference between the schedule applied by the OAS General Secretariat and the United Nations schedule for the period July 1, 1970–January 1, 1971;
B. The difference between salaries liquidated by the General Secretariat of the OAS and the United Nations schedule for the period January 1–June 30, 1972;
C. Any difference that may have resulted between the salary paid by the OAS General Secretariat and the United Nations schedule in force during February, March and April of 1973.[89]

In *Comolli*,[90] where the OASAT found that new salary scales did not apply to a fixed-term contract holder, because his two-year contract governed the terms of his remuneration, the tribunal ordered that the OASAT treat him according to his contract and pay his salary accordingly. The organization was ordered to return to the applicant any sums he may have repaid the organization on the basis that the new scales applied to him.

(d) Specific performance

In virtually all the above cases where salary payments were practically in issue the tribunal ordered some form of specific performance, annulling tainted decisions where appropriate. In one case it remanded the case for rectification of the decision annulled.

---

[87] ILOAT Judgment No. 294 [1977] (FAO) at p. 6.
[88] OASAT Judgment No. 13 [1975].
[89] Ibid. at p. 5.
[90] OASAT Judgment No. 17 [1975].

CHAPTER FORTY-FOUR

The Right of Association

THE right of the staff of international organizations to associate featured in a way in the very first case that was presented to the UNAT in 1950 soon after its creation,[1] in so far as the *locus standi* of the UN Staff Association before the UNAT and the rights of that Association in respect of cases brought before the UNAT was raised as an issue. Subsequently there have been many cases brought before international administrative tribunals in which this right of association has been the subject of litigation in one form or another. The right of the staff of international organizations to associate has often been canvassed strongly by the staff itself and, moreover, it would seem that tribunals have tended to regard this right as of considerable importance, even though they have not always agreed with the views presented by the staff and their Associations.

While tribunals have seldom disagreed among themselves on the more fundamental principles governing the right of the staff to associate and Staff Associations or Unions, it is generally on a few significant points of disagreement between staff and their employers that they have had to pronounce with the result that they have not been able to focus systematically on the subject of the right of association. Thus, they have had to deal with such issues as the right to strike and the right of the organization to make deductions from salary for absence resulting from strikes or the obligation of the organization to consult or negotiate with the Staff Associations before changing salary scales, but they have not had the opportunity of developing a general body of law as such on the subject of the right of the staff of international organizations to associate. Further, in many cases they have been able to settle disputes by interpreting the written law of the organization concerned, albeit sometimes in the light of general principles of law, because the Staff Regulations and Staff Rules of almost all international organizations have fairly substantial provisions on the rights of the staff to associate and the rights of their Associations. In addition, the Statutes of the tribunals themselves are sufficiently clear in regard to the rights of Staff Associations in so far as procedural matters are concerned, even though this results from absence of specific provision rather than from explicit statement. Nevertheless, tribunals have had some interesting cases to decide and have been able significantly to contribute to the development of this area of the law of the

---

[1] *Aubert and 14 Others*, UNAT Judgment No. 1 [1950], JUNAT Nos. 1–70, p. 1.

international civil service, even if they have not had the opportunity to field
all the important questions relating to it.

Staff members of international organizations have had their Associations
or Unions from the early days of the first truly international secretariat, the
League of Nations. From that time on the staff of most international
organizations have had their Associations or Unions, whatever the size and
nature of the organization.[2] What is more, almost all staff members of these
institutions are members of the Associations or Unions belonging to their
organization, even if some of them are members only in name. Thus, in the
UN even Under Secretaries General are members of the UN Staff Association. Staff Associations or Unions have international officials who are paid
employees to present to their employers their views regarding their terms and
conditions of employment and to exert influence and at times put pressure on
the decisions taken by their employers in regard to these. The need for this is
felt all the more in the case of employees of international organizations,
because they do not enjoy the benefit of true parliamentary controls or
generally of the impact of public opinion, as is the case of employees at the
national level. Moreover, the appropriate needs of the function of public
international organizations have not been perceived as being in opposition to
the collective expression of the interests of their employees through such
organs as Staff Associations or Unions.

Provisions of the written law

The written law of most organizations generally recognizes in some form the
right of their staff to associate and to have continuous contact with the
administration of these organizations. The emphasis seems to be on facilitating communication between the representatives of the staff and the
administrative authority, though there is nothing like uniformity in the
manner in which the written law of the various organizations deals with
the issue of the right to associate.

Article 47 of the Staff Regulations of the Council of Europe provides as
follows: 'Staff members shall enjoy the right to associate; they may in parti-

---

[2] On Staff Associations and Staff Unions in general and their history see: Beigbeder, *La
Représentation du personnel à l'Organization mondiale de la santé et dans les principales
institutions spécialisées des Nations Unies ayant leur siège en Europe* (1975); Busch, *Dienstrecht
der Vereinten Nationen* (1981) pp. 227 ff.; Plantey, *The International Civil Service: Law and
Management* (1981) pp. 122 ff.; Szasz, 'Unions of International Civil Servants', 69 *Proc. ASIL*
(1975) p. 100; Szasz, 'Unions of International Officials, Past, Present and Future', 14 *Journal
of International Law and Politics* (1982) p. 807; Lemoine and Maupain, 'Le Défense des intérêts
des agents internationaux par les associations du personnel', *Colloque d'Aix-en-Provence*,
Société française pour droit international (1985) p. 352.

cular, belong to trade unions or professional organizations.'[3] Appendix I to the Staff Regulations deals with staff participation, institutionalizes the association of staff members, and provides for the representation of the general interests of the staff and for the availability of a channel for the expression of its opinions.[4] The Staff Regulations and Staff Rules of the UN attempt, in a different way, to achieve the same objective as the Staff Regulations of the Council of Europe by explicitly setting up a body representative of the staff for the purpose of maintaining contacts with the administrative authority, although they do not specifically refer to the right of association. The Staff Regulations provide:

Regulation 8.1: (*a*) A Staff Council, elected by the Staff, shall be established for the purpose of ensuring continuous contact between the staff and the Secretary General. The Council shall be entitled to make proposals to the Secretary General for improvements in the situation of staff members, both as regards their conditions of work and their general conditions of life.

(*b*) The Staff Council shall be composed in such a way as to afford equitable representation to all levels of the staff.

(*c*) Election of the Staff Council shall take place annually under regulations drawn up by the Staff Council and agreed to by the Secretary General.

Regulation 8.2: The Secretary General shall establish joint administrative machinery with staff participation to advise him regarding personnel policies and general questions of staff welfare and to make to him such proposals as it may desire for amendment of the Staff Regulations and Rules.[5]

Rules 108.1 and 108.2 of the Staff Rules elaborate on the Staff Council and on Joint Committees.[6] Principle 10.1 of the Principles of Staff Employment of the World Bank deals with Staff Consultation. While the right to associate is specifically mentioned therein, the emphasis is on the facilitation of consultation between staff and the administration. The Principle provides that:

The efficient and harmonious conduct of the Organizations' business requires that the President be cognizant of staff views in matters concerning the staff and that these views be given due consideration. In recognition of the right of staff to associate, the President shall establish appropriate mechanisms to consult with representative members of the staff selected by the staff about the establishment of and changes in personnel policies, conditions of employment, general questions of staff welfare, and the establishment, amendment or revocation of Principles and of Staff Rules.[7]

The Staff Rule elaborating on the above Principle of Staff Employment has not been issued yet.

---

[3] See Appendix VI *infra*.
[4] See Appendix VI *infra*.
[5] See Appendix V *infra*.
[6] See Appendix V *infra*.
[7] See Appendix VII *infra*.

The Staff Regulations and Staff Rules of many other organizations contain provisions dealing in effect with the right to associate, although in most cases the emphasis is on the element of consultation.[8] Many of these instruments do not specifically refer to the right of association but some of them elaborate in detail on how representative bodies should be constituted. The fact, however, that the written law of most international institutions has provisions relating to the relations between the staff and the administration through representative bodies testifies to the importance attached to this aspect of the rights of the staff of international organizations even by the organizations themselves.

The right of association

While the fact that the written law of most international organizations has specific provisions relating to the organization of the staff in representative bodies for the purpose of consulting with and expressing the views of staff members to the administrative authorities of these institutions reflects a general recognition of the right of association, it seems to be generally recognized also that a general principle of law concedes to staff members the right of association as a channel for the expression of opinions and to provide consultative mechanisms to the administrative authorities of international organizations. Thus, as early as 1952 the UNAT stated:

The right of association is recognized by articles 20 and 23(4) of the Universal Declaration of Human Rights, adopted by the third General Assembly: The Tribunal notes that the Secretary General has taken steps to make known to the staff his clear views that the staff should be organized in an association with rights of representation to the Administration. The Tribunal is satisfied that the principle of the right of association to which the United Nations are solemnly pledged is admitted on all sides to be a principle which must prevail also inside the organization's own Secretariat.[9]

In addition to the Universal Declaration of Human Rights, Article 8 of the International Covenant on Economic, Social and Cultural Rights recognizes

---

[8] See, e.g., Article 10.1 of the Staff Regulations of the ILO: Amerasinghe (ed.), 4 *Staff Regulations and Staff Rules of Selected International Organizations* (1983) p. 186 at p. 251; Article VIII of the Staff Regulations and Staff Rules 910 to 930 of the WHO: Amerasinghe (ed.), ibid. p. 118 at pp. 166 ff.; Section 4.10 of the Personnel Policies of IFAD: Amerasinghe (ed.), 1 ibid. p. 182 at p. 197; Section 381 of the Personnel Policies of the IDB: Amerasinghe (ed.), 1 ibid. p. 209 at pp. 352 ff.; Rule 9.1 of the Staff Rules of the AFDB: Amerasinghe (ed.), 2 ibid. p. 275 at p. 380; Article 9 and Annex II of the Staff Regulations of the European Communities: Amerasinghe (ed.), 4 ibid., p. 1 at pp. 12, 34; Rules 109.1 and 109.2 of the Staff Rules of the OAS: Amerasinghe (ed.), 3 ibid. p. 214 at p. 261.

[9] *Robinson*, UNAT Judgment No. 15 [1952] JUNAT Nos. 1–70 p. 43 at p. 47.

the right of association.[10] It follows that, once a general principle of law exists recognizing a right to associate, staff members would enjoy that right even in the absence of its incorporation in the statutory law of an international organization. Further, where the written law is absent, the contents of the right of association would derive from the general principle of law.

Other tribunals have not hesitated to emphasize that the right to associate exists as a matter of general principle. In *Connolly-Battisti (No. 7)* the ILOAT said:

The Organization, in common with all others, recognizes the right of the staff in accordance with the principle of freedom of association 'to organize for the purpose of safeguarding and promoting its interests'; MS 301.081. Nor is it disputed that it is for the staff to organise itself and not for the Director General to organise it. It is however generally accepted that the existence of a good and efficient staff association is essential to good staff relations and so is a concern of the Administration. All organisations therefore have in their regulations a section similar to the FAO's Article VIII in which the ways of maintaining contact between the Administration and the staff association are described.[11]

In *García and Márquez (No. 2)* the ILOAT repeated its conviction that the right of association was a recognized general principle of law:

Their claims are only in respect of alleged breaches by the Administration of Staff Rules 910 and 920 and of the principle of freedom of association.

The principle is accepted by the Organization and Article VIII of the Staff Regulations (which is headed 'Staff Relations' and requires the Director to make provision for staff participation in the discussion of policies relating to staff questions) and Staff Rules made thereunder give effect to the principle. The Rules provide inter alia that staff shall have the right to associate themselves together in a formal organisation for the purpose of developing staff activities and making representations to the Bureau concerning personnel policy and conditions of service; that Staff Associations shall have the right to request their membership for voluntary financial contributions; and that the Bureau may give financial assistance to any such Association in the furtherance of activities beneficial to the staff provided the membership of the Association also contributes substantially to such activity. The rights conferred by these rules must be taken together with those that are derived from the general principle; they are referred to below compendiously as the 'right to associate'. By each contract of appointment the Organization accepts as part of the contractual terms the obligation not to infringe the right to associate. Consequently any decision by the Organization which involves an infringement may be made the subject of complaint by any persons holding such a contract.[12]

[10] For the Universal Declaration of Human Rights see Brownlie, *Basic Documents in International Law* (1972) p. 148. For the International Covenant on Economic, Social and Cultural Rights see Brownlie, ibid. p. 154.
[11] ILOAT Judgment No. 403 [1980] (FAO).
[12] ILOAT Judgment No. 496 [1982] (PAHO).

In both these statements there is expressed the understanding that, while the right of association may be recognized in the written law of an organization, it derives from a broader general principle of law and is to be construed in the light of such general principle, particularly where the written law is silent or inadequate. The CJEC has also implied in its approach to the right of association in the European Communities that the right is based on a general principle of law with the result that its scope depends on that general principle, in the absence of specific provision in the written law.[13]

It cannot be disputed that the right to associate, flowing as it does from a general principle of law, will to some extent have a legal dimension of its own, regardless of the statutory or written law of the organization concerned. By the same token, while the written law of an organization may interpret the content of the right in the context of the organization and its needs, since there may be considerable flexibility in this regard, it cannot derogate from or violate the general principle and its contents by reflecting conditions or elements for the exercise of the right of association which are in conflict with the requirements of the general principle. Thus, in an appropriate situation, a tribunal may conceivably be called upon to pronounce as an issue on the compatibility of a statutory or contractual provision with the general principle of law, although thus far no tribunal has had occasion to do so. On the other hand, there have been many occasions on which tribunals have been confronted with situations where they have had to supplement the written law by reference to the general principle in the absence of explicit provision in the written law for what is required by the general principle.

There are several levels at which problems connected with the right of association may have to be solved by tribunals. Where the written law deals with the situation, what may be required is a proper interpretation and application of the written law, particularly where the written law is not incompatible with the general principle of law. On the other hand, where the written law is in conflict with the general principle of law, as already pointed out, the tribunal may have to override the written law and give effect to the general principle of law. Sometimes the written law may be unclear. Then the tribunal will be called upon to interpret the written law, but in conformity with the general principle of law relating to the right to associate. This has happened in some cases. Finally, the written law may simply be silent or inadequate and not reflect the totality of the contents of the general principle of law relating to the right to associate. The tribunal has then had to import the law from the contents of the general principle of law as it understands it and settle the dispute by applying the general principle of law. This also has been done in some cases.

---

[13] See *Willame*, CJEC Case 110/63 [1965] ECR p. 649.

Staff-Association activities

A question that has come before the ILOAT is whether staff members can devote time taken from their hours of duty for the organization to Staff-Association activities. In *Connolly-Battisti (No. 7)*[14] the tribunal found that the applicant had in fact not disobeyed directions given by her supervisor in regard to the amount of time she should have spent on her functions as an office-bearer of one of the Staff Associations of FAO. Hence, she had in any case not acted in such a way as to call for a warning of severe disciplinary measures. However, the tribunal in the course of its judgment made some important general remarks about activities for Staff Associations and facilities available to staff members in respect of their right to associate.

The warning was not given because the complainant had been neglecting her duties out of idleness or truancy. It was given because she was devoting some part of the working day to the affairs of the NLA. The Organization, in common with all others, recognises the right of the staff in accordance with the principle of freedom of association 'to organize for the purpose of safeguarding and promoting its interests'; MS 301.081. Nor is it disputed that it is for the staff to organise itself and not for the Director General to organise it . . . What is not described in the regulations are the facilities which, because of the Administration's interest in the efficient working of the staff association, it is now customary for the Administration to guarantee or provide. The most important of these is permission for the chairman and other officers of the association to take 'time off' within reasonable limits for the association's work.[15]

Two points of significance are made. First, it is recognized that it is for the staff to organize itself and not for the administration to organize it. Second, reference is made to the facility of spending official time on Staff-Association activities.

It will be noted that the ILOAT describes the facility of taking official time off to work for Staff Associations as being subject to permission granted by the organization. It is not clear what the implication of this statement is. It is not specifically stated that the staff members concerned have a right to this facility or that the organization is under an obligation to afford this facility. Perhaps it was regarded as unnecessary to deal with this aspect of the matter, since in fact organizations, as observed, in their own interest guarantee this facility. It would seem that the practice of granting this facility which has become customary among organizations probably reflects an understanding that staff members have a right to it as a matter of general principle. While the right may exist in the abstract, however, it is a matter for decision by the organization how the right is to be given substance in given situations. There

---

[14] ILOAT Judgment No. 403 [1980] (FAO).
[15] Ibid. at p. 8.

may be an element of discretion involved but finally the exercise of discretion would be subject to control by administrative tribunals. While organizations may decide initially how much and when time off may be taken, a decision which is governed both by the interests of the organization in having staff members perform their functions efficiently and by the interests of the staff in having an effective form of association, administrative tribunals would ultimately be able to review the decision taken. There has been no clear instance, however, where a tribunal has in fact reversed a decision of an administration in this regard.

In a general way the CJEC adverted in *Willame*[16] to the issue of the right of staff members to take time off from their official duties for Staff-Association activities. In that case a staff member's dismissal from service was found unlawful. The CJEC, while refusing to base its decision in the case on any denial of this right, because it had other reasons for finding the dismissal unlawful, stated in regard to the issue of staff activities:

The Court merely finds that the Establishment Board was bound to examine the extent to which his activity could, without any fault on his part, have had an unfavourable influence not only on the quantity but also on the quality of the work involved in his post as provided for in the budget.

In fact, the applicant played a very important and permanent role on the staff side; moreover, these activities took place in an institution with a large staff at a time when the entry into force of the Staff Regulations required increased vigilance and activity on the part of the staff representatives. In such a situation it was the duty of the institution to assist the staff representatives as much as possible in order to prevent their having to choose, through no fault of their own, between neglecting to defend the interests of the staff or endangering their own integration by shortcomings in their posts as provided for in the budget.[17]

The Court recognized that there existed an obligation on the part of the organization to make allowance for the performance of functions by staff representatives, especially in the situation in which the organization was placed at the time, so much so that the organization had to enable staff members to perform those functions without causing shortcomings in their work in their substantive positions. The obligation corresponded to a right on the part of the staff to have this facility guaranteed to them and undoubtedly the right flowed from the general principle of law that the staff had a right to associate.

While the Court related the right of the staff member and the obligation of the organization to assist the staff member in respect of activities as a representative of the staff to the particular situation of the organization at the time in question, it did not confine its analysis of the rights of staff members

---

[16] CJEC Case 110/63 [1965] ECR p. 649.
[17] Ibid. at p. 665.

to the special situation that prevailed in the European Communities at the time. The general right of staff members to be able to spend official time on legitimate staff activities was implicitly recognized, although the exact dimensions of this right may not have been specified. As stated already, the content of the right depends on a number of factors, including the particular situation of the organization and of the staff. Furthermore, the Court implied that time spent on staff activities as a staff representative should neither have an adverse effect on the organization's assessment of the quantity and quality of the staff member's work in his substantive position nor should be regarded as derogating from his performance in such position. Thus, time spent on staff activities as a staff representative should be officially regarded as time spent on legitimate activities no different from the functions performed by staff members in their official posts in the organization.

The importance of the facility to spend time on staff activities may be assessed by reference to the fact that organizations generally permit meetings of Staff Associations or their committees to be held during regular office hours without regarding time taken off for this purpose as absence from the office. The UNAT admitted to this practice in *Smith*, a case which concerned deductions from salary for unauthorized absences because of work stoppage or strikes, when it said:

The meeting on Friday, 26 January 1979, which lasted all day, and the meeting during the morning of Monday, 29 January 1979 were, under the terms of the Statute of the Staff Union, 'extraordinary staff meetings'; they were undoubtedly particularly long; the Respondent himself, however, held that attendance at those meetings could not be described as unauthorized absence and the Tribunal recognizes that that interpretation, based as it is on provisions concerning staff members' right of association, must be accepted.

With regard to the unit meetings, the Tribunal finds that their objective was in fact organized work stoppage and that accordingly participation could not be considered as authorized absence inasmuch as no provision concerning unit meetings allows for their having such an objective.[18]

The UNAT conceded that meetings of the Staff Association, even extraordinary meetings which were particularly long, had been considered by the administration of the UN to be legitimate for the purpose of describing attendance at them by the staff as an authorized absence. Further, the tribunal linked this recognition to the right of association which was reflected in the statutory law of the organization. While the absences were specifically recognized as authorized by the administration and the written law was invoked, neither did the written law refer to such absences as authorized nor did the tribunal explicitly predicate on the agreement of the administrative authority

---

[18] UNAT Judgment No. 249 [1979], JUNAT Nos. 231–300 p. 202 at p. 216.

the legality of characterizing those absences as authorized. The tribunal seems to have implied that the administration was acting reasonably and within the bounds of the law in regarding those absences as authorized, the ultimate basis for the legality of those absences being related to the right of association recognized by the written law of the organization and by general principles of law. Effectively, not only is it the agreement of the administrative authority that assures legality to absences for the purpose of attending staff meetings, but the general principles of law relating to the right of association must be regarded as relevant to the question of the legality of absences.

The same reasoning applies to the finding of the tribunal that attendance at the unit meetings could not justifiably be regarded as authorized absences. While reference is made to the absence of a specific provision concerning the legality of such unit meetings for the purpose of claiming an authorized absence, it would seem that it was also the implied view of the tribunal that the right of association recognized by the written law and by general principles of law did not as such require that absences for the purpose of attending such unit meetings be regarded as authorized absences. It is also important to recognize that the absences referred to in *Smith* were occasioned by unit meetings whose objective was work stoppage and this was noted by the tribunal. Thus, it would seem that it is not attendance at all types of unit meetings that will involve unauthorized absences depending on the lack of agreement of the administration, but particularly attendance at those unit meetings of a kind the attendance at which could not legitimately be regarded as unauthorized absences.

In a case concerning promotion, the CJEC held that, in determining that the staff member had several years of experience as head of unit for the purposes of the requirements for promotion of the vacancy notice, it was not an error of law for the administration to ignore continued absences by the staff member from his official duties for duty on the Staff Committee, which resulted in others acting as head of unit for him.[19] Absences caused by duties connected with legitimate staff activities, especially those which involve participation in the work of the administrative authority, cannot but be regarded as authorized. Indeed, it is arguable that such absences should not only be treated negatively as authorized absences but be included as arising from the assigned duties of the staff members.

In *Di Giuliomaria*[20] the issue was whether actions taken by a staff member in his capacity as a staff representative of the Staff Association of FAO could justifiably be regarded by the organization as amounting to serious misconduct warranting summary dismissal. The facts were that (*a*) he had submitted

[19] *Grassi*, CJEC Case 188/73 [1974] ECR p. 1099.
[20] ILOAT Judgment No. 87 [1965] (FAO).

to the General Assembly of the Association motions pertaining to the demands of the staff and (*b*) later, after he had become the chairman of a special salary committee of FAO to which he had been appointed by the General Assembly of the Staff Association, he had carried on his activities as a representative of the Association which had charged him with a specific mission, circulating a statement criticizing the Staff Council and making proposals for the next Assembly. The latter action led to his dismissal. The organization had taken the view that the statement in question manifested the applicant's insubordination and impertinence, misrepresentation of facts and incitement to agitation, and injurious language which amounted to serious misconduct.

The ILOAT stated that as regards the submission to the General Assembly of the Association the applicant was merely availing himself of the right of any member of the staff to defend his occupational interests which was, however, subject to the duty to observe the moderation incumbent on any public official, but did not characterize the action taken by the applicant as having violated the duties owed by him to the organization.[21] Thus, the rights of staff members in this regard were confirmed by the ILOAT.

As regards the general rights of staff members who are staff representatives the ILOAT made the following general statement:

Without it being necessary to consider what the complainant's position would have been as a mere staff member, it may be observed that in his capacity of staff representative Mr. Di Giuliomaria had responsibilities but also enjoyed special rights, such as a considerable freedom of action and expression and the right to criticise the Staff Council and even, to some extent, the F.A.O. authorities; he also had special obligations, such as the obligation to act solely in defence of the interests of the staff and the strict duty not to abuse those rights by using methods or expressions incompatible with the decorum appropriate both to his status as a civil servant and to the functions entrusted to him by his colleagues.[22]

While staff representatives have special rights in regard to freedom of action, expression, and criticism, even of the official authorities of the organization, they also have special obligations in regard to moderation and the abuse of those rights. What is of importance is that the ILOAT recognized that staff representatives had considerable freedom of action, expression, and criticism which could not be impeached or characterized as a violation of their obligations, provided there was no abuse of their rights.

There can be no question that the right to freedom of action, expression, and criticism must be accorded to staff representatives. On the other hand, it is important to recognize that the tribunal placed certain important limitations on this right based on the obligation of staff representatives to act solely

21 Ibid. at p. 4.
22 Ibid. at p. 5.

in the defence of staff interests and on their strict duty not to abuse the right by using methods or expressions incompatible with the decorum appropriate both to their status as international civil servants and to the functions entrusted to them by their colleagues.

On the facts the tribunal found that the applicant in *Di Giuliomaria* had not committed an act of insubordination or impertinence nor had been disrespectful in criticizing the Director General of FAO in the way he did, had not misrepresented facts, and had legitimately exercised his right of criticism of the Staff Council, a staff body. It also held that there was no evidence that the applicant had fostered useless agitation within FAO or that he had urged staff members to join Italian trade unions, regardless of whether staff members of FAO could legally join trade unions in the host country. The tribunal, therefore, reached the conclusion that the applicant had neither abused his rights nor been guilty of serious misconduct. On the particular right of staff representatives to criticize the Staff Council the tribunal said:

[T]he Council's attitude and actions may be criticised, and even sharply criticised by the staff without any restrictions other than those already indicated . . . any member of the staff is entitled to express disapproval of serving members of the Council or to call on them to resign. It does not appear that in his statement Mr. Di Giuliomaria abused his right of criticism or that he used injurious or defamatory language.[23]

The case is undoubtedly a valuable contribution to the law relating to the right of staff members of international institutions to freedom of action, expression, and criticism.

The legality of activities connected with Staff Associations or Unions and the lack of justification for treating time spent in connection with them as being unauthorized absence or time spent on unofficial duties or illegal activities has been confirmed by the attitude of tribunals to certain discretionary decisions taken by administrative authorities in the course of administering the employment relationship. In connection with a decision to terminate employment the UNAT was confronted with the argument that it was the applicant's activities as Chairman of the Staff Association of UNICEF in Lagos that had been the primary cause leading to the termination of his regular appointment. The UNAT examined the facts carefully, thus conceding that, if the applicant's appointment had been terminated for the reason alleged, there would have been an abuse of purpose or *détournement de pouvoir*. On the facts the tribunal found that, even though the respondent had not repudiated various statements made by its responsible officials on the functions of the applicant as Chairman of the Lagos Staff Association, there was ample evidence to show that the real reason for the action taken was the dissatisfaction arising from his performance and from the considerable

[23] Ibid. at p. 7.

friction that had existed between the applicant and his supervisors. Hence, the decision to terminate the appointment had not been taken because of the applicant's activities as a member of the Staff Association.[24] The tribunal did not deny that, if the real reason for the termination decision had been the applicant's activities in connection with the Staff Association, the decision would have been tainted.

In *Robinson*,[25] on the other hand, the UNAT found that the activities of the applicant in the Staff Association were the reason for the non-renewal of his fixed-term contract. It was established that the applicant was an active member of the Staff Association and a member and officer of the Staff Committee and that in those capacities he took part in decisions and representations in which he was opposed to the administration on important and controversial issues. In regard to the right of the administration to consider in taking a decision on the renewal of his contract the activities of the applicant in the Staff Association the UNAT stated:

From what has been said previously about the right of association, it follows in particular that no action must be taken against a staff member either because he has taken a certain position as an officer or representative of the Staff Association or because of his methods of expression or personal behaviour in that capacity.[26]

Thus, it is clear that taking into account Staff-Association activities in deciding not to renew a fixed-term contract was regarded as an infringement of the right of association and, therefore, a *détournement de pouvoir*.

In that case the administration withheld the reason for the non-renewal of the contract and alleged that certain of the facts underlying the decision taken were of a confidential nature. Because of the importance of the right of association, the tribunal held that the burden of proof was upon the respondent to show that the applicant's Staff-Association activities were not the reason for the decision taken. In this connection the UNAT said:

As has been recorded in earlier paragraphs, the Applicant had played a very active part in the work of the Staff Association and above all, as a member of the Staff Committee, had had to take up matters in opposition of the Administration. In the case of such a staff member, the non-renewal of his contract is bound to give rise to suggestions as to the denial of the right of association.

In a situation of this kind, it will normally not be possible for the staff member to produce positive evidence that the reason for the non-renewal of this contract was his Staff Association activities. The most that he can do is to bring evidence to the effect that certain other reasons have not been the cause of the decision, as has been done in this case, that the record of performance of professional functions is satisfactory and that the reports of superior officers are in his favour. If, therefore, his contractual

---

[24] *Fayemiwo*, UNAT Judgment No. 246 [1979], JUNAT Nos. 231–300 p. 161.

[25] UNAT Judgment No. 15 [1952], JUNAT Nos. 1–70 p. 43.

[26] Ibid. at p. 50.

right of association is to be effectively protected, it must be recognized as inherent in that right that the Administration should provide the reason for the non-renewal of his contract.

In view of the Applicant's Staff Association activities, the Tribunal finds that this applies to his case and that the Administration accordingly should have given the reason for its decision not to renew the Applicant's appointment . . .

The Applicant cannot be penalized because certain information is regarded by the Respondent as confidential and the Applicant has no opportunity either of knowing what the reason is or of challenging it. Otherwise in a case of this kind there would be no effective protection of the right of association inherent in the contractual relationship of the Applicant and the United Nations in accordance with the terms of appointment.

The Tribunal finds therefore that the failure to adduce a reason for non-renewal in this case is contrary to the Applicant's right of association and that this entitles him to relief.[27]

In *Olivares Silva*[28] the applicant failed to prove that his having been the Vice President of the Mexican branch of the PAHO Staff Association was the reason for non-renewal of his fixed-term contract, but the ILOAT impliedly accepted the argument that such a reason for the action taken would have vitiated the decision not to renew the contract.

In connection with decisions taken to transfer staff members, the argument has been raised before the ILOAT that the decisions were motivated by the Staff-Association activities of the staff members transferred. But in no case has the applicant successfully proved his allegation, while the tribunal has not denied that such a reason for transfer would result in a *détournement de pouvoir* and vitiate the decision.[29] In *Cowood*[30] the applicant alleged that the failure to promote him was due to his trade-union activity, which was contrary to the Staff Regulations and general principles of law, since it involved an attack on the freedom of trade unions and of opinion. The CJEC went into the facts in great detail and came to the conclusion that the reason alleged by the applicant for his failure to be promoted was not supported by the evidence but that the real reason was objective and was based on the experience and seniority of the person promoted instead of the applicant. The Court implicitly accepted the validity of the contention that to use as a reason for the failure to promote a staff member his Staff-Union activity was a violation of the law.[31]

Interference with Staff-Association activity by punishments meted out by

[27] Ibid. at pp. 50–1.
[28] ILOAT Judgment No. 495 [1982] (PAHO).
[29] See *Quiñones*, ILOAT Judgment No. 447 [1981] (PAHO); *Glorioso*, ILOAT Judgment No. 450 [1981] (PAHO); *Beaudry-Darismé*, ILOAT Judgment No. 494 [1982] (PAHO); *de Groot*, ILOAT Judgment No. 576 [1983] (ITU).
[30] CJEC Case 60/82 [1982] ECR p. 4625.
[31] See also *Gluecksmann*, ILOAT Judgment No. 520 [1982] (PAHO).

the administrative authority to individual staff members cannot be litigated as violations of the right to associate by staff members in general. Legal action must be taken in these cases by the individuals affected by the decision taken. This was asserted by the ILOAT in *García and Márquez (No. 2)*.[32]

Provision of facilities

In *García and Márquez (No. 2)*[33] the ILOAT had to consider the legality of the withdrawal by the administrative authority of facilities provided to the Staff Association of PAHO. The tribunal did not pronounce on the right to have facilities provided for Staff-Association activities but in postulating that such facilities were provided not out of mere benevolence but because it was in the interests of the organization to have Staff Associations perform their functions efficiently, it implied that such a right may exist. The tribunal stated:

The Association exists partly because it is in the interests of the Organization that it should. If it were nothing more than the creation of the staff, the Organization could have no concern with it and there would be no place for it in the Staff Regulations. The Organization does not provide facilities purely out of benevolence but because it is in the interests of the Organization that the functions which the Association discharges should be fully and competently performed. Facilities should be granted only when it is in the interests of the Organization that they should be . . .[34]

The right clearly depends on the interests of the organization but it is not clear whether the determination of what are the interests of the organization and what facilities it is in those interests to provide is an entirely subjective one for the organization. Thus, it is not possible to assert categorically that a Staff Association is entitled to have specific facilities provided in a given situation, though it may have a general right to some facilities.

Once facilities are provided, however, the staff has a right not to have them withdrawn, at least arbitrarily. The view of the law taken by the ILOAT in the same case was stated as follows, in the light of its finding that facilities are provided, because it is in the interests of the organization to provide them:

The Tribunal rejects the Organization's contention that the grant of facilities to the Staff Association is a privilege which can be withdrawn at will. The Association exists partly because it is in the interests of the Organization that it should . . . Facilities should be granted only when it is in the interests of the Organization that they should

---

[32] ILOAT Judgment No. 496 [1982] (PAHO) at p. 16.
[33] ILOAT Judgment No. 496 [1982] (PAHO).
[34] Ibid. at p. 16.

be; likewise, they should be withdrawn, wholly or in part, only when the withdrawal is in the interests of the Organization.[35]

The tribunal continued to elaborate on the obligations of the administrative authority in regard to the withdrawal of facilities by pointing out that:

The Tribunal cannot concern itself with any and every claim by the Staff Association for breaches of agreements for the supply of facilities. Such agreements take effect within the province of labour relations into which the Tribunal does not enter. The Tribunal is concerned only with allegations that the Administration is violating the right to associate; breaches of labour relations may, if sufficiently grave, be relied upon in support of such allegations. In the next two paragraphs the Tribunal considers in what sort of circumstances it can concern itself with such breaches.

First, a wholesale withdrawal of facilities might amount to a violation of the right to associate. The Organization, having in its own interests allowed and encouraged the Staff Association to believe that it could look to it for the provision of certain facilities, upon which the Association has come to depend for its existence, could not, without an amendment to the regulations, withdraw or diminish them to such an extent as to cripple the Association's work. Likewise, it might be shown to be impossible for contact between the members to be maintained if officers were altogether deprived of administrative leave . . .

Secondly, the withdrawal of facilities could violate the right to associate if, irrespective of scale, it was designed to coerce the Association into acting in a way of which the Administration approved or to punish it for having acted in a way of which the Administration disapproved. This would strike at the freedom and independence which is an essential part of the right to associate.[36]

It is clear from what the tribunal said that it is not merely because there is an agreement between the staff and the administrative authority relating to facilities that it will consider the legality of a withdrawal of facilities on the basis of a breach of agreement. It is rather because the withdrawal of facilities turns out to be an infringement of the right to associate that it will determine the legality of such a withdrawal. It is inadequate, therefore, that the staff points to a breach of agreement relating to facilities in order to ground an action brought before the tribunal. It must be shown that the withdrawal of facilities was a violation of the right to associate. Further, breach of an agreement between staff and administration is not by itself the basis for the finding that there had been an infringement of the right to associate. An infringement of the right to associate could occur, as the tribunal pointed out, in two situations which it explained in considerable detail in the text cited above. It would seem to follow from the approach taken by the ILOAT that, though the withdrawal of facilities should be based on the interests of the organization in order to be legally valid, such withdrawal is not within the uncontrolled and

---

[35] Ibid.
[36] Ibid. at pp. 16–17.

subjective discretion of the organization. The tribunal laid down clearly objective conditions for the validity of a withdrawal of facilities in two situations it envisaged.

It will be noted that in the above case the ILOAT related the duty of the administration not to perpetrate a wholesale withdrawal of facilities already granted to the Staff Association to an absence of amendment of the Staff Regulations. Since the Staff Regulations were not amended in the case in question, the statement linking by implication the validity of a wholesale withdrawal of facilities to an amendment of the Staff Regulations was unnecessary. On the other hand, the statement does raise the issue whether such a withdrawal would be justified, even if the Staff Regulations were amended, because there is a general principle of law which recognizes the right of staff to associate from which flows the right of the staff generally not to have their facilities withdrawn in a wholesale manner. In view of the general principle of law which has been acknowledged as fundamental by several tribunals, including the ILOAT, it is submitted that there may well be circumstances in which even an amendment to the written law would not justify a wholesale withdrawal of facilities from a Staff Association, if it resulted in an infringement of the right to associate as it is recognized by a general principle of law.

On the facts of the case the tribunal held that there had not been a wholesale withdrawal of facilities. Hence, the circumstances had to be considered in the light of the second possibility that there had been a partial withdrawal of facilities. The case involved certain incidents which led to the administration's effecting a very substantial curtailment of the facilities previously accorded. The organization substituted for the provision of a full-time secretary at G5 the obligation to pay 50 per cent of the cost of a G4 post; reduced the cash contribution to $750 per annum; limited the use of telex and cables to $250 per annum; limited printing and reproduction, hitherto unlimited, to $500 per annum; and substantially reduced the extent of administrative leave. There was also a form of censorship introduced in so far as it was made a requirement that all communications to and from the Staff Association had to be submitted for inspection by the administration.

The tribunal found that there had been an abuse of purpose or an improper motive in the curtailment of facilities and a direct violation of the right of association in the introduction of censorship. For these reasons it held that the action taken by the administration was unlawful. The reasonsing of the tribunal merits citing in detail. It said:

Within the limits indicated . . . the Director has the widest discretion in determining the extent of the facilities which the Organization offers to the Staff Association and in making from time to time such changes in them as he thinks to be desirable. Changes do not have to be negotiated and agreed; and if the implication in the use of these terms in the dossier is that the Director cannot act unilaterally, it is incorrect. He may not, as is the rule in all his decisions, act without taking all the relevant facts into consideration and he can hardly do that without ascertaining the views of the Staff Association. But after these have been considered, the decision is for him alone. When, however, abrupt, drastic and comprehensive changes are made . . . the Tribunal will normally expect to be informed of the reasons for them. This is especially so when there is evidence that the change is made by the Director's personal decision and is a change in arrangements approved by the Director himself, some of them only six months before.

In the dossier the Organization gives two reasons for the extensive changes that were imposed. The first is the excessive cost which it says was being incurred. The Tribunal does not find this convincing; no figures are given and the topic is not, as is to be expected, one which was ever discussed in the dialogue to which the Staff Committee was invited. The second is the use of the telex facility to communicate grievances to member governments. But it is plain that what is really objectionable here is not the use of the particular facility but the fact of communication. It is unnecessary for the Tribunal to determine whether it is correct or incorrect for the Staff Association to convey its grievances direct to member governments; whether it is or not, it must be legitimate for the Organization to say that it is not providing facilities for that purpose. But although there were a number of communications or attempted communications only one instance is given by the Organization in the dossier of the use of the telex . . . This can hardly be said to justify a curtailment of facilities over the whole range.

It is unnecessary in this case for the Tribunal to determine whether or not the decision [to curtail facilities] . . . was taken without consideration of all the relevant facts. It is enough to say that the absence of any evidence supporting the decision creates the suspicion that it was taken with improper motives and that such a suspicion is amply confirmed by consideration of the events leading up to it . . . The Director wished to get rid of a committee which he believed to be unrepresentative. He attempted to do so by persuasion. The resolutions of 7 September must finally have satisfied him, if he had not been satisfied before, that he had failed. The decision . . . can only be viewed either as an attempt to use coercion where persuasion had failed or as an expression of resentment at the failure. As such it is an abuse of power.

So much for the general decision to curtail. One of the curtailments has been attacked on its own as by itself involving a breach of the right to associate. This was the requirement, rightly described by the Committee as censorship, that all communications to and from the Staff Association should be submitted for inspection by the Administration. This condition, which was still being enforced in June 1981, was justified by Dr. del Cid on the ground that 'factual information which the Staff Association conveys needs discussion between the parties when there are doubts on the accuracy of such information.' This has from time immemorial been the standard excuse for censorship; the alleged object is never to suppress the truth but just to make sure that only the truth is told. Freedom of association is destroyed if communication between the members is permitted only under supervision. A restriction, which would be unjustified if imposed on speech or letters or any other means of communication which the Association found for itself, does not become justified when the means are provided by the Administration.[37]

[37] ILOAT Judgment No. 496 [1982] (PAHO) at pp. 23–4.

Conduct of administrative authorities

Apart from a total or partial withdrawal of facilities, the question whether the conduct of the executive head of the administration or of the administrative authorities in relation to Staff Associations is legal was raised in *García and Márquez (No. 2)*[38] in connection with the right of the staff to associate. The first allegation was that the Director had criticized the leaders publicly. The second was that he had encouraged the creation of a separate Staff Association. The tribunal held that neither of these acts by itself was a violation of the staff's right to associate.[39] The conduct of the administration and its representatives in relation to staff members could not be questioned except in terms of whether it interfered with the right of staff members to associate by, for instance, interfering with the freedom of choice of staff members or reflecting an improper motive. To criticize Staff-Association officials moderately or to work for the creation of separate Staff Associations did not do either.

Recognized and unrecognized Staff Associations

In *Connolly-Battisti (No. 7)*[40] the effect of a distinction made between recognized and unrecognized Staff Associations on the facilities afforded to members of such Associations by the organization was raised as an issue. The ILOAT found it unnecessary to decide the issue on the facts of the case, because the applicant had not disobeyed the instructions given her by her supervisor in regard to time she could spend on the activities of her Staff Association which was unrecognized. However, the issue may be of some importance. The facts of the case, as they are described in the decision, were as follows.

Until 23 September 1974 there was in the FAO a single Staff Association with four constituent bodies representing different interests. One body represented staff serving in the regional offices and in the field. The other three represented staff at headquarters, one for the professional staff and two for the general-service staff. There were two categories of general-service staff, those recruited locally who were all or mostly Italian, and those recruited from abroad; there was then and had been for some time past a significant difference in their terms of service and therefore in their interests. These two bodies were roughly equal in number, each containing seven or eight hundred members. In April 1974 it became clear that the four constituent bodies wished to separate. The administration expressed itself as 'responsive', but made it clear that in its view the right to organize did not

[38] ILOAT Judgment No. 496 [1982] (PAHO).
[39] Ibid. at p. 15.
[40] ILOAT Judgment No. 403 [1980] (FAO).

automatically carry with it the right to bargain with the management nor the
right to use the facilities of the employer or the use of working time: for such
rights to be made operative in practice, it would be necessary to decide which
bodies from among those who might exercise the right to organize were to be
recognized by the management for the purpose of bargaining.

In November 1974 Article VIII of the Staff Regulations was amended to
cover this development. The relevant sections read:

> 301.081   In accordance with the principle that the staff has the right to organize for
> the purpose of safeguarding and promoting its interests, one or more
> representative staff bodies recognized by the Director-General shall main-
> tain continuous contact with and negotiate with the Director-General with
> respect to the terms and conditions of employment of the staff and general
> staff welfare . . .
>
> 301.084   The Director-General, in deciding whether to recognize any group as a
> representative staff body, shall take into account whether:
>> (a)   such body represents a sufficiently large number of staff members or a
>> sufficiently distinct group of staff . . .

The four bodies formed themselves into separate Associations each with its
own statute. By Article 6 of its statute the Non-Local Association, known as
the NLA, declared that its membership should be open to all non-local
general service staff. The other general-service Association, known as the
UGS, although at that time it had few if any non-local members, declared
itself by Article 6 of its statute to be open to all in the general-service category
employed at headquarters.

On 2 December 1974 the Staff Relations Officer of FAO wrote to the chairmen of the four Associations inviting them to put forward their claims for
recognition. On 29 January 1975 the Director General of FAO granted recognition to three of the Associations but refused it to the NLA on the ground
that it did not constitute a sufficiently distinct group. He pointed out that
(a) the claims overlapped since the other general-service Association claimed
representation for the whole general-service category; (b) if both bodies had
been recognized, he would have been placed in the unacceptable position of
having to consult and negotiate with two groups on all matters of concern to
the general-service staff; (c) the conditions of service were now, with one
exception, the same for both categories; and (d) the Council had decided that
no new recruits should be given non-local status. The situation thus created
was for the members of the NLA a very painful one for which the Director
General did not propose any alleviation. They must either apply for membership of the other Association or lose the right to negotiate on terms of
employment and general-service welfare. There was no evidence of any hostility between the other Association and the NLA, but its leaders were not their
leaders; the bonds of loyalty and devotion would have to be broken and
forged anew. This would have been so, even if the members had been

convinced that they had no separate interests, whereas it was because the groups wished each to pursue their separate interests that the old Association had been dissolved. The result was that the NLA adopted a completely intransigent attitude. It refused to accept the Director General's decision and refused the administration's offers to discuss facilities, presumably those which the administration considered to be appropriate for an unrecognized but acknowledged Association. As a result during 1973 it was stripped of virtually all the customary facilities. Nevertheless the NLA continued to function. It claimed to have maintained its membership and it was a fact that even at that time out of a total membership in the other Association of 811 only 56 were non-local.

The argument of the applicant was that, while the relevant Staff Regulations required the administration to maintain contact and negotiate with certain bodies selected and recognized for that limited purpose, there was no justification for discrimination between staff members, whether as individuals or as groups, in regard to the amount of time off allowed to them for staff activities, on the basis of recognition of the Staff Association which they represented. Though the particular issue raised in this argument was not decided in the case, the argument of the applicant merits serious consideration. It is certainly in keeping with the right to associate that staff representatives in unrecognized Associations should be allowed time off for their staff activities, because such Associations are representative bodies and legitimate vehicles for the expression of staff views which could exert an influence on the decisions of the administration, even though they may not be entitled to negotiate or to be consulted by the administration. Since the interests of the organization are crucial to the issue of the right to facilities, as already seen from *García and Márquez (No. 2)*,[41] it may be said that it is certainly in the interests of the organization to have even an unrecognized Staff Association function efficiently, although the administration may not consult or negotiate with it, if it is representative and serves the interests of a special or identifiable group, so that, regardless of other facilities, it is justifiable that the representatives of such an Association should be given time off for staff activities.

Consultation and negotiation: salary scales

There are a few cases decided by the UNAT and the ILOAT in which the issues of collective bargaining, negotiation, and consultation, particularly in connection with the change of salary scales, has been litigated.[42] In

---

[41] ILOAT Judgment No. 496 [1982] (PAHO).
[42] This question has been discussed in brief in Ch. 43 pp. 970 ff. *supra*.

Belchamber[43] the UNAT was faced with a situation in which new salary scales had been introduced for staff in the Geneva office of the UN in the general services category. The questions raised by the applicants related to the procedures followed by the administrative authority in introducing such scales, namely whether the proper staff involvement had been obtained before such scales were instituted.

The first matter of concern to the tribunal in *Belchamber* was whether there was an obligation laid upon the administration to bargain collectively with the staff before introducing the salary scales. The tribunal was quite categorical that there was no general principle of law requiring collective bargaining and that, therefore, it would have to be shown that an obligation to bargain collectively arose from the statutory law of the organization or from a contract or agreement. The tribunal said:

The Application has elaborately dealt with the principles of collective bargaining, with the ILO Convention on Employment in the Public Service and with the need to promote machinery for negotiation in the terms and conditions of employment by public authorities. Without going into the merits of the general proposition, the Tribunal wishes to point out that the legal 'right' and 'duty' to collective bargaining, if any, arises out of statute or contract. Thus there are laws in some countries imposing obligations on employers and employees to bargain in good faith while in some others there are agreements between employers and employees undertaking such obligations. Apart from statutory or contractual obligations, the Tribunal is not aware of an enforceable right to collective bargaining based on general principles of labour law. Therefore the relevant question before the Tribunal is whether such an obligation exists in this case.[44]

The tribunal apparently took the same view of the obligation to negotiate in good faith or consult, although it did not specifically state that there was no general principle of law requiring negotiations in good faith or consultation between the staff and the administration, since it focussed on trying to establish whether such an obligation existed in the statutory law or arose out of agreement or contract.[45]

The UNAT found that there was no statutory or express contractual provision for collective bargaining or negotiation in good faith. It said:

The Tribunal notes that while provisions for consultation with the staff exist in chapter VIII of the Staff Regulations and Rules and in the Statute of the ICSC, there are no provisions in the Staff Regulations and Rules for 'collective bargaining' or 'negotiation in good faith' between the staff and the Administration. Nor is it contended that there is such a statutory obligation on the part of either the staff or the Administration. On the contrary, paragraph 7 of Annex I to the Staff Regulations

[43] UNAT Judgment No. 236 [1978], JUNAT Nos. 231–300 p. 39.
[44] Ibid. at p. 47.
[45] Ibid. at pp. 48 ff.

provides that 'the Secretary General shall fix the salary scales for staff members in the General Service category . . . normally on the basis of the best prevailing conditions of employment in the locality of the United Nations office concerned'. Neither the agreement of 23 April 1976 nor the earlier agreements of 1968–1969 provided *in express terms* for 'collective bargaining' or 'negotiation in good faith' with respect to any future salary agreements. The Tribunal therefore concludes that there is no statutory or express contractual obligation to 'collective bargaining' or 'negotiation in good faith' with the staff representatives prior to the introduction of a salary scale for the staff in the General Service category at Geneva.[46]

The Tribunal then examined whether an obligation to negotiate with the staff was implicit in the agreements made or in the facts and surrounding circumstances, since obligations could arise for the administration in this manner. A detailed examination was made of the past history of the manner in which the salaries of general-service staff were fixed in Geneva.[47] It was found that:

The past history of wage fixing for the General Service staff at Geneva shows that there have been agreements on salary scales on a few occasions and no agreements on others, and that the Secretary-General's authority to fix such salary scales has not been challenged on the ground that there had been no agreement. The Secretary-General has a wide discretion to consult with the staff and he had done so on almost every occasion in the past through the instrument of joint consultative machinery or otherwise. The conduct by the Secretary-General of prior 'negotiations' with the staff does not involve any derogation from his authority.[48]

Finally, although the tribunal did not find that the written law, express or implied, contractual agreements, or the practice of the organization required collective bargaining, it concluded that:

Whether called 'negotiations' or 'joint-consultative machinery', the substance, namely, direct discussion between the representatives of the Executive Heads and of the staff, always took place . . . [W]hether under Staff Regulations and Rules or otherwise, there is a long established practice of joint consultations between the representatives of the Executive Heads and of the staff of the Geneva-based Organizations on the revision of salary scales of the staff in the General Service category at Geneva.[49]

Thus, in this case consultation was required by the written law and had been established as a binding practice. Hence, there was an implied obligation on the part of the administration to hold joint consultations with the staff representatives before revising the salary scales. The situation had not changed after the establishment of the ICSC because then the obligation required consultation after the Commission made its recommendations.

In the circumstances of the case the UNAT concluded that there had been

[46] Ibid. at pp. 47–8.
[47] Ibid. at pp. 48 ff.
[48] Ibid. at p. 50.
[49] Ibid. at p. 51.

no breach by the administration of its obligations, because the absence of consultations was the result of a failure on the part of the staff representatives to co-operate.[50] Thus, while the administration may be under an obligation to consult with the staff on salary scales, the staff must co-operate so that the administration can fulfil this obligation. A culpable failure to co-operate cannot result in the breach of its obligations on the part of the administration.

In three cases decided by the ILOAT similar disputes arose as a result of a change in the salary scales of the general-service staff of three different Geneva-based organizations.[51] The tribunal found that the administrations were not in breach of their respective obligations but made some significant remarks about the differences between negotiation and consultation and about the impact of practice on the obligations of the administration. The questions in all three cases were what were the obligations of the administration in respect of consultation or negotiation with the staff prior to introducing the changes and whether there had been a breach of these obligations.

In *Bénard and Coffino* the tribunal made a distinction between consultation and negotiation. It said:

[T]he Tribunal does not share the view of both parties that there is no difference between consultation and negotiation. While in practice the two often overlap there is a clear distinction between them.

The distinction lies in the situation. If the end-product of the discussions (to use a wide and neutral term) is a unilateral decision, 'consultation' is the appropriate word. If it is a bilateral decision, i.e., an agreement, 'negotiation' is appropriate. Decisions are reached after consultation; agreements after negotiation. Negotiation starts from an equality of bargaining power (i.e., legal equality; economic strength may be unequal); consultation supposes legal power to be in the hands of the decision-maker, diminished only by the duty to consult.

Where there is only a simple obligation to consult, the decision-maker's duty is to listen or at most to exchange views. The object of the consultation is that he will make the best decision and the assumption is that he will not succeed in doing that unless he has the benefit of the views of the person consulted.

The object of negotiation on the other hand is compromise. This object would be frustrated if either party began with the determination not to make any concession in any circumstances, just as the object of consultation would be frustrated if the decision-maker began with a determination not to be influenced by anything that might be said to him. On both these hypotheses there would be lack of good faith.

There is however a situation midway between the two considered in the preceding paragraph. This is where the purpose of what is called 'consultation' is not merely to furnish the decision-maker with the other party's views but also to give him the oppor-

---

[50] Ibid. at p. 55.

[51] *Bénard and Coffino*, ILOAT Judgment No. 380 [1979] (ICITO-GATT); *Domon and Lhoest*, ILOAT Judgment No. 381 [1979] (WHO); *Hatt and Leuba*, ILOAT Judgment No. 382 [1979] (WMO).

tunity of obtaining the assent of the other party to the decision proposed, maybe at the cost of some concessions. When the discussion moves into the second phase it becomes negotiation because it is then in the field of equality of bargaining power. The decision-maker may have the contractual power to command obedience, but he cannot command willing co-operation. Maybe he cannot command co-operation at all. If there is a strike and he is unwilling to discipline the strikers he must settle the dispute by negotiation in which he will start on an equality with the staff. This was the situation in 1976. The ordinary employer, who has no contractual power of fixing wages, is always in this position and always has to negotiate in order to get any agreement at all. The organisations on the other hand, with their reserve power of unilateral decision, are only in that position if they put themselves there voluntarily and because they want an agreed solution in preference to one that is imposed.[52]

On the basis of the distinctions made the ILOAT found that the administration of the organization had consulted with the staff, though not negotiated with them, prior to introducing the changes. According to the Staff Regulations of the organization all that was required was consultation. Hence, there had been no violation of the written law.

The distinction made between consultation and negotiation (which was not even adverted to by the UNAT in *Belchamber*, perhaps because it was clear that the administration had done what it had to under the law, whatever name was given to the procedure) is important from the point of view of what administrations are expected to do where they have an obligation to consult under the written law or by contractual agreement. The Staff Regulations of most organizations provide at the most for consultation with the staff. Thus, administrations are in such a situation only under an obligation to do the minimum described in the judgment of the ILOAT in *Bénard and Coffino*.

In the same case the question was raised of the effect of an agreement between the staff representatives and the administration. The view taken by the ILOAT was that such an agreement did not become part of the contracts of employment of staff members so that it could be relied on as creating an obligation on the part of the administration to negotiate with staff before changing salary scales. Nor could such an agreement result in a term requiring such negotiation being implied in the contracts of employment of staff members. Consequently, the only way in which a term in a collective agreement between staff representatives and the administration could become a part of the law governing the obligations of the administration and the rights of the staff was by its being incorporated in the Staff Regulations by amendment of such Regulations. This was so particularly because the term was of general and not of individual application. In this case the Staff Regulations had not been amended.

A question was also raised about the effect of the practice of the organization in dealing with the staff in the past on creating a duty to negotiate. The tribunal said that if what was relied on was the practice of the organization, it

---

[52] ILOAT Judgment No. 380 [1979] (ICITO-GATT).

would have been necessary to examine minutely how the machinery of Article VIII of the Staff Regulations had been used so as to see what implications could properly be drawn.[53] On examination of the facts it was found that the machinery of the Staff Regulations had not been used as such, an alternative procedure having been employed. The result was that it could not be concluded that practice had altered the Staff Regulation in issue. Thus, it was held that there had been no amendment of the requirement of consultation in the Staff Regulations so as to substitute for it negotiation.[54]

In *Domon and Lhoest*[55] the situation in the WHO was found to be similar to that which prevailed in *Bénard and Coffino*. It was held that a collective agreement between staff representatives and the administration did not become a part of the contracts of employment for all affected staff members, as this would normally require the amendment of the Staff Regulations. As a consequence a term of the collective agreement requiring negotiation could not supplant the provision of the Staff Regulations requiring only consultation. Nor could a term requiring negotiation be implied in the contracts of employment of staff members because of the collective agreement. The tribunal further pointed out in this case that the collective agreement was between the executive heads and Staff Associations of seven separate organizations, so that, even if a term relating to negotiation were to be implied in the individual contracts of employment, problems of meaning would arise. It would not be clear how negotiations were to take place, whether they were to be between each organization and its own Staff Association in defiance of the common system or whether they were to be in conjunction with the other six organizations. If the latter were the correct interpretation, problems would arise if one or more of the executive heads of the organizations refused to negotiate. Thus, there was no room for a clear implication of terms in the individual contracts of employment. As in *Bénard and Coffino*, it was held that the Staff Regulations of WHO expressly required consultation and not negotiation which made it difficult to imply a contradictory term requiring negotiation.

The facts in *Hatt and Leuba*[56] were slightly different. While the circum-

---

[53] Ibid. at p. 20.

[54] The judgment also, in regard to an informal opinion given by three members of the tribunal on a personal basis, pointed out that: 'It has been recorded that the three members of the Tribunal, acting personally, have expressed their opinion that the April Agreement either created an obligation on the executive heads to negotiate *en bloc* with representatives of their staff associations or recognised that one was already in existence. This forms no part of the formal conclusion of the Tribunal in this case, being a matter outside its jurisdiction. The conclusion of the Tribunal in this case is that the breach of such an obligation, if any such obligation exists, would not be a non-observance of the complainant's terms of appointment or of any staff regulation' (ibid. at p. 21).

[55] ILOAT Judgment No. 381 [1979] (WHO).

[56] ILOAT Judgment No. 382 [1979] (WMO).

stances in which the change in salary scales were introduced were similar to those which obtained in the other two cases decided by the ILOAT, the Staff Regulations of the WMO had different requirements from those contained in the Staff Regulations of ICITO-GATT and WHO. Staff Regulation 3.1 of WMO required that the salary scales be determined in accordance with the equivalent scales in the UN office in Geneva. Consequently, it was argued that the salary scales of the UN office in Geneva should have been established by the Secretary General of the UN in accordance with the appropriate procedure and, since he had violated the requirements of the internal law of the UN which dealt with the role of staff representatives, those scales were illegally introduced. The ILOAT disposed of this argument by taking the position that on the issue of the legality of the acts of the Secretary General of the UN, the decision in *Belchamber*, decided by the UNAT, was binding. Since the UNAT had decided in that case that there had been no violation by the administration of the provisions of the Staff Regulations of the UN in regard to the requirement of consultation with the staff, the same conclusion would have to be adopted by the ILOAT. Thus, the salary scales of the UN office in Geneva had been properly established and the applicants had no case.

In the same case the argument was raised that the Staff Committee of the WMO should have been consulted before the change in scales was introduced. The tribunal was of the view that the relevant Staff Regulation required consideration and comment only in connection with questions of policy. Since there was no question of policy involved in the introduction of the new salary scales, because the policy had been settled, there was no breach of the obligation of consultation.[57]

Strikes

Several tribunals have had to deal with questions relating to strikes or work stoppages. Some tribunals have adverted to the question whether strikes are legal and therefore permitted. Most of the questions, however, have concerned the deduction of pay for work stoppages.

(a) Legality of strikes

The ILOAT faced squarely the issue of the legality of strikes in *Berte and Beslier*.[58] The EPO argued in this case that there was no parallel in law between the position of a staff member who willingly joins others in a work

[57] Ibid. at p. 12.
[58] ILOAT Judgment No. 566 [1983] (EPO). See also *Giroud and Beyer*, ILOAT Judgment No. 615 [1984] (EPO); *Kern*, ILOAT Judgment No. 616 [1984] (EPO).

stoppage and that of a staff member who is off work for some fortuitous reason which is invariably peculiar to himself; when there was a strike, the employment relationship was suspended for the duration of the strike and rights and duties arising under it did not directly apply; a new relationship came into being, with rights and duties other than those prescribed in the Staff Regulations and founded on the general principles of law governing strikes; and, lastly, when there was a concerted work stoppage, the administration could decide whatever it thought best for the proper running of the organization. The ILOAT did not accept the implication that a strike resulted in the suspension of the employment relationship with the consequences stated, which was based on the notion that strikes were unlawful. The tribunal said:

The EPO's notion of the right to strike is out of date. As a matter of principle a strike is lawful. It does not break the contract of employment or the administrative link between an organisation and its staff. The employee continues to be a member of the staff and the only provisions of the staff regulations to be suspended are those which are incompatible with the work stoppage. Salary is withheld by virtue of a provision in the Regulations, the requirement for payment of services rendered, and any provision which is not incompatible with the existence of a strike remains in force.[59]

While conceding that in principle a strike was lawful, the ILOAT made it clear that a strike could be unlawful by being an abuse of right or could result in unlawful acts:

If the strike involved the breach of obligations under the rules or contractual obligations or led to unlawful acts, it would be admissible for the administration to take special measures, but in that event there would not be a strike in the proper sense, and the measures would be disciplinary.[60]

Basically, a strike is lawful. It could become unlawful, if it involved a breach of obligation or an abuse of right, the mere absence from work not being a breach of obligation of this kind. But in this case, whether the strike is described as unlawful or the proper view is that there is no strike, the organization must take disciplinary measures. It would appear that in no circumstances can the contract of employment be treated as having come to an end.

    In *Acton and Others*[61] the CJEC avoided giving a categorical answer to the question whether a strike was legal or not. The Court pointed out that deducting pay for days on strike in no way implied any decision in relation to the official's right to strike or in relation to the detailed rules which may govern the exercise of such right and that:

---

[59] ILOAT Judgment No. 566 [1983] (EPO) at p. 5.
[60] Ibid.
[61] CJEC Cases 44, 46 & 49/74 [1975] ECR p. 383.

Although certain Member States deny their public servants or certain categories of public servants the right to strike, whereas other Member States allow it, the Staff Regulations of Officials of the European Communities remain silent on the subject. In the present case it is sufficient to note that the collective stoppage of work in relation to which the decisions in dispute were taken was considered by all concerned to be a method of defending collective interests of the staff and was therefore described as strike action.[62]

Although the underlying idea is that, since there was general agreement that the strike was not unlawful, it could be regarded as a lawful work stoppage, there is no reason to suppose that the Court would not have agreed with the views of the ILOAT referred to above. Strikes are in principle lawful, although they may in certain situations be unlawful. In a comparable way the Appeals Board of the OECD stated that strikes were not authorized by the Staff Regulations of the OECD but that it was unnecessary to examine whether the strike in issue was legal or not, because no sanctions had been imposed for the strike action taken.[63] There was no denial that strikes were legal but in certain circumstances would become illegal. Thus, the approach taken by the Appeals Board of the OECD does not conflict with that of the ILOAT, although there is no explicit statement that in principle strikes are legal.

In *Smith* the UNAT did not pronounce on the legality or illegality of the strike action taken in the case but noted that it 'is aware that the staff has resorted to this means of pressure on various occasions and that such conduct *per se* has not been considered by the Respondent as ground for terminating the employment of the persons concerned or for the imposition of disciplinary measures.'[64] The tribunal, in not commenting on the view taken of strikes by the UN administration, cannot be said to have disagreed with the view that strikes are in principle not illegal and cannot usually be regarded as a cause for terminating employment or imposing disciplinary sanctions.

(b) Penalties

Where a strike is lawfully engaged in, it seems to be accepted that the work stoppage is not a reason for terminating the contracts of employment of staff members who took part in the strike nor is it a ground for taking disciplinary action. This is the implication of the views taken in *Berte and Beslier*, *Acton and Others*, and *Smith*. In *Acton and Others*, in particular, it was said that the provisions of the Staff Regulations dealing with disciplinary sanctions were not relevant to the case in hand,[65] where the strike was considered by all

---

[62] Ibid. at p. 395.

[63] *Domergue*, Decision No. 39, OECD Appeals Board [1965], Recueil des décisions 1 à 62 (1979) p. 110 at p. 111.

[64] UNAT Judgment No. 249 [1979], JUNAT Nos. 231–300 p. 202 at p. 213.

[65] CJEC Cases 44, 46 & 49/74 [1975] ECR p. 383 at p. 396.

concerned not to be illegal. In *Smith*, in so far as it was noted that disciplinary sanctions had not been imposed and that the absence from work had not been regarded as a ground for terminating employment, the tribunal seems not to have disagreed that this was in law the proper approach. The tribunal also stated that such absence from work could not be treated as an abandonment of post which amounts to a separation from service.[66] In *Pibouleau* the applicant argued that the non-renewal of her fixed-term contract was due to her having participated in a work stoppage. The ILOAT did not deny that this would have been an improper motive for dismissal, while it found that the intention had not been proved.[67] Further, it would appear that the absence from work on account of a strike or work stoppage is not to be treated as an ordinary unauthorized absence from work for the purposes of the Staff Regulations which may authorize the set-off of the number of days of unauthorized absence from work against annual leave.[68]

(c) Deductions from pay

The fact that legal strike action does not warrant the imposition of penalties of any kind does not mean that the administration is not entitled to take any measures to protect itself. It is generally accepted that the organization may deduct payments due by way of salary from the emoluments of staff members who engaged in the strike or work stoppage, or refuse to pay for the period during which they did not work. There is no general principle of law that employees are entitled to be paid for the period during which they did not work when they were on strike. Tribunals have expressly or implicitly supported this view of the law. In *Rempp* the ILOAT said: 'According to a principle of international public service salary is generally payable only for services rendered, and so the Institute was right to refuse to pay a staff member who went on strike for the period in which he did not work.'[69] A similar view of the law was taken in principle in *Smith*[70] by the UNAT, in *Acton and Others*[71] by the CJEC, and in *Domergue*[72] by the Appeals Board of the OECD.

The deductions from salary will be validly made if they are made in accordance with the decisions of the legislative body which may also decide

---

[66] UNAT Judgment No. 249 [1979], JUNAT Nos. 231–300 p. 202 at p. 213.
[67] ILOAT Judgment No. 351 [1978] (WHO) at p. 4.
[68] See *Acton and Others*, CJEC Cases 44, 46 & 49/74 [1975] ECR p. 383 at p. 395.
[69] ILOAT Judgment No. 314 [1977] (IPI) at p. 6. See also *Giroud and Beyer*, ILOAT Judgment No. 615 [1984] (EPO) at p. 7; *Kern*, ILOAT Judgment No. 616 [1984] (EPO) at p. 4.
[70] UNAT Judgment No. 249 [1979], JUNAT Nos. 231–300 p. 202 at p. 213.
[71] CJEC Cases 44, 46 & 49/74 [1975] ECR p. 383 at pp. 394–5.
[72] Decision No. 39, OECD Appeals Board [1965], Recueil des décisions 1 à 62 (1979) p. 110 at p. 111.

not to make deductions for certain periods of the strike.[73] But the deductions must be made in accordance with the Staff Regulations in so far as those Regulations specify, for example, how salary is to be calculated. Thus, where the Staff Regulations laid down that a day's wages were to be calculated at the rate of one thirtieth of the month's wages, this measure had to be observed in the calculation of the deduction to be made.[74] The administration may decide how the absence from work is to be measured, in terms of what is to be regarded as illegitimate absence from work, and what is not to be so regarded, provided it does not act arbitrarily. This rule applies where part of the absence from work may be for legitimate reasons. Thus, deducting payments for the time spent during a strike in unit meetings of the Staff Association which were not authorized but not making deductions for time spent during the same strike on extraordinary staff meetings which were unusually long but were, nevertheless, permitted, has been held not to be arbitrary.[75]

Because the administration has not made a deduction from salary on an earlier occasion when there was a strike, the administration is not precluded from making deductions from salary on a subsequent occasion of a strike on the ground that it is estopped from asserting its right not to grant remuneration for services not rendered or work not performed.[76] Though in the administration of deductions from salary for absence from work the organization must not act in a discriminatory manner or treat staff unequally, it has been held not to amount to inequality of treatment that deductions had not been made on earlier occasions because the work stoppages were too short, while deductions were made in respect of longer work stoppages.[77] In the European Communities the fact that some institutions did not make deductions from salary in respect of absence from work because of a strike, while others did, has been held not to have resulted in the discriminatory treatment of staff members of those institutions in which the decision was taken to make deductions.[78]

It has been held that there is no need for the administration to give advance notice of a decision to make deductions from salary in respect of absence on account of a strike, because taking such a measure is within the rights of the

---

[73] See *Rempp*, ILOAT Judgment No. 314 [1977] (IPI).

[74] *Berte and Beslier*, ILOAT Judgment No. 566 [1983] (EPO). See also *Houghton-Wollny*, ILOAT Judgment No. 481 [1982] (FAO); *Giroud and Beyer*, ILOAT Judgment No. 615 [1984] (EPO); *Kern*, ILOAT Judgment No. 616 [1984] (EPO).

[75] *Smith*, UNAT Judgment No. 249 [1979], JUNAT Nos. 231–300 p. 202. See also *Acton and Others*, CJEC Cases 44, 46, & 49/74 [1975] ECR p. 383.

[76] *Smith*, UNAT Judgment No. 249 [1979], JUNAT Nos. 231–300 p. 202.

[77] *Houghton-Wollny*, ILOAT Judgment No. 481 [1982] (FAO).

[78] *Acton and Others*, CJEC Cases 44, 46 & 49/74 [1975] ECR p. 383.

administration.[79] While a staff member must be properly informed of a decision making deductions from his salary on account of a strike and proper substantiation of the decision taken must be made, in *Kern* the ILOAT found that this condition had been satisfied, because the decision:

[W]as notified to him together with all the essential facts which had prompted the EPO to take it. He was given a written explanation with the salary notice recording the deduction and thus had clear and sufficient indication of the reasons for the deductions and of the method of calculating them.[80]

In *Domergue*[81] the Appeals Board of the OECD dealt with the argument that, though the applicant was absent from work during regular working hours during the period of the strike, he could not be regarded as having not performed his duties during that period, because service need not be performed within specific hours during the days of the week. The tribunal answered that salary was paid for the effective performance of duties during specific hours, although exceptionally work may be done at other times. Thus, where the applicant was absent from office during regular working hours because of a strike, deductions could lawfully be made from his salary. It was not an available alternative to the applicant that he could have worked outside regular office hours in order to make up for the regular office hours during which he had been out on strike.

There may be circumstances in which absence from work is not a ground for making deductions from salary, where such absence is connected with a work stoppage. It would appear that there are clearly some situations which cannot be regarded as absences which are not accountable for the purpose of making deductions from salary. Thus, it is not a good excuse where a staff member stayed at home during a strike instead of going to work that he asserted that he was at his supervisor's disposal.[82] Similarly, it is no excuse for absence from work during a strike that the administration of the organization was not altogether opposed to the protest and indeed incited it, since the nature of what happened would be the same in law as an ordinary strike by the staff where such a circumstance did not exist.[83] But where the employer locks out the staff, the circumstances are such that absence from work would be justified with the result that deductions may not legitimately be made by virtue of the absence. The situation was explained by the ILOAT as follows:

Labour law does acknowledge other forms of collective stoppage, brought about by

[79] *Domergue*, Decision No. 39, OECD Appeals Board [1965], Recueil des décisions 1 à 62 (1979) p. 110.
[80] ILOAT Judgment no. 616 [1984] (EPO).
[81] Decision No. 39, OECD Appeals Board [1965], Recueil des décisions 1 à 62 (1979) p. 110.
[82] *Kern*, ILOAT Judgment No. 616 [1984] (EPO) at p. 4.
[83] Ibid.

the employer. In a dispute with staff the employer may, for example, close down the workplace in a lockout . . .

But such tactics are unknown in international organizations . . .

A lockout presupposes a direct instruction or some other form of action by the competent authority to stop the staff from being at work, both in law and in fact.[84]

Staff elections

Tribunals have on occasion been requested to pronounce on the legality or validity of elections, with disparate results. In *Pilleboue*[85] a request was made for a declaration that the UNESCO Staff-Association elections were invalid. The ILOAT did not examine the substance of the case, holding that no provision of its Statute empowered it to adjudicate on such a submission. The Director General of UNESCO had refused to entertain the applicant's request for a declaration of nullity on the ground that he had no jurisdiction to decide such an issue. The ILOAT took the view that the Director General had acted properly because the existing Staff Regulations, and particularly Staff Rule 108.1,[86] did not give him the authority to do so. Hence, the ILOAT could not declare a nullity his decision not to intervene.

The CJEC has taken a different approach and arrived at a different conclusion.[87] The Court, while holding that there were no specific provisions dealing with the admissibility of complaints relating to elections to the Staff Committee in the Staff Regulations of the organization or in the Statute of the Court, concluded that the situation was governed by the general provisions of the Staff Regulations. The Staff Regulations provided for a Staff Committee composed of elected representatives of the staff which would represent the staff in relations with the organization. The Court found that elections to the committee were held to ensure its representative character and that, in order that an application relating to them be admissible, the institution should be able to intervene in order to set the alleged illegality right, because any action must be brought against the institution. The duty of the organization to intervene followed from the Staff Regulations, in general from the powers of the organization and from the duty of the organization to ensure that officials had full freedom to choose their representatives in accordance with democratic rules. Thus, the institutions must not only intervene of their volition but must under the Staff Regulations settle disputes submitted to them. Hence, voters and candidates could bring actions, to dispose of which the Court had jurisdiction. In the decision given subse-

---

84 Ibid.
85 ILOAT Judgment No. 78 [1964] (UNESCO).
86 See Amerasinghe (ed.), 2 op. cit. (note 8 *supra*) p. 1 at p. 61.
87 *de Dapper and Others*, CJEC Case 54/75 [1976] ECR p. 1381.

quently on the merits of the case the Court found that a new method of mechanical counting had been introduced which resulted in serious inaccuracies in the counting and held that the decision of the institution refusing to declare the elections irregular had to be annulled with the result that the election was declared null and void.[88]

The difference in the cases decided by the ILOAT and the CJEC appears to lie in the provisions of the Staff Regulations of the two organizations involved. In the case of the European Communities the Regulations envisaged a more positive role for the institutions in the elections to the Staff Committee, while in the case of UNESCO this was not the case in regard to the elections of the Staff Association. It depends on the Staff Regulations what role the institution should play in such elections. Unless the administration of the organization can be deduced to have some supervisory functions over elections under the Staff Regulations, it would not be able to take decisions in regard to such elections and the staff would not be able to litigate in regard to such decisions.

Locus standi of Associations

Whether Staff Associations can file applications as legal entities before tribunals will depend on the written law of the organizations concerned. There is apparently no general principle of law flowing from the freedom of association or of trade-union activity which entitles a Staff Association to bring an action before a tribunal on behalf of a staff member or in its own right or to intervene in actions brought before a tribunal. Thus, the position would vary from organization to organization and from tribunal to tribunal, depending on the Statutes and Rules of Procedure of tribunals and on the Staff Regulations of the organizations.

The Appeals Board of ESRO has held that, though a staff member cannot bring an action on behalf of the staff, because he has no legal interest in doing so, the Statute of the tribunal permitted the Staff Association of ESRO to do so; indeed, the Staff Association was the only entity entitled to do so.[89] On the other hand, the Appeals Board of the Council of Europe has held in a case relating to an appointment that the Staff Association had no right to intervene under the Statute of the tribunal and the Staff Regulations but could present its views.[90] The latter role would be that of an *amicus curiae*.

---

[88] *de Dapper and Others*, CJEC Case 54/75 [1977] ECR p. 471. The Court made its own count of the votes in order to establish that there had been discrepancies in the count. It also made some positive findings on the legality of the distribution of ballot papers and of mechanical counting.

[89] *Decision No. 32, ESRO/CR/81*, ESRO Appeals Board [1973].

[90] *Lafuma*, Council of Europe Appeals Board, Appeal No. 7 [1972], Case-Law Digest (1985) p. 33.

The CJEC has taken a rather broad approach to the rights of Staff Associations to file applications or intervene before it. In two cases where actions taken against individual staff members were contested by Staff Unions, the CJEC held that they had no standing and made the following general statements of principle:

Under the general principles of labour law, the freedom of trade union activity recognized under Article 24a of the Staff Regulations means not only that officials and servants have the right without hindrance to form associations of their own choosing, but also that these associations are free to do anything lawful to protect the interests of their members as employees. The right of action is one of the means available for use by these associations.

Under the Community legal system, however, the exercise of this right is subject to the conditions determined by the system of forms of action provided for under the Treaties establishing the Communities.

Thus a staff association which fulfills these conditions is entitled, by virtue of the second paragraph of Article 173 of the EEC Treaty, to institute proceedings for annulment against a decision addressed to it within the meaning of that provision.

On the other hand, the bringing of a direct action is inadmissible under the arrangements provided under Articles 90 and 91 of the Staff Regulations for proceedings to be brought before the Court, in so far as these provisions give effect to Article 179 of the EEC Treaty and the corresponding Articles of the ECSC and EAEC Treaties.

Though Article 179 is available as a basis on which arrangement may be made for settlement by the Court of collective as well as individual disputes between the Community and its servants, this does not alter the fact that the procedure for complaint and appeal established by Articles 90 and 91 of the Staff Regulations is designed to deal exclusively with individual disputes.

This means that the channel for appeal provided for under Article 91 is available only to officials or servants.

Under the second paragraph of Article 37 of the Statute of the Court the right to intervene is, on the other hand, open to any person establishing a legitimate interest in the result of any case submitted to the Court, including those coming under Article 91 of the Staff Regulations.[91]

One of the above cases concerned the appointment of staff members. The second concerned deductions from the salary of individual staff members in connection with a strike which were applied generally. In a third case in which a Staff Union attempted to institute proceedings on behalf of the staff in regard to inadequate increases in their salaries which were applied across the board the CJEC held that the Union had no standing for the same reasons.[92]

---

[91] *Union syndicale (Amalgamated European Public Service Union) Brussels, Massa and Kortner*, CJEC Case 175/73 [1974] ECR p. 917; *Syndicat général du personnel des organismes européene*, CJEC Case 18/74 [1974] ECR p. 933.

[92] *Union syndicale—Service public européen and Others*, CJEC Case 72/74 [1975] ECR p. 401.

It would seem that the CJEC was more ready to permit intervention in appropriate cases under Article 37 of its Statute.

The UNAT has held that the Staff Association or Staff Unions have no *locus standi* to bring actions before it or intervene under Article 2.2 of its Statute.[93] Thus, in *Aubert and 14 Others*[94] the tribunal refused to permit the intervention of the Staff Association of the UN, although it was argued that the case concerned the general interest in seeing that the UN observed the contracts of employment and terms of appointment of all staff members. Similarly, the intervention of the Staff Committee represented by its Chairman was disallowed in that case. On the other hand, the UNAT permitted representations to be made by the Staff Association under Article 12 of its Rules and the Staff Association to be heard under Article 17.2 of its Rules.[95] In a subsequent case the Staff Council was allowed to present its views, a written statement on questions of principle being accepted.[96] In another case[97] involving the issue of consultation with the Staff Association, the counsel for the applicant asked the tribunal to note his appearance on behalf of the Staff Council, of the Inter-Agency Defence Committee, and of FICSA. This request was refused by the tribunal. The General Secretary of the Staff Union in Geneva was also refused permission to file a written statement or be heard as the representative of the Staff Union, but he was allowed to file a statement on behalf of the intervenors. The Staff Association does not apparently have a right to make representations or be heard. It is a matter within the discretion of the tribunal whether it will hear or entertain representations from the Staff Association.

There is a similar provision in the Rules of Procedure of the WBAT to that in the Rules of the UNAT. The tribunal may permit the representatives of a Staff Association to participate in the proceedings as an *amicus curiae* or 'friend of the court'.[98] The Staff Association availed itself of this privilege in *van Gent (No. 7)*[99] on the issue of costs which the respondent had requested should be awarded against the applicant.

There are no express provisions governing the role of Staff Associations in litigation before the ILOAT either in the Statute of the tribunal or in its Rules of Court. However, Staff Associations have been permitted to participate in proceedings in several cases. There is clearly no right to participate as such, participation being a privilege accorded by the tribunal in a given case. In

---

[93] See Appendix I *infra*.

[94] UNAT Judgment No. 1 [1950], JUNAT Nos. 1–70 p. 1.

[95] See Article 23.2 of the current Rules: Amerasinghe (ed.), 1 *Statutes and Rules of Procedure of International Administrative Tribunals* (1983) p. 10 at p. 18.

[96] *Crawford*, UNAT Judgment No. 18 [1953], JUNAT Nos. 1–70 p. 65.

[97] *Belchamber*, UNAT Judgment No. 236 [1978], JUNAT Nos. 231–300 p. 39.

[98] Rule 23.2: see Appendix IV *infra*.

[99] WBAT Reports [1985], Decision No. 22 at pp. 2–3.

Garcin[100] the Chairman of the Staff Association of UNESCO submitted an intervention. When the tribunal questioned his right to intervene both in person and ex officio, the intervention was withdrawn. In *McIntire*[101] a memorandum submitted in his own name by the Chairman of the Staff Association of FAO was entertained. In *Beaudry-Darismé*,[102] a case which concerned the transfer of an office-bearer of the Staff Association of PAHO allegedly for unlawful reasons, the Staff Association of PAHO was asked to submit a brief and did so. This was clearly an *amicus curiae* brief. In *García and Márquez (No. 2)*,[103] which concerned the withdrawal of facilities from the Staff Association of PAHO, the application was filed by two staff members in their personal capacity. The tribunal held that the Staff Association of PAHO had no right to intervene, whether it had a collective personality or not, because it had no contract of employment with the organization which was a requirement under Article II of the tribunal's Statute for *locus standi* before the tribunal. The position in the ILOAT, thus, seems to be similar to that in the UNAT and the WBAT. Staff Associations may not file actions or intervene. They may file briefs as *amici curiae* but at the discretion of the tribunal.

Miscellaneous issues

In *de Los Cobos and Wenger*[104] the ILOAT made it clear that it had no competence to pass judgment on the activities of the Staff Union as such. The applicants alleged that the Staff Union had not acted in accordance with its rules in not showing who among the staff were in favour of a proposal, when it had submitted a proposal on behalf of the staff to the management of ILO. The tribunal said of this allegation and its relevance:

The complaints argue that the Staff Union acted at variance with the 'objects' and 'means of action' laid down in its own rules in proposing reductions in salary and in hours of work which, though intended to prevent the dismissal of some of the staff, were to the prejudice of the others. For one thing, they say, the Staff Union ought to have consulted only its own members, not the whole staff, obtained replies which bore officials' names and were signed by them, and so exerted supervision over the voting.

The Tribunal is not competent to pass judgment on the activities of the Staff Union and Staff Union bodies. The complainants' pleas are material only insofar as the Organisation gave weight to the Staff Union's resolutions, and the Tribunal will

[100] ILOAT Judgment No. 32 [1958] (UNESCO).
[101] ILOAT Judgment No. 13 [1954] (FAO).
[102] ILOAT Judgment No. 494 [1982] (PAHO).
[103] ILOAT Judgment No. 496 [1982] (PAHO).
[104] ILOAT Judgment No. 391 [1980] (ILO).

consider those pleas later, if need be, in the context of its review of the impugned decision.[105]

In considering the decision taken by the administration of ILO the tribunal found that, whether the Staff Union resolution was *intra vires* or not, whether it was properly adopted and whether it reflected the wishes of the whole staff or not, the impugned decision was taken not solely on the basis of the Staff-Union resolution but because the administration was influenced by the wishes of a large part of the staff. Hence, the argument relating to the Staff Union's activities was irrelevant.

The case does not deal with the issue how the agreement of the staff may be ascertained or how it should be reflected, particularly through resolutions of the Staff Union, since the agreement of the staff as such was not considered to be relevant in the circumstances. The decision taken by the administration was not dependent for its validity on the agreement of the staff. It was sufficient for the administration to have an indication of the wishes of a large part of the staff. In an appropriate case a tribunal may be called upon to consider whether the agreement of the staff had been obtained and how this could be ascertained through the resolutions of the Staff Association.

Though the application may consist of allegations of infringement of the right of association and the terms of the employment contract safeguarding such freedom, the internal appeals procedure must be exhausted in accordance with the provisions of the Statute of the tribunal. In *García and Márquez*[106] an application was dismissed by the ILOAT in circumstances in which such exhaustion of remedies had not taken place in a case alleging the infringement of the right of association. It was only after internal remedies were properly exhausted that the case was entertained in *García and Márquez (No. 2)*.[107]

In *Alonso (No. 2)*[108] the applicant, as Chairperson of the Staff Association of PAHO, incurred legal expenses on a personal basis in retaining a lawyer on behalf of two staff members who had a dispute with PAHO. The dispute was settled but no mention was made in the settlement agreement of the fees incurred by the applicant. The applicant filed action against PAHO to recover the amount of the fees. The ILOAT dismissed the application, stating that according to Article II of the Statute of the tribunal an injury to the applicant in the course of employment was required to justify an application, unless there had been a breach of the applicant's terms of employment, and that in this case such an injury was not present. Neither was there a physical injury which was what was meant nor was the injury, if there were one caused by the organization, in the course of the applicant's employment.

[105] Ibid. at p. 7.
[106] ILOAT Judgment No. 408 [1980] (PAHO).
[107] ILOAT Judgment No. 496 [1982] (PAHO).
[108] ILOAT Judgment No. 362 [1978] (PAHO).

Remedies

As the above exposé shows, there are few cases in which applicants have succeeded in showing that their rights flowing from the right of association had been violated. Hence, it has been generally unnecessary for tribunals to decide on remedies to be ordered. There are a few cases, however, in which applicants were given remedies.

In *de Dapper and Others*,[109] where elections to the Staff Committee were found to be invalid, the decision of the administration not to declare the elections irregular was annulled. The CJEC ordered that the Staff Committee be disbanded subject to safeguards relating to the legal certainty of acts performed by the Committee between its being set up and the decision of the Court. In *Berte and Beslier*,[110] where deductions from salary on account of a strike had been wrongfully made, the ILOAT ordered that the amounts illegally deducted be repaid with interest at the rate of 10 per cent per annum.[111]

In *García and Márquez (No. 2)*[112] restoration of the status quo ante was not ordered because this would have been improper. The case concerned the withdrawal of certain facilities afforded the Staff Association of PAHO and the imposition of a form of censorship. It was also said that no compensation would be ordered in lieu of rescission of the administration's decisions. However, cash compensation in the amount of $2,250 was awarded. This was to cover for the three years past the reduction of the administration's cash contribution from $1,500 per year to $750 per year. The censorship was also ordered to be withdrawn.

In a case in which the UNAT held that the applicant's contract had wrongfully not been renewed on account of his Staff-Association activities, the tribunal awarded damages.[113] In *Connolly-Battisti (No. 7)*,[114] in which the ILOAT found that the applicant's Staff-Association activities did not warrant the warning given, the decision to issue the warning of severe disciplinary measures was quashed. This was said to be sufficient redress. The applicant's request for the removal from her file of four documents relating to the warning was refused.

In *Hakin (No. 4)*[115] the ILOAT found that the deductions made from the salary of the applicant on account of absences from work resulting from a

---

109 CJEC Case 54/75 [1977] ECR p. 471.
110 ILOAT Judgment No. 566 [1983] (EPO).
111 See also *Giroud and Beyer*, ILOAT Judgment No. 615 [1984] (EPO); *Kern*, ILOAT Judgment No. 616 [1984] (EPO).
112 ILOAT Judgment No. 496 [1982] (PAHO).
113 *Robinson*: see Ch. 37 p. 773 *supra*.
114 ILOAT Judgment No. 403 [1980] (FAO). In *Connolly-Battisti (No. 2)*, ILOAT Judgment No. 274 [1976] (FAO), a decision to issue a written reprimand based on criticism made as a member of the Staff Committee was quashed.
115 ILOAT Judgment No. 437 [1980] (EPO).

strike was justified. The applicant claimed moral damages because he alleged that charges had been made that he did not keep proper working hours. The ILOAT held that the statements made were not of a kind to discredit an official, the applicant had not suffered any emotional disturbance, and in any case the charges were not false. Since falsity of the charges was a *sine qua non* for moral damages, the tribunal said it would not award any.

Appendices

Statute of the Administrative Tribunal of the United Nations

as adopted by the General Assembly by resolution 351 A (IV) on 24 November 1949 and amended by resolution 782 B (VIII) on 9 December 1953 and by resolution 957 (X) on 8 November 1955

Article 1

A tribunal is established by the present Statute to be known as the United Nations Administrative Tribunal.

Article 2

1. The Tribunal shall be competent to hear and pass judgement upon applications alleging non-observance of contracts of employment of staff members of the Secretariat of the United Nations or of the terms of appointment of such staff members. The words 'contracts' and 'terms of appointment' include all pertinent regulations and rules in force at the time of alleged non-observance, including the staff pension regulations.

2. The Tribunal shall be open:

(a) To any staff member of the Secretariat of the United Nations even after his employment has ceased, and to any person who has succeeded to the staff member's rights on his death;

(b) To any other person who can show that he is entitled to rights under any contract or terms of appointment, including the provisions of staff regulations and rules upon which the staff member could have relied.

3. In the event of a dispute as to whether the Tribunal has competence, the matter shall be settled by the decision of the Tribunal.

4. The Tribunal shall not be competent, however, to deal with any applications where the cause of complaint arose prior to 1 January 1950.

Article 3

1. The Tribunal shall be composed of seven members, no two of whom may be nationals of the same State. Only three shall sit in any particular case.

2. The members shall be appointed by the General Assembly for three years, and they may be re-appointed; provided, however, that of the members initially appointed, the terms of two members shall expire at the end of one year and the terms of two members shall expire at the end of two years. A member appointed to replace a

member whose term of office has not expired shall hold office for the remainder of his predecessor's term.

3. The Tribunal shall elect its President and its two Vice-Presidents from among its members.

4. The Secretary-General shall provide the Tribunal with an Executive Secretary and such other staff as may be considered necessary.

5. No member of the Tribunal can be dismissed by the General Assembly unless the other members are of the unanimous opinion that he is unsuited for further service.

6. In case of a resignation of a member of the Tribunal, the resignation shall be addressed to the President of the Tribunal for transmission to the Secretary-General. This last notification makes the place vacant.

Article 4

The Tribunal shall hold ordinary sessions at dates to be fixed by its rules, subject to there being cases on its list which, in the opinion of the President, justify holding the session. Extraordinary sessions may be convoked by the President when required by the cases on the list.

Article 5

1. The Secretary-General of the United Nations shall make the administrative arrangements necessary for the functioning of the Tribunal.

2. The expenses of the Tribunal shall be borne by the United Nations.

Article 6

1. Subject to the provisions of the present Statute, the Tribunal shall establish its rules.

2. The rules shall include provisions concerning:

(a) Election of the President and Vice-Presidents;

(b) Composition of the Tribunal for its sessions;

(c) Presentation of applications and the procedure to be followed in respect to them;

(d) Intervention by persons to whom the Tribunal is open under paragraph 2 of article 2, whose rights may be affected by the judgement;

(e) Hearing, for purposes of information, of persons to whom the Tribunal is open under paragraph 2 of article 2, even though they are not parties to the case; and generally

(f) Other matters relating to the functioning of the Tribunal.

Article 7

1. An application shall not be receivable unless the person concerned has previously submitted the dispute to the joint appeals body provided for in the staff regulations and the latter has communicated its opinion to the Secretary-General, except where the Secretary-General and the applicant have agreed to submit the application directly to the Administrative Tribunal.

2. In the event of the joint body's recommendations being favourable to the application submitted to it, and in so far as this is the case, and application to the Tribunal shall be receivable if the Secretary-General has:

(a) Rejected the recommendations;
(b) Failed to take any action within the thirty days following the communication of the opinion; or
(c) Failed to carry out the recommendations within the thirty days following the communication of the opinion.

3. In the event that the recommendations made by the joint body and accepted by the Secretary-General are unfavourable to the applicant, and in so far as this is the case, the application shall be receivable, unless the joint body unanimously considers that it is frivolous.

4. An application shall not be receivable unless it is filed within ninety days reckoned from the respective dates and periods referred to in paragraph 2 above, or within ninety days reckoned from the date of the communication of the joint body's opinion containing recommendations unfavourable to the applicant. If the circumstance rendering the application receivable by the Tribunal, pursuant to paragraphs 2 and 3 above, is anterior to the date of announcement of the first session of the Tribunal, the time limit of ninety days shall begin to run from that date. Nevertheless, the said time limit on his behalf shall be extended to one year if the heirs of a deceased staff member or the trustee of a staff member who is not in a position to manage his own affairs, file the application in the name of the said staff member.

5. In any particular case the Tribunal may decide to suspend the provisions regarding time limits.

6. The filing of an application shall not have the effect of suspending the execution of the decision contested.

7. Applications may be filed in any of the five official languages of the United Nations.

Article 8

The oral proceedings of the Tribunal shall be held in public unless the Tribunal decides that exceptional circumstances require that they be held in private.

Article 9

1. If the Tribunal finds that the application is well founded, it shall order the

rescinding of the decision contested or the specific performance of the obligation invoked. At the same time the Tribunal shall fix the amount of compensation to be paid to the applicant for the injury sustained should the Secretary-General, within thirty days of the notification of the judgement, decide, in the interest of the United Nations, that the applicant shall be compensated without further action being taken in his case; provided that such compensation shall not exceed the equivalent of two years' net base salary of the applicant. The Tribunal may, however, in exceptional cases, when it considers it justified, order the payment of a higher indemnity. A statement of the reasons for the Tribunal's decision shall accompany each such order.

2. Should the Tribunal find that the procedure prescribed in the Staff Regulations or Staff Rules has not been observed, it may, at the request of the Secretary-General and prior to the determination of the merits, order the case remanded for institution or correction of the required procedure. Where a case is remanded, the Tribunal may order the payment of compensation, not to exceed the equivalent of three months' net base salary, to the applicant for such loss as may have been caused by the procedural delay.

3. In all applicable cases, compensation shall be fixed by the Tribunal and paid by the United Nations or, as appropriate, by the specialized agency participating under article 14.

Article 10

1. The Tribunal shall take all decisions by a majority vote.

2. Subject to the provisions of articles 11 and 12, the judgements of the Tribunal shall be final and without appeal.

3. The judgements shall state the reasons on which they are based.

4. The judgements shall be drawn up, in any of the five official language of the United Nations, in two originals, which shall be deposited in the archives of the Secretariat of the United Nations.

5. A copy of the judgement shall be communicated to each of the parties in the case. Copies shall also be made available on request to interested persons.

Article 11

1. If a Member State, the Secretary-General or the person in respect of whom a judgement has been rendered by the Tribunal (including any one who has succeeded to that person's rights on his death) objects to the judgement on the ground that the Tribunal has exceeded its jurisdiction or competence or that the Tribunal has failed to exercise jurisdiction vested in it, or has erred on a question of law relating to the provisions of the Charter of the United Nations, or has commited a fundamental error in procedure which has occasioned a failure of justice, such Member State, the Secretary-General or the person concerned may, within thirty days from the date of the judgement, make a written application to the Committee established by paragraph 4 of this article asking the Committee to request an advisory opinion of the International Court of Justice on the matter.

2. Within thirty days from the receipt of an application under paragraph 1 of this article, the Committee shall decide whether or not there is a substantial basis for the application. If the Committee decides that such a basis exists, it shall request an advisory opinion of the Court, and the Secretary-General shall arrange to transmit to the Court the views of the person referred to in paragraph 1.

3. If no application is made under paragraph 1 of this article, or if a decision to request an advisory opinion has not been taken by the Committee, within the periods prescribed in this article, the judgement of the Tribunal shall become final. In any case in which a request has been made for an advisory opinion, the Secretary-General shall either give effect to the opinion of the Court or request the Tribunal to convene specially in order that it shall confirm its original judgement, or give a new judgement, in conformity with the opinion of the Court. If not requested to convene specially the Tribunal shall at its next session confirm its judgement or bring it into conformity with the opinion of the Court.

4. For the purpose of this article, a Committee is established and authorized under paragraph 2 of Article 96 of the Charter to request advisory opinions of the Court. The Committee shall be composed of the Member States the representatives of which have served on the General Committee of the most recent regular session of the General Assembly. The Committee shall meet at United Nations Headquarters and shall establish its own rules.

5. In any case in which award of compensation has been made by the Tribunal in favour of the person concerned and the Committee has requested an advisory opinion under paragraph 2 of this article, the Secretary-General, if satisfied that such person will otherwise be handicapped in protecting his interests, shall within fifteen days of the decision to request an advisory opinion make an advance payment to him of one-third of the total amount of compensation awarded by the Tribunal less such termination benefits, if any, as have already been paid. Such advance payment shall be made on condition that, within thirty days of the action of the Tribunal under paragraph 3 of this article, such person shall pay back to the United Nations the amount, if any, by which the advance payment exceeds any sum to which he is entitled in accordance with the opinion of the Court.

Article 12

The Secretary-General or the applicant may apply to the Tribunal for a revision of a judgement on the basis of the discovery of some fact of such a nature as to be a decisive factor, which fact was, when the judgement was given, unknown to the Tribunal and also to the party claiming revision, always provided that such ignorance was not due to negligence. The application must be made within thirty days of the discovery of the fact and within one year of the date of the judgement. Clerical or arithmetical mistakes in judgements, or errors arising therein from any accidental slip or omission, may at any time be corrected by the Tribunal either of its own motion or on the application of any of the parties.

Article 13

The present Statute may be amended by decisions of the General Assembly.

Article 14

The competence of the Tribunal may be extended to any specialized agency brought into relationship with the United Nations in accordance with the provisions of Articles 57 and 63 of the Charter upon the terms established by a special agreement to be made with each such agency by the Secretary-General of the United Nations. Each such special agreement shall provide that the agency concerned shall be bound by the judgements of the Tribunal and be responsible for the payment of any compensation awarded by the Tribunal in respect of a staff member of that agency and shall include, *inter alia*, provisions concerning the agency's participation in the administrative arrangements for the functioning of the Tribunal and concerning its sharing the expenses of the Tribunal.

EXTRACT FROM THE REGULATIONS AND RULES OF THE UNITED NATIONS JOINT STAFF PENSION FUND (JANUARY 1977)

Article 49

Jurisdiction of the United Nations Administrative Tribunal

(*a*) Applications alleging non-observance of these Regulations arising out of a decision of the Board may be submitted directly to the United Nations Administrative Tribunal by:

(i) Any staff member of a member organization which has accepted the jurisdiction of the Tribunal in Joint Staff Pension Fund cases who is eligible under article 21 of these Regulations as a participant in the Fund, even after his employment has ceased, and any person who has succeeded to such staff member's rights upon his death;

(ii) Any other person who can show that he is entitled to rights under these Regulations by virtue of the participation in the Fund of a staff member of such member organization.

(*b*) In the event of a dispute as to whether the Tribunal has competence, the matter shall be settled by a decision of the Tribunal.

(*c*) The decision of the Tribunal shall be final and without appeal.

(*d*) The time-limits prescribed in article 7 of the Statute of the Tribunal are reckoned from the date of the communication of the contested decision of the Board.

Statute of the Administrative Tribunal of the International Labour Organisation

Adopted by the International Labour Conference on 9 October 1946 and Amended by the said Conference on 29 June 1949

Article I

There is established by the present Statute a Tribunal to be known as the International Labour Organisation Administrative Tribunal.

Article II

1. The Tribunal shall be competent to hear complaints alleging non-observance, in substance or in form, of the terms of appointment of officials of the International Labour Office, and of such provisions of the Staff Regulations as are applicable to the case.

2. The Tribunal shall be competent to settle any dispute concerning the compensation provided for in cases of invalidity, injury or disease incurred by an official in the course of his employment and to fix finally the amount of compensation, if any, which is to be paid.

3. The Tribunal shall be competent to hear any complaint of non-observance of the Staff Pensions Regulations or of rules made in virtue thereof in regard to an official or the wife, husband or children of an official, or in regard to any class of officials to which the said Regulations or the said rules apply.

4. The Tribunal shall be competent to hear disputes arising out of contracts to which the International Labour Organisation is a party and which provide for the competence of the Tribunal in any case of dispute with regard to their execution.

5. The Tribunal shall also be competent to hear complaints alleging non-observance, in substance or in form, of the terms of appointment of officials and of provisions of the Staff Regulations of any other intergovernmental international organisation approved by the Governing Body which has addressed to the Director-General a declaration recognising, in accordance with its Constitution or internal administrative rules, the jurisdiction of the Tribunal for this purpose, as well as its Rules of Procedure.

6. The Tribunal shall be open—

(*a*) to the official, even if his employment has ceased, and to any person on whom the official's rights have devolved on his death;

(*b*) to any other person who can show that he is entitled to some right under the terms of appointment of a deceased official or under provisions of the Staff Regulations on which the official could rely.

7. Any dispute as to the competence of the Tribunal shall be decided by it, subject to the provisions of article XII.

Article III

1. The Tribunal shall consist of three judges and three deputy judges who shall all be of different nationalities.

2. Subject to the provisions set out at paragraph 3 below, the judges and deputy judges shall be appointed for a period of three years by the Conference of the International Labour Organisation.

3. The terms of office of the judges and deputy judges who were in office on 1 January 1940 are prolonged until 1 April 1947 and thereafter until otherwise decided by the appropriate organ of the International Labour Organisation. Any vacancy which occurs during the period in question shall be filled by the said organ.

4. A meeting of the Tribunal shall be composed of three members, of whom one at least must be a judge.

Article IV

The Tribunal shall hold ordinary sessions at dates to be fixed by the Rules of Court, subject to there being cases on its list and to such cases being, in the opinion of the President, of a character to justify holding the session. An extraordinary session may be convened at the request of the Chairman of the Governing Body of the International Labour Office.

Article V

The Tribunal shall decide in each case whether the oral proceedings before it or any part of them shall be public or *in camera*.

Article VI

1. The Tribunal shall take decisions by a majority vote; judgements shall be final and without appeal.

2. The reasons for a judgement shall be stated. The judgement shall be communicated in writing to the Director-General of the International Labour Office and to the complainant.

3. Judgements shall be drawn up in a single copy, which shall be filed in the archives of the International Labour Office, where it shall be available for consultation by any person concerned.

Article VII

1. A complaint shall not be receivable unless the decision inpugned is a final decision and the person concerned has exhausted such other means of resisting it as are open to him under the applicable Staff Regulations.

2. To be receivable, a complaint must also have been filed within ninety days after the complainant was notified of the decision impugned or, in the case of a decision affecting a class of officials, after the decision was published.

3. Where the Administration fails to take a decision upon any claim of an official within sixty days from the notification of the claim to it, the person concerned may have recourse to the Tribunal and his complaint shall be receivable in the same manner as a complaint against a final decision. The period of ninety days provided for by the last preceding paragraph shall run from the expiration of the sixty days allowed for the taking of the decisions by the Administration.

4. The filing of a complaint shall not involve suspension of the execution of the decision impugned.

Article VIII

In cases falling under article II, the Tribunal, if satisfied that the complaint was well founded, shall order the rescinding of the decision impugned or the performance of the obligation relied upon. If such rescinding of a decision or execution of an obligation is not possible or advisable, the Tribunal shall award the complainant compensation for the injury caused to him.

Article IX

1. The administrative arrangements necessary for the operation of the Tribunal shall be made by the International Labour Office in consultation with the Tribunal.

2. Expenses occasioned by sessions of the Tribunal shall be borne by the International Labour Office.

3. Any compensation awarded by the Tribunal shall be chargeable to the budget of the International Labour Organisation.

Article X

1. Subject to the provisions of the present Statute, the Tribunal shall draw up Rules of Court covering—

(a) the election of the President and Vice-President;

(b) the convening and conduct of its sessions;

(c) the rules to be followed in presenting complaints and in the subsequent procedure, including intervention in the proceedings before the Tribunal by persons whose rights as officials may be affected by the judgement;

(*d*) the procedure to be followed with regard to complaints and disputes submitted to the Tribunal by virtue of paragraphs 3 and 4 of article II; and

(*e*) generally, all matters relating to the operation of the Tribunal which are not settled by the present Statute.

2. The Tribunal may amend the Rules of Court.

Article XI

The present Statute shall remain in force during the pleasure of the General Conference of the International Labour Organisation. It may be amended by the Conference or such other organ of the Organisation as the Conference may determine.

Article XII

1. In any case in which the Governing Body of the International Labour Office or the Administrative Board of the Pensions Fund challenges a decision of the Tribunal confirming its jurisdiction, or considers that a decision of the Tribunal is vitiated by a fundamental fault in the procedure followed, the question of the validity of the decision given by the Tribunal shall be submitted by the Governing Body, for an advisory opinion, to the International Court of Justice.

2. The opinion given by the Court shall be binding.

ANNEX TO THE STATUTE OF THE ADMINISTRATIVE TRIBBUNAL OF THE INTERNATIONAL LABOUR ORGANISATION

The Statute of the Administrative Tribunal of the International labour Organisation applies in its entirety to these international intergovernmental organisations which, in accordance with their Constitution or internal administrative rules, recognise the jurisdiction of the Tribunal and formally declare that they adopt its Rules of Procedure in accordance with paragraph 5 of article II of the Statute, subject to the following provisions which, in cases affecting any one of these organisations, are applicable as follows:

Article VI, paragraph 2

The reason for a judgement shall be stated. The judgement shall be communicated in writing to the Director-General of the International Labour Office, to the Director-General of the international organisation against which the complaint is filed, and to the complainant.

Article VI, paragraph 3

Judgments shall be drawn up in two copies, of which one shall be filed in the archives of the International Labour Office and the other in the archives of the international organisation against which the complaint is filed, where they shall be available for consultation by any person concerned.

Article IX, paragraph 2

Expenses occasioned by the sessions or hearings of the Administrative Tribunal shall be borne by the international organisation against which the complaint is filed.

Article IX, paragraph 3

Any compensation awarded by the Tribunal shall be chargeable to the budget of the international organisation against which the complaint is filed.

Article XII, paragraph 1

In any case in which the Executive Board of an international organisation which has made the declaration specified in article II, paragraph 5, of the Statute of the Tribunal challenges a decision of the Tribunal confirming its jurisdiction, or consider that a decision of the Tribunal is vitiated by a fundamental fault in the procedure followed, the question of the validity of the decision given by the Tribunal shall be submitted by the Executive Board concerned, for an advisory opinion, to the International Court of Justice.

Statute of the Administrative Tribunal of the International Bank for Reconstruction and Development, International Development Association, and International Finance Corporation

Article I

There is hereby established a Tribunal of the International Bank for Reconstruction and Development (hereinafter referred to individually as the 'Bank'), the International Development Association and the International Finance Corporation (together with the Bank hereinafter referred to collectively as the 'Bank Group') to be known as the World Bank Administrative Tribunal.

Article II

1. The Tribunal shall hear and pass judgment upon any application by which a member of the staff of the Bank Group alleges non-observance of the contract of employment or terms of appointment of such staff member. The words 'contract of employment' and 'terms of appointment' include all pertinent regulations and rules in force at the time of alleged non-observance including the provisions of the Staff Retirement Plan.

2. No such application shall be admissible, except under exceptional circumstances as decided by the Tribunal unless

(i) the applicant has exhausted all other remedies available within the Bank Group, except if the applicant and the respondent institution have agreed to submit the application directly to the Tribunal, and

(ii) the application is filed within ninety days after the latest of the following:

    (a) the occurrence of the event giving rise to the application;

    (b) receipt of notice, after the applicant has exhausted all other remedies available within the Bank Group, that the relief asked for or recommended will not be granted; or

    (c) receipt of notice that the relief asked for or recommended will be granted, if such relief shall not have been granted within thirty days after receipt of such notice.

3. For the purpose of this statute the expression 'member of the staff' means any current or former member of the staff of the Bank Group, any person who is entitled to claim upon a right of a member of the staff as a personal representative or by reason of the staff member's death, and any person designated or otherwise entitled to receive a payment under any provision of the Staff Retirement Plan.

Article III

In the event of a dispute as to whether the Tribunal has competence, the matter shall be settled by the Tribunal.

Article IV

1. The Tribunal shall be composed of seven members, all of whom shall be nationals of Member States of the Bank, but no two of whom shall be nationals of the same State. The members of the Tribunal shall be persons of high moral character and must possess the qualifications required for appointment to high judicial office or be jurisconsults of recognized competence.

2. The members of the Tribunal shall be appointed by the Executive Directors of the Bank from a list of candidates to be drawn up by the President of the Bank after appropriate consultation.

3. The members of the Tribunal shall be appointed for a period of three years: they may be reappointed. However, of the seven members initially appointed, the terms of three members shall expire at the end of two years. The names of those members shall be chosen by lot by the President of the Bank immediately after the first appointments have been completed.

4. A member appointed to replace a member whose term of office has not expired shall hold office for the remainder of his predecessor's term.

5. The members of the Tribunal shall hold office until replaced.

Article V

1. A quorum of five members shall suffice to constitute the Tribunal.

2. The Tribunal may, however, at any time form a panel of not less than three of its members for dealing with a particular case or group of cases. Decisions of such a panel shall be deemed to be taken by the Tribunal.

Article VI

1. The Tribunal shall elect a President and two Vice-Presidents from among its members.

2. The President of the Bank shall make the administrative arrangements necessary for the functioning of the Tribunal, including designating an Executive Secretary who, in the discharge of duties, shall be responsible only to the Tribunal.

3. The expenses of the Tribunal shall be borne by the Bank Group.

Article VII

1. Subject to the provisions of the present Statute, the Tribunal shall establish its rules.

2. The rules shall include provisions concerning:

(a) election of the President and Vice-Presidents;

(b) constitution of panels envisaged in Article V above;

(c) presentation of applications and the procedure to be followed in respect of them;

(d) intervention by persons to whom the Tribunal is open under paragraph 3 of Article II, whose rights may be affected by the judgment;

(e) hearing, for purposes of information, of persons to whom the Tribunal is open under paragraph 3 of Article II; and

(f) other matters relating to the functioning of the Tribunal.

Article VIII

1. The Tribunal shall hold sessions at dates to be fixed in accordance with its rules.

2. The Tribunal shall hold its sessions at the principal office of the Bank, unless it considers that the efficient conduct of the proceedings upon an application necessitates holding sessions elsewhere.

Article IX

The Tribunal shall decide in each case whether oral proceedings are warranted. Oral proceedings shall be held in public, unless the Tribunal decides that exceptional circumstances require that they be held in private.

Article X

1. The Tribunal shall take all its decisions by a majority of the members present.

2. In the event of an equality of votes, the President or the member who acts in such place shall have a casting vote.

Article XI

1. Judgments shall be final and without appeal.

2. Each judgment shall state the reasons on which it is based.

Article XII

1. If the Tribunal finds that the application is well-founded, it shall order the rescission of the decision contested or the specific performance of the obligation invoked. At the same time the Tribunal shall fix the amount of compensation to be paid to the applicant for the injury sustained should the President of the respondent institution, within thirty days of the notification of the judgment, decide, in the interest of such respondent, that the applicant shall be compensated without further action being taken in the case; provided that such compensation shall not exceed the equivalent of three years' net pay of the applicant. The Tribunal may, however, in exceptional cases, when it considers it justified, order the payment of a higher compensation. A statement of the specific reason for such an order shall be made.

2. Should the Tribunal find that the procedure prescribed in the rules of the respondent institution has not been observed, it may, at the request of the President of such respondent and prior to the determination of the merits, order the case remanded for institution or correction of the required procedure.

3. In all applicable cases, compensation fixed by the Tribunal shall be paid by the respondent institution.

4. The filing of an application shall not have the effect of suspending execution of the decision contested.

Article XIII

1. A party to a case in which a judgment has been delivered may, in the event of the discovery of a fact which by its nature might have had a decisive influence on the judgment of the Tribunal and which at the time the judgment was delivered was unknown both to the Tribunal and to that party, request the Tribunal, within a period of six months after that party acquired knowledge of such fact, to revise the judgment.

2. The request shall contain the information necessary to show that the conditions laid down in paragraph 1 of this Article have been complied with. It shall be accompanied by the original or a copy of all supporting documents.

Article XIV

The original copy of each judgment shall be filed in the archives of the Bank. A copy of the judgment shall be delivered to each of the parties concerned. Copies shall also be made available on request to interested persons.

Article XV

The Bank may make agreements with any other international organization for the submission of applications of members of their staff to the Tribunal. Each such agreement shall provide that the organization concerned shall be bound by the judgments of the Tribunal and be responsible for the payment of any compensation awarded by the Tribunal in respect of a staff member of that organization; the agreement shall also include, *inter alia*, provisions concerning the organization's participation in the administrative arrangements for the functioning of the Tribunal and concerning its sharing of the expenses of the Tribunal.

Article XVI

The present Statute may be amended by the Board of Governors of the Bank.

Article XVII

Notwithstanding Article II, paragraph 2 of the present Statute, the Tribunal shall be competent to hear any application concerning a cause of complaint which arose subsequent to January 1, 1979, provided, however, that the application is filed within 90 days after the entry into force of the present Statute.

Rules of the World Bank Administrative Tribunal

As adopted by the Tribunal on 26 September 1980, and amended up to October 8 1982[1]

Chapter 1: Organization

Rule 1: Term of office of members

Subject to any contrary decision of the Executive Directors of the International Bank for Reconstruction and Development (hereinafter referred to individually as the 'Bank' and collectively, together with the International Development Association and the International Finance Corporation, as the 'Bank Group'), the term of office of members of the Tribunal shall commence on the first day of July of the year of their appointment by the Executive Directors of the Bank.

Rule 2: President and Vice-Presidents

1. The Tribunal shall elect a President and two Vice-Presidents for terms of three years. The President and Vice-Presidents thus elected shall take up their duties immediately. They may be re-elected.

2. The retiring President and Vice-Presidents shall remain in office until their successors are elected.

3. If the President should cease to be a member of the Tribunal or should resign the office of President before the expiration of the normal term, the Tribunal shall elect a successor for the unexpired portion of the term. In the case of a vacancy of a Vice-President, the President may arrange for the election of a successor by correspondence.

4. The elections shall be by majority vote.

Rule 3: Duties of President

1. The President shall direct the work of the Tribunal and of its Secretariat. He shall represent the Tribunal in all administrative matters and shall preside at meetings of the Tribunal.

2. If the President is unable to act, one of the Vice-Presidents designated by the President shall act as President. In the absence of any such designation by the President, the Vice-President designated by the Tribunal shall act as President.

3. No case shall be heard by the Tribunal except under the chairmanship of the President or one of the Vice-Presidents.

---

[1] Marginal references are for ease of reference only, do not form part of the rules and do not constitute an interpretation thereof.

Rule 4: Executive Secretary and staff

In addition to an Executive Secretary the Tribunal shall have other staff placed at its disposal by the President of the Bank. The Executive Secretary, if unable to act, shall be replaced by an official appointed by the President of the Bank.

Chapter II: Sessions

Rule 5

1. *Plenary sessions*. The Tribunal shall hold a plenary session once a year on a date fixed by the President for the purpose of hearing cases, forming panels, electing officers and any other matters affecting the administration or operation of the Tribunal. When, however, there are no cases on the list referred to in Rule 12, paragraph 1, which in the opinion of the President would justify the holding of a session for their consideration, the President may, after consulting the other members of the Tribunal, decide to postpone the plenary session to a later date.

2. *Special plenary sessions*. A special plenary session may be convened by the President when, in his or her opinion, the number of urgency of cases requires such a session or it is necessary to deal with a question affecting the operation of the Tribunal.

3. *Notices of sessions*. Notice of the convening of a plenary session or a special plenary session shall be given to the members of the Tribunal at least thirty days in advance of the date of the opening of such a session.

4. *Quorum*. Five members of the Tribunal shall constitute a quorum for plenary sessions.

Rule 6: Panels

1. When the Tribunal decides to form a panel provided for in Article V, paragraph 2 of the Statute, it shall determine the particular case or group of cases for which such panel is formed.

2. A panel when formed shall include the President or one of the Vice-Presidents, who, as the case may be, shall preside over that panel.

3. The presiding member of a panel shall exercise all the functions of the President of the Tribunal in relation to cases before that panel, including determining the dates of sessions of the panel.

Chapter III: Proceedings

Rule 7

1. *Applications*. Applications instituting proceedings shall be submitted to the Tribunal through the Executive Secretary. Such applications shall be divided into four sections, which shall be entitled respectively:

(i)   Information concerning the personal and official status of the applicant;

(ii)   Pleas;

(iii) Explanatory statement; and

(iv)   Annexes.

2. The information concerning the personal and official status of the applicant shall be presented in the form contained in Annex I of these rules.

3. *Pleas* The pleas shall indicate all the measures and decisions which the applicant is requesting the Tribunal to order or take. They shall specify:

(*a*) any preliminary or provisional measures, such as the production of additional documents or the hearing of witnesses, which the applicant is requesting the Tribunal to order before proceeding to consider the merits;

(*b*) the decisions which the applicant is contesting and whose rescission is requested under Article XII, paragraph 1, of the Statute;

(*c*) the obligations which the applicant is invoking and the specific performance of which is requested under Article XII, paragraph 1, of the Statute;

(*d*) the amount of compensation claimed by the applicant in the event that the President of the respondent insititution decides, in the interest of such respondent, to pay compensation for the injury sustained in accordance with the option given under Article XII, paragraph 1, of the Statute; and

(*e*) any other relief which the applicant may request in accordance with the Statute.

4. *Explanatory statement*. The explanatory statement shall set out the facts and the legal grounds on which the pleas are based. It shall specify, *inter alia*, the provisions of the contract of employment or of the terms of appointment the non-observance of which is alleged.

5. *Annexes*. The annexes shall contain the texts of all documents referred to in the first three sections of the application. They shall be presented by the applicant in accordance with the following rules and the form of application appended to these rules:

(*a*) each document shall be annexed in the original or, failing that, in the form of a copy bearing the words 'Certified true copy';

(*b*) documents shall be accompanied by any necessary translations; and

(*c*) unless part of the document is irrelevant to the application, each document, regardless of its nature, shall be annexed in its entirety.

6. *Copies*. The applicant shall prepare eight copies of the application in addition to the original. Each copy shall reproduce all sections of the original, including the annexes. However, the Executive Secretary may grant the applicant permission upon request to omit the text of an annex of unusual length from a specified number of copies of the application.

7. Authentication. The applicant shall sign the last page of the original application. In the event of the applicant's incapacity, the required signature shall be furnished by his or her legal representative. The applicant may instead, by means of a letter transmitted for that purpose to the Executive Secretary, authorize his or her lawyer or the staff member or retired staff member who is representing the applicant to sign in his or her stead.

8. *Filing*. The applicant shall file the duly signed original and the eight copies of the

application with the Executive Secretary. Where the President of the respondent institution and the applicant have agreed to submit the application directly to the Tribunal in accordance with the option given to them under Article II, paragraph 2 (i) of the Statute, the filing shall take place within ninety days of the date on which the President of the respondent institution notifies the applicant of agreement for direct submission. In all other cases, the filing shall take place within the time limits prescribed by Article II, paragraph 2 (ii) of the Statute and by Rule 22.

9. *Corrections*. If the formal requirements of this rule are not fulfilled, the Executive Secretary may call upon the applicant to make the necessary corrections in the application and the copies thereof within a period which the Executive Secretary shall prescribe. He or she shall return the necessary papers to the applicant for this purpose. The Executive Secretary may also, with the approval of the President, make the necessary corrections when the defects in the application do not effect the substance.

10. *Transmission*. After ascertaining that the formal requirements of this rule have been complied with, the Executive Secretary shall transmit a copy of the application to the respondent.

11. *Reservation of application*. If it appears that an application is clearly irreceivable or devoid of all merit, the President may instruct the Executive Secretary to take no further action thereon until the next session of the Tribunal. The Tribunal shall then consider the application and may either adjudge that it be summarily dismissed as clearly irreceivable or devoid of all merit, or order that it should be proceeded with in the ordinary way.

Rule 8: Answer

1. *Answer*. The respondent's answer shall be submitted to the Tribunal through the Executive Secretary. The answer shall include pleas, an explanatory statement and annexes. The annexes shall contain the complete texts of all documents referred to in the other sections of the answer not annexed to the application. They shall be presented in accordance with the rules established for the application in Rule 7, paragraph 5 and Annex I (II).

2. *Copies*. The respondent shall prepare eight copies of the answer in addition to the original. Each copy shall reproduce all sections of the original, including the annexes. However, the Executive Secretary may grant the respondent permission, upon request, to omit the text of an annex of unusual length from a specified number of copies of the answer.

3. *Authentication*. The representative of the respondent shall sign the last page of the original answer.

4. *Filing*. Within sixty days of the date on which the application is transmitted to the respondent by the Executive Secretary, the respondent shall file the duly signed original and the eight copies of the answer with the Executive Secretary.

5. *Transmission* After ascertaining that the formal requirements of this rule have been complied with, the Executive Secretary shall transmit a copy of the answer to the applicant.

Rule 9: Reply

1. The applicant may, within forty-five days of the date on which the answer is transmitted to him or her, file with the Executive Secretary a written reply on the answer.

2. The complete text of any document referred to in the written reply shall be annexed thereto in accordance with the rules established for the application in Rule 7, paragraph 5 and Annex I (II).

3. The written reply shall be filed in an original and eight copies drawn up in accordance with the rules established for the application in Rule 7, paragraph 6. The original shall be signed in accordance with the rules established for the application in Rule 7, paragraph 7.

4. After ascertaining that the formal requirements of this rule have been complied with, the Executive Secretary shall transmit a copy of the written reply to the respondent.

Rule 10: Rejoinder

1. The respondent may within thirty days of the date on which the reply is transmitted to the respondent file with the Executive Secretary a written rejoinder.

2. The complete text of any document referred to in the written rejoinder shall be annexed thereto in accordance with the rules established for the application in Rule 7, paragraph 5 and Annex I (II).

3. The written rejoinder shall be filed in an original and eight copies drawn up in accordance with the rules established for the answer in Rule 8, paragraph 2. The original rejoinder shall be signed on the last page by the representative of the respondent.

4. After ascertaining that the formal requirements of this rule have been complied with, the Executive Secretary shall transmit a copy of the written rejoinder to the applicant.

5. Without prejudice to Rule 11, the written proceedings shall be closed after the rejoinder has been filed.

Rule 11: Additional statements and documents

1. In exceptional cases, the President may, on his or her own initiative, or at the request of either party, call upon the parties to submit additional written statements or additional document within a period which he or she shall fix. The additional documents shall be furnished in the original or in properly authenticated form. The written statements and additional documents shall be accompanied by eight copies. Any document shall be accompanied by any necessary translations.

2. Each written statement and additional documents shall be communicated by the Executive Secretary, on receipt, to the other parties, unless at the request of one of the parties and with the consent of the other parties, the Tribunal decides otherwise. The personnel files communicated to the Tribunal shall be made available to the applicant by the Executive Secretary in accordance with instructions issued by the Tribunal.

3. *Obtaining information.* In order to complete the documentation of the case

prior to its being placed on the list, the President may obtain any necessary information from any party, witnesses or experts. The President may designate a member of the Tribunal or any other disinterested person to take oral statements. Any such statement shall be made under declaration as provided to the parties in accordance with paragraph 2 above.

4. *Delegations of functions.* The President may in particular cases delegate his or her functions under this rule to one of the Vice-Presidents.

Rule 12: Listing of case for decision

1. When the President considers the documentation of a case to be sufficiently complete, he or she shall instruct the Executive Secretary to place the case on the list and to transmit the dossier of such case to the members designated to decide it. The Executive Secretary shall inform the parties as soon as the inclusion of the case in the list is effected. No additional statements or documents may be filed after the case has been included in the list.

2. As soon as the date of opening of the session or panel at which a case has been entered for deciding has been fixed, the Executive Secretary shall notify the parties of the date.

3. Any application for the adjournment of a case shall be decided by the President, or, when the Tribunal is in session, by the Tribunal.

Rule 13: Executive Secretary's functions

1. The Executive Secretary shall be responsible for transmitting all documents and making all notifications required in connection with proceedings before the Tribunal.

2. The Executive Secretary shall make for each case a dossier which shall record all actions taken in connection with the preparation of the case for trial, the dates thereof, and the dates on which any document or notification forming part of the procedure is received in or dispatched from his or her office.

Rule 14: Presentation of case

1. An applicant may present his or her case before the Tribunal in person, in either written or oral proceeding if allowed pursuant to Rule 15, paragraph 1. Subject to Rule 7, paragraph 7, the applicant may designate a staff member or retired staff member of the Bank Group to represent him or her, or may be represented by a lawyer authorized to practice in any country which is a member of the Bank.

2. The respondent institution shall be represented either by one of its officials or retired officials designated for that purpose or by a lawyer authorized to practice in any country which is a member of the respondent institution.

Rule 15: Oral proceedings

1. Oral proceedings shall be held if the Tribunal members hearing a case so decide or if either party so requests and the Tribunal so agrees. The oral proceedings may

include the presentation and examination of witnesses or experts and each party shall have the right of oral argument and of comment on the evidence given.

2. In sufficient time before the opening of the oral proceedings, each party shall inform the Executive Secretary and, through him or her, the other parties, of the names and description of witnesses and experts whom he or she desires to be heard, indicating the points to which the evidence is to refer.

3. The Tribunal shall decide on any application for the hearing of witnesses or experts and shall determine the sequence of oral proceedings. Where appropriate, the Tribunal may decide that witnesses shall reply in writing to the questions of the parties. The parties shall, however, retain the right to comment on any such written reply.

Rule 16: Witnesses and experts

1. The Tribunal may examine the witnesses and experts. The parties, their representatives or lawyers may, under the control of the presiding member, put questions to the witnesses and experts.

2. *Declarations*. Each witness shall make the following declaration before giving evidence: 'I solemnly declare upon my honor and conscience that I will speak the truth, the whole truth and nothing but the truth.' Each expert shall make the following declaration before making a statement: 'I solemnly declare upon my honor and conscience that my statement will be in accordance with my sincere belief.'

3. *Exclusion of evidence*. The Tribunal may exclude evidence which it considers irrelevant, frivolous, or lacking in probative value. The Tribunal may also limit the oral testimony where it considers the written documentation adequate.

Rule 17: Production of documents and inquiry

The Tribunal may at any stage of the proceedings call for the production of documents or of such other evidence as may be required. It may arrange for any measures of inquiry as may be necessary.

Chapter IV: Remand of a Case

Rule 18: Remand

1. If, in the course of the deliberations, the Tribunal finds that the case should be remanded in order that the required procedure may be instituted or corrected under Article XII, paragraph 2 of the Statute, it shall notify the parties accordingly.

2. The Tribunal shall decide on the substance of the case if, on the expiry of the time limit of two working days reckoned from the date of the notification under paragraph 1 above, no request for a remand has been made by the President of the respondent institution.

Chapter V: Intervention

Rule 19: Intervention by individuals

1. Any person to whom the Tribunal is open under Article II, paragraph 2 and Article XV of the Statute may apply to intervene in a case at any stage thereof on the ground that he or she has a right which may be affected by the judgment to be given by the Tribunal. Such person shall for that purpose draw up the file an application in the form of Annex II for intervention in accordance with the conditions laid down in this rule.

2. The rules regarding the preparation and submission of applications specified in Rules 7 through 14 above shall apply *mutatis mutandis* to the application for intervention.

3. After ascertaining that the formal requirements of this rule have been complied with, the Executive Secretary shall transmit a copy of the application for intervention to the applicant and to the respondent institution. The President shall decide which documents, if any, relating to the proceedings are to be transmitted to the intervenor by the Executive Secretary.

4. The Tribunal shall rule on the admissibility of every application for intervention submitted under this rule.

Rule 20: Intervention by organizations

The President of the Bank, the chief executive officer of an international organization to which the competence of the Tribunal has been extended in accordance with the Statute, or the Chairman of the Pension Benefits Administration Committee of the Bank, may, on giving previous notice to the President of the Tribunal, intervene at any stage, if such person considers that his or her respective administration may be affected by the judgment to be given by the Tribunal.

Rule 21: Potential intervenors

When it appears that a person may have an interest in intervening in a case under Rules 19 or 20, the President, or the Tribunal when in session, may instruct the Executive Secretary to transmit to such person a copy of the application submitted in the case.

Chapter VI: Applications Concerning Decisions of the Pension Benefits Administration Committee

Rule 22: Pension cases

Where an application is brought against a decision of the Pension Benefits Administration Committee of the Bank, the time limits prescribed in Article II or the Statute are reckoned from the date of the communication of the contested decision to the party concerned.

Chapter VII: Miscellaneous Provisions

Rule 23

1. *Persons furnishing information.* The Tribunal may, for purposes of information, permit persons to whom the Tribunal is open under Article II, paragraph 3 of the Statute, whenever such persons may be expected to furnish information pertinent to the case, to submit written or oral observations as may be appropriate.

2. *Amicus curiae.* The Tribunal may permit any person or entity with a substantial interest in the outcome of a case to participate as a friend-of-the-court. It may also permit the duly authorized representatives of the Staff Association of a respondent institution so to participate.

Rule 24: Publication of decisions

The Executive Secretary shall arrange for the publication of the decisions of the Tribunal.

Rule 25: Modification and supplementation of rules

The Tribunal, or, when the Tribunal is not in session, the President, after consultation where appropriate with the members of the Tribunal, may:

(i) in exceptional cases modify the application of these rules including any time limits thereunder;
(ii) deal with any matter not expressly provided for in the present rules.

Rule 26: Entry into force

The present rules shall apply to all applications submitted after October 15, 1980 and may apply to applications before that date if both the applicant and the respondent so inform the Tribunal.

ANNEX I

I. Form of first section of application drawn up in accordance with Rule 7

Information concerning the personal and official status of the applicant.

1. Name of respondent.
2. Applicant:
    (a) name and first names;
    (b) date and place of birth;
    (c) marital status;
    (d) nationality; and
    (e) address for purposes of the proceedings.

3. Name and address of lawyer or staff member or retired staff member representing the applicant before the Tribunal.
4. Official status of applicant:
   (a) organization of which the applicant was a staff member at the time of the decision contested;
   (b) date of employment;
   (c) title and level at time of decision contested; and
   (d) type of applicant's appointment.
5. If the applicant was not a staff member at the time of the contested decision, state:
   (a) the name, first names, nationality and official status of the staff member whose rights are relied on; and
   (b) the relation of the applicant to the said staff member who entitles the former to come before the Tribunal.
6. Date of the decision contested.
7. Description of remedies exhausted within the respondent institution.

II. Requirements regarding annexes

1. Each document shall constitute a separate annex and shall be numbered with an Arabic numeral. The word 'ANNEX', followed by the number of the document, shall appear at the top of the first page;

2. The annexed documents shall be preceded by a table of contents indicating the number, title, nature, date and, where appropriate, symbol of each annex; and

3. The words 'see annex', followed by the appropriate number, shall appear in parentheses after each reference to an annexed document in the other sections of the application.

4. Whenever possible, Annexes should be attached in chronological order.

ANNEX II

Form of first section of application for intervention drawn up in accordance with Article 7

Information concerning the personal and official status of the intervenor.

1. Case in which intervention is sought.
2. Intervenor:
   (a) name and first names;
   (b) date and place of birth;
   (c) marital status;
   (d) nationality; and
   (e) address for purposes of the proceedings.
3. Name and address of lawyer or staff member or retired staff member representing the intervenor before the Tribunal.
4. Official status of intervenor:

(*a*) organization of which the intervenor is a staff member;

(*b*) date of employment;

(*c*) title and level; and

(*d*) type of intervenor's appointment.

5. If the intervenor was not a staff member at the time of the contested decision, state:

(*a*) the name, first names, nationality and official status of the staff member whose rights are relied on; and

(*b*) the title under which the intervenor claims he or she is entitled to the rights of the said staff member.

APPENDIX: V

Staff Regulations and Staff Rules of the United Nations (1981)

STAFF REGULATIONS

Contents

Scope and purpose

Scope and purpose

The Staff Regulations embody the fundamental conditions of service and the basic rights, duties and obligations of the United Nations Secretariat. They represent the broad principles of personnel policy for the staffing and administration of the Secretariat. The Secretary General, as the Chief Administrative Officer, shall provide and enforce such staff rules consistent with these principles as he considers necessary.

Article I: Duties, obligations and privileges

Regulation 1.1: Members of the Secretariat are international civil servants. Their responsibilities are not national but exclusively international. By accepting appointment, they pledge themselves to discharge their functions and to regulate their conduct with the interests of the United Nations only in view.

Regulations 1.2: Staff members are subject to the authority of the Secretary-General and to assignment by him to any of the activities or offices of the United Nations. They are responsible to him in the exercise of their functions. The whole time of staff members shall be at the disposal of the Secretary-General. The Secretary-General shall establish a normal working week.

Regulation 1.3: In the performance of their duties members of the Secretariat shall neither seek nor accept instructions from any Government or from any other authority external to the Organization.

Regulation 1.4: Members of the Secretariat shall conduct themselves at all times in a manner befitting their status as international civil servants. They shall not engage in any activity that is incompatible with the proper discharge of their duties with the United Nations. They shall avoid any action and in particular any kind of public pronouncement which may adversely reflect on their status, or on the integrity, independence and impartiality which are required by that status. While they are not expected to give up their national sentiments or their political and religious convictions, they shall at all times bear in mind the reserve and tact incumbent upon them by reason of their international status.

Regulation 1.5: Staff members shall exercise the utmost discretion in regard to all matters of official business. They shall not communicate to any person any information known to them by reason of their official position which has not been made public, except in the course of their duties or by authorization of the Secretary-General. Nor shall they at any time use such information to private advantage. These obligations do not cease upon separation from the Secretariat.

Regulation 1.6: No staff member shall accept any honour, decoration, favour, gift or remuneration from any Government excepting for war service; nor shall a staff member accept any honour, decoration, favour, gift or remuneration from any source external to the Organization, without first obtaining the approval of the Secretary-General. Approval shall be granted only in exceptional cases and where such acceptance is not incompatible with the terms of regulation 1.2 of the Staff Regulations and with the individual's status as an international civil servant.

Regulation 1.7: Staff members may exercise the right to vote but shall not engage in any political activity which is inconsistent with or might reflect upon the independence and impartiality required by their status as international civil servants.

Regulation 1.8: The immunities and privileges attached to the United Nations by virtue of Article 105 of the Charter are conferred in the interests of the Organization. These privileges and immunities furnish no excuse to the staff members who enjoy them for non-performance of their private obligations or failure to observe laws and police regulations. In any case where these privileges and immunities arise, the staff member shall immediately report to the Secretary-General with whom alone it rests to decide whether they shall be waived.

Regulation 1.9: Members of the Secretariat shall subscribe to the following oath or declaration:

'I solemnly swear (undertake, affirm, promise) to exercise in all loyalty, discretion and conscience the functions entrusted to me as an international civil servant of the United Nations, to discharge these functions and regulate my conduct with the interests of the United Nations only in view, and not to seek or accept instructions in regard to the performance of my duties from any Government or other authority external to the Organization.'

Regulation 1.10: The oath or declaration shall be made orally by the Secretary-General at a public meeting of the General Assembly. All other members of the Secretariat shall make the oath or declaration before the Secretary-General or his authorized representative.

Article II: Classification of posts and staff

Regulation 2.1: In conformity with principles laid down by the General Assembly, the Secretary-General shall make appropriate provision for the classification of posts and staff according to the nature of the duties and responsibilities required.

Article III: Salaries and related allowances

Regulation 3.1: Salaries of staff members shall be fixed by the Secretary-General in accordance with the provisions of annex I to the present Regulations.

Regulation 3.2: The Secretary-General shall establish terms and conditions under which an education grant shall be available to a staff member serving outside his recognized home country whose dependent child is in full-time attendance at a school, university, or similar educational institution of a type which will, in the opinion of the Secretary-General, facilitate the child's reassimilation in the staff member's recognized home country. The grant shall be payable in respect of the child up to the end of the fourth year of post-secondary studies or the award of the first recognized degree, whichever is the earlier. The amount of the grant per scholastic year for each child shall be the sum of 75 per cent of the first $3,000 of admissible educational expenses, 50 per cent of the next $1,000 of such expenses and 25 per cent of the next $1,000, up to a maximum grant of $3,000. Travel costs of the child may also be paid for an outward and return journey once in each scholastic year between the educational institution and the duty station, except that in the case of staff members serving at designated duty stations where schools do not exist which provide schooling in the language or in the cultural tradition desired by staff members for their children, such travel costs may be paid twice in the year in which the staff member is not entitled to home leave. Such travel shall be by a route approved by the Secretary-General but not in an amount exceeding the cost of such a journey between the home country and the duty station.

The Secretary-General shall also establish terms and conditions under which an education grant shall be available to a staff member serving in a country whose language is different from his own and who is obliged to pay tuition for the teaching of the mother tongue to a dependent child attending a local school in which the instruction is given in a language other than his own.

The Secretary-General shall also establish terms and conditions under which an education grant shall be available to a staff member whose child is unable, by reason of physical or mental disability, to attend a normal educational institution and therefore requires special teaching or training to prepare him/her for full integration into society or, while attending a normal educational institution, requires special teaching or training to assist him/her in overcoming the disability. The amount of this grant per year for each disabled child shall be equal to 75 per cent of the educational expenses actually incurred up to $5,000, subject to a maximum grant of $3,750.

The Secretary-General may decide in each case whether the education grant shall extend to adopted children or stepchildren.

Regulation 3.3: (*a*) An assessment at the rates and under the conditions specified below shall be applied to the salaries and such other emoluments of staff members as are computed on the basis of salary, excluding post adjustments, provided that the Secretary General may, where he deems it advisable, exempt from the assessment the salaries and emoluments of staff engaged at locality rates.

(*b*) (i) The assessment shall be calculated at the following rates [Table V.1] for staff whose salary rates are set forth in paragraphs 1 and 3 of annex I to the present Regulations.

(ii) The assessment shall be calculated at the following rates [Table V.2] for staff whose salary rates are established under paragraph 7 of annex I to the present Regulations.

(iii) The Secretary-General shall determine which of the scales of assessment set out in subparagraphs (i) and (ii) above shall apply to each of the groups of personnel whose salary rates are established under paragraph 6 of annex I to the present Regulations.

(iv) In the case of staff whose salary scales are established in currencies other than United States dollars, the relevant amounts to which the assessment applies shall be fixed at the local currency equivalent of the above-mentioned dollar amounts at the time the salary scales of the staff concerned are approved.

(*c*) In the case of a person who is not employed by the United Nations for the whole of a calendar year or in cases where there is a change in the annual rate of payments

TABLE V.1.

Total assessable payments ($US)	Assessment (%)	
	Staff member with a dependent spouse or a dependent child	Staff member with neither a dependent spouse nor a dependent child
First $16,000 per year	14.7	19.4
Next $4,000 per year	31	36
Next $4,000 per year	34	39.1
Next $4,000 per year	37	42.1
Next $5,000 per year	39	44.7
Next $5,000 per year	42	47.7
Next $5,000 per year	44	49.9
Next $6,000 per year	47	52.6
Next $6,000 per year	50	55.5
Next $6,000 per year	52	57.5
Next $7,000 per year	53.5	58.9
Next $7,000 per year	55	59.9
Next $7,000 per year	56	60.9
Next $8,000 per year	57	62.1
Remaining assessable payments	59	64.5

TABLE V.2.

Total assessable payments ($US)	Assessment (%)
First $2,000 per year	7
Next $2,000 per year	11
Next $2,000 per year	15
Next $2,000 per year	19
Next $4,000 per year	22
Next $4,000 per year	25
Next $4,000 per year	28
Next $6,000 per year	32
Next $6,000 per year	35
Next $6,000 per year	38
Next $8,000 per year	41
Remaining assessable payments	43

made to a staff member, the rate of assessment shall be governed by the annual rate of each such payment made to him.

(d) The assessment computed under the foregoing provisions of the present regulation shall be collected by the United Nations by withholding it from payments. No part of the assessment so collected shall be refunded because of cessation of employment during the calendar year.

(*e*) Revenue derived from staff assessment not otherwise disposed of by specific resolution of the General Assembly shall be credited to the Tax Equalization Fund established by General Assembly resolution 973 A (X).

(*f*) Where a staff member is subject both to staff assessment under this plan and to national income taxation in respect of the salaries and emoluments paid to him by the United Nations, the Secretary-General is authorized to refund to him the amount of staff assessment collected from him provided that:

(i)   The amount of such refund shall in no case exceed the amount of his income taxes paid and payable in respect of his United Nations income;

(ii) If the amount of such income taxes exceeds the amount of staff assessment, the Secretary-General may also pay to the staff member the amount of such excess:

(iii) Payments made in accordance with the provisions of the present regulation shall be charged to the Tax Equalization Fund;

(iv) A payment under the conditions prescribed in the three preceding subparagraphs is authorized in respect of dependency benefits and post adjustments, which are not subject to staff assessment but may be subject to national income taxation.

Regulation 3.4: (*a*) Staff members whose salary rates are set forth in paragraphs 1 and 3 of annex I to the present Regulations shall be entitled to receive dependency allowances as follows:

(i)   At $450 per year for each dependent child, except that the allowance shall not be paid in respect of the first dependent child if the staff member has no dependent spouse, in which case the staff member shall be entitled to the dependency rate of staff assessment under subparagraph (*b*) (i) of regulation 3.3;

(ii) Where there is no dependent spouse, single annual allowance of $300 per year of either a dependent parent, a dependent brother or a dependent sister. The amount of either of these allowances payable in local currency shall not be less than the local currency equivalent of the dollar amount at the time it was established or last revised.

(*b*) If both husband and wife are staff members, one may claim, for dependent children, under (i) above, in which case the other may claim only under (ii) above, if otherwise entitled;

(*c*) With a view to avoiding duplication of benefits and in order to achieve equality between staff members who receive dependency benefits under applicable laws in the form of governmental grants and staff members who do not receive such dependency benefits, the Secretary-General shall prescribe conditions under which the dependency allowance for a child specified (*a*) (i) above shall be payable only to the extent that the dependency benefits enjoyed by the staff member or his spouse under applicable laws amount to less than such a dependency allowance;

(*d*) Staff members whose salary rates are set by the Secretary-General under paragraph 6 or paragraph 7 of annex I to these Regulations shall be entitled to receive dependency allowances at rates and under conditions determined by the Secretary General, due regard being given to the circumstances in the locality in which the office is located;

(*e*) Claims for dependency allowances shall be submitted in writing and supported by evidence satisfactory to the Secretary-General. A separate claim for dependency allowances shall be made each year.

Article IV: Appointment and promotion

Regulation 4.1: As stated in Article 101 of the Charter, the power of appointment of staff members rests with the Secretary-General. Upon appointment each staff member shall receive a letter of appointment in accordance with the provisions of annex II to the present Regulations and signed by the Secretary-General or by an official in the name of the Secretary-General.

Regulation 4.2: The paramount consideration in the appointment, transfer or promotion of the staff shall be the necessity for securing the highest standards of efficiency, competence and integrity. Due regard shall be paid to the importance of recruiting the staff on as wide a geographical basis as possible.

Regulation 4.3: In accordance with the principles of the Charter, selection of staff members shall be made without distinction as to race, sex or religion. So far as practicable, selection shall be made on a competitive basis.

Regulation 4.4: Subject to the provisions of Article 101, paragraph 3, of the Charter, and without prejudice to the recruitment of fresh talent at all levels, the fullest regard shall be had, in filling vacancies to the requisite qualifications and experience of persons already in the service of the United Nations. This consideration shall also apply on a reciprocal basis, to the specialized agencies brought into relationship with the United Nations.

Regulation 4.5: (*a*) Appointment of Under-Secretaries-General and of Assistant Secretaries-General shall normally be for a period of five years, subject to prolongation or renewal. Other staff members shall be granted either permanent or temporary appointments under such terms and conditions consistent with these regulations as the Secretary-General may prescribe.

(*b*) The Secretary-General shall prescribe which staff members are eligible for permanent appointments. The probationary period for granting or confirming a permanent appointment shall normally not exceed two years, provided that in individual cases the Secretary-General may extend the probationary period for not more than one additional year.

Regulation 4.6: The Secretary-General shall establish appropriate medical standards which staff members shall be required to meet before appointment.

Article V: Annual and special leave

Regulation 5.1: Staff members shall be allowed appropriate annual leave.

Regulation 5.2: Special leave may be authorized by the Secretary-General in exceptional cases.

Regulation 5.3: Eligible staff members shall be granted home leave once in every two years. However, in the case of service at designated duty stations having very difficult or difficult conditions of life and work, eligible staff members shall be granted, respectively, home leave once in every 12 months and once in every 18 months. A staff member whose home country is the country of his official duty station or who continues to reside in his home country while performing his official duties shall not be eligible for home leave.

Article VI: Social security

Regulation 6.1: Provision shall be made for the participation of staff members in the United Nations Joint Staff Pension Fund in accordance with the regulations of that Fund.

Regulation 6.2: The Secretary-General shall establish a scheme of social security for the staff, including provisions for health protection, sick leave and maternity leave, and reasonable compensation in the event of illness, accident or death attributable to the performance of official duties on behalf of the United Nations.

Article VII: Travel and removal expenses

Regulation 7.1: Subject to conditions and definitions prescribed by the Secretary-General, the United Nations shall in appropriate cases pay the travel expenses of staff members, their spouses and dependent children.

Regulation 7.2: Subject to conditions and definitions prescribed by the Secretary-General, the United Nations shall pay removal costs for staff members.

Article VIII: Staff relations

Regulation 8.1: (*a*) A Staff Council, elected by the staff, shall be established for the purpose of ensuring continuous contact between the staff and the Secretary-General. The Council shall be entitled to make proposals to the Secretary-General for improvements in the situation of staff members, both as regards their conditions of work and their general conditions of life.

(*b*) The Staff Council shall be composed in such a way as to afford equitable representation to all levels of the staff.

(*c*) Election of the Staff Council shall take place annually under regulations drawn up by the the Staff Council and agreed to by the Secretary-General.

Regulation 8.2: The Secretary-General shall establish joint administrative machinery with staff participation to advise him regarding personnel policies and general questions of staff welfare and to make to him such proposals as it may desire for amendment of the Staff Regulations and Rules.

Article IX: Separation from service

Regulation 9.1: (*a*) The Secretary-General may terminate the appointment of a staff member who holds a permanent appointment and whose probationary period has been completed, if the necessities of the service require abolition of the post or reduction of the staff, if the services of the individual concerned proved unsatisfactory, or if he is, for reasons of health, incapacitated for further service.

The Secretary-General may also, giving his reasons therefor, terminate the appointment of a staff member who holds a permanent appointment:

(i) If the conduct of the staff member indicates that the staff member does not meet the highest standards of integrity required by Article 101, paragraph 3, of the Charter:

(ii) If facts anterior to the appointment of the staff member and relevant to his suitability come to light which, if they had been known at the time of his appointment, should, under the standards established in the Charter, have precluded his appointment.

No termination under subparagraphs (i) and (ii) shall take place until the matter has been considered and reported on by a special advisory board appointed for that purpose by the Secretary-General.

Finally, the Secretary-General may terminate the appointment of a staff member who holds a permanent appointment if such action would in the interest of the good administration of the Organization and in accordance with the standards of the Charter, provided that the action is not contested by the staff member concerned.

(*b*) The Secretary-General may terminate the appointment of a staff member with a fixed-term appointment prior to the expiration date for any of the reasons specified in paragraph (*a*) above, or for such other reason as may be specified in the letter of appointment.

(*c*) In the case of all other staff members, including staff members serving a probationary period for a permanent appointment, the Secretary-General may at any time terminate the appointment, if, in his opinion, such action would be in the interest of the United Nations.

Regulation 9.2: Staff members may resign from the Secretariat upon giving the Secretary-General the notice required under the terms of their appointment.

Regulation 9.3: (*a*) If the Secretary-General terminates an appointment the staff member shall be given such notice and such indemnity payment as may be applicable under the Staff Regulations and Staff Rules. Payments of termination indemnity shall be made by the Secretary-General in accordance with the rates and conditions specified in annex III to the present Regulations.

(*b*) The Secretary-General may, where the circumstances warrant and he considers it justified, pay to a staff member terminated under the final paragraph of staff regulation 9.1 (*a*) a termination indemnity payment not more than 50 per cent higher than that which would otherwise be payable under the Staff Regulations.

Regulation 9.4: The Secretary-General shall establish a scheme for the payment of repatriation grants within the maximum rates and under the conditions specified in annex IV to the present Regulations.

Regulation 9.5: Staff members shall not be retained in active service beyond the age of sixty years. The Secretary-General may, in the interest of the Organization, extend this age limit in exceptional cases.

Article X: Disciplinary measures

Regulation 10.1: The Secretary-General may establish administrative machinery with staff participation which will be available to advise him in disciplinary cases.

Regulation 10.2: The Secretary-General may impose disciplinary measures on staff members whose conduct is unsatisfactory.
He may summarily dismiss a member of the staff for serious misconduct.

Article XI: Appeals

Regulation 11.1: The Secretary-General shall establish administrative machinery with staff participation to advise him in case of any appeal by staff members against an administrative decision alleging the non-observance of their terms of appointment, including all pertinent regulations and rules, or against disciplinary action.

Regulation 11.2: The United Nations Administrative Tribunal shall, under conditions prescribed in its statute, hear and pass judgement upon applications from staff members alleging non-observance of their terms of appointment, including all pertinent regulations and rules.

Article XII: General provisions

Regulation 12.1: These Regulations may be supplemented or amended by the General Assembly, without prejudice to the acquired rights of staff members.

Regulation 12.2: The Secretary-General shall report annually to the General Assembly such Staff Rules and amendments thereto as he may make to implement these Regulations.

Annex I: Salary scales and related provisions

1. The Administrator of the United Nations Development Programme, having the status equivalent to that of the executive head of a major specialized agency, shall receive a salary of $US125,400 per year; the Director General for Development and International Economic Co-operation shall receive a salary of $US125,400 per year; and Under-Secretary-General shall receive a salary of $US96,765 per year; and an Assistant Secretary-General shall receive a salary of $US85,864 per year, subject to the staff assessment plan provided in staff regulation 3.3 and to post adjustments wherever applied. If otherwise eligible, they shall receive the allowances which are available to staff members generally.

2. The Secretary-General is authorized, on the basis of appropriate justification and/or reporting, to make additional payments to the Director General for Development and International Economic Co-operation, to Under-Secretaries-General and Assistant Secretaries General to compensate for such special costs as may be reasonably incurred, in the interests of the Organization, in the performance of duties assigned to them by the Secretary-General. The maximum total amount of such payments is to be determined in the programme budget by the General Assembly.

3. Except as provided in paragraph 6 of the present annex, the salary scales for staff members in the Director and Principal Officer category and in the Professional category shall be as shown in the present annex.

4. Subject to satisfactory service, salary increments within the levels set forth in paragraph 3 of the present annex shall be awarded annually, except that any increment above step IV of the Principal Office level shall be preceded by two years at the previous step. The Secretary-General is authorized to reduce the interval between salary increments to ten months and twenty months, respectively, in the case of staff subject to geographical distribution who have an adequate and confirmed knowledge of a second official language of the United Nations.

5. The Secretary-General is authorized, on the basis of appropriate justification and/or reporting, to make additional payments to Directors and, where offices are away from Headquarters, to their heads, to compensate for such special costs as may be reasonably incurred in the interest of the Organization in the performance of duties assigned to them by the Secretary-General. The maximum total amount of such payments is to be determined in the programme budget by the General Assembly.

6. The Secretary-General shall determine the salary rates to be paid to personnel specifically engaged for conferences and other short-term service, to consultants, to Field Service personnel, and to Technical Assistance experts.

7. The Secretary-General shall fix the salary scales for staff members in the General Service category and the salary or wage rates for manual workers, normally on the basis of the best prevailing conditions of employment in the locality of the United Nations office concerned, provided that the Secretary-General may, where he deems it appropriate, establish rules and salary limits for payment of a non-resident's allowance to General Service staff members recruited from outside the local area.

8. The Secretary-General shall establish rules under which a language allowance may be paid to staff members in the General Service category who pass an appropriate test and demonstrate continued proficiency in the use of two or more official languages.

9. In order to preserve equivalent standards of living at different offices, the Secretary-General may adjust the basic salaries set forth in paragraphs 1 and 3 of the present annex by the application of non-pensionable post adjustments based on relative costs of living, standards of living and related factors at the office concerned as compared to New York. Such post adjustments shall not be subject to staff assessment. Their amounts shall be as shown in the present annex.

10. No salary shall be paid to staff members in respect of periods of unauthorized absence from work unless such absence was caused by reasons beyond their control or duly certified medical reasons.

[See Tables V.3 to 6]

Annex II: Letters of appointment

(a) The letter of appointment shall state:

(i) That the appointment is subject to the provisions of the Staff Regulations and of the Staff Rules applicable to the category of appointment in question, and to changes which may be duly made in such regulations and rules from time to time;

(ii) The nature of the appointment;

(iii) The date at which the staff member is required to enter upon his duties;

(iv) The period of appointment, the notice required to terminate it and period of probation, if any;

(v) The category, level, commencing rate of salary, and if increments are allowable, the scale of increments, and the maximum attainable;

(vi) Any special conditions which may be applicable.

(b) A copy of the Staff Regulations and of the Staff Rules shall be transmitted to the staff member with the letter of appointment. In accepting appointment the staff member shall state that he has been made acquainted with and accepts the conditions laid down in the Staff Regulations and in the Staff Rules.

Annex III: Termination indemnity

Staff members whose appointments are terminated shall be paid an indemnity in accordance with the following provisions:

(a) Except as provided in paragraphs (b), (c) and (e) below and in regulation 9.3 (b), the termination indemnity shall be paid in accordance with the following schedule [Table V.7].

(b) A staff member whose appointment is terminated for reasons of health shall receive an indemnity equal to the indemnity provided under paragraph (a) of this annex reduced by the amount of any disability benefit that the staff member may receive under the Regulations of the United Nations Joint Staff Pension Fund for the number of months to which the indemnity rate corresponds.

(c) A staff member whose appointment is terminated for unsatisfactory services or who for disciplinary reasons is dismissed for misconduct other than by summary dismissal may be paid, at the discretion of the Secretary-General, an indemnity not exceeding one half of the indemnity provided under paragraph (a) of this annex.

TABLE V.3. *Salary scales for Professional and higher categories showing annual gross and the net equivalent after application of staff assessment ($US). (Effective 1 January 1981)*

Level		I	II	III	IV	V	VI	VII	VIII	IX	X	XI	XII	XIII
Under-Secretary-General USG	Gross	96,765.00												
	NET D	55,076.65												
	NET S	50,011.58												
Assistant Secretary-General ASG	Gross	85,864.00												
	NET D	50,524.52												
	NET S	46,042.46												
Director D-2	Gross	67,009.00	68,931.00	70,908.00	72,927.00									
	NET D	42,172.19	43,051.95	43,941.60	44,850.15									
	NET S	38,626.70	39,407.34	40,200.11	41,009.73									
Principal Officer D-1	Gross	55,919.00	57,732.00	59,531.00	61,342.00	63,193.00	64,998.00	66,755.00						
	NET D	36,939.12	37,809.36	38,672.88	39,537.03	40,397.75	41,237.07	42,054.08						
	NET S	33,997.58	34,768.10	35,532.68	36,297.57	37,058.33	37,800.18	38,522.31						
Senior Officer P-5	Gross	48,661.00	50,086.00	51,495.00	52,856.00	54,218.00	55,605.00	57,005.00	58,405.00	59,818.00	61,231.00			
	NET D	33,318.33	34,041.00	34,745.50	35,426.00	36,107.00	36,788.40	37,460.40	38,132.40	38,810.64	39,485.42			
	NET S	30,776.32	31,420.27	32,047.28	32,652.92	33,259.01	33,864.13	34,459.13	35,054.13	35,654.65	36,251.95			
First Officer P-4	Gross	38,167.00	39,398.00	40,630.00	41,863.00	43,101.00	44,367.00	45,627.00	46,887.00	48,311.00	49,547.00	50,884.00	52,173.00	
	NET D	27,611.52	28,300.88	28,990.80	29,680.72	30,371.53	31,042.51	31,710.31	32,378.11	33,079.83	33,771.50	34,440.00	35,084.50	
	NET S	25,671.67	26,288.40	26,905.63	27,522.87	28,140.88	28,740.96	29,338.20	29,935.44	30,563.02	31,180.42	31,775.38	32,348.99	
Second Officer P-3	Gross	30,518.00	31,589.00	32,648.00	33,713.00	34,814.00	35,939.00	37,055.00	38,157.00	39,202.00	40,237.00	41,282.00	42,315.00	43,375.00
	NET D	23,103.98	23,757.29	24,403.28	25,031.54	25,670.12	26,322.62	26,969.90	27,605.92	28,191.12	28,770.72	29,355.92	29,934.40	30,516.75
	NET S	21,600.46	22,192.72	22,778.35	23,345.90	23,921.73	24,510.10	25,093.77	25,666.66	26,190.21	26,708.74	27,232.29	27,749.82	28,270.75
Associate Officer P-2	Gross	24,233.00	25,097.00	25,967.00	26,832.00	27,706.00	28,589.00	29,492.00	30,387.00	31,285.00	32,184.00	33,078.00		
	NET D	19,194.79	19,739.11	20,287.21	20,832.16	21,382.78	21,927.29	22,478.12	23,024.07	23,571.85	24,120.24	24,663.24		
	NET S	18,026.91	18,527.17	19,030.90	19,531.73	20,037.78	20,533.72	21,033.08	21,528.02	23,024.61	22,521.76	23,013.80		
Assistant Officer P-1	Gross	18,200.00	18,964.00	19,740.00	20,516.00	21,318.00	22,120.00	22,935.00	23,724.00	24,513.00	25,285.00			
	NET D	15,166.00	15,693.16	16,228.60	16,748.56	17,277.88	17,807.20	18,345.10	18,865.84	19,371.19	19,857.55			
	NET S	14,304.00	14,792.96	15,289.60	15,770.25	16,258.67	16,747.08	17,243.42	17,723.92	18,189.03	18,636.02			

D—Rate applicable to staff members with a dependent spouse or child.
S—Rate applicable to staff members with no dependent spouse or child.

TABLE V.4. *Schedules of post adjustments (amount per index point in US dollars). (Effective 1 January 1981)*
(i) Additions (where cost of living is higher than at the base)

Level		Steps I	II	III	IV	V	VI	VII	VIII	IX	X	XI	XII	XIII
Under-Secretary-General														
USG	D	454.19												
	S	412.04												
Assistant Secretary-General														
ASG	D	416.77												
	S	379.37												
Director														
D-2	D	347.25	354.80	362.31	369.82									
	S	318.40	324.91	331.73	338.24									
Principal Officer														
D-1	D	315.32	320.80	325.96	331.42	336.61	342.16	347.44						
	S	290.33	295.35	299.78	304.49	308.95	313.76	318.56						
Senior Officer														
P-5	D	289.79	294.25	298.49	302.78	307.64	311.64	316.55	321.16	325.73	330.02			
	S	267.75	271.75	275.52	279.31	283.70	286.94	291.36	295.46	299.28	303.39			
First Officer														
P-4	D	242.89	248.36	253.86	259.02	265.11	269.72	274.34	278.97	283.81	289.93	295.70	301.26	
	S	225.65	230.61	235.60	240.30	245.58	249.72	253.83	257.96	262.35	267.64	272.98	278.03	
Second Officer														
P-3	D	203.93	209.79	215.03	220.02	225.58	231.16	237.00	242.60	247.34	251.80	256.53	260.99	266.06
	S	190.21	195.56	200.31	204.77	209.84	214.89	220.26	225.35	229.59	233.54	238.06	242.00	246.59
Associate Officer														
P-2	D	169.42	174.53	179.03	183.88	188.67	193.50	198.32	202.84	207.66	212.49	217.00		
	S	159.05	163.32	167.60	171.92	176.50	180.81	185.11	189.40	193.72	198.00	202.30		
Assistant Officer														
P-1	D	135.08	139.65	144.18	148.74	153.30	157.84	162.69	166.66	170.94	175.22			
	S	126.91	131.23	135.53	139.84	144.16	148.19	152.50	156.24	160.29	164.03			

D—Rate applicable to staff members with a dependent spouse or child.
S—Rate applicable to staff members with no dependent spouse or child.

TABLE V.5. *Schedules of post adjustments (amount per index point in US dollars)* (continued)
(i) Deductions (where cost of living is lower than at the base)

Level		Steps I	II	III	IV	V	VI	VII	VIII	IX	X	XI	XII	XIII
Under-Secretary-General														
USG	D	440.37												
	S	399.50												
Assistant Secretary-General														
ASG	D	404.19												
	S	367.96												
Director														
D-2	D	336.77	344.05	351.33	358.70									
	S	308.72	315.14	321.60	328.07									
Principal Officer														
D-1	D	295.35	302.25	309.15	316.05	322.93	329.55	335.97						
	S	291.97	278.14	284.26	290.38	296.46	302.31	308.01						
Senior Officer														
P-5	D	266.47	272.23	277.83	283.20	288.66	293.97	299.38	304.74	310.15	315.51			
	S	246.20	251.36	256.35	261.16	266.04	270.73	275.55	280.33	285.10	289.91			
First Officer														
P-4	D	220.88	226.40	231.92	237.44	242.97	248.25	253.49	258.73	264.23	269.79	275.29	280.54	
	S	205.18	210.17	215.16	220.15	225.09	229.84	234.54	239.24	244.18	249.14	254.08	258.78	
Second Officer														
P-3	D	184.83	190.05	195.22	200.25	205.35	210.75	215.75	220.84	225.52	230.16	234.84	239.47	244.12
	S	172.47	177.22	181.91	186.47	191.11	195.85	200.54	205.14	209.36	213.54	217.80	221.97	226.15
Associate Officer														
P-2	D	153.39	157.91	162.29	166.65	171.06	175.41	179.82	184.19	188.57	192.95	197.30		
	S	143.80	147.88	151.92	155.88	159.93	163.89	167.90	171.91	175.88	179.86	183.83		
Assistant Officer														
P-1	D	121.27	125.47	129.72	133.94	138.15	142.36	146.67	150.74	154.85	158.85			
	S	114.10	118.02	122.00	125.94	129.82	133.66	137.59	141.33	145.12	148.76			

D—Rate applicable to staff members with a dependent spouse or child.
S—Rate applicable to staff members with no dependent spouse or child.

TABLE V.6. *Pensionable remuneration for Professional and higher categories and for purposes of separation payments, net equivalent after application of staff assessment ($US). (Effective 1 January 1981)*

Level		I	II	III	IV	V	VI	VII	VIII	IX	X	XI	XII	XIII
Under-Secretary-General														
USG	PR	114,047.00												
	Net D	62,162.58												
	Net S	56,146.96												
Assistant Secretary-General														
ASG	PR	101,199.00												
	Net D	56,894.72												
	Net S	51,585.76												
Director														
D-2	PR	78,976.00	81,241.00	83,572.00	85,952.00									
	Net D	47,532.85	48,529.46	49,538.99	50,562.40									
	Net S	43,395.98	44,281.61	45,173.81	46,075.84									
Principal Officer														
D-1	PR	65,906.00	68,042.00	70,164.00	72,298.00	74,479.00	76,606.00	78,676.00						
	Net D	41,649.36	42,652.32	43,606.84	44,567.34	45,548.62	46,490.02	47,400.84						
	Net S	38,173.42	39,051.22	39,901.80	40,757.71	41,632.14	42,469.28	43,278.67						
Senior Officer														
P-5	PR	57,351.00	59,031.00	60,691.00	62,296.00	63,901.00	65,536.00	67,186.00	68,836.00	70,501.00	72,166.00			
	Net D	37,626.58	38,433.11	39,229.91	39,980.88	40,727.22	41,487.51	42,254.78	43,009.50	43,758.77	44,508.03			
	Net S	34,606.26	35,320.38	36,025.88	36,689.87	37,349.54	38,021.54	38,669.71	39,369.51	40,037.19	40,704.86			
First Officer														
P-4	PR	44,982.00	46,434.00	47,885.00	49,338.00	50,799.00	52,291.00	53,776.00	55,261.00	56,821.00	58,396.00	59,971.00		
	Net D	31,368.98	32,138.28	32,907.57	33,667.16	34,397.74	35,143.63	35,886.15	36,623.44	37,372.26	38,128.28	38,884.00		
	Net S	29,032.93	29,720.95	30,408.95	31,087.56	31,737.77	32,401.62	33,062.46	33,718.07	34,381.08	35,050.48	35,719.87		
Second Officer														
P-3	PR	35,969.00	37,230.00	38,478.00	39,734.00	41,031.00	42,357.00	43,672.00	44,972.00	46,203.00	47,424.00	48,654.00	49,872.00	51,121.00
	Net D	26,340.36	27,071.67	27,785.72	28,489.36	29,215.44	29,958.13	30,674.36	31,363.36	32,015.90	32,662.82	33,314.74	33,934.06	34,558.62
	Net S	24,526.09	25,185.54	25,827.52	26,457.02	27,106.60	27,771.05	28,411.71	29,027.91	29,611.50	30,190.06	30,773.10	31,325.10	31,880.95
Associate Officer														
P-2	PR	28,560.00	29,579.00	30,604.00	31,624.00	32,654.00	33,694.00	34,759.00	35,814.00	36,872.00	37,932.00	38,985.00		
	Net D	21,910.02	22,531.71	23,156.80	23,779.02	24,407.51	25,021.10	25,638.50	26,250.44	26,864.05	27,478.84	28,069.83		
	Net S	20,518.06	21,081.66	21,648.34	22,212.41	22,782.18	23,336.48	23,893.21	24,445.01	24,998.32	25,552.69	26,081.69		
Assistant Officer														
P-1	PR	21,450.00	22,350.00	23,265.00	24,180.00	25,125.00	26,070.00	27,030.00	27,960.00	28,890.00	29,801.00			
	Net D	17,365.35	17,959.35	18,563.27	19,161.77	19,757.13	20,352.50	20,957.31	21,543.23	22,111.33	22,666.81			
	Net S	16,339.37	16,887.48	17,444.73	17,996.56	18,543.73	19,090.90	19,646.75	20,185.23	20,700.56	21,204.13			

D—Rate applicable to staff members with a dependent spouse or child.
S—Rate applicable to staff members with no dependent spouse or child.

TABLE V.7.

Completed years of service	Months of pensionable remuneration less staff assessment, where applicable		
	Permanent appointments	Temporary appointments which are not for a fixed term	Temporary appointments for a fixed term exceeding six months
Less than 1	Not applicable	Nil	One week for each month
1	Not applicable	1	of uncompleted service
2	3	1	subject to a minimum of
3	3	2	six weeks' and a maximum
4	4	3	of three months' indem-
5	5	4	nity pay
6	6	5	3
7	7	6	5
8	8	7	7
9	9	9	9
10	9.5	9.5	9.5
11	10	10	10
12	10.5	10.5	10.5
13	11	11	11
14	11.5	11.5	11.5
15 or more	12	12	12

(*d*) No indemnity payments shall be made to:

A staff member who resigns, except where termination notice has been given and the termination date agreed upon;

A staff member who has a temporary appointment which is not for a fixed term and which is terminated during the first year of service;

A staff member who has a temporary appointment for a fixed term which is completed on the expiration date specified in the letter of appointment;

A staff member who is summarily dismissed;

A staff member who abandons his post;

A staff member who is retired under the Regulations of the United Nations Joint Staff Pension Fund.

(*e*) Staff members specifically engaged for conference and other short-term service or for service with a mission, as consultants or as experts, and staff members who are locally recruited for service in established offices away from Headquarters may be paid termination indemnity if and as provided in their letters of appointment.

Annex IV: Repatriation grant

In principle, the repatriation grant shall be payable to staff members whom the Organization is obligated to repatriate. The repatriation grant shall not, however, be paid to a staff member who is summarily dismissed. Detailed conditions and definitions relating to eligibility shall be determined by the Secretary-General. The amount of the grant shall be proportional to the length of service with the United Nations, as follows [Table V.8].

TABLE V.8. *Weeks of pensionable remuneration less staff assessment, where applicable*

Years of continuous service away from home country	Staff member with a spouse or dependent child at time of separation	Staff member with neither a spouse nor a dependent child at time of separation	
		Professional and higher categories	General Service category
1	4	3	2
2	8	5	4
3	10	6	5
4	12	7	6
5	14	8	7
6	16	9	8
7	18	10	9
8	20	11	10
9	22	13	11
10	24	14	12
11	26	15	13
12 or more	28	16	14

STAFF RULES

Contents

Article or chapter

Rules

Appendices to the Staff Rules

A. Pensionable remuneration for Professional and higher categories and salary scale and pensionable remuneration for Field Service category
B. Salaries and allowances for other categories at Headquarters
C. Arrangements relating to military service
D. Rules governing compensation in the event of death, injury or illness attributable to the performance of official duties (issued separately as document ST/SGB/Staff Rules/Appendix D/Rev.1 and Amend.1)
E. Medical expense assistance plan for General Service and other local staff of designated United Nations Office (issued separately as document ST/SGB/Staff Rules/Appendix E/Rev.1)

Rule 101.1: Applicability

Staff rules 101.1 through 112.8 are applicable to all staff members appointed by the Secretary-General except technical assistance project personnel, staff members specifically engaged for conferences and other short-term service, and special internes.

Chapter I: Duties, Obligations and Privileges

Rule 101.2: Hours of Work

(a) Normal working hours at Headquarters shall be from 9.30 a.m. to 6 p.m., Monday through Friday, with an interruption of one hour for lunch. Exceptions may be made by the Secretary-General as the needs of the service may require.

(b) The Secretary-General shall set the normal working hours for each duty station away from Headquarters and notify the staff of these hours.

(c) A staff member shall be required to work beyond the normal hour of duty whenever requested to do so.

Rule 101.3: Official Holidays

(a) Official holidays at Headquarters shall be New Year's Day (1 January), Washington's Birthday (third Monday in February), Memorial Day (last Monday in May), Independence Day (4 July), Labor Day (first Monday in September), Thanksgiving Day (fourth Thursday in November), Christmas Day (25 December) and one further day during the Christmas season designated each year by the Secretary

General. If any such day occurs on a Saturday or Sunday, the preceding Friday shall be considered an official holiday in lieu of Saturday and the following Monday in lieu of Sunday.

(b) The Secretary-General shall set the official holidays for each duty station away from Headquarters and notify the staff of these holidays.

(c) Staff members who are nationals of any country which observes a national day may be excused from work on that day.

Rule 101.4: Change of Official Duty Station

A change of official duty station shall take place when a staff member is assigned from one office of the Organization to another for a fixed period exceeding six months or transferred for an indefinite period. Detailment of a staff member from his or her official duty station for service with a United Nations mission or conference shall not constitute change of official duty station within the meaning of these Rules.

Rules 101.5: Interagency Loans

The Secretary-General may loan the services of a staff member to a specialized agency or other intergovernmental organization, provided such loan in no way diminishes the right or entitlements of the staff member under his or her letter of appointment to the United Nations.

Rules 101.6: Outside Activities and Interests

(a) Staff members shall not engage in any continuous or recurring outside occupation or employment without the prior approval of the Secretary-General.

(b) No staff member may be actively associated with the management of, or hold a financial interest in, any business concern if it were possible for the staff member to benefit from such association or financial interest by reason of his or her official position with the United Nations.

(c) A staff member who has occasion to deal in his or her official capacity with any matter involving a business concern in which he or she holds a financial interest shall disclose the measure of that interest to the Secretary-General.

(d) The mere holding of shares in a company shall not constitute a financial interest within the meaning of this rule unless such holding constitutes a substantial control.

(e) Staff members shall not, except in the normal course of official duties or with the prior approval of the Secretary-General, perform any one of the following acts, if such act relates to the purpose, activities, or interests of the United Nations.

(i)   Issue statements to the press, radio or other agencies of public information;
(ii) Accept speaking engagements;
(iii) Take part in film, theatre, radio or television productions;
(iv) Submit articles, books or other material for publication.

Rule 101.7

(Cancelled)

Rule 101.8: Membership in Political Parties and Political Activities

(*a*) Membership in a political party is permitted provided that such membership does not entail action, or obligation to action, contrary to staff regulation 1.7. The payment of normal financial contributions shall not be construed as an activity contrary to staff regulation 1.7.

(*b*) In any case of doubt as to the interpretation or application of staff regulation 1.7 and the present rule, the staff member concerned shall request a ruling from the Secretary-General.

Chapter III: Salaries and Related Allowances

Rule 103.1: Salary Scales for Field Service Personnel

The salary scales and conditions of salary increments for members of the Field Service shall be those set forth in appendix A (Field Service).

Rule 103.2: Salary Scales for General Service Personnel

The Secretary-General shall set the salary scales and conditions of salary increments for staff members in the General Service category at each established office, and these rates and conditions shall be published in appendix B.

Rule 103.3: Wage Rates for Manual Workers

The Secretary-General shall set wage rates and conditions of wage increments for manual workers at each establish office, and these rates and conditions shall be published in appendix B.

Rule 103.4: Salary and Wages for Locally Recruited Mission Personnel

The Secretary-General shall set salary or wage rates for personnel specifically recruited for service with a mission from within the general area of the mission.

Rule 103.5: Non-Resident's Allowance

(*a*) Staff members in the General Service category, who have been recruited from outside the country in which the duty station is located, or in respect of whom the United Nations assumes an obligation to repatriate, shall receive a non-resident's allowance at a rate and under conditions determined by the Secretary-General for the duty station, as shown in appendix B, provided that in no case shall the allowance be paid to a staff member whose nationality within the meaning of rule 104.8 is that of the country of the duty station or to staff member while he or she is excluded under rule 104.7.

(b) Members of the Field Service and staff members recruited specifically for service with a mission shall not be eligible for non-resident's allowance.

(c) The non-resident's allowance shall be taken into account in determining Joint Staff Pension Fund, medical, and group insurance contributions; overtime and night differential compensation; payments and indemnities on separation.

Rule 103.6: Language Allowance

(a) A staff member in the General Service category or in the Field Service category below level 6 shall be paid a language allowance if he or she passes a test, prescribed for this purpose, in any official language other than the language in which the staff member is required to be proficient by the terms of his or her appointment, unless the entitlement is specifically excluded in appendix B. No staff member shall be paid a language allowance for more than two official languages.

(b) Proficiency tests in the use of official languages shall be held not less than once each year.

(c) Staff members in receipt of a language allowance may be required to undergo further tests at intervals of not less than five years in order to demonstrate their continued proficiency in the use of two or more official languages.

(d) The amount of the allowance payable at each duty station shall be determined by the Secretary-General, provided that the amount payable for a second language shall be half the amount payable for one language. The amount of the allowance payable at Headquarters is shown in appendix B.

(e) The language allowance shall be taken into account in determining Joint Staff Pension Fund, medical and group insurance contributions; overtime and night differential compensation; payments and indemnities on separation.

Rule 103.7: Post Adjustment

(a) Subject to paragraph (d) below, post adjustments under annex I, paragraph 9, of the Staff Regulations shall be applied in accordance with the schedules set out in that annex in the case of staff members in the Professional category and above who are assigned to a duty station for one year or more.

(b) (i) The rate of post adjustment shown on the schedules for staff members with dependants shall apply to a staff member if his or her spouse is recognized as a dependant under rule 103.24 or if it is recognized that the staff member provides substantial and continuing support of one or more of his or her children.

(ii) Where both husband and wife are staff members in the Professional category or above, post adjustment shall be paid to each at the single rate unless they have a dependent child or children. In the case the dependency rate of post adjustment shall be paid to the spouse having the higher salary level and the single rate of post adjustment to the other spouse.

(iii) The higher rate of post adjustment shall be paid in accordance with the above provisions, regardless of where the dependants reside.

(*c*) The schedules of post adjustments referred to in paragraph (*a*) above shall be applied to each duty station according to the classification established for that purpose by the International Civil Service Commission.

(*d*) While the salary of a staff member is normally subject to the post adjustment of his or her duty station during assignments for one year or more, alternative arrangements may be made by the Secretary-General under the following circumstances:

(i)   A staff member who is assigned to a duty station classified lower in the schedule of post adjustments than the duty station in which the staff member has been serving may continue to receive for a reasonable period the post adjustment applicable to the latter while the members of his or her immediate family (spouse and children) remain at that duty station.

(ii) When a staff member is assigned to a duty station for less than one year, the Secretary-General shall decide at that time whether to apply the post adjustment applicable to the duty station and, if appropriate, to pay installation grant under rule 107.20 and assignment allowance under rule 103.22 or, in lieu of the above, to authorize appropriate subsistence payments.

(iii) When the Secretary-General designates an assignment as a special mission assignment under rule 103.21 (*a*), with provision for mission subsistence allowance, the post adjustment for the mission area will not be applicable.

(*e*) At duty stations where the average rental cost used in calculating the post adjustment index is based on the cost of housing provided by the United Nations, by the Government or by a related institution, staff members who have to rent housing accommodation at substantially higher commercial rates will be a supplement to the post adjustment in the form of a rental subsidy under conditions established by the Secretary-General.

Rule 103.8: Salary and Wage Increments

(*a*) Satisfactory service for the purpose of awarding a salary increment shall be defined, unless otherwise decided by the Secretary-General in any particular case, as satisfactory performance and conduct of staff members in their assignments as evaluated by their supervisors.

(*b*) Notwithstanding paragraph (*a*) of this rule, in the absence of exceptional circumstances, staff members holding probationary appointments shall become eligible for a second salary increment only after they have been granted permanent or regular appointments or if their probationary periods have been extended. Salary increments granted under this paragraph shall become effective in accordance with the provisions of paragraph (*c*) hereunder.

(*c*) Salary and wage increments shall be effective on the first day of the pay period in which the service requirements are completed, provided that the period of service may be shortened to meet the requirements of rule 103.9 and that such increments shall not be effective earlier than the first day of the day period in which a staff member returns to pay status from a period of leave without pay. No increment shall be paid in the case of staff members whose services will cease during the month in which the increment would otherwise have been due.

(*d*) If a staff member with satisfactory service is changed to a lower salary level, the period of service since the last increment shall be credited towards the next increment within the lower level. If a staff member whose service has not been satisfactory is changed to a lower salary level, the staff member's eligibility for salary increment in the lower level will be based on satisfactory service in the lower level.

Rule 103.9: Salary Policy in Promotions

Staff members receiving promotions shall be paid in accordance with the following provisions:

(i) During the first year following promotion a staff member in continuous service shall receive in salary the amount of one full step in the level to which the staff member has been promoted more than he or she would have received without promotion, except where promotion to the lowest step of the level yields a greater amount. The step rate and date of salary increment in the higher salary level shall be adjusted to achieve this end.

(ii) When, on promotion, a staff member becomes ineligible for payment of non-resident's allowance and/or language allowance which he or she has formerly been receiving, the amount the staff member has been receiving for these allowances shall be added to his or her salary before promotion to establish the step rate and date of next salary increment under (i) above.

Rule 103.10

(Cancelled)

Rule 103.11: Special Post Allowance

(a) Staff members shall be expected to assume temporarily, as a normal part of their customary work and without extra compensation, the duties and responsibilities of higher level posts.

(b) Without prejudice to the principle that promotion under staff rule 104.14 shall be the normal means of recognizing increased responsibilities and demonstrated ability, a staff member who is called upon to assume the full duties and responsibilities of a post at a clearly recognizable higher level than his or her own for a temporary period exceeding six months may, in exceptional cases, be granted a non-pensionable special post allowance from the beginning of the seventh month of service at the higher level.

(c) In the case of a staff member assigned to serve in a mission, or when a staff member in the General Service category is required to serve in a higher level post in the Professional category, the allowance may be paid immediately the staff member assumes the higher duties and responsibilities.

(d) The amount of the special post allowance shall be equivalent to the salary increase (including post adjustment and dependency allowances, if any) which the staff member would have received had the staff member been promoted to the level of the post in which he or she is serving.

Rule 103.12: Overtime and Compensatory Time Off

(*a*) Staff members serving at establish offices in the Manual Worker category, in the General Service category or in the Field Service who are required to work in excess of the working week established for this purpose shall be given compensatory time off or may receive additional payment, under the conditions set forth in appendix B.

(*b*) Should the exigencies of the service permit, and subject to the prior approval of the Secretary-General, occasional compensatory time off may be granted to staff members serving at established offices in the Professional category who have been required to work substantial or recurrent periods of overtime.

(*c*) The Secretary-General may set the conditions for overtime work or compensatory time off for staff members serving on missions or on other assignments away from their duty stations.

Rule 103.13: Night Differential

(*a*) Staff members serving at established offices who are assigned to night-time tours of duty shall receive a night differential at a rate and under conditions set forth in appendix B.

(*b*) When members of the Field Service are serving at an established office they may be paid a night differential in accordance with the conditions applicable to that office.

(*c*) Night differential shall not be paid for the same work for which overtime payment or compensatory time off is allowed or for any hours when the staff member is on leave or in travel status.

(*d*) The Secretary-General shall set the conditions regarding night-time tours of duty in respect of missions.

Rule 103.14: Salary Advances

(*a*) Salary advances may be made to staff members under the following circumstances and conditions:

(i)   Upon departure for extended official travel or for approved leave involving absence from duty for two or more pay days in the amount that would fall due for payment during the anticipated period of absence;

(ii)   In cases where staff members do not receive their regular pay cheque through no fault of their own, in the amount due;

(iii)   Upon separation from service, where final settlement of pay accounts cannot be made at the time of departure, subject to the advance not exceeding 80 per cent of the estimated final net payments due;

(iv)   In case where new staff members arrive without sufficient funds, in such amount as the Secretary-General may deem appropriate;

(v)   Upon change of official duty station or detail to mission duty, in such amounts as the Secretary-General may deem appropriate.

(*b*) The Secretary-General may, in exceptional and compelling circumstances, and if the request of the staff member is supported by a detailed justification in writing, authorize, an advance for any reason other than those enumerated above.

(*c*) Salary advances other than those referred to in subparagraphs '(*a*) (i), (ii) and (iii) above shall be liquidated at a constant rate as determined at the time the advance is authorized, in consecutive pay periods, commencing not later than the period following that in which the advance is made.

Rule 103.15: Retroactivity of Payments

A staff member who has not been receiving an allowance, grant or other payment to which he or she is entitled shall not receive retroactively such allowance, grant or payment unless the staff member has made written claim:

(i)   In the case of the cancellation or modification of the staff rule governing eligibility, within three months following the date of such cancellation or modification;

(ii) In every other case, within one year following the date on which the staff member would have been entitled to the initial payment.

Rule 103.16: Pensionable Remuneration

(*a*) For the purpose of the Regulations of the United Nations Joint Staff Pension Fund, pensionable remuneration shall, subject to paragraphs (*b*) and (*c*) below, consist of the sum of:

(i)   The amount of the gross salary of the staff member established in accordance with staff regulation 3.1;

(ii) The amount of any non-resident's allowance and/or language allowance payable under staff rules 103.5 and 103.6, respectively.

(*b*) In the case of staff members in the Professional and higher categories and Field Service personnel, for each complete 5 per cent by which the weighted average of the post adjustment classifications of the headquarters and regional offices of the member organizations of the United Nations Joint Staff Pension Fund varies from the weighted average as of 1 January 1977, the portion of pensionable remuneration established under paragraph (*a*) (i) above shall be increased or decreased, as the case may be, by a corresponding 5 per cent; for this purpose the weighted average shall be calculated as of March and September of each year, and any consequent variation shall take effect from the following 1 July or 1 January, respectively. The schedule of pensionable remuneration effective 1 January 1977 and any subsequent adjustment shall be shown in appendix A.

(*c*) Where a promotion from the General Service category to the Professional category would result in a reduction of the staff member's pensionable remuneration, the level of pensionable remuneration reached prior to the promotion shall be maintained until it is surpassed by the level based on the staff member's salary in the Professional category.

Rule 103.17: Rule Assessment

(*a*) In application of the staff assessment plan under staff regulation 3.3,

(i)   Salaries for staff members in the Professional and higher categories and for Field

Service personnel shall be subject to the assessment rates specified in paragraph (*b*) (i) of that regulation;

(ii) Salaries or wages for staff members in the General Service category, for Manual Workers and for locally recruited mission personnel shall be subject to the assessment rates specified in paragraph (*b*) (ii) of that regulation.

(*b*) The dependency rates of staff assessment under staff regulation 3.3 (*b*) (i) shall apply when:

(i) The staff member's spouse is recognized as a dependant under rule 103.24; or

(ii) The staff member provides substantial and continuing support to one or more of his or her children.

(*c*) Where both husband and wife are staff members whose salaries are subject to the staff assessment rates specified in staff regulation 3.3 (*b*) (i), staff assessment shall apply to each at the single rate. If they have a dependent child or children, the dependency rate shall apply to the spouse having the higher salary level and the single rate to the other spouse.

Rule 103.18: Deductions and Contributions

(*a*) There shall be deducted, each pay period, from the total payments due to each staff member:

(i) Staff assessment, at the rates and subject to the conditions prescribed in staff regulation 3.3 and rule 103.17;

(ii) Contributions to the United Nations Joint Staff Pension Fund, based on the staff member's pensionable remuneration as defined in rule 103.16.

(*b*) Deductions from salaries, wages and other emoluments may also be made for the following purposes:

(i) For contributions, other than to the United Nations Joint Staff Pension Fund, for which provision is made under these Rules;

(ii) For indebtedness to the United Nations;

(iii) For indebtedness to third parties when any deduction for this purpose is · authorized by the Secretary-General;

(iv) For lodging provided by the United Nations, by a Government or by a related institution.

Rule 103.19

(Cancelled)

Rule 103.20: Education Grant

Definitions

(*a*) For the purposes of this rule:

(i) 'Child' means an unmarried child of a staff member who is dependent upon the staff member for continuing support. 'Disabled child' means a child who is unable, by reasons of physical or mental disability, to attend a normal educational institution and therefore requires special teaching or training to prepare him or her for full integration into society or, while attending a normal educational institution, requires special teaching or training to assist him or her in overcoming the disability.

(ii) 'Home country' means the country of home leave of the staff member under rule 105.3. If both parents are eligible staff members, 'home country' means the country of home leave of either parent.

(iii) 'Duty station' means the country, or area within commuting distance notwithstanding national boundaries, where the staff member is serving.

Eligibility

(b) A staff member who is regarded as an international recruit under rule 104.7, and whose duty station is outside his or her home country shall be entitled to an education grant in respect of each child in full-time attendance at a school, university or similar educational institution. The Secretary-General may also authorize payment of the education grant, during mission service, to a staff member regarded under rule 104.6 as a local recruit as his or her normal official duty station. The grant shall not, however, be payable in respect of:

(i) Attendance at a kindergarten or nursery school at the pre-primary level;

(g) Where the period of service of the staff member does not cover the full scholastic year, the amount of the grant for that year shall normally be that proportion of the grant otherwise payable which the period of service bears to the full scholastic year.

Travel

(h) A staff member to whom an education grant is payable under paragraph (d) or under subparagraph (e) (ii) above in respect of his or her child's attendance at an educational institution shall be entitled to travel expenses for the child of one return journey each scholastic year between the educational institution and the duty station, provided that:

(i) Such travel expenses shall not be paid if the requested journey is unreasonable, either because of its timing in relation to other authorized travel of the staff member or his or her eligible family members or because of the brevity of the visit in relation to the expense involved;

(ii) Where attendance is for less than two thirds of the school year, travel expenses shall not normally be payable;

(iii) Transportation expenses shall not exceed the cost of a journey between the staff member's home country and the duty station.

Tuition of the mother tongue

(i) The Secretary-General will decide in each case whether the education grant shall be paid for tuition of the mother tongue under the second paragraph of staff regulation 3.2.

Claims

(*j*) Claims for the education grant shall be submitted in writing and supported by evidence satisfactory to the Secretary-General.

Rates of exchange

(*k*) For the purpose of applying the scales of reimbursement set out in paragraphs (*d*) and (*e*) above, when the expenses incurred are in a currency other than the United States dollar, the rate of exchange to be used shall be whichever rate yields more units of the other currency: the United Nations operational rate of exchange in effect on 1 January 1977 or on the date when the reimbursement is made.

Special education grant for disabled children

(*l*) A special education grant for disabled children shall be available to staff members of all categories, regardless of whether or not they are serving in their home country, provided that they have an appointment of one year or longer or have completed one year of continuous service.

(*m*) The amount of the grant shall be 75 per cent of the educational expenses actually incurred up to $4,000 per year, the maximum grant thus being $3,000. If the disabled child is eligible for the regular education grant, the total amount payable under the two types of grant shall not exceed $3,000 per year. 'Educational expenses' reimbursable under the special education grant shall comprise the expenses incurred to provide an educational programme designed to meet the needs of the disabled child in order that he or she may attain the highest possible level of functional ability.

(*n*) The grant shall be computed on the basis of the calendar year, if the child is unable to attend a normal educational institution, or on the basis of the school year, if the child is in full-time attendance at a normal educational insitution while receiving special teaching or training. The grant shall be payable in respect of any disabled child from the date on which the special teaching or training is required up to the end of the school year or the calendar year, as appropriate, in which the child reaches the age of 25 years.

(*o*) Where the period of service does not cover the full school year or calendar year, the amount of the grant shall be that proportion of the annual grant which the period of service bears to the full school or calendar year.

(*p*) Claims for the grant shall be submitted annually in writing and supported by medical evidence satisfactory to the Secretary-General regarding the child's disability. The staff member shall also be required to provide evidence that he or she has exhausted all other sources of benefits that may be available for the education and training of the child. The amount of educational expenses used as the basis for the calculation of the special education grant shall be reduced by the amount of any benefits so received or receivable by the staff member.

(*q*) The provision concerning the rates of exchange contained in paragraph (*k*) above shall also apply to the computation and payment of the special education grant for disabled children.

Rule 103.21: *Salary and Allowances during Mission Assignments*

(*a*) The Secretary-General may designate special mission assignments, including assignments for periods of one year or more, during which a mission subsistence allowance shall be authorized in lieu of assignment allowance under rule 103.22, installation grant under rule 107.20 and any post adjustment to the area applicable under rule 103.7 (*a*). Where such a designation has been made, the mission subsistence allowance shall be payable to staff members recruited or assigned from outside the area of the mission, and the salaries of staff members assigned from another duty station shall continue to be subject to the post adjustment, if any, applicable at the duty station from which the staff members were assigned.

(*b*) The Secretary-General shall set at the rates and conditions for the missions subsistence allowances payable on each such assignment. Eligible staff members who have a dependent spouse or one or more dependent children may be authorized to receive a higher rate of mission subsistence allowance than staff members not having such dependants. Where both husband and wife are staff members entitled to missions subsistence allowance, the allowance, will be paid to each at the single rate. If they have a dependent child or children, the allowance will be paid at the dependency rate to the spouse having the higher salary level and at the single rate to the other spouse. The allowance may be paid wholly or partially in the currency of the mission area or in the form of provision of food and/or logding in kind.

(*c*) The Secretary-General may pay a clothing allowance to staff members who are assigned to service with a mission in a tropical or arctic area. The United Nations shall provide uniforms and accessories, but no clothing allowance, to members of the Field Service who are required to wear them.

Rule 103.22: Assignment Allowance

(*a*) Subject to the provisions of rules 103.21 and 107.27, an assignment allowance shall be paid to a staff member in the Professional category and above who is appointed or assigned to a duty station outside his or her home country for a specified period of service under the following circumstances:

(i) The allowance will be authorized when the fixed-term appointment or temporary assignment is for a period of one year or more but less than two years;

(ii) The allowance may be authorized when the fixed-term appointment or temporary assignment is for a period of two years or more but less than five years. Normally, the allowance will be paid in the case of service at a duty station in the field, whereas removal costs under rule 107.27 will be paid in the case of service at a duty station in a city where the headquarters of the United Nations, a specialized agency or the International Atomic Energy Agency is located.

(*b*) The allowance shall not be paid to a staff member for more than five years in respect of service at one duty station, except for service at a duty station outside Europe and North America, where the period of entitlement may be extended beyond five years for a period of service not exceeding two years if the staff members is maintained at the same duty station on the initiative of the Organization. After the staff member has been paid the allowance for five years or more at one duty station, he or she shall not be entitled to any payment of removal costs under rule 107.27 (*a*) to the same duty station.

(c) When a staff member is assigned to a duty station for less than one year, the allowance will normally not be paid. However, appropriate subsistence payments may be made under rule 103.7 (d) (ii) where no assignment allowance is payable.

(d) Where the allowance has been paid for an initial period and the appointment or assignment is extended for additional fixed terms at one duty station, payment of the allowance may be continued.

(e) When an initial fixed-term appointment at one duty station is converted to a probationary appointment, or when an assignment is extended to five years or more, the allowance shall cease, and an entitlement to removal costs shall thereupon commence.

(f) The allowance may, in exceptional cases, be paid to a staff member who, after service of at least two years at a duty station outside his or her home country, is assigned to at duty station within that country.

(g) The assignments of allowance shall be payable at the following annual rates:

(i) For assignments to duty stations in Europe, in Canada, in Cyprus, in Malta, Turkey (European portion) and in the United States of America:

	Single rates $	Dependency rates $
P-1 and P-2	800	1,000
P-3 and P-4	950	1,200
P-5 and above	1,100	1,400

(ii) For assignments to all other duty stations:

P-1, P-2, P-3 and P-4	1,600	2,000
P-5 and above	1,900	2,400

(h) The dependency rates of the assignment allowance shall be paid to a staff member if either the spouse or a child of the staff member is recognized as dependent upon the staff member for main the continuing support. Where both husband and wife are staff members entitled to assignment allowance, the allowance will be paid to each at the single rate. If they have a dependent child or children, the allowance will be paid at the dependency rate to the spouse having the higher salary level and at the single rate to the other spouse.

Rule 103.23: Dependency Allowances

(a) The rates of dependency allowances applicable to the Field Service category and to the General Service and Manual Workers categories shall be set out in appendix A and appendix B, respectively, to these Rules.

(b) Subject to the provisions of staff regulation 3.4 (a), the full amount of the dependency allowance provided under that regulation and the Staff Rules in respect of a dependent child shall be payable, except where the staff member or his or her spouse receives a direct governmental grant in respect of the same child. Where such a governmental grant is made, the dependency allowance payable under this rule shall be the approximate amount by which the governmental grant is less than the dependency allowance set out under the Staff Regulations and Staff Rules. In no case shall the sum of the two payments be less than the rate set out under the Staff Regulations and Staff Rules.

(c) Staff members shall be responsible for notifying the Secretary-General in writing of claims for dependency allowance and may be required to support such claims by documentary evidence satisfactory to the Secretary-General. They shall be responsible for reporting to the Secretary-General any change in the status of a dependant affecting the payment of this allowance.

(d) A dependency allowance shall be paid in respect of not more than one dependent parent, brother or sister, and such payment shall not be made when a payment is being made for a dependent spouse.

Rule 103.24: Definition of Dependency

For the purposes of the Staff Regulations and Staff Rules:

(a) A dependent spouse shall be a spouse whose occupational earnings, if any, do not exceed an amount established by the Secretary-General for the purpose. This amount shall normally be the approximate equivalent of the lowest entry level of the United Nations salary scales for the duty station in the country of the spouse's place of work, provided that, in the case of staff in the Professional category or above, the amount shall not at any duty station be less than the equivalent of the lowest entry level at New York in force on 1 January of the year concerned. The amount established by the Secretary-General shall be published to the staff by administrative instruction or other appropriate means.

(b) A 'child' shall be the unmarried child of a staff member under the age of 18 years or, if the child is in full-time attendance at a school or university (or similar educational institution), under the age of 21 years. If the child is totally and permanently disabled, the requirements as to school attendance and age shall be waived.

A child shall be recognized as dependent for purposes of staff regulation 3.4 when the staff member provides continuing support and submits a claim certifying to this effect; provided that where divorce has occurred and the child does not reside with the staff member, dependency allowance will be payable only where the staff member submits satisfactory documentary evidence that he or she has assumed responsibility for the main and continuing support of the child.

(c) A dependent parent, dependent brother or dependent sister shall be a parent, an unmarried brother or an unmarried sister of whose financial support the staff member provides one half or more, and in any case at least twice the amount of the dependency allowance; provided that the brother or sister is under the age of 18 years or, if in full-time attendance at a school or university (or similar educational institution), under the age of 21 years. If the brother or sister is totally and permanently disabled, the requirements as to school attendance and age shall be waived.

Chapter IV: Appointment and Promotion

Rule 104.1: Letter of Appointment

The letter of appointment granted to every staff member contains expressly or by reference all the terms and conditions of employment. All contractual entitlements of staff members are strictly limited to those contained expressly or by reference in their letters of appointment.

Rule 104.2: Effective Date of Appointment

(*a*) The appointment of every locally recruited staff member shall take effect from the date on which the staff member starts to perform his or her duties.

(*b*) The appointment of every staff member internationally recruited shall take effect from the date on which the staff member enters into official travel status to assume his or her duties or, if no official travel is involved, from the date on which the staff member starts to perform his or her duties.

Rule 104.3: Re-employment

(*a*) A former staff member who is re-employed shall either be given a new appointment or, if he or she is re-employed within 12 months of being separated from service or within any longer period following retirement on disability under the Joint Staff Pension Fund Regulations, he or she may be reinstated in accordance with the provisions of paragraph (*b*) hereunder. If the former staff member is given a new appointment, its terms shall be fully applicable without regard to any former period of service. If the former staff member is reinstated, it shall be so stipulated in his or her letter of appointment.

(*b*) On reinstatement the staff member's services shall be considered as having been continuous, and the staff member shall return to the United Nations any monies he or she received on account of separation, including termination indemnity under rule 109.4, repatriation grant under rule 109.5 and payment for accrued annual leave under rule 109.8. The interval between separation and reinstatement shall be charged, to the extent possible and necessary, to annual leave, with any further period charged to special leave without pay. The staff member's sick leave credit under rule 106.2 at the time of separation shall be re-established; the staff member's participation, if any, in the Joint Staff Pension Fund shall be governed by the Regulations of that Fund.

Rule 104.4: Notification by Staff Members and Obligation to Supply Information

(*a*) Staff members shall be responsible on appointment for supplying the Secretary-General with whatever information may be required for the purpose of determining their status under the Staff Regulations and Staff Rules or of completing administrative arrangements in connexion with their appointments.

(*b*) Staff members shall also be responsible for promptly notifying the Secretary-General, in writing, of any subsequent changes affecting their status under the Staff Regulations or Staff Rules.

(*c*) A staff member who intends to acquire permanent residence status in any country other than that of his or her nationality or who intends to change his or her nationality shall notify the Secretary-General of that intention before the change in residence status or in nationality becomes final.

(*d*) A staff member who is arrested, charged with an offence other than a minor traffic violation or summoned before a Court as a defendant in a criminal proceeding, or convicted, fined or imprisoned for any offence other than a minor traffic violation shall immediately report the fact to the Secretary-General.

(*e*) A staff member may at any time be required by the Secretary-General to supply information concerning facts anterior to his or her appointment and relevant to his or her suitability, or concerning facts relevant to his or her integrity, conduct and service as a staff member.

Rule 104.5: Geographical Distribution

Recruitment on as wide a geographical basis as possible, in accordance with the requirements of staff regulation 4.2, shall not apply to posts in the General Service category or in similar salary levels.

Rule 104.6: Local Recruitment

(*a*) The conditions under which staff members shall be regarded as local recruits for the purposes of these rules at each duty station, including missions, are set forth in appendix B.

(*b*) A staff member regarded as having been locally recruited shall not be eligible for the allowances or benefits indicated under rule 104.7.

Rule 104.7: International Recruitment

(*a*) Staff members other than those regarded under rule 104.6 as having been locally recruited shall be considered as having been internationally recruited. The allowances and benefits in general available to internationally recruited staff members include: payment of travel expenses upon initial appointment and on separation for themselves and their spouses and dependent children, removal of household effects, non-resident's allowance, home leave, education grant and repatriation grant.

(*b*) Members of the Field Service and Staff members recruited specifically for mission service shall not be eligible for non-resident's allowance or removal of household effects.

(*c*) A staff member who has changed his or her residential status in such a way that he or she may, in the opinion of the Secretary-General, be deemed to be a permanent resident of any country other than that of his or her nationality may lose entitlement to non-resident's allowance, home leave, education grant, repatriation grant and payment of travel expenses upon separation for the staff member and his or her spouse and dependent children and removal of household effects, based upon place of home leave, if the Secretary-General considers that the continuation of such entitlement would be contrary to the purposes for which the allowance or benefit was created. Conditions governing entitlement to international benefits in the light of residential status are shown in appendix B.

Rule 104.8: Nationality

(*a*) In the application of Staff Regulations and Staff Rules, the United Nations shall not recognize more than one nationality for each staff member.

(*b*) When a staff member has been legally accorded nationality status by more than one State, the staff member's nationality for the purposes of the Staff Regulations and these Rules shall be the nationality of the State with which the staff member is, in the opinion of the Secretary-General, most closely associated.

Ruled 104.9

(Cancelled)

Rule 104.10: Family Relationships

(*a*) Except where another person equally well qualified cannot be recruited, appointment shall not be granted to a person who bears any of the following relationships to a staff member: father, mother, son, daughter, brother or sister.

(*b*) The husband or wife of a staff member may be appointed provided that he or she is fully qualified for the post for which he or she is being considered and that the spouse is not given any preference by virtue of the relationship to the staff member.

(*c*) A staff member who bears to another staff member any of the relationships specified in (*a*) and (*b*) above:

(i)   Shall not be assigned to serve in a post which is superior or subordinate in the line of authority to the staff member to whom he or she is related;

(ii) Shall disqualify himself or herself from participating in the process of reaching or reviewing an administrative decision affecting the status or entitlements of the staff member to whom he or she is related.

(*d*) The marriage of one staff member to another shall not affect the contractual status of either spouse but their entitlements and other benefits shall be modified as provided in the relevant staff regulations and rules. The same modifications shall apply in the case of a staff member whose spouse is a staff member of another organization participating in the United Nations common system. Where both husband and wife are staff members and maintain separate households because they are assigned to different duty stations, the Secretary-General may decide to maintain such separate entitlements and benefits, provided that this is not inconsistent with any staff regulation or other decision of the General Assembly.

Rule 104.11

(Cancelled)

Rule 104.12: Temporary Appointments

On recruitment staff members may be granted one of the following types of temporary appointments: probationary appointment, fixed-term appointment, or indefinite appointment.

(a) *Probationary appointment*

The probationary appointment may be granted to persons under the age of 50 years who are recruited for career service. The period of probationary service under such an appointment shall normally be two years. In exceptional circumstances, it may be reduced or extended for not more than one additional year.

At the end of the probationary service the holder of a probationary appointment shall be granted either a permanent or a regular appointment or be separated from the service.

The probationary appointment shall have no specific expiration date and shall be governed by the Staff Regulations and Staff Rules applicable to temporary appointments which are not for a fixed term.

(b) *Fixed-term appointment*

The fixed-term appointment, having an expiration date specified in the letter of appointment, may be granted for a period not exceeding five years to persons recruited for service of prescribed duration, including persons temporarily seconded by national Governments or institutions for service with the United Nations. The fixed-term appointment does not carry any expectancy of renewal or of conversion to any other type of appointment.

(c) *Indefinite appointment*

The indefinite appointment may be granted to:

(i) Persons specifically recruited for mission service who are not granted a fixed-term or regular appointment.

(ii) Persons specifically recruited for service with the Office of the High Commissioner for Refugees or any other Agency or Office of the United Nations as may be designated by the Secretary-General.

The indefinite appointment does not carry any expectancy of conversion to any other type of appointment. The indefinite appointment shall have no specific expiration date and, except as provided in staff rule 106.2 (*a*) (iv), shall be governed by the Staff Regulations and Staff Rules applicable to temporary appointments which are not for a fixed term.

Rule 104.13: Permanent and Regular Appointments

(a) *Permanent appointment*

(i) The permanent appointment may be granted to staff members who are holders of a probationary appointment and who, by their qualifications, performance and conduct, have fully demonstrated their suitability as international civil servants and have shown that they meet the high standards of efficiency, competence and integrity established in the Charter.

(ii) Permanent appointments shall be subject to review at the end of the first five years of service under such appointment.

(b) *Regular appointment*

(i) The regular appointment may be granted when warranted by specific circumstances, especially such circumstances of a local nature, to staff members, in the General Service and Manual Worker categories who are holders of probationary appointments and have shown that they meet the high standards of efficiency, competence and integrity established in the Charter.

(ii) The regular appointment shall be for an indefinite period and may last until retirement. It shall be governed by the Staff Regulations and Staff Rules applicable to temporary appointments which are not for a fixed term. Regular appointments shall be subject to review at the end of the first five years.

   (c) (i) Recommendations proposing the grant of permanent or regular appointments on the ground that a holder of a probationary appointment has met the requirements of this rule may be made to the Secretary-General by agreement between the Office of Personnel Services and the Department or Office concerned. Such agreements shall be reported to the Appointment and Promotion Board before submission to the Secretary-General.

      (ii) Affirmative recommendations to the effect that the holder of a permanent or regular appointment under a five-year review has maintained the requisite standards of suitability may similarly be made by agreement between the Office of Personnel Services and the Department or Office concerned and shall be reported to the Appointment and Promotion Board before submission to the Secretary-General.

      (iii) In the absence of an agreed favourable recommendation as provided in (c) (i) or (ii) above, the matter shall be referred to the Appointment and Promotion Board.

(d) Permanent or regular appointments limited to service with the United Nations Children's Fund or the United Nations Development Programme may be granted by the Executive Director of the Children's Fund or the Administrator of the Development Programme, respectively, with the assistance of such boards as may be established in accordance with the provisions of the last sentence of rule 104.14 (a) (i).

Rule 104.14: Appointment and Promotion Board

   (a) (i) An Appointment and Promoting Board shall be established by the

Secretary-General to give advice on the appointment, promotion and review of staff in the General Service and Professional categories and on the appointment and review of staff at the Principal Office level, except those specifically recruited for service with the United Nations Children's Fund, the United Nations Development Programme, the Untied Nations Environment Programme, the United Nations Institute for Training and Research or the United Nations University. The Secretary-General shall also establish appointed and promotion committee and such other subsidiary panels as may be necessary to assist the Appointment and Promotion Board in the performance of its functions. The heads of the organs referred to above may establish boards whose composition and functions are generally comparable to those of the Appointment and Promotion Board to advise them in the case of staff members recruited specifically for service with those organs.

(ii) Subject to the criteria of Article 101, paragraph 3, of the Charter and to the provisions of staff regulations 4.2 and 4.4, the Appointment and Promotion Board shall, in filling vacancies, normally give preference, where qualifications are equal, to staff members already in the Secretariat and staff members in other international organizations.

(b) Composition and procedures of the Appointment and Promotion Board:

(i) The Appointment and Promotion Board shall consist of seven members and seven alternates, at the Senior Officer level and above. The Assistant Secretary-General, Personnel Services, or an authorized representative shall serve *ex officio* as a non-voting member of the Board. The other members and alternates shall be appointed by the Secretary-General after consultative with, and after consideration of a panel of names proposed by, the Staff Council. Such members and alternates shall be appointed for fixed periods, normally of one year, subject to renewal. The Secretary-General will ensure that at least two members and two alternates are appointed from among nominees submitted by the Staff Council.

(ii) The Board shall elect its own Chairman and establish its own procedures.

(c) Composition and procedures of the appointment and promoting committees:

(i) The Appointment and Promotion Committee at Headquarters shall consist of seven members and fourteen alternates, at the Second Officer level and above. A designated official of the Office of Personnel Services shall serve *ex officio* as a non-voting member of the Committee. The other members and alternates shall be appointed by the Secretary-General after consultation with, and after consideration of a panel of names proposed by, the Staff Council. Such members and alternates shall be appointed for fixed periods, normally of one year, subject to renewal. The Secretary-General will ensure that at least two members and four alternates are appointed from among nominees submitted by the Staff Council. The Appointment and Promotion Committees established at other designated offices shall be similarly constituted and shall be composed five or seven members and an equal number of alternates, with at least two members and two alternates appointed from among nominees submitted by the local Staff Council.

(ii) Each committee shall elect its own Chairman and, subject to such general directives as may be issued by the Board, shall establish its own procedures.

(*d*) Subsidiary panels:

As necessary, working groups at Headquarters and in other designated offices, with functions comparable to those of the Appointment and Promotion Board and committees, may be appointed in the same manner by the Secretary-General.

(*e*) For any particular review where promotion is envisaged, the rank of members or alternates serving on the committees or subsidiary panels shall not be below the level to which promotion is contemplated.

(*f*) Functions of the Appointment and Promotion Board:

The function of the Appointment and Promotion Board shall be to make recommendations to the Secretary-General in respect of the following:

(i) Appointment:
Proposed probationary appointments and other proposed appointments of a probable duration of one year or more, excluding the appointment of persons recruited specifically for service with a mission.

(ii) Review:
   (A) The suitability for permanent or regular appointment of staff members serving on probationary appointments, as may be referred to it in accordance with the provisions of rule 104.13 (*c*). Recommendations of the Board may include extension of the probationary period for one additional year or separation from the service.
   (B) The review of appointments of staff members holding permanent or regular appointment as may be referred to it in accordance with the provisions of rule 104.13 (*c*). Upon the completion of the first five years of service under such appointments, for the purpose of determining whether the staff member concerned has maintained the standards of efficiency, competence and integrity established in the Charter.
   (C) The review of proposals for the termination of permanent appointments for unsatisfactory services under staff regulation 9.1 (*a*) in accordance with the special procedure established for that purpose by the Secretary-General.

(iii) Promotion:
   (A) The selection of staff members qualified for promotion. For this purpose, the Board shall normally once a year conduct a comprehensive, grade by grade review of all staff members within its purview. Wherever practicable, it shall develop and maintain promotion registers embodying the results of such a review. These registers shall be established in relation to an estimate of the total number of known and foreseeable vacancies to be filled by promotion at each grade level in the period until the next general review of staff.
   (B) In the event that a particular vacancy cannot, by reason of the nature of the work, by appropriately filled from a promotion register, the Board may recommend exceptionally, in advance of the next regular review, the promotion of a staff member considered by it to be best qualified after review of a relevant group of staff.

(C) Minimum periods of service in the grade shall be established as a normal requirement for consideration for promotion. These normal requirements shall not be less than:

    i. One year for staff members in the Professional category or in the Principal level of the General Service category at Headquarters;

    ii. Six months for all other staff members.

(g) The foregoing functions with respect to staff in the Professional category and at the Principal Officer level will be performed by the Appointment and Promoting Board or, at its request, by the appointment and promotion committees, which will report to the Board. The same functions in respect of staff in the General Service category will normally be performed by working groups, in accordance with the provisions establishing such working groups.

Rule 104.15: Medical Examination

(a) Staff members may be required from time to time to satisfy the United Nations Medical Officer, by medical examination, that they are free from any ailment likely to impair the health of others.

(b) Staff members may also be required to undergo such medical examinations and receive such inoculations as may be required by the United Nations Medical Officer before they go on or after they return from mission service.

Chapter V: Annual and Special Leave

Rule 105.1: Annual Leave

(a) Staff members shall accrue annual leave while in full pay status at the rate of six weeks a year, subject to the provisions of paragraph (f) below, and of rule 105.2 (c) and provided that no leave shall accrue while a staff member is receiving compensation equivalent to salary and allowances under rule 106.4

(b) Annual leave may be taken in units of days and half-days. All arrangements as to leave shall be subject to the exigencies of the service, which may require that leave be taken by a staff member during a period designated by the Secretary-General. Leave may be taken only when authorized, but the personal circumstances and preferences of the individual staff member shall, as far as possible, be considered.

(c) Annual leave may be accumulated, provided that no more than 12 weeks of such leave shall be carried forward beyond 1 January of any year or such other date as the Secretary-General may set for a duty station. However, upon completion of service with a mission (so designated for this purpose by the Secretary General), any accumulation of annual leave which otherwise would have become subject to forfeiture during the mission service, or within two months thereafter, may be utilized to cover all or part of an authorized period of post-mission leave. Any such leave which is not so utilized within four months following departure from the mission area shall be forfeited.

(d) Any absence from duty not specifically covered by other provisions in these rules shall be charged to the staff member's accrued annual leave, if any; if the staff member has no accrued annual leave, it shall be considered as unauthorized, and pay and allowances shall cease for the period of such absence.

(*e*) A staff member may, in exceptional circumstances, be granted advance annual leave up to a maximum of two weeks, provided his or her service is expected to continue for a period beyond that necessary to accrue the leave so advanced.

(*f*) The Secretary-General shall set the terms and conditions under which annual leave may be allowed to staff members recruited specifically for service with a mission from within the general area of the mission and notify the staff of these terms and conditions. These terms and conditions will be set with due regard to local practices in the area of the mission concerned.

Rule 105.2: Special Leave

(*a*) Special leave, with full or partial pay or without pay, may be granted for advanced study or research in the interest of the United Nations, in cases of extended illness or for other important reasons for such period as the Secretary-General may prescribe.

(*b*) A staff member, other than one recruited specifically for a mission, who has completed one year of sastisfactory probationary service or who has a permanent or regular appointment and who is called upon to serve in the armed forces of the State of which the staff member is a national, whether for training or active duty, may be granted special leave without pay for the duration of such military service, in accordance with terms and conditions set forth in appendix C.

(*c*) Staff members shall not accrue service credits towards sick, annual, home and maternity leave, salary increment, termination indemnity and repartriation grant during full months of special leave with partial pay or without pay. Periods of less than one calendar month of such leave shall not affect the ordinary rates of accrual; nor shall continuity of service be considered broken by periods of special leave.

Rule 105.3: Home Leave

(*a*) Staff members, other than those considered as local recruits under rule 104.6 or excluded from home leave under rule 104.7, who are serving outside their home country and who are otherwise eligible shall be entitled once in every two years of qualifying service to visit their home country at United Nations expense for the purpose of spending in that country a substantial period of annual leave. Leave taken for this purpose and under the terms and conditions set forth in this rule shall hereinafter be referred to as home leave.

(*b*) A staff member shall be eligible for home leave provided the following conditions are fulfilled:

(i) While performing his or her official duties the staff member continues to reside in a country other than that of which he or she is a national, or, in the case of a staff member who is a native of a non-metropolitan territory of the country of the duty station and who maintained his or her normal residence in such non-metropolitan territory prior to appointment, he or she continues to reside, while performing his or her official duties, outside such territory;

(ii) The staff member's service is expected by the Secretary-General to continue at least six months beyond the date of his or her return from any proposed home leave, on the understanding that, in the case of the first home leave, the staff member's service is also expected to continue at least six months beyond the second anniversary of the date of his or her appointment or of the date on which the staff member becomes eligible for home leave and that in the case of home leave following the return from a family visit travel under rule 107.1 (*b*), the staff member has completed not less than nine months of continuous service since departure in the family visit travel.

(*c*) Staff members whose eligibility under (*b*) above is established at the time of their appointment shall begin to accrue service credit towards home leave from that date. Staff members who become eligible for home leave subsequent to appointment shall begin to accrue such service credit from the effective date of their becoming eligible.

(*d*) The country of home leave shall be the country of the staff member's nationality, subject to the following terms, conditions and exceptions:

(i)   The place of home leave of the staff member within his or her home country shall be, for purposes of travel land transportion entitlements, the place with which the staff member had the closest residential ties during the period of his or her most recent residence in the home country preceding appointment;

(ii) A staff member who has served with another public international organization immediately preceding his or her appointment shall have the place of home leave determined as though his or her entire previous service with the other international organization had been with the United Nations;

(iii) The Secretary-General, in exceptional and compelling circumstances, may authorize as the home country, for the purposes of this rule, a country other than the country of nationality. A staff member requesting such authorization will be required to satisfy the Secretary-General that the staff member maintained normal residence in such other country for a prolonged period preceding his or her appointment, that the staff member continues to have close family or personal ties in that country and that the staff member's taking home leave there would not be inconsistent with the purposes and intent of staff regulation 5.3.

(*e*) Except in the case of staff members serving on probationary appointments, and subject to the provisions in appendix B, the first home leave for an eligible staff member shall fall due in the second calendar year after the one in which the staff member was appointed or in which entitlement is acquired. A staff member appointed on a probationary basis shall not be entitled to his or her first home leave until the staff member has been granted a permanent appointment or an extension of probationary period, unless the Secretary-General considers that it will not be possible for the Appointment and Promotion Board to review his or her case within six months after the completion of two years' service, in which event, the Secretary-General may grant the home leave subject to the other conditions of this rule. Home leave may be taken, subject to the exigencies of the service and to the provisions above in respect of probationary appointment, at any time during the calendar year in which it falls due.

(*f*) In exceptional circumstances, a staff member may be granted advanced home leave, provided that not less than 12 months of qualifying service have been completed or that not less than 12 months of qualifying service have elapsed since the date of return from his or her last home leave. The granting of advanced home leave shall not advance the calendar year in which the next home leave falls due.

(g) If, excepting as provided hereunder, a staff member delays taking his or her home leave beyond the calendar year in which it falls due, the staff member shall not be entitled to take his or her next such leave until the second succeeding calendar year thereafter. Should, however, the Secretary-General decide that exceptional circumstances, arising out of the exigencies of the service, make it necessary for a staff member's home leave to be delayed beyond the calendar year in which it falls due, such delayed leave may be taken without altering the time of his or her next succeeding home leave entitlements, provided that not less than 12 months of qualifying service elapse between the date of the staff member's return from the delayed home leave and the date of his or her next home leave departure.

(h) A staff member may be required to take his or her home leave in conjunction with travel on official business or change of official duty station, due regard being paid to the interests of the staff member and his or her family.

(i) Subject to the conditions specified in chapter V I I of these rules, a staff member shall be entitled to claim, in respect of authorized travel on home leave, travel time and expenses for himself or herself and eligible family members for the outward and return journeys between the official duty station and the place of residence in his or her home country.

(j) Travel of eligible family members shall be in conjunction with the approved home leave of the staff member, provided that exceptions may be granted if the exigencies of the service or other special circumstances prevent the staff member and his or her family members from travelling together.

(k) If both husband and wife are staff members eligible for home leave, each staff member shall have the choice either of exercising his or her own home leave entitlement or of accompanying the spouse. A staff member who chooses to accompany his or her spouse shall be granted travel time appropriate to the travel involved. Dependent children whose parents are staff members, each of whom is entitled to home leave, may accompany either parent. The frequency of travel shall not exceed once in every two years both with regard to staff members and to their dependent children, if any.

(l) A staff member travelling on home leave shall be required to spend a substantial period of leave in his or her home country. The Secretary-General may request a staff member, on his or her return from home leave, to furnish satisfactory evidence that this requirement has been fully met.

Chapter V I: Social Security

Rule 106.1: Participation in the Pension Fund

Staff members whose appointments are for one or longer or who complete one year of service under shorter appointments without an interruption of more than 30 days shall become participants in the United Nations Joint Staff Pension Fund, provided that they are then under 60 years of age and that participation is not excluded by their letters of appointment.

Rule 106.2: Sick Leave

(*a*) Staff members who are incapacitated from the performamce of their duties by illness or injury or whose attendance is prevented by public health requirements will be granted sick leave in accordance with the following provisions:

(i)   All sick leave must be approved on behalf of the Secretary-General.

(ii)   A staff member holding a fixed-term appointment for less than one year shall be granted sick leave credit at the rate of 2 working days per month of contractual service.

(iii)   A staff member holding a probationary appointment or a fixed-term appointment of one year or longer but less than five years shall be granted sick leave up to three months on full salary and three months on half salary in any period of 12 consecutive months, provided that the amount of sick leave permitted in any four consecutive years shall not exceed 18 months, nine months on full salary and nine months of half salary.

(iv)   A staff member who holds a permanent, regular or indefinite appointment, who holds a fixed-term appointment for five years or who has completed five years of continuous service shall be granted sick leave up to nine months on full salary and nine months on half salary in any period of four consecutive years.

(v)   Staff members shall be responsible for informing their supervisors as soon as possible of absences due to illness or injury. Where practicable, they should, before absenting themselves, report to the United Nations Medical Officer.

(vi)   Except with the approval of the Secretary-General, no staff member may be granted sick leave for a period of more than three consecutive working days without producing a certificate from a duly qualified medical practitioner to the effect that the staff member is unable to perform his or her duties and stating the nature of the illness and the probable duration of incapacity. Such certificate shall, except in circumstances beyond the control of the staff member, be produced not later than the end of the fourth working day following the initial absence from duty of the staff member.

(vii)   After a staff member has taken periods of uncertified sick leave totalling seven working days within a calendar year, any further absence from duty within that year shall either be supported by a medical certificate or deducted from annual leave or charged as special leave without pay.

(viii)   A staff member may be required at any time to submit a medical certificate as to his or her condition or to undergo examination by a medical practitioner named by the Secretary-General. Further sick leave may be refused or the unused portion withdrawn, if the Secretary-General is satisfied that the staff member is able to return to duty, provided that, if the staff member so requests, the matter shall be referred to an independent practitioner or a medical board acceptable to both the Secretary-General and the staff member.

(ix)   A staff member shall not, whilst on sick leave, leave the area of the duty station without the prior approval of the Secretary-General.

(*b*) When sickness of more than three consecutive working days occurs within a period of annual leave, including home leave, sick leave may be approved on production of an appropriate medical certificate or other satisfactory evidence. In such circumstances, a staff member should submit his or her request for sick leave together with supporting certificate or other evidence as soon as practicable, and in any event immediately on his or her return to duty.

(*c*) A staff member shall immediately notify the United Nations Medical Officer of any case of contagious disease occurring in his or her household or of any quarantine order affecting the household. A staff member who, as a result of these circumstances, is directed not to attend the office shall receive his or her full salary and other emoluments for the period of authorized absence.

(*d*) Entitlement to sick leave shall lapse on the final date of a staff member's appointment.

Rule 106.3: Maternity Leave

(*a*) A staff member who will have served continuously for one year at the anticipated time of confinement shall be entitled to maternity leave in accordance with the following provisions:

(i)   The leave shall commence six weeks prior to the anticipated date of confinement upon production of a certificate from a duly qualified medical practitioner indicating the anticipated date of confinement. However, at the staff member's request and upon production of a certificate from a duly qualified medical practitioner indicating that she is fit to continue to work, the absence may be permitted to commence less than six weeks but normally not less than three weeks before the anticipated date of confinement.

(ii) The leave shall extend for a total period of sixteen weeks from the time it is granted. The post-confinement leave shall therefore extend for a period equivalent to sixteen weeks less the period between the commencement of the maternity leave to the actual date of confinement, subject to a minimum of ten weeks. However, the staff member, on request, may be permitted to return to work after the lapse of a minimum period of six weeks following confinement.

(iii) The staff member shall receive maternity leave with full pay for the entire duration of her absence in accordance with (i) and (ii) above. However, if due to a miscalculation on the part of the medical practitioner or midwife as to the date of confinement the pre-confinement leave is more that six weeks, the staff member shall receive full pay to the actual date of confinement and will be allowed the minimum ten weeks of post-confinement leave as provided in (ii) above.

(*b*) A staff member with less than one year of continuous service at the anticipated time of confinement shall absent herself from her duties in accordance with the same schedule and under the same conditions as provided in (*a*) (i) and (ii) above. Where the actual date of confinement falls within the period of sixteen weeks immediately preceding the anniversary date of her continuous service, she shall be granted maternity leave with full pay for a period equivalent to sixteen weeks less the period between the date of confinement and the anniversary date of continuous service. Any absence that cannot be so covered by maternity leave shall be charged to her accrued annual leave or to special leave without pay.

(*c*) Sick leave shall not normally be granted for maternity cases except where serious complications arise.

(*d*) (Cancelled)

(*e*) Annual leave shall accrue during the period of maternity leave, provided that the staff member returns to service for at least six months after the completion of maternity leave.

(*f*) Qualifying service shall not be considered as lost by periods of special leave with partial pay or without pay or suspension from duty without pay, but service credit towards maternity leave shall not accrue during full months in such status. Periods of less than one month in such status shall not affect the ordinary rates of accrual.

Rule 106.4: Compensation for Death, Injury or Illness Attributable to Service

Staff members shall be entitled to compensation in the event of death, injury or illness attributable to the performance of official duties on behalf of the United Nations, in accordance with the rules set forth in appendix D to these rules.

Rule 106.5: Compensation for Loss or Damage to Personal Effects Attributable to Service

Staff members shall be entitled, within the limits and under terms and conditions established by the Secretary-General, to reasonable compensation in the event of loss or damage to their personal effects determined to be directly attributable to the performance of official duties on behalf of the United Nations.

Chapter VII: Travel and Removal Expenses

Rule 107.1: Offical Travel of Staff Members

(*a*) Subject to the conditions laid down in these rules, the United Nations shall pay the travel expenses of a staff member under the following circumstances:

(i)   On initial appointment, provided the staff member is considered to have been internationally recruited under rule 104.7;

(ii)   When required to travel on official business;

(iii)   On change of official duty station, as defined in rule 101.4;

(iv)   On home leave, in accordance with the provisions of rule 105.3;

(v)   On family visit, in accordance with the provisions of paragraph (*b*) below;

(vi)   On separation from service, in accordance with the provisions of chapter IX of the Staff Regulations and Staff Rules;

(vii)   On travel authorized for medical or security reasons or in other appropriate cases, when, in the opinion of the Secretary-General, there are compelling reasons for paying such expenses.

(*b*) Under subparagraph (*a*) (v) above, the United Nations may pay the travel expenses of a staff member to the place of recruitment, to the place of home leave or to the previous duty station for the purpose of visiting his or her eligible family members once every year in which the staff member's home leave does not fall due, provided that:

(i)   The staff member has completed not less than one year of continuous service at the duty station since the initial appointment or assignment or not less than nine months since departure on his or her last home leave journey;

(ii)   The staff member's service at the duty station is expected to continue at least six months beyond the date of return to the duty station;

(iii) During the preceding twelve months, none of the eligible family members has been present with the staff member at the duty station after travel at United Nations expense except education grant travel.

Should a staff member wish to visit his or her eligible family members residing at any other place, the travel expenses borne by the United Nations shall not exceed the maximum amount that would have been payable on the basis of travel to the place of home leave.

(*c*) Under subparagraph (*a*) (vi) above, the United Nations shall pay the travel expenses of a staff member to the place of recruitment or, if the staff member had a probationary appointment or an appointment for a period of two years or longer or had completed not less than two years of continuous service, to the place recognized as his or her home for the purpose of home leave under rule 105.3. Should a staff member, on separation, wish to go to any other place, the travel expenses borne by the United Nations shall not exceed the maximum amount that would have been payable on the basis of return transportation to the place of recruitment or home leave.

Rule 107.2: Official Travel of Family Members—Established Offices

(*a*) Subject to the conditions laid down in these rules, the United Nations shall pay, in the case of service at an established office, the travel expenses of a staff member's eligible family members under the following circumstances:

(i)   On the initial appointment of a staff member who is considered to have been internationally recruited, under the provisions of rule 104.7, provided the appointment is for a period of one year or longer or is a probationary appointment and provided the staff member's services are expected by the Secretary-General to continue for more than six months beyond the date on which travel of his or her family members commences;

(ii)   Following completion by the staff member of not less than one year of continuous service, provided his or her services are expected by the Secretary-General to continue for more than six months beyond the date on which travel of his or her family members commences;

(iii) On change of official duty station, provided the service of the staff member at the new duty station are expected by the Secretary-General to continue for more than six months beyond the date on which travel of his or her family members commences;

(iv)   On home leave, in accordance with the provisions of rule 105.3;

(v)   On separation of a staff member from service, provided the staff member's appointment was for a period of one year or longer or the staff member had completed not less than one year of continuous service;

(vi)   On journeys approved in connexion with the education of a staff member's child;

(vii)   On travel authorized for medical or security reasons or in other appropriate cases, when, in the opinion of the Secretary-General, there are compelling reasons for paying such expenses;

(viii) On travel of the spouse to the duty station, in lieu of the staff member's family visit travel under rule 107.1 (*a*) (v), subject to the same conditions as specified in rule 107.1 (*b*).

(*b*) Under subparagraphs (*a*) (i) and (ii) above, the United Nations shall pay the travel expenses of a staff member's eligible family members either from the place of recruitment or from the place of home leave. Should a staff member wish to bring any eligible family member to the official duty station from any other place, the travel expenses borne by the United Nations shall not exceed the maximum amount that would have been payable on the basis of travel from place of recruitment or home leave.

(*c*) Under subparagraph (*a*) (v) above, the United Nations shall pay the travel expenses of a staff member's eligible family members from the official duty station to the place to which the staff member is entitled to be returned in accordance with the provisions of rule 107.1. Where both husband and wife are staff members and either or both are entitled to the payment of travel expenses on separation from service, travel expenses shall be paid for each only upon their own separation from service, Where both spouses are entitled to return travel expenses, each staff member shall have the choice either of exercising his or her own entitlement or of accompanying the other spouse, provided that in no case shall such expenses be paid for a staff member while he or she remains in the service of the Organization.

Rule 107.3: Official Travel of Family Members—Mission Service

(*a*) Subject to the conditions laid down in these rules, the United Nations shall pay in the case of service with a mission, the travel expenses of a staff member's eligible family members to and from the mission area provided that:

(i)   The staff member is detailed, assigned or transferred from an established office or has been recruited specifically for the mission from outside the area of the mission;

(ii)   The staff member is detailed, assigned or transferred or appointed for an anticipated continuous period of not less than one year, or the staff member's assignment after a shorter period is extended so that the total anticipated period is not less than one year;

(iii)   The staff member's services are expected to continue in the mission area beyond six months after the beginning date of the family member's travel, and they are expected to remain in the mission area for the major part of the staff member's assignment;

(iv)   The Secretary-General has decided that there are no special circumstances or local conditions which make it undesirable for the staff member to be accompanied by his or her family members;

(v) The staff member assumes responsibility for providing living accomodation for his or her family members.

(b) The provisionns of paragraphs (b) and (c) of rule 107.2 shall apply to mission service, provided that, in the case of staff members detailed, assigned or transferred from an established office, travel shall normally be between the established office and the mission area.

Rule 107.4: Loss of Entitlement to Return Transportation

(a) A staff member who resigns before completing one year of service or within six months following the date of his or her return on home leave or family visit shall not be entitled to payment of return travel expenses for himself or herself and family members unless, in the opinion of the Secretary-General, there are compelling reasons for authorizing such payment.

(b) Entitlement to return travel expenses shall cease if travel has not commenced within six months after the date of separation. However, where both husband and wife are staff members and the spouse who separates first is entitled to return travel expenses, his or her entitlement shall not cease until six months after the date of separation of the other spouse.

Rule 107.5: Eligible Family Members

(a) Eligible family members, for the purposes of official travel, shall be deemed to comprise a spouse and those children recognized as dependent under rule 103.24 (b). A son or daughter of more than 21 years of age may also be considered a dependent child for travel purposes if totally disabled.

(b) The Secretary-General may authorize payment of the travel expenses of a child for one trip either to the staff member's duty station or to his or her home country beyond the age when the dependency status of the child would otherwise cease under the relevant Staff Regulations and Staff Rules, either within one year or upon completion of the child's continuous full-time attendance at a university, when the attendance at the university commenced during the period of recognized dependency status.

(c) Notwithstanding rule 107.2 (a) (v) or rule 107.3, the Secretary General may also authorize payment of the travel expenses for repatriation purposes of a former spouse.

Rule 107.6: Authority for Travel

Before travel is undertaken it shall be authorized in writing. In exceptional cases, staff members may be authorized to travel on oral orders, but such oral authorization shall require written confirmation. A staff member shall be personally responsible for ascertaining that he or she has the proper authorization before commencing travel.

Rule 107.7: Travel Expenses

(*a*) Travel expenses which shall be paid or reimbursed by the United Nations under the relevant provisions of these rules shall include:

(i)   Transportation expenses (i.e., carrier fare);

(ii)   Terminal expenses;

(iii) Transit expenses;

(iv)   Travel subsistence allowance;

(v)   Necessary additional expenses incurred during travel.

(*b*) Staff members shall exercise the same care in incurring expenses that a prudent person would exercise if travelling on personal business.

Rule 107.8: Route, Mode and Standard of Transportation

(*a*) Official travel shall; in all instances, be by a route, mode and standard of transportation approved in advance by the Secretary-General.

(*b*) Travel expenses or other entitlements, including travel time, shall be limited to the amount allowable for a journey by the approved route, mode and standard. Staff members who wish to make other arrangements for personal convenience must obtain permission to do so in advance and pay all additional costs.

Rule 107.9: Route and Mode of Travel

(*a*) The normal route for all official travel shall be the most direct and economical route. An alternative route may be approved when, in the opinion of the Secretary General, it is in the best interests of the United Nations.

(*b*) The normal mode of transportation for all official travel shall be by air. An alternative mode of transportation may be approved when, in the opinion of the Secretary General, its uses is in the best interests of the United Nations.

(*c*) If a staff member or family member travels by a more economical mode of transportation than the approved mode, the United Nations shall only pay for the mode of transportation actually used.

Rule 107.10: Standard of Accomodation

(*a*) For all official travel by air, staff members and their eligible family members shall be provided with economy class accommodation or its equivalent, except that Under-Secretaries-General, Assistant Secretaries-General and their family members, other than on travel in connexion with an education grant under rule 103.20, shall be provided with first class accommodation when the duration of a particular flight exceeds nine hours (by the most direct and economical route), including scheduled stops for such purposes as change of planes or refuelling, but excluding travel time to and from airports.

(*b*) The air travel accommodation under paragraph (*a*) above shall be provided at the most economical rate appropriate. Children under two years of age travelling by air shall be provided with a ticket giving entitlement to a seat.

(*c*) For all official travel by sea approved under paragraph (*b*) of rule 107.9, staff members and their family members shall be provided with the standard of accommodation which is, in the opinion of the Secretary-General, appropriate to the circumstances of the case.

(*d*) For all official travel by train approved under paragraph (*b*) of rule 107.9, staff members and their family members shall be provided with regular first class or equivalent accommodation, including sleeper and other facilities, as appropriate.

(*e*) A higher standard of accommodation may be approved when, in the opinion of the Secretary-General, special circumstances warrant it.

(*f*) If a staff member or family member travels by more economical accommodations than the approved standard, the United Nations shall only pay for accommodations actually used at the rate paid by the traveller.

Rule 107.11: Travel by Automobile

(*a*) Staff members who are authorized to travel by automobile shall be reimbursed by the United Nations at rates and under conditions established by the Secretary General on the basis of operating costs in the area in which the travel is undertaken and an appropriate minimum distance for the calculation of the daily subsistence allowance.

(*b*) Reimbursement for travel within a radius of 35 miles of the official duty station shall be based on actual mileage, and for travel beyond a 35-mile radius, on the mileage as shown on official road guides. Commutation between residence and place of business shall not be reimbursable.

(*c*) The mileage rate established by the Secretary-General shall be payable to only one of two or more persons travelling together on the same trip and in the same automobile.

(*d*) The total of mileage rate reimbursement and travel subsistence allowance which a staff member may claim in respect of a particular journey shall be limited to the maximum travel expenses to which he or she would have been entitled had the staff member and eligible family members travelled by the most economical route.

Rule 107.12: Purchase of Tickets

(*a*) Unless the staff member concerned is specifically authorized to make other arrangements, all tickets for transportation involving official travel of staff members and eligible family members shall be purchased by the United Nations in advance of the actual travel or, where circumstances so require, shall be secured by the staff member.

(*b*) When a staff member requests a standard of accommodation in excess of his or her entitlement under rule 107.10 or is authorized to travel, for reasons of personal preference or convenience, by other than the approved route or mode of transportation as provided for under rule 107.9, the staff member shall be required to reimburse the United Nations for any additional costs thus incurred before the United Nations provides him or her with the necessary tickets.

Rule 107.13: Terminal Expenses

(*a*) For all official travel to or from the duty station, a staff member may claim reimbursement of terminal expenses incurred for each outward or return journey and for each authorized intermediate stop up to $12 in respect of himself or herself and up to $4 in respect of each family member authorized to travel at United Nations expense. No expenses shall be reimbursable in respect of an intermediate stop:

(i)   Which is not authorized;
(ii) Which does not involve leaving the terminal; or
(iii) Which is for less than four hours and is exclusively for the purpose of making an onward connexion.

(*b*) When an outward or a return journey is made from or to Headquarters (New York), or when an intermediate stop is made at Headquarters (New York), the limits specified in paragraph (*a*) above shall be $20 and $7, respectively.

(*c*) Terminal expenses shall be deemed to include all expenditures incurred for the means of public conveyance between the airport or other point of arrival or departure and the hotel or other place of dwelling, including transfer of accompanied baggage and other related incidental charges, except the costs provided for under rule 107.19(iii).

Rule 107.14: Expense While in Transit

(*a*) A staff member and his or her eligible family members authorized to travel by sea shall be entitled to a fixed amount to cover transit expenses equivalent to the amount of travel subsistence allowances that would have been payable in respect of the travel if the travel had been by air.

(*b*) When the authorized mode of transportation is other than by sea, full travel subsistence allowance shall be payable for the time spent in transit, subject to the conditions laid down in rules 107.15 through 107.18, and provided that, in the case of travel other than on official business, a maximum of three days' travel time shall be allowed in respect of any specific journey.

Rule 107.15: Travel Subsistence Allowance

(*a*) Except as provided in rule 107.14 (*a*) and in paragraph (*h*) below, a staff member authorized to travel at United Nations expense shall receive an appropriate daily subsistence allowance in accordance with a schedule of rates established from time to time. Such established rates shall be subject to rule 107.16 and to reductions in cases where lodging or meals are provided free of charge by the United Nations, by a Government or by a related institution.

(*b*) The Secretary-General may, in exceptional and compelling circumstances, authorize a reasonable increase in the travel subsistence allowance to be paid to a staff member who is required to accompany a senior official and whose official duties while in travel status require that his or her additional living expense be established at a rate substantially higher than that contemplated in setting the allowance rate for his or her level.

(*c*) Travel subsistence allowance shall be deemed to comprise the total contribution of the United Nations towards such charges as meals, lodging, gratuities, and other payments made for personal services rendered. Except as provided in rule 107.19, any expenditures incurred in excess of the allowance shall be borne by the staff member.

(*d*) Except as provided in rule 107.14 (*a*) and in paragraph (*h*) below, when the spouse or dependent children of a staff member are authorized to travel at United Nations expense, the staff member shall be paid an additional travel subsistence allowance in respect of each of them at half the rate applicable to the staff member.

(*e*) Except for leave taken at a rate not exceeding one and a half days for each completed month on which a staff member is in travel status on official business, travel subsistence allowance shall not be paid in respect of any period of annual special leave. It shall not, in any event, be paid in respect of leave taken at the conclusion of active duty on an assignment but prior to the staff member's return to his or her official duty station.

(*f*) The travel subsistence allowance shall continue to be paid during periods of sick leave while in travel status, except that, if the traveller is hospitalized, only one third of the appropriate daily rate shall be paid.

(*g*) The appropriate travel subsistence allowance shall be paid for any days on which a staff member is required to perform official duties in connexion with travel on home leave.

(*h*) No travel subsistence allowance shall be payable in respect of travel on home leave, family visit or education grant, provided that the allowance may be paid for stopovers actually made on such travel under conditions established by the Secretary-General. Where travel at United Nations expense is authorized for medical, security or other reasons under rule 107.1 (*a*) (vii) or 107.2 (*a*) (vii), an appropriate amount of subsistence allowane may be paid at the discretion of the Secretary-General.

Rule 107.16: Special Rates of Travel Subsistence Allowance

In the event of staff members being assigned to conferences or for other extended periods of duty away from their official duty station, the Secretary-General may establish a special rate of subsistence allowance.

Rule 107.17:

(Cancelled)

Rule 107.18: Computation of the Travel Subsistence Allowance

(*a*) Except during travel by sea, subsistence allowance shall be paid to a staff member, at the rates and under the conditions prescribed in rule 107.15 for each calendar day or fraction thereof involving an overnight stay away from his or her residence, during which the staff member or his or her family members are in official travel status, provided that for a journey of 24 hours or longer a full day's allowance at the appropriate rate shall be paid for the day on which travel is begun and that no allowance shall be paid for the day on which travel is ended. Where travel does not involve an overnight stay away from the residence, no allowance shall be paid for a journey of less than 10 hours, and 40 per cent of the allowance shall be paid for a journey of 10 hours or more.

(b) Where travel is by sea, a full day's allowance at the appropriate rate shall be paid for the day of arrival at the port of disembarkation, provided the traveller remains in official travel status for more than 12 hours thereafter. No allowance shall be paid for the day on which embarkation takes place.

(c) If more than one rate should apply during the course of any one day, the rate applicable to the major portion of the day shall be paid for the entire day. If the traveller completes his or her travel on the same day as he or she commenced it, the rate applicable for the area of the destination shall be paid for that day.

(d) When it is necessary, for the purpose of computing the amount of travel subsistence allowance payable, to specify the 'hour of departure' and the 'hour of arrival', these shall be considered as the time when the train, vessel or airplane used by the traveller actually leaves or arrives at its regular terminal.

Rule 107.19: Miscellaneous Travel Expenses

Necessary additional expenses incurred by a staff member in connexion with the transaction of official business or in the performance of authorized travel shall be reimbursed by the United Nations after completion of travel, provided the necessity and nature of the expenses are satisfactorily explained and supported by proper receipts, which shall normally be required for any expenditures in excess of $2.00. Such expenses, for which advance authorization shall be obtained to the extent practicable, shall normally be limited to:

(i) Hire of local transportation other than that provided for under rule 107.13;
(ii) Telephone, telegraph, radio and cable messages of official business;
(iii) Transfer of authorized baggage by railway express or other appropriate agency;
(iv) Hire or room for official use;
(v) Stenographic or typewriting services or rental of typewriters in connexion with the preparation of official reports or correspondence;
(vi) Transportation or storage of baggage or property used on official business.

Rule 107.20: Installation

(a) Subject to the conditions set forth hereunder and except for mission service, a staff member shall be paid, in respect of himself or herself and his or her eligible family members, an installation grant when the staff member travels at United Nations expense to a new duty station on an assignment expected to be of at least one year's duration. Such payment shall be the total compensation payable by the United Nations towards the initial extraordinary living costs uncurred by the staff member and his or her eligible family members immediately following their arrival at the duty station.

(b) The amount of the installation grant shall be the equivalent of 30 days of subsistence allowance at the appropriate daily rate applicable under subparagraph (c) (i) below in respect of a staff member and at one half that rate in respect of a family member for whom travel expenses have been paid by the United Nations. This amount shall be calculated on the basis of the rate prevailing on the date of the staff member's or the family member's arrival, as appropriate.

(c) (i) The Secretary-General may establish special rates of subsistence allowance for purposes of installation grant for specific categories of staff at the various duty stations and publish such rates by administrative instruction or by other appropriate means. Where such special rates have not been established, the travel subsistence allowance rates have not been established, the travel subsistence allowance rates established under rule 107.15 shall be used in computing the installation grant.

(ii) Under conditions established by the Secretary-General, the limit of 30 days provided in paragraph (b) above may be extended up to a maximum of 90 days. The amount of the grant during the extended period shall be 60 per cent of the appropriate rate applicable to the initial period.

(iii) In addition to any amount of grant paid at the daily rates under this rule, the payment of a lump sum may be authorized at designated duty stations under conditions established by the Secretary-General. The lump sum shall be $300 for the staff member and $300 for each eligible family member who joins the staff member at the duty station, up to a maximum of $1,200.

(d) If a change of official duty station represents a return to a place at which the staff member was previously stationed, the full amount of installation grant shall not be payable unless the staff member has been absent from such place for at least two years. In the case of a shorter absence, the amount payable shall be that proportion of the full grant which the completed months of absence bear to two years.

(e) Where both husband and wife are staff members travelling at United Nations expense to a duty station, installation grant shall be paid to each in respect of himself or herself. If they have a dependent child or children, installation grant in respect of such child or children will be paid to the staff member on whom each child is recognized to be dependent. With regard to the lump sum provided for in (c) (iii) above, the amount payable to both spouses jointly shall not exceed the maximum of $1,200.

(f) Installation grant shall not be payable in connexion with education grant travel.

(g) The Secretary-General may, in appropriate cases, authorize payment of all or part of the installation grant where the United Nations has not been required to pay travel expenses upon the appointment of a staff member regarded as internationally recruited under rule 104.7

Rule 107.21: Excess Baggage and Unaccompanied Shipments

(a) For the purposes of these rules 'excess baggage' shall mean baggage in excess of the weight or volume carried without extra charge by transportation companies, and 'personal effects and household goods' shall be defined in rule 107.27 (d) (ii).

(b) Staff members travelling by air economy class or its equivalent shall be entitled to payment of excess baggage for themselves and their eligible family members to the extent of the difference between the free baggage allowance by first class and by economy class or its equivalent.

(*c*) When baggage is carried without charge by one transportation company, but considered as excess by a company furnishing subsequent transportation other than by air, the traveller may be reimbursed for the charges involved provided he or she obtains a statement from the company making the charges that the baggage was considered as excess.

(*d*) Charges for excess baggage by air, other than those authorized under paragraph (*b*) above, shall not be reimbursable unless, in the opinion of the Secretary General, the circumstances under which the staff members is travelling are of a sufficiently exceptional and compelling nature to warrant such reimbursement.

(*e*) When the authorized travel is by air or by land, charges for unaccompanied shipment of personal baggage relating to travel on home leave, family visit or education grant may be reimbursed as follows:

(i) Up to a maximum of 50 kg (110 lb) or ll cubic feet by surface means per person in respect of each journey, except as provided in subparagraph (ii) below. At the request of the staff member, this entitlement may be converted to 10 additional kg of accompanied excess baggage or its equivalent as established by the Secretary-General;

(ii) For travel on education grant in regard to the first outward journey to, or the final journey from, an educational institution up to a maximum of 200 kg (440 lb) or 44 cubic feet by surface mean in respect of each journey.

(*f*) On travel on appointment or assignment for one year or more, on transfer or on separation from service in the case of an appointment for one year or more, where no entitlement to removal costs exists under rule 107.27, a staff member shall be paid expenses incurred in transporting personal effects and household goods by the most economical means, as determined by the Secretary-General, up to a maximum, including the weight or volume of packing and crating, of:

(i)   1,000 kg (2,200 lb) or 220 cubic feet for the staff member.
(ii)   500 kg (1,100 lb) or 110 cubic feet for the first family member, and
(iii) 300 kg (660 lb) or 66 cubic feet for each additional family member

authorized to travel at the expense of the Organization.

(*g*) Unaccompanied shipments shall normally be made in one consignment and shall be within the limit of costs of transportation between the places of departure and destination of the authorized travel of the staff member or his or her family members. Reasonable costs of packing, crating, cartage, unpacking and uncrating of such shipments under paragraphs (*e*) (ii), (*f*), (*h*) and (i) will be reimbursed within the limits of authorized weight or volume but costs for the servicing, dismantling, installing or special packing of personal effects and household goods shall not be reimbursed. Storage and demurrage charges shall not be reimbursed unless, in the opinion of the Secretary-General, they are directly incidental to the transportation of the consignment.

(*h*) On travel on appointment, assignment, transfer or separation from service, where entitlement to removal costs does exist under rule 107.27, a staff member shall be paid expenses incurred in transporting a reasonable amount of personal effects and household goods, as an advance removal shipment, by the most economical means, as determined by the Secretary-General, up to a maximum, including the weight or volume of packing and crating, of:

(i)   450 kg (990 lb) or 99 cubic feet for the staff member,
(ii)   300 kg (660 lb) or 66 cubic feet for the first family member, and
(iii) 150 kg (330 lb) or 33 cubic feet for each additional family member

authorized to travel at the expense of the Organization. The weight or volume of any shipment under this paragraph shall be deducted from the maximum weight or volume to which the staff member is entitled under paragraph (d) of rule 107.27.

(i) On travel on appointment or assignment for less than one year or on separation from service in the case of an appointment for less than one year, a staff member may be authorized to ship personal effects at United Nations expense by the the most economical means, up to a maximum of 100 kg (220 lb) or 22 cubic feet, including the weight or volume of packing and crating. Where the appointment or assignment is extended for a total period of one year or more, the staff member shall be paid expenses for an additional shipment of personal effects and household goods up to the maximum entitlements established in paragraph (f) above.

(j) Where surface shipment under paragraphs (e) (ii), (f), (h) or (i) is the most economical means of transport, such shipment may be converted to air freight on the basis of one half of the weight or volume of the authorized surface entitlement:

(i)   When a staff member elects to covert the whole surface entitlement to air freight; or
(ii) When, in the opinion of the Secretary-General, the conversion to air freight of a portion of the surface entitlement is necessary to meet urgent needs.

If the entitlement is under paragraph (h) above, twice the weight or volume of the air freight shipment shall be deducted from the staff member's entitlement under rule 107.27.

(k) When the authorized travel is by air, the staff member may elect to convert the whole surface shipment relating to travel on home leave, family visit or education grant under paragraph (e) (i) above to air freight on the basis of the one-half rule. No costs for packing, crating, unpacking and uncrating will be paid, but reasonable costs will be paid for cartage of such air freight shipments.

(l) Notwithstanding the one-half rule laid down in paragraphs (j) and (k) above, conversion to air freight on the basis of the full weight or volume may be authorized in the following cases:

(i)   Where the cost of air freight is lower than surface shipment;
(ii)   Where there is an extraordinary risk of damage to, or loss of, the shipment in transit; or
(iii) Where an excessive shipping delay is expected, particularly for shipment to land-locked countries.

However, for surface shipments under paragraph (e), conversion on the basis of the full weight or volume may be authorized only in the cases indicated in subparagraphs (i) and (ii) above.

Rule 107.22: Insurance

(*a*) Staff members shall not be reimbursed for the cost of personal accident insurance or of insurance of accompanied personal baggage. However, compensation may be paid in respect of loss or damage to accompanied personal baggage, in accordance with such arrangements as may be in force under rule 106.5.

(*b*) In the case of unaccompanied shipments authorized under rule 107.21, except on home leave, family visit or education grant travel, insurance coverage will be provided by the Organization up to the value of $5,000 for a staff member without a spouse or dependent child and $12,000 for a staff member with a spouse or dependent child. Such insurance coverage shall not include articles of special value for which special premium rates are charged. The United Nations will not be responsible for loss or damage of unaccompanied baggage.

(*c*) The cost of insurance of personal effects and household goods in transit (excluding articles of special value for which special rates of premium are charged) under rule 107.27 shall be reimbursed, up to a maximum valuation of $25,000 for a staff member without a spouse or dependent child and $40,000 for a staff member with a spouse or dependent child residing at the official duty station. The United Nations shall in no case be responsible for loss or damage.

(*d*) In the case of unaccompanied shipments under rules 107.21 and 107.27, the staff member shall furnish the Organization, prior to shipment, with an itemized inventory in duplicate of all articles, including containers such as suitcases, and the replacement value in United States dollars of each article in the shipments.

Rule 107.23: Travel Advances

Staff members authorized to travel shall provide themselves with sufficient funds for all current expenses by securing an advance of funds if necessary. A reasonable advance of funds against the estimated reimbursable travel expenses may be made to a staff member or his or her family members for expenses authorized under these rules. An advance of funds shall be considered reasonable if not less than $50.00 or more than 80 per cent of the estimated reimbursable expenditures. If, in the course of travel, the staff member has earned in subsistence allowance an amount equal to the amount advanced, the staff member may be advanced the balance of the estimated reimbursable expenditures.

Rule 107.24: Illness or Accident during Travel

United Nations shall pay or reimburse reasonable hospital and medical expenses, in so far as these are not covered by other arrangements, which may be incurred by staff members who become ill or are injured while in travel status on official business.

Rule 107.25: Reimbursement of Travel Expenses

The Secretary-General may reject any claim for payment or reimbursement of travel or removal expenses which are incurred by a staff member in contravention of any provision of these rules.

Rule 107.26: Transportation of Decedents

Upon the death of a staff member or of his or her spouse or dependent child, the United Nations shall pay the expenses of transportation of the body from the official duty station or, in the event of death having occurred whilst in travel status, from the place of death, to a place to which the deceased was entitled to return transportation under rule 107.1 or 107.2. These expenses shall include reasonable costs for preparation of the body. If local interment is elected, reasonable expenses incurred for the interment may be reimbursed.

Rule 107.27: Removal Costs

(*a*) Subject to the provisions of rule 103.22 on assignment allowance, when an internationally recruited staff member is to serve at an established office for a continuous period which is expected to be two years or longer, the Secretary-General shall decide whether to pay an assignment allowance under rule 103.22 or to pay costs for the removal of the staff member's personal effects and household goods under the following circumstances:

(i)   On initial appointment for a period of two years or longer;

(ii) Upon completion of two years of continuous service;

(iii) On charge of duty station to an established office, provided that the staff member is expected to serve at the new duty station for a period of two years or longer and that, in exceptional cases where the expected period of service is one year or more but less than two years, the Secretary-General may authorize payment of removal costs under this rule in lieu of assignment allowance under rule 103.22;

(iv) Upon separation from service, provided that the staff member had an appointment for a period of two years or longer or had completed not less than two years of continuous service.

(*b*) Under subparagraphs (*a*) (i) and (ii) above, the United Nations shall pay the expenses of removing a staff member's personal effects and household goods either from the place of recruitment or from the place recognized as his or her home for purposes of home leave under rule 105.3, provided that the effects and goods were in the staff member's possession at the time of appointment and are being transported for his or her own use. Payment of removal expenses from a place other than those specified may be authorized by the Secretary-General in exceptional cases, on such terms and conditions as the Secretary-General deems appropriate. No expenses shall be paid for removing a staff member's personal effects and household goods from one residence to another at the duty station.

(*c*) Under subparagraph (*a*) (iv) above, the United Nations shall pay the expenses of removing a staff member's personal effects and household goods from the official duty station to any one place to which the staff member is entitled to be returned in accordance with the provisions of rule 107.1 or any other one place authorized by the Secretary-General in exceptional cases on such terms and conditions as the Secretary-General deems appropriate, provided that the effects and goods were in the staff member's possession at the time of separation from service and are being transported for his or her own use.

(*d*) Payment by the United Nations of removal expenses shall be subject to the following conditions:

(i) The maximum weight and volume for which entitlement to removal at United Nations expense exists shall be 27 measurement tons of 40 cubic feet each (1,080 cubic feet), inclusive of packing crates and lift vans, for a staff member without a spouse or dependent child and 45 measurement tons (1,800 cubic feet) for a staff member with a spouse or dependent child residing at the official duty station. Higher maxima may be authorized if the staff member presents convincing evidence that his or her normal and necessary personal effects and household goods to be removed exceed those limits;

(ii) For the purpose of unaccompanied shipments and removal, personal effects and household goods shall include all effects and goods normally required for personal or household use provided that animals, boats, automobiles, motor cycles, trailers and other power-assisted conveyances shall in no case be considered as such effects and goods;

(iii) Shipments under this rule shall normally be made in one consignment. Reasonable costs of packing, crating, cartage, unpacking and uncrating of such shipments within the limits of the authorized weight or volume will be reimbursed, but costs for the servicing, dismantling, installing or special packing of personal effects and household goods shall not be reimbursed. Storage and demurrage charges shall not be reimbursed unless, in the opinion of the Secretary-General, they are directly incidental to the transportation of the consignment;

(iv) Transportation of personal effects and household goods shall be by the most economical means, as determined by the Secretary-General, taking into account costs allowable under subparagraph (*d*) (iii) above;

(v) In addition to the removal expenses under this rule, the cost of transporting a privately owned automobile to a duty station may be partially reimbursed under conditions established by the Secretary-General, provided that the duty station to which the automobile is transported is one of the duty stations designated for that purpose and that the assignment of the staff member to the duty station is expected to be for a period of two years or more or that the initial assignment for a lesser period is extended so that the total period of assignment becomes two years or more.

(*e*) Removal costs shall not be payable under this rule in the case of mission service.

(*f*) When both husband and wife are staff members and each is entitled to removal of personal effects and household goods or to unaccompanied shipment under rule 107.21 (*f*), the maximum weight or volume that may be removed at United Nations expense for both of them shall be that provided for a staff member with a spouse or dependent child residing at the official duty station.

(*g*) When an internationally recruited staff member is assigned to a duty station where an assignment allowance, rather than payment of removal costs, is authorized, the United Nations shall pay the costs for the storage of personal effects and household goods and other pertinent charges, including the cost of insurance up to a maximum of $25,000 for a staff member without a spouse or dependent child and $40,000 for a staff member with a spouse or dependent child, provided that:

(i) The staff member is assigned from a duty station to which he or she enjoyed removal entitlement under paragraph (*a*) above or would have enjoyed such entitlement had the staff member been recruited from outside the area of the duty station;

(ii) The staff member is expected to return to the same duty station within five years;

(iii) The quantity of personal effects and household goods stored does not exceed the diffference between the maximum allowance under paragraph (*d*) above and the amount actually shipped under rule 107.21. The maximum insurance value shall be reduced accordingly.

In no event shall storage charges be paid beyond the five-year period following the date of assignment. Such charges shall not be paid in the case of mission or other assignments not involving a change of official duty station.

Rule 107.28: Loss of Entitlement to Unaccompanied Shipment or Removal Expenses

(*a*) A staff member who resigns before completing two years of service shall not normally be entitled to payment of removal expenses under rule 107.27 above.

(*b*) Entitlement to removal expenses under rule 107.27 (*a*) (i), (ii) and (iii) shall normally cease if removal has not commenced within two years after the date on which the staff member became entitled to removal expenses or if the staff member's services are not expected to continue for more than six months beyond the proposed date of arrival of the personal effects and household goods.

(*c*) Upon separation from service, entitlement to unaccompanied shipment expenses under rule 107.21 (*f*) and (*i*) or removal expenses under rule 107.27 shall cease if the shipment or removal has not commenced within six months or one year, respectively, after the date of separation. However, where both husband and wife are staff members and the spouse who separates first is entitled to unaccompanied shipment or removal expenses, his or her entitlement shall not cease until six months or one year, as the case may be, after the date of separation of the other spouse.

Chapter VIII: Staff Relations

Rule 108.1: Staff Council

(*a*) The Staff Council shall be consulted, through its elected officers composing the Staff Committee, on questions relating to staff welfare and administration, including policy on appointments, promotions and terminations and on salaries and related allowances, and shall be entitled to make proposals to the Secretary-General on behalf of the staff on such questions.

(*b*) Except for instructions to meet emergency situations, general administrative instructions or directions on questions within the scope of paragraph (*a*) shall be transmitted in advance to the Staff Committee for consideration and comment before being placed in effect.

(*c*) The Staff Council at Headquarters shall be composed of from 39 to 41 representatives elected on the basis of approximately equal electoral units. Any member of the staff shall be eligible for election to the Staff Council.

(*d*) Polling officers elected by the staff shall be responsible for dividing the Departments of the Secretariat into electoral units on the basis of the organizational chart of the Secretariat. The Staff Council shall obtain the approval of the Secretary-General for any rearrangement of electoral units. The polling officers shall organize annually the election of members of the Staff Council in such a way as to insure the complete secrecy and fairness of the vote.

(*e*) Staff members in established offices away from Headquarters may select representatives to make on their behalf proposals to the Secretary-General regarding matters covered by regulation 8.1 (*a*) and regulation 8.2

Rule 108.2: Joint Advisory Committee

(*a*) The joint administrative machinery provided for in regulation 8.2 shall consist of a Joint Advisory Committee composed as follows:

(i)   A Chairman selected by the Secretary-General from a list propoed by the Staff Council;
(ii) Four members and three alternates representing the Staff Council;
(iii) Four members and three alternates representing the Secretary-General.

(*b*) Additional representatives either of the Staff Council or of the Secretary-General may be invited from time to time to participate in the Committee's discussion of particular problems.

(*c*) The Secretary-General shall designate a suitably qualified staff member to act as Secretary to the Joint Advisory Committee and shall arrange for such clerical or other services as may be necessary for the Committee's proper functioning.

(*d*) Special joint committees to advise on special problems may be set up as the occasion arises.

(*e*) Instructions or directives embodying proposals made by the Joint Advisory Committee with the endorsement of the Staff Council representatives shall be regarded as having the requirements of rule 108.1 (*a*) and (*b*).

Chapter IX: Separation from Service

Rule 109.1: Special Advisory Board, Definition of Termination, and Abolition of Posts and Reduction of Staff

(a) *Special Advisory Board*
The Special Advisory Board under staff regulation 9.1 (*a*) shall be composed of a Chairman appointed by the Secretary-General on the nomination of the President of the International Court of Justice and of four members appointed by the Secretary-General in agreement with the Staff Council.

(b) *Definition of termination*
A termination within the meaning of the Staff Regulations is a separation from service initiated by the Secretary-General, other than retirement at the age of 60 years or more or summary dismissal for serious misconduct.

(c) *Abolition of posts and reduction staff*

(i) Except as otherwise expressly provided in paragraph (*b*) below, if the necessities of the service require abolition of a post or reduction of the staff, and subject to the availability of suitable posts in which their services can be effectively utilized, staff members with permanent or regular appointments shall be retained in preference to those on all other types of appointments, and staff members with probationary appointments shall be retained in preference to those on fixed-term or indefinite appointments, provided that due regard shall be had in all cases to relative competence, to integrity and to length of service. Due regard shall also be had to nationality in the case of staff members with not more than five years of service and in the case of staff members who have changed their nationality within the preceding five years when the suitable posts available are subject to the principle of geographical distribution.

(ii) (*a*) The provisions of paragraph (i) above in so far as they relate to locally recruited staff members shall be deemed to have been satisfied if such locally recruited staff members have received consideration for suitable posts available at their duty stations.

(*b*) Staff members specifically recruited for service with a subsidiary organ of the United Nations which enjoys a special status in matters of appointment under a resolution of the General Assembly or as a result of an agreement entered into by the Secretary-General, such as the United Nations Children's Fund, the United Nations Development Programme, the United Nations Environment Programme, the United Nations Institute for Training and Research or the United Nations University, have no entitlement under this rule for consideration for posts outside the organ for which they were recruited.

Rule 109.2: Resignation

(*a*) A resignation within the meaning of the Staff Regulations, is a separation initiated by a staff member.

(*b*) Unless otherwise specified in their letters of appointment, three month's written notice of resignation shall be given by staff members having permanent appointments and 30 days' written notice of resignation by those having temporary appointments. The Secretary-General, however, may accept resignations on shorter notice.

Rule 109.3: Notice of Termination

(*a*) A staff member whose permanent appointment is to be terminated shall be given not less than three month's written notice of such termination.

(*b*) A staff member whose temporary appointment is to be terminated shall be given not less than 30 days' written notice of such termination or such notice as may otherwise be stipulated in his or her letter of appointment.

(*c*) In lieu of these notice periods, the Secretary-General may authorize compensation calculated on the basis of the salary and allowances which the staff member would have received had the date of termination been at the end of the notice period.

Rule 109.4: Termination Indemnity

(*a*) Payment of termination indemnity under staff regulation 9.3 and annex I I I to the Staff Regulations shall be calculated on the basis of the staff members's pensionable remuneration, the amount of which, exclusive of non-resident's allowance or language allowance, if any, shall be subject to staff assessment according to the applicable schedule of rates set forth in staff regulation 3.3 (*b*).

(*b*) Length of service shall be deemed to comprise the total period of a staff member's full-time continuous service with the Secretariat, regardless of types of appointment. Continuity of such service shall not be considered as broken by periods of special leave without pay or in partial pay, but full months of any such periods exceeding one calendar month shall not be credited as service for indemnity purposes; periods of less than one calendar month shall not affect the ordinary rates of accrual.

(*c*) Termination indemnity shall not be paid to any staff member who, upon separation from service, will receive a retirement benefit under Article 29 of the United Nations Joint Staff Pension Fund Regulations or compensation for total disability under rule 106.4.

Rule 109.5: Repatriation Grant

Payment of repatriation grants under regulation 9.4 and annex I V to the Staff Regulations shall be subject to the following conditions and definitions:

(*a*) 'Obligation to repatriate', as used in annex I V to the Staff Regulations, shall mean the obligation to return a staff member and his or her spouse and dependent children, upon separation, at the expense of the United Nations, to a place outside the country of his or her duty station.

(*b*) 'Home country', as used in annex I V to the Staff Regulations, shall mean the country of home-leave entitlement under rule 105.3 or such other country as the Secretary-General may determine.

(*c*) Continuous service away from the staff member's home country shall, for the purposes of this rule, exclude service before 1 January 1951. If at any time the staff member was considered to have acquired permanent residence in the country of his or her duty station and subsequently changed from such status, the staff member's continous service will be deemed to have commenced at the time the change was made. Continuity of such service shall not be considered as broken by periods of special leave without pay or in partial pay, but full months of any such periods shall not be credited as service for the purpose of calculating the amount of the grant payable; periods of less than one calendar month shall not affect the ordinary rates of accrual.

(*d*) Payment of the repatriation grant shall be subject to the provision by the former staff member of evidence of relocation away from the country of the last duty station. Evidence of relocation shall be constituted by documentary evidence that the former staff member has established residence in a country other than that of the last duty station.

(*e*) Entitlement to repatriation grant shall cease if no claim for payment of the grant has been submitted within two years after the effective date of separation. However, where both husband and wife are staff members and the spouse who separates first is entitled to repatriation grant, his or her entitlement to repatriation grant shall cease if no claim for payment of the grant has been submitted within two years after the date of separation of the other spouse.

(*f*) (Cancelled)

(*g*) Payment of the repatriation grant shall be calculated on the basis of the staff member's pensionable remuneration, the amount of which, exclusive of non-resident's allowance or language allowance, if any, shall be subject to staff assessment according to the applicable schedule of rates set forth in staff regulation 3.3 (*b*).

(*h*) Payment shall be at the rates specified in annex I V to the Staff Regulations.

(*i*) No payments shall be made to local recruits under rule 104.6, to a staff member who abandons his or her post or to any staff member who is residing at the time of separation in his or her home country while performing official duties, provided that a staff member who, after service at a duty station outside his or her home country, is transferred to a duty station within that country may be paid on separation a full or partial repatriation grant at the discretion of the Secretary-General.

(*j*) A dependent child, for the purpose of repatriation grant, shall mean a child recognized as dependent under rule 103.24 (*b*) at the time of the staff member's separation from service. The repatriation grant shall be paid at the rate for a staff member with a spouse or dependent child to eligible staff members regardless of the place of residence of the spouse or dependent child.

(*k*) Where both husband and wife are staff members and each is entitled, on separation, to payment of a repatriation grant, payment shall be made to each, at single rates, according to their respective entitlements, provided that, where dependent children are recognized, the first parent to be separated may claim payment at the rate applicable to a staff member with a spouse or dependent child. In this event, the second parent, on separation, may claim payment at the single rate for the period of qualifying service subsequent thereto or, if eligible, at the rate applicable to a staff member with a spouse or dependent child for the whole period of his or her qualifying service, from which shall normally be deducted the amount of the repatriation grant paid to the first parent.

(*l*) Loss of entitlement to payment of return travel expenses under rule 107.4 shall not affect a staff member's eligibility for payment of the repatriation grant.

(*m*) In the event of the death of an eligible staff member, no payment shall be made unless there is a surviving spouse or one or more dependent children whom the United Nations is obligated to return to their home country. If there is one such survivor, payment shall be made at the single rate; if there are two or more such survivors, payment shall be made at the rate applicable to a staff member with a spouse or dependent child.

Rule 109.6: Retirement

Retirement under article 29 of the United Nations Joint Staff Pension Fund Regulations shall not be regarded as a termination within the meaning of the Staff Regulations and Staff Rules.

Rule 109.7: Expiration of Fixed-term Appointments

(*a*) A temporary appointment for a fixed term shall expire automatically and without prior notice on the expiration date specified in the letter of appointment.

(b) Separation as a result of the expiration of any such appointment shall not be regarded as a termination within the meaning of the Staff Regulations and Staff Rules.

Rule 109.8: Commutation of Accrued Annual Leave

If, upon separation from service, a staff member has accrued annual leave, the staff member shall be paid a sum of money in commutation of the period of such accrued leave up to a maximum of 60 working days. The payment shall be calculated on the basis of the staff member's pensionable remuneration, the amount of which, exclusive of non-resident's allowance or language allowance, if any, shall be subject to staff assessment according to the applicable schedule of rates set forth in staff regulation 3.3 (b).

Rule 109.9: Restitution of Advance Annual and Sick Leave

Upon separation, a staff member who has taken advance annual or sick leave beyond that which he or she has subsequently accrued, shall make restitution for such advance leave by means of a cash refund or an offset against moneys due to the staff member from the United Nations, equivalent to the remuneration received, including allowances and other payments, in respect of the advance leave period. The Secretary General may waive this requirement if in the opinion of the Secretary General there are exceptional or compelling reasons for so doing.

Rule 109.10: Last Day for Pay Purposes

(a) When a staff member is separated from service, the date on which entitlement to salary, allowances and benefits shall cease shall be determined according to the following provisions:

(i) Upon resignation, the date shall be either the date of expiration of the notice period under rule 109.2 or such other date as the Secretary General accepts. Staff members will be expected to perform their duties during the period of notice of resignation, except when the resignation takes effect upon the completion of maternity leave or following sick or special leave. Annual leave will be granted during the notice of resignation only for brief periods;

(ii) Upon expiration of a fixed-term appointment, the date shall be the date specified in the letter of appointment;

(iii) Upon termination, the date shall be the date provided in the notice of termination;

(iv) Upon retirement, the date shall be the date approved by the Secretary-General for retirement;

(v) In the case of summary dismissal, the date shall be the date of dismissal;

(vi) In the case of death, the date on which entitlement to salary, allowances and benefits shall cease shall be the date of death, unless there is a surviving spouse or dependent child. In this event, the date shall be determined in accordance with the following schedule:

Completed years of service in the Secretariat (as defined in rule 109.4)	Months of extension beyond date of death
3	3
4	4
5	5
6	6
7	7
8	8
9 or more	9

Payment related to the period of extension beyond the date of death may be made in a lump sum as soon as the pay accounts and related matters can be closed. Such payment shall be made only to the surviving spouse and dependent children and shall be calculated on the basis of the staff member's pensionable remuneration, the amount of which, exclusive of non-resident's allowance or language allowance, if any, shall be subject to staff assessment according to the applicable schedule or rates set forth in staff regulation 3.3 (*b*). All other entitlements and accrual of benefits shall cease as of the date of death.

(*b*) When an internationally recruited staff member is exercising an entitlement to return travel, the last day for pay purposes shall be the date established under subparagraph (*a*) (i), (ii) or (iii) above or the estimated date of arrival at the place of entitlement, whichever is later. The estimated date of arrival shall be determined on the basis of the time it would take to travel without interruption by an approved route and mode of direct travel from the duty station to the place of entitlement, the travel commencing no later than the day following the date established under paragraph (*a*).

Rule 109.11: Certification of Service

Any staff member who requests shall, on leaving the service of the United Nations, be given a statement relating to the nature of his or her duties and the length of service. On the staff member's written request, the statement shall also refer to the quality of his or her work and his or her official conduct.

Chapter X: Disciplinary Measures

Rule 110.1: Joint Disciplinary Committee

A Joint Disciplinary Committee is established and shall be available to advise the Secretary-General at the request of the Secretary-General in disciplinary cases involving staff members serving at Headquarters; comparable committees shall be established in the United Nations Office at Geneva, in UNIDO, Vienna, and at such other offices as may be designated by the Secretary-General.

Rule 110.2: Composition of the Joint Disciplinary Committee

(*a*) The Joint Disciplinary Committee at Headquarters shall consist of three members as follows:

(i) A chairman, selected from a panel appointed annually by the Secretary-General after consultation with the Staff Committee;
(ii) One member appointed annually by the Secretary-General;
(iii) One member elected by the staff.

The staff shall elect annually by ballot three staff members, one from each of the following groups:

Group I   Staff below Associated Officer level or in corresponding salary levels;
Group II   Staff in Associated Officer through Second Officer level or in corresponding salary levels;
Group III   Staff in First Officer through Director level.

The member to sit on the Committee in any case shall be from the group to which the staff member concerned belongs.

(*b*) Alternate members shall be selected in the same manner as the members; an alternate member shall serve during the consideration of any case for which a member is unavailable or disqualified under paragraph (*e*) below, provided that alternate members elected by the staff shall serve in the order in which they received votes in such election.

(*c*) The members and alternate members of the Joint Disciplinary Committees shall be eligible for reappointment or re-election.

(*d*) A member may be removed from the panel of chairmen by the Secretary-General after consultation with the Staff Committee; the member and the alternate members appointed by the Secretary-General may be removed by the Secretary-General; the member and the alternate members elected by the staff may be removed by a two-thirds majority vote of the Staff Council.

(*e*) The Chairman of the Joint Disciplinary Committee, at the request of either party, may disqualify any member or alternate member from the consideration of a specific case, if in the opinion of the Secretary-General such action is warranted by the relation of such member or alternate member to the staff member whose case is to be considered. The Chairman may also excuse any member or alternate member from the consideration of a specific case.

Rule 110.3: Disciplinary Measures

(*a*) Except in cases of summary dismissal, no staff member serving at any duty station where a Joint Disciplinary Committee has been established shall be subject to disciplinary measures until the matter has been referred for advice to the Joint Disciplinary Committee, provided that referral to the Joint Disciplinary Committee may be waived by mutual agreement of the staff member concerned and the Secretary-General.

(*b*) Disciplinary measures under the first paragraph of staff regulation 10.2 shall consist of written censure, suspension without pay, demotion or dismissal for misconduct, provided that suspension pending investigation under rule 110.4 shall not be considered a disciplinary measure.

(c) Written censure shall be authorized by the Secretary-General and shall be distinguished from reprimand of a staff member by a supervisory official. Such reprimand shall not be deemed to be a disciplinary measure within the meaning of this rule.

Rule 110.4: Suspension Pending Investigation

If a charge of misconduct is made against a staff member and the Secretary-General so decides, the staff member may be suspended from duty, with or without pay, pending investigation, the suspension being without prejudice to the rights of the staff member.

Rule 110.5: Joint Disciplinary Committee Procedure

(a) In considering a case, the Joint Disciplinary Committee shall act with maximum dispatch. Normally, proceedings before the Committee shall be limited to the original written presentation of the case, together with brief statements and rebuttals, which may be made orally or in writing, but without delay. The Joint Disciplinary Committee shall make every effort to send its report to the Secretary-General within two weeks after being convened.

(b) The Joint Disciplinary Committee shall permit a staff member to arrange to have his or her case presented before it by any other staff member serving at the duty station where the Committee is established.

Chapter XI: Appeals

Rule 111.1: Joint Appeals Board

(a) A Joint Appeals Board is established to consider and advise the Secretary-General regarding appeals filed under the terms of staff regulation 11.1 by staff members serving at Headquarters.

(b) In case of termination or other action on grounds of inefficiency or relative efficiency, the Board shall not consider the substantive question of efficiency but only evidence that the decision has been motivated by prejudice or by some other extraneous factor.

(c) Where its competence is in doubt, the Joint Appeals Board itself shall decide.

(d) The Joint Appeals Board may make recommendations to the Secretary-General should it desire to change the procedures regarding appeals as set forth in these rules.

Rule 111.2: Composition of the Joint Appeals Board

(a) The Joint Appeals Board at Headquarters shall consist of three members as follows:

(i)   A chairman, selected from a panel appointed annually by the Secretary-General after consultation with the Staff Committee;

(ii) One member appointed annually by the Secretary-General;

(iii) One member elected annually by ballot of the staff.

(*b*) Alternate members shall be selected in the same manner as the members; an alternate member shall serve during the consideration of an appeal for which a member is unavailable or disqualified under paragraph (*e*) below provided that alternate members elected by the staff who are available shall serve in the order in which they received votes in such election.

(*c*) The members and alternate members of the Joint Appeals Board shall be eligible for reappointment on re-election.

(*d*) A member may be removed from the panel of chairmen by the Secretary-General after consultation with the Staff Committee; the member and the alternate members appointed by the Secretary-General may be removed by the Secretary-General; the member and the alternate members elected by the staff may be removed by a two-thirds majority vote of the Staff Council.

(*e*) The Chairman of the Joint Appeals Board, at the request of either party, may disqualify any member or alternate member from the consideration of a specific appeal, if in the opinion of the Chairman such action is warranted by the relation of such member or alternate member to the staff member whose appeal is to be considered. The Chairman may also excuse any member or alternate member from the consideration of a specific appeal. No person who has served on the Joint Disciplinary Committee during consideration of a specific case shall serve on the Joint Appeals Board should it consider an appeal relating to the same case.

Rule 111.3: Procedure of the Joint Appeals Board

(*a*) A staff member who, under the terms of regulation 11.1, wishes to appeal an administrative decision, shall, as a first step, address a letter to the Secretary-General, requesting that the administrative decision be reviewed. Such a letter must be sent within one month from the time the staff member received notification of the decision in writing.

(*b*) If the staff member wishes to make an appeal against the answer received from the Secretary-General, the staff member shall submit his or her appeal in writing to the Secretary of the Joint Appeals Board within one month from the date of receipt of the answer. If no reply has been received from the Secretary-General within one month of the date the letter was sent to the Secretary-General, the staff member shall, within the following month, submit his or her appeal in writing to the Secretary of the Joint Appeals Board.

(*c*) An appeal against the Secretary-General's decision on disciplinary action shall be addressed to the Secretary of the Joint Appeals Board within one month from the time the staff member received notifications of the decision in writing.

(*d*) An appeal shall not be receivable by the Joint Appeals Board, unless the above time have been met, provided that the Board may waive the time limits in exceptional circumstances.

(*e*) Before the Joint Appeals Board undertakes consideration of an appeal, the staff member concerned shall be notified of the composition of the Board.

(*f*) A staff member may arrange to have his or her appeal presented to the Joint

Appeals Board on his or her behalf by another member of the Secretariat. The staff member may not, however, be represented before the Board by a person who is not a member of the Secretariat.

(g) The filing of an appeal with the Joint Appeals Board shall not have the effect of suspending action on an administrative decision which is the subject of the appeal.

(h) In considering an appeal, the Joint Appeals Board shall act with the maximum of dispatch consistent with a fair review of the issues before it. Normally, proceedings before the Board shall be limited to the original written presentation of the case, together with brief statements and rebuttals, which may be made orally or in writing, in one of the working languages.

(i) The Board shall have authority to call members of the Secretariat who may be able to provide information concerning the issues before it and to request the production of documents.

(j) The Joint Appeals Board shall, by majority vote, adopt and submit a report to the Secretary-General. The report shall be considered as constituting a record of the proceedings in the appeal and may include a summary of the matter, as well as the Board's recommendation. Votes on the recommendation shall be recorded, and any member of the Board may have his or her dissenting opinions included in the report.

(k) The Board shall submit its report to the Secretary-General as soon as possible after undertaking consideration of an appeal.

(l) The final decision in the matter, taken by the Secretary-General after the Board has forwarded its report, shall be notified to the staff member, together with a copy of the Board's recommendation. The Secretary-General's decision and a copy of the Board's recommendation shall also be transmitted to the Staff Committee, except in cases of appeals against disciplinary action.

Rule 111.4: Appeals in Offices Away from Headquarters

(a) A Joint Appeals Board generally comparable to that at Headquarters shall be established in the United Nations Office at Geneva and in UNIDO, Vienna, to advise the Secretary-General in the case of any appeal under staff regulation 11.1 by a staff member serving respectively at these duty stations. Appeals submitted by such staff members in accordance with paragraphs (b) and (c) of rule 111.3 shall be addressed to the Secretary of the Joint Appeals Board at Geneva or Vienna, as appropriate.

(b) In the case of any appeal under staff regulation 11.1 by a staff member serving in any other office away from Headquarters or by any staff member after his or her employment has ceased, the Secretary-General shall secure the advice either of the Joint Appeals Board at Headquarters, Geneva or Vienna or of an appropriate *ad hoc* body. Appeals submitted by such staff members in accordance with paragraphs (b) and (c) or rule 111.3 shall be addressed to the Secretary of the Joint Appeals Board at Headquarters.

(c) Staff members serving away from Headquarters, the United Nations Office at Geneva or UNIDO, Vienna, or former staff members may meet the time limits specified in paragraphs (a), (b) and (c) of rule 111.3 by delivering the letter addressed to the Secretary-General and the appeal addresssed to the Secretary of the Joint Appeals Board at Headquarters within the respective specified periods to an office of the United Nations for transmission to Headquarters.

Chapter XII: General Provisions

Rule 112.1: Gender of Terms

In the French text of these rules reference to staff members in the masculine gender shall apply to staff members of both sexes, unless clearly inappropriate from the context.

Rule 112.2: Amendment of, and Exceptions to, Staff Rules

(*a*) These rules may be amended by the Secretary-General in a manner consistent with the Staff Regulations.

(*b*) Exceptions to the Staff Rules may be made by the Secretary-General, provided that such exception is not inconsistent with any staff regulation or other decision of the General Assembly and provided further that it is agreed to by the staff member directly affected and is, in the opinion of the Secretary-General, not prejudicial to the interests of any other staff member or group of staff members.

Rule 112.3: Financial Responsibility

Any staff member may be required to reimburse the United Nations either partially or in full for any financial loss suffered by the United Nations as a result of the staff member's negligence or of his or her having violated any regulation, rule or administrative instruction.

Rule 112.4: Liability Insurance

In accordance with resolution 22 (I) (E) of the 31st plenary meeting of the General Assembly, staff members who own or drive motor cars shall carry public liability and property damage insurance in an amount adequate to insure them against claims arising from injury or death to other persons or from damage to the property of others caused by their cars.

Rule 112.5: Staff Member's Beneficiaries

(*a*) At the time of appointment, each staff member shall nominate a beneficiary or beneficiaries in writing in a form prescribed by the Secretary-General. It shall be the responsibility of the staff member to notify the Secretary-General of any revocations or changes of beneficiaries.

(*b*) In the event of the death of a staff member, all amounts standing to the staff member's credit will be paid to his or her nominated beneficiary or beneficiaries, subject to application of the Staff Rules and of the Joint Staff Pension Fund Regulations. Such payment shall afford the United Nations a complete release from all further liability in respect of any sum so paid.

(*c*) If a nominated beneficiary does not survive, or if a designation of beneficiary has not been made or has been revoked, the amount standing to the credit of a staff member will, upon the staff member's death, be paid to his or her estate.

Rule 112.6: Service and Conduct Reports

In the salary levels below the Director (D-2) level, the service and conduct of a staff member shall be the subject of reports made from time to time by the staff member's supervisors. Such reports, which shall be shown to the staff member, shall form a part of his or her permanent cumulative record.

Rule 112.7: Proprietary Rights

All rights, including title, copyright and patent rights, in any work performed by a staff member as part of his or her official duties shall be vested in the United Nations.

Rule 112.8: Effective Date and Authentic Texts of Rules

Except as otherwise indicated, rules 101 through 112.8 as published in this revised edition (ST/SGB/Staff Rule/1/Rev.5) shall be effective 1 January 1979. The English and French texts of these rules are equally authoritative.

APPENDICES TO THE STAFF RULES

Appendix A

TABLE V.9. *Pensionable remuneration for Professional and higher categories and, for purposes of separation payments, net equivalent after application of staff assessment ($US). Effective 1 January 1980*

Level		Step I	II	III	IV	V	VI	VII	VIII	IX	X	XI	XII	XIII
Under-Secretary-General														
USG	PR	106,442												
	Net D	56,037												
	Net S	50,597												
Assistant Secretary-General														
ASG	PR	94,402												
	Net D	51,221												
	Net S	46,323												
Director														
D-2	PR	73,710	75,824	77,980	80,220									
	Net D	42,918	43,790	44,652	45,548									
	Net S	38,964	39,728	40,493	41,288									
Principal Officer														
D-1	PR	61,446	63,448	65,464	67,466	69,510	71,498	73,430						
	Net D	37,636	38,517	39,404	40,285	41,154	41,989	42,801						
	Net S	34,357	35,127	35,904	36,674	37,431	38,157	38,862						
Senior Officer														
P-5	PR	53,466	55,076	56,644	58,142	59,640	61,166	62,706	64,246	65,800	67,354			
	Net D	33,944	34,715	35,436	36,125	36,814	37,513	38,191	38,868	39,552	40,236			
	Net S	31,103	31,786	32,421	33,028	33,634	34,249	34,842	35,435	36,033	36,631			

	I	II	III	IV	V	VI	VII	VIII	IX	X	XI	XII	XIII
First Officer													
P-4 PR	41,916	43,274	44,632	46,004	47,404	48,804	50,190	51,576	53,032	54,502	55,972	57,372	
Net D	28,236	28,937	29,616	30,302	31,002	31,702	32,371	33,036	33,735	34,441	35,127	35,771	
Net S	26,031	26,657	27,261	27,872	28,495	29,118	29,711	30,300	30,919	31,543	32,149	32,716	
Second Officer													
P-3 PR	33,474	34,664	35,868	37,044	38,220	39,438	40,684	41,916	43,064	44,212	45,360	46,522	47,712
Net D	23,756	24,399	25,049	25,684	26,314	26,948	27,596	28,236	28,832	29,406	29,980	30,561	31,156
Net S	22,015	22,592	23,176	23,746	24,312	24,879	25,458	26,031	26,563	27,074	27,585	28,102	28,632
Associate Officer													
P-2 PR	26,656	27,594	28,546	29,498	30,464	31,416	32,382	33,348	34,342	35,350	36,358		
Net D	19,844	20,406	20,961	21,504	22,054	22,597	23,148	23,688	24,225	24,769	25,313		
Net S	18,478	18,989	19,491	19,981	20,479	20,969	21,467	21,954	22,436	22,925	23,414		
Assistant Officer													
P-1 PR	20,020	20,860	21,714	22,568	23,450	24,332	25,228	26,096	26,964	27,804			
Net D	15,743	16,272	16,810	17,348	17,904	18,449	18,987	19,508	20,028	20,532			
Net S	14,742	15,225	15,716	16,207	16,714	17,211	17,699	18,172	18,645	19,103			

D = Salary rates applicable to staff members with a dependent spouse or child.
S = Salary rates applicable to staff members with no dependent spouse or child.

TABLE V.10. *Pensionable remuneration for Professional and higher categories and, for purposes of separation payments, net equivalent after application of staff assessment ($US). Effective 1 January 1980–30 June 1980*

Level		Step I	II	III	IV	V	VI	VII	VIII	IX	X	XI	XII	XIII
Under-Secretary-General														
USG	PR	102,641												
	Net D	54,516												
	Net S	49,248												
Assistant Secretary-General														
ASG	PR	91,031												
	Net D	49,872												
	Net S	45,126												
Director														
D-2	PR	71,078	73,116	75,195	77,355									
	Net D	41,813	42,669	43,538	44,402									
	Net S	38,003	38,747	39,504	40,271									
Principal Officer														
D-1	PR	59,252	61,182	63,126	65,057	67,028	68,945	70,808						
	Net D	36,636	37,520	38,375	39,225	40,092	40,917	41,699						
	Net S	33,477	34,255	35,004	35,747	36,506	37,225	37,905						
Senior Officer														
P-5	PR	51,557	53,109	54,621	56,066	57,510	58,982	60,467	61,952	63,450	64,949			
	Net D	33,027	33,772	34,498	35,170	35,835	36,512	37,195	37,859	38,518	39,178			
	Net S	30,292	30,951	31,594	32,187	32,772	33,368	33,969	34,552	35,128	35,705			
First Officer														
P-4	PR	40,419	41,729	43,038	44,361	45,711	47,061	48,398	49,734	51,138	52,556	53,973	55,323	
	Net D	27,458	28,139	28,819	29,481	30,156	30,831	31,499	32,152	32,826	33,507	34,187	34,829	
	Net S	25,335	25,944	26,552	27,141	27,742	28,343	28,929	29,517	30,114	30,717	31,319	31,886	

Level													
Second Officer													
P-3 PR	32,279	33,426	34,587	35,721	36,855	38,030	39,231	40,419	41,526	42,633	43,740	44,861	46,008
Net D	23,089	23,730	24,357	24,969	25,582	26,216	26,840	27,458	28,034	28,609	29,170	29,731	30,304
Net S	21,414	21,992	22,555	23,105	23,655	24,224	24,782	25,335	25,850	26,364	26,864	27,363	27,874
Associate Officer													
P-2 PR	25,704	26,609	27,527	28,445	29,376	30,294	31,226	32,157	33,116	34,088	35,060		
Net D	19,272	19,815	20,366	20,904	21,434	21,958	22,489	23,019	23,563	24,088	24,612		
Net S	17,959	18,452	18,952	19,439	19,919	20,391	20,871	21,351	21,841	22,313	22,784		
Assistant Officer													
P-1 PR	19,305	20,115	20,939	21,762	22,613	23,463	24,327	25,164	26,001	26,811			
Net D	15,271	15,802	16,322	16,840	17,376	17,911	18,446	18,948	19,450	19,937			
Net S	14,310	14,796	15,270	15,743	16,232	16,721	17,208	17,664	18,121	18,562			

D = Salary rates applicable to staff members with a dependent spouse or child.
S = Salary rates applicable to staff members with no dependent spouse or child.

TABLE V.11. *Salary Scales for Field Service Category, showing annual gross and net after application. of staff assessment ($US).*
Effective 1 January 1977

Level	Step I	II	III	IV	V	VI	VII	VIII	IX	X	XI	XII	XIII
Principal Field Service Officer II													
FS-7 Gross	26,437	27,277	28,123	29,007	29,891	30,775	31,660	32,544	33,452	34,385			
Net D	19,712	20,216	20,720	21,224	21,728	22,232	22,736	23,240	23,744	24,248			
Net S	18,358	18,816	19,273	19,729	20,184	20,639	21,095	21,550	22,004	22,457			
Principal Field Service Officer I													
FS-6 Gross	20,679	21,392	22,105	22,817	23,530	24,255	25,003	25,752	26,500	27,248			
Net D	16,158	16,607	17,056	17,505	17,954	18,403	18,852	19,301	19,750	20,199			
Net S	15,120	15,530	15,940	16,350	16,760	17,169	17,577	17,985	18,393	18,800			
Senior Field Service Officer													
FS-5 Gross	16,568	17,135	17,702	18,268	18,835	19,402	19,968	20,560	21,154	21,748	22,341	22,935	23,529
Net D	13,465	13,839	14,213	14,587	14,961	15,335	15,709	16,083	16,457	16,831	17,205	17,579	17,951
Net S	12,654	12,997	13,340	13,682	14,025	14,368	14,711	15,052	15,394	15,735	16,076	16,418	16,759
Intermediate Field Service Officer													
FS-4 Gross	13,858	14,319	14,786	15,252	15,719	16,194	16,682	17,170	17,658	18,145	18,633	19,121	19,609
Net D	11,608	11,930	12,252	12,574	12,896	13,218	13,540	13,862	14,184	14,506	14,828	15,150	15,472
Net S	10,926	11,227	11,528	11,828	12,129	12,427	12,723	13,018	13,313	13,608	13,903	14,198	14,493
Junior Field Service Officer													
FS-3 Gross	11,883	12,271	12,664	13,057	13,450	13,843	14,246	14,657	15,067	15,477	15,887	16,311	16,739
Net D	10,182	10,465	10,748	11,031	11,314	11,597	11,880	12,163	12,446	12,729	13,012	13,295	13,578
Net S	9,594	9,858	10,123	10,387	10,652	10,916	11,180	11,445	11,709	11,973	12,237	12,498	12,757

Security Officer										
FS-2 Gross	10,428	10,765	11,103	11,440	11,777	12,119	12,471	12,822	13,174	13,525
Net D	9,091	9,344	9,597	9,850	10,103	10,356	10,609	10,862	11,115	11,368
Net S	8,571	8,808	9,045	9,282	9,519	9,756	9,993	10,229	10,466	10,702
Messenger										
FS-1 Gross	9,255	9,512	9,769	10,029	10,329	10,629	10,929	11,229	11,529	11,829
Net D	8,117	8,342	8,567	8,792	9,017	9,242	9,467	9,692	9,917	10,142
Net S	7,654	7,866	8,079	8,290	8,501	8,712	8,923	9,134	9,345	9,556

D = Applicable to staff members with a dependent spouse or child.
S = Applicable to staff members with no dependent spouse or child.

Dependency allowances.

	$
Dependent child[1]	450
Secondary dependent	300

Language allowance (below level FS-6): First additional language—$480 per year net; second additional language—$240 (to be included in pensionable remuneration).

Increments: Salary increments within the levels shall be awarded annually on the basis of satisfactory service.

---

[1] No allowance is payable for the first dependent child of a staff member without dependent spouse.

TABLE V.12. *Pensionable remuneration for Field Service category and, for purposes of separation payments, the net equivalents after application of staff assessment ($US). Effective 1 July 1980*

Level	Step I	II	III	IV	V	VI	VII	VIII	IX	X	XI	XII	XIII
Principal Field Service Officer II													
FS-7 PR	37,012	38,188	39,372	40,610	41,847	43,085	44,324	45,562	46,833	48,139			
Net D	25,666	26,298	26,913	27,557	28,200	28,843	29,462	30,081	30,717	31,370			
Net S	23,731	24,297	24,848	25,424	25,999	26,573	27,124	27,675	28,241	28,822			
Principal Field Service Officer I													
FS-6 PR	28,951	29,949	30,947	31,944	32,942	33,957	35,004	36,053	37,100	38,147			
Net D	21,192	21,761	22,330	22,898	23,467	24,017	24,582	25,149	25,714	26,276			
Net S	19,700	20,214	20,728	21,241	21,755	22,249	22,757	23,266	23,774	24,278			
Senior Field Service Officer													
FS-5 PR	23,195	23,989	24,783	25,575	26,369	27,163	27,955	28,784	29,616	30,447	31,277	32,109	32,941
Net D	17,743	18,243	18,720	19,195	19,671	20,148	20,623	21,097	21,571	22,045	22,518	22,992	23,466
Net S	16,567	17,024	17,457	17,888	18,321	18,754	19,185	19,614	20,042	20,470	20,898	21,326	21,755
Intermediate Field Service Officer													
FS-4 PR	19,401	20,047	20,700	21,353	22,007	22,672	23,355	24,038	24,721	25,403	26,086	26,769	27,453
Net D	15,335	15,760	16,171	16,582	16,994	17,413	17,844	18,273	18,683	19,092	19,502	19,911	20,322
Net S	14,368	14,757	15,133	15,508	15,884	16,266	16,659	17,051	17,423	17,795	18,167	18,539	18,912
Junior Field Service Officer													
FS-3 PR	16,636	17,179	17,730	18,280	18,830	19,380	19,944	20,520	21,094	21,668	22,242	22,835	23,435
Net D	13,510	13,868	14,232	14,595	14,958	15,321	15,693	16,058	16,419	16,781	17,142	17,516	17,894
Net S	12,695	13,023	13,357	13,689	14,022	14,355	14,696	15,029	15,359	15,689	16,019	16,360	16,705
Security Officer													
FS-2 PR	14,599	15,071	15,544	16,016	16,488	16,967	17,459	17,951	18,444	18,935			
Net D	12,123	12,449	12,775	13,101	13,412	13,728	14,053	14,378	14,703	15,027			
Net S	11,408	11,712	12,016	12,320	12,605	12,895	13,193	13,490	13,789	14,086			
Messenger													
FS-1 PR	12,957	13,317	13,677	14,041	14,461	14,881	15,301	15,721	16,141	16,561			
Net D	10,959	11,218	11,477	11,738	12,028	12,318	12,608	12,897	13,183	13,460			
Net S	10,320	10,562	10,805	11,048	11,319	11,589	11,860	12,130	12,395	12,649			

D = Salary rates applicable to staff members with a dependent spouse or child.
S = Salary rates applicable to staff members with no dependent spouse or child.

TABLE V.13. *Pensionable remuneration for Field Service category and, for purposes of separation payments, the net equivalents after application of staff assessment ($US). Effective 1 January 1980–30 June 1980*

Level		I	II	III	IV	V	VI	VII	VIII	IX	X	XI	XII	XIII
Principal Field Service Officer II														
FS-7	PR	35,690	36,824	37,966	39,159	40,353	41,546	42,741	43,934	45,160	46,420			
	Net D	24,953	25,565	26,182	26,803	27,424	28,044	28,665	29,267	29,880	30,510			
	Net S	23,090	23,640	24,194	24,749	25,304	25,859	26,415	26,951	27,496	28,057			
Principal Field Service Officer I														
FS-6	PR	27,917	28,879	29,842	30,803	31,766	32,744	33,754	34,765	35,775	36,785			
	Net D	20,600	21,151	21,700	22,248	22,797	23,354	23,907	24,453	24,999	25,544			
	Net S	19,165	19,663	20,159	20,654	21,149	21,654	22,151	22,641	23,131	23,621			
Senior Field Service Officer														
FS-5	PR	22,367	23,132	23,898	24,662	25,427	26,193	26,957	27,756	28,558	29,360	30,160	30,962	31,764
	Net D	17,221	17,703	18,186	18,647	19,106	19,566	20,024	20,504	20,968	21,425	21,881	22,338	22,795
	Net S	16,091	16,531	16,971	17,391	17,808	18,225	18,642	19,077	19,497	19,910	20,322	20,735	21,148
Intermediate Field Service Officer														
FS-4	PR	18,708	19,331	19,961	20,590	21,221	21,862	22,521	23,180	23,838	24,496	25,155	25,813	26,472
	Net D	14,877	15,288	15,704	16,102	16,499	16,903	17,318	17,733	18,148	18,548	18,943	19,338	19,733
	Net S	13,948	14,325	14,706	15,069	15,432	15,801	16,180	16,559	16,937	17,300	17,659	18,018	18,377
Junior Field Service Officer														
FS-3	PR	16,042	16,566	17,096	17,627	18,158	18,688	19,232	19,787	20,340	20,894	21,447	22,020	22,598
	Net D	13,118	13,464	13,813	14,164	14,514	14,864	15,223	15,589	15,944	16,293	16,642	17,003	17,367
	Net S	12,335	12,652	12,973	13,294	13,616	13,936	14,265	14,601	14,926	15,244	15,562	15,892	16,224
Security Officer														
FS-2	PR	14,078	14,533	14,989	15,444	15,899	16,361	16,836	17,310	17,785	18,259			
	Net D	11,764	12,078	12,392	12,706	13,020	13,328	13,642	13,955	14,268	14,581			
	Net S	11,072	11,365	11,659	11,952	12,245	12,528	12,816	13,103	13,390	13,677			
Messenger														
FS-1	PR	12,494	12,841	13,188	13,539	13,944	14,349	14,754	15,159	15,564	15,969			
	Net D	10,626	10,876	11,125	11,378	11,670	11,951	12,230	12,510	12,789	13,069			
	Net S	10,008	10,242	10,476	10,712	10,984	11,247	11,508	11,768	12,029	12,290			

D = Salary rates applicable to staff members with a dependent spouse or child.
S = Salary rates applicable to staff members with no dependent spouse or child.

Appendix B
Headquarters

TABLE V.14. *Salary scales for General Service category showing annual gross and net after application of staff assessment ($US).*
Effective 1 February 1980

Level	Step I	II	III	IV	V	VI	VII	VIII	IX	X
Principal										
G-5 Gross	19,434.00	20,345.00	21,255.00	22,165.00	23,075.00	23,986.00	24,972.00	25,957.00	26,943.00	27,930.00
Net	14,432.00	15,024.00	15,616.00	16,207.00	16,799.00	17,391.00	17,983.00	18,574.00	19,166.00	19,758.00
Senior										
G-4 Gross	16,571.00	17,268.00	17,965.00	18,660.00	19,357.00	20,054.00	20,751.00	21,446.00	22,143.00	22,837.00[1]
Net	12,571.00	13,024.00	13,477.00	13,929.00	14,382.00	14,835.00	15,288.00	15,740.00	16,193.00	16,644.00
Intermediate										
G-3 Gross	14,677.00	15,193.00	15,707.00	16,240.00	16,792.00	17,346.00	17,902.00	18,455.00	19,011.00	19,565.00
Net	11,274.00	11,635.00	11,995.00	12,356.00	12,715.00	13,075.00	13,436.00	13,796.00	14,157.00	14,517.00
Junior										
G-2 Gross	13,017.00	13,479.00	13,941.00	14,404.00	14,867.00	15,329.00	15,790.00	16,272.00	16,769.00	
Net	10,112.00	10,435.00	10,759.00	11,083.00	11,407.00	11,730.00	12,053.00	12,377.00	12,700.00	
Messenger										
G-1 Gross	11,527.00	11,940.00	12,354.00	12,769.00	13,183.00	13,597.00	14,011.00	14,426.00		
Net	9,069.00	9,358.00	9,648.00	9,938.00	10,228.00	10,518.00	10,808.00	11,098.00		

Dependence allowances:

	$
Dependent spouse	850
Dependent child	400
Except for first dependent child of a widowed or divorced staff member	850
Secondary dependent	450

Language allowance (to be included in pensionable remuneration):
First additional language—$598 per year net
Second additional language—$299 per year net

Non-resident's allowance (to be included in pensionable remuneration: $200 per year net. In no case shall the amount of the non-resident's allowance, when added to the staff member's salary (exclusive of language allowance, if any), bring the total to more than $16.977 after staff assessment.

Increments: Salary increments within the levels shall be awarded annually on the basis of satisfactory service.

[1] The new step * enters into effect on 1 May 1980. For staff members at step IX of the G-4 level as of 1 May 1980 the increment to the new step X shall be awarded as set out below:

Time spent at Step IX as of 1 May 1980	Date of movement to new Step X
5 years or more	1 May 1980
4 to 4 years and 11 months	1 June 1980
3 to 3 years and 11 months	1 July 1980
2 to 2 years and 11 months	1 August 1980
1 to 1 year and 11 months	1 September 1980
less than 1 year	On completion of 12 months at step IX or 1 October 1980, whichever is later.

TABLE V.15. Salary scales for General Service category showing annual gross and net after application of staff assessment ($US). Effective 1 August 1979 (revised)

Level	Step I	II	III	IV	V	VI	VII	VIII	IX	X
Principal										
G-5 Gross	18,357.00	19,223.00	20,089.00	20,955.00	21,822.00	22,688.00	23,554.00	24,455.00	25,393.00	26,332.00
Net	13,732.00	14,295.00	14,858.00	15,421.00	15,984.00	16,547.00	17,110.00	17,673.00	18,236.00	18,799.00
Senior										
G-4 Gross	15,659.00	16,295.00	16,958.00	17,620.00	18,283.00	18,946.00	19,609.00	20,271.00	20,934.00	
Net	11,961.00	12,392.00	12,823.00	13,253.00	13,681.00	14,115.00	14,546.00	14,976.00	15,407.00	
Intermediate										
G-3 Gross	13,896.00	14,386.00	14,876.00	15,366.00	15,854.00	16,371.00	16,898.00	17,426.00	17,954.00	18,482.00
Net	10,727.00	11,070.00	11,413.00	11,756.00	12,098.00	12,441.00	12,784.00	13,127.00	13,470.00	13,813.00
Junior										
G-2 Gross	12,316.00	12,756.00	13,196.00	13,636.00	14,076.00	14,516.00	14,954.00	15,394.00	15,834.00	
Net	9,621.00	9,929.00	10,237.00	10,545.00	10,853.00	11,161.00	11,468.00	11,776.00	12,084.00	
Messenger										
G-1 Gross	10,899.00	11,291.00	11,686.00	12,080.00	12,474.00	12,869.00	13,263.00	13,656.00		
Net	8,629.00	8,904.00	9,180.00	9,456.00	9,732.00	10,008.00	10,284.00	10,559.00		

Dependence allowances:

	$
Dependent spouse	850
Dependent child	400
Except for first dependent child of a widowed or divorced staff member	850
Secondary dependent	450

Language allowance (to be included in pensionable remuneration):
First additional language—$598 per year net
Second additional language—$299 per year net

Increments: Salary increments within the levels shall be awarded annually on the basis of satisfactory service.

Non-resident's allowance (to be included in pensionable remuneration): $200 per year net. In the case shall the amount of the non-resident's allowance, when added to the staff member's salary exclusive of language allowance, if any) bring the total to more than $16,153 after staff assessment.

TABLE V.16. *Salary scales for General Service category—Security Service showing annual gross and net after application of staff assessment ($US). Effective 1 February 1980*

Level	Step											
	I	II	III	IV	V	VI	VII	VIII	IX	X	XI	XII
Security Lieutenant												
S-5 Gross	24,025.00	24,977.00	25,952.00	26,952.00	27,932.00	28,942.00	29,987.00	31,055.00				
Net	17,415.00	17,986.00	18,571.00	19,171.00	19,759.00	20,365.00	20,992.00	21,633.00				
Security Sergeant												
S-4 Gross	21,177.00	21,988.00	22,811.00	23,668.00	24,628.00	25,615.00	26,662.00	27,685.00				
Net	15,565.00	16,092.00	16,627.00	17,184.00	17,777.00	18,369.00	18,997.00	19,611.00				
Senior Security Officer												
S-3 Gross	19,465.00	20,031.00	20,622.00	21,209.00	21,823.00	22,468.00	23,145.00	23,823.00	24,567.00	25,337.00		
Net	14,452.00	14,820.00	15,204.00	15,586.00	15,985.00	16,404.00	16,844.00	17,285.00	17,740.00	18,202.00		
Security Officer												
S-2 Gross	16,838.00	17,380.00	17,929.00	18,452.00	18,986.00	19,543.00	20,111.00	20,677.00	21,266.00	21,868.00	22,523.00	23,189.00
Net	12,745.00	13,097.00	13,454.00	13,794.00	14,141.00	14,503.00	14,872.00	15,240.00	15,623.00	16,014.00	16,440.00	16,873.00
Security Officer (Probationary)												
S-1 Gross	15,769.00	16,194.00										
Net	12,038.00	12,326.00										

Dependency allowances:

	$
Dependent spouse	850
Dependent child	400
Except for first dependent child of a widowed or divorced staff member	850
Secondary dependent	450

Language allowance (to be included in pensionable remuneration):
First additional language—$598 per year net
Second additional language—$299 per year net

Increments: Salary increments within the levels shall be awarded annually on the basis of satisfactory service.

TABLE V.17. Salary scales for General Service category-Security Service showing annual gross and net after application of staff assessment ($US). Effective 1 August 1979 (revised)

Level	Step I	II	III	IV	V	VI	VII	VIII	IX	X	XI	XII
Security Lieutenant												
S-5 Gross	22,723.00	23,558.00	24,450.00	25,402.00	26,333.00	27,295.00	28,288.00	29,305.00				
Net	16,570.00	17,113.00	17,670.00	18,241.00	18,800.00	19,377.00	19,973.00	20,583.00				
Security Sergeant												
S-4 Gross	20,015.00	20,786.00	21,569.00	22,385.00	23,252.00	24,130.00	25,125.00	26,098.00				
Net	14,810.00	15,311.00	15,820.00	16,350.00	16,914.00	17,478.00	18,075.00	18,659.00				
Senior Security Officer												
S-3 Gross	18,386.00	18,925.00	19,486.00	20,046.00	20,629.00	21,243.00	21,888.00	22,532.00	23,198.00	23,875.00		
Net	13,751.00	14,101.00	14,466.00	14,830.00	15,209.00	15,608.00	16,027.00	16,446.00	16,879.00	17,319.00		
Security Officer												
S-2 Gross	15,896.00	16,402.00	16,925.00	17,423.00	17,931.00	18,460.00	19,000.00	19,538.00	20,100.00	20,672.00	21,295.00	21,929.00
Net	12,127.00	12,461.00	12,801.00	13,125.00	13,455.00	13,799.00	14,150.00	14,500.00	14,865.00	15,237.00	15,642.00	16,054.00
Security Officer (Probationary)												
S-1 Gross	14,934.00	15,326.00										
Net	11,454.00	11,728.00										

Dependency allowances:

	$
Dependent spouse	850
Dependent child	400
Except for first dependent child of a widowed or divorced staff member	850
Secondary dependent	450

Language allowance (to be included in pensionable remuneration):
First additional language—$598 per year net
Second additional language—$299 per year net

Increments: Salary increments within the levels shall be awarded annually on the basis of satisfactory service.

TABLE V.18. *Salary scales for General Service category—Dispatches and Guides in the Visitors Service showing annual gross and net after application of staff assessment* ($US). Effective 1 February 1980

Level	Step I	II	III
Dispatcher			
V-2 Gross	17,469.00	18,400.00	19,374.00
Net	13,155.00	13,760.00	14,393.00
Guide			
V-1 Gross	15,177.00	15,841.00	16,572.00
Net	11,624.00	12,089.00	12,572.00

Dependence allowances:

	$
Dependent spouse	850
Dependent child	400
Except for first dependent child of a staff member without a spouse	850
Secondary dependent	450

Increments: Salary increments within the levels shall be awarded on the basis of satisfactory service, as follows: for Guides, after an interval of six months; for Dispatchers, after an interval of one year.

Non-resident's allowance: Not entitled.

Scheduled work week: The scheduled work week consists of the five days assigned in any calendar week, from Monday to Sunday. Whenever a sixth or seventh consecutive work day is required, regardless of the scheduled work week, a supplementary payment shall be made at the rate of one and one half times the base salary.

Language allowance:
Not entitled.

Half-time Guides:
  (i) Salary: The salary of half-time Guides shall be half that paid to Guides. This salary shall be the basis for determination of payments for annual leave; sick leave; maternity leave; commutation of accrued annual leave; entitlements to termination indemnity; compensation for death, illness or injury attributable to service; and any other compensation determined on the basis of salary.
 (ii) Dependency allowances: Dependency allowances shall be paid to half-time Guides at half the rate applied to Dispatchers and Guides.
(iii) Regular hour of duty: The regular tour of duty of half time Guides shall be half that expected of Dispatchers and Guides.
 (iv) Overtime: Half-time Guides who are required to work in excess of their regular hour of duty shall be remunerated on a pro-rata basis for additional hours worked up to the maximum hours of the normal hour of duty of Dispatchers and Guides; thereafter and for work required on official holidays, they shall be compensated as otherwise provided in Appendix B.
  (v) For purposes of determining service credit for salary increment, maternity leave and sick leave, every two months of continuous service on a half-time basis shall be counted as one month.

TABLE V.19. *Salary scales for General Service category—Dispatches and Guides in the Visitors Service showing annual gross and net after application of staff assessment ($US). Effective 1 August 1979 (revised)*

Level	Step		
	I	II	III
Dispatcher			
V-2 Gross	16,488.00	17,372.00	18,300.00
Net	12,517.00	13,092.00	13,695.00
Guide			
V-1 Gross	14,371.00	15,003.00	15,660.00
Net	11,060.00	11,503.00	11,962.00

Dependency allowances:

	$
Dependent spouse	850
Dependent child	400
Except for first dependent child of a staff member without a spouse	850
Secondary dependent	450

Increments: Salary increments within the levels shall be awarded on the basis of satisfactory service, as follows: for Guides, after an interval of six months; for Dispatchers, after an interval of one year.

Non-resident's allowance: Not entitled.

Scheduled work week: The scheduled work week consists of the five days assigned in any calendar week, from Monday to Sunday. Whenever a sixth or seventh consecutive work day is required, regardless of the scheduled work week, a supplementary payment shall be made at the rate of one and one half times the base salary.

Language allowance:
Not entitled.

Half-time Guides:
  (i) Salary: The salary of half-time Guides shall be half that paid to Guides. This salary shall be the basis for determination of payments for annual leave; sick leave; maternity leave; commutation of accrued annual leave; entitlements to termination indemnity; compensation for death, illness or injury attributable to service; and any other compensation determined on the basis of salary.
 (ii) Dependency allowances: Dependency allowances shall be paid to half-time Guides at half the rate applied to Dispatchers and Guides.
(iii) Regular hour of duty: The regular hour of duty of half time Guides shall be half that expected of Dispatchers and Guides.
 (iv) Overtime: Half-time Guides who are required to work in excess of their regular hour of duty shall be remunerated on a pro-rata basis for additional hours worked up to the maximum hours of the normal hour of duty of Dispatchers and Guides; thereafter and for work required on official holidays, they shall be compensated as otherwise provided in Appendix B.
  (v) For purposes of determining service credit for salary increment, maternity leave and sick leave, every two months of continuous service on a half-time basis shall be counted as one month.

TABLE V.20. *Manual Workers — salaries and allowances showing annual gross and net after application of staff assessment ($US). Effective 1 February 1980*

Level	Step					
	I	II	III	IV	V	VI
General Foreman						
M-7 Gross	28,397.00	29,367.00	30,333.00	31,302.00	32,295.00	33,349.00
Net	20,038.00	20.620.00	21,200.00	21,781.00	22,362.00	22,942.00
Foreman						
M-6 Gross	25,088.00	26,020.00	26,952.00	27,883.00	28,817.00	29,748.00
Net	18,053.00	18,612.00	19,171.00	19,730.00	20,290.00	20.849.00
Leadman						
M-5 Gross	22,594.00	23,431.00	24,290.00	25,197.00	26,103.00	27,010.00
Net	16,486.00	17,030.00	17,574.00	18,118.00	18,662.00	19,206.00
Skilled Worker (Journeyman)						
M-4 Gross	20,395.00	21,180.00	21,968.00	22,754.00	23,542.00	24,355.00
Net	15,057.00	15,567.00	16,079.00	16,590.00	17,102.00	17,613.00
Semi-skilled Worker						
M-3 Gross	18,288.00	19,005.00	19,720.00	20,438.00	21,155.00	21,871.00
Net	13,687.00	14,153.00	14,618.00	15,085.00	15,551.00	16,016.00
Helper						
M-2 Gross	16,374.00	17,025.00	17,677.00	18,328.00	18,980.00	19,632.00
Net	12,443.00	12,866.00	13,290.00	13,713.00	14,137.00	14,561.00
Unskilled Worker						
M-1 Gross	14,731.00	15,281.00	15,829.00	16,408.00	17,000.00	17,589.00
Net	11,312.00	11,697.00	12,080.00	12,465.00	12,850.00	13,233.00

Dependency allowances:

	$
Dependent spouse	850
Dependent child	400
Except for first dependent child of a widowed or divorced staff member	850
Secondary dependent	450

Increments: Salary increments within the levels shall be awarded annually on the basis of satisfactory service.

TABLE V.21. *Manual Workers — salaries and allowances showing annual gross and net after application of staff assessment* ($US). Effective 1 August 1979*

	Step					
Level	I	II	III	IV	V	VI
General Foreman						
M-7 Gross	26,777.00	27,698.00	28,618.00	29,540.00	30,462.00	31,382.00
Net	19,066.00	19,619.00	20,171.00	20,724.00	21,277.00	21,829.00
Foreman						
M-6 Gross	23,657.00	24,515.00	25,402.00	26,288.00	27,175.00	28,062.00
Net	17,177.00	17,709.00	18,241.00	18,773.00	19,305.00	19,837.00
Leadman						
M-5 Gross	21,363.00	22,160.00	22,955.00	23,752.00	24,593.00	25,457.00
Net	15,686.00	16,204.00	16,721.00	17,239.00	17,756.00	18,274.00
Skilled Worker						
(Journeyman)						
M-4 Gross	19,271.00	20,018.00	20,768.00	21,515.00	22,265.00	23,012.00
Net	14,326.00	14,812.00	15,299.00	15,785.00	16,272.00	16,758.00
Semi-skilled Worker						
M-3 Gross	17,266.00	17,948.00	18,629.00	19,312.00	19,994.00	20,675.00
Net	13,023.00	13,466.00	13,909.00	14,353.00	14,796.00	15,239.00
Helper						
M-2 Gross	15,484.00	16,065.00	16,685.00	17,305.00	17,925.00	18,545.00
Net	11,839.00	12,242.00	12,645.00	13,048.00	13,451.00	13,854.00
Unskilled Worker						
M-1 Gross	13,947.00	14,470.00	14,991.00	15,514.00	16,040.00	16,602.00
Net	10,763.00	11,129.00	11,494.00	11,860.00	12,226.00	12,591.00

Dependency allowances:

	$
Dependent spouse	850
Dependent child	400
Except for first dependent child of a widowed or divorced staff member	850
Secondary dependent	450

Increments: Salary increments within the levels shall be awarded annually on the basis of satisfactory service.

* Supersedes the salary scale, effective 1 October 1979, as shown in Appendix B (Headquarters)/Amend.1.

Conditions Governing Compensation for Overtime Work

Pursuant to staff rule 103.12, staff members in the General Service category or in the Manual Worker category who are required to work overtime at Headquaters shall be given compensatory time off or may receive additional payment in accordance with the following provisions:

(i)   Overtime at Headquarters means time worked in excess of the scheduled work day or in excess of the scheduled work week or time worked on official holidays, provided that such work has been authorized by the proper authority.

(ii)   The scheduled work day at Headquarters means the duration of the working hours in effect at the time on any day of the scheduled work week, less one hour for a meal.

(iii)   The scheduled work week at Headquarters consists of the five working days assigned to the staff member during seven consecutive calendar days.

(iv)   Compensation shall take the form of an equal amount of compensatory time off for overtime in excess of the scheduled work day up to a total of eight hours of work on the same day. Subject to the exigencies of the service, such compensatory time off may be given at any time during the four months following the month in which the overtime takes place.

(v)   Compensation shall take the form of payment at the straight time rate in respect of each hour in excess of 40 hours if, at the time of a review to be conducted three times a year, it is ascertained that a staff member has accumulated more than 40 hours of compensatory time off which could not be authorized because of the exigencies of service. The remaining entitlement to 40 hours of compensatory time off will be counted as part of the staff member's accumulated entitlement at the time of the next review.

(vi)   Compensation shall take the form of an additional payment for overtime in excess of a total of eight hours of work of any day of the scheduled work week, or when it takes place on the sixth or seventh day of the scheduled work week.

(vii)   Compensation for overtime shall take the form of an additional payment when it takes place on an official holiday, provided that the Secretary-General may require all staff members at Headquarters to work on a holiday that falls during a period of exigency. In that event, the Secretary-General shall set another working day to be observed as the holiday, and the holiday falling during the period of exigency shall be treated as a normal working day.

(viii) The additional payment referred to in subparagraphs (vi) and (vii) above shall be made at the rate of one-and-one-half times the aggregate of the staff member's base salary or wage and language and non-resident's allowances, if any.

(ix)   Subject to the exigencies of service, compensatory time off may be granted at a time and a half rate in lieu of compensation by additional payment at the time and a half rate under subparagraphs (vi) and (vii) above if the staff member concerned so requests.

(x)   Compensation for overtime shall be reckoned to the nearest half-hour; casual overtime of less than one half-hour on any day during the scheduled work week shall be disregarded. A staff member who is required to work on the sixth or seventh day of the week or on an official holiday shall receive no less than four hours of overtime compensation.

(xi)   In the interests of the health of the staff and the efficiency of the service, supervisors shall not require a staff member to work more than 40 hours of overtime
during any one month, except where unusual exigencies of the service so
require.

Condition Governing Night Differential

(i) Pursuant to rule 103.13, staff members at Headquarters shall receive, for any
regular working hours between 6 p.m. and 9.30 a.m., a night differential at the rate of
10 per cent of the aggregate of their salary or wage of their language and non-
resident's allowances and post adjustment, if any, provided that no such differential
shall be paid for any part of the tour of duty that begins between 6 a.m. and 9.30 a.m.

(ii) Payments shall be reckoned to the nearest hour, and work periods of less than
one half-hour shall not be taken into consideration.

Conditions Governing Local Recruitment

Pursuant to rule 104.6,
(i) Staff members who have been recruited to serve in posts classified in the Manual
Worker category or in the General Service category shall be regarded as having been
locally recruited unless:
(a)   They have been recruited from outside the area of the duty station,
(b)   Their entitlement to one or more of the allowances or benefits indicated under
rule 104.7 has been duly established by the Secretary-General, or
(c)   The post for which the staff member has been recruited is one which, in the
opinion of the Secretary-General, it would otherwise have been necessary to fill
by recruitment from outside the area of the duty station.

(ii) A staff member who is regarded as having been locally recruited in accordance
with the provisions of subparagraph (i) above, shall cease to be so regarded from the
date on which the staff member is (a) reclassified to the Professional category or (b)
reassigned, after an appropriate examination, to a post within the General Service
category which, in the opinion of the Secretary-General, it would otherwise have been
necessary to fill by recruitment from outside the area of the duty station.

Conditions Governing Acquisition of Entitlement to
Benefits of International Recruitment

Pursuant to rule 104.7,
(i) If a staff member in permanent residence status takes up non-immigrant status
in the country of his or her duty station, the staff member shall thereupon be granted
entitlement to such of the allowances and benefits stipulated in rule 104.7 to which he
or she is otherwise entitled and the staff member shall begin to accrue service credit for
such allowances and benefits from the date on which he or she acquires non-
immigrant status.
(ii) (Cancelled)

Appendix C

Arrangements Relating To Military Service

(*a*) In accordance with section 18 (*c*) of the Convention on Privileges and Immunities of the United Nations, staff members who are nationals of those Member States which have acceded to that Convention shall be 'immune from national service obligations' in the armed service of the country of their nationality.

(*b*) Any requests to Governments which have not acceded the Convention to defer or exempt staff members from military service by reason of their employment with the United Nations shall be made by the Secretary-General and not by the staff member concerned.

(*c*) Staff members who have completed one year of satisfactory probationary service or who have a permanent or regular appointment, may, if called by a Member Government for military service, whether for training or active duty, be placed on special leave without pay for the duration of their required military service. Other staff members, if called for military service, shall be separated from the Secretariat according to the terms of their appointments.

(*d*) A staff member called for military service who is placed on special leave without pay shall have the terms of appointment maintained as they were on the last day of service before the staff member went on leave without pay. The staff member's re-employment in the Secretariat shall be guaranteed, subject only to the normal rules governing necessary reductions in force or abolition of posts.

(*e*) In the interpretation of rule 109.1 (*c*), the period of special leave without pay for military service shall be counted for the purpose of establishing seniority.

(*f*) A staff member on special leave without pay for military service shall be required to advise the Secretary-General within 90 days after release from military service, if the staff member wishes to be restored to active duty with the Secretariat. The staff member shall also be required to submit a certificate of completion of military service.

(*g*) If a staff member, after the period of required military service, elects to continue such service or if te staff member fails to obtain a certified release therefrom, the Secretary-General will determine, on the merits of the particular case, whether further special leave without pay will be granted and whether re-employment rights shall be maintained.

(*h*) If the staff member's absence on special leave without pay appears likely to last six months or more, the United Nations will pay, if so requested, for transporting the staff member's spouse and dependent children to the staff member's place of entitlement an for theier return travel after the staff member's return to active duty with the secretariat, provided that the expenses involved will be counted as travel expenses related to the next home leave entitlement of the staff member.

(*i*) The United Nations shall not continue its contribution to the Joint Staff Pension Fund on behalf of the staff member during the staff member's absence on special leave without pay for military service.

(*j*) The provisions of rule 106.4 relating to illness, accident or death attributable to the performance of official duties on behalf of the United Nations shall not be applicable during periods of military service.

(*k*) The Secretary-General may, if the circumstances of the military service appear to warrant it, credit the staff member's period on special leave without pay for military service in fixing the salary step upon the staff member's return to active duty with the Secretariat.

(*l*) The Secretary-General may apply such of the foregoing provisions as are appropriate in the case of a staff member who, with the advance approval of the Secretary-General, volunteers for military service or request a waiver of immunity under section 18(*c*) of the Convention on privileges and Immunities of the United Nations.

APPENDIX VI:

STAFF REGULATIONS OF THE COUNCIL OF EUROPE (1981)

Table of Contents

Part I: General Provisions

Part II: Appointments and Assessment, Termination of Contracts

Part III: Duties and Obligations of Staff

Part VIII: Final Provisions

62 Implementing provisions
63 Amendments
64 Entry into force

Appendices

Part I: General Provisions

Article 1: Scope

1. These Regulations shall apply to any person who has been appointed in accordance with the conditions laid down in them to a permanent post in the Council of Europe (hereinafter referred to as the Council), but shall not apply to temporary staff.

2. The conditions of employment of temporary staff shall be laid down by the Secretary General in standard contracts, which may stipulate that certain provisions of these Regulations shall be applicable.

Article 2: Hierarchical Authority

The staff of the Council shall be under the authority of the Secretary General and answerable to him. Any hierarchical superior in the Secretariat shall exercise his authority in the name of the Secretary General.

Article 3: Non-discrimination

There shall be no discrimination between staff members on the grounds of race, creed, opinions, civil status or sex.

---

[1] This text will be adopted at a later meeting of the Ministers' Deputies.

Article 4: Posts, Grades and Categories

1. Each post shall carry a grade.

  2. The different grades shall be divided among four categories, in accordance with the system in force in all the co-ordinated organisations:

a. category A, comprising staff engaged in administrative, planning and research duties;

b. category L, comprizing staff engaged in interpretation and translation duties;

c. category B, comprising:

  — staff engaged in executive and supervisory duties;

  — staff engaged in secretarial or clerical duties;

d. category C, comprising staff engaged in technical, manual or service duties.

Article 5: Numbers

The total number of staff and the number in each grade shall not be in excess of the figures indicated in the establishment table save where exceptions are authorised by the Committee of Ministers.

Article 6: Staff Participation

Staff members shall be entitled to express their views, in particular in the bodies provided for in these Regulations on any measures in application of these Regulations or amendments to them and on any other measures relating to the conditions of employment of staff members. They shall co-operate through their representatives in the running of the committees set up by these Regulations and the appended regulations and rules.

Article 7: General Meeting of Staff

Members of staff shall be entitled to attend the General Meeting of Staff, whose attributions and functioning are described in Appendix I hereto.

Article 8: Staff Committee

1. The Staff Committee shall represent the general interests of the staff.

  2. It shall be elected by the members of staff in accordance with the provisions of Appendix I to these Regulations which also determines its membership and attributions.

Article 9: Joint Committee

With a view to facilitating co-operation between the administration and the staff on matters of a general nature concerning the staff, there shall be set up a Joint Committee whose attributions and mode of operation are laid down in Appendix I to these Regulations. The Secretary General shall appoint the Chairman of the Joint

Committee. The other members and their substitutes shall be appointed in equal numbers by the Secretary General and the Staff Committee.

Article 10: Functions Performs in Connection with Staff Representation

The functions performed by staff members on the committees and boards dealing with staff matters set up under these Regulations and appended regulations and rules shall be deemed to be part of the services they render to the Council. No staff member shall suffer prejudice as a result of performing such functions.

Part II: Appointments and Assessment, Termination of Contract

Article 11: Authority to Make Appointments

As provided in Article 36.c of the Statute of the Council of Europe and in accordance with the regulations on appointments (Appendix II to these Regulations), the Secretary General shall make appointments to all posts in the Secretariat other than those to which the holders are elected by the Consultative Assembly and shall assign each staff member, in the interests of the service, to a post in his category corresponding to his grade.

Article 12: Recruitment Policy

1. Recruitment should be aimed at ensuring the employment of staff of the highest ability, efficiency and integrity.

2. When vacancies are being filled, due allowance shall be made for the qualifications and experience of serving staff members, the desirability of bringing in fresh talent from time to time, and the need for posts to be distributed fairly among nations of the member states.

3. In the context of the rules set out in the foregoing paragraphs and under the arrangements determined by the regulations on appointments, vacancies in Category A representing the start of a career shall, unless otherwise provided for in those regulations, be filled by recruitment from outside the Council and the other vacancies in this category either by outside recruitment or by promoting. In particular, the Secretary General will seek to secure the services, for a limited period, of civil servants and specialists.

4. No post may be reserved for nationals of any specific member state.

5. Category C staff normally be recruited in the region in which their place of employment is located.

Article 13: Non-discrimination between candidates

Recruitment shall not be subject to any conditions of race, creed, civil status, sex or opinion provided that such opinion is not at variance with the basic principles enshrined in the Statute of the Council of Europe.

Article 14: Recruitment Conditions

1. To be eligible for appointment as a staff member of the Council, a candidate must:

a. be a national of a state which is member of the Council of Europe and have the civic rights enabling him to be appointed to the civil service of that state;

b. produce evidence that he has discharged any obligations imposed on him by the legislation concerning military service;

c. produce satisfactory testimonials of good character;

d. meet the physical requirements of the post;

e. undertake to fulfil the obligations defined in Part III of these Regulations;

f. have been selected by the procedure laid down in the regulations on appointments.

2. If no suitable candidate for a post can be found or should temporary specialist assistance be required, the Secretary General may waive the nationality condition. For staff members concerned this implies a contract of limited duration.

Article 15: Initial Contract

1. A staff member shall be engaged on a contract drawn up in accordance with a standard form and concluded by him with the Secretary General under the conditions defined by the regulations on appointments.

2. The contract shall state the date on which the appointment becomes effective; on no account may this date precede that on which the official takes up his duties.

3. The content of the contract shall be communicated to the candidate in a letter of appointment.

Article 16: Starting Salary

On recruitment, a staff member's basic salary shall be that of the first step in his grade. However, the Secretary General may, in exceptional circumstances, and having stated the reasons for his decisions, allow additional seniority in the grade in order to take account of the staff member's training and special experience.

Article 17: Probationary Period

1. Before a member of staff can be confirmed in his appointment, he must have satisfactorily completed a probationary period, the length of which shall be determined by the regulations on appointments.

2. During the probationary period a contract may be terminated by either party at one month's notice during the first year or at three months' notice thereafter.

3. Staff recruited in the upper two grades of Category A shall not be required to undergo a probationary period.

Article 18: Confirmation of Appointment

The contracts confirming the appointment shall be of indefinite duration or fixed term contracts, as determined by the regulations on appointments without prejudice to Articles 19 and 20 of these Regulations.

Article 19: A7 and A6 Grades

Recruitment on an A6 or A7 post shall be governed by an initial contract of a fixed term of two years. If, on expiry, it is decided to maintain the staff members's appointment, this initial contract may be extended for one year, or renewed, or replaced by a contract for an indefinite duration.

Article 20: Secondment

Any civil servant of a member state or a specialist working on a permanent basis in another body (university, association, firm) who is seconded to the Council for a limited period in pursuance of Article 12, paragraph 3, of these Regulations shall be engaged on a fixed-term contract not exceeding two years. The initial contract shall be renewable until the end of the secondment. The duration of the appointment shall in no case exceed six years.

Article 21: Promotion

1. Promotion consists in the appointment of a staff member to a post in a higher grade. It shall take place after a vacant or regraded post has been thrown open to competition.

2. The Secretary General shall decide on promotions in accordance with the conditions laid down by the regulations on appointments.

Article 22: Assessment

During the probationary period staff shall be assessed in accordance with the regulations on appointments. After confirmation of appointment, they shall be assessed in accordance with the provisions of the regulations on the assessment of staff after confirmation in post set out in Appendix I I I to these Regulations.

Article 23: Termination of Contract

1. Any contract shall terminate at the least on the last day of the month in which the staff member reaches the age-limit laid down in Article 24 of these Regulations.

2. Fixed-term contracts shall terminate on expiry, unless renewed.

3. A contract for either a fixed or an indefinite period may be terminated at the end of a calendar month by:

a the staff member, as a result of his resignation; such resignation shall take effect at the end of a period of notice of at least three months from the date on which resignation was tendered, unless the Secretary General agrees to shorten this period at the request of the staff member, who shall give reasons therefor;

b the Secretary, on one of the folowing grounds:

   i.   abolition of the post, after consultation of the Joint Committee and subject to at least three months' prior notice to the staff member;

  ii.   dismissal for disciplinary reasons;

 iii.   manifest unsuitability or unsatisfactory work on the part of the staff member; termination for either of these reasons may not occur unless the staff member has been formally asked to remedy his shortcomings during a six-month probationary period and the probationary period has not had any positive results;

the decision concerning termination may be taken only after examination of the case by an ad hoc group comprising the Chairman of the Disciplinary Board and two staff members chosen by the procedure laid down for the Disciplinary Board; the staff member shall be given a hearing and may be assisted by a person of his choice; the ad hoc group shall formulate a reasoned opinion for the Secretary General;

the decision to terminate the contract shall carry prior notice of at least three months;

 iv.   permanent invalidity as provided for in the Pension Scheme Rules.

Article 24: Age Limit

A staff member shall retire on reaching the age of sixty-five years.

Part III: Duties and Obligations of Staff

Article 25: Loyalty and Integrity

1. On taking up his duties, every member of the staff shall sign the following declaration in the presence of the Secretary General:

'I solemnly declare that I will carry out the duties entrusted to me as a member of the staff of the Council of Europe loyally and conscientiously, respecting the confidence placed in me. In discharging these duties and in my official conduct I will have regard exclusively to the interests of the Council of Europe. I will not seek or receive any instructions in connection with the exercise of my functions from any government, authority, organisation or person outside the Council. I will refrain from any action which might reflect upon my position as a member of the staff of the Council or which might be prejudicial morally or materially to the Council.'

2. A staff member may not, without the permission of the Secretary General, accept either directly or indirectly any material or other advantage offered in relation to the performance of his duties. This prohibition shall continue after the staff member's employment has terminated:

Article 26: Professional Discretion

A staff member must maintain the utmost discretion in respect of facts and information which come to his notice in, or in connection with, the performance of his duties.

Without the authorisation of the Secretary General he may not communicate in any form whatever to an unauthorised person any document or information which has not been made public. This obligation shall continue after staff member's employment has terminated.

Article 27: Publications

1. A staff member may not publish or have published any text relating to the work of the Council, either on his own initiative or in collaboration with others, nor make public statements or deliver lecturers on such matters, without the authorisation of the Secretary General.

2. The authorisation referred to in paragraph 1 shall be granted if there is no risk of the interests of the Council being affected. The decision shall be taken within thirty days of the staff member's request. In the absence of a reply within that period, authorisation shall be deemed to have been given.

3. In the case of other publications, statements or lecturers, the staff member shall refrain from making use of his status as a staff member of the Council.

Article 28: Giving Evidence in Legal Proceedings

A staff member may not, without the consent of the Secretary General, make use in legal proceedings, for any purpose whatever, of information within the meaning of Article 26 of these Regulations. Consent shall be given if there is no danger of prejudice to the overriding interests of the Council. This prohibition shall continue after the staff member's employment has terminated.

Article 29: Place of Residence

A staff member shall reside in such a place that he is not hampered in the performance of his duties.

Article 30: Responsibility for Peformance of Duties

1. Whatever his rank in the organisation, a staff member is required to assist and advise his superiors. He is responsible for discharging the tasks entrusted to him. The responsibility of his subordinates does not absolve him of the responsibilities which devolve upon himself.

2. Where an order received by a staff member seems to him to be irregular, or if he considers that its execution is likely to have undesirable consequences of a serious nature, he shall convey his opinion to the person giving the order, if necessary in writing. If the latter confirms the order the staff member may refer the question to the hierarchical authority immediately above. If the latter confirms the order, the staff member shall carry it out, unless it execution would constitute an act contrary to criminal law or to the safety regulations applicable to the Council. He may request that he be given such confirmation in writing.

3. However, if the superior giving the order considers that it must be executed promptly notwithstanding the provisions of pargraph 2, the subordinate shall carry it

out unless its execution is contrary to criminal law or to the safety regulations applicable to the Council.

Article 31: Unauthorised Absence

A staff member may not absent himself from his duties without authority. If he does so without valid reason, the Secretary General may deduct and appropriate amount from his remuneration, and discriplinary measures may be taken against him.

Article 32: Secondary Activities

A staff member intending to engage in an occupational activity outside the organisation, whether paid or unpaid, shall seek the permission of the Secretary General. Permission shall be granted only if the activity in question does not interfere with the performance of the staff member's professional obligations and is not incompatible either with the interests of the Council or with his being a staff member of the Council. The Secretary General shall answer his request within thirty days, failing which permission shall be deemed to have been given. Permission may be cancelled if it ceases to meet the above condition.

Article 33: Incompatibilities

1. A staff member may not be member of a national parliament, the Consultative Assembly or any other international parliamentary assembly, or hold a post remunerated by a government.

2. A staff member standing for election to a parliament or assembly as referred to in paragraph 1 must notify the Secretary General, who shall place him on leave for personal reasons for the period of the election campaign. If he is elected and chooses to serve his political mandate he shall resign from the Council.

Article 34: Election Campaign for an Elective Mandate at Regional or Local level

A staff member wishing to stand for public office at regional or local level shall inform the Secretary General, who, in the light of the interests of the Service and the duration of the election campaign, shall decide whether the staff member may be granted leave of absence or whether he must take leave for personal reasons.

Article 35: Acceptance of an Elective Mandate at Regional or Local Level

The Secretary General shall determine whether and to what extent a staff member may, in addition to his official duties, hold an elective mandate at regional or local level or whether he must take leave for personal reasons.

Article 36: Official Matters Impinging on Personal Interests

A staff member to whom it falls, in the course of his duties, to deal with a matter which impinges on his personal interests in a manner which might affect his objectivity shall so inform his immediate superior. He shall be relieved of responsibility for any matter involving himself or a member of his family.

Article 37: Medical Examination

A staff member shall submit to any medical examination provided for in the Regulations or ordered as a general measure by the Secretary General.

Article 38: Recovery of Overpayments

1. Any sum overpaid shall be recovered if the recipient was aware, or should have been aware, that there was no due reason for the payment.

2. The Secretary General may waive recovery of all or part of the amount on social grounds.

Article 39: Privileges and Immunities

1. The privileges, immunities and facilities laid down in the General Agreement on the Privileges and Immunities of the Council of Europe, signed in Paris on 2 September 1949, and in any other agreements relating thereto, are conferred on staff members solely in the interests of the Council of Europe and not for their personal benefit.

2. Privileges immunities and facilities do not absolve staff members from their private obligations, nor from the obligation to observe the laws and regulations in force in the country where they perform their duties.

3. In every case where privileges and immunities are invoked, the staff member concerned shall immediately inform the Secretary General.

4. A staff member may not himself relinquish his immunities without the permission of the Secretary General, who shall if necessary take the decision to waive them.

Part IV: Rights of Staff Members

Article 40: Protection of Staff Members in their Official Capacity

1. A staff member may seek the assistance of the Secretary General to protect his material or non-material interests and those of his family where these interests have been harmed without fault or negligence on his or their part by actions directed against him or them by reason of his being a staff member of the Council.

2. Where the Secretary General deems that the conditions set forth in the above paragraph are met, he shall decide what form such assistance may take and the amount up to which the Council shall pay the costs incurred in the defence of the interests referred to in paragraph 1, including the costs of any legal action taken. If the Secretary General considers that legal action may harm the interests of the Council, he may ask the persons concerned not to take such action; in such cases, if they do take legal action, the Council shall make good the material damage suffered by the persons concerned, provided that they assign their rights to the Council.

Article 41: Remuneration

1. Staff salaries and allowances and the methods of paying them shall be laid down in regulations made by the Committee of Ministers as set out in Appendix IV to these Regulations.

2. The Secretary General may award a special allowance to members of the staff performing duties of special responsibility beyond that normal for their rank.

Article 42: Payment of Expenses by the Council

1. The Council shall pay:

a. the travel and subsistence expenses of a staff member on an official journey;

b. the travel, subsistence and removal expenses incurred by a staff member when taking up his duties, when being subsequently transferred and on termination of his contract;

c. the staff member's travel expenses on the occasion of home leave.

2. Other expenses incurred by a staff member in, or in connection with, the performance of his duties, provided they have been approved, shall be reimbursed.

3. On the death of a staff member to whom expenses covered by the provisions of paragraph 1.*b* above were paid when he took up his duties, the Council shall defray:

a. the cost of transporting the body of the staff member from the place of death to the place of funeral;

b. the cost of transporting the deceased staff member's personal belongings;

c. the travel costs of the survivors who were dependent on the staff member and were part of his household.

4. The Council shall also, in the cases referred to in paragraphs 1.*b* and *c* and 3.a, pay the expenses in respect of—provided they are part of his household—the staff member's spouse, children and other dependent persons as defined in Article 5 of Appendix IV and, where appropriate, of a person accompanying one or more of the staff member's children aged under 10.

5. In the case of home leave as referred to in the second sentence of Article 45, paragraph 2, expenses shall be paid in respect of only journey for each person in any two-year period giving entitlement to home leave.

6. The Secretary General shall issue rules setting forth conditions and limits applicable to payment of the expenses referred to in this article.

Article 43: Social Security

1. Staff members shall be properly covered against the risks of accident, illness, old age, disability and death and for maternity expenses.

2. The Pension Scheme applicable to staff members is set out in Appendix V to these Regulations.

3. Staff members shall pay a reasonable share of the contributions payable. In particular, they shall pay the employee's contribution to the French Social Security Scheme as applicable under the Agreement between the Council of Europe and France and one-third of the cost of their affiliation to the compulsory supplementary

insurance scheme. Constributions for accidents at work and industrial disease risks shall be borne by the Council in full.

Article 44: Indemnity for Loss of Job

An indemnity for loss of job may be awarded to any member of staff confirmed in his appointment, if his contract is terminated in the circumstances provided for in Appendix V I to these Regulations, which also sets out the methods of calculating and paying such indemnities.

Article 45: Leave

1. Staff members shall be entitled to paid leave of two and a half working days per month of service.

2. A staff member in receipt of an expatriation allowance shall be entitled to home leave of eight working days every two years except where, at the time of his appointment or transfer, the staff member had solely the nationality of the country in which he is employed to the exclusion of any other nationality. A husband and wife who are on the staff of the Council, or of whom one is employed by the Council and the other by another international organisation, and who are both entitled to claim home leave, may take such either together in the country where one of them has his/her home or separately in their respective home countries.

3. The provisions governing leave for personal reasons are set out in Appendix V I I to these Regulations.

4. The Secretary General may grant short periods of paid special leave.

5. The Secretary General shall determine the duration of paid sick leave and maternity leave.

Article 46: Personal Administrative Files

1. There shall be established a single personal administrative file for each staff member.

2. The file shall contain solely the documents relating to the application of these Regulations and their implementing provisions to the person concerned and other documents concerning his administrative situation, competence, work and conduct. The file shall be kept by the Establishment Division, with the exception of the medical file, which shall be kept by the Council's doctor.

3. The file shall contain no document unknown to the staff member. The latter may comment on any document submitted to him; any comments shall be attached to the document for inclusion in the file unless the author of the document in question amends the content thereof with the agreement of the staff member.

4. The file shall not refer to the political, philosophical or religious views of the staff member.

5. A staff member or his authorised representative may at any time examine his file, even after the termination of his employment.

6. The file shall be confidential and may only be consulted at the headquarters of

the Secretariat. The Secretary General shall issue rules stipulating which staff members, boards and committees shall, by reason of their official functions, be authorised to consult it.

Article 47: Freedom of Association

Staff members shall enjoy the right to associate; they may, in particular, belong to trade unions or professional organisations.

Article 48: Certificate of Employment

A staff member or former staff member may apply for a certificate of employment stating the length of service and duties performed. He may also request that the certificate include an assessment of his ability and the quality of the work peformed.

Part V: Working Conditions

Article 49: Occupational Hygiene and Safety

The Secretary General shall take appropriate measures to ensure the safety and hygiene of the work premises.

Article 50: Hours of Work

The working week and the hours of work and particular arrangements applicable to expectant mothers and disabled persons shall be fixed by the Secretary General.

Article 51: Overtime and Night Work

A staff member may be required to carry out duties outside normal working hours and to perform night work. The maximum duration of night work and such extra duties and the regulations governing any compensation are set forth in Appendix V I I I to the Regulations.

Article 52: Part-time Work

Subject to the requirements of the organisation, the Secretary General may authorise staff members to work part-time as provided in Appendix IX to these Regulations.

Article 53: Staff Training

1. The Secretary General shall take the necessary steps to promote staff training on the basis of an annual plan drawn up in consultation with the Staff Committee, within the limits of available resources. The plan shall cover the kinds of training provided and the arrangements for its implementation.
   2. The aim of training shall be to maintain and increase the ability of staff to

discharge their duties so as to improve their contribution to the attainment of the Council's aims and objectives.

3. Where this is not incompatible with the smooth running of the Council, the Secretary General may grant special facilities to staff who are studying for a qualification in a field related to the work of the Council.

Part VI: Discipline

Article 54: Disciplinary Measures

1. Any failure by a staff member to comply with his obligations under the Staff Regulations, and other regulations, whether intentionally or through negligence on his part, may lead to the institution of disciplinary proceedings and possibly disciplinary action.

2. Disciplinary measures shall take one of the following forms:

a.   written warning;
b.   reprimand;
c.   deferment of advancement to a higher step;
d.   relegation in step;
e.   downgrading;
f.   removal from post.

3. A single offence shall not give rise to more than one disciplinary measure.

Article 55: Disciplinary Board

1. A Disciplinary Board shall be set up, consisting of a Chairman and four members. The Chairman shall arrange for secretarial assistance.

2. The Secretary General shall each year appoint the Chairman of the Disciplinary Board, chairmanship of the board being incompatible with membership of the Joint Committee. The Secretary General shall also draw up a list containing, if possible, the names of two staff members from each grade in each category mentioned in Article 4. The Staff Committee shall at the same time trasmit a like list to the Secretary General.

3. Within five days of receipt of a report initiating disciplinary proceedings, the Chairman of the Disciplinary Board shall, in the presence of the staff member concerned, draw lots from among the names in the above-mentioned lists to decide which four members shall constitute the Disciplinary Board, two being drawn from each list.

4. Members of the Disciplinary Board shall not be of a lower grade than that of the staff member whose case the Board is to consider.

5. The Chairman shall inform each member of the composition of the Board.

6. Within five days of the formation of the Disciplinary Board, the staff member in question may make objection once to any of its members other than the Chairman.

7. Within the same period any member of the Disciplinary Board may ask to be excused from serving, provided he has legitimate grounds.

8. The Chairman of the Disciplinary Board shall, by drawing lots, fill any vacancies.

9. The Chairman and members of the Disciplinary Board shall be completely independent in the performance of their duties. The proceedings of the Board shall be secret.

Article 56: Disciplinary Proceedings

1. Disciplinary proceedings shall be instituted by the Secretary General after a hearing of the staff member concerned.

2. Disciplinary measures shall be ordered by the Secretary General after completion of the disciplinary proceedings provided for in Appendix X to these Regulations.

Article 57: Suspension

1. In a case of serious misconduct liable to entail a disciplinary measure as referred to in Article 54, paragraph 2.*d*, 2.*e* and 2.*f*, the Secretary General may, after hearing the Chairman of the Disciplinary Board, suspend the presumed author of the misconduct.

2. The decision that a staff member be suspended shall specify whether he is to continue to receive his remuneration during the period of suspension or what part thereof is to be withheld; the part withheld shall not be more than half the staff member's basic salary.

3. A final decision on the staff member's administrative situation shall be taken within four months of the date when the decision to suspend him came into force.

4. If, on the expiry of the time-limit prescribed in paragraph 3, no decision has been taken on his case or if none of the disciplinary measures mentioned in Article 54, paragraph 2.*d*. 2.*e* and 2.*f* has been ordered, the staff member shall be entitled to reimbursement of the amount of remuneration withheld.

Article 58: References in Personal Administrative Files

No reference to a disciplinary measure shall remain in the personal administrative file of the staff member concerned after two years in the case of a written warning or reprimand, and after six years in the case of other measures except removal from post.

Part VII: Disputes

Article 59: Complaints Procedure

1. A staff member who has a direct and existing interest in so doing may submit to the Secretary General a complaint against an administrative act adversely affecting him. The expression 'administrative act' shall mean any individual or general decision or measure taken by the Secretary General. If the Secretary General has not replied within sixty days to a request from a staff member inviting him to take a decision or measure which he is required to take, such silence shall be deemed an implicit decision rejecting the request. The sixty-day period shall run from the date of receipt of the

request by the Secretariat, which shall acknowledge receipt thereof.

2. The complaint must be made in writing and lodged via the Head of Establishment Division:

a.   within sixty days from the date of publication or notification of the act concerned; or

b.   if the act has not been published or notified, within sixty days from the date on which the person concerned learned thereof; or

c.   within sixty days from the date of the implicit decision rejecting the request as mentioned in paragraph 1.

The Head of Establishment Division shall acknowledge receipt of the complaint.

In exceptional cases and for duly justified reasons, the Secretary General may declare admissible a complaint lodged after the expiry of the periods laid down in this paragraph.

3. The Secretary General shall give a reasoned decision on the complaint as soon as possible and not later than sixty days from the date of its receipt and shall notify it to the complainant. The absence of a reply to the complaint within that period shall be deemed an implicit decision rejecting the complaint.

4. Either on the initiative of the Secretary General or if the staff member so requests in his complaint, the complaint shall be referred to the Advisory Committee on Disputes. In that event, the Secretary General shall have ninety days to give a decision on the complaint.

5. The Advisory Committee on Disputes shall comprise four staff members, two of whom shall be appointed by the Secretary General and two elected by the staff under the same conditions as those for the election of the Staff Committee. The committee shall be completely independent in the discharge of its duties. It shall formulate an opinion based on considerations of law and any other relevant matters after consulting the persons concerned where necessary. The Secretary General shall, by means of a rule, lay down the rules of procedure of the committee.

6. The complaints procedure set up by this article shall be open on the same conditions *mutatis mutandis*

a.   to former staff members;

b.   to persons claiming through staff members or former staff members, within two years from the date of the act complained of; in the event of individual notification, the normal time-limit of sixty days shall apply;

c.   to the Staff Committee, where the complaint relates to an act of which it is subject or to an act directly affecting its powers under the Staff Regulations;

d.   to candidates outside the Council who have been allowed to sit a competitive recruitment examination, provided the complaint relates to an irregularity in the examination procedure.

7. A complaint shall not have a suspensive effect. However, the complainant may apply to the Chairman of the Appeals Board. With copy to the Secretary General, for a stay of execution of the act complained of if its execution is likely to cause him grave prejudice difficult to redress. The Secretary General shall, save for duly justified reasons, stay the execution of the act until the Chairman of the Appeals Board has ruled on the application in accordance with the Board's Statute.

Article 60: Appeals Procedure

1. In the event of either explicit rejection, in whole or part, or implicit rejection of a complaint lodged under Article 59, the complainant may appeal to the Appeals Board set up by the Committee of Ministers.

2. The Appeals Board, after establishing the facts, shall decide as to the law. In disputes of a pecuniary nature, it shall have unlimited jurisdiction. In other disputes, it may annul the act complained of. It may also order the Council to pay to the appellant compensation for damage resulting from the act complained of.

3. An appeal shall be lodged in writing sixty days from the date of notification of the Secretary General's decision on the complaint or of the expiry of the time-limit referred to in Article 59, paragraph 3. Nevertheless, in exceptional cases and for duly justified reasons, the Appeals Board may declare admissible an appeal lodged after the expiry of these periods.

4. An appeal shall have no suspensive effect. However, if a stay of execution of the act complained of has been granted by the Chairman of the Appeals Board following an application under Article 59, paragraph 7, that stay of execution shall be maintained throughout the appeal proceedings unless the Board decides otherwise on a reasoned request from the Secretary General.

5. While an appeal is pending, the Secretary General shall avoid taking any further measure in respect of the appellant which, in the event of the appeal being upheld, would render unfeasible the redress sought.

6. Decisions of the Appeals Board shall be binding on the parties as soon as they are delivered. The Secretary General shall inform the Board of the Execution of its decisions within thirty days from the date on which they were delivered.

7. If the Secretary General considers that the execution of an annulment decision is likely to create serious internal difficulties for the Council, he shall inform the Board to that effect in a reasoned opinion. If the Board considers the reasons given by the Secretary General to be valid, it shall then fix the sum to be paid to the appellant by way of compensation.

Article 61: Calculation of Time-limits

The time-limits in Articles 59 and 60 shall run from midnight of the first day of each time-limit as defined in the provision concerned. Saturdays, Sundays and official holidays shall count when calculating a time-limit. However, where the last day of a time-limit is a Saturday, Sunday or an official holiday, the time-limit shall be extended to include the first working day thereafter.

Part VIII: Final Provisions

Article 62: Implementing Provisions

1. The Secretary General shall issue rules, instructions or office circulars laying down the provisions for implementation of these Regulations.

2. Implementing provisions entailing a financial commitment shall be subject to approval by the Committee of Ministers.

Article 63: Amendments

These Regulations may be added to or amended by the Committee of Ministers. Unless otherwise decided, alterations so made to the Regulations shall apply to all staff.

Article 64: Entry into Force

1. The provisions of these Regulations, including their appendices, shall enter into force on 1 January 1982 and rescind the previous Regulations.

2. Any regulations or implementing provisions which conflict with these Regulations shall be rescinded on the same date.

APPENDIX I: REGULATIONS OF STAFF PARTICIPATION

Article 1: Scope

These regulations, issued in accordance with Articles 6 to 9 of the Staff Regulations, concern the attributions and functioning of the General Meeting of Staff, the Staff Committee and the Joint Committee.

Part I: General Meeting of Staff

Article 2: Scope

1. The General Meeting of Staff shall be the organ in which all staff members may express their opinions on their conditions of employment and work. It shall meet at least once a year in ordinary session, and must be convened in extraordinary session if fifty staff members so request in writing, stating their reasons.

2. The General Meeting shall elect its own Chairman and adopt its own Rules of Procedure.

Part II: Staff Committee

Article 3: Membership, Elections, Rules of Procedure

1. The Staff Committee shall comprise members and substitutes, whose term of office shall be two years.

2. All members of the staff of the Council shall be entitled to vote provided that they have been in post for at least six months. All members of staff in post for at least one year shall be entitled to stand for election.

3. The Staff Committee shall be elected by secret ballot. Elections shall be valid only if a majority of the staff entitled to vote takes part.

4. Other conditions for election to the Staff Committee and its composition shall be laid down by the General Meeting of Staff.

5. The Staff Committee shall adopt its own Rules of Procedure.

Article 4: General Attributions

1. The Staff Committee shall represent the general interests of the staff and contribute to the smooth running of the Council by providing the staff with a channel for the expression of their opinions. It may also defend the interests of retired staff and other beneficiaries of the Pension Scheme.

2. The committee shall be responsible for organising elections of staff representatives to those bodies of the Council where provision is made for such representation, unless it is expressly provided that the said representatives shall be appointed directly by the committee.

3. The committee shall participate in the management and supervision of social welfare bodies set up by the Council in the interests of its staff. It may, with the consent of the Secretary General, set up such welfare services.

Article 5: Matters within the Competence of the Secretary General

1. The Staff Committee shall bring to the notice of the Secretary General any difficulty having general implications that concerns the interpretation and application of the Staff Regulations. It may be consulted on any difficulties of this kind.

2. The Staff Committee may propose to the Secretary General any draft implementing provisions relating to the Staff Regulations, as well as any measures of a general nature to be taken by him concerning the staff.

3. The Secretary General shall consult the Staff Committee on any draft provision for the implementation of the Staff Regulations. He may consult it on any other measure of a general kind concerning the staff.

Article 6: Regulations within the Competence of the Committee of Ministers

1. The Secretary General and the Staff Committee shall consult each other on any draft that either intends to submit to the Committee of Ministers on matters which come within the competence of the Committee of Ministers under Article 16 of the Statute of the Council of Europe and which relate to:

— alteration or amendment of the Staff Regulations,
— alteration, amendment or adoption of other regulations concerning the staff.

2. the Secretary General shall keep the Staff Committee informed of any proceedings before the Committee of Ministers in pursuance of Article 16 of the Statute of the Council of Europe which relate to the matters referred to in paragraph 1 above.

Article 7: Relations with the Committee of Ministers

1. The Staff Committee may communicate to the Committee of Ministers any proposal on the matters referred to in Article 6, paragraph 1.

2. The Committee of Ministers may consult the Staff Committee in the most appropriate manner in any proceedings relating to the matter referred to in Article 6, paragraph 1.

3. Any written communication or written consultation between the Committee of Ministers and the Staff Committee shall take place through the Secretary General. Oral consultations shall be held in his presence.

4. Documents drafted by the Staff Committee for the Committee of Ministers shall be transmitted by the Secretary General within one week of his receiving them.

Part III: Joint Committee

Article 8: Membership

1. The Joint Committee shall consist of:
— the Chairman, appointed each year by the Secretary General,
— members and substitutes, appointed each year simultaneously and in equal numbers by the Secretary General and by the Staff Committee.

2. A substitute shall sit on the Joint Committee only in the absence of a member.

Article 9: Attributions

The Joint Committee may be consulted by the Secretary General or by the Staff Committee on questions of a general nature which either of them sees fit to submit to it. It shall also give its opinion on measures for the termination of service within the meaning of the regulations on indemnity for loss of job (Appendix VI).

Article 10: Meetings

1. The Joint Committee shall meet at the request of the Secretary General or of the Staff Committee.

2. The proceedings of the Joint Committee shall be valid only if all members or, in their absence, substitutes are present.

3. The Chairman of the Joint Committee shall not vote except on questions of procedure.

4. the opinion of the committee shall be communicated in writing to the Secretary General and the Staff Committee.

5. Any member of the Joint Committee may require that his views shall be recorded in the said opinion.

Part IV: Time-limits

Article 11

The Secretary General or the Committee of Ministers, as the case may be, shall lay down the time-limits within which the Staff Committee or the Joint Committee must deliver opinions requested of them, which shall be not less than fifteen working days. The time-limit may, however, be shortened by mutual agreement. If no opinion has been delivered within the period laid down, the Secretary General or the Committee of Ministers, as the case may be, shall proceed.

APPENDIX II: REGULATIONS ON APPOINTMENTS

Article 1: Scope

These regulations, issued in accordance with Part II of the Staff Regulations, set out the conditions under which permanent posts are filled by transfer, recruitment or promotion.

Article 2: Definitions

1. Transfer is the appointment of a staff member to another post carrying the same grade.

2. Recruitment is the appointment to a vacant post of a candidate who is not a staff member.

3. Promotion is the appointment of a staff member to a post carrying a higher grade.

Article 3: Qualifications required for Appointment to the Various Categories of Post

1. Candidates for posts in category A, which comprises staff members engaged in administrative, planning and research duties, must have a university education with a suitable degree. Exceptionally, the degree requirement may be waived if the candidate has equivalent professional experience.

2. Candidates for posts as interpreters and translators in category L must have a general education of university standard and appropriate professional training or experience.

3. Candidates for category B posts involving executive and supervisory duties must have reached an educational standard equivalent to a full course of general secondary education and possess appropriate professional qualifications.

4. Candidates for category B posts involving technical, secretarial or clerical duties must have reached an educational standard equivalent to an intermediate level of general secondary education and possess appropriate professional qualifications.

5. Candidates for category C posts, which involve technical, manual or service duties, must have reached an educational standard equivalent to a general primary education and, if need be, possess appropriate professional qualifications.

Article 4: Physical Fitness

The candidate's physical fitness to carry out the duties attaching to the post applied for must be attested by a medical certificate issued following examination by a doctor chosen by the Secretary General.

Article 5: Transfers

1. Any staff member may inform the Secretary General that he wishes to be assigned to another post in the same grade. His request shall be considered when a vacancy arises or when an exchange is contemplated.

2. Before filling a vacant post, the Secretary General shall first consider whether this should be done by way of transfer. If so, he shall approach the staff member considered for transfer in order to allow him to express his views.

3. The Secretary General shall also approach staff members considered for an exchange.

4. In the cases referred to under Articles 25 and 26, the Secretary General shall also comply with the special procedures laid down.

Article 6: Choice of Appointment Procedure

1. In the case of a vacant post which is not being filled by transfer in accordance with Article 5 above and without prejudice to the provisions of Articles 25, 26, paragraph 1, and 27, the Secretary General shall decide, having regard to the provisions of Article 12 of the Staff Regulations, whether the post in question should be filled through recourse to the external recruitment procedure or thrown open to internal competition among existing staff and, in the case of external recruitment, whether it is in principle envisaged that at the end of the probationary period confirmation in post shall be for an indefinite duration or for a fixed term.

2. In the case of beginning-of-career posts in category A, the Secretary General may hold a competitive examination confined to the nationals of one or more of the member states which are underrepresented in the Secretariat. Further, in exceptional cases dictated by the nature of the post, the Secretary General may hold for a vacant post a competitive examination confined to the nationals of one or more member states, whatever the category and grade of the post concerned and regardless of whether the state or states in question are underrepresented.

3. The decision shall be taken on the basis of an opinion of the Bureau of the Appointments Board. This opinion shall be formulated after consultation of the Director or Head of Department responsible for the post to be filled and shall refer to his views.

Article 7: Advertising of Vacant Posts

1. Except in the cases provided for in Articles 5, 15, paragraph 3, 26, paragraph 1, and 27 and subject to the provisions of Article 25 of these regulations, all vacancies shall be advertised in accordance with the provisions of this article.

2. If the external recruitment procedure is followed, the vacancy shall be brought to the knowledge of:

a.   the Permanent Delegations, if the post is in category A, L or B;

b.   members of the Secretariat, by means of a notice posted on the premises, so that they can compete, subject to the provisions of Article 6, paragraph 2;

c.   the public, where necessary, by means of suitable advertisements.

3. If the promotion procedure is followed, the vacant or regraded post shall be suitably notified within the Secretariat. If the post is in category A, L or B, the Permanent Delegations shall receive a copy of the notice for information.

4. The notice shall describe the duties attaching to the vacant post, and state the conditions for eligibility, the qualifications required of candidates and the time-limit for submission of applications. The Secretary General shall determine the time-limit in each case, taking the nature of the vacant post into account ; the time-limit shall be not less than three weeks in the case of internal competition and not less than eight weeks in the case of external recruitment. In the cases of *force majeure* or in exceptional circumstances the Secretary General may extend the time-limit by up to two weeks.

Article 8: Applications

1. Applications shall be admissible only if they comply with the conditions set out in the vacancy notice.

2. If the external recruitment procedure is followed, applications must be made on an official form issued by the Secretariat. Any supporting documents required, including degrees, certificates, etc., must be attached to the form.

3. If the promotion procedure is followed, applications shall also be made on an official form.

4. The receipt of applications shall be acknowledged.

Article 9: Appointments Board

1. The Appointments Board is the Secretary General's advisory body in matters of appointment by recruitment or promotion. Its deliberations, reports, opinions and recommendations shall be confidential.

2. the Board shal be consulted in all cases except in the case of appointments to:

— A6 and A7 posts, which are covered by Article 25;
— posts which are covered by Article 26, paragraph 1;
— posts in the Private Office of the Secretary General, which are covered by Article 27.

3. Every opinion and recommendation submitted to the Secretary General by the relevant section of the Appointments Board shall set out the reasons on which it is based, be signed by all persons having participated in the deliberations and, should the occasion arise, be accompanied by their dissenting opinions.

4. The members of the Appointments Board shall be completely independent in the discharge of their duties: they shall not receive any instructions.

Article 10: Composition of the Board

1. The Appointments Board shall consist of:

a.   the Bureau,
b.   the Recruitment Panel I,

c.   the Recruitment Panel I I,

d.   the Promotions Panel.

2. Their membership and functions are set out in Articles 11 to 18 and Articles 20, 21 and 22 of these regulations.

3. The Secretary General shall lay down the rules of procedure of the different sections of the Board.

Article 11: Bureau of the Board

1. The Bureau of the Appointments Board shall consist of four members:

— the Director of Administration and Finance;

— a staff member of grade A6 and A7 who has completed at least five years' service in the Secretariat, appointed for one year by the Secretary General;

— the Head of Establishment Division;

— a member of the Private Office of the Secretary General nominated by the Secretary General.

2. The Bureau shall ensure observance of Articles 11 to 22 of the Staff Regulations and of these regulations.

3. The Bureau shall:

— verify notices of vacant posts and decide how widely such posts shall be advertised:

— convene the Recruitment and Promotions Panels:

— appoint members of Recruitment Panel I I, in accordance with the provisions of Article 13, paragraph 1;

— supply the Secretary General with the opinion provided for by the provisions of Article 6, paragraph 3.

4. The Bureau shall consult a staff member duly appointed by the Staff Committee before formulating its opinions or taking decisions.

Article 12: Recruitment Panel I

1. The Recruitment Panel I shall comprise:

— the four members of the Bureau;

— two other staff members chosen by the Secretary General with reference to the nature and level of the post or posts to be filled;

— two staff members appointed by the Staff Committee.

2. The Secretary General may, if he sees fit, in view of the nature of the vacant post, invite one or two persons from outside the Council to sit on the Panel in an advisory capacity.

3. The Chairman of the Panel shall be the Director of Administration and Finance.

4. Sessions of the Panel shall be valid only if at least five members are present.

5. The Recruitment Panel I shall be responsible for any competitive examination or selection based on qualifications that is conducted as part of the external recruitment procedure when the post to be filled is in category A or L or of grade B4, B5 or B6, even where the applicants include staff members already in post. The Panel shall:

— draw up a list of applicants invited to compete;
— decide whether tests or examinations are to be held, make arrangements for their organisation, set the subjects of the papers, and appoint the examiners;
— assess the results of such tests and examinations;
— interview the applicants; where written tests or examinations have been held, only those applicants who have obtained satisfactory results shall be interviewed.

   6. At the end of the procedure the Panel, after having listed the applicants in order of merit, shall submit a recommendation to the Secretary General.

Article 13: Recruitment Panel II

1. The Recruitment Panel II shall comprise:
— at least two staff members appointed by the Bureau of the Appointments Board;
— a staff member appointed by the Staff Committee.

   2. In cases of recruitment to vacant posts in grades B1 to B3 and category C, the Establishment Division, in collaboration with the Panel, shall:
— draw up the list of applicants invited to take part in the competitive examination or selection based on qualifications;
— decide, as appropriate, on the holding of tests or examinations, make arrangements for their organisation, set the subjects of the papers and appoint the examiners.

   3. The Panel shall:
— assess the results of such tests and examinations;
— interview the applicants; where written texts or examinations have been held, only those applicants who have obtained satisfactory results shall be interviewed.

   4. At the end of the procedure the Panel, after having listed the candidates in order of merit, shall submit a recommendation to the Secretary General.

Article 14: Promotions Panel

1. The Promotions Panel shall comprise:
— the four members of the Bureau;
— a second staff member of grade A6 or A7, who has completed at least five years' service in those grades, appointed for two years by the Secretary General;
— the Director or Head of Department responsible for the post to be filled;
— two staff members appointed by the Staff Committee.

   2. The Chairman of the Panel shall be the Director of Administration and Finance. However, where a category A post is to be filled, the Deputy Secretary General may also sit on the Panel and take the Chair.

   3. Sessions of the Panel shall be valid only if a least five members are present.

   4. The Promotions Panel shall be responisble for any competitive examination or selection based on qualifications that is conducted as part of the promotions procedure. The Panel shall:
— scrutinise all applications;

— decide whether tests or examinations are to be held, make arrangements for their organisation, set the subjects of the papers and appoint the examiners;

— assess the results of such tests and examinations;

— if necessary, interview the applicants; where written tests or examinations have been held, only those applicants who have obtained satisfactory results shall be interviewed.

5. At the end of the procedure, the Panel shall submit a recommendation to the Secretary General on the basis of all the relevant information at its disposal. Where a number of applicants satisfy the conditions, they shall be listed in order of merit.

A record of the Panel's proceedings, including in particular its recommendation, shall be submitted to the Secretary General. The record shall be signed by all persons who have participated in the deliberations.

6. The Panel shall supply the Secretary General with an opinion on cases of promotion provided for in Article 24.

Article 15: Competitive Examination

1. Competitive examinations shall include written papers and an interview conducted by the appropriate panel. The written papers shall be eliminatory, manuscripts must be anonymous, and must be marked by two examiners.

2. A competitive examination shall be held when posts in the starting grades of categories A, L and B are to be filled by recruitment. When other posts are to be filled by recruitment, the appropriate Recruitment Panel shall consider whether this procedure should be adopted.

3. When the number of applicants having passed a competitive examination conducted as part of the external recruitment procedure exceeds the number of vacant posts thrown open to competition, a reserve list shall be drawn up and notified to the applicants concerned. In the event of a vacancy which is not filled by way of transfer or promotion, the Secretary General shall appoint a suitable candidate named in the reserve list. Reserve lists shall be valid for two years; in exceptional cases, the Secretary General may extend the validity of a reserve list up to one year.

4. When appointments are being made by promotion, the Promotions Panel shall decide whether written examinations should be held; in such cases the examinations shall be designed mainly to test professional ability.

Article 16: Selection Based on Qualifications

1. When selection is based on qualifications, the applicant's qualifications shall be examined and if necessary he shall be interviewed by the appropriate panel.

2. The selection procedure based on qualifications plus an interview shall be followed when recruiting:

— to posts in category L other than those referred to in Article 15, paragraph 2;

— to posts filled by securing the services of civil servants or specialists as provided in Article 12, paragraph 3, of the Staff Regulations;

— to posts in category C.

In other instances of recruitment, the appropriate Recruitment Panel may decide to follow this procedure, in accordance with the discretion conferred on it by Article 15, paragraph 2.

3. When appointments are being made by promotion, the Promotions Panel shall normally examine the applicants' qualifications. However, if it deems necessary, in order to form a more complete opinion of the applicants, it may decide to conduct interviews or hold a competitive examination in accordance with Article 15, paragraph 4.

Article 17: Probation

1. Newly recruited staff shall be appointed provisionally on the basis of a contract whose duration shall correspond to the probationary period laid down in Article 18.

2. During the first year, either side may terminate this contract at one month's notice; after the first year, three months' notice must be given.

3. Termination of the contract on the initiative of the Secretary General shall be decided by him on the advice of Recruitment Panel I or, in the case of B1 to B3 or category C staff, of Recruitment Panel II.

Article 18: Probationary Period

1. The probationary period is a trial and training period and shall last:

a. two years for staff recruited into category A or L, subject to the provisions of Article 17, paragraph 3, of the Staff Regulations concerning staff recruited to grade A6 or A7;

b. one year for staff recruited into category B or C.

The probationary period may be reduced in the case of a contract for a fixed term of less than two years, on the basis of rules laid down by the Secretary General. However, the probationary period may not be shorter than six months.

The probationary period may be extended by one year for staff members referred to in sub-paragraph a and by six months for those referred to in sub-paragraph b, in the cases provided for in Article 20, paragraph 3, and Article 21, paragraph 3.

2. The probationary period shall be reduced in relation to the period of service completed as a temporary staff member in the same or a comparable post, on the basis of rules laid down by the Secretary General.

3. Where the probationary period has been interrupted for reasons outside the staff member's control, the Secretary General may, on the advice of Recruitment Panel I or, in the case of B1 to B3 or category C staff, of Recruitment Panel II, extend it by the length of the interruption.

4. During the probationary period, the staff member shall be assigned to a department or to different departments in turn. He shall be entrusted with duties corresponding to his grade to enable him to acquire the necessary training under the supervision of his superiors. At the šame time, he shall receive instruction from the administrative department responsible for in-service training in the aims, structure and functioning of the Council.

Article 19: Reports on Probationers

1. During the probationary period, the staff member's immediate superiors must report on his performance at the end of the sixth, twelfth and twentieth months, where probation is for two years and at the end of the fifth and eighth months, where it is for one year.

2. The report shall be made known to the staff member who shall receive a copy, during an interview with his Director, Head of Department or, if so authorised, Head of Divison. The staff member may make observations in writing within five working days. The report, to which the staff member's comments (if any) shall be attached, shall be sent to the Secretary General.

Article 20: Confirmation in Post for an Indefinite Duration

1. At least threee months before the probationary period expires, Recruitment Panel I or, in the case of B1 to B3 or category C staff, Recruitment Panel I I shall examine the staff member's file and, in particular, the reports made on him in accordance with Article 19.

2. If the staff member's work and state of health are satisfactory, the Recruitment Panel shall recommend that the Secretary General confirm him in his post with a contract of indefinite duration.

3. If the staff member's work is the subject of conflicting opinions, the Recruitment Panel may, in exceptional cases, recommend that the Scretary General extend the probationary period in accordance with the provisions of Article 18, paragraph 1.

4. If the staff member's work or state of health is unsatisfactory, the Recruitment Panel shall recommend that the Secretary General terminate his employment, subject to the required notice being given. The staff member concerned shall be notified of this recommendation and shall have the right to submit observations to the Secretary General within eight working days.

Article 21: Confirmation in Post for a Fixed Term

1. At least three months before the probationary period expires, Recruitment Panel I or, in the case of B1 to B3 or category C staff, Recruitment Panel I I, shall examine the staff member's file and, in particular, the reports made on him in accordance with Article 19.

2. If the staff member's work and state of health are satisfactory, the Recruitment Panel shall recommend that the Secretary General confirm him in his post with a fixed-term contract.

3. If the staff member's work is the subject of conflicting opinions, the Recruitment Panel may, in exceptional cases, recommend that the Secretary General extend the probationary period in accordance with the provisions of Article 18, paragraph 1.

4. If the staff member's work or state of health is unsatisfactory, the Recruitment Panel shall recommend that the Secretary General terminate his employment, subject to the required notice being given. The staff member concerned shall be notified of

this recommendation and shall have the right to submit observations to the Secretary General within eight working days.

5. In the case of secondment (Article 20 of the Staff Regulations) for a period of less than two years, Articles 17, 18 and 21, paragraphs 1, 2, 3 and 4 shall not apply. However, during the first six months of the contract period, the Secretary General may terminate the contract upon three months' notice, after hearing the person concerned, the latter's superior and the Recruitment Panel.

Article 22: Promotions

1. Under the internal promotions procedure, a staff member may be promoted only to the grade immediately above his present one, save for exceptional cases which are duly justified.

2. In cases of equal merit, preference shall be given to the applicant who has served longer in the grade, and, as a subsidiary criterion, with the Council.

3. The Promotions Panel may recommend that the staff member be required to undergo a probationary period in the higher post for which he has applied before a decision is taken regarding his promotion. This period shall not exceed one year, at the end of which the Secretary General shall take a firm decision on the basis of a report by the staff member's superiors; Article 19, paragraph 2, shall apply by analogy. If the promotion is accorded, it shall have retroactive effect.

4. In the event of a post being upgraded, the Promotions Panel shall first consider whether the incumbent meets the requirements for promotion.

Article 23: Access for Serving Staff to Category A Posts by Competitive Examination

1. Subject to the provisions of Article 6, paragraph 2, any serving staff member may apply for a post in category A thrown open to competition under the external recruitment procedure. If successful, he shall be subject to the provisions of Article 17, 18, 19 and, as appropriate, of Article 20, paragraphs 1, 2 and 3 or Article 21, paragraphs 1, 2 and 3. If his work has not proved satisfactory during the probationary period, he shall revert to his previous administrative status.

2. Staff in grades B4, B5 or B6 may apply for an A2/A3 post if, by decision of the Secretary General under Article 6, the post is, as an exceptional measure, to be filled by internal competitive examination. In addition to the requirements of Article 3 of these regulations, such staff members must have completed at least ten years' service, of which at least four in those grades.

Article 24: Special Conditions for Appointment to Grades A1, A2 and A3

1. Only applicants who are at least 25 years old and have had at least two years' professional experience at a level which is considered adequate may be appointed to A2 posts by recruitment. If these conditions are not fulfilled, they shall be appointed to grade A1.

2. An applicant may only be appointed to an A3 post by recruitment if he is at least 33 years old and has had at least eight years' professional experience in the exercise of functions which are considered equivalent to those attaching to grade A2.

3. Appointment by promotion may be made:

— to grade A2, only if the staff member in grade A1 is at least 25 years old and has had two years' professional experience, including his service with the Council;
— to grade A3, only if the staff member in grade A2 has completed at least four years' service in that grade. This period may be reduced, on the basis of rules laid down by the Secretary General, if the staff member has had at least four years' professional experience prior to his recruitment in the exercise of duties with comparable requirements. In no case, however, may the prescribed period be reduced by more than two years.

Article 25: Procedure for Appointment to Grades A6 and A7

1. Any vacancy at grade A6 or A7 shall be suitably notified to Permanent Delegations and published within the Secretariat unless, where particular circumstances so require, the Committee of Ministers shall decide otherwise on a proposal by the Secretary General.

2. The Secretary General shall make an appointment after an informal exchange of views with the Committee of Ministers, during which he shall make known his intentions and the reasons for his choice.

3. In the case of a post in the Office of the Clerk of the Consultative Assembly, the Secretary General shall also inform the Bureau of the Assembly of his intentions at an informal exchange of views.

4. The procedures provided for in paragraphs 2 and 3 above shall also apply to exchanges of staff members of the same grade.

5. Recruitment to an A6 or A7 post shall be governed by an initial contract of a fixed term of two years. If, on expiry, it is decided to maintain the staff member's appointment, this initial contract may be extended for one year, or renewed, or replaced by a contract for an indefinite duration.

6. Appointment of the Financial Controller[1] and the Secretary to the Committee of Ministers shall not become effective until approved by the latter committee. The Secretary General may terminate their appointments only after consulting that Committee.

Article 26: Special Appointments Procedures

1. The Registrar of the European court of Human Rights shall be elected by the Plenary Court after the President has obtained the opinion of the Secretary General, and the Deputy Registrar shall be elected after the opinions of the Secretary General and of the Registrar have been obtained;[2] the Secretary General shall make the appointment accordingly.

2. Without prejudice to the other provisions of these regulations, appointment of the staff members listed below shall be subject to observance of the following existing procedures:

---

[1] Article 35 of the Financial Regulations.
[2] Articles 11 and 12 of the Rules of the European Court of Human Rights.

a. staff members of the Registry of the European Court of Human Rights other than the Registrar and Deputy Registrar are appointed by the Secretary General with the agreement of the President or Registrar;[3]

b. the Governing Board of the European Youth Foundation chooses the Executive Director of the Foundation;[4]

c. the Head and technical staff of the Secretariat of the European Pharmacopoeia Commission are appointed by the Secretary General on the advice of the Commission.[5]

Article 27: Appointment to Posts in the Private Office of the Secretary General

1. Articles 6 to 21 and Article 25 of these regulations shall not apply to appointments to posts in the Private Office of the Secretary General. Before appointing the Head of the Private Office, the Secretary General shall inform the Committee of Ministers of his intentions.

2. A staff member recruited from outside to a post in the Private Office shall be given a contract of fixed duration for not more than two years, which shall be renewable but whose final date of expiry shall not be later than that of the Secretary General's term of office.

3. A staff member transferred to a post in the Private Office carrying a higher grade than his present one, or an official assigned to a post of a higher grade during his work in the Private Office, shall be paid a personal allowance equivalent to the difference between the salary attaching to the post he occupies in the Private Office and the salary attaching to his grade. He may not be promoted until two years after the date of his transfer.

Article 28: Supernumerary Transfer

1. Where a staff member is to be transferred and there is no vacant post in his own grade, the Secretary General may, with the agreement of the Committee of Ministers, transfer the staff member as an exception and for a limited time to a post in a lower grade without prejudice to his rights and subject to the provisions of Article 5, paragraph 2, of these regulations.

2. The supernumerary staff member shall be transferred to a post in a grade corresponding to his own and in keeping with his qualifications as soon as a vacancy occurs.

Article 29: Exercise of Responsibilities Attaching to a Higher Post

1. A staff member may be called upon by the Secretary General, on an exceptional basis and in the interest of the service, to assume the responsibilities attaching to a post carrying a grade immediately higher than his own which is vacant or whose holder is temporarily unable to carry out his duties.

2. Such a decision shall be reviewed at the end of each financial year.

---

[3] Rule 13 of the Rules Court of the European Court of Human Rights.

[4] Article 5, paragraph 3.a of the Statute of the European Youth Foundation.

[5] Article 9 of the Convention on the Elaboration of a European Pharmacopoeia.

APPENDIX III: REGULATIONS ON THE ASSESSMENT OF STAFF
AFTER CONFIRMATION IN POST

Article 1

These regulations, issued in accordance with Article 22 of the Staff Regulations, lay down the conditions under which staff members are assessed after confirmation in post.

Article 2

1. After confirmation in post, Council of Europe staff members with the exception of those in grades A6 or A7 and those who have reached the age of sixty shall be subject to an assessment report at least every two years.

2. No assessment report may be made unless the staff member concerned has worked for at least six months under the same immediate superior.

Article 3

1. The assessment report shall be drawn up, following an interview with the staff member concerned, by the immediate superior and countersigned by the Director or Head of Department, accompanied, as the case may be, by his comments. The duty of countersignature may be delegated, subject to authorisation by the Secretary General.

2. A standard form of assessment report shall be used for each category of staff.

Article 4

1. An interim assessment report may be made either at the request of the Secretary General or in the circumstances stated in paragraphs 2 and 3 below but not until six months have elasped from the date of the previous report.

2. An interim report may be made at the staff member's request in the following cases:

a.   on his transfer to another department;

b.   if his immediate superior is transferred to another department or leaves the Council.

3. In the circumstances specified in paragraph 2.a and b, the immediate superior may make an interim report if he considers that important additions should be made to the assessment of the relevant member of his staff in the latter's interests or those of the Council.

Article 5

The staff member shall be given a copy of the final assessment report at an interview with the assessors, and he may submit comments in writing within five working days. The report, to which any comments by the staff member shall be appended, shall be sent to the Head of Establishment Division. It shall form part of the staff member's personal administrative file.

Article 6

1. Assessors shall not have access to previous reports nor shall they be allowed to keep copies of reports they make themselves.

2. A Director or Head of Department shall, however, be permitted during a meeting of the Promotions Panel to read assessment reports on candidates for a post in his Directorate or Department.

Article 7

Staff members required to act as assessors shall be briefed on the purpose of assessment reports and how to make assessments.

APPENDIX IV: REGULATIONS GOVERNING STAFF SALARIES AND ALLOWANCES

Article 1: Scope

These regulations, issued in accordance with Article 41 of the Staff Regulations, specify the salaries and allowances of staff members and the procedures for their granting and payment.

Article 2: Basic Salary

Staff members' basic salaries shall be determined in accordance with the scales contained in the tables appended.

Article 3: Steps

1. Each staff member shall advance up the scale for his grade by the steps shown.

2. Such advancement shall be continuous, from one step to the next.

3. For category A staff, advancement to steps 2 to 5 (grades A7 and A6) and 2 to 7 (grades A5, A4, A3 and A2) shall take place after twelve months of service in the step immediately below, and advancement to steps 6 (grade A7), 6 to 8 (grade A6) and 8 to 11 (grades A5, A4, A3 and A2) after twenty-four months of service in the step immediately below. Grade A1 staff shall be promoted from step 1 to step 2 after twelve months' service in the lower step.

4. For category L staff, advancement to the next step shall take place after eighteen months of service in the step immediately below.

5. For staff in categories B and C, advancement to steps 2 to 8 shall take place after twelve months of service in the step immediately below, and to steps 9 to 11 after twenty-four months' service.

Article 4: Household Allowance

1. The household allowance shall be fixed at 6% of the basic annual salary. The

amount of this allowance shall not, however, be less than 6% of the basic salary for grade B3, step 1.

2. The following shall be entitled to the household allowance:

i. married staff;

ii. widowed, divorced, legally separated or unmarried staff who have one or more dependent children as defined in Article 5 or, if applicable, Article 12;

iii any staff member who does not satisfy the conditions under i and ii above but who has one or more dependants as defined in Article 5, paragraph 2.

3. Notwithstanding the foregoing provisions, a married staff member having no dependent children or other dependants as defined in Article 5 or Article 12 of these regulations shall not be entitled to the allowance provided for in paragraph 1 if his/her spouse's income from a gainful occupation is equal to or higher than the basic salary for grade B3, step 1, plus the amount of the allowance.

4. If the spouse's income is between the ceiling referred to in paragraph 3 and the basic salary for grade B3, step1, a reduced allowance equal to the difference between that ceiling and the amount of the said income shall be payable.

5. Where, in accordance with the above provisions, a husband and wife employed by the Council or by the Council and another co-ordinated organisation, are both entitled to the household allowance, the allowance shall be paid only to the person whose basic salary is the higher.

6. The household allowance shall be paid after deduction of any similar allowances to which the official or his/her spouse may be entitled from another source.

Article 5: Allowance in respect of Dependent Children or Other Dependants

1. i. A monthly allowance shall be paid in respect of each dependent child under 18 years of age, in accordance with the appended scale.

   ii. By dependent child is meant any legitimate, natural, adopted or otherwise dependent child who depends on the staff member's child shall be taken as meaning:

   a. a child for whom adoption procedure has been initiated;

   b. an orphan dependent on the staff member.

   iii. The allowance shall continue to be payable until the dependent child reaches the age of 26 if he (or she) is receiving, on a full-time basis, school or university education or vocational training which does not carry a wage or salary properly so called.

   iv. The allowance shall continue to be payable without any age-limit if the dependent child cannot support himself (herself) owing to permanent disablement certified by a doctor approved by the Secretary General.

   v. If a staff member or the spouse of a staff member receives under his/her country's laws or regulations an allowance whose purpose is the same as that of the allowance provided for in this article, the amount of that allowance shall be deducted from the allowance payable by the Council.

   vi. In the case of two staff members employed by the Council or by the Council and another co-ordinated organisation, the allowance in respect of dependent children shall be paid to the official who receives the household allowance.

2. An allowance equal in amount to the allowance payable in respect of a dependent child shall, by decision of the Secretary General for cause shown, be payable to a staff member in respect of any ascendant of either himself or his spouse, where such ascendant is dependent on him for main and continuing support and in respect of any relative by blood or marriage whom he is under a legal obligation to provide with main and continuing support.

Article 6: Expatriation or Residence Allowance

1. i.　The expatriation allowance shall be payable to staff in categories A, L and B, who at the time of their appointment were not nationals of the host state and had not been continuously resident on that state's territory for at least three years, no account being taken of previous service in their own country's administration or with other international organisations.

　ii.　This allowance shall also be paid to staff in the same categories who, although nationals of the host state, had been continuously resident for at least ten years in another state at the time of their appointment, no account being taken of previous service in their own country's administration or with other international organisations.

　iii.　In the event of a staff member who is entitled to the expatriation allowance being transferred to the country of which he is a national, he shall cease to be entitled to the expatriation allowance.

　iv.　When any point on the frontier of the country of which the staff member is a national is within a radius of 50 km from the duty station, such a staff member shall not entitled to the expatriation allowance unless he supplies proof that he has established his actual and habitual residence in the country of service or, exceptionally and subject to agreement by the Secretary General, in another country of which he is not a national, taking account of his family circumstances.

2. The expatriation allowance shall comprise:

i.　for all staff in the above three categories a sum equal to 20% of their basic salaries if they receive the household allowance and to 16% if they do not;

ii.　for staff in category B serving in France, and additional fixed amount depending on their grades and family situation, in accordance with the appended scale;

iii.　a fixed monthly allowance, in accordance with the appended scale, in respect of each dependent child as defined in Article 5 above.

The combined total of the sums specified under sub-paragraphs i and ii above shall in no case be less than the total payable under this head to a staff member in grade B3, step 1.

3. Where a husband and wife, who are both non-resident, are employed in the same country by the Council and another co-ordinated organisation, they shall each be entitled to an expatriation allowance, but at the rate of 16% whether or not they are entitled to the household allowance.

4. Staff in the above categories who cannot claim the expatriation allowance under the provisions of paragraph 1 and who at the time of their appointment were resident at a distance of more than 300 km from their duty station shall be paid an allowance amounting:

i. for staff receiving the household allowance, to 35% of the expatriation allowance payable in the same family circumstances;
ii. for other staff, to 15% of that allowance.

Article 7: Education Allowance

1. Staff members entitled to the expatriation allowance—with the exception of those who are nationals of the country in which they are serving—may request payment of the education allowance in respect of each dependent child, within the meaning of these regulations, regularly attending an educational establishment on à full-time basis.

2. By way exception, resident staff members may request payment of the education allowance provided that the two following conditions are met:

a. the official's duty station is not less than 80 km distant from any school or university corresponding to the child's educational cycle;
b. the official's duty station is not less than 80 km distant from the place of domicile at the time of recruitment.

3. Entitlement to the allowance shall commence on the first day of the month during which the child begins to attend a primary school. It shall terminate when the child ceases full-timed studies, and not later than the end of the month in which the dependent child allowance ceases to be paid.

4. Except where otherwise state, the education allowance shall be granted on production of vouchers certifying that expenditure of the kind mentioned in paragraph 5 has in fact been incurred by and paid for by the staff member.

5. Within the prescribed limits, the following items of expenditure shall be taken into account when calculating the education allowance:

a. school or university registration fees;
b. general fees for schooling and education charged by the educational establishment;
    expenses on special courses and activities that are not normally part of the child's basic course of studies shall not be taken into account; in no circumstances shall the cost of related equipment be reimbursed;
c. examination fees;
d. tuition fees for private lessons on condition that:
    — tuition is given in subjects which are not contained in the child's syllabus but are part of the compulsory national education programme of the country of which the staff member is a national; or
    — tuition is required to enable the child to adjust to the educational curriculum of the institution attended, or to enable the child to become familiar with the language spoken in the area in which the child lives if the education is given in another language;

in all these cases, tuition fees may be taken into account for an adjustment period of not more than two years;

e. daily expenses on travel between the educational institution and home by public transport or school bus. Reduced fares must be taken into consideration. Where a private car is used or when no public transport or school bus is available, an amount equal to 10% of the dependent child allowance shall be taken into account;

f. expenditure on half-board, or on board and lodging in cases where the child does not live at the staff member's home; if vouchers for board and lodging are available, the amount to the taken into account shall not exceed two times the dependent child allowance applying in the country where the studies are carried out. If no vouchers are available, the amount to be taken into account shall be limited to one and a half times the dependent child allowance mentioned above;

g. purchase of school books as required by the curriculum, and compulsory school uniforms.

6. The amount of the allowance shall be 70% of the total expenditure mention under paragraph 5, and in no case more than two and a half times the dependent child allowance applying in the country where the studies are pursued and three times the dependent child allowance applying in the country where the studies are pursued if the child is educated in the country of which the staff member is a national.

7. Staff members whose children carry out their studies at a place more than 300 km away from the duty station shall also be entitled—on condition that the amount does not exceed the cost of a round-trip between the duty station and the place approved for home leave—to the reimbursement of the cost of one round-trip per year between the place of study and the duty station. Nevertheless, staff members who have received such repayment for one or several children may not during the same year request repayment for the round-trip on home leave for the same child or children.

8. The supplement for dependent children, included in the expatriation allowance, and the education allowance shall not be paid concurrently.

9. The actual amount of the education allowance shall be determined after deduction, where appropriate, from the total amount of the expenditure by the staff member for educational purposes as mentioned in paragraph 5 above, of any allowance received from other sources for the child's education (scholarships or study grants). Deducttion shall be made separately for each child.

10. At the beginning of the school year a staff member requesting an education allowance shall inform the administration as fully as possible on the expenditure which will be incurred for the education of each child. On the basis of that information the administration shall provisionally calculate the education allowance as described in paragraphs 6 to 9 above on an annual basis and make it payable at one-twelfth of the total amount from the beginning of the school year.

11. At the end of the school year the staff member shall provide evidence of the total expenditure during the school year in order to facilitate the final calculating of the allowance. Positive or negative discrepancies between the final amount and the total sum of the monthly payments shall be settled as soon as possible.

12. The education allowance as finally settled in accordance with paragraph 11

above may be used as the basis for determining the amount of the allowance to be paid in the next school year provided that the entitlement remains unchanged.

13. The staff member shall inform the administration of any changes of cirumstances which affect the entitlement to and the amount of the education allowance.

Article 8: Settling-in Allowance

1. A settling-in allowance shall be payable to staff who either are in receipt of the expatriation allowance or were, at the time of their appointment to the Council, ordinarily resident more than 100 km from their duty station. This allowance shall also be payable to a staff member who has to change his permanent residence as a result of being transferred from one place of duty to another more than 100 km away.

2. The amount of this allowance shall be proportion of the basic annual salary, as follows:

— for staff receiving the household allowance with two or more dependent children, one-sixth
— for married staff without children or staff receiving the household allowance with only one dependent child one-eighth
— for other staff, one-twelfth

3. The allowance shall be payable when the staff member takes up his/her duties, If the staff member is married, however, it shall not be payable in full until he/she has taken up residence with his/her family at his/her place of duty. If he/she is not joined by his/her family, the amount payable shall be that payable to other staff.

4. A staff member whose contract is terminated during his period of probation or who resigns before completing two years' service shall be require to repay to the Council a sum proportionate to the length of time which he would have had to serve in order to complete two years' service.

Article 9: Language Allowance

1. A language allowance of a sum equal to the value of the increment per step for grade B2 may be granted to staff in grade B1 and B2 having adequate knowledge of the two official languages.

2. A language allowance of a sum equal to the value of the increment per step for grade C3 may be granted to staff in grades C1 to C4 who have an adequate knowledge of the two official languages, and who fulfil the following requirements:

i.   having frequent contacts with persons using exclusively either English or French, and
ii. being required to use both these languages under the terms of their job description.

3. Adequate knowledge of the two official languages shall be established by means of an appropriate test of linguistic proficiency.

Article 10: Payment of Overtime Work

Overtime work by staff in grades, B3, B2 and B1 and in category C shall, where the exigencies of the service preclude their being granted compensatory leave, be payable on the conditions set out at Appendix VIII to the staff Regulations.

Article 11: Rent Allowance

1. Staff members shall be entitled, on production of vouchers, to a rent allowance provided that they satisfy the following conditions:

a. that they do not own in the place of their duty station a dwelling suitable to their grade or family circumstances;

b. that they are the tenants or sub-tenants of furnished or unfurnished premises suitable to their grade or family circumstances;

c. that the rent paid, excluding all charges, exceeds the proportion of their emolument specified in paragraph 3 below.

2. A staff member who is not unmarried shall not be entitled to the allowance unless he/she receives the household allowance.

3. The amount of allowance shall be proportion of the difference between the actual rent paid, excluding all charges, and the following nominal sums:

— 15% of the emolument of category C staff members and staff members of category B up to and including grade B4;

— 20% of the emolument of grade B5 and B6 staff members;

— 22% of the emolument of grade A1, L1 and L2 staff members.

4. This proportion shall be 50% for unmarried staff or married staff with no children, 55% for staff members with one dependant and 60% for those with two or more dependants, provided that in no case shall the amount of the allowance exceed:

— 10% of the emolument of the staff members concerned in the case of staff members in category C and in grades B1 to B4 inclusive;

— 5% of the emoluments of the staff members concerned in the case of staff members in grade B5 and B6, A1 and A2, L1 and L2.

5. For the purposes of this article, emoluments shall mean basic salary, expatriation or residence allowance, household allowance or language allowance, less social security, supplementary insurance and pension scheme contributions.

Article 12: Allowance for Handicapped Child

1. An allowance for a handicapped child shall be paid to any staff member with a dependent child who is handicapped within the meaning of this article, whatever the age of the child.

2. A child shall be deemed to be handicapped if it is established by medical evidence that he or she is suffering from a serious and permanent disability necessitating either special care or supervision not provided free of charge, or special education or training.

3. The decision to pay the allowance shall be made the Secretary General after consulting a board which he shall consitute for the purpose and which shall include not less than one medical practitioner. The Secretary General's decision shall specify the period for which the allowance shall be paid, subject to review.

4. The criterion for entitlement to the benefits specified in these regulations shall be the serious and continuing impairment of physical or mental activities.

5. Children may be deemed to be handicapped where they suffer from:

— serious or chronic affection of the central or autonomic nervous system, however caused, such as disease of the brain, disease or disorders of the spinal cord or bone marrow or autonomic paralysis;
— serious affection of the locomotor system;
— serious affection of one or more sensory systems;
— chronic and disabling mental illness.

6. The above list shall not be deemed to be exhaustive and is given by way of indication only; it shall not be taken as an absolute basis for assessing the degree of disability or incapacity.

7. The amount of the allowance shall be equal to the amount of the allowance for a dependent child and shall be additional thereto.

8. Where the staff member concerned is entitled to a similar allowance under a national or international scheme, the amount of allowance payable by the Council shall be the amount by which the rate payable under paragraph 7 exceeds the amount payable under the national or international scheme.

Article 13: Extra Duties Allowance

1. An extra duties allowance shall be paid to a staff member who is called up by the Secretary General, in application of Article 29 of the regulations on appointments, to assume the responsibilities attaching to a post carrying a grade immediately higher than his own.

2. The amount of this allowance shall correspond to one twelve-month step in the basic salary scale for the grade of the staff member carrying out the extra duties.

3. The allowance shall be paid from the third consecutive month of service in the higher post, without retroactive effect in respect of the first two months.

TABLE VI.1. *Monthly Basic Salary Scale for Grades A, L, B and C Staff Serving in France (French francs)*[a]

Category and grade	Steps 1	2	3	4	5	6	7	8	9	10	11	12	Increment per step of: 12 mth	18 mth	24 mth
A7	24 120	24 928	25 736	26 544	27 756	28 968							808		212
A6	22 033	22 641	23 249	23 857	24 769	25 681	26 593	27 505					608		912
A5	19 292	19 831	20 370	20 909	21 448	21 987	22 796	23 605	24 414	25 223	26 032		539		809
A4	16 656	17 089	17 522	17 955	18 388	18 821	19 471	20 121	20 771	21 421	22 071		433		650
A3	14 486	14 895	15 304	15 713	16 122	16 531	17 145	17 759	18 373	18 987	19 601		409		614
A2	11 741	12 057	12 373	12 689	13 005	13 321	13 795	14 269	14 743	15 217	15 691		316		474
A1	9 190	9 467											277		0
L5	17 609	18 313	19 017	19 721	20 425	21 129	21 833	22 537	23 241	23 945				704	
L4	15 486	16 105	16 724	17 343	17 962	18 581	19 200	19 819	20 438	21 057	21 676	22 295		619	
L3	14 846	15 440	16 034	16 628	17 222	17 816	18 410	19 004	19 598	20 192				594	
L2	11 934	12 411	12 888	13 365	13 842	14 319	14 796	15 273	15 750	16 227				477	
L1	9 719	10 108												389	

Category and grade	Steps 1	2	3	4	5	6	7	8	9	10	11	Increment per step of: 12 or 24 months
B6	10 990	11 353	11 716	12 079	12 442	12 805	13 168	13 531	13 894	14 257	14 620	363
B5	9 590	9 906	10 222	10 538	10 854	11 170	11 486	11 802	12 118	12 434	12 750	316
B4	8 300	8 574	8 848	9 122	9 396	9 670	9 944	10 218	10 492	10 766	11 040	274
B3	7 145	7 381	7 617	7 853	8 089	8 325	8 561	8 797	9 033	9 269	9 505	236
B2	6 105	6 307	6 509	6 711	6 913	7 115	7 317	7 519	7 721	7 923	8 125	202
B1	5 205	5 377	5 549	5 721	5 893	6 065	6 237	6 409	6 581	6 753	6 925	172
C6	8 050	8 292	8 534	8 776	9 018	9 260	9 502	9 744	9 986	10 228	10 470	242
C5	7 205	7 421	7 637	7 853	8 069	8 285	8 501	8 717	8 933	9 149	9 365	216
C4	6 480	6 674	6 868	7 062	7 256	7 450	7 644	7 838	8 032	8 226	8 420	194
C3	5 850	6 026	6 202	6 378	6 554	6 730	6 906	7 082	7 258	7 434	7 610	176
C2	5 310	5 469	5 628	5 787	5 946	6 105	6 264	6 423	6 582	6 741	6 900	159
C1	4 850	4 996	5 142	5 288	5 434	5 580	5 726	5 872	6 018	6 164	6 310	146

[a] Scale applicable as from 1 July 1981.

TABLE VI.2. *Monthly Basic Salary Scale for Grades A, L, B and C Staff Serving in Belgium (Belgium francs)*[a]

Category and grade	Steps												Increment per step of:			Increment per step of:
	1	2	3	4	5	6	7	8	9	10	11	12	12 mth	18 mth	24 mth	12 or 24 months
A7	154 750	159 932	165 114	170 296	178 069	185 842							5 182		7 773	
A6	141 350	145 260	149 170	153 080	158 945	164 810	170 675	176 540					3 910		5 865	
A5	123 760	127 223	130 686	134 149	137 612	141 075	146 270	151 465	156 660	161 855	167 050		3 463		5 195	
A4	106 860	109 642	112 424	115 206	117 988	120 770	124 943	129 116	133 289	137 462	141 635		2 782		4 173	
A3	92 950	95 568	98 186	100 804	103 422	106 040	109 967	113 894	117 821	121 748	125 675		2 618		3 927	
A2	75 330	77 351	79 372	81 393	83 414	85 435	88 467	91 499	94 531	97 563	100 595		2 021		3 032	
A1	58 960	60 734											1 774		0	
L5	113 000	117 520	122 040	126 560	131 080	135 600	140 120	144 640	149 160	153 680				4 520		
L4	99 360	103 334	107 308	111 282	115 256	119 230	123 204	127 178	131 152	135 126	139 100	143 074		3 974		
L3	95 250	99 060	102 870	106 680	110 490	114 300	118 110	121 920	125 730	129 540				3 810		
L2	76 560	79 622	82 684	85 746	88 808	91 870	94 932	97 994	101 056	104 118				3 062		
L1	62 380	64 875												2 495		
B6	75 900	78 405	80 910	83 415	85 920	88 425	90 930	93 435	95 940	98 445	100 950					2 505
B5	66 300	68 488	70 676	72 864	75 052	77 240	79 428	81 616	83 804	85 992	88 180					2 188
B4	58 000	59 914	61 828	63 742	65 656	67 570	69 484	71 398	73 312	75 226	77 140					1 914
B3	50 900	52 580	54 260	55 940	57 620	59 300	60 980	62 660	64 340	66 020	67 700					1 680
B2	44 900	46 382	47 864	49 346	50 828	52 310	53 792	55 274	56 756	58 238	59 720					1 482
B1	39 900	41 217	42 534	43 851	45 168	46 485	47 802	49 119	50 436	51 753	53 070					1 317
C6	54 400	56 032	57 664	59 296	60 928	62 560	64 192	65 824	67 456	69 088	70 720					1 632
C5	49 800	51 294	52 788	54 282	55 776	57 270	58 764	60 258	61 752	63 246	64 740					1 494
C4	46 000	47 380	48 760	50 140	51 520	52 900	54 280	55 660	57 040	58 420	59 800					1 380
C3	42 900	44 187	45 474	46 761	48 048	49 335	50 622	51 909	53 196	54 483	55 770					1 287
C2	40 400	41 612	42 824	44 036	45 248	46 460	47 672	48 884	50 096	51 308	52 520					1 212
C1	38 400	39 552	40 704	41 856	43 008	44 160	45 312	46 464	47 616	48 768	49 920					1 152

[a] Scale applicable as from 1 July 1981.

Table VI.3 Scale of Allowances for Dependent Children and Other Dependants[1]

Staff members serving in France : 672.10 FF per month.
Staff members serving in Belgium : 4 313 BF per month.

Expatriation Allowance

Scale of the additional fixed part applicable to category B staff members serving in France (monthly amount) :

Grades	Recipient of the household allowance	Other staff
B4	12.90 FF	
B1.B2.B3	105.10 FF	57.80 FF

Scale of the fixed monthly allowance paid for each dependent child:
Staff members serving in France: 188.50 FF
Staff members serving in Belgium: 1 210 BF

APPENDIX V: PENSION SCHEME RULES

The staff members covered by Article 1, paragraph 1, of the Staff Regulations shall benefit from the pension scheme described below:

Chapter I: General Provisions

Article 1: Scope

1. The pension scheme established by these Rules applies to the permanent staff, holding indefinite term or definite or fixed term appointments in:
— the Council of Europe;
— the Organisation for Economic Co-operation and Development (OECD);
— the European Space Agency (ESA) (ex European Organisation for the Development and Construction of Space Vehicle Launchers (ELDO) and European Space Research Organisation (ESRO));
— the North Atlantic Treaty Organisation (NATO);
— the Western European Union (WEU).

2. This scheme shall not apply to other categories of personnel defined in each organisation, such as experts, consultants, temporary staff, auxiliary staff, employees and personnel hired under local labour legislation, etc.

3. In these Rules, the term 'organisation' refers to that organisation listed in

---

[1] Scale applicable as from 1 July 1981.

paragraph 1 above which employs the staff member to whom these Rules apply and the term 'staff member' or 'permanent staff member' means the staff referred to in paragraph 1 above.

Article 2: Deferred Entitlement

Where the medical examination which every staff member has to undergo at the time of his appointment shows him to be suffering from an illness or disablement, the organisation may decide that, as regards risks arising from an illness or disablement existing before he took up his duties, the said staff member shall not be entitled to the invalidity or death benefits provided for in these Rules until the expiry of a period not exceeding five years from the date on which he entered the service of the organisation. If a staff member leaves one of the organisations listed in Article 1 and takes up employment in another of those organisations within a period of not more than six months, the time spent in the service of the first organisation shall be deducted from this five-year period.

Article 3: Definition of Salary

1. For the purposes of these Rules, salary shall be the monthly basic salary of the staff member, according to the scales in force in the organisations listed in Article 1.1.

2. The minimum salaries taken into consideration for the calculation of pensions shall be those of serving staff members, whether in respect of pensions to be paid in the future or these actually being paid.

Article 4: Definition of Service Conferring Entitlement to Benefits

1. Subject to the provisions of Articles 5 and 41.1, entitlement to benefit under these Rules shall be determined by the total of the periods actually served in' the organisations listed in Article 1:

i.   as a staff member as defined in Article 1;
ii. in any other capacity prior to permanent appointment, provided any periods so served were not separated by breaks of more than one year.

2. The periods referred to in Article 16.2 shall also be taken into consideration.

Article 5: Calculation of Service Conferring Entitlement to Benefits

1. Where a staff member appointed by the organisation has previously served with one of the organisations listed in Article 1, his entitlement to benefits under the terms of Article 4 shall be conditional upon his paying over to the organisation which re-appoints him the amounts paid to him on leaving his previous service:

i.   pursuant to Article 11,
ii. in respect of his Provident Fund holding, within the limits stated in Article 44.2,

plus compound interest on such amounts at 4% per annum from the date when the staff member received them until the date when they are paid over in accordance with this paragraph.

Should the staff member fail to pay over the amounts in question, reckonable service shall count only as from the new appointment.

2. Where a staff member appointed by the organisation was previously drawing a retirement pension in respect of service with one of the organisations listed in Article 1, payment of that pension shall cease.

If the staff member refunds to the organisation offering him a new appointment the pension payments he has received, the provisions of Article 4 shall apply on termination of his new appointment.

If he does not make this refund, the years of service for which credit was acquired in the employment that originally entitled him to payment of the discontinued retirement pension shall be taken into account, in the calculation of the retirement pension due on cessation of his new employment, by reference to the salary for his last grading in such previous employment; moreover, that part of the final pension figure shall be abated by 5% for each year during which the staff member drew the initial pension before the age of 60.

3. Where a staff member retires at a grade and step lower than that which he had previously held in the organisation or in a previous organisation, his entitlement to benefits under these Rules shall be determined by taking into account the total of his years of service and the benefits shall be calculated on the basis of the salary for the highest grading held by him. However, a reduction shall be made in the number of years of service to be credited to him in respect of time served at a lower grade and step after having held the grade by reference to which benefits are calculated; this reduction shall be proportionate to the difference between the said gradings.

4. For the implementation of paragraphs 2 and 3 above, salaries shall be taken into account in accordance with the scales in force when the final pension assessment is made.

5. The taking into account of the periods referred to in Article 4.1.ii shall be conditional on:

i.   the staff member submitting an application to that effect within six months following his appointment as a permanent staff member governed by the Staff Regulations; the application shall specify the periods of service with which the staff member wishes to be credited;
ii.   the organisation giving its agreement;
iii. the staff member paying, for each month of service with which he is to be credited, a contribution of 7% of his first monthly salary as a permanent staff member.

Article 6: Reckonable Years of Service

1. The benefits provided for under these Rules shall be calculated by reference to reckonable years of service consisting of:

i.   the total length of service in the organisations listed in Article 1, calculated in accordance with Articles 4 and 5;
ii.   service credited in accordance with Article 12.1.

2. Incomplete years of reckonable service shall be taken into account on the basis of one-twelfth of a year for each whole month of service. For pension calculation purposes, the period remaining shall be treated as a whole month if it is equal to or more than fifteen days.

However, the period remaining shall not be taken into account for the purpose of calculating the minimum of ten years' service required for entitlement to the retirement pension provided for in Article 7 of the Rules.

3. The method of reckoning part-time service shall be laid down in the instructions for the implementation of these Rules.

Chapter II: Retirement Pension and Severance Grant

Section 1: Retirement Pension

Article 7: Condition of Entitlement

A staff member who has completed ten or more years actual service, within the meaning of Article 4, in one of the organisations listed in Article 1 shall be entitled to a retirement pension.

Article 8: Age of Entitlement—Deferred Pension and Early Pension

1. A staff member shall become eligible for a retirement pension at the age of 60.

2. Pension rights shall continue to accrue to a staff member continuing to be employed after pensionable age, but his pension shall not exceed the maximum amount laid down in Article 10.2.

3. If a staff member retires before pensionable age, payment of his retirement pension shall be deferred until he reaches that age.

4. However, a staff member who retires before pensionable age may request early payment of his pension provided he is at least 50 years old.

In such case, the retirement pension shall be reduced by reference to the age of the staff member when he starts to draw his pension, as shown in [Table VI. 3].

TABLE VI.3.

Age when payment of pension begins	Ratio of pension on early retirement to pension at 60
50	0.51
51	0.54
52	0.57
53	0.61
54	0.65
55	0.70
56	0.75
57	0.80
58	0.86
59	0.93

Article 9: Commencement and Cessation of Entitlement

1. Entitlement to payment of a retirement pension shall commence on the first day of the month following that in which a staff member became eligible for payment of the pension.

2. Entitlement shall cease at the end of the month in which the staff member dies.

Article 10: Rate of Pension

1. Except where paragraphs 2 and 3 of Article 5 apply, the amount of the retirement pension shall be, per reckonable year of service within the meaning of Articles 4 and 6, 2% of the salary corresponding to the last grade held by the staff member for not less than one year before termination of his appointment and the last step held in that grade.

2. The maximum rate of the pension shall be 70% of this salary, subject to the provisions of paragraph 3 below.

3. The amount of the retirement pension shall not be less than 4% of the salary for grade C1, step 1, per reckonable year of service credited pursuant to Articles 4 and 6 ; it may not, however, exceed the staff member's last salary as defined in Article 3. If the staff member was employed on a part-time basis when he left the organisation, the minimum retirement pension as defined in this paragraph shall be reduced proportionately.

Section 2: Severance Grant

Article 11: Severance Grant

A staff member whose service terminates otherwise than by reason of death or invalidity and who is not entitled to a retirement pension nor to the benefit of the provisions of Article 12.2, shall be entitled on leaving to a payment of:

i. the aggregate amount deducted from his salary in respect of his pension contribution, together with compound interest at the rate of 4% per annum;

ii. a severance grant equal to one month and a half of his last salary multiplied by the number of reckonable years of service credited within the meaning of Article 6;

iii. one-third of the amounts paid to the organisation under the provisions of Article 12.1, together with compound interest at the rate of 4% per annum. Should, however, the whole of these amounts have to be refunded to his previous employer, the reckonable years of service corresponding to those amounts shall be disregarded in the calculation of the severance grant.

Section 3: Inward and Outward Transfer of Pension Rights

Article 12: Inward and Outward Transfer of Pension Rights

1. A staff member who enters the service of the organisation after leaving the service of a government administration or national organisation, or international organisation not listed in Article 1, or a firm, may arrange for payment to the

organisation in accordance with the instructions for the implementation of these Rules, of any amounts corresponding to the retirement pension right accrued under the pension scheme to which he was previously affiliated in so far as that scheme allows such a transfer.

In such case the organisation in which the staff member serves shall determine, by reference to his grade on confirmation of appointment and to the instructions for the implementation of these Rules, the number of years of reckonable service with which he shall be credited under its own pension scheme.

2. A staff member who leaves the service of the organisation to enter the service of a government administration or national organisation, or international organisation, not listed in Article 1.1, which has entered into an agreement with the organisation, shall be entitled to transfer to the pension fund of that administration or orgnisation, either

— the actuarial equivalent of his retirement pension rights accrued under these Rules, such equivalent being calculated in accordance with the provisions for the implementation of these Rules; or,
— in the absence of such rights, the amounts provided under Article 11.

3. If, as a result of a staff member's transfer from one organisation listed in Article 1 to another, the severance grant is paid by an organisation other than that which received the amounts referred to in paragraph 1 above. Article 11.iii shall apply as if the organisation responsible for paying the severance grant had received the amounts referred to.

Chapter III: Invalidity Pension

Article 13: Conditions of Entitlement—Invalidity Board

1. Subject to the provisions of Article 2, an invalidity pension shall be payable to a staff member who is under the age-limit laid down in the Staff Regulations and who, at any time during the period on which pension rights are accruing to him, is recognised by the Invalidity Board defined below to be suffering from permanent invalidity which totally prevents him from performing the duties attached to his employment in the organisation.

2. The Invalidity Board shall consist of three medical practitioners, the first two being appointed by the organisation and the staff member, respectively, and the third one selected jointly by the first two. Cases shall be submitted to it by the organisation either on its own initiative or at the request of the staff member concerned.

Article 14: Rate of Pension

1. Subject to the provisions of Article 5.3 and of paragraph 3 below, the invalidity pension shall be equal to the retirement pension to which the staff member would have been entitled at the age-limit laid down in the Staff Regulations if he had continued to serve until that age and without the need for a minimum of ten years' service under Article 7.

2. However, where the invalidity arises from an accident in the course of the performance of his duties, from an occupational disease, from a public-spirited act or from risking his life to save another human being, the invalidity pension shall be 70% of the salary defined in paragraph 3 below.

3. The salary used as a basis for the calculation of the invalidity pension referred to in paragraphs 1 and 2 above shall be the salary for the grade and step held by the staff member in accordance with the scales in force at the date laid down in Article 17.1.

4. The invalidity pension shall not be less than 120% of the salary for grade C1, step 1, but may not be more than the last salary, such salaries being those which appear in the scales in force at the date laid down in Article 17.1 and are subject to review like the minimum salaries referred to in Article 3.2.

5. In the case of invalidity deliberately brought about by the staff member, the organisation shall decide whether he should receive an invalidity pension or only a retirement pension or a severance grant, depending on his length of effective service.

Article 15: Earnings Rule

Where a person in receipt of an invalidity pension is nevertheless gainfully employed, this pension shall be reduced by the amount by which his pension together with the remuneration he receives for the said employment exceeds the salary for the highest step in the grade he held at the time of his recognition as unfit for service.

This reduction shall apply only up to the age-limit laid down in the Staff Regulations.

Article 16: Medical Examination—Termination of Pension

1. While a staff member drawing an invalidity pension is still under the age-limit laid down in the Staff Regulations, the organisation may have him medically examined periodiclly to ascertain that he still satisfies the conditions for entitlement to such pension.

2. When a staff member who has not reached the said age-limit ceases to satisfy the conditions for entitlement to the invalidity pension, the organisation shall terminate that pension.

The time during which the staff member has drawn his invalidity pension shall then be reckoned, without payment of back contributions, for the calculation of the severance grant or retirement pension, as the case may be.

Article 17: Commencement and Cessation of Entitlement

1. Entitlement to an invalidity pension shall commence on the first day of the month following that in which the staff member is recognised to be permanently incapable of performing his duties.

2. In addition to the cases of cessation of entitlement specified in Article 16.2, entitlement to an invalidity pension shall cease at the end of the month in which the recipient of such a pension dies.

Chapter IV: Survivor's Pension

Article 18: Conditions of Entitlement

1. A person shall be entitled to a survivor's[1] pension if he is the surviving spouse:

i. of a staff member who died in service, provided they had been married to each other for at least one year at the time of the staff member's death, unless the death resulted either from disablement or illness contracted in the performance of his duties, or from an accident;

ii. of a former staff member entitled to a deferred pension, if they had been married to each other for at least one year at the time when the staff member left the organisation; this condition as to a minimum period of marriage prior to the staff member's leaving the organisation shall not apply if the marrige had existed for at least ten years at the time of the death;

iii. of a former staff member drawing an invalidity pension, if they were married to each other at the time of his recognition as permanently unfit for service; this condition as to the existence of the marriage at the time of the recognition of the staff member as permanently unfit for service shall not apply if the marriage had existed for at least five years at the time of his death, or if his death resulted from disablement or illness contracted in the performance of his duties, or from an accident;

iv. of a former staff member drawing a retirement pension, if they had been married to each other for at least one year at the time when the staff member left the organisation; this condition as to a minimum period of marriage prior to the staff member's leaving the organisation shall not apply if the marriage had existed for at least five years at the time of his death.

The last-mentioned period shall be extended to ten years if the staff member had retired before the age of 60.

2. None of the above-prescribed conditions as to the existence of a marriage at the relevant time, or as to the minimum period of a marriage immediately prior to the relevant time, shall apply where there are one or more children of the marriage or of a marriage of the staff member contracted prior to his leaving the organisation, inasmuch as the surviving spouse is providing for their needs; in such case, the survivor's pension shall be payable under the derogation provided for in the present paragraph, for as long as the children are actually being so provided for.

When they are no longer being so provided for, the survivor's pension shall none the less continue to be payable for so long as the surviving spouse does not have an income of his own from the exercise of any occupation, or from any retirement pension or other survivor's pension, equal to at least the amount of the survivor's pension from the organisation.

3. Entitlement to a survivor's pension shall be subject to the provisions of Article 2.

---

[1] Wherever it occurs in the Rules, the term 'survivor' means the widow or widower, as the case may be, of a staff member.

Article 19: Rate of Pension

1. The pension of the survivor of a staff member of former staff member shall be 60% of:

i.   the retirement pension that would have been payable to the staff member, had he not died in service, on the basis of his reckonable service credited up to the time of his death, without the need for a minimum often years' service under the provisions of Article 7;

ii.   the deferred retirement pension that would have been paid to the staff member at the age of 60;

iii. the invalidity pension that was actually being paid to the staff member at the time of his death, no account being taken of reductions under Article 15;

iv.   the retirement pension that was actually being paid to the staff member at the time of his death, no account being taken of any reductions under Article 8.4.

2. Where a staff member has died as a result of an accident in the course of the performance of his duties, from an occupational disease, from a public-spirited act or from risking his life to save another human being, the survivor's pension shall be 60% of the invalidity pension to which the staff member would have been entitled under Article 14.2 had he survived.

3. The survivor's pension shall not be less than 35% of the staff member's last salary; nor shall it be less than the salary for grade C1, step 1.

4. However, the survivor's pension shall not exceed the amount of the former staff member's own pension in the cases covered by paragraph 1. ii, iii and iv above.

Article 20: Reduction for Difference in Age

Where the difference in age between the deceased staff member and the surviving spouse (the latter being the younger), less the length of time they have been married, is more than ten years, the survivor's pension, calculated in accordance with the preceding provisions, shall be subject to a reduction, per year of difference, amounting to:

— 1% for the years between ten and twenty;
— 2% for the years twenty up to but not including twenty-five;
— 3% for the years twenty-five up to but not including thirty;
— 4% for the years thirty up to but not including thirty-five;
— 5% for the years from thirty-five upwards.

Article 21: Remarriage

Entitlement to a survivor's pension shall cease on remarriage. The survivor shall be entitled to immediate payment of a capital sum equal to twice the annual amount of the pension, if there are no dependent children to whom the provisions of Article 25.3 apply.

Article 22: Rights of a Former Spouse (divorced spouse)

1. The former spouse of a non-remarried staff member shall, on the latter's death, be entitled to a survivor's pension, provided that, at the time of his death, the staff member was, by virtue of a Court decision, which has become final and binding, under an obligation to pay maintenance to the former spouse; but the survivor's pension shall not exceed the amount of such maintenance.

This entitlement shall not arise if the former spouse remarried before the staff member died. If remarriage takes place after the staff member's death, the provisions of Article 21 shall apply.

2. Where a staff member dies leaving both a spouse entitled to a survivor's pension and a non-remarried former spouse fulfilling the conditions laid down in paragraph 1 above, the whole of the survivor's pension shall be divided between the before-mentioned persons in proportion to the duration of their marriages.

The amount to which a non-remarried former spouse is entitled shall, however, not be more than the amount of maintenance payable at the time of the death of the staff member.

3. Where one of the persons entitled to a survivor's pension dies or renounces his share or forfeits his rights under Article 35 or where the amount of his pension has been restricted under the terms of the second sub-paragraph of paragraph 2 above, his share shall accrue to the share of the other person, except where pension rights revert to orphans, as provided for under Article 25.2, second sub-paragraph. In such a case the restriction laid down in the second sub-paragraph of paragraph 2 above shall apply.

4. Reductions in respect of difference in age as provided for in Article 20 shall be applied separately to survivors' pensions calculated in accordance with the present article.

Article 23: Commencement and Cessation of Entitlement

1. Entitlement to a survivor's pension shall commence from the first day of the month following that in which the staff member died. However, this pension shall not become payable until payment of the salary of the deceased staff member has ceased under the Staff Regulations and Rules of the organisation.

2. Entitlement to a survivor's pension shall cease at the end of the month in which the recipient of the pension dies or ceases to satisfy the conditions for entitlement to that pension.

Article 24: Incapacitated Widower

1. Where his income does not amount to the survivor's pension provided for in Article 19, the husband of a deceased female staff member who can supply evidence that, at her death, he was permanently incapacitated by disablement or serious illness from engaging in gainful employment, may receive a survivor's pension under the terms of these Rules.

2. If the husband remarries, payment of the pension shall cease.

3. The present provisions shall apply only where the death of the female staff member occurred:

i.   before 1 January 1979;
ii. after 1 January 1979, if the female staff member was already affiliated to the pension scheme before 1 January 1979, and the amendments made with effect from 1 January 1979 to Article 18, paragraphs 1.ii and iv and 2, of the Pension Scheme Rules precluded the surviving spouse from entitlement to a survivor's pension.

Chapter V: Orphan's or Dependants Pension

Article 25: Rate of Pension

1. Where a staff member still serving or entitled to an invalidity or an immediate or deferred retirement pension dies, his children or other dependants shall be entitled to a pension under the terms of paragraphs 2 and 3 below.

2. Where the staff member dies leaving a spouse entitled to a survivor's pension, the pension referred to in paragraph 1 above shall be:

—   40% of the survivor's pension, no account being taken of reductions pursuant to Article 20, but not less than half the salary for grade C1, step 1;
—   increased, in respect of the second and every further beneficiary, by an amount equal to the allowance for a dependent child.

The pensions referred to in this paragraph 2 shall be brought up to the levels provided for in paragraph 3 in the event of the spouse entitled to a survivor's pension dying or remarrying or losing the right to that pension.

3. Where the staff member dies without leaving a spouse entitled to a survivor's pension, the pension referred to in paragraph 1 above shall be:

—   80% of the theoretical suvivor's pension, no account being taken of reductions pursuant to Article 20, but not less than the salary for grade C1, step 1;
—   increased, in respect of the second and every further beneficiary, by an amount equal to twice the allowance for a dependent child.

4. The children or other dependants of a widowed staff member whose deceased spouse was not employed by one of the organisations listed in Article 1 shall each be entitled to a pension of twice the allowance for a dependent child.

5. The total amount of the pensions provided for in the above paragraphs shall be divided equally among all beneficiaries.

6. The expression 'dependent children' shall mean children who were effectively dependent on the staff member or former staff member at the time of his death or were born not more than three hundred days after his death.

The expression 'other dependants' shall mean persons who, exceptionally, had been granted similar rights to dependent children under rules applying in the co-ordinated organisations before the death of the staff member or former staff member.

Article 26: Cessation of Entitlement

Entitlement to one of the pensions under Article 25 shall cease at the end of the month in which the child or other dependant ceases to satisfy the conditions for entitlement to the allowance for a dependent child or dependent person under the Staff Regulations and Rules of the organisation.

Article 27: Beneficiaries of More than One Category

1. Where a staff member leaves a survivor and also children of a previous marriage or other entitled persons, the total pension, calculated as if for a survivor having all these persons dependent on him, shall be apportioned among the various categories of persons concerned in proportion to the pensions which would have been payable to each category if treated separately.

2. Where there are children born of different parents, the total pension, calculated as though all the children were of the same parentage, shall be apportioned among the various categories of beneficiaries in proportion to the pensions which would have been payable to each category if treated separately.

3. For the purpose of calculating these apportionments, all the children who were recognised as dependants of the deceased staff member shall be included in the category of children of the marriage to the staff member.

4. In the case envisaged in paragraph 2 above, persons recognised as dependants, other than children, shall be included in the same group as the children to whom they are assimilated for the purpose of the apportionment.

Chapter VI: Family Allowances

Article 28: Conditions

1. The family allowances comprising household allowance, children's and dependants' allowance, handicapped child allowance and education allowance granted under the organisation's Staff Regulations and Rules shall be paid:

i.   to the recipient of a retirement pension, at the age of entitlement, or later;
ii. to the recipient of an invalidity pension;
iii. to the recipient of a survivor's pension.

The household allowance shall be calculated by reference to the pension of the recipient.

2. The amount of the allowance for a child or other dependant payable to the person entitled to a survivor's pension shall be twice the normal amount.

3. If the recipient of a retirement, invalidity or survivor's pension receives other family benefits in respect of the same children, the amount of the latter benefits shall be deducted from the allowances provided for in this article.

4. Entitlement to the allowances provided for in this article shall cease at the end of the month in which the child or other dependant ceases to satisfy the conditions for entitlement to those allowances under the Staff Regulations and Rules of the organisation.

Article 29: Ceiling for Benefits Payable to Survivors and Orphans

The total amount payable in respect of survivors', orphans' and dependants' pensions and of family allowances shall not exceed the maximum of the retirement pension referred to in Article 10.2, together with the family allowances to which the deceased staff member was entitled.

The amounts payable in respect of survivors', orphans' and dependants' pensions shall, where applicable, be reduced in proportion to the share of each beneficiary.

Chapter VII: Provisional Pensions

Article 30: Conditions of Entitlement

1. Where a serving staff member, or former staff member in receipt of a retirement or invalidity pension, has been missing for more than one year in circumstances justifying a presumption of death, the spouse or persons recognised as dependants may provisionally be awarded a survivor's pension, or orphan's pension, as appropriate.

2. The provisions of paragraph 1 above shall apply to persons recognised as dependants of a widowed spouse in receipt of a survivor's pension, who has been missing for more than one year.

3. Provisional pensions under paragraphs 1 and 2 above shall be converted into definitive pensions when the death of the staff member or spouse has been established officially or when that person has been declared missing by a final Court decision.

Chapter VIII: Determination of the Amounts of Benefits

Section 1: Assessment of Entitlement

Article 31: Organisation Responsible for the Assessment

1. The assessment of entitlement to the benefits payable under these Rules shall be made by the organisation in which the staff member was serving at the time when his active employment ended with the assistance of a joint administrative unit for the organisations listed in Article 1.1, responsible for such part of the work as can be centralised.

2. A detailed statement of the assessment shall be communicated to the staff member or the persons entitled under him at the same time as the decision awarding the pension.

Article 32: No Double Entitlement

Without prejudice to the application of Articles 4 and 5, the following may not be paid concurrently out of the budgets of one or more of the organisations listed in Article 1.1:

i.   a retirement and an invalidity pension as provided for in these Rules;
ii. a retirement or invalidity pension and a loss-of-employment indemnity paid over a period.

Article 33: Basis of Calculation

1. Pensions provided for in these Rules shall be calculated by reference to the salary defined in Article 3 and to the scales applicable to the country of the staff member's last posting.

2. However, if the staff member settles subsequently:

i.   in the country of which he is a national; or
ii. in the country of which his spouse is a national; or
iii. in a country where he has served at least five years in one of the organisations listed in Article 1.1,

he may opt for the scale applicable to that country.

This option shall apply to only one of the countries referred to in this paragraph, and shall be irrevocable except where paragraph 3 below is applicable.

3. On the death of his spouse, a former staff member who settles in the country of which he is a national, or of which such deceased spouse was a national, may opt for the scale applicable in that country.

The same option shall be open to the survivor of a former staff member and to orphans who have lost both parents.

These options shall be irrevocable.

4. Where a country opted for under the provisions of paragraphs 2 and 3 above is not or has not been a member of one of the organisations listed in Article 1.1, the reference scale shall be that applicable in the host country of the headquarters of the organisation responsible for payment of benefits.

5. The scales referred to in this article are those in force on the first day of the month following that in which the staff member left the organisation.

6. The provisions of paragraph 2 above do not apply to the benefits under Article 11. However, a staff member who settles in his country of origin may have the leaving allowance provided for in Article 11.ii calculated in accordance with the scale for that country, subject to the provisions of paragraph 4 above.

Article 34: Re-assessment—Cancellation

1. Pensions may be re-assessed at any time in the event of error or omission of any kind.

2. They shall be subject to modification or cancellation if their award was contrary to the provisions of these Rules.

Article 35: Forfeiture of Rights—Requirement of Evidence

1. Persons who are eligible for benefits under this pension scheme shall furnish such supporting evidence as may be required the organisation and inform it of any facts which may affect their entitlement to benefits.

Should they fail to comply with these obligations, they may be deprived of the right to benefits under this scheme; save in exceptional circumstances, they shall refund any sums received to which they were not entitled.

2. Where the survivor, orphans or other dependants of a deceased staff member fail to apply for their pension within one year from the date of his death, the benefits

under these Rules shall not be payable until the first day of the month following that in which they make their application.

3. Where the former spouse referred to in Article 22 fails to apply for his pension within one year from the date of the death of the staff member, his rights shall be wholly forfeited.

Section 2: Adjustment of Benefits

Article 36: Adjustment of Benefits

Should the council of the organisation responsible for the payment of benefits decide on an adjustment of salaries in relation to the cost of living, it shall grant at the same time an identical adjustment of the pensions currently being paid, and of pensions whose payment is deferred.

Should salary adjustment be made in relation to the standard of living, the council shall consider whether an appropriate adjustment of pensions should be made.

Section 3: Payment of Benefits

Article 37: Mode of Calculation

1. Benefits under these Rules shall be paid monthly in arrears.
2. Benefits shall be paid by the organisation referred to in Article 31.
3. Benefits shall be paid in the currency used in their calculation in accordance with Article 33.

Article 38: Sums Owed to the Organisation

Any sum owed by a staff member to any of the organisations listed in Article 1 at the date when a benefit is payable under these Rules shall be deducted from the amount of his benefits or from the benefits payable to those entitled under him. The deduction may be spread over a period.

Article 39: Right of Subrogation

Where a staff member's invalidity or death is attributable to a third party, the award of the benefits provided for in these Rules shall in principle be made subject to the beneficiary assigning to the organisation his claims against such third party, up to the amount of such benefits.

However, the organisation may waive its right to take action pursuant to such subrogation against the third party concerned where special circumstances justify such a waiver.

Chapter IX: Financing the Pension Scheme

Article 40: Charge on Budgets

1. Benefits paid under this pension scheme shall be charged to the budgets of the organisation responsible for the assessment of these benefits pursuant to Article 31.

2. The member states of the organisation jointly guarantee the payment of these benefits.

3. In the event of a merger, reconstitution or other transformation or in the event of dissolution of the organisation, the council or any ad hoc body set up, where required in one of the aforementioned cases, shall take the necessary measures to ensure uninterrupted payment of the pension scheme benefits until cessation of entitlement of the last beneficiary.

4. Should a country, being a member or ex-member of the organisation, fail to comply with its obligations under this article, the other countries shall meet the cost thereof in proportion to their contribution to the budget of the organisation as fixed annually from and after the said country's default.

Article 41: Staff Members' Contribution—Costing the Scheme

1. The staff members' contribution to this pension scheme shall be 7% of their salary and shall be deducted monthly.

2. Contributions properly deducted shall not be recoverable. Contributions improperly deducted shall confer no rights to pension benefits; they shall be refunded, at the request of the staff member concerned or of those entitled under him, without interest.

3. Should the councils of the co-ordinated organisations listed in Article 1.1 deem it necessary to have an evaluation of the cost of the pension scheme made by one or more actuaries and should this show the staff members' contributions to be insufficient to cover one-third of the financing of the benefits payable under these Rules, the said councils shall decide what changes, if any, are to be made in the rates of contribution.

Chapter X: Provisions Relating to Adjustment of Pensions

Article 42: Pensions which are Subject to National Tax Legislation

1. The recipient of a pension under these Rules shall be entitled to the adjustment applying to the member country of the organisation in which the pension and adjustment relating thereto are chargeable to income tax under the tax legislation in force in that country.

2. The adustment shall equal 50% of the amount by which the recipient's pension would theoretically need to be increased, were the balance remaining after deduction of the amount of national income tax or taxes on the total to correspond to the amount of the pension calculated in accordance with these Rules.

For such purpose, there shall be drawn up, for each member country, in accordance with the implementing instructions referred to in paragraph 6, tables of equivalence specifying, for each amount of pension, the amount of the adjustment to be added thereto. The said tables shall determine the rights of the recipients.

3. In calculating the theoretical amount of income tax or taxes referred to in paragraph 2 of this article, account shall be taken only of the provisions of tax legislation and regulations affecting the basis of liability and the amount of income tax or taxes for all pensioner-taxpayers in the country concerned.

Pensioners without spouse or dependants shall be deemed to be in the position of a pensioner without entitlement to any tax reliefs or allowances for family responsibilities, all other recipients being deemed to be pensioners enjoying the tax reliefs and allowances of a person who is married without children.

No account shall be taken:

— of individual factors related to the personal circumstances or private means of a particular pensioner:
— of the income of the spouse or dependants of the pensioner.

On the other hand, account shall, in particular, be taken of circumstances arising in the course of the year as a result of:

— a change in civil status or settlement in another place of residence with a different taxation system;
— commencement or cessation of payment of the pension.

4. The organisation shall supply the member countries concerned with the names, forenames and full address of pensioners and the total amount of the pension and adjustment.

5. The recipient of an adjustment as specified in this article shall be required to inform the organisation of his full address and of any subsequent change therein.

Such recipient shall produce evidence of his pension and the relative adjustment having been declared or taxed; should he fail to comply with this obligation, he shall be deprived of the right to this adjustment and shall refund any amounts unduly received in this respect.

6. The other procedures for calculating the adjustment and, in particular, those necessitated by the special features of certain national tax laws, and the procedure for payment of the adjustment shall be laid down in the implementing instructions established in accordance with the tax legislation of member countries.

Notwithstanding Article 52, the implementing provisions referred to in this paragraph shall require approval by the councils of the organisations listed in Article 1.1.

Chapter XI: Transitional Arrangements

Section 1: Staff Formerly Subject to the Pension Scheme Introduced on 1 January 1967

Article 43: Credit for Service

a. *Service performed after 1 January 1967*
1. Periods served after 1 January 1967 by staff members in service on 1 July 1974 shall in all cases be taken into account under the pension scheme established by these Regulations.

b. *Service performed prior to 1 January 1967 and credited under the previous pension scheme*
2. Periods of service prior to 1 January 1967 credited to staff under the pension

scheme established by Resolution (66) 39 shall in all cases be taken into account under the pension scheme established by these Regulations.

c. *Service performed before 1 January 1967 and not credited to staff members under the previous pension scheme*

   3. Staff in service on the date of adoption of these Rules

i. Staff members in service on the date of adoption of these Rules who renounced the right to be credited with service performed prior to 1 January 1967 under the pension scheme established by Resolution (66) 39 may, if they so desire, revoke that decision and ask to be given credit for such service within the period of one year laid down in paragraph 7.i. This new option shall be irrevocable both for the staff member concerned and for the persons entitled in respect of him. It shall be made in the conditions laid down in Article 44.a.

ii. Should a staff member become incapacitated without having made the choice referred to in paragraph 3.i above, he shall retain the option of claiming credit for service prior to 1 January 1967 within the period of one year laid down in paragraph 7.i.

iii. Should a staff member die without having exercised the option referred to in paragraph 3, his spouse or, in the event of the latter's death, his orphans or other dependants may exercise the option referred to in sub-paragraph i above but shall do so within the period of six months laid down in paragraph 7.ii.

iv. If the options described in the present paragraph are not exercised within the prescribed time-limits, the staff member or the persons entitled in respect of him shall be deemed to have maintained the option exercised under the pension scheme established by Resolution (66) 39.

   4. Staff who left the organisation between 1 January 1973 and the date of adoption of these Rules

i. Staff members who left the organisation between 1 January 1973 and the date of adoption of these Regulations without having claimed credit for their service prior to 1 January 1967, may apply within the period of one year referred to in paragraph 7.i to have all periods of service performed before the date on which they left the organisation credited to them with a view to benefiting from the pension scheme established by these Regulations, with the exception of the leaving allowance.

ii. Such application shall be granted provided the staff member concerned refunds to the organisation:

   1. for the period before 1 January 1967: the amounts specified in Article 44.a;

   2. for the period between 1 January 1967 and the date of departure: the amount of the allowance paid to him in accordance with Article 16 of the pension scheme established by Resolution (66) 39, less the amount to which he is entitled under Article 44.b.4.

   5. Staff who left the organisation between 1 January 1967 and 1 January 1973

i. Staff who left the organisation between 1 January 1967 and 1 January 1973 at the age of 60 or over after at least ten years' service, without having claimed credit for their service prior to 1 January 1967, may apply within the period of one year referred to in paragraph 7.i to have all periods of service performed before the date on which they left the organisation credited to them with a view to benefiting from the pension scheme established by these Regulations, with the exception of the leaving allowance.

ii. Such application shall be granted provided the staff member concerned refunds to the organisation:

1. for the period before 1 January 1967: the amounts specified in Article 44.a;
2. for the period between 1 January 1967 and the date of departure, the amount of the allowance paid to him in accordance with Article 16 of the pension scheme established by Resolution (66) 39, plus compound interest at 4% per annum until 1 January 1973.

They shall, however, be granted a reduction on the amounts to be repaid, calculated in accordance with Article 49.2 of these Regulations.

d. *Service for less than ten years*

6. i. Staff who left the organisation on reaching the statutory age-limit after 31 December 1966 without having performed ten years' service may apply within the period of one year referred to in paragraph 7.i for a proportional pension calculated according to the provisions of Article 10, subject to their having entered the service of the organisation before 1 July 1974 and having claimed credit for all their service and refunded the amounts referred to in paragraphs 4 and 5 above respectively, in accordance with their date of departure.

ii. If the staff member referred to in sub-paragraph i had already claimed credit for service prior to 1 January 1967, he shall be required when applying for a proportional pension to refund the leaving allowance paid to him plus compound interest at 4% per annum until 1 January 1973, subject to deduction where appropriate of an abatement calculated in accordance with Article 49.2 of these Regulations.

iii. A staff member entering the service of the organisation after 1 January 1967 but before 1 July 1974 and leaving it on reaching the statutory age-limit without having performed ten years' service may also choose between the leaving allowance and a proportional pension.

e. *Time-limits and coming into effect of options*

7. i. The time-limits for options and applications laid down in this article shall expire one year after the final adoption of these Regulations.

ii. However, in the cases of death referred to in paragraph 3.iii, the period during which the option may be exercised by the persons entitled in respect of the staff member shall be six months as from the date on which the organisation has notified them of the pension scheme established by these Regulations.

Similarly, if the former staff member dies without making his application within the time-limit set in paragraphs 4.i, 5.i and 6.i, the persons entitled in respect of him may do so within the six-month period mentioned in this sub-paragraph.

iii. The options provided for in this section shall take effect on 1 July 1974; however, in the cases referred to in paragraphs 4, 5 and 6 the option shall take effect either on the date of award of benefits under the pension scheme or on the date on which the staff member leaves the organisation if he is entitled to a deferred pension, but in no case earlier than 1 January 1973.

f. *Credit for other periods of service*

8. i. A staff member may also claim credit, within the period referred to in paragraph 7.i. above, for periods of service performed in the organisation prior to his appointment as a permanent official, in accordance with the provisions of Article 5.5 of these Regulations.

ii. A staff member who claims credit under these transitional arrangements for service performed in the Council of Europe prior to 1 January 1967 must also claim credit for all service performed as a permanent official elsewhere, in one or more of the organisations referred to in Article 1.1 of these Regulations, on the conditions laid down in the regulations applicable to the said organisations.

However, staff members who have already claimed credit for periods of service in the Council of Europe prior to 1 January 1967 in accordance with the pension scheme established under Resolution (66) 39 shall not be required to claim credit for periods of service performed in other organisations prior to the date of adoption of these Regulations.

Article 44: Conditions for Crediting Periods of Service Performed Prior to 1 July 1974

a. *Service performed prior to 1 January 1967*

1. A staff member credited with service performed prior to 1 January 1967 shall surrender his holding in the Provident Fund. However:

i. A staff member credited with service performed prior to the establishment of the Provident Fund shall retain the difference between:*a*. the amounts contributed by the organisation as a severance allowance plus their yield, and *b*. the aforesaid amounts, plus compound interest at 4% per annum.

If the said period of service has already been credited under Article 76 of the Pension Scheme Regulations established by Resolution (66) 39, subject to payment of a contribution equal to 7% of the salary received in respect of such service, the staff member shall be entitled to have the said contribution refunded with interest at a rate equal to the return on investment in addition to the difference referred to in the preceding sub-paragraph.

ii. For any period of service between 1 January 1953 when the Provident Fund was established, and 1 January 1967 when the pension scheme established by Resolution (66) 39 came into force, the staff member shall retain the difference between:

— his Provident Fund holding at 31 December 1966 plus compound interest at the rates equal to the return on investment, as fixed annually, and

— the amount corresponding to 21% of the salary received in respect of such service, plus compound interest at 4%.

If the staff member has already claimed credit for that period of service under Article 75 of the Pension Scheme Regulations established by Resolution (66) 39, he shall be entitled to reimbursement of the difference referred to in this sub-paragraph ii.

iii. Returns on investments and compound interests as provided for in sub-paragraphs i and ii above shall be calculated:

— up to 1 July 1974 in the case of staff members in service at that date;

— up to the date on which benefits became payable in the case of staff members who retired between 1 January 1967 and 1 July 1974;

— up to the date on which the staff member left the organisation if he was entitled to a deferred service pension prior to 1 July 1974;

— up to the date of death if it occurred before 1 July 1974.

2. The provisions of paragraph 1 above shall also apply to persons in receipt of pensions granted under the Pension Scheme Regulations established by Resolution (66) 39.

They shall not apply to staff who, having claimed credit for service prior to 1 January 1967, left the organisation before 1 July 1974 and received a leaving allowance under the Pension Scheme Regulations established by Resolution (66) 39 unless the staff members in question are granted proportional pensions in accordance with Article 43.6.i and ii.

3. i. Where a staff member has exercised his right to make withdrawals from his Provident Fund holding and where, in consequence, the amount standing to his credit is less than the amount he would have had to surrender under paragraph 1 if he had not made withdrawals, service prior to 1 January 1967 shall be credited only in the proportion these two amounts bear to each other.

ii. This provision shall not apply where a staff member has, within the period referred to in Article 43.7.i, undertaken to refund the difference between the two amounts plus compound interest at 4% per annum as from 1 July 1974.

If the staff member makes only partial repayment, past service shall be credited only in the proportion provided for in sub-paragraph i above.

iii. Should a staff member become incapacitated or die without having exercised the option referred to in Article 43, the figure of 70% provided for in Article 14.2, as well as the minimum pensions provided for in Articles 14.4 and 19.3, shall be reduced in the proportion existing between:

— the total number of years of service reckonable—up to the statutory age-limit in the event of invalidity—allowing for the reductions provided for in this paragraph, and

— the total number of years of service that would have been credited if the staff member had been credited with all service performed prior to 1 January 1967.

iv. The repayments referred to in this paragraph shall be effected within time-limits laid down in the rules for application of these Regulations.

b. *Service performed after 1 January 1967*

4. i. With regard to service performed between 1 January 1967 and 30 June 1974, a staff member shall be paid the difference between:

- his personal contributions for the period concerned plus compound interest at a rate equal to the return on the Pension Fund's investments up to 30 June 1974, and
- the aforesaid contributions plus compound interest at 4% per annum up to the same date.

ii.   However, the said difference shall not be payable to staff who left the organisation before 1 January 1973.

Article 45: Pension Without Credit for Past Service

i. A staff member who does not claim credit for service prior to 1 January 1967 shall be entitled to benefit under these Regulations only in respect of the period of service subsequent to that date.

ii. In the calculation of the minimum retirement pension referred to in Article 10.3, only the years served after 1 January 1967 shall be taken into account.

iii. If a staff member becomes incapacitated or dies while serving after the date on which these Rules are finally approved, the provisions of Chapters III to VI shall apply as appropriate.

Article 46: Bonus for Service After the Age of Sixty

1. A staff member who did not leave the organisation before 1 January 1973, who has chosen one of the options specified in Articles 43, 44 and 45 and who has continued to serve beyond the age of 60, shall, in respect of each year completed after that age, be entitled to an increase in pension corresponding to 5% of the reckonable years of service credited to him at the age of 60, but

i.   the increase granted in respect of each year served after the age of 60 shall not exceed 2% of the salary defined in Article 10.1, and

ii. his total pension shall not exceed 70% of the salary so defined.

2. Within the same limit, pension rights shall continue to accrue as provided for in Article 10.1.

3. This article shall, in the case covered by Article 14.1, apply only in respect of actual service after the age of 60.

Article 47: Compensation for Loss of Previous Pension Rights

A staff member who left the organisation before 1 January 1973 may receive compensation by way of reckonable years of service under the conditions and within the limits laid down in the provisions implementing the Rules if he establishes that, by reason of having joined the pension scheme of the organisation, he has been obliged to forfeit all or part of any pension rights that may have accrued to him previously in his country of origin, without being able to obtain the actuarial equivalent of such rights.

Article 48: Application of the Present Regulations to Pensions Paid Out of the Council of Europe Pension Fund

1. Pensions awarded under the pension scheme established by Resolution (66) 39, shall be subject to the provisions in these Regulations as from the date on which they come into force.

If the amount of these pensions is changed, this change shall take effect as from 1 January 1973 or as from the date on which the aforesaid pensions were granted, if it is later.

2. However, persons in receipt of disablement, survivor's or orphan's pensions may choose, under the conditions laid down in paragraphs 3 and 4 below, between the application of Chapters III to VI inclusive of these Regulations and the continued application of Chapters III to VI inclusive of the pension scheme set up by Resolution (66) 39.

3. If they have not claimed credit for service prior to 1 January 1967, persons in receipt of the pensions referred to in paragraph 2 above who choose the first option, that is the application of Chapters III to VI inclusive of these Regulations, shall be required to pay the amounts necessary for the crediting of this service in accordance with the conditions laid down in Article 44.a.

4. The option provided for in paragraph 2 above shall be exercised within the period of one year from the date on which the organisation has informed those concerned of the provisions of these Regulations.

Should a beneficiary die before exercising his option, his dependants may exercise it within a period of six months as from the date on which the organisation has notified them of the provisions contained in these Regulations.

In the absence of an option within the periods laid down the beneficiary or his dependants shall be deemed to have chosen the maintenance of the application of Chapters III to VI inclusive of the pension scheme set up by Resolution (66) 39.

5. Article 46 of these Regulations shall not apply to the calculation of the pensions referred to under this article if the staff member left the organisation before 1 January 1973.

Section 2: Staff whose Service Terminated Before 1 January 1967

Article 49: Scope

1. As a transitional measure, the provisions of these Regulations shall, if so requested by them, apply to:

i. former staff members with not less than ten years' service who left the organisation at the age of 60 or more and their widows, incapacitated widowers and orphaned children;

ii. the widows, incapacitated widowers and orphaned children of staff members who died while serving;

iii. staff members permanently incapacitated while serving and their widows, incapacitated widowers and orphans,

when the contingencies referred to in i, ii and iii occurred before 1 January 1967.

2. These beneficiaries shall, however, refund to the organisation responsible for payment of benefits the Provident Fund holdings paid at the time of departure, death, or recognition as unfit for service. This refund shall include non-reimbursed withdrawals, under the conditions laid down in Article 44.3.

This refund shall be limited to the amount of contributions paid by the staff member and by the organisation, plus compound interest at 4% per annum; such refund shall be abated, where applicable, by an amount calculated by means of the following fraction:

— numerator: the difference between the age of the staff member on 1 January 1973 and his age at the time of departure, death or recognition as unfit for service;
— denominator: the difference between 80 and the age of the staff member at the time of departure, death or recognition as unfit for service.

3. The request referred to in paragraph 1 above must be made within a period of one year from the date on which the organisation notifies entitled pesons of the pension scheme established by these Regulations, failing which the right to make it shall lapse. The benefits under this article shall be granted with effect from 1 January 1973.

4. Benefits under this article shall be calculated by reference to the staff member's grading when he left the service before 1 January 1967, but on the basis of the corresponding scales in force on 1 January 1973, subsequently adjusted in accordance with Article 36.

5. Staff to whom this article applies shall not benefit under the provisions of Article 46.

Section 3: Hardship Allowance

Article 50: Hardship Allowance

1. As an exceptional measure, when a staff member governed by the transitional arrangements is—or the persons claiming under him are—unable to make the refunds required under Article 44 or Article 49, he—or they—may, if the Secretary General considers this justified in the light of his—or their—overall income, be granted a hardship allowance. This allowance shall not exceed the amount of the minimum pension provided for in the Rules in respect of each category of beneficiary.

A hardship allowance may also be granted on grounds of low level income to the widowers of female staff members who died before 1 January 1979. In this case, any pension granted as the case may be to the children or other dependants shall be reduced to the amount laid down in Article 25.2.

2. The hardship allowance may only be granted as from the first day of the month following that in which the application is made, and in any event not earlier than 1 July 1974; it may not, however, be granted to a former staff member before he has reached the age of 60, unless he is incapacitated.

3. Detailed application of this article will be governed by the instructions referred to in Article 52.

Chapter XII: Final Provisions

Article 51: Co-ordination

These Rules must be applied in a uniform manner by the different organisations listed in Article 1.1. To this end, the Secretaries (and Directors) General of those organisations shall consult among themselves in order to carry out the appropriate co-ordination.

Article 52: Detailed Implementation

Instructions for the implementation of these Rules shall be drawn up by the Secretary General (Director General) of the organisation.

Article 53: Entry into force

These Rules shall enter into force on 1 July 1974.

Implementing Instructions for Article 42 of the Pension Scheme Rules concerning the Tax Adjustment to Pensions

Article 1: Scope and Calculation of the Adjustment

1. Article 42 of the Pension Rules shall apply only if the pension and the adjustment to it are subject to taxes on income levied in a member country of the organisation. The family allowances provided for in Article 28 of the Pension Rules shall be assimilated to pensions in determining the tax adjustment in so far as similar allowances are taxable under the national tax legislation of the member country.

2. The adjustment referred to in Article 42 of the Pension Rules shall be determined on the basis of the legal provisions relating to taxes on income in force in the member country in which the pensioner is legally subject to such taxation. It shall be established in respect of pensions paid during the tax period as determined in that country.

3. Where the pension of a person entitled to the adjustment is paid in a currency other than that of the country in which such person is subject to taxes on income, the adustment shall be determined on the basis of the pension converted into the currency of that country. Such conversion shall be effected at the rate obtaining on the official exchange market.

4. Where the amounts paid during any tax period include arrears of pension relating to any previous period, the adjustment shall be determined or recalculated, as the case may be, with due regard to the tax treatment applicable to such arrears.

Article 2: Establishment of Tables of Equivalence for Payment of the Adjustment

1. Tables of equivalence for payment of the adjustment shall be established for each tax year by the Inter-organisations Section, hereinafter referred to as 'the Section'.

2. The tax authorities of member countries shall provide the Section, at its request, with the details of legislation and regulations necessary for establishing the tables. The tables shall be checked and confirmed by the tax authorities of the member country concerned. In the event of disagreement between such authorities and the Section on the content of the tables, the Secretaries General and the Co-ordinating Committee shall consider the matter on the basis of Article 42 of the Pension Rules and of these implementing instructions.

3. Provisional tables of equivalence shall be drawn up prior to the commencement of the period to which they refer. They shall show, for rounded pension figures and in respect of each member country, an amount equivalent to 90% of the monthly adjustment calculated according to the distinctions contained in Article 42.3 of the Pension Rules and on the basis of the tax legislation in force at the time of drawing up the tables.

4. The provisional tables shall be revised whenever amendments to tax legislation involve a change in the amount of the adjustment. The Secretaries General and the Co-ordinating Committee may however decide by mutual agreement to dispense with the updating of tables in cases where the balance of gain or loss is minimal.

5. As soon as the authorities in member countries have finally adopted the tax legislation applicable to income for the period covered by the provisional tables, these latter shall be replaced by final tables establishing the rights or recipients in accordance with Article 42.2 of the Pension Rules. These final tables shall show the amount of the adjustment for the whole of the period which they cover, as well as the monthly amount of the adjustment.

6. The provisional and final tables of equivalence shall be accompanied by all such information as is necessary for their use. Such information shall include:

— the rules to be observed in cases where changes in family status, dependants or permanent address ('domicile') of the person entitled to the adjustment may affect the amount of the adjustment which the person concerned may claim;
— the names and addresses of the tax authorities to which the organisations supply the information specified in Article 42.1 of the Pension Rules;
— the evidence to be supplied by persons entitled to the adjustment as proof of the declaration for tax purposes, or the taxation, of their pension and the adjustment relating thereto;
— the dates for making such declarations and for paying the tax in those member countries which have been authorised to avail themselves of the provisions of Article 3.2 of these implementing instructions.

Article 3: Method of Payment of the Adjustment

1. The adjustment shall be paid by monthly instalments by way of advance at the same time as the pension and in an amount corresponding to that appearing in the provisional tables of equivalence referred to in Article 2.3 of these implementing instructions. The amounts of pension, arrears of pension and adjustment shall be shown separately on the intrument of payment issued to the recipient.

2. At the request of a country, the Secretaries General and the Co-ordinating Committee may, by mutual agreement, decide that, by way of exception to paragraph

1, there shall be a time-lag in payment of the monthly instalments of the adjustment relating to that country, provided however that payment of the whole of the monthly instalments shall be finalised before the ultimate date for payment of the tax to which they refer.

3. As soon as the final tables of equivalence are available, the total amount of the monthly instalments paid in respect of the tax period shall be compared to the final amount of the adjustment due for the whole of that period. Any excess or shortfall shall be rectified but so, however, that the amount involved shall not be taken into account in determining the adjustment in respect of the following tax year.

4. The adjustments shall be paid in the currency of the country in which the recipient is subject to taxes on income.

Article 4: Information to be Supplied to Member Countries by the Organisation

1. The particulars specified in Article 42.4 of the Pension Rules shall consist of the following:

a. a personal particulars form giving the names and forenames, full address and, where applicable, the residence for tax purposes (*domicile fiscal*), of the pensioner, the total amount of pension paid for the period constituting the tax year, the final amount of the adjustment arrived at for such period and the amount of arrears of pension, identifying the year to which such arrears relate;

b. a master list reproducing, for each country, the information contained in the personal particulars forms.

2. The particulars listed in paragraph 1 of this article shall be supplied to the tax authorities of the country in which the persons concerned are subject to taxes on income. A copy of the personal particulars form shall be sent to the pensioner and a copy of the master list shall be sent to the representative of the country in question to the organisation.

3. The obligations specified in this article shall be complied with at the time of the rectification referred to in Article 3.3 of these implementing instructions.

Article 5: Evidence of Payment of Tax

The tax authorities referred to in Article 2.6 of these implementing instructions shall inform the Section of the evidence by which, in accordance with Article 42.5 of the Pension Rules, recipients of the adjustment may establish that their pension and the relevant adjustment have been declared for tax purposes or have been taxed.

Article 6: Financing the Adjustment

1. The cost of the adjustment provided for in Article 42 of the Pension Rules shall be borne by the country in which the recipient thereof is subject to taxes on income of the period considered.

2. Expenditure arising under paragraph 1 of this article shall be the subject of a separate budget which shall be drawn up at the same time as the other budgets of the organisation. Final settlement of the contributions to this separate budget shall be made at the end of the period to which it relates.

Article 7: Transitional Measures

1. Arrears of pension relating to tax periods prior to the approval of the Pension Rules by the Council shall be treated as contributions towards the purchase of pension rights to the extent that they are set off against capital due for the crediting of the pensioner's past service.

2. The effect of this provision on the amount of the adjustment shall be determined by the tax authorities mentioned in Article 2.6 of these implementing instructions, in collaboration with the Section.

Article 8: Date of Effect

These implementing instructions shall take effect on the date of entry into force of the Pension Rules.

APPENDIX VI: REGULATIONS ON INDEMNITY FOR LOSS OF JOB

Article 1: Scope

These regulations, issued in accordance with Article 44 of the Staff Regulations, lay down the conditions in which the Secretary General may grant an indemnity for loss of job.

Article 2: General Principles

An indemnity may be granted to a staff member who holds a firm contract[1] and whose services are terminated for any one of the following reasons:

a. suppression of the budget post occupied by the staff member;

b. changes of such a nature in the duties of the budget post occupied by the staff member that he no longer possesses the required qualifications;

c. general staff cuts including those due to a reduction in or termination of the activities of the Council;

d. the withdrawal from the Council of the member state of which the staff member is a national;

e. the transfer of the headquarters of the Council or any of its units to another country and the consequent transfer of the whole staff concerned;

f. the refusal by the staff member, where his contract does not cover the point, to be permanently transferred to a country other than that in which he is serving;

and

a. who is not offered a post in the same grade in the Council; or

---

[1] A firm contract shall mean a contract made with a staff member on completion of the probationary period. A staff member who has held a firm contract in a Co-ordinated Organisation and who has subsequently been offered, either in that organisation or in another Co-ordinated Organisation, a contract involving a probationary period, shall be deemed to

b. who is not appointed to a vacant post in one of the other Co-ordinated Organisations at a comparable remuneration; or

c. who, if employed in the public service, has not been immediately reintegrated in·his national civil or military administration.

Article 3: Calculation of Indemnity

The method of calculating the indemnity differs as between contracts of limited duration and contracts of indefinite duration.

Article 4: Contracts of Limited Duration

The amount of indemnity for loss of job shall be equal to half the product of the monthly emoluments of the staff member (basic salary increased by 14%, plus, where appropriate, the household allowance and allowance for dependent child or other dependant) multiplied by the number of months remaining up to the expiry of the term of his contract, provided that it shall in no case exceed:

— five months' emoluments in the case of a contract for three years or less;
— eight months' emoluments in the case of a contract for four years, or for any term between three years and four years;
— ten months' emoluments in the case of a contract for more than four years.

Article 5: Contracts of Indefinite Duration

1. The amount of the indemnity, expressed in months or fractions of a month of emoluments (basic salary increased by 14%, plus, where appropriate, the household allowance and allowance for dependent child or other dependant) shall be one month's emoluments for each year of service from the date when the staff member joined the Council. However, the amount of indemnity so calculated shall be subject to a ceiling of twenty-four months. Furthermore, the amount of indemnity shall not represent a number of months, or fractions of a month, in excess of the period which the staff member would still have to serve before reaching the age-limit specified in Article 24 of the Staff Regulations.

2. In calculating the amount of indemnity for loss of job under paragraph 1, account shall be taken, where appropriate, of any years of service previously performed by the staff member concerned in other Co-ordinated Organisations and in respect of which he has not received any indemnity for loss of job under the present regulations or the previous regulations[1] provided, however, that no account shall be taken of any years of service preceding:

1. an interruption of the service of the staff member concerned with the Co-ordinated Organisations;
2. the termination for disciplinary reasons of his services with any Co-ordinated Organisation.

---

satisfy this condition if such contract is terminated during or on completion of such probationary period.

Article 6: Successive Contracts with Several Organisations

Any staff member who has served not less than ten consecutive years with one or more Co-ordinated Organisations and whose services are terminated in the conditions specified in Article 2 shall be entitled to an indemnity for loss of job under the provisions of Article 5, whatever the nature of the contract held by him at the time when his appointment is terminated.

Article 7: Emoluments Taken into Consideration

The emoluments to be taken into consideration when calculating the indemnity are those of which the staff member concerned was in receipt when he left the Council.

Article 8: Payment of the Indemnity

The indemnity shall be paid to the staff member in full at the time he leaves the Council.

Article 9: Transitional Provisions

Staff members serving with the Co-ordinated Organisations at the time when the regulations of 19 September 1972 (Resolution (72) 33) came into effect shall have the right to opt for the continued application to them of the previous regulations adopted by the Committee of Ministers on 22 January 1966 (Resolution (66) 17).

Article 10: Final Provisions

These regulations supersede those adopted by the Committee of Ministers on 19 September 1972 (Resolution (72) 33).

APPENDIX VII: REGULATIONS ON LEAVE FOR PERSONAL REASONS

Article 1

These regulations, issued in accordance with Article 45, paragraph 3, of the Staff Regulations, set out the conditions under which a staff member may be given leave, or shall be *ex officio* placed on leave, for personal reasons by the Secretary General.

Article 2

A staff member shall be *ex officio* placed on leave in the cases and conditions set out in Articles 33, 34 and 35 of the Staff Regulations.

Article 3

1. Leave may be granted at the staff member's request for the following reasons, in particular:

a. to bring up a child or to look after a child suffering from a disability requiring continuous care:

b. on account of an accident to or serious illness of the spouse, a child or an ascendant;

c. for study or research work of value for the staff member's training and the Council;

d. because of establishment of the staff member's usual residence elsewhere than at the place where he is serving, when such residence is determined by the spouse's occupation.

2. In taking his decision the Secretary General shall have regard to the exigencies of the service and the nature of the reasons adduced.

Article 4

1. Except in special circumstances, such leave shall not exceed a total of three years in the staff member's entire career. Each period of leave shall be limited to one year, but may be renewed for not more than one year at a time. An application for renewal should normally be submitted two months before the end of the current period of leave.

2. Leave shall not be granted until after expiry of the period of probation, save on one of the grounds mentioned in Article 3.*a* and *b* above.

3. The staff member shall take all the annual leave to which he is entitled before being granted leave for personal reasons.

4. Paragraphs 1 to 3 shall not apply in the cases described in Article 2.

Article 5

1. The staff member shall inform the Secretary General of any change in the situation that gave rise to his application for leave for personal reasons.

2. The Secretary General may at any time verify that the situation in respect of which the leave was granted continues to exist.

3. Should it transpire that such is no longer the case, the decisions to grant leave may be revoked immediately.

Article 6

1. During the period of such leave the staff member shall not be entitled to any of the elements entering into his remuneration, although when such leave is granted the Secretary General may, for one of the reasons referred to in paragraph 1.*a* and *b* of Article 3 and in deserving cases, arrange for the allowance in respect of dependent children or other dependants and the education allowance to continue to be paid.

2. The staff member shall not qualify for any increment or promotion.

3. The period of leave shall not be taken into account in calculating the dates laid down for advancement from one step to the next.

Article 7

1. Affiliation to the social security and supplementary insurance schemes shall be suspended.

2. The pension rights of the staff member and of persons entitled under him shall be governed by the Pension Scheme Rules[1] and the relative implementing instructions.[2]

Article 8

The vacancy in staff numbers left by the staff member may not be filled except by temporary staff.

Article 9

A staff member who without due cause has not resumed his duties on expiry of the period of leave shall be deemed to have resigned.

Article 10

In exceptional cases the staff member may, at his request, be reinstated before the end of the period of leave.

Article 11

In determining the date of the staff member's resumption of duties the Secretary General shall have regard to the interests of the Council, the staff member concerned and the person replacing him.

Article 12

A staff member on leave for personal reasons shall remain subject to all administrative regulations except as otherwise provided in these regulations.

---

[1] See Article 13.

[2] See instructions 4.1/1.iv, 14/1 and 19/1.

APPENDIX IX: REGULATIONS ON PART-TIME WORK

Article 1

These regulations, issued in accordance with Article 52 of the Staff Regulations, specify the conditions on which a member of staff confirmed in his appointment may, at his request, be authorised by the Secretary General to work half-time provided that such an arrangement is compatible with the exigencies of the service.

Article 2

Authorisation to work half-time shall be granted only on duly attested grounds of a family or medical nature. In the latter cases a certificate from the Council's medical officer is required.

Article 3

A staff member who is authorised to work half-time shall work each day or each week, as the case may be, for half the official working hours, in accordance with a timetable laid down by the Secretary General.

Article 4

1. Permission to work half-time shall be given for a maximum period of one year but may be renewed on the same conditions. Application for renewal must be made at least one month before the expiration of the period for which authorisation was originally given, and the staff member concerned must set out the reasons in support of the request for renewal.

2. The total period of half-time work shall not exceed six years throughout the whole of the staff member's career, except where permission is granted for reasons of the staff member's own health.

Article 5

1. When the reasons justifying authorisation to work half-time cease to exist, such authorisation shall be withdrawn before the end of the period for which it was granted, subject to not less than one month's notice.

2. At the staff member's own request, the Secretary General may authorise him, subject to the same period of notice, to resume full-time work.

Article 6

In calculating the seniority for an increment, the period during which the staff member was assigned to half-time work shall be counted as full-time work.

Article 7

1. A staff member who works half-time shall receive 50% of the various components of his remuneration. The minima fixed for the household allowance (Article 3, paragraph 1, of the regulations governing staff salaries and allowances) and for the expatriation or residence allowance (Article 6, paragraph 2, of the same regulations) shall be reduced by half.

2. The allowance in respect of dependent children or other dependants and the education allowance shall continue to be paid in full.

Article 8

1. A staff member working half-time shall be entitled to the leave provided for in the relevant regulations on the same basis as staff working full time. A day's leave shall be understood as being half a day, remunerated as specified in Article 7 above. However, the staff member shall receive full remuneration for those days of leave to which he is entitled in respect of a period of full-time work.

2. His entitlement to refund of travelling expenses for home leave shall be reduced by 2% for each month of half-time work falling within the period of two years in respect of which he is entitled to home leave.

Article 9

The arrangements applicable to pensions shall be as provided in the Pension Scheme Rules (Appendix V).[1]

Article 10

Staff working half-time shall continue to be subject to such rules and regulations as are not waived by these regulations.

APPENDIX X: REGULATIONS ON DISCIPLINARY PROCEEDINGS

Article 1

These regulations issued in accordance with Article 56 of the Staff Regulations, govern disciplinary proceedings.

Article 2

1. No warning or reprimand shall be ordered by the Secretary General before hearing the staff member concerned.

2. If the misconduct of which the staff member is accused may warrant one of the disciplinary measures provided for in Article 54, paragraph 2.*c*, *d*, *e* and *f*, the Secretary General shall lay before the Disciplinary Board a report clearly specifying

---

[1] See Article 6, paragraph 3.

the reprehensible acts and the circumstances in which they were allegedly committed.

3. The said report shall be transmitted to the Chairman of the disciplinary Board, who shall bring it to the knowledge of the Board members and of the staff member.

Article 3

On receipt of the report, the staff member charged shall be entitled to see his complete personal file and to take copies of all documents relevant to the proceedings.

Article 4

At the first meeting of the Disciplinary Board the Chairman shall appoint one of its members to prepare a general report on the matter.

Article 5

1. The staff member concerned shall have not less than fifteen days from the date of receipt initiating disciplinary proceedings to prepare his defence.

2. When the staff member appears before the Disciplinary Board he shall have the right to submit written or oral observations, to call witnesses and to be assisted in his defence by a person of his own choice.

Article 6

The Secretary General shall likewise have the right to call witnesses.

Article 7

1. If the Disciplinary Board requires further information concerning the facts of or the circumstances in which they arose, it may order an enquiry in which each side can submit its case and reply to the case of the other side.

2. The enquiry shall be conducted by the rapporteur. For the purpose of the enquiry the Disciplinary Board may call for any document relating to the matter before it.

Article 8

1. After consideration of the document submitted and having regard to any statements made orally or in writing by the staff member concerned and by witnesses, and also to the results of any enquiry undertaken, the Disciplinary Board shall, by majority vote, deliver an opinion, stating its grounds, on the disciplinary measure appropriate to the facts complained of, and transmit the opinion to the Secretary General and to the staff member concerned within one month of the date on which the matter was referred to the Board. The time-limit shall be three months where an enquiry has been held on the instructions of the Disciplinary Board.

2. The Secretary General shall take his decision within one month; he shall first hear the staff member concerned.

Article 9

1. The Chairman of the Disciplinary Board shall not vote on matters before the Board save on procedural questions or in case of a tie.

2. He shall ensure that the Disciplinary Board's decisions are implemented and shall bring all the relevant information and documents to the attention of each of its members.

Article 10

1. The Chairman shall be responsible for the minutes of meetings of the Disciplinary Board.

2. Witnesses shall sign the minute recording their deposition.

3. The opinion stating grounds provided for in Article 8 shall be signed by all members of the Disciplinary Board.

Article 11

Costs incurred on the initiative of a staff member in the course of disciplinary proceedings, and in particular fees to a person chosen for his defence from outside the Council of Europe, shall be borne by the staff member when the disciplinary proceedings result in any of the measures set out under Article 54, paragraph 2.*c* to *f* of the Staff Regulations.

Article 12

Where there are new facts supported by relevant evidence, disciplinary proceedings may be re-opened by the Secretary General on his own initiative or on application by the staff member concerned.

APPENDIX XI: STATUTE OF THE APPEALS BOARD

Article 1: Membership of the Board

1. The Appeals Board (hereinafter referred to as the Board) shall be composed of three members, who shall not be staff members of the Council of Europe. One member shall be appointed by the European Court of Human Rights (hereinafter referred to as the Court) from among its own members; the remaining members shall be appointed by the Committee of Ministers among jurists or other persons of high standing, with great experience in the field of administration. The members of the Board shall be appointed for a term of three years and shall take up office on the same date. They may be re-appointed.

Three substitute members shall be appointed by the Court and the Committee of Ministers, on the same conditions.

The six members and substitute members must be nationals of different member states.

2. In the event of the death or resignation of a member or substitute member during the three-year term for which he was appointed, the Court or the Committee of Ministers, as the case may be, shall appoint a replacement to serve for the remainder of the term of office of his predecessor.

Article 2: Chairman

The member of the Board appointed by the Court shall be the Board's Chairman. If the Chairman is unable to act, he shall be replaced by the substitute member appointed by the Court.

Article 3: Independence of Members

The members of the Board shall be completely independent in the discharge of their duties; they shall not receive any instructions.

Article 4: Jurisdiction

The jurisdiction of the Board is provided for in Article 60 of the Staff Regulations. Any dispute concerning the scope of its jurisdiction shall be settled by the Board itself.

Article 5: Admissibility

1. An appeal shall not be deemed admissible unless it complies with the conditions laid down in Article 60, paragraphs 1 and 3, of the Staff Regulations.
2. If the Chairman states, in a reasoned report to the members of the Board, that he considers the appeal to be manifestly inadmissible, and if the members raise no objections within two months, the appellant shall be informed without delay that his appeal has been declared inadmissible for the reasons stated in the report, a copy of which shall be communicated to him.

Article 6: Working Languages

The official languages of the Board shall be English and French.

Article 7: Preparation of Case-files

1. The notice of appeal must indicate its purpose, set out the facts and grounds of appeal and be accompanied by all supporting documents. Two copies thereof shall either be sent by registered post or handed to the Secretary of the Board, who shall acknowledge receipt and communicate them to the Chairman and to the Secretary General.
2. The Chairman shall set a time-limit for the submission by the Secretary General of his observations in writing, to which all supporting documents not already submitted by the appellant shall be attached. The observations of the Secretary General shall be communicated to the appellant, for the submission of whose reply, if any, a time-limit shall also be set by the Chairman.

3. The appeal, together with the memoranda and other supporting documents, the comments of the Secretary General and the appellant's reply, if any, shall be communicated to the members of the Board at least fifteen days before the date of the session at which it is to be considered.

4. If the Advisory Committee on Disputes has been asked for an opinion under Article 59, paragraph 4, of the Staff Regulations, the opinion shall be communicated to the Board as part of the case-file. However, evidence given before the Advisory Committee shall not be binding on the parties, nor may it be raised against them in the proceedings before the Board.

5. The Board may request any other document it considers necessary for the consideration of the appeal.

6. Every document included in the case-file shall be transmitted to the parties or made available to them for consultation in the offices of the Board's Secretariat.

7. The Secretary to the Board shall be responsible for communicating documents to the parties.

Article 8: Stay of Execution

1. The Chairman shall rule within fifteen days on applications made under Article 59, paragraph 7, of the Staff Regulations for a stay of execution of an administrative act.

2. The Chairman may make his decision subject to certain conditions.

Article 9: Meetings of the Board

1. The Board shall not be validly constituted unless a Chairman and two members or substitute members are present.

2. The Board shall be convened by the Chairman.

3. The Board's hearings shall be public unless the Board itself decides otherwise.

4. The Secretary General and the appellant may attend the hearing and make any oral submissions in support of the arguments put forward in their written statements. They may be assisted and represented for that purpose by one or more persons of their choice.

5. The Board shall hear any witnesses whose evidence it considers relevant to the hearing. The Board may require any official of the Council to appear before it as a witness.

6. The members of the Board shall deliberate in private.

Article 10: Intervention

1. Any natural person to whom the Board is open for the purposes of lodging an appeal and who establishes a sufficient interest in the result of a case submitted to the Board may be authorised by the Board to intervene in that case.

2. Submissions made in an intervention shall be limited to supporting the submissions of one of the parties.

Article 11: Costs of the Appeal

1. The Board may, if it considers that an appeal constituted an abuse of procedure, order the appellant to pay all or part of the costs incurred.

2. In cases where it has allowed an appeal, the Board may decide that the Council shall reimburse at a reasonable rate properly vouched expenses incurred by the appellant, taking the nature and importance of the dispute into account.

3. In cases where it has rejected an appeal, the Board may, if it considers there are exceptional circumstances justifying such an order, decide that the Council shall reimburse in whole or in part properly vouched expenses incurred by the appellant. The Board shall indicate the exceptional circumstances on which the decision is based.

4. The Board may decide that the Council shall reimburse justified travel and subsistence expenses incurred by witnesses who have been heard, within the limits of the rates applicable to staff on official journeys.

Article 12: Decisions of the board

1. The Board shall reach its decision by a majority vote. Reasons shall be given for decisions.

2. No appeal lies from decisions. In the event of a clerical error in a decision, it may be rectified by the Chairman either *ex officio* or at the request of one of the parties.

3. A copy of the decision shall be delivered to each of the parties. The original shall be deposited in the archives of the Secretariat of the Board.

4. Decisions of the Board shall be published in *extenso* by the Secretary General.

Article 13: Internal Rules of Procedure

The Board shall adopt its own Rules of Procedure.

Article 14: Secretariat and Budgetary Arrangements

1. The Secretary General shall make the necessary administrative arrangements for the functioning of the Board.

2. The Secretary General shall appoint a secretary and a deputy secretary to the Board. In the discharge of their duties they shall be responsible only to the Board.

3. Subject to the provisions of Article 15, any compensation awarded by the Board shall be borne by the budget of the Council.

4. Travel and subsistence expenses incurred by members of the Board shall be refunded according to the rules in force in the Council and at the rates determined by the Committee of Ministers.

Article 15: Organisations Attached to the Council of Europe

1. The jurisdiction of the Board may be extended to cover disputes between organisations attached to the Council of Europe and their officials, should the appropriate authorities of such organisations so request.

2. In such cases, an agreement governing administrative procedure and arrangements shall be concluded between the Secretary General and the organisation concerned. The agreement shall expressly provide that the latter organisation shall itself bear the cost of compensation awarded by the Board to any of its officials and the cost of sessions occasioned by such disputes.

Principles of Staff Employment of the World Bank (1983)

Table of Contents

Preamble

The Articles of Agreement of the International Bank for Reconstruction and Development and of the International Development Association (together referred to as The World Bank), and the Articles of Agreement of the International Finance Corporation (IFC) provide respectively that, subject to the general control of the Executive Directors of the Bank and the Association and of the Directors of the Corporation (all referred to as the Executive Directors), the President is responsible for the organization, appointment and dismissal of officers and staff.

Moreover, the fact that The World Bank and the IFC (the Organizations) are not subject to the employment legislation of any of their member countries imposes a special obligation on the Organizations in the relationship between them and their staff. Therefore, and without enlarging or restricting the constitutional or delegated authority of the President, the Executive Directors, upon the recommendation of the President, have adopted the following Principles of Staff Employment, which may be amended from time to time.

These Principles of Staff Employment embody the general conditions and terms of employment with the Organizations and the duties and obligations of the Organizations and of staff members. They set forth the broad policies in accordance with which the President shall organize and manage the staff of The World Bank and the IFC.

Chapter 1: Application and Authority

1.1 These principles apply to all staff members, that is, all persons appointed by the President to perform services for The World Bank of the IFC, except that, considering the particular characteristics of their appointments, the President may vary the application of these Principles to persons on Part Time, Temporary, Trainee, Consultant of Executive Director's Assistant appointments, or to any new types of appointment that may be established. The President shall ensure the observance of these Principles and shall develop, provide, and maintain such programs and Staff Rules consistent with these Principles, as he considers necessary to the efficient conduct of the Organizations' business.

Chapter 2: General Obligations of the World Bank and IFC

2.1 The Organizations shall at all times act with fairness and impartiality and shall follow a proper process in their relations with staff members. They shall not differentiate in an unjustifiable manner between individuals or groups within the staff and shall encourage diversity in staffing consistent with the nature and objectives of the Organizations. They shall respect the essential rights of staff members that have been and may be identified by the World Bank Administrative Tribunal. Furthermore, the Organization shall:

(a) establish and maintain appropriate safeguards to respect the personal privacy of staff members and protect the confidentiality of personal information about them;

(b) make all reasonable efforts to ensure appropriate protection and safety for staff members in the performance of their duties;

(c) refrain from any action that would deprive staff members retroactively of compensation in any form for services already rendered;

(d) provide staff members security in their employment consistent with the terms of their appointments, their satisfactory performance and conduct and the efficient administration of the Organizations;

(e) develop and maintain compensation and personnel management policies and practices designed to help create an environment conducive to the high standards of performance required by the Organizations in the interests of their member countries; and

(f) take such measures as may be necessary to protect the international character of the staff in discharging their duties.

Chapter 3: General Obligations of Staff Members

3.1 The sensitive and confidential nature of much of their work requires of staff a high degree of integrity and concern for the interests of the Organizations. Moreover, as employees of international organizations, staff members have a special responsibility to avoid situations and activities that might reflect adversely on the Organizations, compromise their operations, or lead to real or apparent conflicts of interest. Therefore, staff members shall:

(a) discharge their duties solely with the interest and objectives of the Organizations in view and in so doing shall be subject to the authority of the President and responsible to him;

(b) respect the international character of their positions and maintain their independence by not accepting any instructions relating to the performance of their duties from any governments, or other entities or persons external to the Organizations unless on secondment to them or employed by them while on leave of absence from The World Bank or the IFC. Staff members shall not accept in connection with their appointment or service with the Organizations any remuneration, nor any benefit, favor or gift of significant value from any such governments or other entities or persons, nor shall they, while in the service of The World Bank or the IFC, accept any medal, decoration or similar honor for such service. Staff members may retain reemployment rights or pension rights acquired in the service of another organization;

(c) conduct themselves at all times in a manner befitting their status as employees of an international organization. They shall not engage in any activity that is incompatible with the proper discharge of their duties with the Organizations. They shall avoid any action and, in particular, any public pronouncement or personal gainful activity, that would adversely or unfavorably reflect on their status or on the integrity, independence and impartiality that are required by that status; and

(d) observe the utmost discretion in regard to all matters relating to the Organizations both while they are staff members and after their service with the Organizations has ended. In particular they shall refrain from the improper disclosure, whether direct or indirect, of information related to the business of The World Bank or the IFC.

3.2 All rights in any work produced by staff members as part of their official duties shall belong to The World Bank or the IFC unless such rights are explicitly relinquished.

Privileges and Immunities

3.3 Staff members shall enjoy, in the interest of their Organizations, privileges, immunities, and facilities to which the Organizations, their officers and employees are entitled under their respective Articles of Agreement or other applicable treaties or international agreements or other laws. Such privileges, immunities, and facilities shall not excuse staff members from the performance of their private obligations or from due observance of the law. Having regard to the particular circumstances, the

Organizations may decide whether, in the interests of the Organizations, an immunity shall be waived or invoked.

Chapter 4: Entering Employment

4.1 The Organizations' recruitment policy shall be to seek to attract staff members of the highest caliber appropriate to job requirements under employment terms and conditions that are responsive both to the Organizations' needs and the staff member's well-being. To that end, the Organizations shall:

(*a*)   give paramount importance to securing the highest standards of efficiency and technical competence in appointing staff members and, within that parameter, pay due regard to the importance of recruiting staff on as wide a geographical basis as possible. To this end, rules shall be established under which, depending on the need of the Organizations for particular skills, positions may be filled by international or other types of recruitment;

(*b*)   establish rules and conditions regarding medical standards and age limits for appointments to the staff and for continued employment, and rules governing employment of close relatives, whether by blood or marriage; and

(*c*)   appoint staff members by letter of appointment, which shall specify the type of the apppointment. Unless otherwise specified in such letter, the appointment shall be subject to those Principles and Staff Rules applicable to he staff member's type of appointment, to amendments to those Principles and Staff Rules, and to other written agreements, if any, with the staff member. An appointment for more than a year shall normally commence with a probationary period to allow The World Bank or the IFC and the staff member to assess their suitability to each other.

Chapter 5: Organization and Personnel Management

5.1 The efficient administration of the Organizations require that their work be conducted within certain generally applicable standards and conditions. At the same time, it is recognized that the changing demands on the Organizations require that they adapt to meet evolving needs and circumstances. To enable the Organizations to respond effectively in such circumstances, and at the same time in a manner considerate of the needs and aspirations of their staff, the Organizations shall:

(*a*)   organize, assign and transfer staff to meet the needs of The World Bank or the IFC (with due consideration for the qualifications and wishes of the staff members concerned, and determine the terms and conditions under which staff members may be seconded or released to work for another entity or organization;

(*b*)   establish types of appointment and determine their characteristics, including whether they shall be for a definite or indefinite term or full-time or part-time;

(*c*)   establish procedures for the periodic review of staff members' work performance in order to promote the most effective use of their expertise, to determine the quality of their service, to recognize their achievements, and to identify training and development needs of staff members in the interests of the Organizations;

(*d*) establish programs and arrangements for staff training and development for the purpose of updating and improving staff skills to meet the needs of the Organizations;

(*e*) establish procedures for the promotion of staff members without prejudice to external recruitment at all levels;

(*f*) establish procedures and conditions under which staff members may be assigned to positions graded at various level, while providing reasonable measures to alleviate adverse effects on staff members assigned to positions graded or regraded at a lower level;

(*g*) establish the conditions and limits under which staff members may be required to travel, at the Organizations' expense, on official business; and

(*h*) establish rules and procedures regarding working hours, including conditions and limits for overtime work, and official holidays.

Chapter 6: Compensation

6.1 The basic objectives of the Organizations' compensation policy shall be to:

(*a*) enable the Organizations to recruit staff members of the highest calibre appropriate to job requirements and to retain them so long as there is reasonable coherence between their career interests and the evolving mission and circumstances of the Organizations;

(*b*) help motivate staff members to perform to the best of their abilities;

(*c*) provide levels of compensation that are equitable internally; and

(*d*) achieve these objectives with due regard to cost, bearing in mind the responsibility of the Organizations to their member countries.

6.2 With these objectives in view, the Organizations shall:

(*a*) establish and periodically review the general levels of staff compensation and adjust such levels, as appropriate;

(*b*) institute and maintain programs of systematic job evaluation, the purpose of which is to grade jobs according to their purpose, function, and level of responsibility so as to provide a sound and equitable basis for the remuneration of staff members;

(*c*) institute and maintain programs which permit the Organizations to reward staff members according to their performance and contribution to the Organizations' objectives;

(*d*) establish and maintain programs to promote the health and well-being of staff members and to provide financial protection and assistance for staff members and their families, including but not limited to annual, maternity and sick leave, coverage for medical and hospitalization expenses, accidents and loss of life, and provisions for retirement through lump sum or periodic payments;

(*e*) in view of the importance to the Organizations, given their international role, of expatriate staff members maintaining their cultural, professional and personal links with their home countries, establish and maintain programs for staff members, including the periodic travel of such staff members and their families

to their home countries and assistance with the education of their children, and
determine the eligibility for such programs;

(*f*) provide reasonable assistance, depending on the type of recruitment, to staff
members required to relocate to take up their appointments or new assignments,
or who resettle under rules established by the Organizations upon ending
employment, including the payment of travel expenses for staff members and
their families, and the shipment of their personal and household effects; and

(*g*) pending the necessary action being taken by member governments to exempt
their nationals from taxation on their incomes from the Organizations when paid
on a net of tax basis, provide a tax allowance determined by the Executive
Directors to be reasonably related to the taxes required to be paid by staff
members on those incomes.

Chapter 7: Ending Employment

7.1 The Organizations' separation policy shall seek to maintain their vitality and
integrity while paying due regard to the special circumstances faced by staff members
of international organizations. Accordingly:

(*a*) Separation from service may occur by resignation, with due notice, expiration of
an appointment in accordance with the terms of that appointment, retirement,
mutual agreement, or upon reaching the upper age limit for employment, unless
this limit has been waived in the interests of The World Bank of the IFC;

(*b*) Separations may also be initiated by The World Bank or the IFC. They shall be
based on the needs for efficient administration and for upholding the standards of
the Organizations. Staff members separated at the initiative of the Organizations
have the right to be notified in writing of the decision and the reason for it, which
shall be based on the following:

(i)   a decision not to confirm a staff member's appointment at the end of or
during probation; or

(ii) grounds of health; or

(iii) when the Organizations determine that a position or positions are no longer
necessary, or that the responsibilities of a position have changed so that the
staff member is not qualified to fill it, provided that no vacant position in
the same type of appointment exists for which the Organizations determine
that the staff member is eligible and has the required qualifications or for
which he or she can be retrained in a reasonable period of time; or

(iv) unsatisfactory service, personal or professional misconduct, abandonment
of duties, or action adversely reflecting upon the reputation and integrity of
the Organizations of their staff.

(*c*) A staff member separated at the initiative of the World Bank or the IFC under
b(i), (ii), or (iii), above shall receive financial and/or other assistance on
conditions and within limits established by the Organizations, which shall include
consideration of the reason for such decision, the length of service, as well as other
relevant factors. The World Bank or the IFC may also grant financial and/or

other assistance to staff members separated at the initiative of The World Bank or the IFC under b(iv) above or by mutual agreement, depending on the individual circumstances.

Chapter 8: Disciplinary Measures

8.1 A staff member who fails to observe the standards of conduct established pursuant to these Principles, who engages in misconduct, or who neglects to perform assigned tasks without reasonable excuse, may be subject to disciplinary measures. Depending on the seriousness of the offense and other relevant factors, the disciplinary measures taken in a particular case may be censure, suspension from duty with or without pay or with reduced pay, demotion, reduction in pay, or separation of the staff member from the service of the Organizations as provided in Chapter 7 above. A staff member may also be suspended from duty with pay, without prejudice, pending investigation of a charge under this paragraph.

8.2 Staff members have the right to be notified in writing of the grounds for disciplinary action.

Chapter 9: Appeals

9.1 Staff members have the right to fair treatment in matters relating to their employment. Where disputes arise, staff members shall have full opportunity to present their case without fear of reprisal. To this end:

(a) the President shall establish mechanisms, with staff participation as appropriate, to assist in the resolution of such disputes; and

(b) the World Bank Administrative Tribunal shall, as prescribed in its Statute, hear and pass judgment upon applications from staff members alleging non-observance of their contracts of employment or terms of appointment, including these Principles and all pertinent Staff Rules of the Organizations.

Chapter 10: Staff Consultation

10.1 The efficient and harmonious conduct of the Organizations' business requires that the President be cognizant of staff views in matters concerning the staff and that these views be given due consideration. In recognition of the right of the staff to associate, the President shall establish appropriate mechanisms to consult with representative members of the staff selected by the staff about the establishment of and changes in personnel policies, conditions of employment, general questions of staff welfare, and the establishment, amendment or revocation of Principles and of Staff Rules.

Chapter 11: General Provisions

Delegation

11.1 The President may delegate to any staff member, committee or unit of the Organizations the authority to perform any of the functions referred to in these Principles.

Transition Provision

11.2 Pending the issuance of Staff Rules, the Organizations' Personnel, Administrative, and Field Office Manuals shall remain in effect to the extent they are not inconsistent with these Principles. However, for the types of appointments in Chapter 1 to which the application of the Principles may be varied, those Manuals continue to apply until superseded by Staff Rules. Staff Rules may provide that they supersede any part or all of those Manuals.

SELECT BIBLIOGRAPHY ON INTERNATIONAL CIVIL SERVICE LAW

A. Reference Works

Amerasinghe, C.F., *Case Law of the World Bank Administrative Tribunal*, World Bank Administrative Tribunal, Washington, DC (1983).

—— (ed.), *Staff Regulations and Staff Rules of Selected International Organizations*, 5 vols., World Bank Administrative Tribunal, Washington, DC (1983).

—— (ed.), *Statutes and Rules of Procedure of International Administrative Tribunals*, 2 vols., World Bank Administrative Tribunal, Washington, DC (1983-4).

—— and Bellinger, D., *Main Points in the Decisions of the World Bank Administrative Tribunal*, 2 vols., World Bank Administrative Tribunal, Washington, DC (1983-5).

—— and Bellinger, D., *Index of Decisions of International Administrative Tribunals*, World Bank Administrative Tribunal, Washington, DC (1985).

—— and Bellinger, D., *Index to Decisions of the World Bank Administrative Tribunal*, World Bank Administrative Tribunal, Washington, DC (1985).

World Bank Legal Department, *Lawsuits against International Organizations: Cases in National Courts involving Staff and Employment*, Washington, DC (1983).

B. International Court of Justice Documents

Application for Review of Judgment No. 158 of the United Nations Administrative Tribunal: Pleadings, Oral Arguments, and Documents, International Court of Justice (1973).

Effect of Awards of Compensation made by the United Nations Administrative Tribunal: Pleadings, Oral Arguments, and Documents, International Court of Justice (1954).

Judgments of the Administrative Tribunal of the ILO upon Complaints made against the United Nations Educational, Scientific, and Cultural Organization: Pleadings, Oral Arguments, and Documents, International Court of Justice (1956).

C. Books

Akehurst, M.B., *Les Sources et la nature du droit appliqué par les tribunaux administratifs internationaux*, Paris (1964).

—— *The Law Governing Employment in International Organizations*, Cambridge (1967).

Balladoud, Jacques, *Le Tribunal administratif de l' Organisation Internationale du Travail et sa jurisprudence*, Paris (1967).

Basdevant [= Bastid], Suzanne, *Les Fonctionnaires internationaux*, Paris (1931).

Bleckmann, Albert, *Internationale Beamtenstreitigkeiten vor Nationalen Gerichten: Materialien zum Recht der internationalen Organisationen und zur Immunität: Rechtsgutachten für die Union Syndicale, Section Eurocontrol*, Berlin (1981).

Bowett, D.W., *The Law of International Institutions*, 4th edn., London (1982).

Comba, Andrea, *Le giurisdizioni administrative delle organizzazioni internazionali*, Turin (1967).

Del Vecchio, A.M., *Il Tribunale Administrativo delle Nazioni Unite*, Milan (1972).

Durante, Francesco, *L'ordinamento interno delle Nazione Unite*, Milan (1964).

Graham, Norman A., and Jordan, Robert S., *The International Civil Service: Changing Role and Concepts*, New York (1980).

Hammarskjöld, Dag, *The International Civil Servant in Law and in Fact: A Lecture delivered to Congregation on 30 May, 1961*, Oxford (1961).

Heyman, Jean-François, *Les Juridictions administratives internationales*, Dijon (1958).

Ho, Cheng-Hao, *Illusion of Justice: A Critical View of the UN Administrative Tribunal and Appeals System in Staff Grievance*, Brooklyn, N.Y. (1978).

Jenks, C. Wilfred, *The Proper Law of International Organizations*, London (1962).

Napoletano, Guido, *La cessazione de rapporto di lavoro dei funzionari internazionali*, Milan (1980).

Plantey, A., *Droit et pratique de la fonction publique internationale*, Paris (1977).

—— *The International Civil Service: Law and Management*, New York (1981).

Ranshofen-Wertheimer, Egon F., *The International Secretariat: a Great Experiment in International Administration*, Washington, DC (1945).

Rolin, H., Perasi, T., and Rousseau, Ch., *Avis consultatif sur les droits et obligations des fonctionnaires internationaux*, Geneva (1953).

Rogalla, Dieter, *Beamtenmitsprache im Neuner-Europa*, Baden-Baden (1978).

Ruzié, David, *Les fonctionnaires internationaux*, Paris (1970).

Schermers, Henry G., *International Institutional Law*, 3 vols., Leiden (1972-4).

Schreuer, Christoph, *Decisions of International Institutions before Domestic Courts*, Dobbs Ferry, N.Y. (1981).

Seidl-Hohenveldern, Ignaz, *Die Immunität internationaler Organisationen in Dienstrechtsstreitfällen: Rechtsgutachten zur Eurocontrol*, Berlin (1981).

Weil, Prosper, *Le Droit administratif international, bilan et tendances*, Cours I.H.E.I., The Hague (1963).

Wriggins, H., and Bock, E.A., *The Status of the United Nations Secretariat: Role of the Administrative Tribunal*, New York (1954).

D. Articles and Papers

Akehurst, M.B., 'Unilateral Amendment of Conditions of Employment in International Organizations', 41 *British Yearbook of International Law* 286 (1964).

—— 'Renewal of Fixed-Term Contracts of Employment in International Organizations', 31 *Revue internationale des sciences administratives* 83 (1965).

—— 'Le Principe de l'estoppel en droit administratif international', 96 *Journal du droit international* (*Clunet*) 285 (1966).

Amerasinghe, C.F., 'The World Bank Administrative Tribunal', 31 *International and Comparative Law Quarterly* 748 (1982).

—— 'The Implications of the *de Merode Case* for International Administrative Law,' 43 *Zeitschrift für ausländisches öffentliches Recht und Völkerrecht* 1 (1983).

—— 'Termination of Permanent Appointments for Unsatisfactory Service in International Administrative Law', 33 *International and Comparative Law Quarterly* 859 (1984).

—— '*Détournement de pouvoir* in International Administrative Law', 44 *Zeitschrift für ausländisches öffentliches Recht and Völkerrecht* 439 (1984).

—— and Bellinger, D., 'Non-Confirmation of Probationary Appointments', 54 *British Yearbook of International Law* 167 (1983).

Amphoux, Jean, 'L'Arrêt de la Cour de Justice des Communautés européennes du 16 décembre 1960 dans l' affaire Humblet', 65 *Revue générale de droit international public* 564 (1961).

Andrae, K.W., 'Das Dienstrecht der NATO', 4 *Recht und System des öffentlichen Dienstes* 263 (1973).

Apprill, C., 'La Notion de "droit acquis" dans le droit de la fonction publique internationale', 110 *Journal de droit international* 316 (1983).

Aronstein, Georges, 'Les tribunaux administratifs et le statut des fonctionnaires internationaux', *Journal des tribunaux* 561 (1955).

Baade, H.W., 'The Acquired Rights of International Public Servants', 15 *American Journal of Comparative Law* 251 (1967).

Bastid, Suzanne, 'Le Statut juridique des fonctionnaires de l'ONU', in *The United Nations: Ten years' Legal Progress. Collection of Essays*, 145, The Hague (1956).

—— 'El Tribunal Administrativo de las Naciones Unidas', in *Cursos y conferencias, Año academico 1956–7*, 5, Madrid (1957).

—— 'Les tribunaux administratifs internationaux et leur jurisprudence', 92. 2 *Academie de droit international de la Haye: Recueil des cours* 374, La Haye (1958).

—— 'Le Tribunal administratif des Nations Unies', in *Études et documents du Conseil d'État*, 15, Paris (1960).

—— 'Have the U.N. Administrative Tribunals contributed to the Development of International Law?', in W. Friedmann (ed.), *Transnational Law in a Changing Society* 288, New York (1972).

Bedjaoui, Mohammed, 'Jurisprudence comparée des tribunaux administratifs internationaux en matière d' excès de pouvoir', 2 *Annuaire français de droit international* 482 (1956).

—— 'Application de la loi locale aux fontionnaires internationaux. Notes sur les jugements du Tribunal administratif des Nations Unies des 7 décembre 1956 et 12 juillet 1957', 86 *Journal de droit international* (*Clunet*) 216 (1959).

Beigbeder, Y., 'La Commission de la fonction publique internationale', 41 *Revue internationale des sciences administratives* 385 (1975).

—— 'Individual Grievance Procedures in United Nations Secretariats', 37 *Industrial Relations* 328 (1982).

Benar, G., and Hémand, J.F., 'Le Comité chargé des demandes de réformation des jugements du Tribunal administratif des Nations Unies', 6 *Annales de la faculté de droit d'Istanbul* 511 (1957).

Cahier, Philippe, 'Le Droit interne des organisations internationales', 67 *Revue générale de droit international public* 563 (1963).

Carlston, Kenneth S., 'International Administrative Law: A Venture in Legal Theory', 8 *Journal of Public Law* 329 (1959).

Carneiro, L., 'Competencia do Tribunal Administrativo das Naçoes Unidas', 10 *Boletim da Sociedade Brasileira de Direito Internacional* 119 (1954).

Crozat, Charles, and Benar, Georges, 'La Jurisprudence du Tribunal administratif des Nations Unies', 18 *Annales de la faculté de droit d'Istanbul* 373 (1963).

Dehaussy, Jacques, 'La Procédure de réformation des jugements du Tribunal administratif des Nations Unies', *Annuaire français de droit international* 460 (1956).

Dreyfus, F., 'L'Application du principe de la proportionnalité: à propos de trois jugements du Tribunal administratif de l'O.I.T.', 90 *Revue du droit public et de la science politique* 691 (1974).

Drummond, Sir Eric, 'The Secretariat of the League of Nations', 9 *Public Administration* 228 (1931).

Focsaneanu, Lazar, 'Le Droit interne de l'O.N.U.', *Annuaire français de droit international* 315 (1957).

Friedman, Wolfgang, and Fatouros, Arghyrias A., 'The United Nations Administrative Tribunal', 11 *International Organization* 13 (1957).

Green, L.C., 'The International Civil Servant, his Employer and his State', 40 *Grotius Society Transactions* 147 (1954).

Grunebaum-Ballin, P., 'De l'utilité d'une juridiction spéciale pour le réglement sement des litiges intéressant les services de la S.D.N.', *Revue de droit international et de législation comparée* 67 (1921).

Guillaume, Gilbert, 'La Commission de recours de l'Organisation du Traité de l'Atlantique Nord et sa jurisprudence', *Annuaire français de droit international* 322 (1968).

—— 'Les Commissions de recours des organisations coordonnées', *Études et documents du Conseil d'État* 73, Paris (1969).

—— 'La jurisprudence de la Commission de recours de l'OTAN de 1968 à 1972', *Annuaire français de droit international* 392 (1972).

Hahn, H.J., 'Einführung in die typischen Elemente des Dienstrechts der internationalen Einrichtungen', 4 *Recht und System des öffentlichen Dienstes* 25 (1973).

—— 'Das Dienstrecht der Organisation für wirtschaftliche Zusammenarbeit und Entwicklung (O.C.D.E.)', 4 *Recht und System des öffentlichen Dienstes* 159 (1973).

—— 'Das Recht des internationalen öffentlichen Dienstes', *Jahrbuch des öffentlichen Rechts* 357 (1973).

Honig, F., 'Awards of the United Nations Administrative Tribunal, The Advisory Opinion of the I.C.J.', 104 *Law Journal* 192, 534 (1954).

Huet, Pierre, 'Les Tribunaux administratifs des organisations internationales (statuts des Tribunaux de la S.D.N., des Nations Unies et de la C.R.O.E.C.E.)', *Journal du droit international* (*Clunet*) 336 (1950).

—— 'La Commission de recours de l'O.E.C.E.', 80 *Journal du droit international* 256 (1953).

Jenks, C. Wilfred, 'Some Problems of an International Civil Service', 3 *Public Administration Review* 93 (1943).

—— 'Some Constitutional Problems of International Organizations', 22 *British Yearbook of International Law* 11 (1945).

—— 'Due Process Law in International Organizations', *International Organization* 163 (1965).

Jiménez de Aréchaga, Eduardo, 'The World Bank Administrative Tribunal', 14 *New York University Journal of International Law and Politics* 759 (1982).

Koh, Byung Chul, 'Administrative Justice in the United Nations: an Appraisal of its Administrative Tribunal', 31 *Revue internationale des sciences administratives* 210 (1965).

Ladreit de Lacharrière, René, 'Note sur l'avis consultatif de C.J.I. du 23 octobre 1956', *Annuaire français de droit international* 383 (1956).

Langavant, Emmanuel, 'Le Fonctionnaire de la C.E.C.A. devant la Cour de Justice de Luxembourg: l'arrêt Kergall', 83 *Journal du droit international* (*Clunet*) 650 (1956).

—— 'L'Arrêt Algera et autres du 12 juillet 1957 de la Cour de Justice de la C.E.C.A.', 85 *Journal du droit international* (*Clunet*) 372 (1958).

Langrod, Georges, 'L'Aspect administratif de l'organisation internationale', 2 *Revue hellénique de droit international* 183 (1949).

—— 'Le Tribunal administratif des Nations Unies', 67 *Revue du droit public et de la science politique* 71 (1951).

—— 'La Jurisprudence du Tribunal administratif des Nations Unies, 37 *Rivista di diritto internazionale* 243 (1954).

—— 'Les Réalisations jurisprudentielles du Tribunal administratif international de Genève', 32 *Revue de droit international et de droit comparé* 7 (1955).

—— 'La Reforme du Tribunal administratif des Nations Unies', 17 *Zeitschrift für ausländisches öffentliches Recht und Völkerrecht* 249 (1956).

Lemoine, Jacques, 'La Commission paritaire du B.I.T.', 15 *Annales de la faculté de droit d'Istanbul* 343 (1960).

—— 'Le Contrôle judiciaire des modifications de conditions de service des fonctionnaires internationaux', *Annuaire français de droit international* 407 (1962).

—— and Maupain, Francis, 'La Défense des intérêts des agents internationaux par les associations du personnel', in *Les Agents internationaux: Colloque d'Aix-en-Provence, Societé française pour le droit international*, 352, Paris (1985).

Letourneur, M., 'Le Tribunal administratif de l'O.I.T.: quelques aspects de sa jurisprudence', in *Mélanges Waline: Le Juge et le droit public*, 203, Paris (1974).

—— 'La Jurisprudence du tribunal administratif de l'O.I.T.', in *Mélanges Couzinet*, 449, Paris (1974).

Lukianov, V.V., 'On Administrative Justice in the United Nations Organisation', *Soviet Yearbook of International Law* 110 (1980), Summary in English.

Mann, F.A., 'The Proper Law of Contracts concluded by International Persons', 35

British Yearbook of International Law 34 (1959).

Manzanares, J., 'La Représentation du personnel dans les Communautés européennes', in *Mélanges Langrod: Pour un droit juste et une gestion moderne*, 247, Paris (1969).

Margiev, V.I., 'On Legal Nature of Internal Law of International Organisations', *Soviet Yearbook of International Law* 99 (1980), Summary in English.

Maupain, F., 'Une nouvelle dimension jurisprudentielle du droit de la fonction publique dans la famille des Nations Unies', 84 *Revue générale de droit international public* 794 (1980).

—— 'L'Élargissement du contrôle judiciaire des modifications unilatérales des conditions d'emploi des fonctionnaires internationaux et la notion des droits acquis', *Revue internationale des sciences administratives* 33 (1985).

'The Meller Conference on the International Civil Service: Selected Papers' (New York, 20–2, Nov. 1981), 14 *New York University Journal of International Law and Politics* 759 (1982).

Meron, Theodor, 'Status and Independence of the International Civil Servant', 167 *Académie de droit international de la Haye: Recueil des Cours* 285 (1980). See Ch. 5, pp. 354–62.

—— '*In re* Rosescu and the Independence of the International Civil Service', 75 *American Journal of International Law* 910 (1981).

—— and Elder, Betty, 'The New Administrative Tribunal of the World Bank', 14 *New York University Journal of International Law and Politics* 1 (1981).

Moderow, Włodzimierz, 'Observations sur l'affaire des fonctionnaires américains congédiés par le Secrétaire général à la demande du gouvernement des États-Unis', *Politique étrangère* 501 (1954).

Morgenstern, Felice, 'The Law Applicable to International Officials', 18 *International and Comparative Law Quarterly* 739 (1969).

—— 'Das Dienstrecht des internationalen Arbeitsamtes', 4 *Recht und System des öffentlichen Dienstes* 65 (1973).

Padilla, David J., 'Administrative Tribunal of the Organization of American States', 14 *Lawyer of the Americas* 259 (1982).

Pellet, A., 'La Grève des fonctionnaires internationaux', 79 *Revue générale de droit international public* 932 (1975).

—— 'Les Voies de recours ouvertes aux fonctionnaires internationaux', Parts 2 and 3, 85 *Revue générale de droit international public* 657 (1981).

Peuch, Jacques, 'Le Contrat de fonction publique internationale des Nations Unies', *Annales de la faculté de droit de Beyrouth* 147 (1957).

Phelan, E.J., 'The New International Civil Service', *Foreign Affairs* 307 (1932).

Prygoski, P.J., 'Due Process and Designated Members of Administrative Tribunals', 33 *Administrative Law Review* 441 (1981).

Ranshofen-Wertheimer, Egon F., 'International Administration: Lessons from the Experience of the League of Nations', 37 *American Political Science Review* 872 (1943).

—— 'The Position of the Executive and Administrative Heads of the United Nations International Organizations', 39 *American Journal of International Law* 323 (1945).

Raton, P., 'Travaux de la commission juridique de l'Assemblée générale des Nations Unies', *Annuaire français de droit international* 426 (1967).

Renninger, J.P., 'Staffing International Organizations: the Role of the International Civil Service Commission', 37 *Public Administration Review* 391 (1977).

Reymond. H., 'The Coordination of Personnel Policies and Administration in the United Nations System', 48 *International Review of Administrative Sciences* 19 (1982).

Richardson, I.L.M., The Legal Relation between an International Organization and its Personnel,' 2 *Wayne Law Review* (1956) p. 75.

Robert, J., 'Les tribunaux administratifs dans les organisations européenes', *Annuaire européen* 125 (1972).

Rogalla, Dieter, 'Das Dienstrecht der Europäischen Gemeinschaften', 4 *Recht und System des öffentlichen Dienstes* 305 (1973).

Ruzié, David, 'Le Non-renouvellement des contrats à durée déterminée et l'ingérence des États (à propos de l'affaire Ballo)', *Annuaire français de droit international* 426 (1967).

—— 'Les Relations entre l'administration et le personnel des organisations internationales', *Annuaire international de la fonction publique* 309 (1972).

—— 'L'Avis consultatif de la Cour internationale de Justice du 12 juillet 1973 dans l'affaire de la demande de réformation du jugement no. 158 du Tribunal administratif des Nations Unies', *Annuaire français de droit international* 320 (1973).

—— 'La Condition juridique des fonctionnaires internationaux', 105 *Journal du droit international* 868 (1978).

—— 'Le Pouvoir des organisations internationales de modifier unilatéralement la condition juridique des fonctionnaires internationaux. Droits acquis ou droits essentiels: à propos d'une jurisprudence du Tribunal administratif de la Banque Mondiale', 109 *Journal du droit international* 421 (1982).

—— 'Le Recours à l'arbitrage dans le contentieux de la fonction publique internationale: l'exemple du personnel local de l'U.N.R.W.A.', 113 *Journal de droit international* 109 (1986).

Seyersted, Finn, 'Settlement of Internal Disputes of Intergovernmental Organizations by Internal and External Courts', 24 *Zeitschrift für ausländisches öffentliches Recht und Völkerrecht* 1 (1964).

Sizaret, Louis, 'Une disposition curieuse, l'article 65 du statut des fonctionnaires des Communautés européenes', 2 *Revue trimestrielle de droit européen* 181 (1966).

Strohl, Pierre, 'La Réforme de la Commission de Recours de l'O.E.C.E.', in *Recueil de la Fonction Publique internationale* 97 (1958).

Taijudo, Kanae, 'The Protection of International Civil Servants and the Role of Administrative Tribunals', *Hogaku Ronso (Kyoto Law Review)* 1 (1962). In Japanese.

—— 'The United Nations Administrative Tribunal', *Kokusai rengo no kenkyu* 190 (1963). In Japanese.

Valticos, Nicolas, 'Le développement d'une jurisprudence internationale au sujet des normes établies par les organisations internationales', in In Memoriam *Sir Otto Kahn-Freund*, 717, London (1980).

Vandersanden, Georges, 'La Commission de Recours de l'O.T.A.N., son fonctionnement à la lumière de sa jurisprudence', 10 *Revue belge de droit international* 90 (1974).

Velasco, Engenio, 'Los Tribunales Administrativos en general y el del Banco Interamericano de Desarrollo en particular', IDB paper (1984).

Vignes, Daniel, 'Un tribunal administratif international juge de litiges de droit privé du travail', 37 *Revue de droit international et de droit comparé* 233 (1960).

—— 'Les delais des recours judiciares ouverts aux fonctionnaires internationaux: à propos de la décision du 20 août 1968 de la Commission de Recours du Conseil de l'Europe', *Annuaire français de droit international* 346 (1969).

Von Oertzen, Hans Joachim, 'Die Entsendung von Beamten in die Europäischen Gemeinschaften', *Die öffentliche Verwaltung* 533 (1966).

Weil, Prosper, 'La Nature du lien de fonction publique dans les organizations internationales', 67 *Revue générale de droit international public* 273 (1963).

Vuyst, B.M., de 'The Use of Discretionary Authority by International Organizations in their Relations with International Civil Servants', 12 *Denver Journal of International Law and Policy* 237 (1983).

—— 'The World Bank Administrative Tribunal', 16 *Revue belge de droit international* 81 (1981-2).

Wierringhaus, Hans, 'Une nouvelle juridiction administrative en Europe: la Commission de recours du Conseil de l'Europe', *Annuaire français de droit international* 379 (1965).

Wolf, Francis, 'Le Tribunal administratif de l'O.I.T.', 63 *Revue générale de droit international public* 279 (1954).

—— 'Le Tribunal administratif de l'Organisation internationale du Travail: origine et évolution', *Études et documents du Conseil d'État (Paris)* 33 (1969).

TABLE OF CASES

(Volume II begins at page 637)

(Volume II begins at page 637)

(Volume II begins at page 637)

(Volume II begins at page 637)

(Volume II begins at page 637)

(Volume II begins at page 637)

(Volume II begins at page 637)

(Volume II begins at page 637)

(Volume II begins at page 637)

(Volume II begins at page 637)

(Volume II begins at page 637)

(Volume II begins at page 637)

(Volume II begins at page 637)

(Volume II begins at page 637)

(Volume II begins at page 637)

(Volume II begins at page 637)

(Volume II begins at page 637)

(Volume II begins at page 637)

(Volume II begins at page 637)

(Volume II begins at page 637)

(Volume II begins at page 637)

(Volume II begins at page 637)

(Volume II begins at page 637)

(Volume II begins at page 637)

(Volume II begins at page 637)

(Volume II begins at page 637)

(Volume II begins at page 637)

(Volume II begins at page 637)

(Volume II begins at page 637)

(Volume II begins at page 637)

(Volume II begins at page 637)

(Volume II begins at page 637)

(Volume II begins at page 637)

(Volume II begins at page 637)

(Volume II begins at page 637)

(Volume II begins at page 637)

(Volume II begins at page 637)

(Volume II begins at page 637)

(Volume II begins at page 637)

(Volume II begins at page 637)

(Volume II begins at page 637)

(Volume II begins at page 637)

(Volume II begins at page 637)

(Volume II begins at page 637)

(Volume II begins at page 637)

(Volume II begins at page 637)

(Volume II begins at page 637)

(Volume II begins at page 637)

(Volume II begins at page 637)

Index

(Volume II begins at page 637)

(Volume II begins at page 637)

(Volume II begins at page 637)

(Volume II begins at page 637)

(Volume II begins at page 637)

(Volume II begins at page 637)

(Volume II begins at page 637)

(Volume II begins at page 637)

(Volume II begins at page 637)

(Volume II begins at page 637)

(Volume II begins at page 637)

(Volume II begins at page 637)

(Volume II begins at page 637)

(Volume II begins at page 637)

(Volume II begins at page 637)

(Volume II begins at page 637)

(Volume II begins at page 637)

(Volume II begins at page 637)

(Volume II begins at page 637)

(Volume II begins at page 637)

(Volume II begins at page 637)

(Volume II begins at page 637)

(Volume II begins at page 637)

(Volume II begins at page 637)

(Volume II begins at page 637)

(Volume II begins at page 637)

calling of witnesses 626-8: *see also* Calling of witnesses
composition of tribunal 632-3: *see also* Composition of Tribunal
deferral or suspension 628-9: *see also* Deferral or suspension
disciplinary, and détournement de procédure 276, 278, 279, 282
disciplinary measures and 815, 816, 838
discretionary powers and 258
discretion as to 609
equity and 191
general principles of law and 609
international administrative tribunals and 75-6
intervention 609-14: *see also* Intervention
joinder of cases 614-16: *see also* Joinder of cases
judicial precedent and 193-4
new issues 635: *see also* New issues
obligatory powers and 257
oral proceedings 623-6: *see also* Oral proceedings
preliminary measures 618-21: *see also* Provisional measures
production of documents 621-3: *see also* Production of documents
provisional measures 618-21: *see also* Provisional measures
representation 616-18: *see also* Representation
Rules of Procedure on 609
separation of issues 633-5: *see also* Separation of issues
Staff Regulations and 144-5
Statutes on 609
withdrawal of suit 630-2: *see also* Withdrawal of suit
Production of documents 618-19, 621-3
as provisional measure 618-19
confidential information and 623
equity and justice and 622
inherent powers to order 621, 622
interests of applicant and 623
Rules of Procedure on 621, 622
Statutes on 621, 622
Professional organizations, right of association and 977
Promotion 4, 355, 909-41
abolition of post and 920, 935
acquired rights and 415, 932-3
annulment and 449, 452, 538
appraisal reports and 925, 928, 937
arbitrariness and 353, 354
classification and 849, 851, 862, 934
compensation and 485, 525
costs and 570
delay and 928

détournement de pouvoir and 292, 298, 917, 918-21, 937
discretion on 259, 270, 913-17, 935, 939
discrimination and 317, 326-7, 720-1, 920-1, 937-8
due process and 928-30
error of fact and 914, 924, 937
error of law and 335, 914, 917, 921-3, 939, 940
expectancy of 912-13, 940
fixed-term contracts and 750
general principles of law on 910
geographical distribution and 919
highest standards and 909, 934
illegality and 940
interests of service and 919
irrelevant facts and 349, 924
merits and 921, 924, 925, 934
mistaken conclusions and 351, 352, 914, 926
nationality and 921
non-retroactivity and 406
omission of facts and 914, 924-6, 937, 940
prejudice and 920, 935
probation and 775, 916
procedural irregularity and 356, 358, 360, 363, 364, 369, 377, 381, 384, 386, 389, 914, 926-32, 937, 939, 940, 941
qualifications and 924, 926
quantum of compensation and 470, 495
reasons for 930-1, 938
remedies and 937-41
right to 910-13
right to associate and 395, 919, 935
right of defence and 929
salary and 935-7, 938, 949
seniority and 917, 921, 924, 926
specific performance and 451, 480, 938, 939
Staff Regulations and Staff Rules on 909-10, 912, 913, 922, 923, 929, 936, 938
substantive irregularities and 921-6, 937
substitution of judgment and 916
temporary staff and 935
termination and 664-5
time limits and 220
transfer and 908, 916, 934, 935
written law and 927-8, 935, 936, 938
Proof of abuse of purpose 300-5: *see also* Abuse of purpose
arbitrary decision 301
hostility and 301
improper motive 300, 301, 303, 304, 305
job performance 301, 304
nationality 301
right of association 302-4
Staff Regulations and Staff Rules 301
Proper law of contract: *see also* Contract of Employment, Terms and conditons of employment

(Volume II begins at page 637)

(Volume II begins at page 637)

(Volume II begins at page 637)

(Volume II begins at page 637)

(Volume II begins at page 637)

(Volume II begins at page 637)

(Volume II begins at page 637)

(Volume II begins at page 637)

(Volume II begins at page 637)

(Volume II begins at page 637)

(Volume II begins at page 637)

(Volume II begins at page 637)

(Volume II begins at page 637)